The Soviet Economy
A BOOK OF READINGS

THE IRWIN SERIES IN ECONOMICS

Consulting Editor   LLOYD G. REYNOLDS   Yale University

The
Soviet
Economy

A BOOK OF READINGS

Edited by

MORRIS BORNSTEIN
Professor of Economics

and

DANIEL R. FUSFELD
Professor of Economics

Both of the University of Michigan

Fourth Edition · 1974

RICHARD D. IRWIN, INC.   Homewood, Illinois   60430
IRWIN-DORSEY INTERNATIONAL   London, England   WC2H 9NJ
IRWIN-DORSEY LIMITED   Georgetown, Ontario   L7G 4B3

Fourth Edition

First Printing, April 1974

ISBN 0-256-01519-8
Library of Congress Catalog Card No. 73–90600

Printed in the United States of America

PREFACE

THERE ARE two principal reasons to study planned economies, particularly that of the Soviet Union. First, to understand planned economies as such: how they operate, how they are organized, their successes and failures, their problems and achievements. Second, because of the information such study provides about the basic economic principles applicable to any modern economy. Contrast and comparison with the American economy throw those basic principles into sharp focus. Courses in comparative economic systems in American colleges have long had these goals.

In recent years the clash of ideologies and the world rivalry of the Soviet Union and the United States have created both greater interest in the Soviet Union and a greater need for more students to understand its economy and how it compares with ours. Courses on comparative economic systems and the Soviet Union and its economy have multiplied.

At the same time that interest has been growing, a large volume of research on the Soviet economy has become available. Much of the research has been presented in articles which make admirable supplementary reading for courses on the Soviet economy, courses in comparative economic systems, and introductory courses in economic principles. It is the purpose of this volume to present material that would be particularly appropriate for such use.

Part I examines some basic features of Soviet economic planning. It includes a summary view of the principles by which resources are allocated, a survey of the evolution of planning, and studies of the problems of achieving consistent plans in a "high-pressure" economy.

Part II goes into greater detail about the operation of the economy. It covers the role of prices, finance, enterprise management, labor, and agriculture.

Part III deals with economic growth. It begins with a brief evaluation of Soviet statistics and an analysis of the sources of economic growth in the USSR. A survey of trends in consumption and an account of the new automobile program follow. The the new Soviet Methodology for Investment Allocation and an evaluation of it are presented. The next two selections discuss problems of technological change. The last article considers environmental problems associated with growth.

Part IV examines Soviet economic relations with other Comecon countries, with the industrialized non-Communist nations, and with the less developed areas.

Part V considers efforts at reform of the system of planning, administration, and management. In the first selection, the prominent Soviet economist E. G. Liberman evaluates the 1965 economic reform. The second article analyzes recent developments in planning and incentives. The last discusses the latest reorganization of industrial administration.

Of the 26 articles in this fourth edition, only eight appeared in the third edition. In part this reflects the rapid changes taking place in the Soviet economy and the advances in Soviet studies of recent years. It also reflects the many suggestions made by the users of earlier editions. The editors are grateful to them for their invaluable help. We also wish to express our thanks to Phyllis J. Romo for expert secretarial assistance.

Wherever possible full articles have been included. The editors feel that students benefit from seeing how a scholar wrestles with the implications of his topic. Except for the elimination of excessively technical matters, references to foreign-language sources, and some outdated material and other minor deletions, the articles have been left as the authors intended. At the same time, we have selected only articles that are written in a lucid style and get to the essential matters effectively.

March 1974   MORRIS BORNSTEIN
                                                       DANIEL R. FUSFELD

CONTENTS

I
BASIC FEATURES OF SOVIET ECONOMIC PLANNING

When the Bolsheviks attained power in Russia in 1917 they took over a nation which was largely agricultural, with a backward technology and illiterate peasantry. Yet, according to their ideology, a large wage-earning working class was essential to the building of a society based on social ownership of the means of production. If only for ideological reasons, the leadership was bound to push for large-scale industrialization and the creation of an urban working class. In addition, the economic basis for national power had to be created, the working class of the rest of the world had to be convinced of the superiority of socialism, and economic abundance ultimately had to be achieved as the basis for a fully communal society. Considerations of both ideology and power brought the Soviet leadership to advocate large-scale industrialization as rapidly as possible.

By the mid-1920s, when the economy had largely recovered from war and revolution, a lively public policy debate broke out over the proper growth strategy for the country. Out of that debate, and the political rivalries it involved, came the growth policies which have characterized the Soviet economy ever since. They involved high rates of saving and investment, the mobilization of an economic surplus to be used to achieve the national purpose, and a deliberate effort to hold back consumption. These objectives required economic planning, for the normal adjustment mechanism of a consumer-oriented market system would not ordinarily be expected to achieve these goals. The added requirement of maximum speed in economic development meant that the economy had to be driven forward as fast as possible—that planning had to be "taut."

The Soviet leaders also chose planning for ideological reasons. Their socialist orientation and Marxist beliefs meant rejection of capitalist insti-

1

tutions and substitution of planning for the market system. But, in many ways, the solutions to problems facing the Soviet leadership were practical ones, rooted in everyday reality, rather than in ideology.

The articles in this section analyze the basic features of Soviet economic planning. The first examines the fundamentals of the system of centralized decision-making under "planners' sovereignty." The second provides a critical historical survey of the evolution of Soviet planning. The next investigates the special feature of "tautness" in planning, arising from the regime's desire for full use of resources for rapid growth. The last considers the problems involved in achieving consistency in ambitious and detailed plans.

1. HOW DOES THE SOVIET ECONOMY FUNCTION WITHOUT A FREE MARKET?

Z. M. Fallenbuchl

Americans are so familiar with the functioning of our market economy that we find it hard to understand how any other system might work effectively. The tendency of a market economy, operating through the motive of profit maximization by producers, to produce the commodities demanded by consumers, has an internal logic which has been recognized for centuries. Yet this "consumers' sovereignty" has been replaced by a "planners' sovereignty" in the Soviet Union.

The following article explains how the Soviet system has been made to work through a series of interrelated policy decisions on the part of the planners, without relying extensively on the market mechanism as a means of making basic economic decisions. The author is Professor of Economics at the University of Windsor (Canada). The article is reprinted with permission from *Queens Quarterly*, Vol. LXX, No. 4 (Winter 1964), pp. 559–75.

IN A FREE enterprise economy the basic economic problems of what to produce, how to produce, and for whom to produce are decided through the operation of a market. In the Soviet-type economy these problems are solved through a combination of administrative commands, and market forces which are allowed to operate within certain limits in respect of some economic activities.

Administrative commands can effectively be applied because the state and the party exercise an enormous degree of control over the economy. This control is based on the three main institutional features of the system.

INSTRUMENTS OF CONTROL

There is, first of all, the totalitarian political power and the state monopoly of information and education which give the leaders a considerably greater freedom of decision than that which would ever be possible under political democracy, at least in peace time.

Another feature is the state ownership of the great majority of the means of production. The state sector is responsible for about 92 percent of the gross value of industrial output. All of the land is owned by the state and 16 percent of the total area under cultivation belongs to state farms while over 80 percent of the area is allocated to collective farms over which the state has complete control. In addition, the government has at its disposal nationalized banking and finance, transportation, the monopoly of international trade, domestic wholesale trade, and over 90 percent of the retail outlets.

The third feature of the system is centralized planning with economic plans which are enacted as law and which are therefore backed by legal sanctions, supplemented by various kinds of administrative pressures and numerous economic and non-economic incentives.

This institutional framework enables the leaders to make some basic economic decisions in accordance with their own scales of preferences and to ignore, up to a certain point, the preferences of the consumers. It is impossible to understand the working of the Soviet economy without realizing that dictatorial objectives are the dominant force determining the direction of a great deal of economic activity.

However, not even the most autocratic leaders and the best planners can solve millions of detailed economic problems in a completely centralized way. Moreover, an excessive centralization and bureaucratization have serious drawbacks. The maintenance of an extensive bureaucratic machine is expensive, rigidity and inertia tend to develop, and economic efficiency of the system declines. Hence the perennial dilemma of the Soviet economic organization: how to decentralize some economic activities without losing the control over the economy and the possibility of central planning.

Some decentralization on a regional basis was introduced by the industrial reorganization of 1957 but the majority of basic economic decisions are still highly centralized. It is possible that Professor G. Grossman is correct in saying in *Value and Plan* that "from the regime's point of view the feasibility of any further overall decentralization in economic affairs rests largely on the degree of spontaneous and complete commitment to the official values on the part of the executants or, in Soviet parlance, on state discipline."[1] On the other hand, one can expect that with the improvement of the system of material incentives and

[1] *Value and Plan: Economic Calculation and Organization in Eastern Europe*, ed. Gregory Grossman (Berkeley: University of California Press, 1960), p. 6.

the development of more sophisticated planning methods a greater degree of decentralization will be possible.*

CONSUMER CHOICE

The communists have rejected consumer's sovereignty but they have left consumers with some degree of free choice in the market for consumption goods. Contrary to the early communist dreams, the consumers receive their incomes not in the form of allocation of various consumption goods but in money form. They are free to decide what they want to buy within the limits imposed by the existing quantities of commodities which have been produced in accordance with the planners' decisions.

Two problems are involved here. The first is the maintenance of an overall balance between the effective demand of the population, i.e., the sum of personal incomes which are likely to be spent on consumption, and the aggregate supply of consumption goods available. Any discrepancy between the two can be eliminated by adjustments in the general price level which can easily be effected by changes in the rates of the sales tax, in the total wage bill, or in the aggregate supply of consumption goods, if the authorities are prepared to do it.

The second problem is that of maintaining balance between demand for and supply of particular commodities. If there are discrepancies, then adjustments in relative prices, changes in the production plans, and, in the case of some serious shortages, rationing can be introduced.

Although the consumers are free to choose among the produced consumption goods, they have only a very limited opportunity to influence the production pattern, which is mainly determined by the planners. The planners decide whether or not the consumers should have more textiles or electrical appliances, for example. They can assess the strength of demand on the basis of changes in the stocks of particular commodities and they can order changes in the production plans, but the process is lengthy and clumsy. The managers of the state enterprises can possibly adjust the product mix, but the system by which demand is transmitted to the producers is very inadequate. Not only has the wholesale trade organization no material incentive to effect the required adjustments, but even if it would report the pattern of demand, the state enterprises have usually no material incentive to make changes in the product mix which would lead to an underfulfillment of the gross output plan or, at least, to additional efforts and complications.

How is it possible for the Soviet planners to leave the freedom of choice to consumers and, at the same time, to deny them the power to decide the pattern of production?

The answer can be found in the maintenance of a permanent state of full employment on the one hand and the ability to control inflation

---

* Editors' note: Recent developments are discussed below in Selection 24.

on the other. In all communist countries the leaders try to achieve the fastest possible economic growth by directing a huge proportion of resources to investment while, at the same time, they tend to increase "communal consumption" (education, health, social welfare, entertainment, public administration) and to maintain a high level of defense expenditures. As a result of this policy, there is a chronic shortage of producers goods in relation to the amounts which are needed. The producers goods industries have permanently more than sufficient demand for their output.

A relatively small proportion of resources is left for consumption and this relative shortage creates sellers' market conditions. Under these conditions the possibility of insufficiency of the overall effective demand for consumption goods is eliminated, and the maintenance of balance is reduced to guarding against inflation, i.e., an excess effective demand in relation to the aggregate supply of consumption goods. The problem is not how to stimulate effective demand but how to reduce it without reducing the output of capital goods by not providing incentive to work in the form of satisfactory wages and the ability to spend them on consumption goods.

The existence of the sellers' market makes it easy to sell anything which has been produced, and the planners do not have to fear any serious overproduction of individual commodities. Although cases of the overproduction of some particular commodities have occurred from time to time in the Soviet Union, and other communist countries, so far these cases have been relatively insignificant under the conditions of general scarcity.

The degree of scarcity has now slowly been reduced, but so long as the communist countries maintain their determination to achieve the highest possible rates of growth, to have a relatively large proportion of total consumption in the communal form and to spend a large proportion of their national income on armaments, space programs, and similar types of expenditures, the planning of the production of consumption goods will remain relatively easy.

It is only when there is a saturation of the market with consumption goods that the planners have to take fully into consideration consumers' tastes to avoid both an overall relative overproduction and unsold quantities of some particular commodities. But as soon as the planners start to consult the consumer, the plans are likely to be upset by unexpected changes in demand. The planners have to depend then on estimates of the future changes in demand. Mistakes are possible and the economy may find itself with an overcapacity in one industry and an undercapacity in another.

One can venture a hypothesis that two alternative situations are possible in the future. One is that the West will be faced with a more or less permanent cold war, peaceful or less peaceful competition, and a gigantic Soviet space program. The second alternative is that, if political changes in the Soviet Union induce a transfer to a mass consumption economy in that country, the Soviet economy will experience oscillations and disturbances not unlike those known in the West, although perhaps somewhat more moderate in the absence of other sources of instability which are present in a free enterprise economy.

The policy of over-committing the resources eliminates the danger of insufficiency of aggregate demand and reduces the importance of over-production of particular commodities, but it also has its disadvantages.

First of all, it implies a relatively low standard of living. It creates inconvenience for the consumers who are faced with various shortages, delays, and difficulties. In addition to these there are also some serious dangers involved.

Although the danger of balance of payments difficulties which is usu-ally associated with such conditions is not great in the case of the Soviet Union because of its self-sufficiency and the state monopoly of interna-tional trade, the danger of inflation is always present. There have been periods of open inflation in the Soviet Union and other communist coun-tries, but as the planners have some effective means to fight inflation, it is a suppressed inflation rather than an open inflation which is more typical for the Soviet-type economy. The anti-inflationary means include a complete control over almost all prices and a high degree of control over wages. The danger of a cost-pushed inflation is therefore relatively unimportant. As a British economist, A. K. Cairncross, has observed, "the Soviet authorities can afford to ignore the side of wages as opposed to the side of demand. They can, therefore, allow demand to press supply to a degree that would be highly explosive in this country [i.e., Britain] except perhaps in war-time."

The existence of suppressed inflation is, however, responsible for a number of inefficiencies. It leads to hoarding of machines and raw mate-rials by state enterprises, to a deterioration in the quality of both con-sumers' and producers' goods, to bottlenecks and interruptions in the productive process, and to the "take it or leave it" mentality in the distribution process.

PLANNING

The communists have rejected not only consumers' sovereignty but also the maximization of consumers' satisfaction (at least the present consumers' satisfaction) as guiding principles for the planners, and they have rejected maximization of profits as a guiding principle for produc-tive enterprises.

Stalin in his last work on economics referred to the "highest form of lasting and permanent profitability" which replaced profitability of individual enterprises. This concept, which has not been denounced by his successors until now, stresses that planning of production and investment should be based on long-run macroeconomic considerations instead of short-run microeconomic ones or, as Stalin has expressed it, "profitability is seen not from the point of view of individual enterprises or branches of production, and not in the context of a single year, but from the point of view of the whole national economy and in the context of, say, 10–15 years . . ."

Planning is based on some general decisions as to the rate of growth of the economy as a whole and its structure, as well as various political, military, and other non-economic considerations.

These decisions are expressed in general directives and tentative long-run targets which form a part of the Party program. On this basis the general plans are constructed, representing a fairly detailed, and integrated list of output targets, and the investment program to create the productive capacity necessary for the achievement of these targets.

Since 1928, when the planning era began, there have been seven such plans. Six of them were of five years duration and the most recent one covers the period of seven years. Four five-year plans were completed: the first (in four years), second, fourth and fifth. The third plan was interrupted by the Second World War and the sixth was abandoned in 1958 and replaced by the seven-year plan.*

The operational orders are prepared in the form of annual, quarterly, and monthly plans, which represent subdivisions of the five- or seven-year plans with such changes as may be necessary to improve planning. These short-run plans attempt to coordinate the production process in various sectors of the economy. They are very detailed and their preparation has sometimes been delayed with the result that enterprises were given their production plans and allocation of inputs after the beginning of the planning period.

The method which is used in the preparation of the plans is the so-called "planning by material balances"—a crude input-output process expressed mainly in physical terms.

Because of the enormous practical difficulty of considering all interrelationships within the economy, the planners' approach has been, until now, to concentrate on certain key branches of material production which are selected by the Party leaders as the priority branches. The whole plan is built around output goals and investment projects in these key branches. The other branches of the economy are developed only to the extent which is required in order to achieve the main goals. This approach was recommended by Lenin who called it the principle of "decisive links." It simplifies planning and makes sure that the most important goals are achieved. Whenever their implementation requires more resources than have been planned for, the low-priority sectors are

---

* Editors' note: The Eighth and Ninth Five-year Plans covered, respectively, 1966–70 and 1971–75.

sacrificed. At the same time when plans were fulfilled, or even over-fulfilled in heavy industry, such branches of the economy as agriculture, housing and light industry were seldom able to fulfill their plans, although these plans were usually less ambitious than those for the high-priority branches of the economy.

In this way some serious errors in planning were often cushioned by the existence of such non-priority branches and this seems to be the main reason why relatively unsophisticated methods are sufficient to enable the economy to function.

As a result, the Soviet economy has been developing through a series of leaps forward with successive concentration of the main efforts on some particular sectors, maintaining always, however, the priority of the production of producers' goods, and eliminating successive bottlenecks. The process has been very uneven and wasteful, but it has worked, and it resulted in very high rates of growth.

The following description of Soviet pre-war planning by a Polish Marxist, Professor O. Lange, explains very well the nature of the process which has not changed since.

> The Soviet economy was planned not for the harmony of the different branches, but for one single purpose, namely the most rapid industrialization and preparation of effective national defense . . . The fact that over-fulfillment of the production plans is regarded as a virtue, instead of an upsetting of the general economic plan, shows clearly that Soviet- economic planning did not serve the objectives of a harmonious socialist welfare economy, but served political and military objectives to which all other aspects of economic planning were sacrificed.[2]

The Soviet economy is often referred to as "a war economy" because of this concentration on a few major goals, breaking of successive bottlenecks, general scarcity, and the mobilization of all efforts and resources irrespective of costs. Just as its happens during a war in any country, decisions of central authorities in respect of major goals and corresponding resource allocation are decisive throughout the whole economy.

This type of economic system is well adapted to achieve the selected goals but it cannot usually secure economic efficiency. In other words, it can solve the problem of "what to produce" in accordance with the planners' scale of preferences but it is not completely successful in solving the problem of "how to produce" the required product mix.

INCENTIVES

Whereas prices of consumption goods are usually adjusted to eliminate discrepancies between demand and supply, prices of producers' goods

---

[2] O. Lange, "The Working Principles of the Soviet Economy," in *The USSR Economy and the War* (New York: Research Bureau for Postwar Economics, 1944), p. 43.

are used as accounting prices and as indicators of the planners' wishes as to the use of inputs by the state enterprises. In this way the planners can induce the solution of the problem of "how to produce." Prices are utilized, for example, to spread new technology, to economize scarce raw materials or even simply to cover the costs of inefficient plants.

As it is impossible for the central planning office to specify all details concerning the desired assortment and methods of production, a certain number of decisions have to be left to the management of the productive enterprises.

The managers' first duty is to maximize gross value of output and also to fulfill other tasks specified by the plan, such as, for example, reduction of costs, increase in labor productivity, and others. There is a whole system of material incentives, the purpose of which is to induce enterprises to conform to the plan.

Piece rates and bonuses are used to induce greater efforts by workers. A certain percentage of planned and a somewhat higher percentage of extra profits are left within the enterprise in the form of the so-called "enterprise fund," while enterprises expected to make losses receive part of any saving resulting from the reduction in the planned loss. This fund can be used in part for small investments within the enterprise, improvements in working conditions, housing and amenities, and in part for the payment of bonuses. It was, however, one of the findings of Professor J. S. Berliner in his study of informal organization of the Soviet firm, that "profits play a rather secondary role as incentive to Soviet plant management." Fulfillment of the planned profit target, which is fixed as the residual between the planned value of sales and planned costs of production, is only one of several criteria according to which the performance of the firm and its manager is assessed. The other "quantitative indices," like volume of output and total wage bill, and "qualitative indices," like reduction in costs and increase in labor productivity, are equally or even more important.

For the achievement of planned tasks and, above all, for the fulfillment of output plans, managers receive bonuses which form a considerable proportion of their total incomes. In addition to material incentives there are a number of non-economic incentives and administrative pressures.

Evaluating the effects of the existing system of incentives, Berliner concludes that it "has created a corps of managers dedicated to their work and responsive to the production demands made upon them" by the planners, but that at the same time certain features of the system are "directly responsible for motivating management to make a variety of decisions contrary to the intent and the interest of the state."

Together with excessively high targets and general full employment conditions, the system induces some undesirable changes in the product mix (for example, when the target is expressed in tons there is a tendency to produce a heavier product), the concealment of the real productive capacity of enterprises (to make the fulfillment of high targets easier), and the falsification of reports and the deterioration of quality.

The system, as it exists now, tends to encourage the largest possible output but it does not provide a sufficient inducement to ensure the most efficient ways of producing this output.

In a free enterprise economy a product which is better from the users' point of view will sell at a higher price and will bring a higher profit to the enterprise, encouraging in this way production of this product. In the Soviet-type economy the preferences of the users of producers' goods will not be transmitted through the price mechanism to the producer. As a result, the users have often to produce with equipment and raw materials which may not be the best from the users' point of view but which bring the highest bonus to the enterprises producing them. This practice obviously has an adverse effect on the efficiency of the enterprises using this equipment and raw materials.

The system also induces waste of raw materials. When, for example, the enterprises producing a variety of products have their plan targets expressed in value terms, the incentive system works in such a way as to induce the use of more expensive materials as the cost, plus a fixed margin of planned profit, will add up to a higher price in this case and will automatically increase the value of production, thus helping fulfill the plan.

The induced changes in the product mix may lead to shortages of some types of producers' goods. The following description of the situation by a Polish economist explains this effect of the bonus system:

> The plan must not only be fulfilled, but it must even be surpassed . . . In such a case the plan, and not production, becomes the aim of the enterprise. The management makes great efforts in order to reach 100 percent of the plan, or even 103 percent (a greater excess does not bring a bonus and it leads to an increased target in the future . . .). This system is responsible for a situation where everybody has fulfilled the plan, but there is a shortage of those goods which were planned. Some goods . . . have been produced in excess . . . whereas other goods are missing, creating slowing down effects in many interrelated branches of the economy or making satisfaction of many urgent needs impossible.

Another illustration may be quoted from the experience of East Germany:

> In spite of overfulfillment of the plan, in spite of an increase of production by a fifth, there is much that is not in order. Neither the plan of final production nor of the production of spare parts was fulfilled either in timing or as to assortment. What good is it if an additional D.M. 5 million worth of more spare parts is produced but not in the desired assortment?[3]

[3] W. F. Stolper, *The Structure of the East German Economy* (Cambridge, Mass.: Harvard University Press, 1960), p. 7.

The communist leaders are now aware of the problem and economists are discussing the ways in which the system could be made more efficient. At least some economists are sceptical whether any solution other than introduction of the principle of profitability will give the required results.

The distortion of the price mechanism is another factor which tends to reduce efficiency of production. As prices of producers' goods are fixed at artificially low levels, they do not reflect real costs of production of these goods and they do not induce their economical use. There is no reason, for example, why an enterprise should increase its labor costs in order to eliminate a wasteful use of a particular raw material which is inexpensive from the enterprise's point of view, although it may be expensive to produce.

Also, the differentials between prices of various producers' goods do not reflect their relative scarcities. In the absence of the market for producers' goods, and because prices of these goods have been often used to achieve various goals, the price system in the Soviet Union and other communist countries cannot be used as a guiding device for efficient allocation of resources.

The distortion of the price system is now officially recognized as a great obstacle to efficient planning and it has been admitted that "an improvement in price formation is of great importance."

Some other factors adversely affecting efficiency of production are the practice of allocating funds for fixed and, partly, for working capital of enterprises in the form of free grants, limiting the use of the rate of interest to relatively unimportant bank loans and even less important private savings, fixing low depreciation reserves, and not utilizing the concept of land rent.

Especially difficult under these conditions is the choice among alternative investment projects, and among different methods of production, as well as replacement of old machines and equipment by new. For this reason, these problems have been discussed in the Soviet Union and other communist countries for years. The great debate concerning the methods of calculation of the economic efficiency of investment started in the late 1940s and despite a mass of articles, numerous conferences, and the publishing of several official instructions, it has not resulted in finding a completely satisfactory solution. A planning device similar to the rate of interest has finally been introduced, although this interest is not actually charged to the enterprises, and some further improvements in investment planning will probably be introduced in the future.

Although some serious mistakes have been made in the field of investment planning, the importance of the inefficiency of the system should not be overestimated. The Soviet economy has not been fully efficient, but it works and it has been able to produce very high rates of growth.

One can only speculate that with improved efficiency these rates would have been even greater.

INCOME DISTRIBUTION

The problem of "for whom the economy produces" is again solved mainly by leaders' decisions in accordance with what they believe is in the interest of the nation and partly by market forces operating within certain limits.

The division of national income into accumulation fund and consumption fund is basically a political decision in the Soviet-type economy, although a number of important economic factors have to be taken into consideration.[4] This division determines how big a proportion of the annual total production is used for current needs and how much will be devoted for the expansion of the total product in the future.

The accumulation fund is, in turn, divided into (a) investment in the so-called "productive sphere" (i.e., funds for the expansion of productive capacity in industry, agriculture, and transportation), (b) investment in the "unproductive sphere" (funds for the expansion of building and equipment in connection with education, health, social welfare, research, the arts), and (c) the state reserves.

The consumption fund is divided into (a) the wage fund of those employed in material production, (b) current expenses on education, health, art, and similar activities, (c) the social insurance fund (pensions, benefits etc.), and (d) the state administration fund.

The decisions concerning the division of the consumption fund determine the proportions of the total product which are produced for those who work in the "productive sphere," those who are employed in the "unproductive sphere," and that which is used by the state for its administrative expenses.

Within the "productive sphere" the distribution of income among the state sector, collective sector, and a rather insignificant private sector, composed mainly of private plots of collective farmers, some craftsmen and professional people, is effected through budgetary grants and loans, the manipulation of prices, the rates of turnover tax, and deductions from profits. In this way, considerable funds have been transferred from collective farmers to the state industry and from light industry to heavy industry.

The distribution of income among members of the industrial labor force depends on the wage scale, which is sharply differentiated in accordance with the relative scarcity of a particular skill, the importance of an industry (the high priority industries have higher wage scales

---

[4] Z. M. Fallenbuchl, "Investment Policy for Economic Development: Some Lessons of the Communist Experience," *Canadian Journal of Economics and Political Science,* Vol. XXIX, No. 1 (February 1963), pp. 26–39.

than the low priority industries), and the geographical area (higher wages are paid in remote areas).

In agriculture, workers employed by the state farms receive wages based on the same principle as industrial wages, while members of collective farms receive their remuneration in accordance with the nature of the work, which determines the allocation of work-day units.*

Although the general level of wages and wage differentials are determined by the central authorities, a certain flexibility exists in practice.

Under the 1940 decrees, unauthorized leaving of a job, as well as absenteeism or lateness, were treated as criminal offenses punishable by imprisonment, forced labor, or fines. These decrees were not, however, applied in practice after 1953 and they were cancelled in 1956. At present the labor market is free in the sense that people can move to enterprises which offer higher wages. There is a penalty, however, if someone leaves his job and does not take another one within a month. Labor does not have the right to strike or to collective bargaining for wage increases.

Market forces operate in reality in a stronger way than it would appear on the basis of the study of existing regulations. In various ways managers are able to compete for better workers or scarce skills by offering higher wages than the official rates. This is often done by reclassifying upward a particular worker or by manipulation with bonuses and piecework arrangements. There exists, therefore, a discrepancy between official and actual rates.

The labor market is, however, highly imperfect. There is usually only very limited knowledge of existing openings elsewhere. Geographical mobility is limited by housing shortages, the rigid system of housing allocation, and administrative restrictions imposed on moving to some areas. In addition, moving is complicated by the fact that usually more than one member of the family is working.

As a result of the imperfections of the market, workers with exactly the same skill have different wage rates in different industries, different geographical areas, or even within the same industry and within the same area.

CONCLUSIONS

Summarizing, we may say that the decisions of the central authorities determine, to a considerable extent, the solution of what? how? and for whom? These decisions are mainly enforced by direct controls, but market forces are also utilized in some areas to strengthen these orders or, sometimes, to replace them. In some cases market forces act, however, against the wish of the planners and create undesirable results.

On the whole the Soviet-type economy can solve the problem of "what

---

* Editors' note: Recent changes are discussed below in Selection 9.

to produce" rather well in the sense that it secures the priority of the production of producers' goods and high rates of growth. It makes possible the concentration of huge resources on some selected goals and, in general, the required composition of output is produced, although some distortions of the product mix of both consumption and producers' goods tend to occur.

The solution of the problem of "how to produce" seems to be much less satisfactory. The system involves considerable waste and inefficiency, some of which will, no doubt, be eliminated in the future with a further improvement in planning methods, decentralization of economic administration, and introduction of a better system of material incentives.

The problem of "for whom the system produces" is solved well in the sense that the state can secure for investment, communal consumption, public administration, and defense a very high proportion of national income. It does not seem to secure to labor, however, that part of the value of the total product which labor contributes and it does not always secure equal pay for equal skill and equal effort.

As quite a lot has been said about the defects of the system, wastes and inefficiencies, it is perhaps necessary to comment on how, despite all these drawbacks, the Soviet economy has been able to achieve such high rates of growth, and spectacular scientific and technological achievements.

The main reason for fast Soviet economic growth is the channeling of as large a part of income as possible into productive capital investment. This is the result of an ability to reduce consumption to an extent which would not be possible under a democratic political system. Until now the Soviet Union has also been able to borrow foreign technology from the more advanced countries, at least in the majority of fields. The natural possibilities of the country have also to be taken into consideration. Russian rates of growth at the end of the 19th century and the beginning of the 20th century were also very high. Perhaps the most important factor is, however, a firm determination to catch and surpass the capitalist countries and to enforce fast economic growth, whatever the cost in terms of human suffering and economic waste.

The well known scientific and technological achievements can, similarly, be explained by the determination of the government and the possibility of concentrating huge resources in this field, refusing at the same time any more significant improvement in consumption. The level of technology is extremely uneven in the Soviet Union. While in some high-priority sectors the most advanced technology, sometimes the best in the world, is used, the majority of non-priority sectors are very backward. The Soviet Union leads in the space program and, at the same time, very primitive methods are used, for example, in building-construction. It is pioneering in space travel and, at the same time, it has an extremely poor road system.

In conclusion it can be said that with time the impact of factors adversely affecting efficiency will probably tend to decline, although certain features of the system make improvement difficult. On the other hand, it may not be possible to maintain present high rates of accumulation and the present pattern of investment allocation with the increasing maturity of the country and political pressure for a higher standard of living.

What the net result of these two forces will be is difficult to foresee. Although there are some grounds for expecting that Soviet rates of growth will perhaps be lower in the future than in the past, they will still remain relatively high.

2. ECONOMIC PLANNING IN THE USSR

R. W. Davies

Comprehensive central planning and administrative control were adopted in the USSR in the late 1920s to mobilize resources for rapid industrialization. The planning process embraced the allocation of material inputs and outputs, the regulation of money flows, and the use of the labor force. Although these methods worked imperfectly, they did succeed in achieving some of the main objectives of the Soviet regime. However, after the death of Stalin in 1953, it became increasingly evident to the Soviet leadership, as well as to Soviet economists and administrators, that this "mobilization" model was less suitable for the more "mature" contemporary Soviet economy. In an attempt to adapt the economy to meet its current problems, the Soviet government has altered resource allocation, economic organization, and planning techniques. Economic reformers have advocated even more drastic changes, but there are a number of obstacles to further improvements in Soviet economic planning and management.

This selection provides a critical historical survey of the evolution of Soviet planning. It explains why comprehensive planning was adopted, the forms it took, and its advantages and disadvantages. It shows why the "Stalinist model" had to be modified and discusses the changes adopted. It concludes with a discussion of factors affecting the future development of Soviet economic planning.

R. W. Davies is Professor and Director of the Centre for Russian and East European Studies at the University of Birmingham, England. The selection, which is reprinted by permission, was originally published as "The Soviet Planning Process for Rapid Industrialization," *Economics of Planning,* Vol. 6 (1966), No. 1, pp. 53–67, and "Planning a Mature Economy in the USSR," *Economics of Planning,* Vol. 6 (1966), No. 2, pp. 138–52.

17

THE SOVIET PLANNING PROCESS FOR
RAPID INDUSTRIALIZATION

An Outline of the System

THE SOVIET government set itself the objective of a more rapid rate
of industrialization, with a greater investment in capital-consuming industries and processes, than could be achieved within the framework
of the market economy of the 1920s. The main objective was achieved,
but with a much slower increase in living standards (consumer goods,
agricultural output) than had been intended. To enforce its priorities,
the Soviet government abandoned the major assumptions of its earlier
policy:

1. A market relationship with the peasant was replaced by administrative or coercive control over his output. The centers of economic
and political resistance in the rural commune were destroyed, the hundreds of thousands of *kulak* families were expelled from their home
villages. Twenty-five million individual peasant farms were combined
into 250,000 collective farms (*kolkhozy*), one or several to each village.
The old boundaries and strips were destroyed, and most land and cattle
were pooled and worked in common. Agricultural machinery was gradually made available from several thousand state-owned Machine and
Tractor Stations (MTS). The *kolkhoz* was required to supply a substantial part of its output to the state collection agencies at low fixed prices
in the form of compulsory deliveries. These supplies were then used
by the state (*a*) to make available a minimum amount of foodstuffs
to the growing urban population, and (*b*) for export. Exports of grain
fell from 9 million tons in 1913 to 2 million tons in 1926–27 and 178
thousand tons in 1929; they rose (temporarily) to 4.8 million tons in
1930 and 5.1 million tons in 1931, and this increase was used to pay
for imports of equipment and industrial materials. . . .

2. Inflation was permitted to develop: The wages of the expanding
industrial and building labor force were partly met by increasing the
flow of paper money. Prices began to rise, but the inflation was partly
repressed through price control in both the producer goods market and
the retail market (private shops and trading agencies were taken over
by the state to facilitate this). For several years (1929–35) a rationing
system was introduced in the towns, supplemented by state sales of
goods above the ration at high prices. In this way, the available supply
of consumer goods and foodstuffs was distributed over the old and the
new urban population, and consumption per head in the towns was forced
down. This was then an extreme form of the "regime of economy."

3. Within industry, the system of physical controls which had already existed during the 1920s was greatly extended. Prices were fixed,

and there was no market for producer goods; instead, materials and equipment were distributed to existing factories and new building sites through a system of priorities, which enabled new key factories to be built and bottlenecks in existing industries to be widened. The plan set targets for the output of major intermediate and final products, and the physical allocation system was designed to see these were reached.

To sum up these first three points: the policy of 1928–32 enabled a new allocation of GNP to be imposed on the economy. The discussions of the 1920s had assumed that savings would be made by the state within the framework of a dynamic equilibrium on the market between agriculture and industry. This placed a constraint on the proportion of GNP which could be invested, and on the allocation of that investment (investment in consumer goods industries would need to be sufficient to enable the output of consumer goods to increase at the rate required for equilibrium). Now this constraint was removed; urban and rural living standards could be temporarily depressed, and physical controls used to divert resources to the establishment of new capital-intensive industries and techniques which gave no return during the construction period and were relatively costly in the medium-term. This method of obtaining forced savings through physical controls resembled the wartime planning controls used in capitalist economies to shift resources towards the end product of the armament and maintenance of the large armed forces. In the Soviet case, the end product was the capital goods industries and the maintenance of the workers employed in building and operating them. But in both cases a shift in the allocation of resources which could not easily be achieved through manipulating the market mechanism was achieved through direct controls.

4. However, the system was not one simply of physical controls. Within a few years, the following features, stable over a long period, supplemented the system so far described:

a. Each peasant household was permitted to work a private plot and to own its own cow and poultry. After obligations to the state had been met, the separate households and the *kolkhoz* as a unit were permitted to sell their produce on the free market ("collective farm market"), on which prices were reached by supply and demand. Here an important part of all marketed foodstuffs was bought and sold.

b. With some important exceptions, the employee was free to change his job. A market for labor existed, if a very imperfect one, and wage levels were formed partly in response to supply and demand. A corollary of this was that cost controls and profit-and-loss accounting were introduced in industry to supplement the physical controls.

c. Rationing of consumer goods was abolished, and an attempt was made to balance supply and demand on the consumer market, as a whole and for individual goods, through fiscal measures, notably a purchase tax (the "turnover tax") differentiated according to commodity.

5. A large variety of unplanned and even illegal activities between firms supplemented and made feasible the rather crude controls of the central plan and must be considered as part of the logic of the system.

The Planning Process

We have so far established that Soviet plan controls may be divided schematically as in Figure 1. Each enterprise receives a set of output

FIGURE 1
Principal Planning Controls Over Industrial Activity

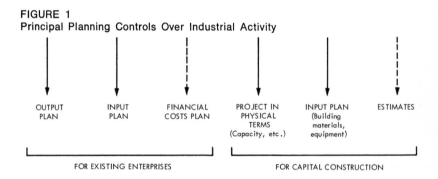

targets and input allocations with which to fulfill them; at the same time its monetary expenditures are controlled by financial or cost plans, which are less important to it than its output plan, but which come into operation if the pressure from above for higher output leads the enterprise to increase its money expenditures excessively.

Disaggregation. A key problem for the central planners is to disaggregate their major decisions so that they will be enforced at the plant level and to aggregate information and proposals so as to be able satisfactorily to take into account the effect of their past and present decisions on different parts of the economy. In Soviet planning, this has normally been dealt with in the following ways:

1. Economic organization is adapted to handle this problem.

a. Factories are placed under the control of ministries or subministries, each of which is responsible for a particular group of products (e.g., iron and steel, motor vehicles). Each ministry is given very considerable control over its enterprises. The government is therefore to a considerable extent concerned only with handling transfers *between* industries.

b.   Smaller factories producing low priority items are placed under the control of the government of one of the constituent republics, or under local authorities. In the past, the government tended not to bother with them, and to treat allocations to them as a residual.

c.   Within the State Planning Committee (Gosplan), which is an advisory body to the government, and within each ministry or subministry, departmental organization mirrors the planning arrangements. In the iron and steel industry, for example, there are separate departments of the ministry responsible for sales of the industry's product, for supplies to the industry, for production plans of iron and steel works, and for capital construction. Within Gosplan, there are separate departments concerned with production, allocation, and construction. This is illustrated schematically in Figure 2.

FIGURE 2
Central Economic Administration

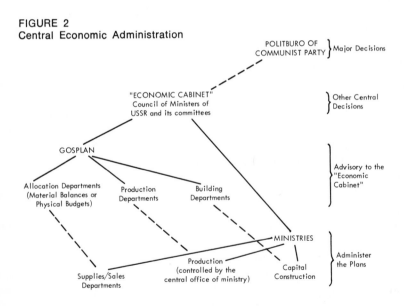

2.   The time-horizon is divided so as to disaggregate. Five-year plans set broad rates of growth for GNP by sector of origin and end use, state output targets for important intermediate and final products, and list the location and intended capacity of all major construction projects. Annual plans (known as "operative" plans) handle the detailed application of these longer term plans in a particular year; quarterly and even monthly partial plans handle particular industries or aspects of planning.

3.   Planning procedures are designed so as to enable more or less systematic aggregation and disaggregation. We give the procedure for the annual plan as an example:

FIGURE 3
Procedure for Annual Planning

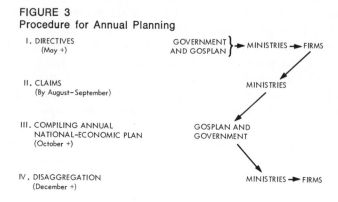

Stage I. Gosplan possesses a mass of data on past performance, and it or the government issues a statement about the principal economic magnitudes to be aimed at for the following year. These directives indicate the main proportions and principal production targets, the proposed investment allocation for each ministry, and proposals for the growth of output per man-year ("labor productivity," in Soviet terminology) and the reduction of costs.

Stage II. Ministries have already prepared a skeleton production program and set of claims for materials and equipment; this is now adjusted in the light of the directives and of information received from the firms. The forms on which claims are submitted are approved by Gosplan: The products itemized generally correspond to the nomenclature of the national production and supply plans, which have included up to 5,000 product groups. There are usually substantial differences between the ministries' output proposals and supply claims and the original directives.

Stage III. Gosplan now has the job of fitting together the ministry plans and its own draft plans: We enter the "period of coordination and reconciliation," in which the heads of firms and ministries negotiate with the government in Moscow. From this there emerges the national economic plan, with its constituent production, supplies (allocation), and investment plans. This whole negotiation is conducted in terms of, say, 30 times as many major indicators as were set out in the original directives.

Stage IV. The ministries now disaggregate the national economic plan to firm level.

4.   These aggregation and disaggregation procedures are assisted by two important sets of what might be termed "control coefficients":

a. Output targets (or success indicators). The fulfillment of these has been the main driving motive of the Soviet firm and even ministry (managerial promotions and salaries tended to be related to success in fulfillment of output targets). Output targets were given for very broad groups of products at the national level, and they were supplemented by the sales departments of each ministry, whose disaggregation of the planned output target for a product group is supposed in theory to be binding on the firm. We return to the difficulties involved here later.

b. Norms or consumption standards. At the shop-floor level, hundreds of thousands of specific consumption standards are used to control the production process and to cut down waste. But at the plant level, discussion already proceeds on the basis of aggregated standards; a further aggregation takes place between plant and ministry. Gosplan uses overall input coefficients to check the claims of ministries, and many of these are incorporated in the plan. These may be of the form

> x physical units of input of A for y physical units of output of B; e.g., tons of crude steel per ton of rolled steel.

or

> x physical units of input of A for y value-units of output of B; e.g., tons of cement per 1 million rubles' building and assembly work.

Different consumption standards will be applied to different processes and even to different plants; these are probably quite reliable as a rough measure of efficiency and of reliability of claims, and a useful device for handling complex production activities centrally.

Coordination. The outline so far given of the planning process is unrealistic, for it assumes much smoother control than is possible in practice. Smooth planning has been vitiated by:

1. Uncertainty. Innovations, mistakes, and bottlenecks were not predicted with any accuracy; future proportions of coal and oil output, for example, were quite wrongly predicted even after World War II.

2. "Tight" planning. The plan was used as an instrument for forcing up production, and all targets were deliberately strained, all stocks minimized. This reinforced uncertainty and encouraged the emergence of unexpected bottlenecks. (In the early 1930s annual as well as five-year plan targets were sometime wildly exaggerated.)

Moreover, we have so far been writing as if planning started from a clean sheet with each planning period. In fact, of course, planners work *at the margin*. Of a steel output of 12 million tons, as much as 10 million tons in an annual plan may be irrevocably committed to existing activities. Even in a five-year plan, possible shifts may be small: during the second five-year plan, for example, most capital investment was devoted to completing projects already started during the first plan or earlier.

The "coordination and reconciliation" activities undertaken by Gosplan in drawing up the annual plan are therefore limited by uncertainty, by the consequences of tight planning, and by existing commitments. Gosplan has two functions here. First, it seeks to balance programs by eliminating existing or potential bottlenecks due to the excess of demand over supply. To do this it follows a regular procedure and uses a list of priorities. Thus it may cut cement supplies to housing in order to have enough to push through a crash program to complete a steel foundry needed to produce certain types of steel required by priority industries. Second, it tries to inject into departmental programs the priorities and investment programs favored by the government. Thus it may increase cement supplies to the constructors of new chemical factories which are regarded as urgent.

In the coordination procedure, a great deal of use has been made by Gosplan of "material balances" or physical budgets, showing supplies and requirements for different product groups or types of equipment. These physical budgets were adjusted by the appropriate Gosplan through a fairly crude procedure of rule-of-thumb iteration. These were not input-output tables, for no technical coefficients had been calculated; sometimes a rough allowance was made for indirect outlays (e.g., of steel needed to make more machinery for motorcar factories if the output of motorcars was increased, as well as direct outlays of steel on the motorcars themselves). The procedure was therefore slow and inexact. At present, input-output tables and the traditional "material balances" are used side by side.

Financial Planning

1. Our account so far has been primarily concerned with physical planning. But as we have seen, a money flow corresponded to all the physical flows, and some of the money transactions in the system (e.g., wage payments, sales on the collective-farm market, sales on the retail market generally) were not accompanied by physical controls. Once the inflationary process had led to the initial reallocation of GNP in 1928–30, financial equilibrium was a subsidiary goal of the government. What was required was that money payments to the population (wage payments by the state, payments by the state to *kolkhozy* which were then distributed to their members, etc.) should not exceed the value of the supply of commodities available on the state-controlled market at fixed prices and on the collective-farm market at market prices. As outpayments by the state included the earnings of persons employed in the investment goods industries, in the social services, and in the armed forces, a gap existed between the cost-price of consumer goods (equal

to the cost of wages in that sector and the materials, etc., it employed) and the total monetary demand.

This gap needed to be covered by taxation, and could be met in principle in one or all of three ways: (*a*) by direct taxation, (*b*) by allowing the profits of enterprises to rise and then taxing them, or (*c*) by an indirect tax: this could be an equiproportional markup on all goods, or imposed only on consumer goods.

a. Direct taxation has been of minor importance: there are no incomes uncontrolled by the state available to tax, and high income tax on state employees is regarded as undesirable.

b. Profits tax has been of some importance, but in the early stages the authorities feared that the monetary pressure on the retail market would lead to very high profits in the consumer goods industries (this pressure was not held back after 1935 by the rationing procedures which still operated in the case of producer goods).

c. The misnamed "turnover tax" therefore became the main source of tax: it is a markup on the wholesale price of consumer goods and the low delivery price of foodstuffs. The markup is differentiated by product for social reasons and to bring about a rough equality between the supply and the demand for each product. It was argued that a high level of tax on producer goods, which were mainly sold to the state, would only require the state to reimburse itself from a still higher tax rate on consumer goods.

Figure 4 (on p. 26) illustrates the principal money flows in the system.

2. Prices in the producer and the consumer goods industries therefore had a common base; they were reached as follows:

a. costs of production, including wages, the cost of materials, overheads, a small allowance for depreciation, but no interest charge on capital;

b. a small markup for profits;

c. trade and transport costs.

To these was added in the case of consumer goods

d. turnover tax (differentiated by product) to reach the retail price.

Profits are partly taxed, partly retained by the firm or industry; a high proportion of profits in excess of the plan is placed at the disposal of the firm in the "Director's Fund" (now the "Enterprise Fund").

It will be noted that the prices of producer goods are unresponsive to supply and demand, and could remain stable for many years. Each industry receives a price for its product equal to average costs for the industry plus a small margin for profit; but the industry itself can

FIGURE 4
Soviet Financial Planning: A Simplified Picture (not to scale)

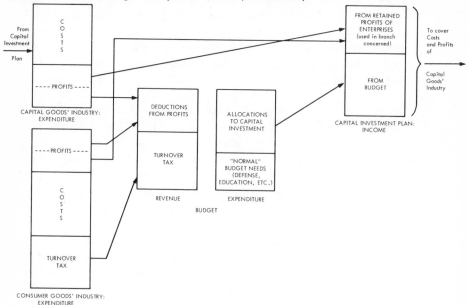

pay differential prices, offering high prices to high-cost firms and low prices to low-cost firms. However, prices include no systematic allowance for the varying richness of the capital stock of firms producing similar products. In practice, the rate of profit earned on different products varies enormously, owing to the hit-and-miss way in which prices were fixed.

3.   Elaborate arrangements are made to control the flows of (a) short-term loans (for seasonal stocks, goods in transit, etc.), (b) wages, (c) allocations to investment (mainly financed by the budget), and (d) cash through the State Bank (responsible for working capital) and specialized investment banks (responsible for allocations to fixed capital). All these devices aimed at maintaining the financial equilibrium, which was secured through balancing money incomes against money expenditures through the fiscal system. In the end, inflation was repressed over a short period before World War II (1935–37) and in a more systematic way after the war (1948–   ). Between 1948 and 1953, retail prices were even substantially reduced.

Labor and Labor Controls

1.   The following are the principal devices used by the government to control the urban labor force:

   a. Once unemployment had been absorbed (by about 1932), recruitment of labor from the villages to the towns was organized systematically on contract with the collective farms.

   b. Training and education of semiskilled, skilled, and technical manpower are systematically planned.

   c. At various stages (particularly in the war and postwar years from 1940 to 1951), scarce grades or types of manpower were restricted in their movement or even subject to allocation.

   2. In spite of these measures, labor was highly mobile, particularly in the early 1930s, and both central planners and factory managements utilize money wages to influence the allocation of labor—hence a form of labor maket emerged, though recent studies of Soviet production functions have confirmed that it was highly imperfect:

   a. The government approves national scales for different grades and types of labor in different areas, and adjusts these from time to time to take account of demand and supply; there is a high differential for skill.

   b. There is an elaborate piece-rate and bonus system to encourage higher productivity.

   c. Management can in practice manipulate bonuses and classifications to attract scarce kinds of labor.

   3. Unskilled and even semiskilled labor are not basically a scarce factor of production (owing to the existence of a large stock of labor in the countryside). There has therefore been a recurrent tendency to substitute labor for capital.

   4. The need for labor coupled with the pressure to fulfill the output plan encouraged management to overspend its allocation for wages and made for an inflationary situation. Control by the State Bank over wage payments is the most important single element in maintaining wage stability.

   5. Government control over trade unions has greatly assisted wage policy. The central wage bargaining process was very tenuous from 1929 onward. At the same time, a policy of cutting the rate for the job as techniques and organization improved was systematically enforced, so that money wages rose *less* rapidly than output per man.

   6. But the government, as well as firmly controlling wage rates, also took responsibility for social conditions. Hours of work were restricted to seven to eight hours daily. Pensions, sickness and maternity benefits, holidays with pay, and welfare services (crèches, factory clubs, canteens), largely administered through the trade unions, were more generous than was the case in many Western countries at a similar stage of industrialization. These social benefits (particularly housing tied to the factory) were used to influence the movement of labor (high

priority factories tended to have better facilities and housing; benefits were partly dependent on length of service at the particular factory).

Strengths and Weaknesses of the Soviet Planning System

No adequate "cost-benefit analysis" of the Soviet system or its constituent parts has yet been attempted. Here we simply list some of its principal achievements and failures:

Advantages.   1.   The system succeeded in enforcing allocation of a very high proportion of GNP to investment over a long period; within this allocation resources were concentrated on the growth-inducing producer goods industries, which were transformed from high-cost to low-cost industries. In general, it is possible with this kind of mechanism to enforce successfully high priority crash programs (e.g., the sputniks).

2.   A high degree of centralization enabled the planners to inculcate the latest technology, imported from more advanced economies, into the whole economy at a rapid rate: project institutes, such as *Gipromez* (the State Institute for Projects of Iron and Steel Works), were able to plan large-scale technological advance for a whole industry on a national scale. For many major technological problems, the Soviet system of centralized research also carries great advantages at a more advanced stage of development (e.g., nuclear research).

3.   Considerable economies of scale (including economies from standardization) and economies of effort are possible in nationally planned industries.

4.   The output drive from above, characteristic of Soviet planning until recently, provides a powerful instrument for enforcing high capacity utilization, and for keeping management and men working at a high pace.

Disadvantages.   1.   The cost of concentrating resources on producer goods industries was very high. Thus the policy adopted towards the peasantry led to a drastic decline in peasant holdings of working livestock and forced the state in fact to reallocate unexpected resources to the agricultural equipment industry and hence to the high-grade steel industry. It also had a drastic long-term effect on peasant morale.

2.   When the central planners make a *wrong* technological choice, the cost (because the policy is carried out on a national scale) is proportionately heavy; for example, there has been overinvestment in the coal industry and underinvestment in oil and chemicals.

3.   When controls are highly centralized, initiative and innovation at the plant level are cramped. But decentralization of a system of administrative planning is difficult. If the success indicators are not very detailed, managements will produce what it is easier to produce rather than what is wanted. Control of quality through success indicators is very difficult. The sellers' market which was coupled with Soviet adminis-

trative planning reinforced these difficulties. At the same time it led to the tendency for each industrial ministry to become a self-contained "empire," carrying out wasteful backward integration in order to control its supplies. If advertising and inflated sales organizations are a high cost of modern capitalism, inflated supplies organizations were (and are) a high cost of Soviet central planning.

To sum up with an example: Central planning enabled the emergence of steel foundries and rolling mills, using home-manufactured equipment, which are technologically as good as those in the United States and are worked at a much higher capacity. It also produced a situation where Soviet bedsteads were the heaviest in the world (because planned in tons), were produced on too small a scale (because made under several ministries) and therefore costly, and owing to the sellers' market could be made of iron, when the consumer would have preferred something more modern.

This is a mere list of factors. Economists need to ask themselves: *how* costly and beneficial were these various factors? How far were the advantages and disadvantages of the system inextricably tied together? Could the Soviet strategy for rapid growth, or some features of it, be employed without the disadvantages? How many of the unsuccessful features were due to the special conditions of Russia (including the difficult external and internal position of the government) and to the inexperience and imperfect knowledge of the people who made the system?

PLANNING A MATURE ECONOMY IN THE USSR

Economic Theory and the Soviet Economy

1. Traditional economic theory contrasts two types of system: the competitive or market system, with its "ideal type" of perfect competition, and "command economy," or "planning under a dictator." These are treated as two possible alternative methods of allocating resources.

  a. The *market economy* is divided into competing units: a large number of individual consumers bargain with a large number of producers on the market. The goal of the producer is to maximize his profit; the goal of the consumer is to maximize his satisfaction. The resulting demand and supply are equated through price.

  The decisions on the consumer market are reflected back into the factor market, where a similar bargaining process settles the distribution of incomes between factors and the distribution of the factors.

  As a result, resources in such an economy are allocated "rationally," by which the economist means "in accordance with the desires of the consumers."

    b. In the *command economy* (often referred to as *"planning under a dictator"*), final demand is determined not by individual consumers but by the decision of the central authority, as "dictator's preferences" or "planners' preferences" replace "consumers' preferences." The central authority also controls the allocation of all factors of production and the distribution of income. The system is completely centralized: its difficulty lies in the ability of the "dictator" to work out the "thousands of equations" involved in transforming his preferences into practical economic decisions.

2. How far does this theory provide an effective framework of analysis for contemporary capitalism and for Soviet planning?

    a. The development of economic analysis in the past forty years has involved a number of realistic modifications of the original theory as applied to modern capitalism:

        i. In many cases free entry into industries will be restricted and a state of imperfect competition will exist; at equilibrium, output may be lower and price higher than under perfect competition. However, economies of scale may make for lower costs in a highly organized oligopolistic industry: advantage and disadvantage must be carefully examined.

        ii. While consumer *choice* exists, advertising, imperfect knowledge, and the power of initiative of the large firm mean that consumer *sovereignty* is quite restricted.

        iii. The assumption of permanent equilibrium in the system is a microeconomic one. At the level of macroeconomics, supply does not create its own demand and hence the possibility of underemployment of factors exists. Macroeconomic equilibrium requires government intervention.

        iv. The large government sector requires separate analysis. Nationalized industries produce as monopolies, but often with their "maximum profit" goal constrained; and as consumers they control a large part of the market for certain intermediate goods (e.g., an electricity board purchasing power-station equipment). The defense, education, and health departments of central and local governments are also large buyers and often act as oligopsonies. State fiscal and monetary and tariff policy regulates the market.

        v. The view that a firm's economic behavior can be understood solely in terms of aiming at maximum profit in response to market price is an insufficient one. Within the large firm, decisions will be taken administratively (through the hierarchy) or by a cooperative or bargaining process; and much interfirm behavior may also be explained in this way. Industry is not an infinite number of atoms responding to price, but a finite number of blocs: The bloc as a whole reacts to price, but also has dealings with other blocs which are to be explained in terms of organization theory rather than of the price mechanism; and bargaining and administrative processes help to explain economic behavior within each bloc.

However, even with these modifications the original theory retains much validity:

    i. If firms do not always aim at maximizing their profits, they are concerned with making a satisfactory level of profits ("satisficing").

    ii. There is consumer choice, and a market process also operates for intermediate goods and (partly) on the factor market.

    iii. In spite of the considerable role of the government, a large segment of investment is still determined by the decisions of individual entrepreneurs (or entrepreneurial firms).

b. These developments of Western economic theory are of direct relevance to our understanding of the Soviet system:

    i. Physical planning is not something unknown in capitalist economies. In the Soviet economy, relationships between firms are regulated by administrative and bargaining processes; in a competitive system they are largely regulated by the market. But analogies to all the administrative and bargaining processes described in the section on "the planning process" above may be found within the capitalist firm, and within the government sector (compare the process for making fiscal estimates in a market economy with the procedures for plan compilation in Soviet industry). The "thousands of equations" of Western economic theory are simplified by the existence of "administrative decentralization": subsystems of economic administrators share decision making with the Council of Ministers; and bargaining and pressure from lower units assist the decision-making process. Moreover, like decisions by private entrepreneurs, planners' decisions are made only "at the margin."

    ii. Some important economic activity in the USSR is to be explained in terms of a market mechanism, though most Soviet markets are highly imperfect. As we have seen, there is a partial market for labor, a fixed-price market for retail consumer goods, a free market for part of retail food sales; and various unofficial or illegal markets operate in practice.

Modern capitalist economies are imperfectly competitive and have important elements of administrative control; the Soviet economy is not entirely "planned from the center," and imperfect markets exist for certain purposes.

The Soviet Economy as a Special Case of Planned Economy

The Soviet planning system of the 1930s–1950s is not the only possible form of planned economy. In Soviet experience alone, at least two other forms of planning system have existed. In the period of *War Communism* (1918–20), industry was nationalized and industrial output was allocated physically. Owing to inflation the economy was virtually moneyless; labor was directly controlled, consumer goods were rationed and agricultural output subject to requisition. However, peasants continued to work their own land and no serious attempt was made to socialize agriculture. This system was the closest approach in principle to the "ideal form" of the command economy in the history of the Soviet system. In the period of the *New Economic Policy* (1921–29), as in present-day Poland, state ownership of industry was combined with private agriculture through a regulated market. The effectiveness of planning was constrained by the existence of the market, but central goals were to some extent enforced.

A considerable variety of forms of central planning is to be found in Eastern Europe.

The systematic study of forms of economic organization has so far been little developed. One may distinguish two basic ways of classification.

Ownership.   A planned economy is unlikely to be one in which all economic activity is nationalized. It will be a "mixed economy," combining private ownership with state ownership and possibly embracing different forms of state ownership (very varied forms of public ownership have been experienced, incorporating different degrees of state, consumer, and workers' control). In this spectrum, the Soviet economy lies considerably toward the "state" end, particularly as far as industry is concerned. Nearly all industrial activity is nationalized, and since 1918 forms of syndicalism or "guild socialism" have been firmly rejected in favor of "one-man management" by administrators appointed by the state and . liable to instant dismissal. The argument for this has always been in terms of economic efficiency and of the need to enforce a central state policy.

Allocation of Resources.   Various forms of "market socialism" are in principle conceivable, and have been much discussed among economists (especially in Poland and Yugoslavia). To what extent can a scale of preferences (of planners or individual consumers or a combination of both) be put into effect through a market, on which state firms aim to maximize their profits in simulation of private enterprises? In a variation of this, suggested by Kornai and others, the state would use its regulatory powers only to counter inefficient decisions due to the existence of state monopolies. Prices in "market socialism" might be formed freely, or might be fixed by the planners, but would, of course, need to reflect the chosen preference-scale more or less exactly, as they would indicate to the producer what he should produce, and how he should allocate resources (including investment). In its extreme form, the economic behavior of "market socialism" ought not to differ from that of a private market economy.

The alternative approach is the one followed by the Soviet government: to allocate resources by direct physical controls, and to allow some degree of decentralization in decision making to other controllers at industry, region, or plant level.

Planning systems might be classified (*a*) by the relative strengths in them of the "market principle" and the "physical planning principle," (*b*) by the degree to which, within the market sector, the government regulates the market (imposes its preferences), and (*c*) by the degree to which decision making is decentralized within the physical planning sector.

We have not made any allowance for the *effectiveness* of controls. Should not the degree of planning be measured not only by the all-embracingness of the planners' goals and the detailedness of their controls but also by the extent to which the planners succeed in fulfilling their goals in the actual allocation of resources? For instance, War Communism was in principle a highly centralized system. But in practice central decisions were usually ineffective; illegal barter and local quasi markets tended to dominate economic life: what was the "real" economic system? Again, where was there more planning—in industry under War Communism, where detailed orders were not enforced, or in agriculture under the New Economic Policy, where indirect controls succeeded to some extent in moving agriculture in the direction desired by the central government? Further, good planners of course incorporate their knowledge of their objective possibilities into their goals: but is a planner whose goals are very limited, but successfully achieved, as "effective" as, say, the Soviet planners in 1929–31, who set quite impossible goals but did succeed in reallocating resources very drastically in the desired direction?

Planning a More Mature Economy

The basic allocation decisions and the planning process in the USSR in 1928–53 probably had stronger "functional" elements than "dysfunctional" elements in the stage of moving the Soviet economy from a semiagrarian economy to an industrialized economy. But as the economy matured, the "dysfunctional" elements certainly became more prominent. The changed context may be summarized as follows:

1. Industrial output per head is now above the British level and moving towards the U.S. level for some important producer goods. The economy is vastly more complex than it was in the 1930s.

2. The Industrial Revolution has been accompanied by major social changes:

   a. In 1928, two thirds of the population were illiterate; now, nearly everyone can read and write.

   b. In 1928, some 3 million persons were employed in industrial labor; it is now (1965) over 25 millions.

   c. In 1928, some 5 percent of the state-employed labor force (i.e., excluding peasants and collective farmers) had received professional or semiprofessional education; the figure now (1965) is about 15 percent.

3. The technological situation is different: as the economy becomes more mature, the amount of technological borrowing it can do tends to decline, and the amount of innovation required increases. This is reinforced by the long-term trend for labor to become a more scarce factor of production: the economy must increasingly come to rely on higher labor productivity and hence on more capital-intensive production (and/or on technical progress) rather than on increasing the industrial labor force.

In this new situation, changes in both allocation and organization are required. It is not easy to demonstrate that industrial efficiency is hampered by a relatively low standard of living (the Soviet average real wage is probably about a quarter that of the United States, but labor productivity may be over half the U.S. level). But in any case political and social pressures have dictated a shift in resources towards consumption. Such a shift requires a much greater output of food; and in agriculture it is very probable that the low return to the peasant for the output of the collective farm has held down productivity. And certainly as the economy has grown, the highly centralized planning structure has become less efficient and less workable.

Here we summarize the principal changes so far made in both respects since 1953.

Allocation of Resources. 1. There has been a relative and absolute increase in the resources devoted to consumer goods (manufactures, manufactured foodstuffs). In the 1930s and in 1946–50, the output of producer goods increased much more rapidly than that of consumer goods; the gap is now much narrower.

2. A much higher proportion of total investment has been allocated to urban housing construction.

3. In 1953–58, the prices paid by the state for agricultural products were very substantially increased; according to official figures, the money incomes of collective farms rose from 5 billion new rubles to 13.2 billion new rubles between 1953 and 1958. At the same time, the total annual

investment in agriculture (state plus collective farm) increased from 2.1 to 5.1 billion new rubles. This double shift was accompanied by a rapid rise in agricultural output—by some 50 percent, according to official figures (i.e., a greater increase than in 1928 to 1953).

Between 1958 and 1965 agriculture tended to stagnate (even ignoring the bad harvest of 1963). Recent studies have shown that this stagnation has occurred simultaneously with a falling-off in peasant incomes and in the rate of growth of investment in agriculture. It seems likely that agricultural difficulties are at least in part due to the failure of the state to allocate a share of GNP to agriculture adequate enough to enable the goals of the planners to be achieved (organizational weaknesses may also have played a part).

4. There has been a significant shift in the distribution of income. The incomes of peasants tended (until 1958) to increase more rapidly than those of the urban population. Within the urban population, there has been a process of leveling up: the minimum wage has been increased, wage differentials have been narrowed, social benefits such as pensions have been substantially increased.

5. Nevertheless, the priorities have not been reversed. It seems certain, however the measurement is done, that a higher proportion of GNP is allocated to net investment than in the U.S., and that a higher proportion of this investment is allocated to the producer goods industries. As a result, the rate of industrial growth has remained high (7–9 percent a year), though less high than a decade ago.

Organization.   Attempts to improve the working of Soviet planning have followed two main lines simultaneously: (1) improvements in central planning; (2) attempts to decentralize.

1. Improvements in central planning. Central decision making has undoubtedly tended to be more consistently thought out, and to become more logical and consistent.

Long-term technological decisions have been reconsidered, and a bold policy of technical change has been embarked upon. Thus oil has been given preference to coal, and the transfer of the railways to the diesel has been undertaken; this reverses previous policy. The development and manufacture of prefabricated reinforced concrete components and other building materials have been given preference over traditional materials like brick and timber. Plastics are being developed in preference to steel and other metals.

In the discussions about all these changes, most of which had previously been undertaken in capitalist economies in response to market criteria, there has been a great deal of emphasis on economic arguments. The question of the appropriate criteria to use in making investment choices has been predominant here. Thinking has moved in the direction of adopting a single rate of return for the whole economy (the rate

of return is, of course, the inverse of the so-called "recoupment period"):
the standard formula now used is

$$\frac{I_1 - I_2}{C_2 - C_1} \leq R.P.$$

where I_1 and I_2 are the investment alternatives being compared and
C_1 and C_2 are the costs of production in the two alternatives, and $R.P.$
is the maximum permissible period in which the investment may be
recouped. (This has tended to vary by industry, from 4–5 years in light
industry, i.e., a rate of return of 20–25 percent, to 16–17 years in electric
power, i.e., a rate of return of about 6 percent.)

The adoption of a standard rate for all industries would require the
use of something like a cost-benefit analysis if the social welfare problem is to be taken into account; Soviet thought is moving cautiously
in this direction.*

A stumbling block to consistent macroeconomic decision making is
the inconsistency of the prices in which goods are valued. Investment
decisions, and indeed all multiproduct decisions, have to be discussed
not in physical terms but in value terms. As we have seen, Soviet prices
are an inadequate indicator of real costs; they do not include a capital
charge (so capital-intensive production is relatively undervalued), they
do not vary with the scarcity or abundance of the goods, the rent element
for use of natural resources is inconsistent, and the price incorporates
a profit markup which is more or less arbitrary. Rule-of-thumb adjustments are made by the central planners, but decisions are clumsy and
often inaccurate.

A second line of approach to the improvement of central planning
has been the attempt to improve knowledge at the center by use of
mathematical methods. Technical coefficients have been worked out so
that the consequences of alternative production policies may be taken
into account more systematically; national and some regional input-output tables have been constructed (among the largest is the 438-sector
matrix for planning purposes of 1964–65). The central planning of supplies and requirements seems still to be carried out by rule-of-thumb
methods, but these are now supplemented by improved information. At
the same time various methods of mathematical programming, such as
the transportation algorithm, have been used to improve traffic flows
(e.g., truck transport in Moscow, scheduling of Baltic steamers, timber
and coal hauls), bringing savings of about 10 percent in costs for each
problem.

2. Attempts at decentralization. Three major attempts have been
made since 1953 to devolve some of the decision-making powers of the
central authorities. But these attempts have been conducted within the

---

* Editors' note: Recent changes in investment criteria are discussed below in
Selections 15-A and 15-B.

framework of the physical planning system, rather than representing an increase in the market sector of the economy.

a. 1954–56: "step-by-step" decentralization. The Gosplan-Council of Ministers central organization attempted to shed some of its powers by reducing the number of indicators in the national output, supply and capital investment plans; thus product groups, for which output targets were laid down, were made more aggregative. The intention was that each ministry, possessing more flexibility itself, would devolve some of its authority to its departments, which in turn would increase the decision-making powers of economic units.

The reform was on the whole unsuccessful. Ministries failed to pass down their powers to the factory; instead, they tended to use their increased authority to bind their own "empires" more closely together. At the same time, the reduction in the number of central output targets (success indicators) revealed clearly a dilemma inherent in administrative planning. The enterprise is required to maximize its output in terms of the output targets. If the targets are broad or loose, it will try to follow the "easiest" course within the target. If the target is merely for "tons of nails shorter than 2 inches" the factory will try to produce all $1\frac{9}{10}''$ nails, because this is easiest. If it is for "numbers of nails," the factory will try to produce all $\frac{1}{2}''$ nails. But if the plan is set in terms of $\frac{1}{2}''$, $1''$, $1\frac{1}{2}''$ and $1\frac{9}{10}''$ nails, there will be overcentralization. If the target is set in terms of gross value of output, the factory will maximize its use of materials and semifabs and minimize the net value it adds to each product (this has been dealt with by using a new indicator of "standard cost of work done to the product," but this has involved further—if smaller—difficulties).

b. 1957–65: regionalization. In 1957, industry was "regionalized": the industrial ministries were abolished, 104 regions were set up and all factories in each region were put under the regional economic committee. However, much of the central machinery was retained, particularly the sales organizations which control product mix, and gradually committees for each industry were reestablished, with research organizations attached. What emerged was a mixture of area-by-area and industry-by-industry control. This probably gave the factory manager greater effective power, if only because he no longer had one unambiguous boss; it also led to the breakup of the ministerial "empires" and a more effective consideration of regional factors in central decision making. But it also made economic administration very much more complicated.

c. September, 1965–   : more authority to the factory. The reforms introduced by Kosygin contained two main elements. First of all, they abandoned the attempt at regional organization and returned to control by industrial ministries. More important, they made the first serious attempt to increase greatly the powers of the factory management. The most important measures are the following.

i. The importance of profits as a success indicator is intended to be greatly increased. Profits retained by factories are to be large and will be related to planned profit (if achieved) rather than actual profit so as to discourage firms from trying to keep their plan low. Bonuses to management and workers will be paid from and related to the amount of profit.

ii. Various measures are to be adopted to encourage the efficient use of capital investment.

iii. The powers of the factory management to determine the way in which it spends the total allocation for wages are greatly increased; the manager may divide up the total allocations as he wishes between classes of employee—he may, for instance, reduce the total number of persons employed in order to increase the portion of highly paid workers.*

iv. The main global indicator of output is to be "actually marketed production" rather than "gross production"; it is hoped that this will force factories to produce goods for which there is a high demand.

However, the main physical indicators are retained, including both the plan of supplies in physical terms and the itemization of production items in physical terms in the national-economic plan; Kosygin merely expressed the hope that the degree of detail would be gradually reduced. The success of the reforms in moving away from administrative planning will depend on the extent to which a linear relationship can be established between the preferences of the planners and the profits earned by the factory; if such a linear relationship exists, and the factory aims at maximizing its profit, then the desired pattern of production will be achieved without administrative orders.

But the achievement of such a "linear relationship" requires a radical reform of the price system. The main suggestions for reform have been: make turnover tax into an equiproportional markup on the wholesale price (or value added) of all products; give higher profits for scarce products and negative profits for surplus products; include an interest charge on capital stock. But so far only the last of these proposals appears to be likely to be achieved in the near future.† The prices which the planners are to establish have not been worked out in detail, and even the method by which they could be reached is unclear. Kosygin

---

* Editors' note: For recent changes curtailing enterprise powers, see Selection 25 below.

† Editors' note: Such a change was introduced in 1967.

has announced an impending price reform, but it seems unlikely to be a radical one.

Three things seem to block a major price reform: (1) fear that an increase in market forces, or the use of profit as a "universal regulator" in a socialist economy, may diminish the control of the center over the allocation of resources; it is for this reason that proposals permitting a kind of "market socialism" to develop have been firmly rejected; (2) a feeling that profit will not be so powerful an incentive to managers to increase output as output targets in physical terms have been; and (3) inability (as yet) to arrive at the actual prices required.

The weakness of the reforms of the planning system we have so far discussed is, then, that they do not tackle the problem of *valuation* systematically or integrally. The reforms are essentially *ad hoc.* Thus all the proposals for improving the allocation of investment incorporate a required rate of return which is arrived at more or less empirically or even arbitrarily: The choice between investments is not consistently interwoven with long-term production planning. The result is likely to be that the approved pattern of planned investment is not entirely compatible with the approved production targets, so that adjustment by rule-of-thumb will still need to follow. Similarly even the most radical reforms proposed for short- and medium-term production and supply planning depend on the availability of a system of prices which systematically reflect the aims or preferences of the planners; prices must favor a production pattern which not merely widens present bottlenecks but also makes its contribution to the dynamic goals of the planners.

A far-reaching proposal such as Liberman's could worsen the operation of the system rather than assist it, if put into effect without an appropriate set of prices being available. This does not mean that the partial reforms which have been proposed or undertaken would not improve the operation of the present system. Waste and inconsistency have been reduced both by the use of better investment criteria and by the application of linear programming techniques to partial problems.

One general solution—much discussed and partly attempted in Poland and Yugoslavia—is for the required scale of prices to be reached by permitting state enterprises to compete on a market. The central planners would restrict themselves to controlling the general level of investment and to intervening in order to ensure that the market was as perfect as possible. The principal economic objection to this solution is that it would incorporate into the planned economy most of the disadvantages of modern capitalism, in a situation in which the imperfections of the market would be more considerable than in a privately owned economy.

Mathematical methods. An increasingly influential school of Soviet economists holds that with the application of mathematical methods and the use of the computer the major dilemmas of central planning can be solved. Computers make it possible to examine the properties of a very large number of economic variables: With the aid of appropriately designed mathematical models, economic processes can be simulated on the computer so that plan variants can be tested for feasibility and consistency. The core of the method is that objective functions are set up which indicate what is to be maximized or minimized within a system of constraints. The functions yield a system of imputed values (efficiency prices or shadow prices), and these for the problem concerned are the consistent system of prices which, as we have seen, the nonmathematical proposals lacked.

Soviet mathematicians and mathematical economists believe that this technique can be applied to the planning of the entire economy. What is proposed is a "unified and automatized system of national economic planning and management" which would seek to optimize the achievement of goals set by the government. The economy would be divided for planning purposes into a number of blocs or subsystems (both by area and by sector); for each bloc an appropriate programming model would attempt to optimize subgoals consistent with and integrated with the overall national goals, which would in turn be incorporated in a macromodel for the economy as a whole. For each bloc, a set of shadow prices would emerge which would indicate its "best" economic behavior in the planning period. A measure of decentralization is inherent in the system: The elements in each subsystem would be free to move so as to optimize their subgoals within constraints obtained from the larger bloc of which the subsystem formed a part.

A requirement for the efficient working of the new system is the establishment of a consistent computerized system of information flows. All economic information (for instance, all inputs and outputs) will need to be classified by a unified system for the entire economy, so that data may be processed in forms suitable for feeding in to the planning models on which the system is to be based. A chain of computer stations is being established for assembling and processing economic information. (This is a long and arduous business; it is likely to take about 10 years.) *

For the efficient operation of the system, actual economic forms need to be adapted as far as possible to the solutions found on the computer (inflexibilities in institutions and arrangements constitute constraints on optimization). In particular, actual prices, it is hoped, will be made to correspond more closely to the shadow prices obtained from the computations. This does not mean that all prices would necessarily need to be fixed by the state; actual market arrangements in a subsystem could be made consistent with the larger economic models (in principle, a private and uncontrolled sector could be incorporated as a stochastic element in the overall system).

---

* Editors' note: Recent developments in the use of mathematical models and computers in planning are discussed below in Selections 4 and 24.

If prices thus correspond to the preferences stated in the models, they would be appropriate for Liberman's proposal that profit should indicate to an economic unit how it should behave. But in the light of Western studies of the behavior of the private firm, it seems likely that the Soviet firm cannot be expected to behave as though maximizing profits were its sole goal; as part of the restructuring of planning, an appropriate system of incentives would be needed to ensure that decisions are executed.

So far we have spoken simply of models which would optimize the achievement of government-fixed goals; we have evaded the problem of the preference functions which would convert those goals into meaningful quantities. At present, the goals of the Soviet government are stated in terms of a long series of targets for investment goods, intermediate goods, and final consumption goods. These targets, as we saw earlier, are reached both for five-year and for annual plans as the result of a long bargaining process and reflect both the need to overcome expected bottlenecks and the major investment projects and priorities which the government intends to encourage. To optimize the achievement of these targets (as is for example the aim in Hungary) is only to maximize the achievement of a network of decisions reached by a rule-of-thumb process. The alternative is to persuade the politicians to reformulate their goals in more general or more operational terms. A satisfactory outcome will obviously only be achieved as a result of a long and difficult dialogue between the politicians and the mathematically trained planners. One element in this dialogue must be a discussion on the extent to which the preference functions of the planning models should incorporate the preferences of the individual consumer. Some Soviet and East European economists would be prepared to go a very long way in the direction of consumer sovereignty; others have suggested that zones of state influence, individual influence, and mixed influence would need to be determined. One considerable weakness of present Soviet discussions is that they have paid little attention to techniques such as cost-benefit analysis which are needed in order to bring social and other noneconomic factors more consistently into the considerations of planners and politicians: the rationale of economic policy making has not been carefully considered, and hence goals may remain inconsistent or ill-defined.

Conclusion

Few of the techniques of planning we have now been considering were available to the Soviet economist during the period of intensive industrialization; those which were available were worked out only in elementary form. In any case, the gap between the goals of the politicians and the assumptions of the economists was so great that little dialogue was possible. The politicians, and the politically minded economists, undertook the elaboration of their own system of planning and their own rule-of-thumb methods of quantifying their goals to make them operational. In doing this, they acquired a rich fund of valuable experience about the problems of development through central planning; the lessons from this experience, both successful and unsuccessful, could save resources in other economies where central planning is being used for development. Unfortunately, it is information about formal mechanisms for planning and financial control which has until now tended to be communicated from the Eastern bloc to the developing countries, rather than a realistic account of problems and achievements. For the developing countries, the further question exists: now that the new techniques for planning are available, can they be coupled with planning for a high rate of growth in conditions of rapid social change? If so, some of the successes of Soviet-type central planning may be achieved at less cost.

3. PRESSURE AND PLANNING IN THE SOVIET ECONOMY

Herbert S. Levine

A distinctive feature of Soviet central planning is the "tautness" which results from the regime's pressure to set and strive for very ambitious targets which intentionally strain the ability of the economy to achieve them. In this selection, Levine argues that the pressure imposed on and built up within the economic system, rather than centralized planning as such, accounts for many of the observed characteristics of the Soviet economy. He explains the sources of pressure on enterprises and the effects, including distortion of managerial incentives, inadequate inventories, and a sellers' market. He concludes by evaluating the prospects for planning without pressure.

Herbert S. Levine is Professor of Economics at the University of Pennsylvania. The article is reprinted by permission from *Industrialization in Two Systems: Essays in Honor of Alexander Gerschenkron*, ed. Henry Rosovsky (New York: John Wiley & Sons, Inc., 1966), pp. 266–85, with the omission of some references to Russian-language sources. Copyright by the President and Fellows of Harvard College.

I. INTRODUCTION

THIS PAPER is about the Soviet experience with centralized planning and the significance of this experience for our general understanding of the functioning of economic systems. Building on a well-known Gerschenkronian hypothesis about Russian economic history, the paper argues that because Soviet centralized planning is so enmeshed with the exertion of pressure on the internal economy by the Russian State, it is difficult clearly to ascribe causes to observed effects. Therefore, the Soviet experience should be used with care by economists in discussions of the characteristics and consequences of centralized economic planning. The argument is to some extent modified toward the end of the paper owing to the possibility that there may exist a somewhat general joint-productness about pressure and centralized planning. But more about that in awhile.

Among the "hypotheses" of Professor Gerschenkron—those broad, insightful generalizations so cautiously wrung from masses of carefully collected empirical evidence—there is one describing a pattern of Russian economic development which is observable on a number of occasions in the course of Russian history.[1] The history of Russia, for the past five hundred years, is dominated by the theme of territorial expansion: from the small principality of Muscovy just emerging from Mongol rule, Russia grew to its present great size. During this process of expansion, the Russian State frequently came into contact and conflict with Western nations more advanced and more powerful than she. Such confrontations forced upon the leaders of Russia the painful realization that they would not be able to attain what they wanted to attain because of the extreme backwardness of the Russian economy. In such situations, Gerschenkron asserts, the Russian State would take on the role of initiator of economic development. The State would apply pressure to the internal economy to get it to grow rapidly and thus be able to support the foreign policy aims of the State in as short a period as possible. This relationship between military affairs and economic growth was the cause of the fitful nature of economic development observed in Russian economic history. When the military needs of the State were pressing, the economy was pressured into rapid growth. When a degree of power parity was reached, the need for further rapid growth subsided and the State removed its pressure for growth. Because so much growth was compressed into such short periods, the burden of sacrifice borne by the people living in Russia during those periods was great. To exact this sacrifice, extremely oppressive means and institutions were employed. The increase of pressure and the exaction of sacrifice were often so intense that they led to the exhaustion of the internal population; consequently, a period of rapid growth was very likely to be followed by a long period of little or no growth.

This was the pattern of Russian economic development described by Gerschenkron. It should be added that he was careful to point out that the pattern was intended as a framework for understanding the forces at work in Russian economic growth and was not meant to describe "some iron law of evolution" through which Russian development had to proceed:

> What is implied is that the actual development seems to conform to a certain pattern and that such conformities and uniformities as can be observed do help us understand the course of events . . . That the development followed a certain course does not preclude the possibility of alternative routes, but it does suggest that the forces which propelled the Russian economy along its actual course must have been strong indeed.[2]

---

[1] See Alexander Gerschenkron, *Economic Backwardness in Historical Perspective* (Cambridge, Mass.: Harvard University Press, 1962), pp. 17–18.

[2] Ibid., p. 157.

The pattern is most clearly and fully seen in the period of Peter the Great. It is also observable in the period of rapid growth of the 1890s, although this spurt of development is not followed by a long period of relative stagnation.[3] Finally, it is seen in the massive industrialization drive launched under the Soviets.

This last period is still in progress, and, whereas it remains to be seen whether future events will conform to the pattern, it is evident that the course of past events, since the end of the 1920s, does clearly conform.[4] The key role played in the pattern by the conflict between military needs and economic backwardness is graphically illustrated in a famous speech delivered by Stalin, at the beginning of the industrialization drive, in which he said:

> One feature of the history of old Russia was the continual beatings she suffered for falling behind, for her backwardness. She was beaten by the Mongol Khans . . . the Turkish beys . . . the Swedish feudal lords . . . the Polish and Lithuanian gentry . . . the British and French capitalists . . . the Japanese barons. All beat her . . . for her backwardness: for military backwardness, for cultural backwardness, for political backwardness, for industrial backwardness, for agricultural backwardness. . . . Do you want our socialist fatherland to be beaten and to lose its independence? If you do not want this you must put an end to its backwardness in the shortest possible time . . . We are fifty or a hundred years behind the advanced countries. We must make good this distance in ten years. Either we do it, or they crush us.[5]

In the Soviet industrialization drive, the State has been the initiator and controller of economic growth. To force the speed of this growth, it has applied pervasive pressure on the entire internal economy. Cruelly oppressive means have been used to exact severe sacrifice from the Russian people.

Soviet economic development and Soviet economic institutions can best be understood against the background of this pattern in Russian economic history. Stalin's use of collectivization is in many ways a functional analogue of Peter the Great's use of serfdom. Centralized planning is the means by which the State exerts its control over the economy and through which it transmits pressure for rapid growth.[6] To see Soviet

---

[3] For discussion, see Ibid., pp. 130–42.

[4] Ibid., pp. 147–51.

[5] J. Stalin, *Selected Writings* (New York: International Publishers, 1942), p. 200.

[6] This is not the place for a full discussion of the definition of the term *centralized planning*. Briefly speaking, what is meant is a system wherein the major economic decisions are made by central authorities and are communicated to the periphery by means of directives; the units at the periphery act in response to these directives, or "commands," rather than in response to parameters such as prices. See Janusz G., Zielinski, "Centralization and Decentralization in Decision Making," *Economics of Planning*, Vol. 3, No. 3 (December 1963), pp. 196–208, and Gregory Grossman, "Notes for a Theory of the Command Economy," *Soviet Studies*, Vol. XV, No. 2 (October 1963), pp. 101–23.

collectivization merely as a device to increase production is to miss its vital function in exaction of sacrifice from the peasantry. Further, to see Soviet centralized planning merely as a Marxian device to eradicate the disproportions resulting from the anarchy of market systems is to miss its role both in giving the political leaders control over the course of Soviet development and in giving them a means of forcing rapid structural change on the economy, in order to modernize it and so bring it up to parity with the West.

The Soviet economy in the Plan Era is often taken as *the* case study of centralized planning, and the operating characteristics of the Soviet economy (as described in the works of Berliner, Granick, Nove and others)[7] are often taken as *the* necessary consequences of centralized planning. It is the argument of this paper that such views of the economic significance of the Soviet experience with centralized planning ignore the background of the Soviet use of centralized planning. They ignore, specifically, the role played by pressure, that pressure exerted on the economy by the political leaders through the means of centralized planning. It will be argued that the observed operating characteristics of the Soviet economy can be said to be as much if not more a result of the pressure in the system than they are of the mechanism of centralized planning itself.

II. SOURCES OF PRESSURE

When the Russian economy, at the end of the 1920s, had reattained its pre-World War I levels, the Soviet leaders turned away from the loose policies of the NEP period and toward the highly centralized means of economic planning and control which have marked the Plan Era. Undoubtedly, centralized planning had certain political and ideological attractions for the Soviet leaders,[8] but it also had important economic attractions. Having made the decision to embark upon forced draft industrialization—to close the "fifty to one hundred year-gap" between Russia and the advanced nations of the West in ten years—the regime needed economic organization methods appropriate to the task. In a situation wherein the aim of the State is to make a rapid and massive structural change in the economy, when this aim is clearly the dominant aim and when the priorities, the things that have to be done to accom-

---

[7] Joseph S. Berliner, *Factory and Manager in the USSR* (Cambridge, Mass.: Harvard University Press, 1957); David Granick, *Management of the Industrial Firm in the USSR* (New York: Columbia University Press, 1954), and "An Organizational Model of Soviet Industrial Planning," *Journal of Political Economy*, Vol. LXVII, No. 2 (April 1959), pp. 109–30; and Alec Nove, *The Soviet Economy: An Introduction* (New York: Frederick A. Praeger, Inc., 1961), chap. 6 and *passim*.

[8] See Alexander Gerschenkron, *The Stability of Dictatorships* (Harvard Lecture, Yale University, April 3, 1963); and Abram Bergson, *The Economics of Soviet Planning* (New Haven, Conn.: Yale University Press, 1964), pp. 173–74.

plish the aim (the concentration on basic industrial commodities and machinery), are also clear, then direct centralized planning commends itself.[9] In such situations, indirect, decentralized methods of economic organization and control, relying on the price mechanism and marginalist calculations, can be said to work too slowly, moreover, not very effectively. When concentration is on new products, new industries, and new regional complexes, the constants needed to make close marginal decisions are themselves variables. Uncertainty runs rampant, and externalities, which cannot easily be internalized by individual decision makers, become of major importance.[10] Under such circumstances, centralized planning offers the state in some ways a more promising means of effectuating its control over the economy, for it is both a means of directly concentrating economic efforts on high priority sectors and diverting the impact of mistakes onto low priority sectors and a means of transmitting pressure and urgency to the economy.

The pressure transmitted by the Bolshevik regime to the Soviet economy was essentially of two different types. One was the pressure on the living standards of the Russian people, which was manifested in the rising rate of investment out of GNP, falling rate of consumption, and, for long parts of the Plan Era, falling levels of per capita consumption.[11] The second was the pressure exerted on the producing units in the economy to increase output. This pressure for more output per unit of input, this search for reserves of productivity was ubiquitous, and it was supported by a multitude of economic, social, and political incentives: the monetary rewards for surpassing production targets, the red banners for victory in interplant competitions, the political promotions (or demotions) for production successes (or failures). It imparted to all the producing units in the economy a constant and omnipresent condition of excess effective demand.

Although it is the first type of pressure, the pressure on the living standards of the people, which is of major interest to Gerschenkron in his pattern of Russian economic development, it is the second type of pressure, the pressure on the productive capacity of the basic enterprises, which is of major interest in this paper.

"Taut" Planning

The pressure on producing units was a result not only of the conscious policy on the part of the regime; it was also intensified, consciously

---

[9] Compare the United States' and United Kingdom's uses of centralized techniques during World War II.

[10] See Tibor Scitovsky, "Two Concepts of External Economies," *Journal of Political Economy,* Vol. LXII, No. 2 (April 1954), pp. 143–51.

[11] See Janet G. Chapman, "Consumption," in *Economic Trends in the Soviet Union,* ed. Abram Bergson and Simon Kuznets (Cambridge, Mass.: Harvard University Press, 1963), pp. 236–44.

and unconsciously, in the process of plan construction and implementation. A Soviet plan is not intended as a tool to achieve harmonious operation of the economy, but as a tool to mobilize resources for the attainment of a rapid rate of growth.

> State plans established for the enterprises must mobilize all workers, manual and professional, in the struggle for the plan, in the movement forward toward the conquering of difficulties and the attaining of new growth in the national economy.[12]

Therefore, at the very beginning as a matter of policy, the intention is to give the enterprise a "taut" plan.[13] There is to be little slack between the full productive capacity of the enterprise and the output demanded of it. In fact, the intention is to set the target somewhat beyond the "full capacity" so as to force the enterprise to seek out reserves of increased output.

In the process of plan construction—speaking now of the annual plan, and primarily of the industrial plan—the conscious policy of putting pressure on all producing units is embodied in the control figures, the preliminary aggregate targets constructed by the state planning committee (Gosplan)[14] after consultation with the political leaders, and communicated by Gosplan down through the planning-control hierarchy to the producing units.[15] The input norms used in the construction of the control figures are highly optimistic ones, in this way imparting a significant degree of tautness to the plan at its inception.[16] This pressure is undoubtedly relieved somewhat in the counterplanning and bargaining as the

---

[12] *Pravda*, March 1, 1947, p. 1.

[13] See Holland Hunter, "Optimal Tautness in Developmental Planning," *Economic Development and Cultural Change*, Vol. IX, No. 4 (July 1961), Part I, pp. 561–72.

[14] We will use the term *Gosplan* to refer to the central planning body responsible for the construction of the annual plan even though at various times a different organization had this responsibility.

[15] For a description of the process and chronology of plan construction, see Bergson, *The Economics of Soviet Planning;* Herbert S. Levine, "The Centralized Planning of Supply in Soviet Industry," in *Comparisons of the United States and Soviet Economies* (papers Submitted by Panelists Appearing Before the Subcommittee on Economic Statistics, Joint Economic Committee, 86th Cong., 1st sess.) (Washington, D.C.: U.S. Government Printing Office, 1959), Part I, pp. 151–76; and Herbert S. Levine, *A Study in Economic Planning* (unpublished Ph.D. thesis, Harvard University, 1961).

[16] In actuality, the conscious policy of pressure appears even earlier than the control figures in the chronology of plan construction. In the first stage, that of preparing the statistical base, done in the first part of the planning year, the planners have to project available data to the end of the planning year, that is, to the eve of the planned year. To assure the discipline of the plan, this projection should be done on the basis of all the growth rates planned for the (planning) year, but by the time these projections are undertaken, some knowledge is available on how the plan for the planning year is going. Thus, to the extent that current failures are ignored in the statistical projections, the plans for some sectors and some enterprises are extra taut.

plan comes back up the planning-control hierarchy. The enterprises seek to implant protective fat in the plan; although the superior organs do cut out some of the fat, they are restrained somewhat by the "family relationship" which exists between the superior body and the enterprises subordinate to it.[17] A considerable amount of pressure is reinstated in the plan when it comes back into Gosplan, for the central planners are not part of the same family as are those directly responsible for production, and therefore they are free to bargain for the degree of tautness in the now much more detailed plan that they had originally put in the aggregate plan when it first began its journey down the administrative hierarchy. We would probably be safe to assume that when the plan is accepted back into Gosplan, it is in general less taut than when it began but not substantially so.

At this point, it is the task of Gosplan to work out the internal consistency of the plan. The method used is that of the material balances, in which an accounting balance, listing planned sources and uses of a product, is constructed for each of a large number of major products. The consistency of the plan is achieved by forging a balance between planned sources and uses in each and every material balance.[18] The material balances are often said to resemble aspects of input-output tables. This is true, although it should be noted that a material balance is similar to a row, not a column, of an input-output table and thus does not explicitly reflect the production technology of the economic plan.

The material balance method and Soviet planning practice do have a spiritual kinship with the input-output approach insofar as the assumption of fixed input coefficients is concerned (or, in the Soviet case, at least temporarily fixed coefficients). The production function used in the construction of a Soviet plan is of the following nature:

$$X_k = \min \left(\frac{x_{1k}}{a_{1k}}, \frac{x_{2k}}{a_{2k}}, \cdots, \frac{x_{ik}}{a_{ik}}, \cdots, \frac{x_{nk}}{a_{nk}} \right),$$

where, X_k = the planned output of the kth good,

x_{ik} = the planned flow of the ith good to the kth sector,

a_{ik} = the planned input of the ith good per unit of output of the kth good.

This function states that the output of any good is equal to the smallest ratio of an input flow divided by that input coefficient.[19] Aside from

---

[17] The aspect of the "family relationship" important here is that the performance of the superior organ is a sum of the performances of the subordinate enterprises.

[18] This process is discussed in the sources in Footnote 15 above. The number of material balance has varied in the postwar period from approximately 760 to 1600.

[19] For example, if $x_{1j} = 10$, $a_{1j} = 2$, $x_{2j} = 28$, $a_{2j} = 4$; then, $X_j = \min (10/2, 28/4) = 5$. (This means that 8 units of x_{2j} are in "excess" supply.)

questions of inventory planning, it is the aim of planners to get all the relevant ratios equal to each other and equal to the desired level of output.

If the planned level of output of, say, the kth good turns out, on first inspection of the kth good's material balance, to be less than the planned uses of the kth good $\left(\sum_{i=1}^{n} x_{ki}\right)$, as is generally the case, how do Soviet planners achieve the required balance? That is, how do they increase the planned output of k and/or decrease the planned uses of k? One possible approach is to increase X_k by increasing each x_{ik} (in proportion to each fixed a_{ik}) and/or to decrease Σx_{ki} by decreasing all or some of the x_{ki}'s. This approach, however, requires that a multitude of subsequent changes be made. As each input flow into $k(x_{ik})$ is increased, each input into each input (x_{vi}) has to be increased, and this has to be done a number of times before each material balance in the set will be sufficiently balanced (and similarly, *mutatis mutandis*, on the down side). I have argued in detail elsewhere that, although Soviet planners do go back a few levels when the output of a key product is increased, this iterative approach is not the sole nor probably even the primary method they use to attain a consistent set of material balances.[20] Briefly put, the computational requirements of the iterative approach, given the form of the material balances and the computational technology in use (desk calculators at best), make it clear that this is an infeasible approach, and it is confirmed by the Russians' own statements.

Adjusting Imbalances

How, then, are the output levels of deficit products increased and/or demand requirements decreased?[21] It appears that much reliance is put on methods which avoid the necessity of making secondary changes, thus avoiding reverberation of a change through the entire set of material balances. Output levels are increased, without increase in inputs; planned distributions to users are decreased, without decreasing the output levels of the user sectors. The approach is not to change the x_{ik}'s and the x_{ki}'s, but to change the input coefficients, the a_{ik}'s and the a_{ki}'s. This adds to the tightness of the plan, to the pressure on the producing enterprise. This increased pressure may at times be applied where protective fat still exists, and thus it may not be undesirable or unrealistic pressure. However, since buildup of pressure at this stage is not a result of conscious effort to remove fat but, rather, a by-product of a primitive plan-

---

[20] See Levine, "Centralized Planning of Supply. . . ," pp. 163–67. For a somewhat divergent view, see J. M. Montias, "Planning with Material Balances in Soviet-Type Economies," *American Economic Review,* Vol. XLIX, No. 5 (December 1959), pp. 963–85.

[21] The phrase "deficit product" is used here to mean a product for which demand is greater than planned supply during the process of plan construction.

ning technique used by harried planners to hammer out consistency in the plan, it must be assumed that in many instances it will be applied where there is not an ample layer of fat. That this is so is attested to by the statements of many Soviet authorities, including an official statement of the Communist Party to the effect that planned input relationships are often unrealistic, leading to "excess tension in the fulfillment of plans." Furthermore, it should not be thought that perhaps the excess pressure on some enterprises is "balanced off" by the excess fat of others. The pressure on an enterprise is not easily relieved by the presence of fat at another enterprise because in an atmosphere of heavy pressure an enterprise jealously guards whatever surplus resources it might have in anticipation of needing them itself someday (soon).

There are several other nonsecondary effect steps taken to reduce imbalances in the material balances which are worth discussing. Planned levels of input stocks are often cut down excessively in an effort either to increase the output of a deficit product into which the stock in question is an input or to reduce the demands on a deficit input. In practice, stocks actually held are usually significantly greater than planned levels. The proclivity of Soviet enterprise managers to hoard inventories is well known, and we will discuss this further on. However, here we wish to point out that one reason Soviet managers hold above-norm stocks is simply that the planned levels of these stocks are set too low. At times when inventories of input materials are even twice as high as planned levels, these inventories prove to be insufficient to prevent production stoppages. Actually, Soviet inventory levels (related to flow of output) should be higher than those in say the United States. This is so because to a certain extent inventories and unused productive capacity are substitutes for each other and because under Soviet conditions of general plan tightness there is a relative unavailability of excess productive capacity in the Soviet economy. Another balancing technique which avoids secondary effects is to accelerate the introduction of new productive capacity and include its planned output flow in the material balance of a deficit product. Under the best of conditions, the precise scheduling of the introduction of new capacity is difficult to accomplish; but under Soviet conditions, it is well nigh imposible, for with the tightness of plans, the consequent unreliability of supply, and the general deficiencies of excessive centralization (see below), the introduction of new capacity is almost always held up for want of one or another needed material or piece of equipment. Under such conditions, the reliance on output from new capacity to be introduced during the planned year, a fortiori when the introduction schedule is artificially speeded up, constitutes an element of "paper consistency" and thus adds to the pressure built up in the plan.

Further pressure is put on the enterprise by certain indirect ways of reducing input coefficients. For example, the planned flow of materials to be used in maintenance work is often reduced below required levels. Thus, when the need for maintenance becomes pressing, the enterprise must shift materials from direct production work to maintenance, in this way increasing the pressure in its production plan.

The buildup of pressure in the process of plan construction does not end with the working out of the internal consistency of the plan but continues into and through the stage at which the plan is officially reviewed and confirmed and also in the stage wherein the confirmed plan is brought down through the administrative hierarchy to the producing unit.

When the draft of the plan has been reviewed and altered by the political leaders it is not clear whether the changes made are mostly increases or decreases in outputs—whether they are intended to increase or relieve pressure on the specific sectors involved. Perhaps the approach varies both at a given time and over time. What is clear, however, is that when the political leaders make changes in outputs, it is hardly possible for the planners, in the short time they have at this stage (normally about two weeks), to work out the indirect consequences of these changes. Therefore, even if they were able to forge a consistent draft of the plan to present to the political leaders, it comes back unbalanced and remains unbalanced. To the extent, then, that the plan is more inconsistent than it was, the pressure in it is further increased.

The confirmed plan contains output, input, and other types of commands addressed primarily to the high-level administrative bodies. Before 1957 these were the ministries; at this writing they are mainly the administrative-planning bodies at the republic level (also the remaining and recreated ministries and the state committees). In the pre-1957 period, for which the picture is clearer than now, the relevant parts of the plan were sent to the ministry involved, and the ministry and its intermediary organs were supposed to subdivide the ministerial output targets and input allotments among the subordinate enterprises. In order to give themselves more maneuverability and thus more protection, the ministries practiced what the Russians call reinsurance planning and reserving.[22] Reinsurance planning describes the ministerial practice of assigning output targets to subordinate enterprises so that the total assignments totaled more than the ministerial output assignment. By increasing targets in this way, the ministries put pressure on all enterprises to produce at higher levels (with lower targets, they might have stopped at producing at lower levels), thus giving themselves more of a protective cushion against the possibility that some of their enterprises would not fulfill even the lower targets. This practice was officially recognized by

---

[22] Reinsurance planning is what Berliner refers to as clearance planning. See Berliner, *Factory and Manager in the USSR,* pp. 83–85, 257–259. It is to be assumed that these practices were continued by the relevant administrative bodies after the 1957 reorganization.

the government, which set a limit of 10 percent on the amount by which the sum of assignments to enterprises could exceed the ministerial output assignment.

Reserving was another form of ministerial self-protection. This refers to the practice whereby a ministry did not distribute to its subordinate enterprise all the input allotments it received. The ministry reserved to itself a part of the allotments which it could then dispatch to trouble spots as they appeared during the course of the planned year. This practice too was officially recognized by the government, which permitted the ministry the right to reserve no more than 5 percent of the total ministerial allotment.

Although these practices added to the maneuverability of the ministry and in this way may have reduced the pressure on it, they added substantially to the pressure on the enterprise. They may be viewed as a means of redistributing some of the slack the ministry previously permitted enterprises to retain (in the bargaining process when the plan was coming up the hierarchy). By these methods such slack was transferred from the individual enterprises to the ministry as a whole, leaving the enterprise in a more highly pressured condition.

III. IMPACT OF PRESSURE

The question now to be faced is how all this pressure built up in the system leads to the observed characteristics of the Soviet economy. In this discussion, we do not intend to deny the role played by centralized planning itself and its many deficiencies. However, many of the characteristics, although related to the deficiencies of centralized planning, have been brought to their observed intensity by the presence of pressure in the system, and in addition there is a set of observed characteristics which are more directly related to pressure than they are to the presence of centralized planning.[23] We will examine the impact of pressure on Soviet economic activity under three major headings: the incentive system, the empty economy, and the seller's market. These are not three separate, airtight compartments, nor do they all operate at the same analytical level. They are at best loose classifications, and their effects are in many ways interrelated. But they are, nevertheless, useful categories with which to develop the argument.

Before proceeding to an analysis of the impact of pressure, let us look first at the impact of the direct deficiencies of centralized planning. The Soviet economy suffers from many ills of overcentralization, of which the major cause is that the planners at the center do not know and indeed cannot be expected to know all the details of the real situa-

---

[23] Somewhat similar ideas are discussed in Granick, "An Organizational Model . . ."

tions at the basic producing units.[24] The information required by central planners in the Soviet system of centralized planning is monumental.[25] Moreover, because the information which the enterprise supplies has an important effect on the tasks and resources given to the enterprise, the enterprise will distort the information; for example, it will "pad" its requests for materials (this is of course a generally observed characteristic of bureaucracies which operate under analogous conditions). It appears that Soviet central planners at times try to avoid confrontation of masses of information, of doubtful reliability at that, and try to conduct their business without being burdened by too much information from the enterprises. Under such conditions plans are constructed with even less knowledge of real conditions at the periphery. As a result of the limited knowledge at the center, enterprises often receive detailed plans which do not take into account either the actual production capabilities and specialities of producing-enterprises or the specific input needs of consuming-enterprises. There is a frequent lack of coordination among the different plans (outputs, inputs, deliveries, finances, etc.) given to the enterprise by different superior planning organs. It is commonplace to see complaints in Soviet economic literature about enterprises' being given delivery assignments which are greater than their output targets, or allocations of input materials without sufficient allocation of financial means to purchase them. Moreover, this problem is aggravated by the great number of changes in the plans for enterprises made by superior organs during the course of the planned year (see below), for it often happens that changes are made in one set of plans without compensating changes being made in the others. All this creates a general condition of unreality in plan assignments and unreliability of planned inter-enterprise relationships.[26]

In addition to the above, centralized planning visits upon the Soviet economy the multitude of maladies flowing from the overgrowth of

---

[24] See Bergson, *Economics of Soviet Planning*, pp. 331–32; and Leon Smolinski, "What Next in Soviet Planning?" *Foreign Affairs*, Vol. 42, No. 4 (July 1964), pp. 602–13.

[25] As an extreme example, to supply the information requested by its supply administration for the central construction of input norms, the Ural Machine Building Factory submitted a document 17,000 pages long.

[26] The following blistering attack is by a prominent Yugoslav economist, quoted in Bela A. Balassa, *The Hungarian Experience in Economic Planning* (New Haven, Conn.: Yale University Press, 1959), p. 79:

> The balancing of supply and demand in a centrally planned economy occurs in offices where a few people unaware of the real effects of their authoritarian plan become the supreme judges of the destinies of all producers and consumers through their bureaucratic machine. From this source of authority, plans lead further down to smaller bodies, splitting unrealistic averages into still smaller averages, according to norms born in offices which, when they reach the enterprise level, have little resemblance to the conditions of actual life.

(Perhaps centralized planning in the Soviet Union was not quite so bad as it apparently was in Yugoslavia—H.S.L.)

bureaucratic administration: red tape, delays in reaching decisions and getting things done, multiplicity of paper work, conflicting and overlapping lines of authority, and so forth.

There are other disadvantages directly attributable to centralized planning, but these are the most important ones. Keeping them in mind, let us go on to our argument that it is the pressure imposed on and built up within the economic system rather than centralized planning per se that to a significant extent accounts for many of the observed characteristics of the Soviet economy.

Incentive System

The pressure in the plan is communicated to the directors of enterprises through the application of the system of rewards and penalties. The Soviet incentive mechanism, with its high rewards for successful fulfillment and overfulfillment of plan assignments and its monetary and position penalties for failure, is clearly geared to transmit the pressure in the plan. And since bonus rewards for plan fulfillment are not an insignificant part of managerial income, accounting for about 40 percent of that income, the incentive system transmits the pressure in an intensified way.[27] Its impact is pervasive, but closely interwoven with the operation of the other categories we will consider, and thus often difficult to distinguish. Nevertheless, many of the things discussed by Berliner and Granick are clearly related to the pressure transmitted by the incentive system.[28]

First of all, there is the search for safety. Since success is a function of performance relative to expected (or commanded) performance, rewards can be acquired not only by performing on a high level, but also by being assigned low expectations. Therefore, the pressure on the enterprise in the plan, magnified by the incentive mechanism, greatly intensifies the general bureaucratic tendency to seek out ways of increasing security by understating productive capacity, by overstating input requirements, and by hoarding hidden inputs. Furthermore, the pressure transmitted by the reward and penalty system leads also to a group search for safety, the protective family circle.

Another aspect of the search for safety in the face of pressure from the incentive system is the operation of the "ratchet principle"[29]: the enterprise manager tempers his rate of plan overfulfillment in order not to get too high a plan the following year, and he resists innovation (which always entails some risks) because the penalty for failure is great, and the reward for success short-lived.

---

[27] See especially Berliner and Nove in Footnote 7 of this chapter.

[28] See Footnote 7 of this chapter.

[29] Berliner, *Factory and Manager in the USSR,* pp. 78–79.

Many familiar operating characteristics of the Soviet economy are primarily responses to the pressures communicated by the incentive system. The pressure to fulfill the dominant physical output plans is so great that enterprises ignore costs, "storm" at the end of the accounting period, falsify output data, skimp on quality, distort the planned output mix by emphasizing those outputs where the bonus per unit of available resources is highest.[30]

"Empty Economy"

The second of our categories is the "empty economy." The heavy pressure leads to a situation of general tautness in the Soviet economy. There is an absence of slack, and reserve stocks of resources are not easily available. This condition is what Hicks referred to as the "empty economy" when describing the post-World War II English economy. In such a situation, he said, the economy becomes accident prone, and minor mishaps become major crises.[31] This is just what happens in the Soviet economy; since there are insufficient protective reserves, even a minor shortage of an important material often becomes a major bottleneck.[32] This not only calls for the pursuit of bottlenecks in the construction of Soviet plans, but also leads to the great number of changes which are made in the operating plans during the course of the planned year in an effort to attack bottlenecks as they appear. The unavailability of reserves coupled with frequent unrealistically tight plans, leads to the unreliability of the Soviet materials supply system and its consequences: work stoppages, use of inferior but available substitute inputs, and the enterprise's network of expediters searching for needed inputs in all parts of the country. It also intensifies the tendency toward the hoarding of input materials, and it encourages producing units to integrate vertically, to produce as many of the needed inputs as possible; thus the economy loses the potential economies of specialization.

Sellers' Market

The pressure in the system and the way rewards are established in relation to the physical output plan have led to a chronic condition of sellers' market in the Soviet economy. This term means simply the

---

[30] This distortion of the product-mix is associated with the absence of a meaningful price system in the centralized economy. However, the enterprise's need to engage in such activity is greatly intensified by the pressure in the system.

[31] J. R. Hicks, "The Empty Economy," *Lloyds Bank Review*, No. 5 (July 1947), pp. 1–13. I am indebted to Prof. F. Holzman for calling my attention to this article. See also H. K. Charlesworth, *The Economics of Repressed Inflation* (London: Macmillan, 1956).

[32] Shortages may arise because enterprises failed to operate properly or because the plans themselves were unrealizable.

situation wherein demand, under the given "rates of exchange," is consistently greater than supply.

This seller's market has had a marked effect on the operation of the Soviet economy. Moreover, its impact was intensified during the pre-1957 period (and to some extent afterward) by the strategic role of producers' organizations in the construction of the central plan. It was the sales administration of the producing ministry which, in the final stages of plan construction, was responsible for setting the highly detailed production plans for enterprises within its ministry and for establishing detailed product flows from producing-enterprises to consuming-enterprises, all within the bounds set by the official annual plan. (After the 1957 reorganization these tasks were performed by Gosplan organs, entitled main administrations of interrepublican deliveries and based upon the former ministerial sales administrations.) This arrangement intensified the influence of the sellers' market because the ministerial sales organs were concerned with interests of the producers, the group with strong market power, rather than with the interests of the purchasers, the group with weak market power, thus in many situations adding a contributing force to the sellers' market rather than a countervailing one.

Given the sellers' market and the dominance of the physical output targets, the Soviet enterprise does not have to worry at all about being able to sell its output; it can concentrate its efforts on getting its needed inputs and making sure it is able to meet its output targets. Among other things, this accounts for the Soviet enterprise's greater aversion to innovation in products than to innovation in processes. Under the conditions stipulated, the producing-enterprise has no incentive to improve its product in order to make it more useful to the consuming-enterprise (as we saw before, it has little incentive to improve its production processes because of the operation of the "ratchet principle"). Furthermore, it is not pressed to do so by the sales administration of its ministry because the sales administration is more concerned with the production problems of its own ministry than with the needs of consumers.

The producer's one-sided concern with its own production needs and lack of concern for the needs of consuming enterprises lead also to a lowering of the quality of output and to a failure to produce the output assortment most needed by the users, the producer concentrating on the output mix most easy to produce and yielding the highest bonus. In addition, the sellers' market affects the timing of output and deliveries. Soviet steel-rolling mills, for example, tend toward long, uninterrupted runs of individual items of their output mix, which is fine for meeting their output targets but is highly detrimental to the interests of, say, a machine plant customer who needs a number of different types of rolled steel to produce a machine. Finally, because of the lack of attention paid by the sales administration of the producing-ministries to the needs of individual consumers, a consuming-enterprise is often assigned an irrational array of suppliers; its orders are spread out among a large number of them rather than concentrated in a few, and it also is often assigned different suppliers from year to year. This contributes further to the unreliability of inter-enterprise relations in the Soviet economy.

Before leaving this question, let us look briefly at some of the methods which are used to counteract the deleterious effects of the sellers' market. One important method is vertical integration but here with a slightly different focus from the one we discussed in relation to the "empty economy." Here the aim is to make sure that the quality and mix of inputs are in accord with the needs of the consumer. Furthermore, it is sometimes used to foster product innovation as was done when the coal ministry produced its own coal cutting machinery.

Another method is the fairly frequent use of wholesale prices established f.o.b. point of destination, that is, one price for all consumers or for all consumers in a given region.[33] By including transportation charges in the price, an incentive for achieving a rational geographic distribution of orders is given the producers rather than the consumers. This is wise, both because it is the sales administrations of the producers that play the dominant role in fixing producer-consumer ties and because under conditions of a sellers' market, purchasers may be willing to buy from any producer no matter what the extra transportation cost, whereas sellers, if they have to cover transportation costs, might be more apt to try to minimize these costs.

The most formal effort to counteract the uneven market power of sellers and buyers is the attempt to gain legal protection of the rights of buyers through the use of legal contracts enforced by the system of arbitration courts. However, its effects are somewhat reduced by the reluctance of buyers to apply contractual sanctions against suppliers violating these contracts, because of the fear of antagonizing suppliers they may be dependent upon in the future.

IV. PLANNING WITHOUT PRESSURE?

The hypothesis put forth in this paper has concerned the role and impact of pressure in the Soviet economy. It has been argued that the pressure on the basic producing units exerted by the political leaders and built up in the process of plan construction is manifested through and intensified by the incentive system, the "empty economy," and the sellers' market, and is responsible to a great extent for many of the observed characteristics of the Soviet economy frequently attributed to the mechanism of centralized planning itself.

---

[33] See Morris Bornstein, "The Soviet Price System," *American Economic Review*, Vol. LII, No. 1 (March 1962), p. 77, and the sources listed there.

The hypothesis has been argued; what is needed to test it are some observations on the operation in the Soviet economy of a system of centralized planning without pressure. Is such a situation possible? More practically, is it to be expected?

Theoretically it appears feasible, although some problems of incentives would need discussion. In the realm of Marxian theory, it fits well with what Marx and Engels seemed to have had in mind on the rare occasions when they spoke of planning in a socialist society. To Marx, the aim of having a central plan was the eradication of anarchy and the gearing of the economy to the wants of society.[34] There was no thought of using it to apply pressure to the economy.

After the death of Stalin and especially after his removal from the ranks of the deities in 1956, Soviet leaders began to talk about the reduction of pressure on producing units. In discussing the draft of the Seven Year Plan, Khrushchev said that "the Seven Year Plan is being drawn up in such a way that it can be implemented without overstrain," and he went on to describe some of the negative features of overly tight plans. Others have also spoken about the dangers of overstrain and complained of its presence, but at the same time, complaints are also heard about excessive looseness in the plans. The debate continues and it is not clear yet to what extent there has been a change in the amount of pressure in the plan.

By extending the Gerschenkron pattern of Russian economic development, with which this paper began, to the present period, it might be argued that the time is ripe for the removal of pressure. Russia has built up its economic base. It has achieved a state of military parity with the West. There is no longer the gnawing tension between what the State wants to do and what it can do because of a relatively backward economy, for the economy is no longer so relatively backward. Furthermore, the leader associated with the economic development drive is dead, and his political influence removed. In the past workings of the pattern, it was after the death of Peter the Great and after the removal of Count Witte, that the State withdrew its pressure from the economy. Perhaps such political events are important for changing the atmosphere. The period of pressure has been long, and it has included a terribly destructive war; certainly the people must be exhausted. There are signs now that the pressure on the standard of living of the Russian people has been reduced. For example, consumption levels have grown significantly in the decade of the 1950s,[35] and now many notable Russian political figures and economists are calling for a relative increase in

---

[34] "(Labor's) apportionment in accordance with a definite social plan maintains the proper proportion between the different kinds of work to be done and the various wants of the community." Karl Marx, *Capital,* Vol. I (Moscow: Foreign Languages Publishing House, 1954), p. 79.

[35] Chapman, "Consumption."

the growth of consumption. Perhaps one of the strongest statements and most pertinent for our purpose was made recently by a leading Soviet economic official:

> In the period of the construction of the material and technical base of socialism, the industrialization of the country entailed sacrifices; it was necessary to economize on everything, including personal consumption. Today our economy is so healthy and industry is so well developed that we have every possibility of successfully solving the problem of creating the material and technical base for communism and, on this basis, strengthening defenses and simultaneously stepping up the personal consumption of the Soviet people.[36]

It must be noted that Professor Gerschenkron has never, to our knowledge, extended his pattern of Russian economic development to the point of using it to indicate the strong possibility of the Soviet political leaders' withdrawal of pressure from the economy. The extension is the author's. Gerschenkron has in fact put forth an hypothesis on dictatorships which to a significant extent runs counter to this. In his 1963 Harvard Lecture at Yale University, he argues that modern dictatorships must continuously legitimatize themselves in order to remain in power. They do this by (among other things) the "maintenance of a permanent condition of stress and strain," and by the "incessant exercise of dictatorial power."[37] He does not go so far as to deny that the Soviet leaders have not or may not reduce stress and strain but to the extent that they do, he argues, their power will erode.[38]

Do the recent signs of the reduction of pressure indicate that nonpressure centralized planning in the Soviet economy is just around the corner? We do not think so. At the same time the degree of pressure may be changing, the forms of planning and control are also changing. This is so not only because the Soviet economy today is larger and more complex and thus more difficult to plan, but also because there has been change in economic focus. Centralized planning has accomplished what its use was intended to accomplish: the radical and rapid structural transformation of the Soviet economy. On almost all counts (with the exception of proportion of labor force in agriculture and also, perhaps, the overall level of technology), Russia is today a highly industrialized nation. The aim now is to improve the efficiency of the economy, to get more output per unit of input, and to change the product mix in a slower and not altogether predetermined way. This is not a situation in which the brute force methods of centralized planning recommend themselves. When the task is to improve economic efficiency, decision making must be moved to the level of the producing units, and useful

---

[36] Academician A. Arzumanian in *Pravda,* February 24, 1964, as translated in the *Current Digest of the Soviet Press,* Vol. XVI, No. 8 (March 18, 1964), p. 4.

[37] Gerschenkron, *Stability of Dictatorship,* p. 5.

[38] Ibid., pp. 34–36.

choice parameters (prices) must be provided so that relative benefits and costs can be compared and economically meaningful choices made.

That this situation calls for an increase in decentralized methods of planning and control is apparent, and it is also apparent from the current discussions (Libermanism, and so forth) and from some current actions that this is the direction the Soviets are taking. However, since the Soviet leaders undoubtedly want to maintain control over the general path and pace of development (including avoidance of glaring disproportions, maintenance of full employment, and so forth), reform will undoubtedly stop far short of complete decentralization. At a minimum, the political leaders will retain control over the amount and direction of investment. Also, they will most likely retain some power to assure aggregate sectoral balancing and the production and inculcation of major elements of technical change.[39] The development of computers and computer techniques for data collection, processing, and use will help the centralized aspects of such a mixed system operate more effectively than would be the case in the absence of these computational devices.

What is in store, then, is a Soviet economy with perhaps less pressure but also with less centralized planning. It appears that we may never get to observe real nonpressure centralized planning in the Soviet economy. For that matter (and for similar reasons), the entire subspace of economies with nonpressure centralized planning may be empty. Thus we are left with an hypothesis about the separate effects of the separate components, pressure and centralized planning, when in reality the two components may be a joint product. They appear together, both in relation to dynamic, determinate structural change, and they fade together when the economic focus switches to the channels of slower growth, less determinate and more moderate structural change. The analysis presented here is, hopefully, of analytical interest, but to the extent that pressure and centralized planning do operate as a joint product, the value of treating them separately may, we regret to say, be somewhat limited.

Before closing, a word on non-joint responsibility. We have in this paper used—or misused—some of the hypotheses of Professor Gerschenkron. It should be clear, however, that all responsibility for what has been said here lies with the author. It is the task of the apprentice to learn the master's methods, but the master should never be held responsible for the foolishness of the apprentice. A wrathful God once spoke of *poked awon avoth al banim*, but even he did not countenance, *poked awon banim al avoth*.[40]

---

[39] The power to assure aggregate sectoral balancing and sectoral technical change may require the reintroduction of branch line ministries. This may appear to be a contradiction of decentralization, but it is not necessarily so.

[40] For those who, unlike Alexander Gerschenkron, cannot handle a multitude of foreign languages: A wrathful God once spoke of "visiting the sins of the fathers upon the sons," but even he did not countenance "visiting the sins of the sons upon the fathers."

4. THE CONSISTENCY
OF SOVIET PLANS

Michael Ellman

A basic test of good planning is "consistency"—whether supplies and uses of resources balance without shortages or surpluses. Consistency is a necessary condition for "efficiency"—obtaining the maximum output from given resources and technology. In turn, "optimality" in planning involves selecting, from among a number of alternative "efficient" variants of the plan, the variant which best satisfies the ruling social preferences. A common criticism of Soviet planning is that it fails to achieve consistency and thus, also, efficiency and optimality. Despite this, the planners may still succeed in accomplishing important governmental objectives, such as rapid industrialization and national power. However, because of shortcomings in the planning process, they use resources less effectively and fulfill targets to a lesser extent that if resource allocation were guided by consistent, efficient, and optimal plans.

This article analyzes the obstacles to attaining consistency in Soviet planning. After a careful definition of consistency, it examines the two main instruments used in seeking consistency in Soviet planning—material balances and input-output methods. It explains the nature of these tools, their limitations, and their use in the USSR It concludes that although the application of input-output has not by itself greatly reduced inconsistencies in planning, the related introduction of mathematical models and modern computing techniques may significantly improve planning in the future.

Michael Ellman is a Research Officer in the Department of Applied Economics, Cambridge University. The article is reprinted by permission from the *Scottish Journal of Political Economy*, Vol. XVI, No. 1 (February 1969), pp. 50–74, with the omission of citations to Russian-language sources and the appendix table.

I. INTRODUCTION

THERE ARE a number of questions which can be asked about a national economic plan. What are its objectives? Were they achieved? Is the plan comprehensive? Is the plan optimal? A question which is often asked and which seems prima facie to be rather important is that of whether the plan is consistent, i.e., are its various sections compatible with one another? The purpose of this paper is to examine the consistency of Soviet plans. This question is very closely linked with the classic debate on the economics of socialism.

In a famous paper Barone argued that the Ministry of Production in the Collectivist State would have to solve the millions of equations of the Walrasian general equilibrium system, that this would be extremely difficult, and that there was not much point in abolishing capitalism as capitalism automatically solves the equations. In addition the collectivist solution would be very costly (employing an army of bureaucrats) and for the sake of rationality would have to employ the same instruments of economic calculation (e.g., the rate of interest on capital) as capitalism.[1]

An examination of the consistency of Soviet plans leads the present author to the conclusion that Barone and Robbins[2] were right to emphasize the difficulty of drawing up even consistent, let alone optimal, central plans, but that the moral that they drew from this was false. Planning and the market are not alternative roads to the same destination. Planning is advocated by those who wish to achieve a very different distribution of goods among the population than would have been achieved by the market, and to allocate resources, in a dynamic economy, in a direction which the market, left to itself, would not have chosen. The market, left to itself, will allocate resources in a direction determined by the preferences of individuals weighted by the distribution of income and wealth, by the preferences of firms weighted by the distribution of initiative and assets between firms, and by technology. Planning is advocated by those who want to allocate resources in some other direction. Soviet planning has been primarily concerned with the rapid industrialization and modernization of a backward country, and the only sensible way of judging its record is by analyzing its achievements in this field and their costs. The question of the consistency of the plan is much less important than the question of the goals of the plan and their achievement. Nevertheless, the question of the consistency of Soviet plans is of interest in itself, and it is to this question that the present paper addresses itself.

One of the conclusions that is arrived at is that Soviet plans are normally inconsistent. It should be borne in mind that this only means that the plans for at least some of the many thousands of centrally planned commodities are in fact inconsistent, and that the plans for

---

[1] E. Barone, "The Ministry of Production in the Collectivist State," *Collectivist Economic Planning,* ed. F. A. Hayek (London: Routledge & Kegan Paul Ltd., 1935), pp. 245–90.

[2] Robbins repeated the Barone argument in his book, *The Great Depression* (London: Macmillan, 1934).

at least some of the many thousands of enterprises are in fact inconsistent. It does not mean that the main proportions of the plan are inconsistent with each other (a subject outside the scope of this paper). Neither does it mean that it is unimportant for countries with a very highly aggregated framework plan to try and ensure that this plan is consistent.

II. THE PROBLEM

Consider an output plan

$$
\begin{array}{ll}
a_{11}\ a_{12}\ldots & a_{1n} \\
\qquad\qquad\qquad\quad & m \longrightarrow \infty \\
\ldots\ldots\ldots\ldots\ldots\ldots & n = 200{,}000 \\
a_{m1}\ a_{m2}\ldots & a_{mn}
\end{array}
$$

where each column represents the productive activity of an enterprise, and each row represents a separate commodity, so that a_{ij} is the output of the ith good produced by the jth enterprise.

Consider a supply plan

$$
\begin{array}{ll}
b_{11}\ b_{12}\ldots & b_{1n} \\
\qquad\qquad\qquad\quad & m \longrightarrow \infty \\
\ldots\ldots\ldots\ldots\ldots\ldots & n = 200{,}000 \\
b_{m1}\ b_{m2}\ldots & b_{mn}
\end{array}
$$

where each column represents the input requirements of an enterprise, and each row is a commodity, so that b_{ij} is the amount of the ith good required by the jth enterprise.

Consider a delivery plan

$$
\begin{array}{ll}
c_{11}\ c_{12}\ldots & c_{1n} \\
\qquad\qquad\qquad\quad & m \longrightarrow \infty \\
\ldots\ldots\ldots\ldots\ldots\ldots & n = 200{,}000 \\
c_{m1}\ c_{m2}\ldots & c_{mn}
\end{array}
$$

where c_{ij} is the amount of the ith good delivered to the jth enterprise.

The problem of compiling a consistent plan can be represented as the problem of choosing

a) A matrix a_{mn} $m \longrightarrow \infty$
$n = 200{,}000$

b) A matrix b_{mn} $m \longrightarrow \infty$
$n = 200{,}000$

c) A matrix c_{mn} $m \longrightarrow \infty$
$n = 200{,}000$

such that

1) $c_{ij} = b_{ij}$ $i = 1 \ldots \infty$
                          $j = 1 \ldots 200{,}000$

i.e., each enterprise should receive the goods it requires.

2) $a_{ij} \leq \bar{a}_{ij}$

where $\bar{a}_{ij}$ is the full capacity output of the ith good by the jth enterprise, i.e., no enterprise should receive a plan to produce more of a good than is possible.

$$3) \quad \sum_{j=1}^{n} a_{ij} = \sum_{j=1}^{n} b_{ij}$$

i.e., the output of each good should equal requirements.

A plan that meets these requirements is "consistent" in only the weakest of Stone's seven senses of the word.[3] Soviet plans are often inconsistent even in this sense. According to the late Academician Nemchinov, the doyen of Soviet economists, "The plans for production, labor, finance, and supply are often inconsistent."

The chief difficulties in compiling a consistent plan are:

1. Collecting the necessary data. Accurate data on capacity and input requirements are hard to obtain in an economy where enterprises have an incentive to minimize capacity and maximize output needs in their reports to the center.

2. Aggregation. The process of aggregation and disaggregation is a major source of inconsistencies. The author has analyzed this elsewhere.[4]

3. Processing the necessary data. A limited number of officials, divided into numerous departments, and armed with abacuses, pens and telephones—or more sophisticated equipment—have only a limited time to solve the problem, which is excessively complicated both because of its huge dimensions and because the variables are interrelated. When, during the course of plan calculations a_{ij} altered, its input requirements b_{ij} ($i = 1 \cdot \cdot \cdot \infty$) are altered, which alters the necessary outputs of other enterprises.[5]

---

[3] Richard Stone, "Consistent Projection in Multi-sector Models," in *Activity Analysis in the Theory of Growth and Planning,* ed. E. Malinvaud and M. O. L. Bacharach (London: Macmillan, 1967), pp. 232–44.

[4] Michael Ellman, "Aggregation as a Cause of Inconsistent Plans," *Economica,* Vol. XXXVI, No. 141 (February 1969), pp. 69–74.

[5] A prominent Soviet economist has explained that: ". . . every year it becomes more difficult to balance the economy, to compile a plan for its development, to control it . . .

. . . the chief difficulty is that with the existing system of planning and control, based on manual calculations and the perception of a limited amount of information by a planner, it is difficult not only to find an optimal solution to the development of an economy, but physically impossible to balance the plan. For the compilation

III. MATERIAL BALANCES

Nature

An essential requirement for successful government regulation of an economy is a statistical picture of the economy arranged in a way compatible with the instruments of regulation which the government uses. In Britain such a statistical picture is provided by the national accounts, which provide the information necessary for the regulation of the economy by fiscal means. In the Soviet Union the necessary statistical information is arranged in a series of "balances," the "balance of the national economy" and its subdivisions. The nature of the Soviet planning system in which the central authorities give detailed orders for the production of specific items to the enterprises, and allocate to them specific quantities of goods, is such that the most important subdivision of the balance of the national economy is the set of "material balances." These are the instruments used to ensure consistency, i.e., a state of affairs in which producers produce the quantities of goods required by consumers, without shortages or waste.

A material balance shows, on the one hand the economy's resources, and on the other hand the economy's needs, for a particular product for a specified period of time. A material balance can be arranged schematically as in Table 1.

TABLE 1
Material Balance for Product X for 1968
(million tons)

Resources	*Distribution*
1. Production (subdivided by republics)	1. Production needs (subdivided by republics and by ministries)
2. Imports	2. Free market allocation
3. Other sources	3. Exports
4. Stocks at suppliers at beginning of plan period (subdivided by republics)	4. Other needs
	5. Stocks at suppliers at end of year
	6. Reserves

The entries are reasonably self-explanatory. The free market allocation is the amount of the good which goes outside the state sector, e.g., to collective farms or to consumption.

---

of such a plan for the tens of thousands of products for which the USSR state plan sets targets, requires the carrying out of billions of calculations (mathematically this is a problem of solving a system of linear equations), whereas a man equipped with a desk calculator can do 1,000–2,000 calculations per day. Even if the infinite splitting up of the work were possible (which is impossible with these relationships), the whole apparatus of Gosplan could not do one hundredth part of the necessary calculations for this group of plan indices."

The material balances are used in the following way. In April–May of the year preceding the planned year (the planning year) Gosplan, after consultation with the republican gosplans and the USSR ministries, drafts a preliminary plan. It usually contains between 110 to 170 commodities, the exact number varying from year to year. In August, Gosplan compares its preliminary plan with the counter plan that has emerged from below. It draws up material balances for 1,300–1,500 products, to ensure consistency and spot any glaring disproportions. At the end of the year about 2,000 material balances are worked out by Gosplan, and many more disaggregated balances by the State Committee for Material-Technical Supply and its chief administrations. The precise details of the system are in continual flux. Until 1963 there were 24,790 centrally planned products. Of these, Gosplan itself worked out the plans and balances for 3,308, various USSR ministries and departments for 1,331, the union republics for 704, and the chief administrations for interrepublican supply worked out the plans and balances for 19,447 commodities. After the September (1965) Plenum the number of centrally planned commodities was reduced.

The crucial problem in material balance methodology is the equation of planned resources and planned distribution. Usually at the beginning of the balancing work, the prospective demand for a product is greater than the prospective supply. What steps are taken in these circumstances? The basic principle is that the plan is not reduced to accommodate a bottleneck. ("Don't plan on the bottleneck, plan to widen the bottleneck," was a familiar slogan of the 1930s.) This is regarded by the planners and Party leaders as sheer opportunism. What is done is that the corresponding industrial department attempts to increase the supply of the deficit commodity. One way of doing this would be to reduce stocks held by suppliers. Another would be to raise planned imports. The major effort is directed to increase current production by more efficient use of resources. Sometimes the planned introduction of new capacity is speeded up. Remorseless pressure will be transmitted to the enterprises to raise efficiency.

Simultaneously the summary department is attempting to decrease the demand for the deficit material. The basic principle is to accomplish this without lowering the output targets of the users. Pressure is applied to decrease the norms. Another possibility is the substitution of non-deficit materials for the deficit one. Throughout the balancing process, the priority principle is at work, for the emphasis is on guaranteeing the supply of goods to the priority sectors. It is the sectors of secondary importance that have their allocations cut, or are called on to use substitutes. (As a result of the multiplication of objectives from the middle of the 1950s onwards, strict application of the priority principle had perforce to be relaxed, with consequent difficulties.) When a summary department makes a change which reduces the flow of the deficit commodity to other sectors, it notifies the corresponding industry department, and vice versa.

The process of concurrent adjustment of the supply and demand for each balanced commodity ends with the "closing" of the balance, when the sum total of the allocations matches the total planned supply. Before all the balances can be closed simultaneously, it is often necessary to go up and down the administrative hierarchy several times. (The process is similar to that in the UK Ministry of Supply in World War II.)

Problems

The method of material balances suffers from a number of weaknesses:[6]

1. Material balances are not worked out for all goods. This reduces the dimensions of the problem from millions of equations to thousands of equations, but it means that there may well be shortages or waste in non-balanced commodities.

2. Often material balances do not cover the entire output of the good in question. For many kinds of products material balances embrace little more than 60 percent of production. When commodity A is produced as a subsidiary product of enterprise X belonging to industry B, then X's output of A may not be known to the central planners or to the sectoral planners responsible for the A industry. Consequently, even when the balance is closed on paper, the plan may well be inconsistent.

3. If the compilers of different balances use different assumptions, then inconsistencies will result.

4. Most of the data on stocks which the center has are on the stocks of producers. Its data on consumers' stocks are scanty and unreliable.

5. It is well known that the concept of "capacity," data on which are basic to the construction of material balances, is imprecise. The data available to the planners is of doubtful reliability because the enterprises have an incentive to minimize their capacity in reports to the center.

6. When output is measured by the "gross-value-of-output" index, its volume depends, *inter alia*, on the degree of vertical integration.

7. Input norms are basic to the calculations. These too, the enterprises have a direct incentive to falsify.

8. When during the course of the material balance calculations, the output of one product is altered, it is necessary to alter the outputs of all the products that, directly or indirectly, are used in the production of that product. For example, an increase in the production of cars

---

[6] For a discussion of the problems of the material balance technique, see N. K. Chandra, *Some Problems of Investment Planning in a Socialist Economy with Special Reference to the USSR and Poland* (unpublished Ph.D thesis, University of London, 1965).

entails an increase in the production of steel, which in its turn entails
an increase in the production of electricity, which in its turn requires
an increase in the production of coal, which in its turn . . . In practice,
however, Efimov has explained that:

> Because of the great labor intensity of the calculation of changes in the
> material balances and the insufficiency of time for the completion of
> such work in practice, sometimes only those balances which are linked
> by first-order relationship are changed. As regards relationships of the
> second order, and especially of the third and fourth order, changes in
> the balances are made only in those cases where the changes are
> conspicuous.

In other words, whereas consistency requires the evaluation of the con-
vergent series

$$X = (I + A + A^2 + A^3 \cdots)Y$$

the traditional Soviet practice is to approximate X by considering the
first two terms only. In view of the fact that the process of calculation
is often cut short, inconsistencies are to be expected, in principle. The
practical importance of this depends on the ratio of full inputs to direct
inputs, and the number of iterations required for consistency. The Soviet
Central Statistical Administration, working on the 1959 input-output
table for the USSR in value terms, found that usually this ratio was
between 1 and 2, but that much larger values occurred quite frequently,
ranging up to 54.7! The number of iterations required has been estimated
by Levine at between 6 and 13.[7]

On the other hand, it has been shown, using Soviet data, that in
most cases two rounds of interation were enough to bring direct input
norms quite close to full input norms. Furthermore, the number of iterations required is reduced by the existence of bottlenecks. The planners
can arrive at a consistent plan without matrix inversion, through iterations, provided that the outputs in the excess capacity sectors are adapted
to the potentials of the bottleneck sectors.[8] Furthermore, in practice
the planners can use the experience of previous years to offset the difficulties listed above. In addition, if the planners have available to them
an input-output table, they can use the full input coefficients derived
from it in their calculations.

---

[7] Herbert S. Levine, "The Centralized Planning of Supply in Soviet Industry,"
in *Comparisons of the United States and Soviet Economies* (papers Submitted
by Panelists Appearing Before the Subcommittee on Economic Statistics, Joint
Economic Committee, 86th Cong., 1st sess.) (Washington, D.C.: U.S. Government
Printing Office, 1959), Part I, pp. 151–76.

[8] See John Michael Montias, *Central Planning in Poland* (New Haven: Yale
University Press, 1962), pp. 339–45, and J. M. Montias, "On the Consistency and
Efficiency of Central Plans," *Review of Economic Studies,* Vol. XXIX, No. 4
(October 1962), pp. 280–90.

IV. INPUT-OUTPUT

Nature and Problems

An input-output table is a way of arranging the national accounts which focuses attention on productive relationships between industries. In Soviet statistical practice an input-output table is regarded "as an organic part of the balance of the national economy, as its further development, and above all as the development and disaggregation of the balance of the production, consumption, and accumulation of the social product and the national income."

The concept of an economy as a circular flow of commodities goes back to Quesnay's *Tableau Economique.* The first set of national accounts providing data on productive relationships between industries was compiled by the Soviet Central Statistical Administration in the 1920s. Leontief, aware of the Soviet work,[9] subsequently developed in the United States a mathematical model which provides a convenient way of arranging, and a useful method for analyzing and extrapolating, statistics on inter-industry relations.

The construction of input-output tables gives rise to numerous problems. "The most complicated and labor-intensive part of the work on an ex post input-output table is to obtain and process the necessary statistical information." As the statistical information which enterprises send to the Central Statistical Administration is inadequate, the necessary additional information is obtained by sample surveys. The existing data on the production and consumption of agricultural products produced on private plots by collective farmers and others, are not very reliable.

Economic activity takes place in enterprises, which are grouped into administrative units (firms in capitalist countries, economic ministries in the USSR). As input-output is concerned with data about technological relationships between industries to be used in planning, it is desirable that data be collected about the enterprises, and not about the administrative units into which they are grouped.[10] Where an enterprise produces, in addition to its main product, subsidiary products, it is desirable that the subsidiary output, and the inputs necessary to produce it, be transferred to the appropriate industry.[11] (The proportion of "foreign" output depends on the detail of the classification.) In this way it is possible to arrive at a "commodity-commodity" table. Call the

---

[9] He reviewed it in a German journal. There is an English translation in *Foundations of Soviet Strategy for Economic Growth: Selected Soviet Essays, 1924–1930,* ed. Nicolas Spulber (Bloomington, Ind.: Indiana University Press, 1964), pp. 88–94.

[10] Richard Stone, *Input-Output and National Accounts* (Paris: Organization for European Economic Co-operation, 1961), pp. 34–35.

[11] Ibid., pp. 35–36.

method of classification which does not take into account the fact that enterprises may produce more than one commodity, the "industry-industry" classification. The difference between the two can be very great, as Table 2, which refers to Lithuania in 1961, clearly shows.

TABLE 2
The Relationship between a "Commodity-Commodity" and "Industry-Industry" Calculation of the Outputs of Particular Industries, with a 239 Industry Classification

(1) Industry	(2) Volume of Pro- duction of the Industry's Product Produced in En- terprises Belonging to the Industry Itself	(3) Volume of Production of "Foreign" Products Produced by Enter- prises Belonging to the Industry, as a Percentage of Column (2)	(4) Volume of Production of the Given Industry Produced by Enter- prises Belonging to Other Industries, as a Percentage of Column (2)
Wine making.	100	0.5	139.9
Non-alcoholic drinks	100	–	128.0
Yeast	100	1.9	92.4
Medical instruments and equipment	100	331.2	90.4
Concentrated feeds	100	–	87.0
Equipment for the building materials industry	100	202.3	81.0
Electricity and thermal power generation	100	1.3	66.7
Tractors and agricul- tural machinery	100	40.6	64.0
Constructural engi- neering.	100	72.8	48.2

Either those inputs which come to the enterprise from outside, or all inputs regardless of whether they come to the enterprise from outside or from an earlier stage of production within the enterprise itself, can be considered as inputs. (In Soviet statistical practice, the former is known as the "gross output" [*valovaya produktsia*] method, the latter as the "gross turnover" [*valovoi oborot*] method.) Input coefficients calculated from statistics gathered using the former method are determined not only by technology, but also by the extent of vertical integration, and therefore the latter method is preferable for planning.

In general, it is desirable that statistics for input-output purposes be collected from enterprises and not from groups of enterprises, that they allocate subsidiary activities correctly, and that the gross turnover method is used. These points are more important in the USSR than they would be in say, the UK, because Soviet enterprises are less specialized. All Soviet input-output tables are based on data collected from enterprises and are "commodity-commodity" tables rather than "industry-industry" tables. In some cases the gross output method is used, in others the gross turnover method. The latter is favored by most economists in this field and by the Central Economic Mathematical Institute (TSEMI), the former by the Central Statistical Administration.

The question of which prices to use in value input-output tables has been much debated in the Soviet Union. The Central Statistical Administration uses the prices actually paid by consumers. TSEMI prefers producer prices (i.e., costs plus profits and turnover tax but excluding trade and transport expenses). The use of value input-output tables will only result in the compilation of consistent plans if the prices in which the tables are compiled reflect relative consumers' valuations.[12] Soviet prices often do not.

Another problem concerns the units to be used in physical input-output tables. In the input-output model it is assumed that each industry produces only one product, and that every product is uniform, and therefore it is possible to sum the rows in physical units. In all the input-output tables which it is feasible to construct, however, each industry produces a physically heterogeneous collection of goods. In Soviet practice, output is measured not only in natural physical units, but also in conventional physical units, and money. Conventional physical units (e.g., the measurement of various fuels in tons of coal equivalent) are used where it is clear that natural physical units do not reflect consumers' valuations. As a Soviet expert in this field puts it, "Physical measures (weight, volume, area, and so on) often cannot reflect quantitatively the consumers' value of goods. . . . The establishment of conventional units for the measurement of output, which convert physical measures to volumes of consumers' value, has a progressive significance. Such indices are widely used in the input-output table."

Where the output of an industry is very heterogeneous, e.g., the engineering industries and the furniture industry, output is measured in money, using constant prices. In general, the use of physical input-output tables composed of "commodities" aggregated in this way will not lead to the compilation of consistent plans.[13,14]

The input-output model assumes that all inputs are proportional to outputs. In fact in many industries this is not so, as a number of writers

---

[12] Ellman, "Aggregation as a Cause of Inconsistent Plans."

[13] Ibid.

[14] In accordance with normal Soviet practice, the top left hand quadrant of Soviet input-output tables only embraces "material production," and excludes "nonproductive" branches of the economy. (A recent booklet has argued, however, that "all work in a socialist society is productive, that there are no unproductive classes or social groups." An approving reviewer comments that "from the point of view of optimal planning the division of labor into productive and simply socially useful is senseless. All kinds of labor, satisfying a social need, i.e., making a definite contribution to the criterion of optimality, receive shadow prices corresponding to the quantity of their contribution.")

have pointed out.[15] In some of the Soviet regional tables attempts have been made to isolate the non-proportional inputs.

The input-output model assumes that each output is produced by only one technique. In fact many goods are produced by several techniques, e.g., electricity from coal, oil, or uranium. Similarly the input structures of the extractive and agricultural industries vary according to the location of the industry. This can be allowed for by setting out each technique in a column of its own and expanding the matrix from a square into a rectangle.

The compilation of ex ante input-output tables raises a number of further problems: how to estimate future technology, future personal consumption, future capital investments, and future exports and imports. The task of projecting the technological coefficients is rendered much easier by the fact that the vast majority of them are either zero or of negligible importance. "Calculations by the Economic Research Institute of the State Economic Council showed that in the ex post input-output table 10–15 percent of the coefficients in each industry embraced 90–95 percent of all the inputs."[16] Gosplan's Economic Research Institute analyzed the input coefficients of the 83 × 83 1959 all-Union table to find out by what percentage it was necessary to alter the input coefficients of each industry in order to produce a 1 percent change in the output of that industry. It turned out that 86 percent of the non-zero coefficients had to be altered by more than 100 percent to produce such a 1 percent change in the output of the industry concerned.

There are three methods of projecting the important coefficients: by extrapolation,[17] by the use of a model which embodies some theory of how technology may be expected to alter,[18] or by direct estimation by experts in the different technologies. The third method is the one normally used in Soviet practice. For example, when calculating the 1970 all-Union input-output table, more than 200 industrial research and project institutes were asked to estimate future technology in their industries. Experience has shown that the big problem in projecting the technical coefficients is not in estimating technical progress in the production of goods already in production, but in estimating changes in the structure of production, i.e., the "birth" of new products and the "death" of old ones.

---

[15] Hollis B. Chenery and Paul G. Clark, *Interindustry Economics* (New York: John Wiley and Sons, Inc., 1959), p. 144.

[16] The reference is to the 1959 all-Union table in value terms.

[17] See for example Cambridge University, Department of Applied Economics, *A Programme for Growth*, Vol. 3: *Input-output Relationships 1954–1966* (London: Chapman and Hall, 1963); or C. B. Tilanus, *Input-output Experiments: the Netherlands 1948–1961* (Rotterdam: Rotterdam University Press, 1966).

[18] L. L. Pasinetti, "A New Theoretical Approach to the Problems of Economic Growth," in *The Econometric Approach to Development Planning* (Amsterdam: North-Holland Publishing Co.; Chicago: Rand McNally, 1965), pp. 571–688.

The volume and assortment of future final product is determined partly by political choices and partly by technology. To assist in determining the volume and structure of final product for the Union as a whole, 20 variants of the 1970 all-Union input-output table were drawn up (of which two were selected for further study). The main differences between these variants were the result of different assumptions as to the volume and structure of final output. Similarly, when working out the 1970 input-output table for Estonia, 15 variants of final product were tried.

The structure of personal consumption is arrived at using the methods of extrapolation, rational consumption norms,[19] and elasticity coefficients. The projections for social consumption, on the other hand, are based on plan estimates. These are based on plan norms, for example the number of hospital beds required per thousand inhabitants.

Accurate estimation of future capital investment is particularly important in a country where gross capital formation amounts to 35 percent of the national income. The input-output projections used are based on plan estimates. Calculation of the physical composition of investment is considerably simplified for those regions for which capital stock matrices have been compiled. Trade projections are based on plan estimates.

Input-output tables are a valuable source of information about the structure of an economy. They give a vivid picture of inter-industry flows, the commodity composition of imports and exports, and the commodity structure of accumulation and consumption; and they indicate the main proportions of the economy. Analysis of the 1961 input-output table for Lithuania, for example, showed that only a very small proportion of Lithuanian industrial production flowed into Lithuanian agriculture. Since Lithuania is a mainly agricultural republic, it was decided that this was unsatisfactory and that the proportion ought to be increased. The all-Union tables have provided data for an analysis of the efficiency of production and for price calculations.

Use in Soviet Planning

Economic planning is a hierarchical, or multi-level, process. At the top, the time path of a few summary indicators, e.g., national income, is decided; at the bottom, the expansion plans of every enterprise. The

---

[19] Rational consumption norms (an approach which H. S. Houthakker has termed "the technology of consumption" in "The Present State of Consumption Theory: A Survey Article," *Econometrica,* Vol. 29, No. 4 [October 1961], pp. 704–40) are extensively used in projecting personal consumption. In one variant of the Estonian calculations, norms of the consumption of food products, suggested by the Laboratory for the Study and Planning of Nutrition of the Academy of Sciences of the USSR, and consumption norms of non-food products recommended by the Scientific Research Institute of Trade and Social Nutrition, corrected for Estonian conditions, were used.

calculations made at every stage can be summarized in a model, which indicates the assumptions made, the data required, and the steps in the process. The strategy of development can be decided with the help of an extremely aggregated growth model. A classic case is the Feldman model, which brings out clearly (on the assumptions made) the advantages of concentrating on heavy industry.* More recently, Mikhalevsky has attempted to use a number of tools borrowed from Western economic thought (e.g., production functions) to explain past Soviet economic growth and lay the foundation for planning the macrosummary indices. Input-output is a tool to be used at a lower level of the hierarchy to plan the relations between the various industries. It forms a link between plans for the basic national economic indices and the plans for separate industries and regions. Use of input-output in planning is illustrated below:

FIGURE 1
The Use of Input-Output in Economic Planning

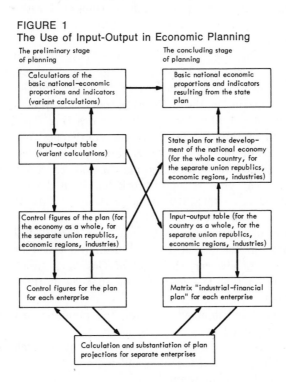

At the present time, both the underlying economic system and the techniques used to plan it are in a state of transition. On the one hand, the September (1965) Plenum inaugurated the transition from the administrative allocation of commodities to inter-enterprise trade. On the other hand, the balance of the national economy and the material bal-

---

* Editors' note: A translation of Feldman's model appears in Spulber, *Foundations of Soviet Strategy for Economic Growth,* pp. 174–99 and 304–31.

ances are still being compiled, an ex ante input-output table in physical terms is drawn up annually by Gosplan's Chief Computing Center to assist in current planning, and ex ante input-output tables in both monetary and physical terms for some years ahead are drawn up by Gosplan's Research Institute and Gosplan's Chief Computing Center to assist in perspective planning.

The use of input-output has important advantages when compared to traditional planning methods:[20]

1.   It shows clearly the relationship between the macroeconomic summary indicators and the physical structure of production.

2.   Being a mathematical method which can be solved on a computer, it is much less laborious than traditional methods, enabling consistency to be achieved in a shorter time and many plan variants to be experimented with. These plan variants can be compared with regard to the values assumed by a number of important economic indices, and the best one picked.

In principle, the use of input-output in current planning promises to improve the consistency of plans and the use of input-output in perspective planning promises to improve the planning of the relative sizes of different industries in the national economy. In practice, the use of an ex ante input-output table for 1970 in drafting the five-year plan for 1966–70 for Lithuania, to check the consistency of the projected national income of the republic with the projected industrial outputs, appears to be something of an exception. In connection with the 1966–70 all-Union five-year plan, a lot of work has been done in drawing up an input-output table for 1970. At a meeting in July 1966, Professor Alter correctly pointed out that this was the first time that ex ante coefficients for an input-output table had been compiled on such a wide scale, not only in the Soviet Union but in the world as a whole. At the same meeting, however, the head of Gosplan's Input-Output Subdepartment stated that the practical significance of this table has not been very great.

The integration of input-output into the planning mechanism gives rise to numerous problems:

1.   The results of input-output calculations may be irrelevant to planning because the indices of the plan and those of the input-output table are non-comparable.[21] For example:

---

[20] For a comparison of the traditional balances and input-output as techniques for arriving at a consistent plan, see S. S. Ahluwalia, "Balancing versus Input-Output Techniques in Ensuring the Internal Consistency of a Plan," in Warsaw Center of Research on Underdeveloped Economies, *Essays on Planning and Economic Development,* Vol. 2 (Warsaw: Polish Scientific Publishers, 1965).

[21] The input-output tables may themselves be non-comparable because different methods are used in their compilation. The all-Union tables compiled by the Central Statistical Administration are in consumer prices. The input-output tables for the Baltic Republics, compiled under the aegis of the Central Economic Mathe-

a. Input-output tables include all the output of particular products. Plan calculations ignore the small industrial enterprises of state farms; building, trade, and transport organizations; collective farms; and consumer cooperatives.

b. The product classification of the plan and the input-output table may be different. When comparing the 1959 all-Union physical input-output table with the basic indices of the seven-year plan, it was found that only 77 products were comparable, 80 products in the input-output table were not in the plan nomenclature, and 33 products in the plan nomenclature were not in the input-output nomenclature.

It is clearly necessary for the Central Statistical Administration and Gosplan to agree on a single industrial classification which will provide control over enterprises and which will be used in planning and in compiling input-output tables.

c. Plans and input-output tables are calculated in different prices. Enterprise wholesale prices + turnover tax = producer prices (industry wholesale prices). Producer prices + trade and transport costs = final consumer prices.

According to a 1966 Soviet source:

In plan calculations, output is calculated in enterprise wholesale prices, and social product in industrial wholesale prices. The method of compiling ex ante input-output tables used at the present time is such that in them products are reckoned in those prices at which were calculated the ex post input-output tables. Because the first, and last, ex post input-output table was worked out by the Central Statistical Administration in final consumer prices of 1959, all the ex ante input-output tables are calculated in those prices. In this way, as a result of using different prices, "output" in the input-output calculations exceeds "ouput" in the plan calculations by the extent of turnover tax and the trade-transport markup.

Consequently, the volume of output of an industry for the planned year arrived at by input-output calculations must be translated from final consumer prices of 1959 to producer prices of 1959, and finally, to enterprise wholesale prices of that year, the prices of which are accepted as comparable to those of the planned period. (Up to 1966 comparable prices for the measurement of the gross output of industry are the enterprise wholesale prices of July 1, 1955.) Such a three-stage re-estimation of the volume of output can scarcely avoid lowering the reliability of the results.

---

matical Institute, are in producer prices. The compilers of the 1959 all-Union value and physical tables used different methods of calculating inputs. In the value table, only those inputs were calculated which came from outside the enterprise concerned, whereas in the physical table all inputs, including those produced within the enterprise itself, were included.

Bringing the prices used in the regional input-output tables into line with plan prices is simpler because the former are in producer prices.

d. Soviet input-output tables are based on a "commodity-commodity" classification, whereas plans are drawn up for industries (where by "industry" is meant a totality of enterprises) and for enterprises. This is a more serious difficulty in the Soviet Union than it would be in Britain because the Soviet industry is less specialized.

e. In planning, a group of industries (sewn goods, footwear, woollens, cotton cleaning, wool scouring, artificial leather, celluloid materials) have their gross outputs calculated differently from all other industries, certain items (raw materials, basic already processed materials, and profits) being excluded.

f. There are also other differences between input-output indices and those used in planning practice. "At the present time to liquidate fully the inconsistencies between the indices of the ex ante input-output table and the national economic plan, which have been mentioned, is extraordinarily difficult in connection with the lack of the necessary ex post and ex ante information."

2. A major difficulty in reconciling input-output with the traditional system of planning by material balances, let alone superseding the latter by the former, is that the latter are worked out for many more products than the former. The Soviet economist Shvirkov wrote in 1963:

> At the present time the USSR Council of Ministers approves in the annual plan for the development of the national economy the volume of production in physical terms of more than 600 types of industrial output. Moreover, about 400 indices which are subdivisions of these 600 products are confirmed in addition. Thus Gosplan USSR must calculate the volume of production of more than 1,000 products for submission to the Council of Ministers of the USSR. Naturally, the volume of production of these products must be coordinated. Such balancing can most effectively be carried out with the help of an input-output table.

Pursuing this line of thought would require an input-output table of order $1,000 \times 1,000$. Shvirkov suggests 800×800 on the ground that this is the upper limit possible with existing computer technology. This approach seems unsatisfactory. Such tables would be difficult to compile and invert. In addition, it would leave open the relationship between Gosplan's input-output table and the many thousands of material balances compiled at lower levels of the planning hierarchy. A much more promising approach has been outlined in an important paper by Dudkin and Yershov. They suggest an iterative method by the use of which it is possible to arrive at a consistent plan for all the products for which material balances are compiled. They do not prove, however, that the iterative process must speedily converge, merely providing an arithmetical example which happens to do so. This approach has been developed further in a book by Dudkin. There is no evidence that these ideas have had any impact on planning in the USSR.

3. There has been a tendency in input-output calculations to use "progressive" coefficients, regardless of the production possibilities for "progressive" goods in short supply, resulting in impossibly high outputs of some goods in the input-output calculations. For example, comparison of necessary output levels as calculated using the physical input-output tables and using the traditional methods in 1962 and subsequent years generally showed close agreement. Where there were divergences, this generally showed not the inadequacy of the traditional methods but the folly of using input coefficients for mineral fertilizers into agriculture, or aluminum into cables, which reflected a desirable, but unfeasible input structure. These problem arises from the fact that in the input-output model technology is fixed and output levels flexible, whereas in planning practice technology is flexible and output levels constrained by resource availability.

4. In order that the enterprise plans be consistent with the national or regional input-output tables, it is desirable that the enterprise plans be drawn up in matrix form using the same statistical conventions as are used in compiling the input-output tables.

5. There is a shortage of economists competent in this field.

6. The most important practical obstacle to the use of physical input-output tables in planning is that the ones so far compiled fail to account for a large proportion of the ouput of important products. For example in the plan table for 1963 one-third of electricity went to "other productive uses."

7. The input-output model assumes that constant returns to scale prevail throughout the economy. In fact, however, increasing returns to scale are normal in manufacturing industry, diminishing returns to scale in extractive industry, and agricultural production is heavily dependent on "chance inputs" (e.g., rain, wind, and sunshine). Consequently it is not normally possible to rely on an input-ouput coefficient when the output under consideration is substantially different from the output for which the coefficient was calculated.

One important difference between planning by material balances and planning by input-output is that the former is concerned with gross production and gross consumption of commodities, and focuses attention on supply bottlenecks, whereas the latter focuses attention on the net output available for final consumption. As Dadayan has remarked, "The production and consumption of coal and steel are significant not in themselves, but only to the extent that they provide for the production of products intended for final consumption. . . . Society does not become one iota richer if the industrial apparatus devours not 300 but 500 million tons of coal or 90 and not 50 million tons of steel."

The use of input-output has provided interesting data on inter-industry relations, which has been of use in economic analysis and policy-making, which has improved the planning of inter-industry proportions, and which supplements existing methods of checking the consistency of highly aggregated plans.

The construction of input-output tables on varying assumptions leads to an immense accumulation of data on possible worlds, and this, together with experiments on inter-industry models, has served to emphasize the need for, the potential utility of, optimal planning. The main gain from the use of input-output in Soviet planning has not been its contribution to reducing inefficiency, but the fact that it has introduced mathematical models and modern computing technology into Soviet planning and that important gains in efficiency may well follow from this.

V. CONCLUSION

It has not been possible to ensure that the plans for all the many thousands of centrally planned commodities and all the many thousands of enterprises are consistent, using material balances or input-output or a combination of these techniques. How, it may be asked, does the economy manage if the plans are normally inconsistent?

The answer seems to be as follows. The last stage of the process of planning supplies is the conclusion of contracts between supplier and user. This stage gives the supplier and user the possibility of bringing the plan into line with real possibilities and needs. One of the features of the reform inaugurated by the September (1965) Plenum is the increased emphasis placed on these contracts and generally on direct contacts between suppliers and users, often of a long-term nature. Furthermore, scarce inputs can often be obtained from those who have them by direct contacts outside the formal planning system, by activities of a quasi-market type. Impossible output plans can generally be avoided by understating possibilities in reports to the center, by representations to the center when impossible output plans are received, or by some mixture of the two strategies. Both of them are customary gambits in the long process of "planning and counter-planning" (i.e., the negotiations between the center, intermediate bodies such as the industrial ministries, and the enterprises over preliminary drafts of the plan, which precede the compilation of the final version of the plan). During the year as inconsistencies come to light, the plans can be, and frequently are, altered, sometimes repeatedly. Frequent alterations to the plan during the "planned" period are often attacked in the Soviet press, but they would seem to be an integral part of a system of inconsistent central planning. Moreover, it is important to remember that the enterprises do not start off each year *ab initio*. Most enterprises produce this year very much what they produced last year, relying on the same suppliers. The changes to the previous year's output envisaged in the plan are normally only of a marginal character. The planners themselves expect inconsistencies to arise. In the annual plan, part of the output of each product is allocated to reserves and as shortages become apparent during the course of the year, the planners allocate these reserves to the priority enterprises. Furthermore, the material balances are most detailed for those products in which the planners are most interested, reducing the dangers of inconsistency in commodities important to the planners.

Although Soviet plans have normally been inconsistent, this has not prevented the economy's flourishing. The planners have not been much troubled by the consistency problem, as they were primarily concerned with strategic problems, for example the relationship of industry to agriculture, the allocation of investment between industries, and the development of specific products (e.g., tanks), specific plants (e.g., the Dnieper and Bratsk hydro stations and the Magnitogorsk iron and steel complex), of specific programs (e.g., the space program), and of specific industries (e.g., oil). In all these their successes were striking. (It was the non-priority sectors that suffered from inconsistencies.) Compared to these crucial questions the calculations necessary to ensure consistency were regarded as a mere "game with figures."[22] The annual plan for the production and distribution of commodities serves to coordinate the plans of individual enterprises and projects. The primary objective of the planners is to fulfill the plans for these separate enterprises and projects, or at any rate for the priority ones among them, and if the annual plans for the production and distribution of commodities are inconsistent, then this does not matter to the planners provided that the priority projects do not suffer and the shortages are felt by non-priority sectors, such as personal consumption. By the 1960s this traditional attitude had begun to alter. The economy had become so complex that the gains from the administrative allocation of resources to the key sectors began to be rivaled by the losses from the misallocation of resources throughout the economy. Furthermore, the planners began to attach importance to the satisfaction of consumers. Hence the discussion of reform, the very limited reforms introduced by the September (1965) Plenum, and the experiments in replacing the centralized administrative allocation of resources by inter-enterprise trade.

It is no more surprising that the Soviet economy functioned and in a number of respects performed extremely well, when the plans were inconsistent, than that the British economy has been as stable as it has in the post-war period given the crudity of the instruments of control used.

---

[22] The phrase is Stalin's. See J. Stalin, *Pravda,* December 29, 1929, translated in *Works,* Vol. 12 (Moscow: Foreign Languages Publishing House, 1955), p. 178.

In summary:

1. The important things about a plan are its objectives, whether or not they are attained and whether or not there existed a more efficient way of attaining them than that chosen by the planners. Consistency is a secondary matter.

2. To ensure that the plans are consistent, Soviet planners have traditionally used material balances and now supplement this with input-output.

3. These techniques have been unable to ensure consistency, and Soviet plans have always been inconsistent.

4. Traditionally the inconsistency of the plans has not worried the planners very much as they were primarily concerned with the achievement of the plan for specific, priority sectors of the economy. The administrative allocation of resources, the core of the traditional economic system, greatly facilitated the concentration of resources according to the priorities of the planners. The inconsistencies of the plans were felt by non-priority sectors about which the planners were not much concerned.

5. The inconsistency of Soviet plans is relevant to discussion of economic reform.

II
HOW THE SOVIET ECONOMY OPERATES

Although the Soviet economy is usually considered to be "planned," nevertheless money, prices, and markets play significant roles in the operation of the economy. Indeed, how to coordinate these "economic levers" with centralized physical planning is one of the major problems facing Soviet economic administrators.

Part II discusses the nature of the problem, the solutions attempted in various sectors of the economy, and the results. The first selection analyzes the principal types of Soviet prices, their shortcomings, and proposals for changes. The second provides a general survey of the financial aspects of the economy and a more detailed explanation of the banking system. The following article examines the motivation and performance of industrial managers in response to physical and financial targets and monetary incentives linked to them. The next dicusses the many facets of the urban labor market, in which wage differentials are used to implement plans for the distribution of labor and for productivity increases. The last two selections explain recent developments in agriculture, where output depends on administrative allocation of material inputs, prices and monetary incentives to the peasantry, and the weather.

5. SOVIET PRICE THEORY AND POLICY

Morris Bornstein

In a market economy, the level and composition of production, the allocation of resources, and the distribution of income and output are determined primarily by market forces whose decisions are expressed through prices. In this sense, "the price system" and "the market" are often used interchangeably to explain the operation of the economic system. In the Soviet planned economy, the role of prices is much more limited, reflecting the prevalence of planners' (rather than consumers') sovereignty and the reliance of the planners on physical planning and administrative commands to execute their decisions.

This selection examines the functions of prices in the Soviet economy and the characteristics of the major types of wholesale and retail prices. It analyzes recent proposals for reforms in the price system and evaluates the measures actually taken.

Morris Bornstein is Professor of Economics at The University of Michigan and one of the co-editors of this volume. The selection is a revised version of his "Soviet Price Theory and Policy," in *New Directions in the Soviet Economy* (Studies Prepared for the Subcommittee on Foreign Economic Policy, Joint Economic Committee, 89th Cong., 2d sess.) (Washington, D.C.: U.S. Government Printing Office, 1966), Part I, pp. 65–94. Citations of Russian-language sources are omitted.

IN THE SOVIET UNION, as in all modern, complex economies, prices play an important part in the guidance of economic activity.[1] However, their role in the Soviet economy is different both from their role in a capitalist market economy and from their role in the socialist market economy described in the theoretical models of Lange, Taylor, and Lerner.[2] In

---

[1] This paper is based in part on research supported by The University of Michigan Center for Russian and East European Studies, whose assistance is gratefully acknowledged.

[2] Oskar Lange and Fred M. Taylor, *On the Economic Theory of Socialism,*

the Soviet economy (and in the Soviet-type economies of Eastern Europe and Communist China), prices are not an autonomous force determining production, resource allocation, and consumption. Instead, prices are manipulated by the central authorities as one of various instruments intended to accomplish their planned goals.

Following a summary view of the various functions of prices in the Soviet economy, this paper deals in turn with the three major subsystems of the Soviet price system: industrial wholesale prices, agricultural procurement prices, and retail prices. The discussion focuses on current pricing practices, theoretical controversies among Soviet economists about price reforms, and recent and pending changes in price policies. Certain types of prices—such as wages, transportation rates, and foreign trade prices—are not considered here. The paper also does not treat in any depth such aspects as the historical evolution of the price system in the 1930s and 1940s, narrowly technical aspects (such as the construction of price lists), or minor types of prices (such as those which collective farms charge their members).

I. ROLE OF PRICES IN THE SOVIET ECONOMY

The functions of the Soviet price system may be classified under three very broad headings: control and evaluation, allocation, and income distribution.[3]

Control and Evaluation

Prices are used by the central planners to secure compliance by enterprise managers with the plans elaborated by the former, and to evaluate the performance of the managers in the execution of their assigned tasks. Although resource allocation is determined by the planners largely in physical terms, it is necessary for them to express complex input and output targets for the enterprise in value terms in order to have a common denominator for physically dissimilar units of raw materials, labor, and capital goods. Thus the enterprise plan contains targets for the value of output, sales, cost, profits, tax payments, etc.

Allocation

Although physical allocation by administrative commands predominates in the Soviet economy, prices do influence the allocation of resources, and thus the pattern of production, in various ways.

---

ed. Benjamin E. Lippincott (Minneapolis: University of Minnesota Press, 1938), and Abba P. Lerner, *The Economics of Control* (New York: Macmillan, 1944).

[3] Here and elsewhere in this paper I draw upon Morris Bornstein, "The Soviet Price System," *American Economic Review*, Vol. LII, No. 1 (March 1962), pp. 64–103.

1. At the central planning level, prices are used to construct macro-economic balances, such as national product and intersectoral accounts, and capital-output ratios to supplement the basic physical planning tools. In addition, the relative pricing of substitutes may have some influence on the selection of technological coefficients for physical planning, as the planners substitute more abundant for scarcer materials during the successive iterations of the balancing process. Finally, project designers use value calculations in choosing among alternative variants of a given-output investment project and in assessing the benefits of modernization or innovation.

2. It is impossible for the central authorities to specify in complete detail the inputs and outputs of each enterprise. As a result, managers have a limited range of choice regarding both inputs and outputs. The relative prices of inputs and outputs influence the choices which managers make in trying to increase the value of output, sales, and profits.

3. Prices affect both the total supply of labor and its distribution. The state relies on low real wages, resulting from the relationship of money wages and consumer prices, to evoke a high rate of participation of the population in the labor force. Wage differences, in turn, are the principal means of securing the distribution of the labor force (by skill, industry, enterprise, and geographical location) desired by the planners.

4. In the collective farm sector, the central authorities use prices, along with delivery quotas, to influence the allocation of resources to certain crops and products in preference to others. (In addition, prices are used, along with delivery quotas, to stimulate total output, but in this case the aim is primarily to raise the productivity of given resources engaged in agriculture, by increasing real compensation and thus incentives.)

Income Distribution

In the Soviet economy, the basis of income distribution is the "social-ist" principle of unequal monetary compensation according to labor ser-vices rendered, rather than the "communist" principle of distribution according to need; and the promise of unequal monetary compensation is the basis of production incentives. The wage (i.e., price) system—together with transfer payments and income taxes—determines the distribution of (disposable) money income. The Soviet government en-deavors to make the distribution of real income less unequal than the distribution of money income by two chief methods. One is a broad program of "free" health and education services financed from general budget revenues. The second is to fix relatively low prices for mass consumption goods and relatively high prices for luxury goods by means of differentiated turnover taxes. The distribution of real income is also made less unequal than the distribution of money income through the administrative allocation of housing and through the informal rationing of queues and empty shelves when retail prices are fixed below the market-clearing level.

II. INDUSTRIAL WHOLESALE PRICES

Nature and Trends

Industrial wholesale prices are those at which goods are transferred or evaluated within the state sector of the Soviet economy.[4] The term covers prices of producer goods, including raw materials, semifabricates, and machinery, as well as manufactured consumer goods. It excludes prices at which agricultural products are obtained by the state from collective farms but includes prices at which procurement agencies sell agricultural products to state enterprises for processing or to trade organizations for retail sale without further processing. It also excludes foreign trade prices, although it includes the prices at which foreign trade organizations buy from and sell to Soviet enterprises. Since 1958, collective farms have been permitted to buy various producer goods at wholesale prices, rather than at retail prices, as previously.

The Soviet industrial wholesale price system is composed of three types of prices. The "enterprise wholesale price" is the price at which a producing enterprise sells its output. The "industry wholesale price" is paid by the state-enterprise buyer and includes, in addition to the enterprise wholesale price, (1) the turnover tax, if any, on the product; (2) the markup of the branch sales organization; and (3) transportation charges if these are borne by the sales organization rather than the buyer. Finally, a settlement or "accounting" price is used in some branches where production costs diverge widely, notably the extractive branches. Individual enterprises or groups of enterprises receive different settlement prices, rather than a single, uniform enterprise wholesale price, from the branch sales organization. The latter, however, sells to customers of the branch at a single industry wholesale price.

Enterprise wholesale prices are composed of the planned branch average cost of production (*sebestoimost'*) and a profit markup. The former has no exact equivalent in Western cost accounting. It includes direct and indirect labor, materials (including fuel and power), depreciation allowances, and various overhead expenses, but excludes both rental and capital charges. The profit markup is supposed to provide a "normal" profit, which until the 1967 wholesale price reform (discussed below) was planned at 5 to 10 percent of *sebestoimost'*. This profit markup is not intended to allocate resources among alternative uses, but rather

---

[4] Ibid., p. 69, and Morris Bornstein, "The Soviet Price Reform Discussion," *Quarterly Journal of Economics*, Vol. LXXVIII, No. 1 (February 1964), pp. 18–19.

is to provide a source of "net income" or accumulation to the state, to serve as an instrument of financial control, and to promote the "businesslike" operation of Soviet enterprises.

Another source of accumulation is the turnover tax, which is levied primarily on consumer goods and included in the wholesale prices of the light and food industries, and thereby in retail prices. As a result, there is a great disparity between producer and consumer goods in the relationship between their "costs" and their wholesale prices. In 1970, for example, in heavy industry, production and marketing costs accounted for 77.0 percent of the value of output in industry wholesale prices; profit, 18.1 percent; and the turnover taxes, 4.9 percent. In contrast, the corresponding figures for the light and food industry branches were 68.0, 9.3, and 22.7 percent.

The main trends in Soviet industrial wholesale prices from 1949 to 1970 are shown in Tables 1 and 2. In the price reform of January 1, 1949, heavy industry prices were raised sharply (on the average by 58 percent above the 1948 level) to eliminate most subsidies and to remove the turnover tax from all producer goods except electric power, natural gas, and petroleum products. As a result of subsequent cost reductions, heavy industry prices were later reduced through comprehensive price revisions in 1950, 1952, and 1955, and through more limited adjustments in particular industries from 1958 to 1966. A comprehensive revision of light industry prices was undertaken in two installments, on October 1, 1966, and January 1, 1967, but the aggregate effect was relatively small. In contrast, the reform of heavy industry prices introduced

TABLE 1
Indexes of Soviet Industrial Prices: Enterprise Wholesale Prices (Excluding Turnover Tax), Selected Years, 1950–70
(1949 = 100)

Commodity Group	1950	1952	1955	1958	1962	1966	1967	1970
All industrial production	83	72	68	67	71	71	77	77
Heavy industry	80	68	61	58	57	55	65	64
Chemical industry	84	76	67	67	67	64	66	66
Ferrous metallurgy	71	63	60	60	60	60	90	90
Coal industry	100	91	84	84	84	84	152	152
Petroleum refining	85	72	65	65	63	63	90	89
Electric power	92	82	74	70	61	61	83	83
Machine-building and metal-working	76	60	52	45	44	40	40	39
Timber industry	85	85	85	107	107	107	128	128
Cellulose and paper industry	81	68	65	65	65	65	81	80
Construction materials industry	82	67	57	57	57	57	68	68
Light and food industry	91	82	86	93	110	114	113	115
Light industry	91	83	80	80	81	84	84	85
Food industry	91	81	91	104	135	140	139	140

TABLE 2
Indexes of Soviet Industrial Prices: Industry Wholesale Prices (Including Turnover Tax), Selected Years, 1950–70
(1949 = 100)

Commodity Group	1950	1952	1955	1958	1962	1966	1967	1970
All industrial production.	80	69	61	60	61	59	64	65
Heavy industry	80	68	61	59	59	57	66	67
Chemical industry	84	76	67	67	67	62	62	62
Ferrous metallurgy	71	64	60	60	60	60	88	88
Coal industry	100	91	84	84	84	84	152	152
Petroleum refining	85	72	65	72	66	66	71	91
Electric power	92	82	74	70	70	69	80	80
Machine-building and metal-working	76	61	52	45	45	42	42	40
Timber industry.	85	85	85	107	107	107	125	126
Cellulose and paper industry. . . .	81	68	65	65	65	65	80	79
Construction materials industry. .	79	67	57	57	57	57	68	68
Light and food industry	80	70	59	61	61	60	59	60
Light industry.	88	88	70	70	70	67	67	68
Food industry.	77	62	54	57	59	58	57	58

on July 1, 1967, significantly raised the average level of heavy industry prices and of all industrial production.[5]

A comparison of Tables 1 and 2 shows how the cushion of the turnover tax makes it possible to alter enterprise wholesale prices without equivalent changes in industry wholesale prices. In the food industry, enterprise wholesale prices (Table 1) have been raised several times since 1952 to cover higher costs from successive increases in agricultural procurement prices. Industry wholesale prices (Table 2) do not show a corresponding rise, however, because these cost increases have been largely offset by reductions in turnover taxes, intended to prevent the higher agricultural procurement prices from affecting industry wholesale prices and thus retail prices. Similarly, the enterprise wholesale prices of refined petroleum products rose 43 percent from 1966 to 1967 (Table 1), in connection with the partial introduction of marginal cost pricing and rental payments, but industry wholesale prices increased less than 8 percent (Table 2). A cut in turnover taxes permitted this increase in prices received by producers without a corresponding increase in prices

[5] The increase was greater than appears from Tables 1 and 2, in which the figures for 1967 are averages of the first half of the year at old prices and the second half at new prices. A more precise measure of the increase is provided by a comparison of prices in the second half of 1967 with those prevailing in 1966. The comparison shows that enterprise wholesale prices rose 9 percent for industry as a whole and 17.5 percent for heavy industry, while the respective increases in industry wholesale prices were 7 and 15 percent. For a detailed description and evaluation of Soviet price statistics, see Morris Bornstein, "Soviet Price Statistics," in *Soviet Economic Statistics*, ed. Vladimir G. Treml and John P. Hardt (Durham, N.C.: Duke University Press, 1972), pp. 355–96.

charged consumers. The opposite occurred in 1970, when industry whole-sale prices of petroleum products were raised 20 percent while enterprise wholesale prices showed a slight reduction.

Price Reform Discussion

In the lengthy discussion on price reform which began in 1956, Soviet economists have criticized the industrial price system on various counts and have advanced different proposals for price reform.[6]

Criticisms. The chief criticisms include the following:

1. Many Soviet economists believe that producer goods prices do not properly reflect their "values," in the Marxian sense of the term. In Marxian value theory it is possible for the actual prices of commodi-ties, whether determined by market forces of administratively, to differ ("deviate") from their values, which in a long-run, "normal" sense are regarded as determined by the amount of past and present socially neces-sary labor embodied in them. ("Socially necessary" labor is the amount used with average skill, intensity of work, and conditions of production.) According to Marxian value theory, the value (*stoimost'* in Russian) of a commodity is regarded as composed of three parts: (a) the value of past labor embodied in the materials and that portion of plant and equipment (as measured by depreciation charges) used up in producing the commodity, (b) the value of current labor for which workers receive compensation in the form of wages, and (c) the value of current labor for which workers are not compensated ("surplus value" or "surplus product"). In Marxian terminology, these components of value are desig-nated, respectively, c for constant capital, v for variable capital, and m (or s) for *mehrwert* (or surplus value or product).

In applying this value $= c + v + m$ formula to the Soviet economy, Soviet economists usually take *sebestoimost'* as equivalent to the sum of c and v, and they regard the sum of total profits and turnover taxes as equal to total surplus product or aggregate m. One criticism of indus-trial price formation is that, because (as noted above) prices of producer goods contain significantly less profits and turnover taxes (m) in relation to *sebestoimost'* ($c + v$) than do prices of consumer goods, producer goods as a group are "priced below their value." In addition, this criti-cism asserts, because surplus value is not properly distributed in the prices of different commodities, relative prices of producer goods do not correspond to their relative values. That is, both the level and the struc-ture of producer goods prices are held to deviate from their Marxian value.

2. In turn, because producer goods prices fail to correspond to their values, either in some aggregate sense or relative to each other, they

---

[6] Bornstein, "The Soviet Price Reform Discussion."

furnish unreliable guides for choices by planners and enterprise managers. If relative prices are not correct, then incorrect choices will be made regarding alternative inputs and outputs. Because producer goods as a group are considered underpriced relative to consumer goods, in the calculation of production expenses both materials and machinery are undervalued relative to labor—whose wage rates are related to the price level of consumer goods—leading to the unjustified substitution of materials and machinery for labor. Similarly, the shortcomings of producer goods prices distort the comparisons of internal and external prices on imports and exports which are made in planning foreign trade.

3. The defects of industrial wholesale prices impede the effective use of value targets in the control and evaluation of enterprise operations. For example, they cause differences in the level or rate of profits (or losses) which are unrelated to the performance of enterprises or their contribution to the economy.

4. Soviet economists agree that this scheme of industrial pricing causes part of the value created in producer goods branches of industry to be "realized" in the prices of consumer goods. Thus, the calculation of various macroeconomic relationships using these prices does not give an accurate picture of the structure and development of the economy. For instance, the share of heavy industry is understated in the distribution of national income by sector of origin, while the share of accumulation (i.e., investment) is understated relative to consumption in the distribution of national product.

Reform Proposals. On the issue of what reforms should be made in the industrial price system, Soviet economists are divided into three main schools: a traditionalist school, a surplus product markup school, and an opportunity cost school.

1. Traditionalist school. One group upholds the essentials of the traditional scheme of industrial price formation but suggests relatively modest adjustments in order to improve the structure of producer goods prices without altering their level significantly. It believes that the use of prices as instruments of economic control requires many deviations of price from "value," in order to promote the efficient operation of enterprises, recognize supply and demand factors in certain cases, promote or discourage consumption of certain goods, etc. The traditionalists see no justification for a large increase in the overall level of producer goods prices to incorporate more "surplus product" in them. Instead, they stress selective adjustments in the structure of producer goods prices to eliminate losses and excessive profits, establish the "correct" price relationships between substitutes, encourage the introduction of new models of machinery, etc.

2. Surplus product markup school. Another group of Soviet economists favor pricing on the basis of "value" by adding a uniform, proportional surplus product (m) markup to *sebestoimost'* $(c + v)$ to derive

a price equal to value (i.e., to the sum of $c + v + m$). They propose to raise the level of wholesale prices of producer goods without altering the general level of wholesale prices (or retail prices) of consumer goods. This would be accomplished by a partial shift of surplus product (profits and turnover taxes) from consumer goods prices to producer goods prices in order to raise the latter relative to the former.

The members of this school differ among themselves, however, on the manner in which surplus product should be distributed in the prices of goods. One view favors using labor cost as the base to which the markup would be applied; a second, *sebestoimost'*; a third, capital; and the fourth, a combination of labor cost and capital. Each of these will be discussed briefly in turn.

The most orthodox position advocates relating the surplus product markup to labor cost—i.e., the wage bill—in order to obtain prices that are truly based on "labor value" (*trudovaia stoimost'*). It proposes a uniform surplus product markup related to the wage bill, according to the following formula:

$$p = c + v + v\frac{M}{V} = c + v\left(1 + \frac{M}{V}\right) \tag{1}$$

where p represents the price of a commodity, c the branch average materials costs (including also depreciation charges) per unit of the commodity, v the branch average wage cost per unit of the commodity, M the total surplus value to be distributed among goods, and V the total wage bill for workers engaged in "material production." The prices of the material inputs (and capital equipment to be depreciated) in c would themselves be calculated in the same way.

Another formula relates the markup to total *sebestoimost'* ($c + v$) rather than to labor cost (v) alone. With p, c, v, M, and V defined as before and C representing the total materials cost (including also depreciation) of aggregate "material production,"

$$p = c + v + (c + v)\frac{M}{C + V} = (c + v)\left(1 + \frac{M}{C + V}\right) \tag{2}$$

This formula resembles the traditional price-setting practice in relating the surplus product markup to *sebestoimost'*, but it differs from it in calling for the uniform application of the same percentage markup to all producer and consumer goods.

A third position relates the markup to capital. With p, c, v, and M defined as before and k representing the average amounts of fixed and working capital per unit of the commodity and K the total fixed and working capital used in "material production," the corresponding formula is

$$p = c + v + k\frac{M}{K} \tag{3}$$

The supporters of this position hold that the magnitude of surplus product depends not only on the quantity of live labor used in production but also on its productivity, which in turn depends on the capital with which it is equipped. They believe that capital investment should be reflected in prices in order to promote the economization of capital in choices between more and less capital-intensive goods and methods of production. Likewise, enterprises should pay capital charges to the State, because such charges would lead them to request less fixed and working capital and to use more effectively the capital they have.

A fourth position offers a compromise between the first and third formulas, by relating part of the surplus product markup to labor cost and part to capital. According to this position, with p, c, v, k, and K defined as before and M_1 representing the part of surplus value to be distributed in proportion to the wage bill and M_2 the part of surplus value to be distributed in proportion to capital,

$$p = c + v\left(1 + \frac{M_1}{V}\right) + k\frac{M_2}{K} \tag{4}$$

It is suggested that M_1 correspond to the portion of the total "surplus product" devoted to "social-cultural expenditures" (health, education, and social welfare measures) and that M_2 correspond to the portion devoted to investment, defense, and general administration. In some variants of the formula, an additional price-forming element D is added to include differential rent on natural resources. Also, some proponents favor a single rate for the capital charge M_2/K, while others prefer a charge differentiated by branches of industry according to the structure of capital and the rate of return on capital.

It should be noted that all of these formulas are cost-oriented, neglecting demand as a basic element in value and price. They do not recognize a connection between value and allocation. The allocation of resources would still be accomplished by directives in physical terms, supplemented by selected divergences of price from the "value" result yielded by the particular formula—for example, in order to secure the correct relative price structure for substitute fuels or machines.

3.   Opportunity cost school. The members of this school, in contrast, advocate, explicitly or implicitly, efficiency prices which reflect relative scarcities and include capital and rent charges. These prices would, ideally, be the shadow prices obtained from the formulation of an "optimum" plan by mathematical programming techniques. Such an optimum plan would achieve as fully and as efficiently as possible a set of final output goals specified by the political leadership. The members of this school recognize that such a plan, and its shadow prices, cannot be formulated at present because of the absence of the necessary detailed information on many millions of economic relationships and lack of the necessary data processing and computing facilities to handle this

information if it did exist. However, they believe that it is still possible at present to improve the existing price system by incorporating, if only imperfectly, some of the features of the ideal prices of the optimum plan.

The advocates of this approach—particularly V. V. Novozhilov and L. V. Kantorovich—have been attacked on the ground that they reject the Marxian labor theory of value by recognizing land and capital as factors of production, relating value to scarcity, and using the "notorious" bourgeois marginal analysis. However, they steadfastly deny any deviation from Marxian value theory, asserting that their prices are different from capitalist prices, that land and capital are considered only insofar as they affect the productivity of labor, etc.

Recent Changes

1961–64 Price Revision. The July 1960 Plenum of the Central Committee of the CPSU called for a revision of heavy industry prices and freight rates during 1961–62, with the aim of introducing the new prices in 1963. The main features of the revision, as disclosed while the work was in progress, indicated that it would conform to the views of the traditionalist school.

The principal objective was to adjust prices and costs (i.e., *sebestoimost'*) in heavy industry to provide a "normal" level of profitability, in relation to *sebestoimost'*, of about 9 percent. The general level of wholesale prices for heavy industry was to remain virtually unchanged, being reduced by only about 3 percent. However, the structure of heavy industry prices was to be altered markedly, by price increases in most extractive branches and price reductions in the secondary branches, such as machine building and chemicals. The revision thus sought to recognize and ratify wage and cost increases in the extractive branches, on the one hand, and productivity gains and cost reductions in the manufacturing branches, on the other, since the last general price revision in 1955. In some cases (e.g., coal and petroleum), relative prices of substitutes were to be changed to adjust demands on the part of the users to the planned supplies. The effects of the producer goods price revision on other sectors of the price system—such as wholesale prices of consumer goods, agricultural procurement prices, and retail prices—were to be negligible.[7]

Work on the price revision was not completed on schedule, however, because of the huge volume and great complexity of the work. One source estimates that the total volume of price lists amounted to 38,400 printed pages containing several million prices. By the end of 1962,

---

[7] Morris Bornstein, "The 1963 Soviet Industrial Price Revision," *Soviet Studies,* Vol. XV, No. 1 (July 1963), pp. 43–52.

price lists had been completed for raw materials and fuels, chemicals, construction materials, and electric power, but not for machine building, in which, because of technological developments some 40 percent of the entries in the price lists were new items. Nevertheless, it appears that by late 1963 or early 1964 the new price lists were ready, as instructions were issued in June 1964 to recalculate the 1964 plan and budget in the new prices, as a basis for calculating the 1966 plan and budget and the five-year plan for 1966–70 in the new prices.

The actual promulgation of the new heavy industry price lists was successively postponed, however. According to S. G. Stoliarov, Chief of the Department of Price Statistics of the Central Statistical Administration, one reason was the opposition of critics of the traditional scheme of price formation, particularly those who favored the surplus product markup approach instead. After the ouster of Khrushchev in October 1964, the adoption of new prices was delayed while the new leadership formulated its economic program, including the decisions on economic planning and management announced in Kosygin's speech to the Central Committee on September 27, 1965.

1966–67 Price Reform.   The principal features of the reform of industrial management are as follows. (1) Sales and profitability, rather than total output, were designated as the main enterprise performance indicators. (2) To encourage enterprises to economize on capital, they are required to pay a charge on fixed and working capital, their profitability is now calculated in relation to capital rather than cost, and a greater part of new investment is to be financed from bank credits instead of budget grants. (3) Enterprises retain a larger share of their profits for investment and the payment of bonuses to both workers and management. (4) Enterprise managers were granted some additional authority over the composition of labor inputs.

To implement these objectives, industrial wholesale prices were revised effective October 1, 1966, and January 1, 1967, in light industry, and July 1, 1967, in heavy industry.[8] The main aim in fixing the new prices was to enable most enterprises to cover production costs and earn enough profit to pay a 6 percent charge on capital, establish incentive funds, and expand their capital. In general, prices are intended to cover branch average costs of production, plus a "normal" profit markup, estimated, for industry as a whole, at approximately 12–15 percent on fixed and working capital. However, profit rates vary by branch of industry. For example, in heavy industry, in order to cover costs in the coal industry and at the same time secure the proper relative prices for substitute fuels, accumulation (in the form of both profits and turnover taxes)

---

[8] The "several million" new prices were published in 679 price handbooks. The main features of the reform are summarized in Gertrude E. Schroeder, "The 1966–67 Soviet Industrial Price Reform: A Study in Complications," *Soviet Studies,* Vol. XX, No. 4 (April 1969), pp. 462–77.

must be higher in the petroleum and gas industries than in the coal industry. In light industry, accumulation (particularly in the form of turnover taxes) will be higher on alcoholic beverages and tobacco than on other products. In the extractive industries, two methods were used to deal with large differences in costs due to natural conditions. In iron ore and coal mining, group settlement prices vary by regions. In the petroleum and gas industries, on the other hand, a type of marginal cost pricing was introduced, under which prices are based on the costs of high-cost enterprises, and rents are charged producers with lower costs and higher profits. Finally, in most industries prices were adjusted to encourage enterprises to improve quality and to adopt new technology.

The revision of industrial wholesale prices was not accompanied by changes in the level or structure of retail prices. Likewise, the prices of industrial producer goods sold to agriculture were not altered, so as not to affect the terms of trade for agriculture. Instead, turnover tax rates were reduced, or the differences were charged to various budget accounts. However, the losses in budget revenue from turnover tax reductions are to be recovered from increased profits taxes and rental payments by enterprises.

The price reform was conducted by a new State Price Committee (SPC), created late in 1965 by the merger of the Price Bureau of USSR Gosplan with the Commission on Prices of the Presidium of the USSR Council of Ministers. The new Committee is a union-republic body with counterparts in the republic Gosplans and departments for prices in the provincial and city planning commissions. Its functions are to establish the principles for fixing all types of prices, to direct the actual setting of prices, and to supervise the enforcement of prices once established. The SPC itself fixes the wholesale prices on all important producer and consumer goods, including 75–80 percent of the value of output of heavy industry and about 50 percent of the value of output of the light and food industries. Price committees in the republics set prices covering nearly 20 percent of the value of output in heavy industry and over 40 percent in consumer goods industry. Enterprises themselves may set prices only for goods whose prices are not fixed by higher organs. In practice, this means that enterprise can negotiate prices with customers only on some kinds of new products and special orders. However, enterprises do have some influence on the prices fixed by the price committees because the enterprises prepare the initial cost estimates on which final prices are based.

The wholesale price reform was successful in making all major branches of industry profitable and in reducing the spread in profitability among industries and enterprises within industries. However, the new prices have been criticized in the Soviet press on many counts, including the following. (1) For many goods, the costs on which prices are based are incorrectly calculated, and often inflated. (2) Relative prices of different varieties frequently conflict with the pattern of production specified in the enterprises' "assortment" plans. (3) Quality differentials are imperfectly reflected in price differentials. (4) Relative prices of substitutes often do not promote consumption in the same proportions as outputs are produced. (5) The SPC has not established the methodological guidelines needed to permit ministries and even enterprises to fix more prices themselves.

The new prices represent an improvement over the previous prices, set in 1955, because they incorporate changes in labor and materials costs which have occurred since then, thus permitting the reduction or elimination of subsidies. In addition, as a result of the inclusion of explicit, though arbitrary, capital charges—and in some cases rents—prices now reflect total costs to a greater, though still incomplete and imperfect, extent. However, the new prices are still largely based on average rather than marginal costs and are not intended to be scarcity prices capable of allocating resources in an efficient way. Thus, they will not contribute much to improving those choices which enterprise managers, seeking sales and profits, are able to make regarding current inputs and outputs and investment. Nor are they likely to enhance significantly the ability of higher administrative authorities to evaluate enterprise performance. In short, the price reform, like the reform of industrial management, is of restricted scope, and its beneficial effects will also be limited.

III. AGRICULTURAL PROCUREMENT PRICES

Agricultural procurement prices are those at which collective and state farms sell to state procurement agencies. Collective farm market prices, at which agricultural producers sell to households, are analyzed in the following section on retail prices.

Nature and Trends

Collective Farm Prices.   In setting procurement prices for collective farms, the Soviet government has pursued two conflicting objectives: (1) to fix the terms of trade for the collective farm peasantry so as to make it bear a large share of the burden of industrialization, and (2) to provide incentives to produce. The former objective clearly dominated during the Stalin era. Since 1953, the latter has been more characteristic of collective farm price policy.

The terms of trade and real income of the peasantry depend on the relationship between agricultural procurement prices paid to the collective farms, on the one hand, and prices paid by collective farms for materials inputs and prices paid by collective farmers for consumer goods, on the other. The terms of trade for the peasantry were extremely unfavorable during the Stalin era. Procurement prices for grain remained almost unchanged from 1929 to 1953. Livestock prices doubled from 1929 to 1940 but remained unaltered from 1940 to 1953. Over the same period, retail prices (at which collective farms also bought many of their industrial inputs) rose many fold. In 1952, the level of retail prices was 10 times the 1940 level. Grain and livestock production was very unprofitable, and the price of potatoes did not even cover the cost of delivery to the city. For technical crops, such as cotton, sugar beets, and tobacco, the situation was more favorable, as procurement price increases after 1940 had kept pace with increases in the prices of consumer goods and industrial inputs.[9]

One of the first steps taken by Stalin's successors in 1953 was to embark on a broad program to increase agricultural output, involving changes in planning and administration, delivery obligations, taxes, investment, and prices. The changes in agricultural procurement prices included a large increase in the general level of prices, regional differentiation of prices, a revision in the relative price structure in favor of food crops, a greater effort to relate prices to costs, and the unification of multiple prices into single procurement prices for each crop. Major price increases were made in 1953, 1956, 1958, 1962, 1963, and 1965. Table 3 shows the trend of collective farm procurement prices from 1952 to 1966. Comparable more recent data unfortunately are not available.

In 1953 the government increased sharply both obligatory delivery prices and state purchase prices. The former applied to the delivery quotas fixed for each farm, and the latter to additional sales to the state above the quota. Although state purchase prices were higher than obligatory delivery prices, they were still below collective farm market prices, and hence sales at state purchase prices were in most cases not voluntary but compulsory. In addition to increasing both types of prices, the government further raised average realized prices on vegetables and potatoes by reducing obligatory delivery quotas, thereby releasing more of their output for sale at the higher state purchase and collective farm market prices. In 1956, procurement prices were again increased. and in some cases the differential between the basic and the higher incentive price was reduced.

Prices were again changed in 1958, when multiple pricing was replaced by a single state purchase price for each product. Concurrently, the

---

[9] On trends in prices and terms of trade from 1928 to 1953, see Jerzy F. Karcz, *Soviet Agricultural Marketings and Prices, 1928–1954*, RM-1930 (Santa Monica, Calif.: RAND Corporation, 1957); and Nancy Nimitz, "Soviet Agricultural Prices and Costs," in *Comparisons of the United States and Soviet Economies* (papers Submitted by Panelists Appearing Before the Subcommittee on Economic Statistics, Joint Economic Committee, 86th Cong., 1st sess.) (Washington, D.C.: U.S. Government Printing Office, 1959), Part I, pp. 249–55. For an accurate picture of the peasantry's terms of trade one must, of course, also consider trends in prices of collective farm market sales, which account for an important share of the incomes of producers of meat, milk, eggs, fruits, and vegetables.

TABLE 3
Indexes of Soviet Agricultural Procurement Prices, Selected Years, 1953–66*
(1952 = 100)

Commodity Group	1953	1954	1955	1956	1958	1962	1965	1966
All agricultural products	154	207	209	251	296	332	404	412
Grain†	236	739	553	634	695	840	1024	1113
Technical crops‡	115	111	117	147	143	143	174	169
Sunflowers	528	626	987	928	774	859	1046	1122
Fruits§	119	135	138	192	179	167	165	157
Potatoes	316	369	368	814	789	1043	1374	1299
Cattle.	385	579	585	665	1175	1523	1980	2103
Milk	202	289	303	334	404	434	521	528
Eggs.	126	135	152	155	297	339	342	343
Wool	107	146	158	246	352	346	379	376

*Average state procurement-purchase prices on agricultural products procured from collective farms and private plots.
†Wheat, rye, barley, oats, maize, millet, buckwheat, and rice.
‡Raw cotton, flax fiber, hemp fiber, sugar beets, and tobacco.
§Including wine grapes.

machine-tractor stations (MTS's) were abolished and their machinery sold to the collective farms. For the first time, prices of all crops were revised at the same time, providing an opportunity for a comprehensive adjustment of relative prices. However, the new prices could not be accurately related to costs (even if this had been intended) because of a lack of appropriate cost data. For decades, as long as average procurement prices were extremely low, reference to costs was politically inexpedient, and collective farms did not calculate their production costs. The notion was even widely accepted that the concept of cost was not applicable to collective farms. Only in 1955 did the state begin to investigate the level and structure of collective farm costs, and only in 1958 did farms begin to calculate their costs.[10] The 1958 prices were therefore not based on costs. Instead they were set on the principle that the total bill to the state for procurements from the collective farms should not exceed the previous bill for procurements plus the bill for MTS operations and investment. Thus, basically, the existing terms of trade between

---

[10] The calculation of collective farm costs was, furthermore, complicated by the question of how to value labor inputs, which were reckoned not in money wage payments or even man-days, but in "labor-day" accounting units. The payments made in money and in kind per labor-day varied widely from one farm to another, and from year to year on the same farm. Moreover, since payments for a labor-day were greater on the more successful farms, to use actual labor-day payments would make it appear that the more efficient farms had higher costs. For purposes of comparison, therefore, it was decided to assign a fixed notional value to collective farm labor inputs, namely, to value them at state farm wage rates. Some Soviet economists, however, favored valuation of collective farm labor inputs at actual labor-day payments. See Nimitz, "Soviet Agricultural Prices and Costs," pp. 256–57, and Frank A. Durgin, Jr., "Monetization and Policy in Soviet Agriculture since 1952," *Soviet Studies*, Vol. XV, No. 4 (April 1964), pp. 389–91.

the agricultural and industrial sectors were left unchanged; as one Soviet economist put it, "only the channels of exchange were altered."[11]

In the case of livestock products, it was not intended that the 1958 prices should cover costs. Instead it was "supposed" that collective farm losses on livestock products would be covered from earnings on grain, sunflowers, and other crops. The ratio of prices to costs in 1960, for example, was 155 percent for grain (excluding corn), but only 65–67 percent for meat and eggs and 86 percent for milk.[12] This relative price-cost structure provided little incentive to collective farms to increase livestock production, and they instead emphasized the more profitable plant crops. In 1962, the government raised purchase prices on cattle and poultry by an average of 35 percent. It also took the politically unpopular step of raising retail prices of meat products by an average of 30 percent and of butter by 25 percent. However, despite the substantial increase in livestock prices, they still failed to cover costs.

In 1965, as part of the broad Brezhnev-Kosygin agricultural program, prices for milk, livestock, and grain were raised, and above-quota premium prices were re-established for wheat and rye, cotton, and sunflowers. Table 4 shows the ratio of the new prices to the average of

TABLE 4
Ratio of 1965 Prices to Average 1963–65 Production
Costs* of Selected Commodities on Soviet Collective
Farms and State Farms
(percent)

Commodity	Collective Farms	State Farms
Grain	184	118
Potatoes	153	114
Vegetables	99	125
Sugar beets	140	107
Sunflowers	589	430
Raw cotton	157	131
Milk	98	93
Cattle†	109	87
Sheep†	113	98
Pigs†	104	96
Poultry	118	98
Eggs	83	112
Wool	134	114

*Sebestoimost', including material inputs, depreciation, and labor costs.
†Weight gain.

---

[11] Another Soviet economist reports that the 1958 prices took into account only state expenditures on the current operations of the MTS's, excluding state investment in them.

[12] In these figures collective farm labor inputs are valued at state farm wage rates.

costs in 1963–65 on collective and state farms. These figures indicate that for all collective farms as a group the new prices made production of cattle barely profitable, while milk, eggs, and vegetables were still produced at a loss.

In addition to these changes since 1953 in the level and structure of procurement prices, the terms of trade of collective farm agriculture have been improved through reductions in the prices of industrial inputs and in the prices of consumer goods sold to the peasantry. Until 1958, machinery, trucks, spare parts, and fuel were available to collective farms only at retail prices, while state farms bought these goods at much lower wholesale prices. In 1958, uniform wholesale prices for state and collective farms were established on trucks, machinery, and spare parts. But this concession was offset, at least in part, by an unpublicized increase in the same year in the wholesale prices of farm machinery and spare parts and in the retail price of gasoline.

This measure was reversed in 1961, when the government reduced retail prices on gasoline and wholesale prices on trucks, machinery, and spare parts. In 1962 it authorized collective farms to buy construction materials at wholesale, rather than retail, prices. Prices of trucks, farm machinery, and spare parts were again reduced at the beginning of 1966.

Though no precise calculations are available, it is evident that successive increases in agricultural procurement prices, together with adjustments in prices of industrial inputs and of consumer goods, have markedly improved the collective farm peasantry's terms of trade since 1953. The general price increases from 1953 to 1958 helped, in conjunction with other measures, to bring about a large increase in agricultural output. Subsequent price increases have been more selective, focusing on lagging commodities, particularly livestock products. However, the introduction of guaranteed pay, at state farm wage rates, for collective farmers beginning in 1966 raised costs. As a result, purchase prices of various products, especially livestock, fail to cover costs on many farms.

State Farm Prices.   State farm delivery prices have been essentially different in nature from the prices paid to collective farms. State farms are "factories in the field" similar to state enterprises in industry, transportation, trade, etc. Their employees receive money wages on a piece-rate basis, and they calculate cost of production (*sebestoimost'*) in essentially the same way as other state enterprises. If—as was commonly the case—sales revenue failed to cover *sebestoimost'*, the deficit was met by redistributions of profits within the state farm network or by operating subsidies from the budget. (In addition, investment has been financed by budget grants.) Because state farm costs are reimbursed by the combination of delivery prices and subsidies, the failure of prices to cover costs does not restrain output. In contrast, for the collective farms, prices are the sole source of compensation for production expenses and productive effort.

Until 1954, state farm prices were based on (but were lower than) the corresponding state purchase prices for collective farms. As these prices did not cover production costs, a subsidy was planned for each type of state farm output. In 1954, with the announced objective of eliminating subsidies, state farm delivery prices were raised and differentiated by geographic zones. The new prices were supposed to yield an overall profit of 7.7 percent on *sebestoimost'*, although it was expected that livestock would still be produced at a loss, to be covered from earnings on crops. But by 1956 the overall profit rate was only 5.6 percent, and by 1958 crop profits failed to cover livestock losses, resulting in an overall loss rate of 1 percent. By 1960, net losses of the state farm system covered by budget subsidies amounted to 600 million rubles (in terms of "new" rubles after the 1961 monetary reform). To eliminate these subsidies, the government in 1961 reduced the state farms' input prices and raised their output prices. State farm costs were cut by about 300 million rubles per year through a reduction of prices on machinery, spare parts, and fuel. State farm revenues were augmented by 500 million rubles through higher prices for livestock products, grain, sugar beets, and fruits. In 1962, state farm livestock prices were raised again, concurrently with the increase in collective farm livestock prices. However, the new prices still failed to cover costs for cattle, pigs, poultry, and eggs. In 1963, along with collective farm prices, state farm prices were raised on cotton, sugar beets, and certain vegetables.

The state farms also benefited from price increases under the new agriculture measures announced in 1965, although their prices remained below collective farm prices by 10 percent on meat, 15 percent on wool, 17 percent on cotton, 39 percent on grain, and 55 percent on sunflowers. As Table 4 shows, the new prices failed to cover costs, and losses were therefore planned, for meat and dairy production.

The principles of the industrial reforms announced in 1965 were first applied to state farms in 1967, when, by way of experiment, 390 of the most profitable state farms (out of a total of 15,000) were transferred to the new system of management. These state farms were paid collective farm prices for their deliveries, in order to provide them profits to finance not only all current expenses but also most of their investment expenditures. The experiment was considered successful; a second group of 400 farms was shifted in 1968, and 9,000 farms were operating on the new system in 1972.

Price Reform Discussion

Beginning in 1958, defects in agricultural procurement prices have been criticized and suggestions for improvement have been advanced at scholarly conferences and in Soviet economic journals and news-papers.[13] The agricultural price reform discussion has been more cautious than the industrial price reform discussion, because agricultural price changes are politically sensitive measures which directly affect the distribution of income between the rural and urban populations. Changes in industrial prices, in contrast, primarily affect financial relationships within the state sector.

Criticisms. The principal criticisms concern price-cost relationships for different products, defects in geographical differentiation of prices, and the failure of prices to promote a rational pattern of specialization.

1. One criticism is that both the level and the structure of procurement prices have been set without adequate regard for production costs (including reasonable compensation for the labor of collective farm members). As a result, incentives to expand collective output are lacking, and collective farmers instead devote as much effort as possible to their private plots. On the one hand, more accurate calculations of costs are needed. On the other, the government should fix prices so as to make the production of each product profitable, rather than expecting profits on plant products to compensate losses on livestock products.[14]

2. Prices of individual crops are differentiated geographically in an effort to skim off differential rents arising from more favorable natural conditions. However, the variation in prices is not as great as the variation in costs in the different zones.[15] As a result, the profitability of a given crop varies greatly from zone to zone. For some crops, such as potatoes, flax, and wool, prices are not differentiated geographically, even though they are produced in different areas with widely varying costs. In addition, there are large differences in costs and profitability within price zones, some of which cover a very large area. For example, grain price zone IV stretches from the shores of the Arctic into southern Siberia, comprising an area 10.3 times that of France, with extreme variations in soil, rainfall, temperature, and length of growing season. One consequence of these defects in price zoning is large differences in the incomes of collective farmers in different regions, and even in the same region, due to natural conditions, rather than to differences in equipment, productive effort, or managerial skill. Another consequence is that the state does not obtain the maximum results from a given

---

[13] For a comprehensive discussion of the issues and reform proposals, see Morris Bornstein, "The Soviet Debate on Agricultural Price and Procurement Reforms," *Soviet Studies,* Vol. XXI, No. 1 (July 1969), pp. 1–20.

[14] According to some recent estimates, profitability rates of 40 to 60 percent on *sebestoimost'* (including reasonable compensation to collective farm members) would be necessary if collective farms are to pay income taxes, make contributions to pension and welfare funds, and carry out planned expansion of fixed and working capital.

[15] According to one estimate, the differences in *sebestoimost'* in different natural zones range from 180 to 600 percent for different agricultural products, while the maximum differentiation of procurement prices is 116 percent (for rye).

total expenditure on agricultural procurements. By increasing prices in some zones and reducing them in others, the state could secure a net increase in the volume of procurements without any increase in total procurement expenditures.

3. Many collective and state farms operate at low profitability or losses because they are required, by their delivery plans, to produce products for which they are not suited. It is not unusual for collective farms to receive procurement plans for 15 or 20 different products, some of which they are expected to produce at a loss. Often the quotas exceed the farm's capabilities, forcing it to request loans in kind for seeding or planting purposes. In part, the lack of rational specialization is the result of the low level of agricultural production: the state is afraid to reduce or eliminate delivery plans from low-yield areas lest it lose badly needed supplies. On the other hand, the requirement that farms produce and deliver products for which they are not suited prevents them from specializing in those crops in which their yields would be much higher.

Reform Proposals. Various proposals have been advanced to deal with shortcomings in the level, structure, and regional differentiation of agricultural procurement prices. They include the following: (1) basing prices on marginal rather than average costs, (2) revising the boundaries of price zones, (3) using instruments other than price differences to take differential rent, and (4) varying prices in accordance with harvest fluctuations.

1. At present, the zone price of a product is supposed to be based on the average cost of production in that zone. As a result, collective farms with higher than average costs for the zone have difficulty covering expenses, and the incomes of their members are correspondingly low. The supporters of marginal cost pricing argue that if the state requires a farm to produce and deliver a commodity, the state should pay the farm a price adequate to cover costs (including reasonable compensation for the labor of its members) and provide a profit for expansion. Although a few members of the marginal cost school favor basing price on the national marginal cost of the product, most accept the principle of zonal price differentiation and urge instead that price be based on the marginal cost of the zone. More precisely, they advocate basing the price on the cost of production of farms with the worst land in the zone (in terms of fertility and location) but with average conditions of production in regard to mechanization, labor productivity, and managerial efficiency. The differential rent accruing to farms with better land would be taken by taxation.

Prices based on marginal costs would, of course, mean a much higher bill for state procurements—double, or for some products or zones even triple, the bill with prices based on zonal average costs. However, there need not be a corresponding increase in wholesale and retail prices. As noted, additional tax revenues would be collected on the differential rent of farms on inframarginal land. These revenues would be allocated to subsidies to the light and food industries and the trade network intended to keep wholesale and retail prices below the level of procurement prices. Opponents of this approach object that it is undesirable to set retail prices below procurement prices, as this situation encourages farms to buy agricultural products at retail prices in order to resell them to the state at procurement prices. Critics also point out that it would be difficult to determine the correct amount of differential rent to be taken through taxation from all but the highest cost farms.

2. Suggestions for improving price zoning include the following. The number of zones should be increased to make them more homogeneous and to reduce intrazonal differences in cost and profitability. Zone prices should be introduced for such crops as potatoes, flax, and wool. The revision of zone boundaries should consider both natural factors (such as soil, temperature, precipitation, topography, etc.) and economic factors (such as the structure of output, extent of mechanization, income per acre and per man-day, etc.). Price zoning should promote rational specialization through higher profitability for crops in the zones most suited to them, but prices should be high enough to cover costs and provide a profit even in the less suitable areas when farms are assigned a delivery quota for the product.

3. Even with improvements in the delineation of price zones, intrazonal differences in cost and profit would continue to exist. To take some of the differential rent of farms with better than average, or better than marginal, land in the zone, income taxes and/or land taxes are recommended. An income tax has been levied on collective farms for a number of years, not only to take differential rent but also to exert control over the fulfillment of production and financial plans. However, the tax was levied on gross income (including labor-day distributions to members) rather than on net income, and with virtually no progression in rates. Reform proposals recommended using net rather than gross income as the base and introducing a progressive scale of rates. In 1965, the base was shifted to net income, and an element of progression was introduced through the exemption from taxation of the first 15 percent of net income. An alternative, or supplementary, method of taking rent is direct money rent payments varying with the quality of the land. However, this method requires a land cadaster, which is not likely to be available for many years.[16]

4. Another reform proposal is that, instead of keeping prices stable despite variations in harvests, the government raise them temporarily when harvests are especially poor. Under this proposal, in bad harvest

---

[16] Despite several conferences and much discussion in the technical literature, Soviet economists are not agreed on the basic principles of the cadaster, the concrete steps to compile it, or the uses to be made of it.

years both agricultural procurement prices and state retail prices would be increased. The 1958 agricultural price revision was supposed to have introduced flexible procurement prices varying with harvests, but in practice flexibility operated in only one direction: prices were reduced for very good harvests but not raised for bad harvests.

1965 Revisions. The 1965 agricultural price revisions reflect these reform proposals only to a very limited extent.[17] Prices are still based on zonal average costs, except in the case of grain procurements in the main grain areas, where the new prices seem to be related to cost conditions on farms located on the least favorable land. While some price zone boundaries were altered, there was no comprehensive revision based on a careful study of natural and man-made factors affecting costs. The nature of the collective farm income tax was significantly improved, but it is still an imperfect instrument for taking differential rent—inferior to explicit rental payments, which are precluded by the absence of a land cadaster. Prices are not to vary inversely with the size of the harvest. Rather, the reintroduction of premium prices for above-plan deliveries of wheat, rye, cotton, and sunflowers will make their average realized prices higher when harvests are good.

On balance then, the 1965 price changes appear to be another desirable, but still relatively modest, step on the road to guiding Soviet agriculture through prices and monetary incentives, rather than administrative commands. Soviet agriculture still lacks sound prices capable of securing rational specialization of production through decentralized decisions of farm managers. Moreover, it is important to recognize that although higher prices, properly related to costs, can stimulate production, the development of Soviet agriculture also requires a steady and adequate flow of industrial inputs (including investment goods) at reasonable prices and on reasonable credit terms, as well as adequate and guaranteed remuneration for farm members.

IV. RETAIL PRICES

Nature and Trends

There are two principal types of retail prices at which goods are sold to households in the Soviet Union: state retail prices and collective farm market prices.[18]

State Retail Prices. The state retail price is charged by state retail stores, consumer cooperative stores, and state and cooperative service

---

[17] For a detailed discussion of the 1965 agricultural program, see Jerzy F. Karcz, "The New Soviet Agricultural Programme," *Soviet Studies,* Vol. XVII, No. 2 (October 1965), pp. 129–61; and Roger A. Clarke, "Soviet Agricultural Reforms since Khrushchev," *Soviet Studies,* Vol. XX, No. 2 (October 1968), pp. 159–78.

[18] The following discussion draws on Bornstein, "The Soviet Price System," pp. 88–97.

establishments, such as restaurants, laundries, theaters, etc. The consumer cooperatives, which operate primarily in the rural areas, are closely supervised by the state, which determines their number, size, location, etc.; allocates goods to them; and establishes sales plans for them. Of total state, cooperative, and urban collective farm market sales in 1971, the respective percentage shares of the three types were 68.8, 28.8, and 2.4 percent.

State retail prices supposedly are fixed with the aim of clearing the market both in aggregate terms and for each commodity. In aggregate terms, the objective is to set the general level of state retail prices so that total retail sales at that price level will absorb the money income which the population is expected to want to spend at state and cooperative retail outlets. For individual goods, the objective is to fix the price of each at a level which equates planned supply and expected demand.

The general level of retail prices depends upon both tax and wage policies. The Soviet government relies primarily on price-increasing taxes, namely the turnover and profits taxes, to finance investment, military programs, and social services. As a result, the general retail price level is higher than it would be if direct taxes on households were used to a greater extent. Planned increases in private consumption can be distributed among households by reducing retail prices or by increasing money incomes (or by a combination of the two). The first method distributes the increase in consumption among the population as a whole, while the second is more selective. With stable retail prices, money incomes of different segments of the population can be increased by different degrees (and at different times) to provide selective incentives for increased production and for occupational and geographical shifts.

The first method was used from 1948 to 1954, when retail prices were reduced each spring. As Table 5 shows, since 1954 the state retail price level has been relatively stable, although there have been adjustments in the prices of individual goods. In addition to a moderate rise in the general wage level,[19] there have been selective increases in the money incomes of particular segments of the population, through increases in agricultural procurement prices, pensions, minimum wages, and the wages of selected occupations (miners, teachers, etc.).

Under planners' sovereignty in the USSR, the basic method of eliminating a disequilibrium in the market for a particular good is to adjust demand to supply, in contrast to the adjustment of supply to demand which characterizes the response under consumers' sovereignty. The latter kind of adjustment occurs in the USSR only to a limited extent when, in response to evidence in the form of shortages or surpluses at the prevailing prices, planners modify the composition (types, models, etc.)

---

[19] Average monthly wages of workers in the state sector rose from 71.8 rubles in 1955 to 130.3 rubles in 1972, for an average annual increase of 3.6 percent over the period.

TABLE 5
Indexes of Soviet State Retail Prices, Selected Years, 1952–71
(1950 = 100)

Commodity Group	1952	1955	1958	1962	1963	1967	1971
All commodities	87	74	76	76	76	75	75
Food	82	70	73	75	75	74	75
Meat	74	60	66	78	85	85	85
Fish.	88	79	77	76	76	70	69
Butter	74	64	65	76	83	83	83
Vegetable oil	84	65	65	65	65	65	65
Sugar.	91	80	80	77	75	74	73
Bread and bread products . . .	73	60	59	59	59	59	59
Potatoes	n.a.*	n.a.	92	100	112	106	106
Vegetables.	n.a.	n.a.	88	84	90	86	98
Alcoholic beverages	88	78	94	94	94	94	91
Non-food commodities	95	81	80	79	78	75	75
Cotton fabrics.	98	71	71	71	71	68	68
Woolen fabrics	97	92	92	89	89	82	82
Silk fabrics.	99	91	89	80	77	68	68
Clothing	98	90	90	86	86	81	81
Knit goods.	99	88	87	87	87	86	86
Leather footwear.	98	81	81	82	83	81	81
Rubber footwear	99	76	75	76	76	74	74
Tobacco products	87	82	81	82	82	82	82
Watches	86	82	79	54	54	46	46
Bicycles	87	78	78	60	60	57	57

*Not available.

of the output of the various kinds of consumer goods which can be produced with the resources which they have allocated to those lines of production.

On some goods, retail prices are set with other objectives which conflict with the aim of clearing the market. One such additional objective, stemming from administrative considerations, is to avoid changing prices very often. This objective clearly conflicts with the aim of balancing demand with supply.

Another objective is to make the distribution of real income less unequal than the distribution of money income. To do this, the government fixes lower prices for mass consumption goods (such as basic foodstuffs) which predominate in the budgets of lower income groups, and higher prices for goods (e.g., consumer durables and luxury foodstuffs) which are relatively more important in the budgets of higher income groups. In pursuit of this objective, prices of some food products, such as meat, have been deliberately set below the equilibrium level (even below the corresponding agricultural procurement prices in some cases), as persistent shortages attest. In this way, the informal rationing of queues and empty shelves helps to modify the distribution of real income from the initial distribution of money income.

Relative prices are also used to pursue other objectives of social policy. For example, low prices are set on books in order to promote indoctrination and education, and on children's apparel in order to aid large families, while high prices are intended to curb the consumption of vodka.

The turnover tax, which now provides about one third of total budget revenue, is the principal device used by planners to secure the desired level and structure of retail prices. The principal components of the state retail price are (1) the enterprise wholesale price (or the agricultural procurement price plus the markup of the procurement agency), (2) the turnover tax, (3) the wholesale trade margin, and (4) the retail trade margin. In addition, there are transportation charges. The wholesale and retail margins are intended to cover expenses and provide a profit at the respective stages. The respective shares of enterprise wholesale prices, turnover taxes, and the two trade margins in the total value of state retail sales in recent years may be estimated very roughly at 60, 30, and 10 percent. Their relative importance in the prices of individual goods differs markedly, however, precisely because the turnover tax is used to fix the retail price at the desired level.

The turnover tax thus serves as a cushion which separates the retail prices paid by households and the wholesale prices received by producing enterprises in industry and agriculture. It permits the planners to alter consumer prices without changing producer prices correspondingly, and vice versa. Retail price reductions need not be accompanied by wholesale price reductions, and wholesale price increases need not be followed by retail price increases. The turnover tax separates not only the levels but also the structures of consumer and producer prices, since the different rates of taxation on different goods cause their relative retail prices to differ from their relative wholesale prices. For most goods the turnover tax is set as a specific ruble amount, and there are separate wholesale and retail price lists. For a limited group of goods, chiefly intended for local markets, the turnover tax is levied as a percentage of the enterprise wholesale price. These goods include some types of haberdashery, household items, and recreational and educational items. For certain nonfood consumer goods, the turnover tax is calculated as a percentage of the retail price. This scheme is used for consumer goods produced by the paper, chemical, and radio industries, as well as for sewn and fur items.

Collective Farm Market Prices.   The collective farm market price of goods is determined by supply and demand in the individual collective farm markets, varying from market to market and from day to day in the same market. There are about 7,300 collective farm markets, approximately 70 percent of them in towns of various sizes and 30 percent in rural areas. The markets occupy designated trading areas and are equipped with a varying number of stalls, benches, tables, storage bins, meat and milk control points, etc. Sellers are charged a small daily fee for the right to offer their wares. About 600,000 peasants are estimated to participate in the markets each day.

Although urban collective farm market sales represented less than 3 percent of total state, cooperative, and urban collective farm market sales in 1971, their importance in Soviet retail trade is greater than this figure suggests. In relation to total trade of the three channels in the same food goods, the collective farm market share in 1971 was 8 percent. In some important cities the collective farm markets account for 20 to 40 percent of total sales of major food products.

Collective farm market prices are set by supply and demand, but both supply and demand are strongly influenced by the state. Demand on the collective farm market depends on the extent to which the state retail network is able, with available quantities at the established prices, to satisfy the effective demand of households. The excess purchasing power remaining after household expenditures in the state retail trade sector finds an outlet in the collective farm market. The supply offered by agricultural producers (collective farms, peasants, and urban workers with garden plots) depends on the amount of output they have left after selling to state procurement agencies.

In contrast to the relative stability of state retail prices (see Table 5), collective farm market prices fluctuate with the size of the harvest, increasing sharply when harvests are poor and supplies are reduced in both state stores and collective farm markets. Collective farm market prices exceed state retail prices on the same commodities by substantial amounts, although the extent varies from item to item. In part the difference reflects below-equilibrium pricing in state stores, but in part it also reflects a premium paid for better quality and freshness in the collective farm market.

Price Reform Discussion

At scholarly conferences and in the economic literature of the last decade, Soviet economists have criticized a number of aspects of retail price formation and have advanced suggestions for changes.

Criticisms.   Among the criticisms of retail prices are the following: (1) prices diverge from a market-clearing level, (2) prices are set without adequate study of demand, (3) rural price differentials are unjustified, and (4) price lists are outdated and too complex.

1. For decades, many state retail prices have been too low, and demand has exceeded supply, giving rise to shortages and queues. Among the causes responsible are the effort to modify income distribution in favor of lower income groups, underfulfillment of ambitious production plans, and the failure to meet assortment plans. In addition, local shortages often exist because of errors in the distribution of goods by

the trade network. A general situation of excess demand was even justified by Stalin on the ground that it was a "law" of socialism that demand should outstrip supply.[20] This position has now been condemned as theoretically unsound and undesirable in practice. Nevertheless, prices remain below the market-clearing level for various goods, particularly meat and certain consumer durables, and for certain services, notably housing.

While there are shortages of these goods, at the same time there are large excess inventories of yard goods, clothing, footwear, cameras, bicycles, watches, and sewing machines. In part, these surpluses are due to overpricing, but they also are due to poor estimates of demand and to the failure to adjust production to changes in consumer tastes. Thus, sharp price cuts on sewing machines and outmoded clothing failed to liquidate excess stocks.[21]

2. If it is intended to strive for market-clearing prices, then accurate estimates of current and future demand are essential. But such studies of consumer demand are lacking. Only in the last few years has serious attention been devoted to demand studies, and work on the subject is still in the early stages. In particular, demand estimates are too aggregative, covering excessively broad categories of goods and very large geographic areas, and neglecting differences in the demands of different income groups. There has been relatively little application of mathematical techniques to the analysis of retail trade problems.

3. Beginning in 1949, prices on various goods in rural areas exceeded urban prices for the same items by about 7 percent. This differential was justified on the ground that marketing and transportation costs are higher for rural trade. However, such a price differential tends to divert peasant purchases from rural to urban retail outlets, and to encourage "speculation," i.e., resale of goods bought in the city to other peasants at higher prices.

4. Many retail price lists are out of date. Retail price lists on some goods, especially fabrics and sewn goods, were fixed in 1954 on the basis of 1939–40 prices. Retail price lists are so numerous and so complex that only a small group of specialists understands them. For example, there are over 90,000 price lists for clothing and over 7,000 for footwear.

Reform Proposals. Various suggestions to improve retail prices have been advanced, including (1) more intensive study of demand, (2) greater flexibility of prices, (3) more decentralization of price fixing, and (4) wider use of the two-price-list scheme.

[20] Abram Bergson, *The Economics of Soviet Planning* (New Haven, Conn.: Yale University Press, 1964), p. 70. For an evaluation of Soviet retail prices from the standpoint of welfare economics, see ibid., chap. 4.

[21] Marshall I. Goldman, "The Reluctant Consumer and Economic Fluctuations in the Soviet Union," *Journal of Political Economy*, Vol. LXXIII, No. 4 (August 1965), pp. 372–73.

1. As a basis for improved price-setting, consumer demand studies should be intensified. In particular, more attention should be devoted to income as well as price elasticities of demand, rural versus urban demand, and the long-term evolution of demand and prices. The work of the various research institutes studying different aspects of demand should be more closely coordinated.

2. Price flexibility should be increased in various ways. Clothing and footwear prices should be raised more often and more quickly on fashionable items in high demand, and reduced on slow-moving, out-of-style items. To adjust production to sales, wholesale prices of producers should be varied in the same direction as retail prices. Seasonal prices, now used for a limited number of food products (such as eggs, fruits, and vegetables), should also be applied to yard goods, clothing, and footwear. When harvests are poor, both retail and agricultural procurement prices should be raised.

3. Since 1957, the union republic and regional authorities have been responsible for fixing retail prices on a group of goods accounting for about 45 percent of retail sales. This group includes sausage and confectionery articles, eggs, milk, sewn goods, furniture, toys, and non-alcoholic beverages. The central authorities in Moscow set prices on the remainder of retail trade, including such important goods as bread, meat, fish, butter, cloth, footwear, knit goods, tobacco, vodka, and most consumer durables. It has been suggested that further decentralization of price fixing is desirable, in order to increase price flexibility and bring prices closer to a market-clearing level. In particular, it has been proposed that producing enterprises, in conjunction with the trade network, fix prices on new items in line with prices on analogous existing items.

4. In the case of sewn goods, china and earthenware, glass articles, and pots and pans, it is proposed that the two-price-list scheme be adopted instead of the present arrangement of levying the turnover tax as a percentage of the retail price. When the tax is levied as a uniform percentage of the retail price for an entire class of goods, the relative structure of retail prices also determines the relative structure of enterprise wholesale prices. In many instances, items which are more complex and more expensive to manufacture do not have correspondingly higher retail and wholesale prices. As a result, the profitability of different items to the producing enterprise varies, and it is inclined to depart from its assortment plan by producing more of the "advantageous" items and less of the "disadvantageous" items. By adopting the two-price-list scheme—that is, by fixing the turnover tax as a specific ruble amount for each item—the government could adjust the wholesale price structure independently of the retail price structure and thus reduce or eliminate differences in the profitability of producing different items in the assortment. To adopt this scheme in the case of clothing, however, it would

be necessary to shift the turnover tax, now levied on the cloth rather than on the finished garment, to the final product.

Recent Changes

Recent measures in the sphere of retail price formation show a limited response to these criticisms and recommendations. For example, in 1965 the State Committee on Trade of the USSR Council of Ministers was instructed to establish an All-Union Scientific Research Institute to study the demand for consumer goods and the problems of trade fluctuations, with branches in the union republics. Organizations to study demand have been created in trade organizations, republic ministries of trade, and at various levels of the consumer cooperative system.

In 1963 a scheme of temporary prices was established under which temporarily high prices are set for new fabrics, clothing, footwear, and furniture in high demand. At the end of one year (or sooner if the demand declines), prices are reduced to their "permanent" level. The temporary surcharge of 10 to 15 percent applies to enterprise wholesale prices as well as to retail prices, because the enterprise wholesale prices of these goods are set as a percentage of their retail prices. This scheme has been criticized because of lengthy delays in setting the new prices, which are fixed at the republic level. Another criticism is that the resulting enterprise wholesale prices do not always make the new goods as profitable to produce as the older items which they replace, causing the enterprise's profits to fall.

In the now famous Bolshevichka-Maiak experiment, the pricing of new goods was decentralized to the enterprise level. The RSFSR Ministry of Trade authorized the factory and its retail outlets jointly to establish retail prices on new garments, on the basis of prices of existing goods but with due recognition of demand factors and additional costs incurred in producing the new garments. Because there is no turnover tax on clothing, enterprise wholesale prices were increased in the same proportion as retail prices. However, the factories found that the new models were less profitable to produce than the old ones, and their profits declined. While price setting (on new goods) was decentralized to the enterprise level during this experiment, when the scheme was extended to a large part of the light and food industry in 1965, enterprises were not given the right to fix prices on new products, and this right was taken away from the two experimental firms. This retreat from decentralized price setting was not publicized or explained in connection with the announcement of the "success" of the experiment and its extension to other enterprises.

Other developments in retail pricing worthy of brief mention are the elimination of the rural price differential and the revision of long-neglected prices on services. As part of the effort to improve the peasantry's terms of trade, beginning in 1959 the rural price differential was successively eliminated on a number of products and was abolished completely in 1966. During 1962-65, a comprehensive revision of prices on personal services (laundry; haircuts; clothing, shoe and appliance repairs; etc.) was conducted in the Ukraine, and served as a guide to similar revisions in other areas.

These measures indicate a new interest on the part of the Soviet government in setting better retail prices—an interest stimulated by the dramatic buildup of unsold goods, after a long period of excess demand conditions when improper relative prices could be tolerated. However, the government has been reluctant to move toward more flexible prices responsive to supply and demand conditions. The use of temporary prices has been limited, and the decentralization of price fixing to the enterprise level, tried in the Bolshevichka-Maiak experiment, has been rescinded. In sum, it appears that the central authorities are much more concerned about retail prices than ever before, but they are hesitant to surrender control over retail prices to the enterprise and through it to the market.

V. CONCLUSION

Soviet economists, planners, and political leaders have been devoting growing attention to prices as the Soviet economy slowly moves toward a greater role for market forces and money flows, rather than administrative commands in physical terms, in guiding production and resource allocation. A broad critical discussion of industrial prices, at scholarly conferences and in the economic press, began in 1956. Similar, though more cautious, discussions of agricultural and retail prices started a few years later. These discussions have exposed many defects in the price system and have produced a wide variety of suggestions for improvements, ranging from minor technical revisions to sweeping changes of a basic character.

It is clear that the highest levels of the Communist Party and the government are now concerned with price problems. Yet the central authorities have shown great reluctance to embark on major reforms in the price system in order to secure prices which reflect scarcity and can allocate resources efficiently. One reason, surely, is resistance to such reforms by members of the planning and administrative bureaucracy, who are used to, and comfortable with, command economy methods which do not depend on sound prices. They have a personal stake in the preservation of the traditional approach to resource allocation. They also genuinely distrust moves toward reliance on market forces and scarcity prices, fearing that they inevitably will bring inflation, on the one hand, and unemployment, on the other.

Because the political leadership and the central planners are unwilling to surrender control over the economy to consumers' sovereignty, they hesitate to let flexible scarcity prices determine output, allocate resources, and distribute income. Thus, it is not surprising that, despite the changes in enterprise performance indicators, managerial powers, and incentives, price setting remains centralized and largely follows traditional patterns. As a result, the planners continue to be faced with the impossible task of regulating the approximately nine million prices in the Soviet economy.

6. FINANCE AND BANKING IN THE USSR

George Garvy

In the Soviet economy, money is supposed to be "neutral" or "passive" rather than "active." Soviet planners endeavor to adjust financial flows to carry out physical plans for allocating resources and distributing output. The budget implements macroeconomic decisions about the division of national product among investment, consumption, and military programs, as well as microeconomic decisions about the allocation of investment among different branches of the economy and regions of the country. The main functions of the banking system are to finance planned inventories at various levels of production and distribution and to supervise the adherence of enterprises to their plans (i.e., to exercise "control by the ruble"). Thus, the banking system plays a derivative, supporting role, and there is no independent monetary policy.

This selection provides both a general survey of the financial aspects of the Soviet economy and a more detailed study of the banking system. The first part explains the separation between the money and payments of households, and those of producing units. It analyzes the nature of financial planning, monetary policy, and the relationship between the banking system and its clients. It points out the many differences in these respects between the economies of the socialist countries of Eastern Europe and regulated capitalist market economies in the West. The second part examines in detail the organization and activities of the Soviet banking system, Soviet monetary theory, and recent changes connected with the current economic reforms.

George Garvy is Economic Adviser at the Federal Reserve Bank of New York. The selection is reprinted by permission from his monograph, *Money Banking, and Credit in Eastern Europe* (New York: Federal Reserve Bank of New York, 1966), pp. 12–27 and 122–36, and his paper, "Policies and Mechanics Relating to Money" presented at a NATO Colloquium on Banking, Money and Credit in Eastern Europe, Brussels, January 24–26, 1973, with further changes by Dr. Garvy to bring the data up to date. Citations to Russian-language sources have been omitted.

I. FINANCIAL CHARACTERISTICS OF THE CENTRALLY PLANNED ECONOMY

ALL THE COMMUNIST countries of Eastern Europe are now attempting, in various degrees, to make use of the market process. Many of the changes are being introduced only gradually, however, in the Soviet Union and to a varying extent in each of the smaller countries in Eastern Europe. In the meantime, the basic features of centrally planned economies remain intact. Production targets, formulated mainly in physical terms, are set by the central government and embodied in specific directives, usually cast in the form of output plans. Designated governmental agencies specify for each enterprise, or group of enterprises, the kinds and sources of inputs and the destination of outputs. Since all basic planning is in real magnitudes ("material balances"), the role of money is mainly to provide a common denominator (*numéraire*) for aggregation and projection. The allocation of resources is determined by the central plan and not through the price system. All prices are set by authority, and wage rates and total payroll costs of individual enterprises are strictly controlled. Consumer prices and transfer prices among producers are seldom changed because stable prices facilitate global planning and an orderly distribution and redistribution of the national product. Administrative decisions, and not market adjustments, are relied upon to correct disequilibria and deviations from plans. Until experiments with more flexible policies were begun in recent years, individual enterprises in the government-owned sector of the economy (which, in each country, accounts for all but a small percentage of total output outside agriculture) had little scope for deciding between production alternatives or for making investment decisions.

The Central Role of the Budget

All financial flows in the Eastern European countries, whether related to the movement of goods or to the flow of investment, are influenced by output plans and by direct controls over funds spent. They are not market determined and, indeed, there are no credit or capital markets. Instead the budget of the national government assumes the key role in the distribution of the national product. All major macroeconomic decisions—such as the division of current output between investment and consumption—are embodied in the government budget. In particular, the financial counterpart of the flow of real resources into investment is for the most part channeled through the budget. The national budget also fulfills an important allocative function with regard to investment flows (between industry and agriculture, among industries and regions), which in the free market economies is performed largely through the market process.

The budget is thus the most important funnel for all payments flows and the most important component of overall financial planning. Receipts of the state-owned enterprises in excess of expenditures for direct costs (mainly labor and materials) are siphoned off into the budget, either through taxes or by the transfer of profits (except for a relatively small part to be invested or spent for collective consumption by the enterprises themselves). About half of the national income of each country flows through the budget, a much larger proportion than in the United States and the other leading industrial countries of the West. This higher proportion results primarily from two facts: first, the channeling through the budget of the bulk of all investment (in working as well as fixed capital), and, second, the financing of a very large part of expenditures of all lower units of government through transfers from the national budget. Moreover, the bulk of "collective consumption"—which includes not only free educational, health, and other services, but also subsidies for housing, transportation, and the like—is budget financed.

Financing of investment in the government sector of the economy involves essentially transfers from the accounts of enterprises to the budget (and vice versa). Voluntary savings provide a very minor though growing counterpart of real investment. The, in effect, forced sale of government bonds to the population, resorted to in the Soviet Union until 1957, must be regarded as a measure for preserving monetary equilibrium by reducing consumption, rather than as a normal means of financing investment.

The Separation of Payments Circuits

One important aspect of the Soviet monetary and banking system, and a main tool of monetary control, is the separation of all payments into two circuits by the use of two different kinds of money. The difference between them is both physical and functional. Household money (currency) is different from enterprise money (bank deposits), and household banking from enterprise banking. Before 1965, a further institutional separation of the flow of payments had been implemented by the assignment to the State Bank of all payments related to current production, while the Investment Bank handled the accumulation and disbursement of all funds related to fixed capital formation in the state-owned sector. The deposit money circuit serves to implement the microeconomic plan of each enterprise and provides the basis for close monitoring ("control") of its performance by the State Bank.

For the population, currency alone serves as a medium of payment, except for a relatively small amount of payments from and through savings accounts. In contrast, all payments among enterprises, economic organizations, and the government (except for petty cash disbursements) involve deposit transfers on the books of the banking system. Currency and deposit money are not interchangeable. Deposits are transformed into currency almost exclusively through payroll withdrawals.

The two circuits correspond to separate markets for consumer and producer goods. In the Soviet Union as well as in other socialist countries, separation of payments flows is a basic mechanism for avoiding excess demand. Separation into two circuits also facilitates financial planning as well as central accounting controls over the flow of resources within the socialized sector, prevents leakages of goods and services from this sector into private consumption, and assures on-schedule transfers from enterprise to budget accounts. It also makes easier the prompt detection of disequilibria, bottlenecks, and various shortfalls in the execution of economic plans. It gives consumers a choice within the range of goods and services offered by planners (which may guide future production) while preserving the planning authorities' freedom of choice with regard to the inputs and outputs for the enterprise sector.

The State Bank is the focal point of the two circuits; management of the two circuits absorbs a large part of the bank staff's time, particularly at the local branch-office level.

The savings bank system provides banking services for the population, including transfer and payments services. Savings bank deposits (or at least some portion) should thus be considered part of the active money supply, in addition to deposit and note liabilities of the State Bank. However, because of the separation of the payments streams into two compartments, and the considerable differences between the functions of money in the two sectors, the concept of a total money supply has limited analytical significance in the Soviet-type economy. Manipulation of the total quantity of money (as contrasted with currency in circulation) is not a policy objective. Thus, what would seem to be a standard Western procedure for testing monetary aspects of the economic process is not applicable to the Soviet reality, because of the basic differences in the motivations underlying the behavior of basic economic units ("enterprises") and also because required data are lacking.

Monetary flows include three distinct types of transactions:

1. The receipt of income by the population from, and its expenditure in, the state-owned and cooperative sectors of the economy;
2. the movement of goods within the state-owned sector; and
3. the transfer of the bulk of "social income" (roughly, the excess of receipts over factor costs other than depreciation) to the budget, from which the bulk of expenditures for fixed investment and for collective consumption are met.

Each of these types of flows will be discussed in turn.

1. Wages and other monetary income are paid in currency, except for a relatively small amount paid directly into savings accounts. As a result, all consumer expenditures are also made in currency. The popu-

lation acquires consumer goods and services almost entirely from state-owned retail stores (the network of "cooperative stores" in villages is, in fact, state-operated).

Collectivized farmers now receive a very large part of their income in cash, but prior to 1953 payments in kind were prevalent. The remonetization of relations between the collective farms (kolkhozes) and the state, and the shifting of the remuneration of their members from an annual distribution of mostly products, on the basis of work performed, to periodic payments in money, have increased the circulation of currency within the rural population as well as its rate of turnover. Members of collective farms and workers on state farms (as well as the insignificant number of still existing independent farmers) receive currency also through direct sales of the output of their privately cultivated small plots.

Farm products purchased directly from the rural population substitute for similar goods that urban consumers would otherwise have purchased from the socialized sector. On the other hand, farmers use the proceeds of sales to the urban population to acquire goods and services from stores of the socialized sector. As long as claims on the socialized sector are merely transferred from one group of the population to another, few problems arise for planners and controllers of currency flows, even though the resulting shifts in the structure of demand require adjustments in the bill of goods produced for the consumer sector.

The bulk of the demand for currency is met from currency returning to the monobank when individuals make retail purchases or service expenditures, pay income taxes, and add to their savings accounts. Prompt recapturing of as large an amount as possible of the currency put into circulation is one of the shibboleths of Soviet monetary management. Continuous efforts are made to prevent consumers from hoarding currency, which might spill over into black market and other illicit activities. These hoards also make possible sudden surges of spending that typically create shortages in retail stores.

State-owned and cooperative retail stores or service establishments are required to deposit daily all currency receipts in excess of a stipulated amount of petty cash[1]. Inordinate emphasis is placed on channeling the cash receipts of trade and service establishments into State Bank offices as promptly as possible and on minimizing the amount of till cash that such establishments (and also industrial establishments) are

---

[1] While, normally, currency returns to the State Bank after only one transaction (when currency paid out as wages is spent in retail stores and redeposited with the Bank), some part changes hands within the population itself, with one group purchasing goods from another. Within the nonsocialized sector, the main kinds of such transactions include, in addition to direct sales of farm products, sales by artisans and cooperative producers, sales of second hand goods, and payments for services of domestics and other individuals (including moonlighters) and for various forms of illicit activities and transactions. Of these, the first is by far the most important.

permitted to hold. Any inflow of currency that results in vault cash holdings ("operational reserves") at a local bank office that exceed stipulated maximum levels is transferred to the centrally controlled "general reserves," from which notes and coins can be released only on specific orders from the head or regional offices of the State Bank. Conversely, elaborate precautions are taken to prevent issuance of currency to enterprises and government units, except in strict conformity with the cash plan.

2. The deposit transfer circuit (the "non-cash circuit" in Soviet terminology) encompasses all payments related to the production and disposition of the entire value of the gross national income other than wages and the channeling of capital consumption allowances. Claims among socialist enterprises arising from production and distribution can give rise to settlements through deposit transfers between the accounts of the buyer and the seller or through mutual offsetting of claims. Such payments are automatically linked to the movement of goods, and involve a minimum of delays and no vendor credit. The related payments instruments are non-negotiable and non-assignable.

Payments between enterprises or various "economic organizations" are made as goods move through channels, for purposes determined by the planners and according to rigid schedules requiring settlement within a stipulated short time after receipt of shipping documents and frequently before the goods have actually been received by the purchaser. Delays in paying for goods occur mainly when consumer goods reaching retail outlets are not accepted due to being unsatisfactory. The greatest use of short-term bank credit is for speeding up transactions in the deposit transfer circuit. It takes the form of automatic extension of loans either to the seller to bridge the settlement gap, or to the purchaser, if his balance is insufficient to pay on the date due.

Deposit transfers are made on the basis of a variety of drafts and other payment orders and standing instructions, with cheques playing a very minor role. With minor exceptions,[2] only amounts needed for meeting payrolls can be converted into currency.[3] However, purchases by state procurement agencies of the output of collective farms are paid for largely in currency.[4]

---

[2] Payments not exceeding a small specified amount (currently 100 rubles) may be made in currency. Trade organizations are authorized, in strictly circumscribed situations, to make payments in cash for certain direct purchases.

[3] Since enterprise profits now average about 20 percent of sales at factory prices, perhaps four fifths of additional credit injected into the non-farm economy normally results in currency withdrawals for payrolls at various stages of production and distribution. Largely because of cumulative currency withdrawals as a result of the continuous increase in aggregate loan volume, at the end of 1969 deposit balances of enterprises were equal to only about one tenth of the loans extended to them.

[4] While the use of deposit transfers is obligatory for the socialized sector only, collective farms must use them in their relations with the budget, with state-owned

3. Transfers of profits, turnover taxes, and other revenues to the Treasury account and the channeling of these revenues to various union ministries (including those concerned with investment) and to the constituent republics requires a complex system of frequent transfers of deposits. Some of these are designed to assure that the government receives its share prior to any other claimant, while others are intended to facilitate current control.

The volume of deposit transfers has risen much more rapidly than GNP, reflecting in part the growing complexity of the production process, but in part also the changes in industrial organization, financial flows, and banking techniques. The total volume of payments grew more than 15-fold between 1940 and 1970, from 95 billion to 1,480 billion rubles (excluding repayments of loans), almost twice as rapidly as GNP.

Deposit transfers within the socialized sector of the economy have no direct effect on equilibrium conditions as long as the total availability of consumer goods and their prices are determined by output plans, administered factory prices, and the applicable turnover tax for each product. Prices of investment goods and transfer prices for all intermediate goods have limited significance as long as the allocation of the total final output is determined by planners in physical terms, although transfer prices within the state enterprise sector may affect the profitability of individual enterprises and branches of industry.

Equilibrium through Planning

Maintenance of equilibrium conditions and achievement of growth objectives are supposed to result from proper overall planning of material resources and not from influencing, indirectly, aggregate pecuniary demand and its structure or the cost and availability of money and capital. From its very origin, Soviet financial planning has been "derivative"—based on material balances, in which specific kinds of physical resources are allocated to achieve growth under conditions of overall equilibrium. Monetary flows are planned as the counterpart of physical flows and adjusted to changes in such flows. Equilibrium between supply and monetary demand for consumer goods and services is to be attained by production, price, and wage decisions taken by the planning authorities. Equilibrium in the cash circuit is achieved when wage and other payments to the population equal the monetary value of the consumer goods and services that are to be produced by the economy at established prices, which, ideally, remain stable for relatively long periods of time. Adjustments needed to maintain such an equilibrium are taken by the planning, not by the monetary, authorities.

---

enterprises, and with the credit system, and for all accounts related to capital formation, which they must keep at the State Bank. The collective farms, however, may keep their funds also in currency or in savings accounts.

Planning for growth under conditions of overall equilibrium of monetary demand and supply takes the form of an interlocking system of financial plans. In effect, these plans are projections, in the form of balances, of sources and uses of funds in the various sectors of the economy. They vary in their makeup—some flows are on a gross, others on a net basis and a few are drawn up in stock terms. Some are, in effect, detailed operating plans while others are more in the nature of broad guidelines for the use of policy-making bodies. There are also considerable differences among countries in the number and articulation of such plans and in the extent to which the plans represent merely internal working documents or approach the status of binding operational directives. Moreover, the role of financial planning itself has been undergoing important changes in recent years.

Whatever the official status of the monetary plans, actual performance measured against plan figures provides a day-to-day check on the working of the economy—indeed the only overall check. Monetary flows in the socialized sector, recorded through the banking system (by entries in the appropriate accounts), reveal deviations from planned real flows and thus mirror disequilibria and bottlenecks in the real processes. Money thus performs an important signal function, but it is not relied on to any significant degree as an adjuster.

The control of individual enterprises is shared among national, regional, and local authorities. As a general rule, enterprises producing basic materials, capital goods, or consumption goods for the national market are subordinated to a ministry. The other enterprises, which tend to be smaller, are responsible to regional political entities (federated republics in the Soviet Union) or to municipalities (which typically have jurisdiction over such enterprises as local retail and service establishments, bakeries, utilities, or movie theaters). Several enterprises of national significance, or even all units in the same industry, are frequently joined for administrative purposes into organizations variously called trusts, combines, groups, firms, aggregations, associations, and the like. (For the sake of consistency, these will hereafter be uniformly referred to as associations; they are normally subordinated to a ministry in charge of a given group of industries.)

The Roles of Money and Credit

Because of the basic reliance on planning in terms of real flows, and the central importance of the national budget for financial planning, the functions of money and credit in Eastern Europe are radically different from the roles they play in free market economies. Ownership of money does not give an absolute command over resources. The individual can acquire only consumer goods and strictly limited categories of property for personal use. Small service establishments, artisans, and independent farmers also can acquire producer goods—and this is of some importance in countries like East Germany and Poland; but these non-socialized sectors are not significant (with the major exception of agriculture in Poland). In the state sector, money may be used only in conformity with the plan; credit gives command over resources only if acquisition of the resources is foreseen in the plan, while plan allocation of resources carries with it an almost automatic claim on credit. The role of monetary flows is to implement the planners' intentions, not to invoke response or to correct movement away from equilibrium ("neutral money"). The power of money to influence real processes is severely limited by direct administrative controls. Attempts to use monetary incentives in order to guide economic activity have been made in recent years, but so far on a limited scale only.

The countries of Eastern Europe know no credit-granting institutions other than banks. To a very limited extent, banks have been used since the mid-1950s to finance certain minor kinds of fixed investment, but the main role of credit under the standard system is to provide the bulk of the financing of inventories at the various levels of production and distribution. Consumer credit and financing of cooperative and individual home building have become important only in recent years. Where a significant part of agriculture remains in private hands, notably in Poland, some efforts have been made since the mid-1950s to provide credit to farmers, both for seasonal needs and for improving technology. Except in East Germany, Czechoslovakia, and Poland, practically no credit is available to private enterprise in the other sectors of the economy. Changes of a rather marginal nature in credit policy and techniques, intended to provide somewhat greater flexibility, were made in the Soviet Union in 1954. These were also copied in the other countries, although in some cases in a modified form, and some changes were introduced for which there was no Soviet example. Until very recent years, however, such divergences involved chiefly techniques and details, rather than a fundamental reappraisal of the potentialities of monetary and credit policy.

The aggregate volume of credit is determined almost automatically by the production and distribution goals set in real terms. The proper amount of total working capital and the extent to which it consists of the enterprises' own resources (designated as "own funds") are determined by the central authorities for each individual industry. Thus changes in the volume of credit are, for the most part, the counterpart of changes in the volume of inventories, unless planning authorities decide to change the relative share of enterprise funds and bank credit in the carrying of inventories. Under the standard system, the granting of credit is almost automatic, once the borrower's output plan has been approved, and the mechanics of credit granting is geared to rigid rules. Changes in the cost and availability of credit are not relied on as the means of achieving changes in resource use, although in recent years differentiation in interest rates has been increasingly used to achieve greater efficiency and to favor socially desirable activities. The prevailing official view is that the essential function of the credit system is the redistribution of cash balances (temporarily redundant enterprise balances, budget surpluses, and consumer savings) rather than credit creation.

During the first 25 years after the credit reforms of 1930–32, the credit policy of the Soviet Union was concerned exclusively with providing the payments counterpart of the movement of real goods through the production and distribution process. The other countries originally copied the Soviet credit system to the smallest details. In very recent years, however, at least some of the countries have begun to explore the possibility of adapting credit administration techniques as instruments of active credit policy.

Liquidity Position of Enterprises

Since the ability of enterprises to acquire goods depends, theoretically at least, on the planners' intent and not primarily on liquidity, the liquidity position of the enterprise sector is ostensibly of no concern to credit policy. In effect, however, administrative and financial controls have not proved sufficient to prevent "unplanned" spending: enterprises have frequently made use of their financial resources to support their operations, as dramatically evidenced in several instances of inflationary outbursts—especially in 1950–53—in all the smaller communist countries with the exception of East Germany. Thus, while the monetary system has no way of influencing the liquidity of the socialized sector on a day-to-day basis, some countries have at times resorted to the device of temporarily sterilizing (blocking) enterprise balances or imposing limitations on their use.

The individual enterprise, which under the standard system has very limited latitude in managing its working capital, is rarely confronted with liquidity problems in the same sense as firms in capitalist countries. Its liquidity position has no direct bearing on its fixed investment plans, since these are, with negligible exceptions, implemented by financing from budgetary resources. Loans are made automatically on bills of lading to cover the standard collection period, and usually provision is made for easy access to bank credit in order to finance unforeseen expenditures, such as bulges in inventories of raw materials due to deliveries ahead of or beyond schedule. At the same time, considerable emphasis is placed on "improving the payments discipline," since failure to pay on time is tantamount to extending interunit credit; it disrupts the circular flow of capital and creates payments difficulties all down the line.

While the management of an enterprise has usually little difficulty in temporarily replenishing working funds through bank loans, its ability to use its own bank balance is strictly circumscribed. In communist countries the absolute order to pay is unknown; all payments must be documented as consistent with the applicable plan, and the purpose of the payment is normally verifiable from the underlying documents. Interenterprise payments are usually made not by check but on the basis of drafts supported by documents related to the shipment of goods, and collection of payments for shipments (or services rendered) requires time-consuming movement of documents. Claims arising from production and distribution are nonnegotiable and nonassignable: they can give rise only to deposit transfers (settlements) between the accounts of the actual buyer and seller.

A shortage of funds normally results in difficulties of one sort or another, but the accumulation of free funds (excess liquidity in Western terms) confers little advantage, since it does not in itself entitle the enterprise to purchase additional resources. It may actually lead to a loss of working capital (if the superior economic authority directs the enterprise to relinquish the excess to other enterprises), or failure to obtain an additional allocation ("replenishment") of working capital from the budget next year, or even a permanent reduction of allotted working capital. Policymakers in communist economies have an interest in keeping the enterprises' own working funds at a minimum, so that extension of credit would give the bank a greater lever to exert tighter controls over each enterprise.

Indeed, the total volume of credit does not have the same significance that it has in the Western countries. The dividing line between credit and working capital owned by the individual enterprise is fluid and not of great significance in itself. The choice between more "own" capital and more credit hinges on overall policy considerations, embodied in industrywide "norms" (prescribed standard ratios). Since all capital in the state enterprise sector is owned by the government and is merely assigned to individual enterprises, a working-capital shortage in any given enterprise can be remedied either by granting it more credit or by adding to its capital (through budgetary resources or through transfers from other enterprises administered by the same ministry or from other "higher echelon" organizations in the economic administration). In principle, all state enterprises operate in part with borrowed funds, mainly because it is desired to increase control by the banking authorities, but the precise share of loans in working funds varies.

The Role of the Banking System

Even before he took power, Lenin envisaged the banking system as becoming the backbone of the socialist state's administrative apparatus.

Nationalization of private banking and establishment of a government monopoly of all foreign exchange transactions were among the first economic measures taken by the Bolshevik government in 1917. In the other Eastern European countries, foreign exchange transactions were virtually a government monopoly at the time the communists obtained a dominant position, and nationalization of banks and other financial institutions was uniformly one of the first actions of the new governments. Centralization of bank credit appeared to be a logical concomitant of centralized planning and management of production and distribution.

The particular form of banking organization developed originally in the Soviet Union combines in the state bank most of the attributes of a central bank with those functions of commercial banking that are relevant in the communist economy, and also with a wide range of activities related specifically to the characteristics of such economies. The term "monobank" fits well this type of banking institution. The monobank is supplemented by a small number of banks that serve special functions, including an investment bank, which is a key institution for channeling funds into fixed capital.

In specific terms, the monobank is the *bank of issue* and is responsible for the regulation of note circulation. It manages the gold and foreign exchange reserves, in close cooperation with (and in some cases under the direction of) the Ministry of Finance and the Ministry of Foreign Trade (which in all countries of Eastern Europe is responsible for administering the foreign trade monopoly). In most of the countries, the financing of foreign trade, and even of related domestic activities, has in recent years been shifted to special foreign trade banks.

The monobank (along with the other banks, to the limited extent that they extend short-term credit) is the sole *source of short-term credit*, as the extension of direct interenterprise ("commercial") credit is forbidden. The bank is not the ultimate but the only lender. Since control of credit is exercised directly, the monobank is not concerned with the same problems (such as controlling the reserves or liquidity of independent commercial banks) or activities (such as discounting and open market operations) as central banks in Western countries. As there are no financial markets or instruments (except savings bonds held by individuals), authorities do not have to worry about the prices of financial assets.

The monobank services the *currency needs* of the entire economy, including the savings banks and all specialized banks, where these exist as separate entities. Its offices act as *agents for specialized banks* in localities where these are not represented.

Since all payments within the socialized sector are transfers on its books, the monobank is the one and all-encompassing *settlements and clearing center* of the country. It keeps the accounts of the national government and of all subordinate government units, and performs all the usual *fiscal agency functions* carried out by central banks in Western countries (e.g., the collection and disbursement of revenue to support regular government activities, the issue and redemption of public loans). Of the proceeds deposited at the monobank from the sale of goods by the state enterprises, a part is paid out in cash for wages and the remaining part is credited to various accounts through book transfers. Thus it functions as a *social accounting center,* which not only keeps track of payments flows but, in many cases, also allocates single payments among several special-purpose accounts.

Because payments flows are planned and tied to plan fulfillment, all such monobank operations as cash withdrawals, book transfers, and credit extensions involve an *audit function* to check conformity of payment to underlying authorization. This important activity—essential to what is called "control by the ruble" (or the forint, or the koruna), which is a basic feature of centrally planned economies—entails more than financial supervision; indeed, it makes the monobank a key part of the policy and administrative apparatus of the communist state.

In view of its manifold functions, it is logical that the monobank is an active participant in all phases of economic planning. It is also a major, and frequently the main, channel through which any failures in the meshing of gears come to the attention of the authorities. But the monobank raises the flag without cracking the whip; when the signals it transmits require corrective action, this is normally taken through policy measures that emanate from the higher authorities of the state.

The difference between the monobank and both the central and the commercial banks of capitalist countries is reflected in the structure of the balance sheet. The assets side of the monobank's balance sheet consists mainly of loans to the various segments of the economy (possibly including a small amount of housing loans to individuals), in addition to gold and foreign exchange; it contains no government or private securities. Among the monobank's liabilities (in addition to capital accounts and note liabilities) are the free balances of its clients—the counterpart of demand deposits in capitalist countries. These balances are owned mainly by economic or governmental units and, to a lesser extent, by cooperative farms and nonprofit organizations. The only counterpart of the interbank balances held by banks in Western countries is the uncommitted deposits of specialized banks. There are no time deposits and only a negligible amount of deposits of individuals.

The monobank's activities have some similarities to those of central banks in underdeveloped countries, with their rudimentary or nonexistent money and capital markets, their reliance on government for the bulk of capital formation, the relatively large volume of lending either by the central bank directly or through development banks, and largely fixed or stable rates of interest. Differences between Eastern Europe and the West in regard to the functions of money and credit and the central bank are considerable and basic.

No state bank of any country of Eastern Europe currently publishes data on the liabilities side of its balance sheet. It is known, however, that in addition to the expansion of credit, reflected in an increase in note circulation and an increase in balance of enterprises, funds for lending are also acquired each year from a combination of the following sources (disregarding any resources of foreign origin): cumulative budget surpluses of previous years (a main means of achieving equilibrium in the economy), an increase in capital resources (from profits or transfers from the budget), funds held at the state bank by the specialized banks, reserves of social insurance funds (where they exist as separate entities, as in Czechoslovakia), and deposits of savings banks (particularly where, as in the Soviet Union, they have no lending business of their own), and an increase in balances of enterprises and organizations. The last of these, being strictly controlled and kept at a minimum, is likely to be of greater significance from a seasonal than from a longer run point of view. In the Soviet Union, industry balances at the end of 1970 stood at 14 billion rubles, which, in relation to the value of industrial output, is considerably below the ratio between the level of commercial bank balances maintained by United States corporations and the value of the corporate product.

Even though the banking literature of the communist countries keeps repeating that the state bank can make loans only within the limits of resources at its disposal, and though considerable day-by-day efforts are made to attract ("mobilize") additional resources (for instance, by inducing farm cooperatives to keep their free funds with banks), the implied analogy with commercial banks in capitalist countries is misleading. The state bank cannot lose funds to any other bank, since it accounts for 95 percent or more of total credit and is the depository of the uncommitted funds of all other banks. Issue of additional currency may be, and almost certainly will be, the result of any additional lending, but this merely represents a shift in the composition of the liabilities that match the loans added to the assets side of the balance sheet. The real, indeed the only, limit to the extension of bank credit in communist countries—where bank liabilities are not subject to reserve requirements and there is full administrative control of foreign payments—is determined by macroeconomic decisions made by the political and planning authorities and embodied in the financial plans.

The Bank and Its Clientele

The relationship between the monobank and its clientele also bears little resemblance to the corresponding relationship in capitalist countries. Rather than being an agent of the depositor, the monobank, when dealing with the individual enterprise, is, in fact, the representative of the state; the population at large has no direct contact with it. It protects the interests of the state by debiting from the depositor's account—in most cases, automatically—the various payments due the treasury. If necessary, it extends credit to meet such payments. More generally, criteria that the bank applies in relations with its clientele are tied to the borrower's execution of the economic plan, to which the meeting of the borrower's financial obligations to the bank is subordinated. Each enterprise, unit of government, or nonprofit (voluntary) organization has to bank with the single office in whose territory it is located. This arrangement obviously provides no incentive for the management and personnel of any unit of the banking system to improve service in order to retain or attract depositors.

Until the emergence of new trends in recent years, the bank and its customers were merely involved in a web of impersonal accounting relationships, embracing set, uniform, and rigid rules, few alternatives, a minimum of flexibility, and supervision that reached into the minute details of an enterprise's activities and amounted in effect to a continuous and detailed audit of physical and financial performance. The monobank used no other criterion for measuring performance than the degree of success with which an enterprise discharged its current financial obligations (maintained a sufficient balance to pay bills and loans when due) and avoided exceeding norms—most importantly, the inventory norms—imposed from the outside by planning authorities and various economic administrations, including ministries.[5]

Monetary Policy in a Planned Economy

From the foregoing brief summary it is clear that the functions of monetary policy in planned economies are very different from those it serves in the West. In the communist countries, as elsewhere, the basic objective of economic policy is to achieve optimum growth rates without exposing the existing price structure to pressures caused by imbalances between the flow of consumer purchasing power and the availability of consumer goods. And the underlying analysis of capabilities—in terms of available real resources—and of the required changes in money supply, credit, and financial flows resulted in procedures not much different from those used in making macroeconomic projections in Western countries. But in formulating and implementing monetary policies that will serve their objectives, the two types of economies differ completely, reflecting their fundamental differences in capital ownership, economic organization, and political and social philosophy.

---

[5] See Robert W. Campbell, *Accounting in Soviet Planning and Management* (Cambridge, Mass.: Harvard University Press, 1963), pp. 205 ff.

In Western countries the formulation of monetary policy is a continuous process, responding flexibly to changes in the performance of the market economy. In communist countries, monetary policy is embodied in all-embracing financial plans, which carry final authority and are changed only at fixed intervals. Although one can identify the nature of credit and note issue policies pursued by a communist country, and show what policies it follows with regard to encouraging personal saving, providing financing for small-scale capital improvements, or managing foreign exchange reserves, it is difficult to tie these separate aspects into something that would add up to a socialist monetary policy. But in all such matters the banking system acts merely as a vehicle for the execution of broader government decisions as embodied in the detailed plans; monetary action is not geared to the market but is determined by administrative processes centered on the planned allocation of resources. The familiar tools of monetary policy available to Western central banks are irrelevant. In communist countries, monetary policy is concerned primarily with assuring the efficiency of currency circulation and of the payments mechanism and with facilitating the economic performance of enterprises, while fiscal policy is heavily relied upon to assure balance between aggregate demand and supply.

In fact, one would look in vain in the writings of Soviet economists, who so far have been setting the tone in the other countries of Eastern Europe as well, for an explicit discussion of monetary policy. Typically, Soviet textbooks and treatises merely discuss the various functions of credit in the socialist economy. The more sophisticated treatment makes a distinction between the "functions" and the "role" of credit, reserving the first term for the place of credit in the socialist economy and equating "role" with the results achieved in accelerating growth and output. Economic literature in Eastern Europe deals with the practical problems of controlling monetary circulation, crediting production and trade, and financing capital investment, usually under separate headings, but it does not discuss monetary policy, as such, or its relationship to fiscal policy, even though in the communist countries the two are closely integrated and the relationship between the monobank and the Ministry of Finance is at least as close as between central bank and government in Western countries. Similarly, banking officials, in their published speeches and articles, typically focus on how the state bank can best implement the economic plan or party decisions. Such statements clearly reflect the implementary nature of the monobank's activities and characteristically treat the monetary aspects of those activities (credit, currency circulation) on the same footing as routine operations (mutual offsets) or control functions (control over payroll disbursements).[6]

---

[6] In the authoritative Soviet two-volume *Dictionary of Finance and Credit* (issued by the official publishing house specializing in financial literature), there is no entry for "monetary policy." "Credit policy" is defined as "a system of

Even though the monobank plays essentially the role of an implementing agency, it has significant functions in the central administration's efforts to influence aggregate demand and stimulate growth. It contributes—to an extent that varies from country to country—to the determination of realistic plan targets and of the proper magnitudes that will "correctly" implement them, as well as serving indispensably in furthering the proper execution of the various financial plans. The monobank's role in economic administration is enhanced by an organizational advantage: in contrast to the various ministries, organized on an industry principle, and to regional economic bodies, it has a close and continuous contract, not only with specific branches or areas, but with the entire economy.

Nevertheless, the fact remains that, when the level and distribution of spending power do not conform with the underlying plan, the means used to correct the disequilibria are not changes in the cost and availability of credit but administrative improvisation by the monobank—unless the matter is so serious that higher echelon government or party authorities step in with a change in the ground rules. The monobank is an adjuster, not a steerer; its role, to borrow Robert V. Roosa's terminology, coined in a different context, is defensive rather than dynamic.

Communist countries have no effective means of controlling the excess liquidity of the population sector and its threat to price stability, except through the harsh and dramatic measures of currency conversions and upward price adjustments (and in some cases, until the mid-1950s, through forced loans placed with the population).[7] Thus a primary objective of financial planning and action is to prevent excess liquidity of consumers from coming into existence and in general to avoid inflation, both overt and repressed (though the word "inflation" is banned from the vocabulary of Soviet economists, at least in relation to their own economy). Nevertheless, inflationary pressures have recurrently arisen in all the countries of Eastern Europe. To combat inflationary tendencies,

---

measures in the area of credit, designed to secure the economic interests of the ruling class." There is no definition for a socialist economy, but a short review of the tasks of credit policy is prefaced by the statement that "In the Soviet Union credit policy corresponds to the tasks that the government places before the country in each phase of the construction of socialism and communism." "Credit restrictions" are described as "limitations or reductions in the volume of credit, which are put into effect by capitalist banks and the bourgeois state," and correspondingly, "credit expansion" is "enlargement of credit, put into effect by capitalist banks and the bourgeois state, which exceeds the growth of production, stimulates overproduction and the coming about of economic crises." There is no reference to a possible role of either process in a socialist economy.

[7] The experience of currency conversion, common to all these countries in the first postwar years, left few fond memories, though the 1947 conversion in the Soviet Union, and some others, did produce a more favorable ratio of exchange for small savings and for certain groups of account holders. See Edward Ames, "Soviet Bloc Currency Conversions," *American Economic Review*, Vol. XLIV, No. 3 (June 1954), pp. 339–53.

to remove their causes, and to re-create conditions favorable to maintenance of price stability, centrally planned economies rely on a combination of fiscal, price, wage, foreign trade, and monetary and credit measures, and also on administrative shifts in the allocation of resources (and, if necessary, changes in plan targets).[8]

The nature of the monobank's role in monetary policy has been clearly stated in an interview given by Dr. O. Pohl, former President of the State Bank of Czechoslovakia: "Of decisive importance for the expansion of an active financial policy is a structurally sound and well-balanced plan. Once the material resources have been incorrectly employed, the bank will be too late with whatever measures it could take." Increased bank participation in the preparation and drawing-up of the plan is desirable, he said, "to enable the bank to step in with its own knowledge and demands when there is still time to influence the anticipated employment of material means, in other words to strengthen the preventive character of the bank's role." After the plan is accepted, the monobank's efforts are directed toward keeping the monetary variables in line with the projections that relate changes in credit and currency circulation to real targets. Within the framework of the plan, credit policy can help bring about a more efficient use of the resources that the plan provides, and thus contribute to lowering costs. But the monobank will automatically validate any of the plan's misjudgments and shortcomings that are binding for it. And although it is expected to prevent spending in excess of stipulated amounts—particularly for wage disbursements and inventory building—it can do little to bring inadequate spending to target levels.

Toward Greater Reliance on "Economic Levers"

With the new policies that began to emerge in the post-Stalin era but which became generally accepted throughout Eastern Europe only by 1965, the role of the banking system has begun to change. In general, the new developments involve a downgrading of physical indicators and an elevation of profitability to a position as an indicator of success—in

---

[8] Even a cursory review of the Eastern European countries' efforts to neutralize the inflationary overhang of World War II and to combat the subsequent succession of inflationary threats would exceed the limits of this study. Fortunately, adequate accounts of these developments are readily available. See John M. Montias, "Bank Lending and Fiscal Policy in Eastern Europe," pp. 38–56, and Andrzej Brzeski, "Forced Industrialization with Unlimited Supply of Money, Poland, 1945–1964," pp. 17–37, in *Money and Plan,* ed. Gregory Grossman (Berkeley and Los Angeles: University of California Press, 1968), and T. M. Podolski, *Socialist Banking and Monetary Control: The Experience of Poland* (Cambridge, England: Cambridge University Press, 1973). See also Franklyn D. Holzman, "Soviet Inflationary Pressures, 1928–1957: Causes and Cures," *Quarterly Journal of Economics,* Vol. LXXIV, No. 2 (May 1960), pp. 167–88. For an (unorthodox) communist view of this problem, see Bronislaw Oyrzanowski, "Problems of Inflation under Socialism," in *Inflation,* ed. Douglas Hague (New York: St. Martin's Press, Inc., 1962), pp. 332–41.

other words, a differentiation between good and poor performers; a more liberal treatment of the former; increased stress on financial performance, as compared with physical output; and greater reliance on initiative and on material incentives. Although the new policies that have been taking shape in recent years give greater latitude to the local bank official, they by no means change his position as agent of the state: the difference lies in a shift from the state's exclusive reliance on administrative controls to a system that makes increasing room for "steering by self-regulation," in which "economic levers" are assigned an active role.

The degrees to which the individual countries have at this writing moved away from the Soviet prototype vary greatly. It is clear that much greater variety in institutional arrangements and policies is developing as each country's specific conditions and experience, as well as the differing views on the way in which a communist economy can make use of the market mechanism and dispense with detailed administrative controls, are gradually being embodied in new banking legislation and regulations. It appears that any further moves in individual countries toward greater reliance on the impersonal mechanism of the market for achieving a more rational and more effective allocation of resources and greater efficiency in their use will be accompanied quite generally by an increased role assigned to financial criteria (including profits) and incentives. Credit policy is likely to play a greater and, in some respects, different role, losing much of its purely implementary character. In this process the bank official will become less concerned with the interpretation of regulations and gauging plan performance and more with evaluating the profitability of alternative uses of credit.

II. BANKING AND CREDIT IN THE USSR

The monetary and credit system of the Soviet Union was rebuilt from scratch after the victory of the Bolshevik revolution. One of the first acts of the new government was to nationalize all domestic and foreign banking institutions, their head offices in the capital having been taken over by armed detachments on a single day. December 14, 1917. Subsequently the monetary system underwent a series of radical changes. These included: attempts during 1918–21 to abolish money; the introduction in 1924 of a uniform and stable currency, after the astronomical inflation and monetary disorganization of the civil war and the following years; and a reform in 1947 designed to mop up the excess consumer liquidity resulting from World War II. The revaluation of the ruble in terms of the dollar in 1961 was, however, of little practical significance. Fundamental credit reforms in 1930–32 put an end to the substantial circulation of trade bills and direct extension of interunit credits and centralized practically all short-term credit activity in the Gosbank. Since then the credit system, though it has undergone further developments, has remained basically unchanged. There has been, however, a good deal of organizational restructuring of banking, reflecting the changes over the years in economic policy and organization and persistent efforts to tighten the Gosbank's control over payments flows.[9]

The development of Soviet financial arrangements has been hampered all along by adherence to theoretical views derived from the writings of Karl Marx, which relate to a capitalist financial environment of a century ago. The checkered history of the banking system over half a century of evolution can be viewed as a struggle to forge an effective tool for monitoring the fulfillment of economic plans and to preserve price stability by controlling payments flows. Although that system served as a model for all communist countries, the Soviet Union has lagged behind the others in the attempts to make money and credit play a more active part in the transformation of the economy away from a rigidly centralized form.

The standard system discussed in Part I is, in essence, the system originally developed in the Soviet Union. All that need be added is a brief description of the evolution of its banking structure, of the modifications that have occurred in recent years, and of those that are currently under way.

The Banking System

Since World War II there has been a strong tendency in the Soviet Union toward consolidation of banking institutions. Even before the war, notably in 1932 and 1936, various banks were consolidated that had been originally created to finance capital formation in specific economic sectors, including agriculture. Subsequently, in 1959, further mergers and reassignment of activities occurred, and as a result the Investment Bank (Stroibank) emerged as the single conduit of budgetary appropriations into fixed investment. And since the beginning of 1963 the savings bank system, with over 78,000 branches (including agencies in factories, offices, and farms), has been part of the Gosbank, operating as a separate department that is also in charge of selling government bonds. Apart from the Gosbank and the Investment Bank, the only other banking institution now in existence is the Bank for Foreign Trade (Vneshtorgbank),[10] whose scope of operations was considerably increased in 1961. Originally, it was concerned mainly with currency exchange

---

[9] The history of developments before World War II is readily available in English; see Arthur Z. Arnold, *Banks, Credit, and Money in Soviet Russia* (New York: Columbia University Press, 1937).

[10] See M. Poliakov, "USSR Bank for Foreign Trade," *American Review of Soviet and East European Foreign Trade*, Vol. 1, No. 1 (January–February 1965), pp. 63–67.

for tourists and diplomatic missions and with remittances, since payments for commercial transactions with foreigners were handled by the Gosbank. After its reorganization the Foreign Trade Bank has been handling all foreign settlements and also the crediting of foreign trade. Since the Investment Bank is essentially an administrative organization supervising the disbursement of government budget grants, and the Foreign Trade Bank is actually only a headquarters organization, the Gosbank is the purest example of a monobank, as it virtually alone services the cash, credit, and payments needs of a country with a population now exceeding 250 million.

In its organization the Gosbank corresponds to the standard type of monobank. In addition to its policy-making head office and its principal offices in the various republics, it has two levels (in some of the smaller republics, only one level) of regional office and a network of about 3,500 local branches which are its main points of contact with enterprises, collective farms, and lower level government units. To service the urban population it maintains nearly 2,000 collection offices (originally part of the network of communal banks abolished in 1959), which receive payments for rent and service bills, taxes, and other compulsory payments and contributions. The office network also includes a small number (currently fewer than thirty) of special cash service agencies in large industrial establishments and construction projects. Seasonal agencies are operated at remote points where large purchases of farm products are made.

Little statistical information is available on the operations of the Gosbank. Its more than 150,000 employees service about 660,000 clients: the bulk of all banking operations is with the approximately 260,000 enterprises that operate on the basis of cost accounting, or *khozraschet* (enterprises that have their own working capital, prepare a balance sheet and an income statement), and borrow regularly or occasionally. There are about 30,000 collective farm accounts. Nearly 270,000 clients are various government units and organizations (such as party, trade union and cultural organizations) that have no access to credit.

Aggregate balances maintained by Gosbank clients are small in comparison with cash balances held by business and government units in the United States. At the beginning of 1971, total balances in accounts of all *khozraschet* organizations amounted to only 11 billion rubles[11] (compared with 4.7 billion rubles ten years earlier), and deposits of collective farms come to about 4.2 billion rubles. It is not known how the sum of these two amounts (which corresponds approximately to demand deposits in the United States, including Treasury deposits at Federal Reserve and commercial banks) compares with note circulation data, as these are considered a state secret.

---

[11] All amounts in this paper are in post-1961 currency reform rubles.

The operation of a centralized payments system poses many problems in a country the size of the Soviet Union, with its diverse economy and its comparatively small degree of industrial integration. The system is based in the main on documentary drafts and involves processing a large number of items. In very recent years this operation has begun to be automated, but the use of electronic equipment is still very limited.

The rapid increase in transactions by individuals—which has occurred even though consumer loans are extended by stores rather than by banks—has been a consequence of rising incomes, a rise in savings, provision of facilities for depositing wages in savings accounts and making periodic payments from them, and the growing importance of housing loans and of tourism. Since savings bank offices handle virtually all accounts and transactions of individuals, the great increase in these transactions seems to have been a main reason for the incorporation of the savings bank system into the Gosbank.

Of even greater importance as an operating problem has been the rise in transactions involving the collective farms. The relationship between the collective farms and the state, and between the farms and their members, began to be monetized in 1953. Under the system hitherto in force, the collectives paid in kind for the services perfomed by the state-owned tractor and farm machinery stations and had to deliver a large part of their output to the state at relatively low prices fixed by the government, which were in fact a form of taxation. In connection with the changes that started in 1953, the tractor and machinery stations were liquidated and their equipment was sold to the collectives. The farms then had to pay in cash for all machinery and fuel, as well as for building materials, fertilizer, and other supplies; on the other hand, they could sell their output to the state on contract, at significantly higher prices.

Since the early fifties, a gradual shift has been made toward remunerating members of collective farms in cash, rather than in kind, even though until recently they received their income annually, after the end of the crop year. In 1953 only one third of the compensation for work contributed by members was in cash; five years later the proportion had risen to more than half, and it was nearly three fourths in 1963. Since the beginning of 1965 the flow of money income to the farm population has been further increased by the introduction of state pension payments to the aged members of collective farms. The introduction in the summer of 1966 of minimum monthly payments to the members of collective farms also resulted in greater use of money in the farm sector.

The substantial growth of payments flows and bank lending in rural areas and the need to service an ever-growing clientele in villages have added to the complexity of Gosbank operations, traditionally geared to the needs of industry and government which are concentrated in urban areas. Thus the Gosbank has continuously attempted to simplify payments procedures. Efforts to speed up payments through local and industrywide compensation arrangements—whereby mutual claims were offset—have not been successful, and separate compensation offices were abolished in 1955. Other forms of compensation arrangements are now in effect, and local and regional offices have been experimenting on and off with a variety of procedures for accelerating payments, at least for certain categories of transactions. Yet the Soviet banking and economic publications continue to devote much space to the need to improve the settlements mechanism, which seems to represent one of the major operating problems of the Gosbank.

The activities of the Gosbank are not limited to purely financial operations. Despite recent changes in other communist countries, the Soviet economy still does not provide the managers of enterprises with direct and powerful incentives or rewards for maximum performance. In fact, managers have no authority to innovate or even to make quite small modifications in established technology and procedures, as they are confronted with bureaucratic hurdles if they attempt any change, however small it may be. In such a system, a considerable part of improvements must be initiated by persons or organizations outside the enterprise. Ever since the creation of the Soviet regime, various techniques have been tried to provide such outside "assistance" for improving performance. Professional employees of the Gosbank take active part in "voluntary" and auxiliary control organizations attached to the lower territorial units of the government and the party. In the words of an article in the bank's official publication:

> Economists[12] of the Gosbank are widely used by the control organs of the party and of the government to check the state of affairs in trade, in public eating places, in various establishments that service the population, and in the development of the network of movie theaters, and to conduct complex investigations of the business and financial activities of enterprises and organizations in the fields of production, trade, procurement, and other branches of the economy.

Credit Planning and Practices

Little need be added here to the discussion of planning above. Credit planning in the Soviet Union goes back to 1924, immediately after the introduction of a stable currency but several years before the extension of short-term credit became a monopoly of the Gosbank. The form and structure of the various monetary plans in use in the Soviet Union have changed little over time, but such changes as have taken place reflect

---

[12] In Eastern Europe the word "economist" has a much broader connotation than in the West, in terms of both training and occupation. In all agencies concerned with the administration of economic activities, a large proportion of the professional staff are classified as "economists."

in the main administrative changes rather than attempts at integration or at increasing the analytical value of the plans. In recent Soviet economic literature one encounters increasing recognition that financial planning involves more than mere balancing of accounting statements, and that the interrelationship of all financial accounts does not necessarily mean they are either integrated among themselves or consistent with the underlying physical balances. Some contemporary Soviet writers on banking subjects are aware of the need to extend financial analysis to deposit money, to the factors that determine the demand for such balances, and to money flows and velocity. So far, however, monetary planning has been limited, in effect, to currency circulation and, in view of the prevailing monetary arrangements, this is equivalent to saying it has been confined to the consumer sector.

Soviet economists have long denied the monetary nature of bank deposits. Most of them consider such balances to be merely a settlement fund, a liability of the Gosbank, or a potential claim of the depositor to currency. The relationship between credit and money creation is only dimly perceived, and the view is widely held that resources of the Gosbank determine its ability to expand credit.[13] The "real bills" doctrine continues to be extolled, and great pains are taken to explain any departures as consistent with it. In Soviet monetary literature the relationship between the balance of international payments and domestic monetary equilibrium and money supply is generally ignored. Only recently a leading authority had to plead for recognition of the fact that the sale of foreign exchange proceeds by exporters, or their purchase by importers, may lead to a change in the volume of money in circulation.

The heavy burden of orthodoxy is evident in the Gosbank's lending activities. Since the end of the Stalin era there has been some tendency toward greater flexibility, but the bank's credit practices have been conservative and unimaginative when compared with those of most other communist countries. Until the announcement of more significant changes in the fall of 1965, progress was mainly in reducing the excessive compartmentalization of lending and in simplifying accounting procedures. Little was accomplished, even tentatively, toward using credit as a constructive tool for influencing the processes of production and distribution, rather than merely as an implementation of higher level decisions. It is difficult to say to what extent this lag vis-à-vis the other countries reflects a hesitancy resulting from the cumulative experience of disastrous effects from sudden and frequent changes in economic policy and organization, and how far it reflects a reluctance to give up monetary

---

[13] An earlier attempt by Professor Kronrod to have bank balances at least recognized as "money of the banking circuit" met with widespread opposition. By 1973, the credit origin of all money and the equivalence of deposits and currency was somewhat more widely recognized.

and credit theories that the Soviet Union itself has generated and elevated to the status of inviolability.

The present loan administration is a patchwork of procedures introduced to supplement the original system of gearing credit to financing the movement of real assets through the economic system. The proliferation of separate "objects of crediting," originally accompanied by the opening of a separate loan account, began almost with the establishment of the Gosbank: "production credit for specific purposes" made its appearance in the bank's balance sheet in 1922. Subsequently, whenever a new pressing need was identified, a new object of crediting was added. Thus, a pharmacy may now obtain loans under 17 different purpose headings, and an alcohol distillery can apply for a bank loan on not fewer than 23 different grounds. As a result, many items of small quantitative significance emerged in Gosbank statistics, including such entries as "loans for the construction of movie theatres." The trend toward compartmentalization of loans was not reversed until the mid-fifties. Since then the loan and current accounts of some enterprises have been merged, and various other simplifications that have increased the flexibility of credit administration have been adopted.

At the end of 1970, the latest year for which data are available, the total volume of short-term credit outstanding amounted to 108 billion rubles, compared with 17 billion rubles in 1950 (see Table 1). Loans directly secured by physical collateral accounted for three fourths of the 1970 total, and with the addition of credit documents in process of collection (covering goods shipped) the figure rises to over nine tenths, leaving less than 8 percent for all other types of credit. These percentages are very close to those for the immediately preceding years, and not much different from the corresponding proportions at the end of 1950.

Industry and retail trade each accounted for one third of the total volume of short-term credit outstanding at the end of 1970, and most of the remaining third was divided between wholesale trade and agriculture. More than 45 percent of the short-term credit to industry, after subtracting the loans to finance collection float, was for carrying inventories of agricultural origin. Both cooperative and state farms are heavily dependent on credit, which currently meets about two thirds of all their production expenses apart from labor costs. Advance payments by state purchasing agencies account for a large part of the production credit extended to cooperatives, including (to the extent that the farms have shifted to the payment of money wages) the credit needed to finance the cost of labor. A gradual shift toward direct Gosbank lending to the cooperatives—for labor as well as other costs—is now under way.

Long-term credit has so far been available mainly to agriculture, where it is the main means of financing capital formation in collective farms, and for construction of dwellings. At the end of 1970 (see Table 2) the outstanding amount of such credit extended by the Gosbank

TABLE 1
Short-Term Credit Outstanding in the USSR, 1950 and 1970

	Year-end 1950	Year-end 1970
Total outstanding (in billions of rubles)	17.3	108.2
By type of loan (in percent of total):		
Raw materials and fuel.	16.7	22.6
Goods in process	2.7	2.0
Finished goods	4.2	3.3
Construction equipment.	0.9	2.7
Trade inventories	36.7	42.8
Including:		
Wholesale trade.	(3.3)	(4.9)
Procurement of farm products	(2.4)	(6.9)
Retail trade	(25.7)	(26.6)
Other real assets.	1.3	3.4
Secured by items in process of collection	28.8	15.3
Other types of loans	8.7	7.9
By economic sector (in percent of total):		
Industry	40.3	33.6
Agriculture (including collective farms)	3.3	8.8
Transportation and communications	1.3	1.3
Construction.	3.5	7.6
Wholesale trade	11.4	7.8
Procurement of farm products	4.4	7.7
Retail trade	35.2	32.2
Other sectors	0.6	1.0

and the Investment Bank, combined, was less than one tenth of the outstanding short-term loans, a proportion that has prevailed during most of the years since 1950. Certainly, the amount of credit extended to stimulate capital investment in agriculture is pitifully small in relation to needs. By the beginning of 1965, 2,700 new construction and building-material–producing enterprises had been created for the specific purpose of promoting the construction of farm buildings (particularly barns), but the aggregate amount of credit made available to them in the preceding year amounted to only 38.4 million rubles. However, the total volume of long-term loans, including credit to agriculture, increased sharply after 1964.

The Reform

In contrast to the path taken in Yugoslavia, Hungary, and also in 1968 in Czechoslovakia, the emphasis of the "reform of economic steering mechanism" (subsequently referred to as "the reform") launched in 1965 in the Soviet Union was not on substituting pecuniary processes for administrative allocations, but rather on a limited restructuring of the price system by explicitly recognizing the cost of capital as one of the elements of production costs, by partially rechanneling financial flows,

TABLE 2
Long-Term Credit in the USSR, 1970
(in millions of rubles)

Type of Loan	*Outstanding at Year-end*		*Loans Granted During Year*
Loans to collective farms	10,296		2,183
For construction of farm buildings and mechanization			881
For equipment			480
For electrification			70
For wage payments.			166
For other purposes			586
Loans to the population	646		
Urban		135	
Rural.		511	
Loans to state and cooperative enterprises and organizations.	7,117		
Housing cooperatives.		2,069	
Other.		5,048	
Total	18,059		

and by offering inducements designed to stimulate personal incentives and performance by making compensation more dependent on profits achieved. None of these have either changed significantly the relative degree of reliance on money versus administrative controls or provided much room for flexibility by using money as an agent of change rather than a registering mechanism. The relationship between enterprises and the various state organizations which supply raw materials and certain intermediate goods and direct the distribution of finished products continues to be controlled by the planning authorities. Contracts merely formalize these relationships and fix details, and financial penalties still play a very modest role in enforcing fulfillment of obligations undertaken. Financial planning has not been abolished, but its detail has been reduced and it has been made somewhat more flexible. The broad categories of credit use continue to be centrally planned in order to maintain a balance between resource availability and demand for resources, and thus to preserve monetary equilibrium.

As a result of the reform, a certain number of detailed decisions were shifted from state to State Bank bureaucracy. The range of alternatives and the scope of discretion available to the Bank remain severely circumscribed by the plan and by minute regulations regarding the form and terms of payments and the extension of credit. Lending procedures have been changed, and usually simplified in detail, but all basic features of the standard system remain. In particular, the reform has not followed the example of East Germany and Czechoslovakia, which have shifted to credit extension on the basis of contracts between banks and individual enterprises.

The reform has significantly increased the role of the banking system in channeling investment funds. Even though credit has been elevated to the position of a key "economic lever," and is expected to play a major role in improving the performance of the economy, it is to be a tauter string rather than a looser leash. The reform has further simplified financing of working capital along the lines of various steps taken in this direction since the middle fifties. In particular, the availability of bank financing for investment as well as for working capital purposes has been liberalized by making loans available in anticipation of retained earnings in future years, thus bridging the time gap between current spending and future income.

Credit on the basis of "norms" established for specific categories of inventories, with a specific ceiling for each, has now been replaced by loans for broad inventory categories, in most cases without specific upper limits. The more recent tendency toward crediting on the basis of total sales turnover makes funds available to pay for deliveries, as attested by shipping documents, with credit no longer being dependent on inspection reports based on actual visual checking of the level of inventories. In fact, this new method of crediting makes bank loans available for the financing of all production costs, including wages. Such loans (known as extending "credit on turnover") are made available to cover normally between 40 and 50 percent of the planned level of working capital. This percentage can vary for individual categories of working capital used by an enterprise, with stipulated exclusions. The reform, as well as earlier efforts to make extension of credit more flexible, appear to have mainly added to the cumbersomeness of procedures and rendered the analysis of the effectiveness of the use of credit more difficult.

Working capital will no longer be replenished in case of need from budget grants or administrative transfers from other enterprises. Enterprises which have depleted their working capital must now obtain bank credit on which interest rates are relatively high and which must be repaid from future profits.

Under the standard system, interest on bank loans was not differentiated as a function of the financial position of the enterprise or by maturity. It was treated as legitimate expenditure and included in the planned unit cost. To induce enterprises to avoid building up excessive inventories—typical of the "protective" techniques of Soviet production management—interest is now charged against actual gross profits, thus diminishing funds available for bonus payments and other enterprise uses. Modest steps have been taken to differentiate interest rates. Bank officials have no authority to change rates fixed for each specified category.

The most important change brought about by the reform is the restructuring of monetary flows. This is the only significant change that has occurred in the financial area in 40 years. The reform involved changes in the role assigned to financial processes and flows without, in fact, changing their character; it has modified the composition rather than the level of financial flows. The main changes can be summarized under three headings: (1) distribution of profits; (2) charges on invested capital; and (3) changes in the financing of investments.

1. *Distribution of profits.* Various changes in the distribution of "planned" profits and those exceeding these targets aim at increasing individual as well as collective incentives. From the point of view of monetary flows, the most significant effect of the reform in this area is the greater volume of retained profits available for decentralized capital investment at the initiative of the individual enterprise, although under close supervision of the various administrative organs.

2. *Charge on invested capital.* Interest, under the name of "charge on capital," is now charged on both fixed and working capital. To equalize the cost of new and existing fixed capital originally supplied on a grant basis, a charge has been imposed on the depreciated value of capital assets in use at the time of the change. Under the standard system, no charge was made for capital—the most precious resource in all developing countries—because it was public property. Considerable misallocation and wasteful use of investment funds resulted, as a larger investment per unit of output was not automatically reflected in higher costs. Failure to include the cost of capital also led to distortions of prices for producer and consumer goods and to large disparities between domestic and foreign prices. Capital now has been recognized as a cost factor, and a charge has been introduced for its use.

The charge on capital may be regarded as a property tax, or, alternatively, as the minimum socially acceptable rate of return on productive assets, or as the minimum share of government in enterprise revenues. Charges on capital are differentiated by industry (although the degree of differentiation has been modest so far), and units with a favorable cost structure (mostly in extractive industries) may be charged quasi-rents. The introduction of differentiated capital charges and of quasi-rents has resulted in narrowing in many cases the considerable differences in profit rates within the same branch of industry and among its individual products. Producers' wholesale prices have been recalculated to reflect the cost of capital. While the introduction of the capital charge is important for the structure of prices, its significance for the flow of funds is limited as long as such payments flow into the same national pool of funds as profits—the budget.

3. *Financing of investments.* A significant change in the financing of investment involves a shift from grant financing to repayable loans, while at the same time increasing the availability of decentralized resources by permitting retention of a greater share of profits and of a large part of depreciation reserves by individual enterprises.[14]

---

[14] Partial shifting to loan financing has been discussed at least since 1957.

The financing of fixed capital investment from budgetary resources on a non-returnable grant basis involved considerable misallocation of resources and costly delays in the completion of construction projects. The financing of the bulk of fixed investment should, therefore, gradually shift to a combination of bank loans, retained enterprise profits, and depreciation reserves. The bulk of investment funds originating in the budget is now channeled through the banking system, while investment from retained earnings of enterprises has gained in relative importance. As a result, the proportion of national income redistributed through the budget should tend to decline, and that of self-investment and bank loans increase. With the reduction in the portion of investment funds channeled through the national budget, the budget will become somewhat more similar in scope to that of the Western countries.[15] However, greater decentralization of investment funds does not necessarily mean greater decentralization of decision making.

The allocation of investment resources remains, however, with the bureaucracy under the control of planners. The state continues to determine the level and the broad distribution of investments.[16] In the new scheme of things there is no more room for anything even remotely resembling a capital market than under the old system. The principal channel for enterprise initiative is arguing it out with the supervisory and planning authorities. The amount which individual enterprises can expand independently for capital projects, including those required to upgrade technology, and even for maintenance and repairs, has not been significantly increased.

Changes in the flow of investment funds (including depreciation reserves) and credit are bound to affect to a certain extent patterns of real investment and inventory behavior—in addition to the level and structure of producer as well as consumer prices—and thus consumer welfare. The broad question is, indeed, whether reforms in the areas of finance will increase the efficiency of the Soviet economy. So far, there is hardly any evidence that this has been the case.

Even in the limited field of financing and credit, the reform has revealed its limitations. Although by now virtually all enterprises have

---

[15] So far, the reform has had only a very slight influence on the sources of budgetary income and on the structure of expenditures. In 1970, the percentage of national income channeled into the budget was essentially the same (52.7 percent) as in the year the reform was initiated (52.9 percent, in 1965). Almost as high a percentage (90.6 percent as compared with 91.8 percent) of the budgetary receipts was derived from payments of the socialized sector of the economy; and the expenditures for the economy, overwhelmingly for investment purposes, declined only slightly, from 45.7 percent in 1965 to 43.9 percent in 1970 budget appropriations, in spite of all the emphasis on decentralized investments from profits retained by individual enterprises.

[16] Thus, since 1971 even in the case of decentralized investment, the upper limit is set by the competent ministries of the individual constitutent republics of the Soviet Union, depending on who supervises the individual enterprise.

been shifted to the new system, the results achieved have clearly fallen far short of original expectations. In many important recent policy statements on economic issues, the very term "reform" has been studiously avoided. However, in the field of enterprise finances and with regard to the redirection of investment funds and extension of credit to agriculture, there has been no retreat. The reforms initiated more than seven years ago remain the only significant change in the standard system, but these changes, as I tried to point out, affect more the form rather than the essence of the relationship of credit to the allocation of resources and their effective use.

Only time will tell whether and when the Soviet Union will be willing to follow the more imaginative and flexible policies of the smaller socialist countries.

7. THE INDUSTRIAL MANAGERS

John P. Hardt and Theodore Frankel

As the Soviet economy has developed and changed, so has the group that manages the enterprises of the planned economy. During the Stalin era, the Communist Party leadership built a group of professional managers which was politically reliable and oriented to the goals of rapid industrialization and fulfillment of production targets. In recent years, however, the changing nature of the economy has placed more emphasis on economic efficiency and the wants of consumers, and less on quantity of output, although the latter is still very important. These economic changes are bringing corresponding changes among the managerial cadres, according to this article by Hardt and Frankel. The managers are becoming more professional in their outlook, seek greater autonomy, and are strongly motivated by bonuses and status. They have become a distinct interest group in the Soviet economic order.

John P. Hardt is Senior Specialist in Soviet Economics, Congressional Reference Service, Library of Congress. Theodore Frankel, now deceased, was editor of *Problems of Communism* at the time of his death. From *Interest Groups in Soviet Politics,* ed. H. Gordon Skilling and Franklyn Griffiths (copyright © 1971 by Princeton University Press), published for the Centre of Russian and East European Studies, pp. 171–76 and 189–208. Reprinted by permission of Princeton University Press. Some footnotes have been omitted, together with some material on the industrial managers in the Stalin era.

THE SOVIET INDUSTRIAL managerial group is large, currently numbering over 100,000. For several reasons this group of industrial enterprise managers continues to be more homogeneous in training, performance, and behavior than the more extensive group of Soviet managers and planners as a whole. But whereas there has been considerable continuity in the characteristics and group identification of those industrial managers who came onto the scene during the Stalin era, in recent years a Soviet version of the entrepreneur with a more sophisticated knowledge of management science has become increasingly important, as the simple and overriding gross output criterion has been progressively replaced by multiple criteria, including sales and profit.

During the course of Stalinist rule a professional management group was built up whose degree of autonomy was related to its political reliability. The Stalinist model of economic planning and management shaped a class of production-engineer managers well suited to the narrowly defined goals of forced industrialization.[1] The establishment of the professional Stalinist manager has not, however, met the requirements of management in the post-Stalin economic system. The new manager required is more of a demand-oriented businessman and less of a supply-oriented production engineer. The emerging comprehensive, optimal approach to planning is responsive to the needs of improved economic efficiency that also generate pressures for a new system of economic management. However, it is likely that the implementation of an optimal planning system for the economy as a whole will have to precede changes in management, if only because the professional economists and statisticians appear to be available to staff the transition, while a comparable supply of appropriately trained professional managers for managerial reform does not appear available. The complex and time-consuming task of creating a new class of businessmen-managers to replace the entrenched production-engineer managers is proceeding very slowly. The increasing divergence which results between the characteristics of the existing managerial and the required managerial group may be a central source of conflict within the Soviet management group as a whole. A proper response to the new requirements of the economy may necessitate both a very large educational effort in management science and the replacement of the majority of the current managerial cadres.

Other issues are emerging between the managers and other large groups such as the top party leadership, the party apparatus, the military, and the security forces. Unsatisfactory economic performance accounts for the persistence and general acceptance of a need for planning and management reform. All groups would share in the advantages of improved economic performance if the management group were modernized or appropriately professionalized. At the same time, professionalization of managerial or other groups resulting in possibly improved efficiency needs to be weighed against a diminution in direct party control and

---

[1] There are a number of studies available on the Soviet manager which focus primarily on the Stalinist period. See Joseph Berliner, *Factory and Manager in the USSR* (Cambridge, Mass.: Harvard University Press, 1957); David Granick, *Management of the Industrial Firm in the USSR* (New York: Columbia University Press, 1954); Jeremy R. Azrael, *Managerial Power and Soviet Politics* (Cambridge, Mass.: Harvard University Press, 1966); Barry M. Richman, *Soviet Management: With Significant American Comparisons* (Englewood Cliffs, N.J.: Prentice-Hall, 1965); and Barry M. Richman, *Management Development and Education in the Soviet Union* (East Lansing, Mich.: Michigan State University, Institute for International Business and Development Studies, 1967).

a reduction in the influence of governmental organs, including the security and police groups, whose *raison d'etre* is to carry out party control. Moreover, the changes apparently required in the managerial group seem to be so extensive as to put in question the ability of many senior managers, who are also members of the party elite, to survive as active members of the group. Whereas the parochial production-oriented professionalism of the Stalinist period generated little group conflict with other institutions, the new professionalism cuts across institutional lines—a fact which impedes its acceptance. Similarly, those features of the economic reform that aim at reducing party control do not produce guaranteed results in improved economic performance, especially in the short-run.

Despite what may be interpreted as significant changes or the beginning of significant changes in the Soviet managerial group since Stalin, a case can still be made from available empirical evidence that only a modification of the Stalinist approach to planning and management has occurred. Thus, modest changes to date could be viewed as reversible and indirect in their impact on the managerial group in terms of its enduring character and relationship to other elite groups. In our view, however, although minor reversals may occur, the trend of change in the managerial group is not likely to be turned back—not as long as the pressures for improved economic performance continue, and particularly if these pressures heighten.

In spite of many changes in personnel and in the characteristics of the managerial group as a whole, the core of managerial cadres in industry appears to represent a group with common interests and identification. Although not having direct channels of access to the top leadership, as a group they have usually had elite representation. Moreover, in the post-Stalin period the core group has begun to represent a broader, larger group of managers and planners.

Conflict within the managerial group may well build up to a point where much more rapid and sudden alteration in management is likely if the pace of Soviet social change is not accelerated. Moreover, among the institutional groups influencing Soviet policy, the managers and the economists, as interest groups, may represent forces of institutional change, as contrasted with groups such as the military and the police which stand for the *status quo*. Hence in the broader context of conflict and change, the managerial group may in future prove to be a significant factor in Soviet political development. Accordingly, our approach in the pages that follow is to appraise conflict within the Soviet management group as a whole and between the managers and other institutional groups in the Soviet elite. In this, reference will first be made to the Stalinist manager and then to the changing role of the industrial manager since 1953.

THE STALINIST MODEL OF ECONOMIC PLANNING
AND MANAGEMENT

Management in the USSR is not conducted *in vacuo*, but in the context of the economic planning process. It is primarily through the plan that priorities for resource allocation are set and criteria for performance are established. The manager receives his guidance concerning the top leadership's economic decisions through the plan. To this extent then the economic planning process developed during the period of Joseph Stalin's power had a pattern and an internal rationale. It is conventionally referred to as the Stalinist model.

To plan in the Stalinist context meant, in effect, to mobilize and concentrate all the resources in the society for the purpose of *maximizing* one primary set of economic goals. This was not in any conventional sense comprehensive planning of the production and distribution processes throughout the economy but rather a form of selective, controlled mobilization of certain key products that may be described in the following fashion:

In implementing the Stalinist economic model Soviet planners have acted "as if" the maximization of output of only *one* sector of the economy—heavy industry—were important. They have acted "as if" the interest of the other sectors could be safely ignored or held constant (*ceteris paribus*) while heavy industrial output was expanded as rapidly as possible. And finally, they have acted "as if" production of the other sectors was of value only insofar as it provided additional increments of materials, labor, and capital for the expansion of the heavy industrial sector. These "as ifs" gave the Soviet planner a set of simple imperatives in planning resource allocation:

First, allocate to the military establishment the resources (labor, materials, capital) needed to fulfill strategic requirements. Also, lay aside the minimum amounts of resources needed for consumption and the preservation and necessary growth of the infrastructure.

Second, maximize the flow of resources into the heavy industrial sector. Then specify how resources are to be combined to maximize output. (The Soviet planner assumed that fixed, functional relationships held between units of steel, energy, and machine equivalents. A simple application of these production functions helped him determine the crude end-product mix, as well as proportions between factors and production. These production functions changed little over time.)

Third, distribute residuals of unrequired or unsuitable resources among other sectors such as agriculture and light industry.[2]

---

[2] John P. Hardt and Carl Modig, "The Industrialization of Soviet Russia in the First Half Century," in *The Soviet Union: A Half-Century of Communism*, ed. Kurt L. London (Baltimore: Johns Hopkins Press, 1968), pp. 295–326.

The application of this plan involved primarily the systematic expansion of the priority industrial sectors through a detailed control and allocation mechanism. Administratively centralized day-to-day management was possible as it only had to be applied within the selected priority sectors. Moreover, during the early stage of industrial development of the Soviet Union in the twenties and thirties, the primary goal was the establishment of a coal, steel, and simple machine-building base, and for that purpose the political leadership could employ a simple physical output criterion of performance for administering management.[3] The characteristics and attitudes of the managerial group during the Stalinist period were consistent with these planning and management criteria.

The operational center of the industrial group directing the Soviet economic planning and management system under Stalin was the director of the industrial enterprise. Although loosely representative of a much more extensive group of managers and planners, the industrial group itself was large in number; under Stalin, tens of thousands, and in recent years, over 100,000. This central management group grew increasingly homogeneous in training, performance, and behavior in the Stalinist period. Detailed plans were formulated and published in many other areas, but these were described by Soviet and Western economists alike as "buffer sectors" or areas in which planning was less consistent in formulation, implementation, and control.[4] Success was well rewarded in the industrial enterprise (and more particularly so in heavy industry), while failure was severely punished. The use of criminal law to control and enforce the management system reached its extremity with the development of the forced labor camp system in the late thirties.

Specifically, the terms "industrial enterprise directors" or "industrial managers" used in this chapter correspond to the Soviet term "directors, leaders, and managers of enterprises," as used in the 1959 Census, which apparently covers the managers of all Soviet enterprises in heavy and light industry. It does not cover the 120,000 managers of enterprises in construction, transportation, and forestry nor the more than 1,200,000 managers in trade, public dining, supply, housing, communal economy, day-to-day services, health, culture, and education. It will be assumed, however, that the group of industrial enterprise directors serves as a reference group (and acts in some ways as a spokesman) for the total

---

[3] John P. Hardt, "Soviet Economic Development and Policy Alternatives," in *The Development of the Soviet Economy: Plan and Performance,* ed. Vladimir G. Treml (New York: Praeger, for the Institute for the Study of the USSR, 1968), pp. 1–23.

[4] See John P. Hardt, Dimitri M. Gallik, and Vladimir G. Treml, Institutional Stagnation and Changing Soviet Strategy," in *New Directions in the Soviet Economy* (Studies Prepared for the Subcommittee on Foreign Economic Policy, Joint Economic Committee, 89th Cong., 2d sess.) (Washington, D.C.: U.S. Government Printing Office, 1966), Part I, pp. 19–62.

group of managers. The 1959 Census lists 128,712 directors, leaders, and managers of enterprises in industry; within this group there is a leading subgroup comprising the directors of the some 43,000 enterprises operating on economic accountability, with the core group constituted by the 11,000 directors of those enterprises which produce 75 percent of Soviet industrial production. Practically all enterprise directors in heavy industry are party members.

While it seems safe to conjecture that the group of industrial enterprise directors is subdivided along branch and regional lines and is further split on such matters as investment and labor resources allocation, there is insufficient evidence to pursue the matter in this essay. For the same reason, the generational conflict, which can be expected to reach a high point within the next decade, will not be treated here.

POST-STALIN CHANGES

Circumstances after the death of Stalin and particularly after the abortive Sixth Five-Year Plan of the mid-fifties made necessary a new and more complex system of planning and management. Comprehensive economic planning became mandatory as the requirements of light industry, consumers, and infrastructure of the Soviet economy, especially transportation and housing, became relevant elements of economic demand. At the same time, the traditional military requirements for resources became dramatically more expensive as nuclear missilery provided a new and costly set of military demands on top of the continuing conventional armaments needs. Moreover, the preferred industrial sector could be, and indeed needed to be, converted from a simple coal/steel type economy to one more consistent with the industrial technology of other countries using more sophisticated energy and metal sources. These increasingly complex supply requirements in the traditional heavy industrial-military sectors of the Soviet economy had also to be reconciled with the burgeoning requirements of consumer-goods and housing materials production. Incentives were required to provide a basis for improved labor and management productivity. The population appeared to be less willing to accept stable or declining living conditions, whether in the city or the countryside.

These problems of expanding demand and diminishing supply were reflected in a reduction of the overall indices of Soviet economic growth, either calculated in terms of the annual rate of increase in the gross national product (GNP) or simply in terms of annual increments in industrial output segments of GNP. The rate of increase in the early sixties was substantially less than the average during the fifties (4.5 percent per annum as compared with about 7 percent).[5] This retardation

---

[5] See Stanley H. Cohn, "Soviet Growth Retardation: Trends in Resource Availability and Efficiency," in *New Directions of the Soviet Economy*, Part II-A, pp. 99–132.

could be explained partially by poor harvests, bad weather, and other factors not directly relevant to the system of planning and management. However, the slowdown in industrial growth which persisted through most of the sixties cannot be explained by factors external to Soviet economic planning and management. The hard choices were between changes in the resource allocation pattern (e.g., reducing the military budget) or improved efficiency in economic administration. The *ad hoc* solutions imposed at the top by Nikita Khrushchev in his agricultural "campaigns," including the new lands policy, fertilizer expansion, the abolition of the machine tractor station, etc., were followed by a more comprehensive approach to pricing and enterprise management under the leadership of Brezhnev and Kosygin, which promised a change from maximal to optimal planning. These changes may be viewed at best as modest, and the unsatisfactory performance of the economy continues to provide a source of pressure for further movement away from the Stalinist system of planning and management toward a different approach.

These changing aspects of demand and supply have directly challenged the central features of the previous economic model, as may be noted by contrasting the following remarks on the post-Stalin situation with the Stalinist model described above.

> First, military allocation levels can be only provisionally set aside, both in the aggregate and in the trade-off between alternative military uses (e.g., missiles *vs.* conventional divisions). The fluctuating military budgets of Khrushchev and his successors bear witness to the fact that defense is now a variable rather than a preferred "given."
>
> Likewise, consumption is no longer a nonpreferred "given." Production to provide for improved living conditions is a variable—if only as a stimulant to productivity.
>
> Second, the simplifying assumptions of fixed product relationships are increasingly untenable as the structure of heavy industry becomes more complex, servicing technologically advanced space programs, traditional military and investment projects, and new requirements in the economic infrastructure.
>
> Third, no longer can Soviet planners treat light industry, transportation, and agriculture as though they were primarily suppliers of "surplus" labor, raw materials, and capital for heavy industry—and consumers of whatever residuals are left after heavy industrial output is maximized.

The old system of economic planning and management has been eroded and in some ways changed basically. A new system, however, has not yet emerged. The possibility of the development of comprehensive optimal planning and management based on a marketlike system seems to be accepted by many Soviet economists, and by some Western economic specialists, including the authors of this paper. It is both theoretically possible and rational in the context of the Soviet system. However, these factors do not alone guarantee its existence. The system to date is still much closer to maximal Stalin-type planning and day-to-day centralized management.

Against this background one might expect to observe a change in the behavior and interests of the managerial group. This expectation would be all the stronger in view of the changes in the institutional environment of the Soviet managers, such as Khrushchev's 1957 decentralization which abolished the industrial ministries, the 1962 split of the party (at the oblast level and below) into industrial and agricultural organizations, as well as the economic reforms effected by his successors. Before addressing ourselves to this question, it might be useful first to consider the basic characteristics of the managerial group as a whole in terms of size, composition and education.

The size of the enterprise directors' group during and since the Khrushchev period has stabilized or even declined. Thus, the 1957 figure for enterprise directors may be estimated as 131,000,[6] while the 1959 Census gave a figure of 128,712.[7] Although hard data are not available, some surmises can be made concerning the composition and social background of today's managers. The first is that with the disappearance of the older groups (Red Directors, Mensheviks, and "bourgeois" specialists) the present group is rather homogeneous. Both those members recruited in the 1940s and the emergent new generation were born under Soviet rule and are the products of Soviet training and indoctrination. The second is that of today's top group of managers approximately half come from white-collar families[8] so that their backgrounds are rather similar. Presumably, white-collar origin and social background are no longer the outsider's mark as they were in the 1920s and 1930s, and consequently enterprise directors feel less uncertain about their social status. Their sense of security is probably also boosted by the greater homogeneity of the group's composition.

There is little question that the educational qualifications of enterprise directors, as a group, were improved during and after the Stalin period. In 1967, 68 percent of industrial directors had a higher education, with the percentage significantly higher in heavy industry and perceptibly lower in light industry, particularly in the provinces. There can be little doubt that of the enterprise directors with higher education, the majority had specialized in engineering rather than in economic or business management. De Witt's figures show that the number of professional engineers and other specialists working in industrial enterprises grew from

---

[6] Nicholas De Witt, *Education and Professional Employment in the U.S.S.R.* (Washington, D.C.: National Science Foundation, 1961), p. 498.

[7] The diminution of the group of enterprise directors is, of course, closely connected with the long-term trend toward the merger of small plants which apparently overbalances the effect of the addition of new plants.

[8] David Granick, *The Red Executive* (Garden City, N.Y.: Doubleday, 1960), p. 40.

153,000 in 1941 to 442,000 in 1959; by contrast, the economists are shown working in state ministries and state agencies other than enterprises.[9]

In view of the preponderance of engineers among enterprise directors it is worth noting that only 7–8 percent of the curriculum time at higher engineering institutions is devoted to political and socio-economic subjects,[10] and of this time probably a high percentage goes to the study of Marxism-Leninism. Even the courses in engineering economics (which are designed to train planners rather than engineers) offered by the Moscow Institute of Engineering Economics devote 40 percent of curriculum time to "hard" science and engineering subjects, 17 percent to political courses, and 36 percent to business administration (production, management, accounting, business law, finance). In the light of the foregoing it seems safe to conclude that the arts of management still occupy second place to the science of engineering in the education and orientation of enterprise directors.

The current economic reform has changed this picture in only one major respect: the party has been running hundreds of seminars and courses for directors, deputy directors, and other leading personnel designed to orient managers away from the old goals of quantity production toward profits and sales.[11] It is too early to say to what extent courses embodying the goals of the new economic reform (managerial initiative, attention to consumer demands, cost efficiency) have been incorporated into the curricula of Soviet schools. Should such courses be added, it would take a number of years before they could significantly affect the attitudes of incumbent directors.

The tenure of enterprise directors has been relatively long and steady since Stalin's last decade. It was disturbed briefly in 1959 when Khrushchev embarked upon a "renewal of cadres" at the middle and lower levels of the industrial establishment, on the grounds that these cadres were not able to cope with the new requirements imposed upon Soviet industry. By the end of 1962, he seemed ready to apply his policy of replacement to the enterprise director, only in turn, at the last minute, against the party cadres proper in his bifurcation of the party in November 1962. However, lately there have been scattered indications of fairly severe managerial shake-ups in the provinces. Thus, in one raion of

[9] De Witt, *Education and Professional Employment in the U.S.S.R.*, pp. 794–98.

[10] Ibid., p. 283.

[11] To give one example of many: In February 1967, the Lvov Gorkom, in conjunction with the Lvov Division of the Economic Institute of the Ukrainian Academy of Science, the Philosophical Institute of the Ukrainian Academy, and the Lvov Polytechnical Institute, sponsored a scientific conference on "Social Problems of the Economic Reform." The First Secretary of the Lvov Gorkom, in his address, stressed that a manager accustomed to operate only under instructions from above or on the basis of his experience and intuition cannot manage properly. He called for better training and more initiative for management cadres.

Volgogradskaya oblast, 43.5 percent of directors and chief engineers were changed in the last two years; and in another raion, during the same time, 32 managers of industrial enterprises were changed, 10 of them for unsatisfactory work.

In conclusion, the post-Stalin period continued the stabilizing trend of the last decade of Stalin's rule, despite the rather drastic institutional rearrangements by Khrushchev and their reversal by his successors. The size of the managerial group, its composition and background, its education and tenure have remained stable or altered only slightly. More important, the image which the directorial group has of its functions and the nature of its interests has remained largely unchanged, despite the slow emergence of a fresh generation of directors and the very considerable pressure toward change exerted by the party. It is too early to say whether the party is willing and able to effect a more rapid transformation in managerial attitudes by a rejuvenation of managerial ranks.

Group Attitudes

Operational Autonomy. While there is little direct evidence of managerial self-assertiveness in the post-Stalin years, there are many indications of a continued desire to achieve operational autonomy—particularly in the reactions of Khrushchev and his successors to the managers. Specifically, in the 1957 reorganization, which formally subordinated industry to the obkom first secretaries, Khrushchev was very careful to concentrate his fire on the central ministries and to reassure the enterprise directors. Thus, in the Central Committee decree of February 14, 1957, repeated reference was made to the need for raising the role of local organs in the economy. Khrushchev's speech in the Supreme Soviet on May 7, 1957, again emphasized the desirability of enlarging the rights of the local economic, administrative, and party organizations. These assurances to the local economic organs, including the enterprises, followed sweeping decrees in 1955 and 1956 giving enterprise directors additional rights in initiating production plans and in recruiting personnel. It is no surprise then that the enterprise directors, believing that Khrushchev was bolstering their autonomy, reacted favorably to the 1957 reorganization, at least at the outset.[12]

Subsequently, beginning as early as 1958, the creeping recentralization of industry cut back whatever gain in authority may have been achieved by the directors in 1957. For one thing, the various divisions of Gosplan, bypassing the *sovnarkhozy*, kept a tight control over the enterprises;[13] for another, the many new State Committees assumed in substance many

---

[12] Wolfgang Leonhard, *The Kremlin Since Stalin* (New York: Praeger, 1962), p. 241.

[13] Alex Nove, *The Soviet Economy: An Introduction*, rev. ed. (New York: Praeger, 1966), pp. 79–80.

of the supervisory functions of the disestablished ministries;[14] and finally, the *sovnarkhoz* system itself was progressively centralized, with the establishment of regional *sovnarkhozy* and ultimately a national *sovnarkhoz*. The 1962 bifurcation of the party further undermined the grant of authority to the enterprise directors and alienated this group from Khrushchev.

Khrushchev's successors, too, played up to the directors' desire for autonomy. The reform of 1965 reinstituting the economic ministries was explicitly intended to enlarge the operational autonomy of the enterprise directors, both by keeping down the ministries' control (through reduction of the number of performance indices set by the ministries) and by changing the style of guidance from direct administrative interference to indirect guidance via financial incentives and penalties. The initial reaction of the enterprise directors to the proposed buildup of their autonomy was, surprisingly enough, negative. There is ample evidence that the directors, as a group, were timid in asserting the additional rights granted to them and that they permitted the ministries to encroach steadily upon enterprise autonomy.[15]

On the face of it, this reaction would seem to contradict the thesis of the desire of directors for autonomy, but a closer look reveals that what the incumbent directors objected to was not autonomy per se, but the conditions under which that autonomy was being offered. This involved the speedy replacement by more modern entrepreneurs of the engineering managers who were bound to the production process and were oblivious to cost and marketing considerations. What made the situation serious for the incumbents was that it was the party which set this high price for entrepreneurial independence. Thus, V. Akhundov, First Secretary of the Central Committee, CP of Azerbaidzhan, has written that the old type of manager, the thoughtless performer and pusher, will disappear. The new type of manager will be a man capable of thinking and acting according to scientific data, a resourceful man with a mercantile spirit. F. Tabeyev, First Secretary of the Tatarskaya ASSR, noted for his willingness to encourage economic experimentation, called for party encouragement of a new style of managerial leadership. Similarly, Professor L. Leontyev stipulated that the success of the economic reform was contingent upon major changes in managerial psychology: "The personnel of enterprises must be freed from the habit of waiting for or requiring instructions from above on the questions which now come within their competence." V. Firsov, director of the V. I. Lenin

---

[14] Ibid., p. 75.

[15] *Soviet Economic Performance, 1966–67* (materials Prepared for the Subcommittee on Foreign Economic Policy, Joint Economic Committee, 90th Cong., 2d sess.) (Washington, D.C.: U.S. Government Printing Office, 1968), pp. 131–32; Theodore Frankel, "Soviet Economic Reform: A Tentative Appraisal," *Problems of Communism*, Vol. XVI, No. 3 (May–June 1967), pp. 32, 34–35.

Machine-building Plant, excoriated the old timid "psychology" which had not changed.

If the initial reaction of enterprise directors to the reform was hesitant because it did not offer them autonomy on their own terms, recent responses seem more positive and more assertive. In February 1966, when most of his fellow directors were still defensive about the economic reform, G. Kulagin, director of the Sverdlov Production Association for Construction of Machine Tools in Leningrad, demanded that while "orders issued by higher administrative organs should be binding upon the enterprises, the specific methods, ways and means of implementation be left to the enterprises themselves." By August 1967 he was loudly demanding that the investment funds allocated to enterprises be increased ten times. K. Rudnev, Minister for Instrument Building, Means of Automation and Control Systems, has written half-jokingly about one of his directors who refused for months to work according to the reform and had to be "coaxed" by the ministry. Many directors now complain publicly about being deprived by their ministries of funds for the assimilation of new technology. One director has asserted his independence to the point of denying workers of the staffing section of the oblast finance department access to his records and refusing to divulge information on the structure of the enterprise administration. A recent article by Ye. Liberman mentioned the attitude of enterprise directors who defend the economic interests of their enterprises against encroachment from the ministry. Finally, in a recent study of 2,000 "middle-level" managers at machine-building factories in Moscow and Kharkov, "almost all expressed their dissatisfaction about the insufficient degree of independence given to them in their work."

More important, enterprise directors have been successful in asserting their autonomy vis-à-vis the primary party organizations in their factories. A recent article in the party journal stated unequivocally that "in accordance with the principle of one-man leadership the right to appoint, shift or dismiss a worker belongs exclusively to the economic manager, whether he is a member of the party or not. . . . If the party organization [differs with the manager] on an issue, it may raise the question with higher party and economic bodies." In the same vein, a local procurator's office in the Ukraine countermanded the veto rights ceded to several factory Komsomol organizations on personnel questions.

At present, then, managers' aspirations for autonomy seem to be more openly avowed and more stubbornly defended than at the beginning of the economic reform of 1965. The reason for this turnabout in attitude may lie in their growing appreciation of what can be gained from even the present limited autonomy.

It should be noted that at least one student of Soviet affairs has detected a somewhat longer-range trend (1952–1965) for Soviet elite groups, and particularly the economic elite, to assert themselves. Professor Lodge finds that the economic elite has increasingly articulated a conviction that it should participate in decision-making and has pressed this claim, with ever greater assertiveness, in the technical press.[16]

Professionalism.   To judge from directorial contributions to public discussions of the economic reform, directors have strong feelings as to the importance of expertise, pride in professionalism, and a warm desire to make professional judgment rather than political needs decisive in industrial operations. It is less certain that this professionalism is of a kind designed to fit the reform's requirements for "business administration" and "industrial management," for it is predominantly of the engineering type. Barry Richman has shown that in 1960, of all professionals employed in industrial enterprises, 76.5 percent had graduated from engineering programs and only 9.8 percent from economics programs.[17] In this connection it is worthy of note that in the technical institutes for engineers, the economic disciplines occupy only 5 percent of all class time. Richman also estimates that at least 90 percent of all enterprise top executives are engineers by vocation and training, although many have not received a higher education.

It is this continuing engineering orientation which is one of the reasons why the incumbent industrial managers—largely the products of the Stalinist period—oppose the current economic reform with its abandonment of "hard criteria," such as volume of production, and its switch to "soft" nonengineering criteria, such as profits and sales. There can be little question that the necessary shift in managerial attitude is being accomplished at a slow rate despite the party's crash program to orient hundreds of thousands of leading industrial cadres toward greater independence and profit-mindedness.

Nor does it seem likely that a new generation of managers can be educated quickly. For one thing, the magnitude of the task is staggering. Soviet sociologists have estimated that 60 percent of all administrative personnel in industry—including directors, deputy directors, chief engineers, heads of service departments, and shop foremen—are in their fifties and sixties. It is estimated that in the next five to ten years, when thirty- and forty-year-olds will move into responsible positions, approximately 4 million people will have to be trained for administration. This will amount to 40 percent of all such positions in industry. The number of managerial specialists (presumably above the shop level) to be brought into industry is estimated at 1½ million.

Moreover, there are still no institutes wholly devoted to problems of industrial management, despite the frequent discussions of American schools of business and recurring proposals to establish Soviet counter-

---

[16] Milton Lodge, "Soviet Elite Participatory Attitudes in the Post-Stalin Period," *American Political Science Review,* Vol. LXII, No. 3 (September 1968), pp. 827–39.

[17] Richman, *Management Development and Education in the Soviet Union,* p. 67.

parts. To be sure, the State Committee for Labor and Wages Questions has founded an "All-Union Scientific-Methodological Center for the Organization of Labor and Production Management," and numerous engineering and economics institutes have introduced courses designed to acquaint the students with problems of management. These innovations, however, cannot be expected to change the basic engineering orientation of the students, as can be seen from the following citation from a recent article on managerial training:

> Enterprise managers in industry and construction are now being trained in faculties for organizers of industrial production associated with the Moscow, Leningrad, Kharkov, and Sverdlovsk engineering economics institutes. Specialists with higher education, *as a rule engineering education*, who have worked for a number of years in enterprises as supervisors of shops, divisions and other services, are being trained in these faculties for work as enterprise directors.

In the same vein, two authors demanding the establishment of a Higher Academy of Management, for "command personnel" of the economy, still insist that management students should initially be trained for production-specialization, to be followed by a postgraduate course in management.

Personal Enrichment and Status. While some qualified Western observers have come to doubt that the "bonus drive" is a distinctive trait of the Soviet managerial class, the top political leadership since Stalin has always acted as if the pursuit of the ruble and the desire for status are *the* keys to managerial motivation. Khrushchev continued Stalin's policy of paying managers in heavy industry high salaries (as much as ten times the average wage of unskilled workers), bonuses amounting to 30–50 percent of basic salaries, plus benefits such as the use of company cars and preferential housing.[18] It has been assumed in the West that such emoluments were given on the premise that they would induce enterprise directors to fulfill and overfulfill what was then the regime's primary target: maximum quantitative output.[19]

It seems to the writers of this essay that Brezhnev and Kosygin rely for the success of the current economic reform primarily on the manipulation of the managers' presumed propensity for bonus maximization. The current reorientation of production from the maximization of physical output to considerations of enterprise efficiency and consumer demand has been accomplished by linking the size of the managers' bonuses to enterprise sales and profits (the latter are now the only source of managerial bonuses). Indeed, the structure of the incentives system under the reform is such that a highly qualified observer has concluded

---

[18] Ibid., pp. 124–25.

[19] Abram Bergson, *The Economics of Soviet Planning* (New Haven: Yale University Press, 1964), p. 75.

that it purpose is to induce the manager to maximize the incentive fund (or funds).[20] And the plethora of instructions that come from the Soviet press concerning the incentive funds testifies to their importance in the present scheme of things.

Interest Articulation and Channels of Access

The extent of interest articulation can safely be assumed to have increased since Stalin. While personal confrontation between individual managers and their superiors in economic councils and ministries probably continued much as before, large-scale inter-personal meetings of managerial personnel vastly increased in frequency over the post-Stalin period. The transition to the current economic reform, in particular, witnessed a veritable explosion of conferences and professional forums, bringing together hundreds and thousands of directors with representatives of state executive organs, soviets, and the professions. In one recent series of meetings, close to 9,000 personnel of this description met in 10 zonal conferences in the RSFSR. Similarly the All-Union Conference on Perfecting Planning and Improving Economic Work in the National Economy (May 14–17, 1968) brought together 5,000 planners, administrators, and economic managers. There can hardly be any doubt that such meetings offer ample opportunities for directors to exchange opinions and to form a consensus or divide into factions, as the case may be. There has been increased opportunity for the ventilation of managers' views in the columns of technical journals, and while many of these views pertain to the technicalities of the reform, they presumably contribute to the establishment of a group opinion and to the rise of group spokesmen.[21]

Significant also is the recent report on a "Club for Professional Meetings" in Leningrad, bringing together the city's top directors for informal get-togethers and discussions on topics ranging from the impact of the price reform on production and matters of personnel morale to enterprise relations with state organs. A recent series of formal talks dealt with the topic: "The Modern Director: What He Is and What He Ought To Be." It is noteworthy that no party sponsorship was mentioned in connection with these meetings.

Stalin's death may be said to have drastically improved the managers' access to the seats of power, because the liquidation of his one-man command immediately upgraded the power of the state officials to whom enterprise directors had routine approach. Conversely, Khrushchev's reorganization of 1957, which well-nigh destroyed the central state

---

[20] Gertrude E. Schroeder, "Soviet Economic Reforms: A Study in Contradictions," *Soviet Studies,* Vol. XX, No. 1 (July 1968), pp. 1–21.

[21] A good example is A. Rudkovsky, director of the S. M. Kirov turbine plant in Kharkov, who has repeatedly been a coauthor of articles with Ye. Liberman.

apparatus in industry, abolished the central contacts established by enterprise directors in Moscow. With the reestablishment in 1965 of the central ministries, the directors' access to the highest state executives (or at least to their deputies in the ministries' main administrations) was reestablished. While the ministers do not share—as many Western observers seem to assume—a complete community of interests with the directors, the similarity of interests is sufficiently large to ensure easy entrée of the directors to the ministers. It can, therefore, be assumed that the Council of Ministers, of which these ministers are members, is quickly cognizant of directors' demands and grievances.

The general relationship of "mutual involvement" between party functionaries, particularly at the local level, and enterprise directors has not changed in its essentials from the Stalin period—despite the very extensive structural changes in party and industry organization effected by Khrushchev and revoked by his successors. The 1957 reorganization of Soviet industry should have led, on the face of it, to a much closer access of enterprise directors to the party, particularly to the oblast apparatus which patently was intended to take over much of the policy and guidance function formerly exercised by the central ministries. However, the 1958 reduction of the party apparatus (possibly in excess of 25 percent) and the concomitant recentralization of the industrial administrative apparatus had the paradoxical effect of overburdening the apparatus and making party functionaries less accessible than before.

Likewise, the results of the 1962 bifurcation of the party were not what might have been expected. Here again the system on paper favored an almost total control of industry by the oblast apparatus—with a resultant increase in accessibility of party functionaries to enterprise officials. As matters worked out, the split of the party organs at the oblast level and below into industrial and agricultural bodies and the continuing recentralization of industry destroyed the parallelism between party and industry structures (i.e., there were close to 90 oblast industrial party committees and fewer than 50 economic councils) and seriously hampered the access of enterprise directors to their party contacts. It also seriously eroded the apparatus's ability to fulfill its economic function of assisting enterprise directors in procurement and coordination problems, due to the disruption of the party's horizontal links to the state apparatus.[22]

Against this background, the current regime's liquidation of Khrushchev's reorganization of the party (1964) and industry (1965) restored, *inter alia*, the access of enterprise directors to both party and state. It is all the more important to stress this point since it was at first believed by Western and certain Soviet observers that the economic reform was undercutting the party's ties to industry. Similarly, there

---

[22] Cf. Jerry F. Hough, "A Harebrained Scheme in Retrospect," *Problems of Communism*, Vol. XIV, No. 4 (July–August 1965), pp. 26–32.

was considerable anxiety in the lower ranks of the party that the economic reform, with its emphasis on material incentives, would do away with the need for the kind of propaganda and agitation which had been their *raison d'être*. However, it has become apparent that the hold of the party, at least at the oblast level and below, has been strengthened rather than weakened by the economic reform. Once again, the united party apparatus—particularly at raion and city level—functions as expediter and trouble shooter along horizontal lines of communication (which are being neglected by the vertically structured state apparatus). Furthermore, continued stress on propaganda and agitation, and the organization of "socialist competitions" has reassured the local cadres that they are still necessary. More important, the party as a whole has been invested with the responsibility for the success of the reform, specifically for the retraining of the management cadres. All these developments entail strong and close relationships between party and enterprise managers and a degree of access which is far closer than in Khrushchev's time and more meaningful than in Stalin's.

The post-Khrushchev period has seen an increase in the strength of the managerial group, as far as numbers, level of education, social homogeneity, and security of tenure are concerned, as well as in the attainment of some of their most cherished objectives: increased income and status, and greater autonomy. At the same time, their freedom to articulate their interests (within limits) and the opportunity to bring them to bear on the powers that be at all levels of the party and government structure have also improved. But even as it improved its capability and in many ways showed willingness to play the role of an interest group, the managerial group has not experienced changes in self-image or in the concept of its interests to match the changes that have occurred in the economy and those that must occur sometime in the future.

Prospects for the Managerial Group

It is paradoxical that at a time when many of the long-term aims of Soviet managers are being met their future seems to be especially uncertain. The requirement for a more professional type of manager has spread from heavy industry to light industry and indeed throughout the economy. Managers have been granted a degree of autonomy, at least from direct party intervention, that would seem more than satisfying, considering their past experience. Moreover, their living conditions have improved. If the Fiat auto deal of 1966 was designed to provide the material basis for more incentives to managerial performance, then we may assume that both the real income and the range of expenditure choice are improving.[23] Yet the managerial group may be less satisfied with its rising income than with stable income and the assured status of the past. The general rise in real income—the average increase in

---

[23] *Soviet Economic Performance, 1966–67* (cited in footnote 15), p. 105.

personal disposable money income has been 7.5 percent from 1964 to 1967—probably exceeded price changes and narrowed the differential advantage of managers over others in the labor force.[24] Similarly, in spite of the passenger car example, the widening of the managers' choice of remuneration has apparently been slow. Continued slow improvements in housing and other aspects of communal living may lead expectations to run ahead of opportunities. David Granick likened the Stalinist "Red Executive" to a skilled American black in a northern city who had an increasing income but suffered sharp restrictions on choice of expenditure outlets, e.g., for housing.[25] We might speculatively posit another parallel between the two groups in the fact that the quantitative measures of income and expenditures may run sharply counter to the psychic satisfaction of the recipient. Of course, satisfaction and performance are not necessarily directly related. Dissatisfaction may indeed spur performance, although this does not appear to be the case.

More disturbing to the Soviet managers is the prospect that their professionalism may become obsolete just when they may be allowed to employ it with less external intervention. A leading article in a prominent Soviet economic journal illustrates this:

> At present the economic managers who grew up in the days when administrative methods were supreme, do not meet the new requirements of the economic reform and the technological revolution. . . . To be a "manager" under present-day conditions means having a special profession, means having a post that can no longer be held by an engineer or an academic economist. The personal capabilities of a man are the conditions for practicing this profession, and these capabilities can only be brought to perfection by hard practice, combined with a constant broadening of one's knowledge of the theory of management.

This situation poses difficult problems for the managerial group. The leading managers may endanger their own careers by pressing for change in the managerial group. Moreover, if they attempt to conform to policy directives to encourage the development of a new managerial style, they must realize that there is no quick and efficient way to change from a Stalinist production engineer into a management "businessman." The old Stalinst problems of relieving bottlenecks in the production process were relatively straightforward technical and administrative ones. The new manager has to deal with problems that require improved data and modern systems of analysis. He may have to be familiar with linear programming and the use of digital computers.

Furthermore, managers' success indicators are derived not from supply considerations, as in the past, but from demand. Sales, quality, and profits—the demand-derived criteria—are more than a set of new administrative indicators; they call for a change of psychology which must

---

[24] Ibid., p. 91.

[25] Granick, *The Red Executive,* p. 123.

accompany the transition from a seller's to a buyer's market. And the buyer may now be increasingly the individual citizen in the market place, rather than another enterprise director or his expediter. Thus, demand-related criteria may be replacing supply in Soviet enterprise management as constraints and measures of performance. This was illustrated in a keynote speech by N. K. Baibakov, the Chairman of Gosplan (State Planning Commission) in May 1968: ". . . We consider that in future the order book should be the starting point for the long-term plan of the factory. Long-term direct links create the conditions for the gradual reduction and consolidation of the assortment of products laid down in the state plan, and for the development of wholesale trade in the means of production." Clearly the market mechanism has not yet taken over,[26] but it is evident that the administratively centralized method of detailed day-to-day management in the key sectors of Stalinist planning is being challenged, perhaps irreversibly. Cleavages within the managerial group have thus developed along educational, generational, and functional lines. If the leadership chooses to move ahead in replacing the old production-engineer type of manager with another generation of managers schooled in a Soviet version of management science, then the fissures will probably deepen within the managerial group.

The Soviet leadership also has its dilemmas. The old manager cannot be easily replaced by one trained in management science. The Soviet educational system does not appear to be geared either qualitatively or quantitatively to supply thousands of "businessmen" managers. The decision of the Stalinist leadership to replace managers and economists with politically reliable production engineers provided some options.[27] These less well-trained engineers "learned en route" to relieve production bottlenecks in the important industrial sectors. The economic costs incurred in the form of inevitable delays and shoddy output could be absorbed by the lower priority, consumer-oriented activities. At present there may be no buffer areas left, and the cost of mistakes in management and planning is increasingly visible in the form of poor products and unclaimed inventories in the capital goods as well as consumer sectors. Adoption of criteria based on profits, sales, and other monetary considerations would surely be more accurate and useful in the context of comprehensive financial planning than as disconnected parts of the *ad hoc*, selective approach of the current reforms. This leads us to look for changes toward comprehensive optimal, financial planning to *precede* significant changes in management.

[26] See especially Schroeder, "Soviet Economic Reforms," and "The 1966–67 Soviet Industrial Price Reform: A Study in Complications," *Soviet Studies,* Vol. XX, No. 4 (April 1969), pp. 462–77.

[27] Gregory Grossman, "Scarce Capital and Soviet Doctrine," *Quarterly Journal of Economics,* Vol. LXVII, No. 3 (August 1953), pp. 311–43.

In turn, the problem of reforming economic planning may lie less in the development of the appropriate professionalism than in allocation changes. The military-heavy industry establishment may oppose the adoption of a new planning system, promising long-run improvements in efficiency, if it threatens them with budget reductions. This broader constraint may be the kind of factor which slows the introduction of comprehensive planning and thereby impedes progress toward improved management. Therefore, given the interrelationship between managerial planning and broader Soviet policy, it is important for us to put the manager-planning changes in a broader societal context.

The emerging pluralism within the Soviet elite has produced conflict between contending groups, most evident in decisions on resource allocation. Some liberal professional economists tend to favor investment in industry and agriculture over further increases in military outlays, so that they may have common cause with the new managerial group. Economic professionalism has not only resource implications, for the professional attitude is itself a common bond among professionals in different spheres. For instance, it is interesting to note the number of articles on economic reform that find their way into the pages of such liberal literary journals as *Novy mir* and other wide-ranging specialized publications. Professionalism in the arts may be less portentous in practical life than the application of professional economic standards in comprehensive planning, but it reflects a common interest in the delegation of party decision-making power. A common *laissez-faire* attitude of professionals throughout the Soviet elite may press effectively for changes in the relationship of the party to the various key institutional groups. As a result not only the monopoly of power in the hands of the top party leaders but their intimate involvement in decisions and policy implementation may be at stake. Thus, through economic reform the changing role of the manager may be linked to more general challenges to the overextended control system of the Soviet government.

Conflict concerning professionalism, however, cuts across institutional lines and ranges some professionals and party generalists on one side against a similar grouping on the other side. The managerial elite is probably involved in interaction with other elites ranging from support of significant change in Soviet society to defense of the *status quo*. Nonetheless, the longer-run interest of the managers would appear to be in an increase in professionalism within a context of more limited party control. The development of a new kind of Soviet manager may be interwoven with a similar development of other new groups, such as planners and the military, throughout the whole fabric of the Soviet elite and may be tied to fundamental changes in the top leadership. When and if a new managerial group finally emerges it may be a part of a very different Soviet society.

8. CONTINUITY AND CHANGE IN THE SOVIET LABOR MARKET

Emily Clark Brown

The allocation of the Soviet labor force is accomplished by a combination of central planning and market forces. The distribution of the labor force by region, branch of the economy, occupation, and skill level is centrally planned in physical terms. However, the planners rely primarily on wage differentials in a largely free labor market to draw labor into the jobs created by the plans. Wage differentials also provide incentives to managers to economize on scarce labor skills. The characteristics of the Soviet labor market are examined in the following article. It depicts the labor market in recent years, as the Soviet planners have faced problems of persistent labor shortages and the need for more efficient use of workers in an economy whose emphasis is slowly shifting away from its former single-minded emphasis on quantity of output.

Emily Clark Brown is Professor Emeritus of Economics at Vassar College, and a leading American expert on Soviet labor. An earlier version of this article was published in the *Industrial and Labor Relations Review,* Vol. 23, No. 2 (January 1970), pp. 171–90. Copyright © 1970 by Cornell University. All rights reserved. This article was thoroughly revised for this book, to reflect developments through 1972.

DURING THE past decade, Soviet experts and policy makers have turned increasing attention to manpower problems.[1] Though seeking to stay

[1] For my earlier analysis, see "The Soviet Labor Market," *Industrial and Labor Relations Review,* Vol. 10, No. 2 (January 1957), pp. 179–200; "A Note on Employment and Unemployment in the Soviet Union in the Light of Technical Progress," *Soviet Studies,* Vol. 12, No. 3 (January 1961), pp. 231–40; and *Soviet Trade Unions and Labor Relations* (Cambridge, Mass.: Harvard University Press, 1966), chap. 2.

For a detailed analysis of some labor supply problems, see Janet G. Chapman, "Labor Mobility and Labor Allocation in the USSR," Association for Comparative Economics, *Proceedings of National Meetings,* July 1971, pp. 1–26.

within the framework of Marxist-Leninist theory, they have had to come to grips with serious problems. They continue to avoid the term "labor market" on the assumption that socialist society manages the development and distribution of the labor force by planning rather than by selling labor power on the market. They also emphasize that Soviet citizens are free to choose their type and place of work and that both public and private interests are served by the incentives under the system of pay, "according to the quantity and quality of work."

Manpower policies and management thus involve both central planning and more or less free choices by individuals and by employing enterprises and organizations under the influence of the whole economic and social planned and unplanned environment. That is, manpower is affected by market forces as well as by planning. Socialist planning has wide influence on the market and modifies the harsh effects of unplanned labor markets; socialist orthodoxy, however, sometimes hampers and slows adoption of needed policies and methods.

Developments in the past decade reflect manpower problems familiar to other industrialized countries but not always acknowledged in the Soviet Union: (1) the threat of unemployment; (2) the existence of local surpluses of labor and underemployment, seasonal and structural; (3) severe shortages of labor in certain occupations and areas; (4) wastes of manpower in many enterprises, due to poor utilization of labor and keeping redundant workers in reserve for emergencies, and because of hindrances to displacement; and (5) the need for improved mechanisms for the distribution of labor, specifically, better planning and the long-delayed establishment of an effective well-coordinated employment service.

The commitment of the Soviet state to full employment has been fulfilled only in part, and the dilemma of conflict between the needs of efficiency and the protection of individuals has not been resolved. Nevertheless, at important points and after long discussion, policies designed to deal with these problems have been adopted.

THE QUESTION OF UNEMPLOYMENT

Soviet economists protest Western talk of unemployment in the USSR as unfounded.[2] They insist that under socialism there is no objective basis for unemployment, even with rapid changes in technology and industrial structure. Full employment of the able-bodied population is said to be assured by continued rapid growth of industry, by increased development of the service fields, by longer education for increasing

---

[2] Among many such statements, *Izvestia,* Feb. 4, 1968, in *Current Digest of the Soviet Press,* Vol. 20, No. 5 (Feb. 21, 1968), pp. 7–8; E. Manevich, "The Management of Soviet Manpower," *Foreign Affairs,* Vol. 47, No. 1 (October 1968), pp. 176–84.

numbers of youths, and by shortened hours of work. The problem, as they see it, is to achieve the most rational and effective distribution and redistribution of labor resources, but this has been increasingly recognized as not as simple as some had thought.

Soviet denial of unemployment is, in considerable part, a matter of definition. When, as currently, there are serious labor shortages of many types and in many regions, it is held that jobs are available; thus no problem of unemployment exists. There is concern over difficulties described as the result of poor organization of the distribution of labor, errors in planning, and unnecessary mobility. People who for any reason are temporarily or permanently out of work are said to be "not occupied in the public economy," or rarely, "needing placement," but never "unemployed." By Western definitions some of them are victims of seasonal, structural, or frictional unemployment; underemployment; or are not in the labor force at all.[3] Considering these difficulties, M. Sonin, a leading expert on manpower, has said, "It would be wrong to suppose that the urgency with which the problem of labor redistribution is being tackled in the USSR is in any way due to the appearance of unemployment."[4] The trade union journal asserted that these problems, though complicated, are fully solvable in theory and are being solved successfully in practice.

The Duty and the Right to Work

In all thinking on manpower, the constitutional right and duty of the citizen to work continues to be basic. It is the obligation of all able-bodied people to engage in "socially useful work" or study. The 1970 Census found that over 91 percent of the able-bodied population of working age—practically all of the men and four fifths of the women—were engaged in the public economy or study, though participation, especially of women, differs by regions. Women engaged only in household activity and family care have been viewed as an important source of additional workers. Increasingly now the care of children is recognized as a normal and useful function; the number of housewives not now in the labor force who could be enlisted in jobs is limited, depending on age and health, availability of nurseries and kindergartens, consumers' services to make family duties easier, the proximity of suitable

---

[3] P. J. D. Wiles, in "A Note on Soviet Unemployment by U.S. Definitions," *Soviet Studies*, Vol. XXIII, No. 4 (April 1972), pp. 619–28, found the data "tricky and nebulous," and the unemployment rate quite unreliable, but he considered more significant a small average duration of unemployment of only three weeks for job changers. See also Carmelo Mesa-Lago, *Unemployment in Socialist Countries* (unpublished Ph.D. dissertation, Cornell University, 1968), chap. 2.

[4] M. Sonin and E. Zhiltsov, "Economic Development and Employment in the Soviet Union," *International Labor Review*, Vol. 96, No. 1 (July 1967), p. 90.

work. Employment in private subsidiary agriculture also has long been considered contrary to the public interest; now it is seen as only a small possible source of additional labor and is expected so to continue for considerable time. It includes mainly older people or young women with family responsibilities, and this type of activity has helped to meet people's needs for food and income.[5]

The citizen's right to work means his right to choose the place and the type of work consistent with his training and ability. Accordingly, he has a right not to be involuntarily unemployed, and the state, in effect, has taken on the obligation of assuring that jobs are available. This does not mean a specific guarantee of job placement to individuals, since such guarantees have been established by law only in special cases, i.e., for youths, invalids, demobilized soldiers, and people displaced by government action such as abolishing central ministries or removing women from underground work in mines. All workers are protected by the requirement that enterprises may discharge only with agreement of the plant trade union committee and on bases specified by law. In reducing staffs, enterprises are obligated to make provisions for other jobs and any necessary retraining before workers are displaced. Claims of illegal discharge reaching the courts result in many reinstatements. Thus the individual's right to his job is traditional. Though the right is not always protected in practice, the obligation is one of many factors leading managements to keep redundant workers on payrolls.

Lacks in Manpower Statistics

A major difficulty in efforts to achieve the most effective and rational use of the labor force is the surprising lack of adequate statistics. Refusal to acknowledge the possibility of an unemployment problem set roadblocks in the way of fact finding. Sonin points out that with the abolition of the labor exchanges and the Commissariat of Labor in the 1930s (on the assumption that unemployment had come to an end), the collection of current statistics on movement of workers and on redundancy was dropped.[6] Since at least 1959, there have been continued criticisms of the Central Statistical Administration for failure to provide needed data. The CSA does not report regularly on the labor force and the "unoccupied population" for cities and districts: reports are for larger territories and regions, within which local shortages and surpluses often balance out. More detail is wanted in reports on displacement, past or planned, and on numbers needing placement. In addition, reports

---

[5] Sonin and Zhiltsov, "Economic Development and Employment in the Soviet Union," pp. 79–80; Chapman, "Labor Mobility and Labor Allocation in the USSR," pp. 16–18.

[6] Sonin and Zhiltsov, "Economic Development and Employment in the Soviet Union," p. 84.

on the unoccupied population have been only estimates, with not enough attention to seasonal variations and to the actual makeup of those occupied in household activity or individual agriculture.[7] Therefore, local authorities lack the data on the demand and supply of labor which they need for rational planning.

The CSA promised in the 1970 Census a more detailed study of population movements, of the makeup of the labor force, and of those not in the public economy. A sample census of about one fourth of the population obtained additional data on occupation, place of work, work record for those who worked less than a full year, and reasons for changing jobs. Census data are to be processed for all districts, cities, and other territorial units.[8] It remains to be seen how much data will be made public, but presumably this will provide a basis for more effective analysis of the balance of labor and better planning for the use of labor resources.

In a decade of increasing concern over labor resources, significant contributions have been made by research in the universities and the Academy of Sciences, and more recently by the new State Committees of the republics on the Utilization of Labor Resources (to be discussed later). For example, an inter-university conference in Moscow in 1969 was told that a survey of 778 small and medium-sized cities in the Russian Republic found 100,000 people in need of jobs. An all-Russian three-day conference in Moscow in June 1971 brought over 400 people together to consider problems of the rational utilization of labor resources and to make recommendations for future studies and policies. Calling for full interdisciplinary investigations to provide bases for rational decisions, Vice-Chairman Maikov of the State Committee declared that a "science of labor resources" was only now coming into being.

The Labor Shortage

Shortages of labor are currently the greatest worry of manpower experts and managers. Shortages are said to be "almost universal," especially in big cities, on big construction projects, and in the East and North.[9] Annual reports on fulfillment of the economic plans continue to

---

[7] V. Churakov, "Problems Concerning the Use of Rural Labor Resources," *Problems of Economics,* Vol. 11, No. 4 (August 1968), pp. 26–34.

[8] *Economic Performance and the Military Burden in the Soviet Union.* (A Compendium of Papers Submitted to the Subcommittee on Foreign Economic Policy of the Joint Economic Committee, 91st Cong., 2d sess.) (Washington, D.C.: U.S. Government Printing Office, 1970), p. 62.

[9] For valuable statistical analyses see *Economic Performance and the Military Burden,* pp. 60–84; Sonin and Zhiltsov, "Economic Development and Employment in the Soviet Union, pp. 67–91; V. Perevedentsev, "Migration of the Population and the Utilization of Labor Resources in the U.S.S.R." *Problems of Economics,* Vol. 13, No. 11 (March 1971), pp. 40–57.

assert that there is full employment, and to point to shortages of labor in some industries and areas. Newly developing industries and enterprises need workers, and even with the emphasis on improving technology and productivity, the total demand for labor in the Ninth Five-Year Plan (1971–1975) is expected to surpass the natural growth in the population of working age. Rapid development of the service fields, in an effort to improve the level of living, contributes to shortages. The increased number of young people who continue education beyond elementary and secondary school reduces the intake of young workers into the labor force. The drift into the cities from agriculture has decreased markedly, reflecting both the drive to increase agricultural production and gains in incomes and living conditions of rural people. While five million people were expected to have been brought into the national economy from household work and individual agriculture from 1966 to 1970, further possibilities were very limited in many areas. During the Ninth Five-Year Plan only 1.5 percent of the growth in the labor force was expected to come from these sources, as against 25 percent in the previous five years. According to the plan, more than four fifths of the five-year growth in national income was to come from increasing productivity of labor rather than the number of workers; in existing industrial enter-prises, in railroad transport, and in agriculture, the entire increase in production should come without additional workers. At the Fifteenth Congress of Trade Unions in March 1972 Chairman Shelepin declared that the main direction of socialist competition should be to mobilize the working people to achieve production plans without increasing the labor force.

Fruitful sources of workers for new enterprises and for developing industries and areas are seen in reducing wastes of labor: in localities where women, young people, or men have difficulty in finding employ-ment because of the lack of balance in industrial development; among seasonal workers in agriculture and other fields; in hidden surpluses of unneeded workers and of inefficiently used hand labor on plant payrolls; and in losses of time between jobs when there is excessive turnover or when necessary displacement occurs. Release of workers by technical and other changes increasingly should provide labor for expanding fields. All this encourages serious attention to the question of how to achieve the most rational utilization of labor resources.

LABOR SUPPLY PROGRAMS

Currently, four main groups of programs to deal with the urgent problems of labor supply are emphasized. The first involves planning the development and location of industry with increased attention to the availability of workers, in order to reduce underutilization of labor in many towns and in agriculture and other seasonal occupations. Second, increased wage incentives and other benefits aim to influence choice of fields and places of work, in order to relieve serious shortages. Third, major efforts are being made to deal with the redundancy problem by providing incentives to management and workers to increase efficiency in the use of labor and to accept displacement of unneeded workers as necessary and desirable. And fourth, there is being developed, at long last, a system of employment exchanges to be accompanied by improvements in planning for the training, distribution, and redistribution of labor.

Location of Industry

Many small and medium-sized cities, as well as rural places, have lacked employment opportunities for part of their population. Textile cities with few jobs for men and heavy industry centers with few places for women are examples, among many, which for years led experts to call for more balanced planning of development by both central and local authorities. In 1965, the Communist party provided that in the Eighth Five-Year Plan new enterprises should be built chiefly in smaller cities with available labor resources. The State Planning Committee (Gosplan) and the Councils of Ministers of the republics compiled recommended lists of such cities; in the Russian Republic, 265 cities with available labor supply were listed, while in 27 cities labor was so scarce that additional construction by new or existing enterprises was forbidden. According to the 1968 plan, 60 percent of all industrial construction was to be in the smaller cities. In addition to the development of local enterprises using local resources and of service establishments, large enterprises were urged to set up affiliated plants or shops to produce component parts in these localities. The Ninth Five-Year Plan similarly aimed to limit the growth of new enterprises in the larger cities, except for those serving the population, and to consider local labor resources in locating new plants, especially in the food and light industries and machine building. How much has been accomplished is not known. There were early complaints of delays in carrying out the directives, but apparently a substantial amount of construction has proceeded in cities of under 100,000 population. One old textile town, Ivanovo, reportedly achieved a balance in job opportunities by bringing in machine-tool, truck building and furniture enterprises employing men. Another, in Vladimir province, was seeking to attract young male workers and to reduce the annual loss of young female workers by building new plants producing textile machinery and lighting fixtures and by increasing the supply of housing available for young workers and families. A complaint from the Tadzik Republic, on the other hand, reported that while many new plants were being built, some managers continued to hire workers from other areas, instead of recruiting and training local people, especially from the large numbers of non-working women in the cities and rural places.[10] Many ministries also were said to have continued to build in big cities, regardless of prohibitions—sometimes on the pretext of reconstructing old plants—and in disregard of difficulties in getting workers, their housing, and other needs.

Central planning has not been able to avoid contradictions between the objectives of the central planners, the departmental concerns of ministries, and large enterprises which make decisions according to their special interests. These interests, which lead to increasing concentration of production, include the advantages of the super-cities both for production and for offering variety of choices to workers, as pointed out by V. Perevedentsev.[11]

Underutilization of rural labor is to be remedied, according to plans, by providing work for collective and state farmers who have little to do in winter and by developing service shops and centers offering employment to women and providing needed services to consumers.[12] A 1966 decree of the USSR Council of Ministers authorized subsidiary enterprises in the villages, with emphasis on processing local food products and developing local building materials and other products for consumers, and also authorized more day nurseries, public catering, and other shops and services. Without harm to agricultural work, these could use otherwise wasted off-season work time and could release labor for the harvest. Again, how much has been accomplished is not known, but such developments probably played a part in the improved incomes and conditions of life in rural places on which experts comment. Reportedly services to the population increased in rural places by 23 percent in 1968 over 1967; for the whole country the increase reported was 17 percent. The Ninth Five-Year Plan, for 1971–1975, called for tripling these services for rural people, doubling for the country as a whole.

Wages and Other Incentives

Those measures attempted to bring jobs to workers. A second group of changes in the planned market included wage adjustments and improvements in financial incentives and living conditions, designed to be more effective in attracting workers to occupations and areas where they were needed and in promoting stability in labor forces. Thus it was hoped to make workers' choices coincide more often with social interests. Associated with this was a new emphasis on improving voca-

---

[10] *New York Times*, April 1, 1969; *Current Digest of the Soviet Press*, Vol. 24, No. 37 (October 11, 1972), pp. 3–4; *Current Digest of the Soviet Press*, Vol. 25, No. 4 (February 21, 1973), pp. 11–12.

[11] Perevedentsev, "Migration of the Population and the Utilization of Labor Resources in the U.S.S.R.," pp. 47–48.

[12] Sonin and Zhiltsov, "Economic Development and Employment in the Soviet Union," pp. 79–80.

tional counseling to help young people choose their future work with knowledge of the growing fields. Dissatisfaction with their occupations has been found to be one of the major reasons for turnover among young workers, and many fail to continue work in the fields in which they were trained.[13]

Particular shortages were attacked by the central authorities through selective increases in wage rates and by special regional benefits. Occupations with the greatest labor shortages included some of the highly skilled (especially machine-tool workers) and lower-paid mass occupations in trade, transportation, construction, and the service fields. A joint decree of the Central Committee of the Communist Party and the USSR Council of Ministers in September 1967 raised the minimum wage rate in all branches of the economy, effective January 1, 1968, from 40–45 rubles a month to 60–70. At the same time, wage scales for machine-tool workers in all branches were increased by 15 percent. A year later wage-rate increases averaging 23 to 25 percent were decreed for construction materials and construction workers, in the hope that this would help provide more stable and efficient labor forces. Later there were special increases in transportation, health and education, and other fields. Revision of the entire wage system is in process in the interest of improving incentives and compensation for difficulties in work and living conditions. Rules permitting working pensioners to retain all or part of their pensions were liberalized in February 1969 for certain industries, occupations, and areas.[14]

The perennial problem of labor shortages in Siberia and the Far East and North also was tackled in 1967. Despite huge numbers of young people and others who went to these regions, turnover continued so high that some areas lost more workers in a year than came in. Young workers typically went out on term contracts, and chiefly, it is said, for the high earnings, but upon completion of the term most of them settle in regions with more favorable living conditions.[15] The zonal wage system, providing compensatory additions to wage rates in hardship regions, had not been effective when the differentials were not enough to compensate both for price differences and for other difficulties in life and work, and when the benefits covered only workers in certain major industries. Accordingly regional wage differentials were now to be applied in all industries and services in the Far East and North, and were later extended to West Siberia and some other areas. For workers in the Far

---

[13] *Current Digest of the Soviet Press*, Vol. 25, No. 2 (February 7, 1972), pp. 12–14.

[14] Sonin and Zhiltsov, "Economic Development and Employment in the Soviet Union," p. 90; *Current Digest of the Soviet Press*, Vol. 21, No. 13 (April 16, 1969), pp. 26–27.

[15] L. Kuprienko, "Influence of the Standard of Living on the Movement of Labor Resources," *Problems of Economics*, Vol. 15, No. 5 (September 1972), pp. 61–77, esp. pp. 75–76.

North, improved benefits, including wage increases based on length of service, were extended to all occupations. Further improvements in regional differentials for these areas of tight labor supply were promised in the Ninth Five-Year Plan. A December 1972 decree of the Supreme Soviet established a schedule for the gradual introduction for different regions, starting with the Far North in that month, of the minimum wage of 70 rubles for production branches, with elimination or reduction of income tax for different wage levels.[16]

These steps towards proper relationships between living standards for different areas and different groups of workers already had helped by 1970 and would unquestionably exert a great influence on labor supply, according to Perevedentsev. He pointed out, however, the complexity of the problems involving different natural and social living conditions, rural and urban life, and different occupational levels. He urged the need for providing higher living standards for groups and areas where there were labor shortages, with strict consideration of all the regional particulars, but the problem of how to measure all these factors and arrive at proper real wage levels remains unsolved. He suggested that the movement of people themselves is the best indication of flaws in the existing conditions. In some areas, despite the financial incentives, efforts to procure and keep workers are still hampered by poor housing, lacks in consumer supplies, and deficiencies in educational, cultural, recreational, and other services.[17]

Redundancy and Displacement of Workers

Perhaps the most significant attack on problems of labor shortages involves efforts to promote more efficient use of existing labor forces by enterprises. As in the past, criticisms continued that much labor time is wasted—by stoppages due to mismanagement, by unnecessary meetings, by permitting people on plant payrolls to spend all or much of their time on sports, music, or other programs, and by the tendency to keep surplus workers as a reserve for emergencies as well as by continued use of unmechanized hand labor, and by absences and lack of discipline.[18] Meantime, the worry about turnover continues; there is a reported loss of an average of 30 days between jobs and much more time in retraining and adjusting to new employment. Proposals to crack down on "flitters" are countered by the argument that many shifts are

---

[16] *Current Digest of the Soviet Press,* Vol. 25, No. 2 (February 7, 1973), p. 10; for further details, see Chapman, "Labor Mobility and Labor Allocation in the USSR," pp. 12–16.

[17] Perevedentsev, "Migration of the Population and the Utilization of Labor Resources in the U.S.S.R.," pp. 40–57.

[18] E. Manevich, "Problems in the Reproduction of Labor Power and Ways of Improving the Utilization of Labor Resources in the U.S.S.R.," *Problems of Economics,* Vol. 12, No. 11 (March 1970), pp. 3–26, esp. pp. 18–20.

justified for personal or social reasons and more result from poor planning and management which fail to provide satisfying work and living conditions.[19] Length of service in an enterprise is a factor in awarding bonuses, also in the Far North in wage and salary levels. Although there is much talk of a need to tighten labor discipline in the interest of stable and productive labor forces, currently reliance appears to be more on efforts to improve management by changes in planning and incentives than in tightening control over workers.[20]

The presence of surplus workers in many plants has long been criticized by economists. Even when technical progress reduces the need for labor, several factors tend to slow displacement. There is a traditional reluctance to discharge people, a feeling that people have a right to their jobs and need to work; management often wants to maintain good relations with "the collective." Besides, with uncertainties in the planning system, it is considered wise to keep a reserve for emergencies; and reducing the size of the labor force and of the wage fund may have adverse effects on management bonuses.[21] For discharges to reduce staff, the law requires agreement of the trade union committee as to whether the reduction is necessary and whether the proper conditions are observed. The needs of production are supposed to rule, but in selecting workers to be released there must be consideration (among those of equal qualifications) of family circumstances; number of dependents; prior rights for sole wage earners, pregnant women, and single mothers with children under one year old; long-service workers; and others. In addition, it is not always easy for the manager to fulfill his obligation to find other jobs for those displaced, especially if there are no local enterprises needing workers of the sort released; until very recently organizations for helping in this responsibility have been neither general nor adequate.

Efforts to maintain a high rate of economic growth under increasing difficulties have led to great emphasis on introduction of new technology and scientific organization of production. Productivity of labor grows at an average rate of about 5 percent a year in industry, faster in many plants which have operated under new conditions of management since 1965. Displacement of workers made redundant by the new conditions is expected to increase significantly. An economist cited the iron and steel industry, which had released 6,000 workers annually between 1959 and 1965 and expected to release up to 14,000 per year in the

---

[19] *Current Digest of the Soviet Press,* Vol. 20, No. 42 (November 6, 1968), pp. 22–23.

[20] For the law as to labor discipline under the all-union principles of labor legislation adopted in 1970, see Emily Clark Brown, "Fundamental Soviet Labor Legislation," *Industrial and Labor Relations Review,* Vol. 26, No. 2 (January 1973), pp. 786–87.

[21] M. Sonin, "Some Problems in Increasing the Efficiency of Utilization of Labor Forces," *Problems of Economics,* Vol. 9, No. 8 (December 1966), pp. 8–10.

Eighth Five-Year Plan, and commented, "Not one of them had any idea that they faced unemployment, since the demand of metallurgy for workers significantly surpassed those figures."

Special studies of groups of plants by the Urals branch of the Academy of Sciences and others help to answer the question of what happened to the workers. Redistribution within the enterprise had been most typical, but studies in 1960–1962 in metallugical and machinery plants found that in one third of the plants studied, up to 20 percent of the workers displaced were discharged. In 1964, in Urals plants studied, 46 percent of those displaced were shifted to other similar jobs in the plant, but this was a decrease from 58 percent in 1960. Another 32 percent were retrained for other occupations in the plant, compared to only 23 percent in 1960. Of those who shifted to other plants, up to 70 percent also changed their occupations, although many of them could have been used at their former skill without retraining. More recent studies found that from two thirds to three fourths of the workers displaced in machine-tool plants remained in the same enterprise, only half of them needing retraining for new specialties.

The extent of release and shifts of workers as a result of technical progress differed greatly between industries and enterprises. It depended on local situations, the balance of labor supply and demand, the level of technical equipment, investment, and specialization and concentration of production, the relation of growth of production and of labor productivity, and the economic interest of the management in reducing the number of workers. The most extensive release of labor had been in the extractive industries, the result both of technical progress and of availability of resources. Reduction of the numbers employed occurred less often in the processing industries, food, textiles, and other light industries, although in some enterprises reconstruction of old plants led to reductions. The largest part, 60–65 percent of the released personnel, came from production work, as greater attention was given to improving technology and organization here than for the auxiliary labor staff where unmechanized hand labor continued to be extensive. One critic suggested that the failure to direct more investment toward the unmechanized auxiliary processes and other low-paid workers is related to the fact that low wages do not cover the total social costs; accordingly further incentives are needed to induce economy in use of such labor.

To realize the full possibilities of such sources of labor supply, the surplus workers in existing enterprises, it was essential to overcome inertia and other hindrances to the release of workers by improvements in planning and in incentives.

The Economic Reform: Incentives to Release Workers. By improving enterprise performance, the "new system of planning and economic incentives" was expected to raise the rate of growth in labor productivity and free many workers for other jobs. Beginning in 1966 in 43 large plants, the reform included 7,000 enterprises by the end of 1967, by April 1969 a total of 32,000, and by January 1973 over 43,000 enterprises, or 87 percent of all industrial enterprises, with 94 percent of the total production.[22] Freedom of action by enterprises was to be increased by reducing the number and detail of central directives in the annual plans, by simplifying success indicators, and by emphasizing growth of profits. Increased incentives for successful performance were to be provided by deductions from profits for a fund for material incentives—bonuses for management and workers—and for a fund for social-cultural uses and housing. In practice the changes in methods of planning and management were less drastic than had been forecast, and many problems hindered the expected progress.

Management received somewhat increased autonomy on labor questions, although the wage fund still was established by central authorities, and wage and salary rates still were centrally controlled. The manager was given the right to decide the number and distribution of workers and staff, subject always to a degree of check by the local trade union, and to work out with the union the details of bonus systems, subject to general regulations. In theory, the manager could release unneeded workers, but the limitations indicated earlier continued to slow the process. Also, as pointed out by Soviet and Western experts, there were built-in disincentives, since the additions to the incentive funds were linked to the amount of the wage fund or to total employment, and plans for reduction of the number employed reduced the wage fund and so hampered growth of bonuses.[23]

The Shchekino Plan.   One difficulty was failure to enlist full cooperation from workers. They had seen little gain in earnings under the reform, and many enterprises had been unable to use their funds for social-cultural purposes and housing because of lack of allocation of materials and wages for construction. A drastic experiment to provide more incentive for increasing productivity and releasing personnel began in 1967 in a rapidly growing chemical combine at Shchekino near Tula. After the manager's request for an additional 400 workers was refused, the ministry, in agreement with the State Committee on Labor and Wages, proposed that the wage fund be frozen for several years at the 1967 level. Then any economies in the wage fund resulting from decreases in the number employed would be left with the enterprise to increase rates of pay and premiums for workers and administration. After a study within the combine it was decided to increase production by 1970

---

[22] On the economic reform and its results see Theodore Frankel, "Economic Reform: A Tentative Appraisal," *Problems of Communism*, Vol. XVI, No. 3 (May–June 1967), pp. 29–41; Keith Bush, "The Reforms: A Balance Sheet," *Problems of Communism*, Vol. XVI, No. 4 (July–August 1967), pp. 30–41; Gertrude E. Schroeder, "Soviet Economic 'Reforms': A Study in Contradictions," *Soviet Studies*, Vol. XX, No. 1 (July 1968), pp. 1–21.

[23] *Current Digest of the Soviet Press,* Vol. 19, No. 19 (May 31, 1967), p. 7.

to 73 percent over 1966 and increase the productivity of labor by 98 percent while decreasing the number employed by 1,000.

By July 1968, 800 people had been released: 343 in 1967 and 457 in 1968; another 200 were expected to be released in 1969. About one fourth of them were engineering and technical workers and office employees, the rest manual workers. The number employed decreased from 200 above the planned limit to 600 below, with a resulting economy in the wage fund of 36,000 rubles per month. Fifty percent of the savings was distributed by decision of the shop chief and the union shop committee in the shops or sections where the economies occurred; the rest was distributed by the director and the plant committee. More than half of those employed received pay increases—raises in wage and salary rates up to 30 percent for combining jobs or increasing the volume of work with fewer workers and up to 20 percent in rates and bonuses for maintenance and repair personnel. Part of the savings were added to the general fund for material incentives for later use. In comparison with 1966, average earnings by the end of 1968 were reported to have increased 24.4 percent, productivity of labor 86.6 percent, and the volume of production 73.3 percent.[24]

These results were achieved by the combined efforts of workers and staff in improving the organization of work, chiefly by combining jobs and widening the area of an individual's responsibility, accompanied by any necessary training and with a tightening of production standards. The incentive of increased pay for those who contributed to the program was considerable. As to those displaced, it was reported that none of the people released were left jobless. Since normal turnover amounted to about 800 annually and new hirings decreased, vacancies absorbed 550 of the first 1,000 released. People were needed also in other enterprises in the city, and the ministry made arrangements for those who wished to shift to plants elsewhere. Fifty-eight people left for the army, study, or pensions, but for 96 who left "by their own choice," or 50 who were discharged "in reduction of staff," there is no indication whether those who wanted jobs got them immediately. Some sceptical workers were quoted as saying, "What, my comrade dismissed and I get higher wages?" But it is said that few conflicts arose, since dismissals were handled with care. Of the first 515 people released, only seven or eight appealed to the factory committee; three lost their cases and the dismissals were approved, but one of these took his appeal to court and was reinstated.

Since these achievements came largely from improved organization rather than from technical progress, the prospects for further gains by the same means were limited. Accordingly the combine was reported to be asking the ministry to support a program for more mechanization

---

[24] *Current Digest of the Soviet Press,* Vol. 20, No. 40 (October 23, 1968), pp. 13–14.

and complex automation. How this would affect their wage and incentive plans is not known. The experiment seems to have demonstrated that with effective financial incentives and with assurance of jobs for those displaced, workers of all levels could be induced to cooperate in increasing efficiency and in the release of redundant labor for use where needed. Government and party officials hailed this as an important method and urged its widespread use. Similar experiments were introduced in other industries: chemical, metallurgical, textile and other light industries, and even in trade. In 1970, sixty enterprises involved were said to have released almost 12,000 people. Two years later there were 300 plants on such plans, and the enterprises had pledged to release 65,000 people or one tenth of their labor forces in the first three years of the Five-Year Plan.[25]

As other enterprises sought to shift to the Shchekino method of using economies in the wage fund for the benefit of those who brought them about, changes were necessary to fit particular conditions, and difficulties in making such adjustments slowed the spread of the experiment. There were many questions, both in theory and in practice, as to the general applicability of the plan. Were the gains primarily from one-shot improvements that could not be repeated? How long would the increased wage and salary rates paid from the economies be continued? What of the already efficient plant with good organization and tight production standards, where further economies in the wage fund were not easy to achieve? Would the plant with slack plans find it more easy to economize and increase production above its planned level than would better run plants? What of enterprises where no further expansion of production was desirable? There was also the broad question of how the gains of productivity should be distributed. An economist pointed out that the questions and contradictions had not been resolved; further theoretical and methodological consideration was needed to remove obstacles to the further implementation of such plans.[26]

One variation, following the lead of the Bashkir oil industry, was for a group of enterprises in one locality, under a common administration or ministry, to pool economies in their wage funds into a common incentive fund, which was then redistributed among the plants according to indicators of their success, such as their level of productivity compared to the standard levels, the extent of technically based production norms, and the number of personnel compared to standards for the industry. In other cases wage funds could not be frozen since changes were taking place in products, equipment or prices. Formulae were developed to measure the extent of reduction in labor costs per unit of product, and to assure that an enterprise gained from economies in its wage fund

---

[25] *Current Digest of the Soviet Press,* Vol. 24, No. 21 (June 21, 1972), pp. 9–10.

[26] Ibid., p. 10.

only if it was up to expected standards on staffing and production. General conditions for following the Shchekino method were established in December 1970 by the USSR Council of Ministers, and elaborated by joint decision of the State Committee on Labor and Wages, Gosplan, the Ministry of Finance, and the Central Council of Trade Unions. The ministries were obligated to verify carefully how an enterprise was using labor and its provisions for training and job placement of those displaced, before it was allowed to shift to this system. While the Shchekino experiment continued to receive favorable comment, more emphasis came to be put on other methods and incentives to increase productivity. Changes in the rules for incentive funds seek to ensure a sound relationship between growth of productivity and earnings. A renewed emphasis on the introduction of "scientifically-based norms" in all enterprises has also developed. Gosplan and the State Committee on Labor and Wages have been told to work out an improved method of determining labor productivity at the enterprise level.[27]

Distribution and Redistribution of Labor: Some Problems. Whatever the success of the programs discussed above, there remains the problem of effective mechanisms for placement and redistribution of labor, training and retraining, and minimization of transitional losses. Several studies have shown that of people changing jobs, only a minority (not over one third) did so with the help of public organizations, i.e., on a planned basis. More often it was by their own search for jobs, a process sometimes resulting in unnecessary lost time and retraining and not conducive to the most effective utilization of labor. For example, a query at four large enterprises in Gorky found that of all workers hired in the prior three months, 24 percent got their new jobs within three days, but 43 percent spent more than ten days looking.[28]

A worker discharged in a reduction of staff has the protection of two weeks' dismissal pay (though before the 1970 basic labor legislation this could be replaced by two weeks' notice) and the right to retraining if needed. For special groups there have been further regulations. A 1961 decree provided a guarantee for displaced skilled workers of at least their former average wage for three months in their new enterprise. Pay during retraining is subject to regulation—with the costs of the retraining and shift borne in part by the state but sometimes in part by individual workers. In the case of the shift of railroads to diesel and electric engines, the Ministry of Transport and the Central Council of Trade Unions provided for pay during one-year training programs for not over 100 rubles a month, only half the average pay on steam locomotives. By a 1970 decree of the Council of Ministers, people released as a result

---

[27] *Current Digest of the Soviet Press,* Vol. 24, No. 31 (August 30, 1972), p. 6; and Vol. 24, No. 35 (September 27, 1972), pp. 17–18.

[28] *Current Digest of the Soviet Press,* Vol. 17, No. 52 (January 19, 1966), pp. 8–10.

of improvements in the administrative apparatus were to have their average pay and their uninterrupted work records maintained during retraining, for up to three months; if they were transferred to other regions, state and party agencies were required to provide housing and priority in provisions for pre-school care of children.[29]

The organization of training and retraining is a matter of growing concern. Free education includes vocational and professional training, with stipends for students in higher and specialized education. The system of training provided in vocational-technical schools, specialized secondary schools, and universities and institutes is criticized as inadequate in many areas and insufficient for the needs of newer fields. For workers, both newly hired and those preparing for new or combined jobs, the most extensive training and retraining is done by enterprises themselves. In 1972, training directly in enterprises (in individual, brigade, and course programs) covered more than 20 million people, including some on collective farms. Vocational schools in that year graduated 1.8 million young skilled workers, secondary specialized schools 1.1 million, and higher education 700,000. An April 1969 decree of the Central Committee of the Communist Party and the USSR Council of Ministers provided for upgrading the vocational-technical schools (to give full secondary education as well as training for the most complicated trades in three to four year courses and evening courses) and for expanding the network of schools with more attention to their rational distribution.

Planning for development and distribution of the labor force is supposedly carried out at each governmental and administrative level, but practice is far from the textbook pattern. Local and regional authorities are often criticized for lack of sufficient attention to working out sound plans for labor, including training and retraining, but they have been hampered by lack of adequate data on trends and needs. Frequently managements fail to plan in advance for training or retraining workers and fail to keep local and educational authorities informed of future needs. One consequence is the considerable number of reports of difficulty in placing young workers and graduate specialists in jobs. In 1968 the department for the placement of young specialists in the Russian Republic reported a constant problem in refusals of organizations to accept graduates in the number they had previously requested. For example, it was impossible to find jobs in their specialty for fourteen workers trained in Kaliningrad as planners for machine-building enterprises. The narrow specialization of such training appears to add to the problem. Complaints continued that frequently neither the requests of enterprises nor the numbers trained in certain specialties were properly based on study of needs. Some fields lacked adequate information service to help

---

[29] Sonin and Zhiltsov, "Economic Development and Employment in the Soviet Union," pp. 87–88; *Current Digest of the Soviet Press,* Vol. 23, No. 18 (June 1, 1971), pp. 5–8.

place graduates in other than local areas. There were problems especially for the less well-trained graduates of correspondence and evening courses. There are also reports of problems of local authorities in finding jobs for youngsters leaving school after the eighth grade or secondary school. Quotas given enterprises, requiring them to hire certain numbers of these children, are supposedly adjusted to the needs and possibilities of the enterprise, yet some plants refuse to take those sent to them. A report in *Izvestia* spoke frankly of "serious flaws in the technology of placement, lack of coordination, absence of flexibility and efficiency," all related to the lack of scientific forecasts of requirements for cadres and of a full nationwide plan for training and placing specialists."[30] In 1969 the Council of Ministers sought to improve the planning of training and assignment of graduates by charging the State Committee on Science and Technology and the Ministry of Higher and Specialized Education to work out annual and long range plans for assigning specialists on the basis of proposals from republic and all-union ministries and departments as to the numbers needed. The educational institutions were then to make their assignments in accordance with approved plans.[31]

The Need for Employment Services

All such discussions pointed toward the need for better coordinated, nation-wide planning for the labor force and its utilization and for employment services with adequate information and powers—despite any resistances by Marxist bureaucrats who fear to admit the possibility of unemployment.

In 1959 the usual opinion among local officials and economists was that there was no need for employment services since there was no unemployment. Nevertheless, in that and succeeding years, leading manpower authorities pointed out wastes resulting from lack of information on openings and on workers wanting jobs and called for a coordinated system with centers where information would be available both for enterprises and for workers, to bring jobs and workers together more efficiently.

Aids in placement had not been entirely lacking. Enterprises listed "workers needed" in newspaper, radio, and TV ads and on the large public street bulletin boards. City information bureaus had lists of openings. Local party committees and trade union offices often knew of people needing jobs. Among official agencies were district commissions on job placement of youths. The district soviet executive committees also were

[30] *Current Digest of the Soviet Press,* Vol. 20, No. 34 (September 11, 1968), pp. 27–28; also Vol. 19, No. 26 (July 19, 1967), pp. 19–20, Vol. 20, No. 7 (March 6, 1968), pp. 8–9, Vol. 23, No. 38 (October 19, 1971), pp. 7–8.

[31] *Current Digest of the Soviet Press,* Vol. 21, No. 39 (October 22, 1969), p. 19.

expected to find jobs for demobilized soldiers and other special groups. State commissions at all higher educational institutions placed graduates for their three years of required employment where needed. Orgnabor, the Administration for Resettlement and Organized Recruitment, was still recruiting people for remote areas. Yet even locally there was no one center to coordinate information and placement services.

The urgency of the problem grew as it became evident that increasing numbers of workers would be released, or at least should be released, by improvements in technology and by the impact of the economic reform. In 1965, Sonin made a detailed proposal for a system of agencies from the local to the national level, to provide job placement services as well as make studies of the labor force and coordinate efforts for better use of labor. Other experts made similar suggestions. An experiment in the city of Gorky was reported approvingly about this time. To help in quicker matching of workers and jobs, in one district the functions of the commission on job placement of youths were broadened. After two years' successful experience as a general employment service, its extension to all districts and to a city-wide office was suggested by citizens.[32]

STATE COMMITTEES ON THE UTILIZATION OF LABOR RESOURCES

The precedent-breaking decision of the central authorities to at last begin a broad employment service was given no special announcement. It was included only as a small section of a December 1966 decree of the Central Committee of the Communist Party and the USSR Council of Ministers "on measures to secure the greatest growth of productivity of labor in industry and construction." The Councils of Ministers of the republics were authorized to set up State Committees on the Utilization of Labor Resources. Gosplan USSR was to be the coordinating agency, with a department on labor resources, and with responsibility for working out the balance of labor and deciding other questions regarding the rational utilization of labor resources.

A brief report in *Pravda* in February 1967 disclosed the formation of a Committee on the Utilization of Labor Resources in the Russian Republic. Publication of the decrees and of the Council of Ministers' regulation for the new state committee provided details on this potentially major development. The establishment of departments on the utilization of labor resources was authorized, in soviet executive committees, for the various governmental levels down to the large cities and districts. Duties of the state committee and its agencies included working with ministries and administrations on plans for retraining and

---

[32] *Current Digest of the Soviet Press*, Vol. 17, No. 52 (January 19, 1966), pp. 8–10.

redistributing labor; supply of information on demands for labor; job placement both locally and for distant jobs, taking the place of Orgnabor; study of the makeup of the unoccupied population; and participation in working out plans for the distribution of industrial construction and the growth of cities, with a view to rational use of labor resources and ensuring full employment. The mandate appeared to be broad, both for an employment service and for sharing in analysis and planning. The Russian committee and those soon established in other republics were only republicwide in scope, however, and the extent of their authority and their relation to other agencies were not defined.

According to scattered reports on experience in the first years, the committees established networks with offices or agents, or points managed only by volunteers, throughout their areas. By 1972 in the Russian Republic there was a central bureau in Moscow with local bureaus in 88 large cities. Leningrad and Moscow had placement offices or agents in every district of the city. In 1971 in all of Russia the bureaus reportedly placed about half a million workers in jobs, and in six months of 1972 more than 300,000. State Committees in Russia, the Ukraine, Kazakhstan, and other republics spoke of their work with enterprises and other agencies in studying labor resources and in planning. In the Ukraine about 100,000 local placements were reported in a year in addition to the placement of 300,000 youngsters from secondary school. Women had been helped to get part-time work or work at home, and jobs had been found for some hard-to-place specialists. The committees reported special success in helping new enterprises get needed labor. Many reported that time lost between jobs decreased; in Russia in 1971 the loss of time in cities with employment bureaus had been reduced to 12 to 15 days, from an average of 28 days. Kazakhstan claimed that its 14,000 placements in two years were made typically in a day or two, compared with the former 30 day loss. Turnover also is said to decrease, as a result of more information and vocational counseling made available to workers. Another gain reported was a substantial reduction in the number who changed occupations when shifting to other enterprises. Thus, in Leningrad in 1972, of those placed through the bureaus only 24 percent changed their type of work, compared with 56 percent in a 1958 study. In 23 Russian cities in 1972 a Teletype system for intercity information on vacancies was operating in connection with the central bureau in Moscow. Several committees spoke of card systems which made it possible to study the makeup of applicants and their reasons for leaving jobs. This was useful for the planning agencies and for agents of the State Committees in working with enterprises to improve their utilization of labor.

Efforts were made, with some success, to induce enterprises to recruit only through the labor resource agencies. Some plants, however, failed to use the service. Those with overplan numbers of workers probably preferred to avoid contact with the agency. In some cities, advertising of vacancies in newspapers and on radio and TV was decreased by agreement with the enterprises. Some managers considered such advertising conducive to wasteful turnover and competition for workers, though there were objections to the restriction from others and from workers who preferred to keep these channels of information open. Plant bulletin boards still served the purpose and hirings at the gates were numerous, as before, despite the desire of some spokesmen for the committees for a monopoly position in the field.

In several cities efforts to improve service both to enterprises and to workers seeking jobs led to experiments dealing with hiring practices and with freedom of choice among workers. In Kazakhstan, in place of recruiting by the separate enterprises and organizations, the information on vacancies was centralized and published only by the employment bureaus, without identifying the location of openings. Interested workers had to come to the bureaus, instead of shopping around among places that advertised. Also, the agencies sent to jobs only workers who had already resigned, to reduce thoughtless turnover by increasing the risks in leaving a job. In Russia the bureaus are said to have close relations with enterprises and to receive systematic information in their demand for labor. Except for two cities, however, enterprises also recruit directly, a practice felt by the agencies to hamper their job of judging the true demand for particular types of labor and sending workers where most needed. The bureaus are said to receive full information on the need for workers, and they may check on the use of labor, make recommendations, and refuse to send workers where there are overplan numbers. Enterprises may accept or reject the people sent them. Workers get full information on openings and have the right to choose among them. Counseling is provided, and when the worker lacks a skill the bureau can arrange in-plant or other types of training for him. Workers' records make it possible to spot problems of frequent changes of jobs or discharges for discipline. The bureaus work with enterprises on any conditions that interfere with efficient use of labor. The information obtained by the agency is used in planning training for specialties having a shortage of labor. The Kaluga bureau claimed in 1972 that it had helped relieve the local labor shortage by as much as 3,300 additional workers, through reducing surplus staffs in some enterprises, shortening the time lost between jobs, and bringing housewives into the public economy. These experiments were reported approvingly as a stage in widening the field of the placement services.

The State Committees emphasize their value for workers as well as for enterprises, by offering full information on possible openings and thus saving time in finding satisfactory jobs. Often they emphasize the voluntary character of their operations. Yet in some districts efforts have been made to use the placement office for control and discipline, by refusing service to people who had jobs or who left jobs for reasons not considered valid. The vice-chairman of the Russian State Committee commented that for those who want an easy life and for violators of labor discipline the bureaus might have a sobering effect. The Leningrad bureaus in 1970 had a system whereby those fired for lack of discipline could be hired only through the placement offices, at lower pay than on former jobs, and with a restriction on any bonuses for three months. Those who changed jobs more than twice a year also were to be restricted, given jobs in their specialty but only at certain plants, and with restrictions as to pay and other benefits.[33] General policy was still undecided as to whether these agencies were to become instruments for control as well as for planning in the interest of more rational utilization of the labor force or whether they were to emphasize voluntarism in a free labor market under the influence of rationally planned incentives and aids.

Problems

The reports, on the whole optimistic, suggest that the first years had brought a degree of improvement in many regions in local agencies for aiding placements and some gains in coordinating efforts to study labor supply and demand and to make rational plans for developing and distributing labor forces. Many problems remained, as shown in reports of officials of state committees and in other reports and letters in the press.[34] Efforts to develop effective local placement and information services and to gain acceptance from enterprises and workers were hampered by lack of clear policy as to the powers of the State Committees and their relations with other agencies, from enterprise up to ministries and other authorities.

Recruitment for distant jobs, the Orgnabor function, continued through the agencies of the committees, though at times this work received much the same criticism as had Orgnabor in the past. Some committees, however, threatened to refuse enterprises more recruits in the future unless they improved their methods. The Chairman of the Russian State Committee admitted excessive mobility when workers were sent to construction sites as others left, but he pointed to the need for more labor in most of the European parts of the RSFSR, while the benefits provided for these areas were "negligible."[35] For more efficient work in guiding mobility, it was frequently pointed out that better nationwide planning and information were needed. Some agencies were hampered even locally by the absence of an effective clearing system for the entire

---

[33] *Current Digest of the Soviet Press,* Vol. 22, No. 6 (March 10, 1970), p. 18.

[34] *Current Digest of the Soviet Press,* Vol. 20, No. 20 (June 5, 1968), pp. 5–6.

[35] *Current Digest of the Soviet Press,* Vol. 24, No. 48 (December 27, 1972), pp. 14–15.

city or between the city and other areas. Gosplan, even with its department on labor resources, apparently did not satisfy the need for a coordinating agency.

The major function of aiding the redistribution of displaced workers was proving complicated and difficult, as reported by the vice-chairman of the Russian state committee in the Gosplan journal. With the committee's participation, measures were being worked out for redistributing 50,000 workers in a year, the larger part of them still in the extractive industries. In the coal industry, which expected to release over 30,000 miners by 1970, programs were said to be underway in all basins for the redistribution of those released. In 1967 and 1968, the ministry and the state committee had arranged for miners in declining basins to go to others where they were needed or for retraining them for local enterprises—thus avoiding the difficulties of some areas early in the 1960s when some miners lost up to a month's work or had to take lower-paying jobs. In lumber and woodworking, where failure to plan in advance had lost many experienced workers to other industries, the ministry and the state committee were at last planning for rational redistribution of workers to fill needs in growing areas. In the oil industry, in non-ferrous metallurgy, iron and steel and construction, plans were underway or being developed to ensure jobs for workers to be released.

Work of committees and their agencies continued to be hampered by the failure of many ministries and their enterprises and of local authorities to cooperate, though careful planning for retraining was sometimes reported. Surprisingly, it was necessary for experts from Gosplan to point out that it would be helpful to know in advance how much the volume of work was to decrease and which specialties were involved; they had found ministries and departments which failed to plan for the redistribution of labor when working out their economic plans. The state committee of Russia and local planning organs of the Bashkir autonomous republic learned of the release of 400 workers only on the eve of the metal mines' closing; the Ministry of Light Metallurgy had not bothered to find jobs for those displaced or to inform the committee. The Russian committee is reported to have had a six-month battle with the Ministry of Transport, which was planning to displace many conductors and trackmen; the committee was unable to procure the information needed from the ministry to plan for transfers—the ministry insisted it had no personnel to prepare the figures.[36]

In October 1967, Gosplan ordered all ministries to inform the State Committees on Utilization of Labor Resources of the planned numbers and makeup of labor forces to be released from 1968 to 1970. The ministries were instructed to obligate their enterprises to work out with the agencies of the state committees measures for redistribution of workers,

---

[36] *Current Digest of the Soviet Press,* Vol. 20, No. 43 (November 13, 1968), pp. 26–27.

but not all ministries and departments carried out the orders. To what extent this problem has been alleviated is not known.

Proposals for New Powers for State Committees

The issue of the powers of the state committees remained undecided. In 1972, they seemed still primarily to be only organizations for coordinating activities. Perhaps this was inevitable while they gathered experience in analysis and planning and in placement services. The fact that they were only agencies of the republic councils of ministers, not of the all-union government, and had undefined powers put them at a disadvantage in dealing with central ministries and large enterprises. Among proposals frequently made was one for an all-union organization, a USSR State Committee on Utilization of Labor Resources, or even Ministry of Labor Resources, with power to coordinate the work of the republican state committees and to work with Gosplan in developing a scientific balance sheet of labor supply and demand for the entire country. Regional planning organizations would be obligated to include programs for labor in their annual and Five-Year Plans. Improved statistical reporting would be essential. It was argued that ministries and enterprises should by law be required to provide the necessary facts to the planning organs and to the state committees and to work out in advance, with agencies of the committee, plans for redistributing released workers. Upgrading of the status of the committees was needed to enable them to speak as peers with ministries and enterprises in negotiating and planning for workers to be released. Only then could the agencies of the state committees require the release of redundant labor, and take on the responsibility for retraining and redistributing displaced workers, an obligation which enterprises were increasingly unable to meet when it meant shifting workers to other enterprises and areas. Many proposals were made for legislation dealing with the release of workers, including provisions as to "the rights and benefits" of those affected. There also were calls for better financing of the state committees and their agencies, i.e., improved facilities and trained personnel and more sophisticated equipment.[37]

SOCIAL AND INDIVIDUAL COSTS

Reduction of the cost to society of underemployment, redundancy, loss of time between and on jobs, wasteful mobility, and unnecessary retraining is the aim of the battery of methods outlined above. Another proposal to accomplish more rational utilization of labor resources came

[37] Among leading experts who made such proposals were Manevich, "Problems in the Reproduction of Labor Power," and V. Korchagin, "Utilization of Manpower Resources in the New Five-Year Plan," *Problems of Economics*, Vol. 14, No. 6 (October 1971), pp. 40–50.

from the mathematical economist, Kantorovich,[38] who suggested a tax on the use of labor in regions of labor shortage or on the use of special types of labor in short supply. The funds would then be used to subsidize enterprises in locating plants or widening production in places with labor surpluses, for improving living conditions in areas of labor shortage, and for retraining workers for the fields where needed. It was held that enterprises should pay the state for the use of labor resources as they do for the use of capital, since such compensation for society's outlays in training labor would encourage economies in the use of this scarce and valuable resource, as well as help in evaluating the economic effectiveness of production.

Attention has turned also to the possible divergence between social and individual interests in technological change which displaces workers. Since 1965 several experts have argued that society should carry the full cost of the shifts. The matter of costs to individuals affects workers' attitudes and, thus, the extent of their cooperation. Some theorists appear to regard this also as a challenge under the Marxist doctrine of the absence of unemployment. They argue that shifts usually are to the advantage of the worker, with better conditions of work and pay on the new job, as well as contributing to the general rise in incomes; yet the change is not always painless. In general, costs of retraining are covered by the enterprise which releases the worker, but pay during training is often less than former wages. Delays occur in finding new jobs, especially when the worker finds his own rather than being placed by organized procedures, and dismissal pay lasts only two weeks.

A nationwide system of material protection for displaced workers has been suggested by an increasing number of experts. In 1968, two Gosplan writers proposed national legislation to ensure that people shifting to other work because of changes in industry do not suffer, materially or morally. Among proposals made are a legal requirement that enterprises give advance warning (perhaps as much as six months) to workers who are to be displaced, with notice to the agencies on utilization of labor resources; a guarantee of placement and of retraining when necessary; protection against financial loss during retraining; dismissal pay for longer than the present limit of two weeks and (at least implied) some form of benefit as long as necessary until placed; protection of the continuous work record; and guarantees that working and living conditions are not worsened. Manevich pointed out that considering the cost to the state of surplus workers on payrolls, the cost of providing material security to workers displaced would be economically justified.[39]

---

[38] *Current Digest of the Soviet Press,* Vol. 20, No. 20 (June 5, 1968), pp. 3–4; N. Fedorenko, "Questions Pertaining to Optimization of the Growth and Location of Production," *Problems of Economics,* Vol. 11, No. 9 (January 1969), p. 20.

[39] Among many such discussions, Manevich, "Problems in the Reproduction of Labor Power," p. 22; Korchagin, "Utilization of Manpower Resources in the New Five-Year Plan," p. 46.

Sonin and others strongly suggested to the trade unions that they also should be active in the plants in seeing that there is good planning for retraining and placing released workers, to avoid breaking their material security. The urgency of the problem increases as more pressures are brought on enterprises to improve their use of labor, though facts are still lacking on the extent of losses incurred by displaced workers. The matter of national standards on all these issues would seem an appropriate area for the trade unions to use their "right of legislative initiative," but there has been no public indication of action pending a green light from high authority in the party or government. It seems to be difficult for the Soviet state to admit that individual workers displaced from jobs sometimes suffer in the transition to other work and need additional protection. Here again the dogma of "no unemployment" is a barrier to full and realistic implementation of the basic promises made to citizens.[40]

CONCLUSIONS

On the whole, in more than a decade of intensive concern over manpower problems, the Soviet authorities continued their traditional policies, combining central planning with market-influenced decisions by individuals, enterprises, and local authorities. Changes in policy, even innovations, usually amounted to improving methods, sharpening tools which had been designed to influence choices in desired directions, increasing incentives, and, only in rather small degrees, decentralization of decision-making powers. Only in one area was there a sharp break with tradition: the start of a comprehensive employment service.

In these developments care was taken to stay within the bounds of Marxist-Leninist terminology; perhaps warnings from above were being

---

[40] In general, the rights and protections of workers were clarified and to some extent widened in the Principles of Labor Legislation of the USSR and the Union Republics, adopted in July 1970, as the first all-union labor legislation, replacing the 1922 labor code of the RSFSR, which with many revisions and supplements had continued to provide the basic standards, The new legislation did not touch the major issues discussed above, either the status and powers of the State Committees of the republics on Utilization of Labor Resources, or the question of further country-wide standards for protecting workers displaced by technological progress. For details see Brown, *Industrial and Labor Relations Review*, Vol. 26, No. 2 (January 1973), pp. 778–92. Among changes in standards that affect the labor market and job protection were a strengthening of the regulations as to discharge, the extension of back pay in case of illegal discharge to three months, and the removal of two weeks' notice as a substitute for two weeks' dismissal pay. Length of continuous service was given increased emphasis as a factor in determining many benefits, including promotion; but the worker who changes jobs in most cases keeps his record of uninterrupted service if he takes a job within thirty days. Establishment of the five-day week as the basic standard for work schedules, the authorization for part-time work, and a number of improvements in protection and benefits for women workers were partly in response to the need to attract women and pensioners into the labor market.

heeded, such as Gosplan Chairman Baibakov's criticism that some economists had indulged in non-Marxist analysis of the economic reform. The
annual reports on the economy continued to state flatly, "This year
as in previous years there was no unemployment in the country," and
this despite press reports of time losses between jobs and of placements
by local employment agencies of people who had experienced difficulty
in finding work.

Strenuous efforts to maintain high rates of growth in the economy
included attention to the need for full and rational utilization of labor
resources. Although the doctrine holds that a socialist system is not
subject to the evils of unemployment, as are capitalist systems, many
experts have pointed out that thought needs to be given to working
out the measures required to assure full employment. Acting as a "self-
fulfilling prophesy," the doctrine stimulates attention to the solution
of manpower problems. In the process, difficulties appear over sometimes
conflicting aims or over inadequacies in their implementation. Neither
at national nor local levels has the planning been adequate to solve
the problems of lack of balance between labor supplies and demands.
Central authorities call for building industry where there are unused
labor resources, but ministries and enterprise managements often find
it more efficient to build in the big centers, and planning authorities
do not always make resources available for developing local enterprises.
Central planners want initiative and enterprise on the part of managements but are hesitant to allow them freedom to make decisions on
market bases. Enterprises are required to hire young people sent to them,
though they also are urged to reduce their staffs. The needs of efficiency
call for displacement of labor, but the human and constitutional rights
of workers hinder the process. The trade union's function of promoting
the interests of production may conflict with the function of protecting
workers. Concern over the costs of turnover leads to proposals to crack
down, but the interest in workers' freedom of choice prevails. The need
for a comprehensive employment service was long pointed out by experts
before the central authorities took the perhaps embarrassing step of
authorizing a limited system; but in 1972 there still was no all-union
organization nor clear definition of the functions and powers of the State
Committees on Utilization of Labor Resources. Thus, both ideology and
human weaknesses hamper attainment of the goal of full and rational
utilization of the labor force.

Socialist doctrine, nevertheless, has positive influences on manpower
policies and practices. For many years central planning has brought
a high enough rate of growth in the economy to create relatively full
employment, despite social and individual losses in seasonal, structural,
and frictional unemployment, and in underemployment; and central
planning is developing policies which should decrease such losses. The
other side of the doctrine is the humanist commitment to individual

rights and freedom of choice in the labor market. The commitment to the right to work slows the process of displacement and obligates the state to see that jobs are available and to assist workers in getting jobs. Nevertheless, the doctrine that there is no unemployment apparently delayed recognition that full facts on employment (and on unemployment, if any) were essential. This doctrine also hindered acceptance of the need for unified employment services and still hampers the improvement of this essential mechanism for effective location of displaced workers. Divergencies between individual and social interests in this field have long been pointed out. Proposals to reconcile them by increasing protection of individual interests, without interfering with the needs of efficiency, are still in the discussion stage.

9. SOVIET AGRICULTURE UNDER BREZHNEV

Alec Nove

Soviet agriculture is backward both in comparison with Soviet industry and in comparison with agriculture in North America and Western Europe. In the USSR 31 percent of the labor force is engaged in agriculture, compared with 4 percent of a smaller labor force in the United States, and output per farm worker in the USSR is only about 10 percent of the U.S. level. The low level of Soviet agricultural productivity is due in part to unfavorable natural conditions of temperature, soil, and rainfall. The principal causes, however, are inadequate investment in agriculture and the lack of incentives for peasants on collective farms.

Immediately after Stalin's death in 1953, his successors embarked on a broad program to increase agricultural output and marketings. Some of the measures taken under Khrushchev's direction, including higher agricultural procurement prices and expansion of crop acreage, raised output. But others—such as unrealistic plans, unsound high-pressure "campaigns," and frequent reorganization of state agricultural administration—hurt agricultural production, which failed to rise significantly after 1958. Therefore, following Khrushchev's ouster, the new leadership gave prompt attention to resuming agricultural growth.

In this article, Alec Nove, Professor of International Economic Studies at the University of Glasgow, briefly examines Khrushchev's agricultural measures and their results. He then analyzes in detail the promise and performance of the new agricultural program announced by Brezhnev in 1965. Nove finds that, although some increase in agricultural production and peasant incomes has been achieved, progress has been, and will continue to be, slow—because of irrational incentives, excessive farm size, administrative interference in farm management, and the lack of labor-saving equipment.

The selection is reprinted by permission from *Slavic Review,* Vol. 29, No. 2 (January 1970), pp. 379–410, with the omission of references to foreign-language sources and most of the tables.

IT IS NOW well over five years since Khrushchev fell. The long-delayed kolkhoz congress has met, and a new statute has been adopted. It seems right, therefore, to examine the policies of the Brezhnev regime, the results achieved, the problems encountered.

Because a number of the measures taken since 1964 were closely connected with—or were deliberate reversals of—Khrushchevian policies, it will be necessary to begin with a brief look at what Khrushchev tried to do and how he tried to do it. The picture that follows is not controversial. It would be largely if not wholly accepted by Brezhnev and Matskevich, as well as by Western specialists. In retrospect it is interesting to note that much of the evidence on which Khrushchev's policies could be criticized was published in the USSR during his reign. For example, the present author's "Soviet Agriculture Marks Time," published in *Foreign Affairs* as long ago as July 1962, was based on printed Soviet criticisms. Of course, none of these Soviet authors named Khrushchev personally, and a systematic critical analysis of his errors and omissions had to await his fall. But the evidence was available earlier, particularly in literary journals. Credit must be given to such conscientious and bold spirits as Ovechkin, Abramov, Dorosh, and economists such as V. G. Venzher. (For all we know, others also tried to protest, but were censored.)

KHRUSHCHEV'S POLICIES AND THEIR CONSEQUENCES

It will be recalled that Khrushchev's first appearance as a party *leader* was at the so-called September plenum of 1953, when he subjected the state of Soviet farming to vigorous criticism. We do not know how many of the policies he then initiated were his own, or whether any leader in the immediate aftermath of Stalin would have made similar proposals. We do know that he proposed substantial increases in agricultural prices, in investments, and in pay for collective work. Taxes on private plots and livestock were greatly reduced. The false claim to have "solved the grain problem" was abandoned along with the biological yield statistics on which it was based, and to provide the necessary grain Khrushchev launched campaigns to expand the sown area ("virgin lands campaign") and to grow more corn for much-needed fodder. The net effects of these measures were positive. Output in 1958 was, according to the official statistics, over 50 percent above that of 1953.

It was in 1958 that things began to go wrong. At about that time Khrushchev eliminated that "antiparty group" and took more direct charge of affairs in general, and agriculture in particular. Though—as we shall see—he was not always able to get his own way, the policies and responsibility for errors must largely be treated as his. Let us look, then, at the reasons for the disappointing performance of Soviet agriculture in his last years of power.

First, there were the consequences of the "campaign" methods, allied with the adoption of exaggerated or impossible plans. The party machine in rural areas was used to imposing a cropping pattern and delivery obligations that had little to do with local conditions or the realities of the given situation. The campaigns were many, and some of them were begun in the earlier years. The virgin lands and corn campaigns were in full swing by 1955–56, and they were persistently continued thereafter—with increasingly unfortunate results. Despite warnings by experts concerning the danger of monoculture in Kazakhstan, Khrushchev insisted that the area sown to grain must 'not be diminished, thereby causing a trend toward falling yields and the threat of a dust bowl. Corn was imposed in areas quite unsuitable for it. "Corn, comrades, is a political crop" was a saying of the times. It was grown to order regardless of the availability of labor, machines, and seed. In the statistics, unripe corn was equated with ripe grain (a practice that was dropped in 1965). A farm chairman was reprimanded for "political underestimation of silage." Campaigns were waged also to secure the adoption of two-stage harvesting (separating the stages of reaping and threshing), the planting of corn in square clusters,[1] the use of peat compost pots, and the reduction of the area of fallow. Another "political" campaign aimed at the drastic reduction of sown grasses (so that some party secretaries treated clover as a "forbidden crop"), and oats were semi-outlawed. Absurdities appeared also in the livestock campaign. The plan to overtake America in the production of meat and milk within two to three years led at first to overslaughtering in order to beat records in sales of meat; then pressure to build up herds led to unnecessary survival of aged cows solely for statistical purposes, and to a fodder shortage, since grain output was static and hay and natural pasture were neglected. Milk yields per cow fell sharply. The list of campaign distortions is a long one.

No doubt Khrushchev would say in his own defense that he did not wish his decrees to be misapplied by the local comrades. Did he not urge that local circumstances be taken into account? No doubt he did, but the whole training and *modus operandi* of party officials led them (as Khrushchev surely knew) to devote their energies to Moscow-directed campaigns, paying much more attention to the report to their superiors (*svodka*) than to the real needs of agriculture—hence the saying that the two main evils in rural Russia are vodka and *svodka*. If it is understood that Moscow expects less oats or more corn, then the *raikom* secretary well knows that he will be reprimanded by the *obkom* secretary if he does not reduce oats and increase corn acreage,

---

[1] At the March 1965 Plenum of the CPSU Central Committee, I. Kebin was bitterly humorous about how his Estonians were deprived of the prize for the highest corn harvest because they did not use square clusters.

because in his turn the *obkom* secretary knows that *his* superior . . . , and so on.

Khrushchev's unrealistic plans included exaggerated state procurement quotas. It is a particularly well-established habit of rural party official-dom, going back all the way to the earliest days of collectivization, to give priority to procurements regardless of any other consideration. Even seed grain is taken. Therefore, despite Khrushchev's own criticism of the practice of arbitrarily varying compulsory procurement quotas, his own plans compelled the secretaries to demand and insist upon over-plan "voluntary" deliveries. These demands played havoc with the farms' own plans and also adversely affected incentives in the form of payments in kind (some farms had little left for this purpose). Bodiul, the Mol-davian party secretary, was particularly eloquent about this at the March 1965 plenum,[2] but he was only one of many. (Yet total procure-ments of grain did not in fact show any sharp rise; presumably the trou-ble lay in arbitrariness plus regional disparities.) Here again Khrushchev was contradictory. In 1955 he had spoken up for autonomy of farms: interference in their affairs was declared to be wrong, apart only from ensuring that they were able to meet fixed and reasonable delivery quotas. But all this was disregarded, and under Khrushchev the degree of arbi-trary interference may have reached record heights. It is hard to blame the party secretaries for this. We must presume that they had no wish to harm agriculture, but that pressure from above left them with little alternative.

After 1958, efforts were made, on Khrushchev's initiative, to restrict the private activities of peasants, especially their ownership of livestock. This pressure took a variety of forms, probably depending on how the local secretaries interpreted the will of Moscow. In some areas they "persuaded" peasants to sell their cows to the collectives; in others, they restricted fodder or pasture rights. Tax regulations were altered to penalize some categories of livestock owners. These restrictions were exceedingly unpopular and affected incentives and morale adversely.[3]

The massive increase in the number of state farms (sovkhozes) that occurred at this time cannot be "blamed" mainly on Khrushchev—if indeed any blame attaches, since most of the peasants who were affected benefited materially from the change. The increase was so great partly because the virgin lands campaign was largely based on state farms and partly because of the conversion (voluntary and "voluntary") of collectives into state farms. This last process went further than Khru-shchev wished, for he blamed local party secretaries for pressing on

---

[2] "In six years output rose by only 21 percent, procurements by 70 percent."

[3] See, for instance, Fedor Abramov's 1973 story *Vokrug da okolo*. [Translated into English by George Reavey as *The New Life: A Day on a Collective Farm* (New York: Grove Press, Inc., 1963).—Editors.]

with these conversions for administrative reasons (including the ease of getting more investment funds for *state* farms out of the central budget).[4]

Khrushchev relied heavily on the party machine, but in the process confused and muddled the administrative mechanism of both state and party. By a complex process, which cannot be described in detail here, he got rid of the minister of agriculture, Vladimir Matskevich, and eliminated by 1961 almost all the powers of the ministry. He reorganized repeatedly. The abolition of the Machine Tractor Stations (MTS) in 1958 eliminated an important link in the party and state control mechanism, which Khrushchev himself had strengthened in 1953. The local party secretaries, who were oriented above all to current campaigns, were no longer counterbalanced by any effective ministerial structure. New bodies were set up with partial responsibilities: the State Committee on Procurements, and *Sel'khoztekhnika* (responsible for supplies of equipment and many other items to agriculture). Some of the ministry's powers were transferred to Gosplan. Then in 1962 a new hierarchy of control was devised, based upon the Territorial Production Administrations, whose territories were not coincident with the raions (the territories in which the party secretaries operated). Above this level were oblast, republican, and all-union agricultural committees, with a special role within the republics and oblasts for the first secretary of the party. The resultant confusion was made worse by two other measures: the separation in 1962–63 of the agricultural from the urban party organizations and the proposal in 1964 to set up all-union organizations for particular products (one such for poultry and eggs, *Ptitseprom*, actually came into existence). It is clear that Khrushchev's reorganization antagonized many influential persons. Thus there were protests from party secretaries at the raion level, and the all-union and republican agricultural committees seem not to have functioned.

The abolition of the MTS had adverse consequences in several respects. Though it eliminated the much-criticized "two masters in the field," it also disrupted the material basis of maintenance and repair. In Matskevich's words, "In these years the repair base of agriculture was weakened." Repairs were to have been handled by state Repair Technical Stations (RTS), but the RTS were not allowed to develop. Some 2,300 repair shops were sold to kolkhozes and sovkhozes, many of which could not fully utilize them, and finally "the [state] repair service was virtually liquidated. The largest repair enterprises were handed over to *sovnarkhozy* and converted to other forms of productive activity." In a conversation with this author, a Soviet agronomist said: "What was wrong with the MTS was that their use was compulsory. Instead of allowing farms to buy machines if they wished, and turning

---

[4] The conversions were supposedly "voluntary."

the MTS into bona fide rental and repair agencies, it was decided to abolish them. This was a grave error."

So were the terms on which the farms had to buy the machines. To quote Matskevich again, "heavy loss was imposed on the collective-farm economy" because "prices for tractors, trucks, and spares were increased," while state procurement prices for farm products were fixed at a level at which they could not cover the increased costs of buying, operating, and replacing the equipment; the problem was further compli-cated by "an unsound decision to reduce the period of payment for ma-chinery," as a result of which the financially weaker farms had to devote to this purpose all available money resources, a condition which affected both their "productive activities and payment for collective labor." At the plenum it was stated that the costs of capital repairs had doubled. A sower that cost 180 rubles in 1955 was repriced at 340 rubles, and prices of spare parts were doubled at a blow.

A reduction of procurement prices was achieved by using a provision in the 1958 price decree that allowed variations of 15 percent according to the size of the harvest. Because 1958 was a good-weather year, prices were duly reduced by 15 percent—only they "forgot" to increase them again afterward. Prices during this period were exceedingly irrational, in that the profitability of different products varied widely and bore no relationship to either plan or need. The campaign to increase output of meat and milk, already in full swing in 1958, was accompanied by prices at which (as all published evidence showed) farms selling to the state did so at a heavy loss. This situation contrasted with the profitabil-ity of nearly all crops in most areas.[5]

There were wide regional variations between prices and costs, and the northern and western regions, with their relatively higher costs, were least favored. Some prices were increased before Khrushchev's fall. Thus meat and milk prices went up in 1962, and in 1963 cotton prices were raised by 12 to 20 percent and sugar beet prices by about 25 percent. It is worth noting that certain perquisites and bonuses which encouraged specialization in these two industrial crops had been abandoned in 1958, with unfortunate results.

Peasant pay for collective work undoubtedly fell in these years in some areas, apparently reaching a low point in 1960. Pay in 1960 in the USSR as a whole, according to unofficial Soviet sources, was 8 percent below 1958 levels. The largest fall, by 29 percent, was in Moldavia; the Ukraine showed a drop of 18 percent. In Moldavia, according to the already quoted speech by Bodiul, distribution of grain to peasants fell from 580,000 tons in 1958 to only 211,000 tons in 1964, owing to

---

[5] The terms "profit" and "loss" have no precise meaning at this period in kolkhozes because payment to labor was still a residual. But prices were below costs on almost any reasonable assumption about what costs were.

excessive state procurements. But pay, at least in cash, did rise substantially after 1960, as will be shown in detail later.

Investments fell also. This was partly the result of the financial burdens on farms associated with the purchase of the MTS, but there was also a cutback in output of farm machinery. Matskevich attributed the fall to overconfidence resulting from the good harvest of 1958, which led to a downgrading of agriculture's priority. Ezhevsky, head of *Sel'khoztekhnika*, advanced the explanation that some comrades believed that the kolkhozes would use the former MTS equipment so much more productively that less of it would be needed. There was, it is true, a renewed upswing in subsequent years, which Matskevich does not mention, because it does not fit his argument. In fact, there was an ambitious investment program launched in 1963, but it was far behind schedule when Khrushchev fell.[6] In any case, harm was done by the precipitate decline of 1958–59.

The same rather depressing picture can be drawn for housing, except that the decline came later. The highest figure was in 1959—802,000 houses were erected "by the rural population." In 1960 the total fell to 618,000. In subsequent years it fell still further: in square meters the figure for housing erected "in kolkhozes" fell from 26.8 million in 1960 to only 18.3 million in 1965.

Finally, as Brezhnev pointed out, there was systematic neglect of the northern and western areas of European Russia. These areas lacked fertilizer and equipment, but with proper drainage and good husbandry they have great potential and are drought-free. Yields in such oblasts as Kostroma, Pskov, Novgorod, and Vladimir were exceedingly low. Of course, the vast virgin lands campaign greatly increased the total sown area and produced results, but this did not excuse the overconcentration on the south and east. In a particularly bitter speech, the Pskov party secretary, I. Gustov, spoke of a decline in deliveries of fertilizers since 1957, even though output of fertilizer was rising. Yields were appallingly low—a mere 5 or 6 quintals of grain or 60 to 70 quintals of potatoes per hectare, year in and year out. The rural population was fleeing to town.

These, then, were the principal reasons for agriculture's failure to make significant progress after 1958. The very bad weather of 1963 hit a weakened agriculture, which had few reserves and an excessive livestock population (excessive, that is, in relation to the fodder available even in an average year). A heavy blow to morale was struck when the USSR had to import grain from the capitalist West. Khrushchev's fall had many causes, but the 1963 fiasco certainly contributed. It so happens that 1964 was a favorable year, so favorable that Khrushchev's successors found it embarrassing to admit how good it was so soon after

---

[6] Thus the plan for state investments for 1964 was 5.4 billion, the actual was 4.4 billion (productive investments).

having got rid of Khrushchev.[7] (The heavens then mocked Brezhnev and his colleagues by providing another year of poor weather in 1965, necessitating still more purchases of grain abroad.)

BREZHNEV'S NEW LINE

The March (1965) plenum indicated that the new management had learned from Khrushchev's mistakes. In Brezhnev's speech there were criticisms of his predecessor, and the following changes were announced.

(1) *No more "campaigns."* Indeed, Brezhnev saw fit to warn local officials against rushing to the other extreme and instructing farms to reduce corn acreage. The emphasis was on farm autonomy, on the methods and pattern most suitable for local conditions, subject only to the requirement that certain products be delivered to the state. Fallow, grass, and oats were no longer to be barred.

(2) *Moderate and fixed procurement quotas.* Resisting proposals to remove compulsion from procurements, Brezhnev undertook to ensure that delivery quotas would be reasonable and stable. For grain he laid down a quota, unchanged for six years ahead, at a level below the known needs of the economy. The state would have to buy more, and it would do so at higher prices for many grains in order to make such additional sales genuinely voluntary and attractive. The annual delivery quotas for livestock products, though fixed in advance, would be increased with the hoped-for expansion of production.

(3) *Restrictions on private plots eased.* The extra taxes on private plots were abolished, and rights to collective pastures and adequate supplies of hay were reasserted. It was a return to the status quo ante 1958.

(4) *Administrative order restored.* Back into its usual role came the Ministry of Agriculture, and the minister whom Khrushchev had dismissed, Matskevich, resumed his functions. The confusions of the local organs were sorted out. Oblast and raion agricultural administrations were again made responsible for local planning under the supervision of the appropriate party secretary. The division of the party was also abandoned.

(5) *Better maintenance and repair facilities.* The task of ensuring repairs, providing large workshops, and renting out special-purpose equipment was given to *Sel'khoztekhnika*. There would be 200 new "repair factories" and over 1,000 specialized workshops. This body, which was vigorously criticized at the plenum, undertook to improve supplies of all kinds and its links with industry.

(6) *Price increases* for many categories of farm products were decreed, with higher prices for some over-quota deliveries. The increase

---

[7] For the story of successive upward amendment of the 1964 statistics, see A. Nove, "Some Thoughts While Reading the Soviet Press," *Soviet Studies,* Vol. XVII, No. 1 (July 1965), pp. 97–102, and "Statistical Puzzles Continue," *Soviet Studies,* Vol. XVIII, No. 1 (July 1966), pp. 83–85.

brought the procurement price of meat to a level actually above retail prices in some instances, necessitating a large subsidy (hence the impossibility of paying still more for over-quota sales, though this was asked for). Prices in higher-cost areas were, as a rule, increased by particularly large amounts. The price change involved a number of anomalies, which will receive more thorough examination later on. At the same time, prices of industrial goods used by agriculture were reduced. Some of these reductions were substantial. For example, "before 1960 kolkhozes paid four times as much as industrial enterprises for one kilowatt-hour of electricity. In 1961 the price was halved. . . . From 1966 it was again halved . . . and became equal to prices charged to industrial enterprises." Thus there was to be a sharp rise in net revenues of farms.

(7) *Increases in pay* of peasants for collective work were already considerable after 1960, and Brezhnev intended to ensure their further rise. As we shall see, the overdue and much-discussed step of paying guaranteed incomes to kolkhoz peasants was taken the next year. Old-age pensions for peasants, announced by Khrushchev before his fall, also began to operate.

(8) *Increased investments* were firmly promised. Total state and kolkhoz agricultural investments of 71 billion rubles were planned for the 1966–70 quinquennium, as against 34.2 billion in 1961–65.[8] More would be financed by the state. Brezhnev's regime also undertook to improve rural amenities and housing, well realizing the danger of an outflow of the energetic and skilled young men needed to work in a more modern and mechanized agriculture. Fertilizer presents a special case. Khrushchev had launched a huge plan—80 million tons by 1970—in December 1963, although even the production plan originally set for 1965 (35 million gross tons) could not be fulfilled.[9] Such plans were impossible, and under Brezhnev the plans were made more modest. But this did not imply a change of policy so much as a realization of what was and was not feasible. Supplies of fertilizer, much of it the result of investments started in Khrushchev's time, increased very rapidly, as will be shown later. It must be said that the failure to fulfill farm investment plans may have been due to restrictions by Khrushchev's colleagues and insistent claims by other sectors, rather than conscious decision by Khrushchev himself.

(9) *Other measures* included a major effort to expand irrigation and drainage, and also a drive to apply lime to acidic soils at government expense. Special attention would be paid to the neglected nonblack-earth areas of the center and west. Kolkhoz debts to the state were written off. Taxes on kolkhozes were redefined and revised downward. Farms were to be encouraged to undertake small-scale manufacture, to provide

---

[8] Note that these investment data are not comparable with statistics published in earlier years.

[9] Fertilizer output in 1965 was 31.3 million tons.

employment in slack periods, and also to process foodstuffs, make bricks, generate electricity, and so forth.

THE NEW POLICY IN PRACTICE

Organization and Methods

The restored Ministry of Agriculture has been operating smoothly enough, through local agricultural bodies of the pre-Khrushchevian pattern. The Territorial Production Administrations became the raion agricultural administrations, and the party *raikomy* also resumed their "normal" functions. True to promises made, there have been no central campaigns designed to impose any particular crop pattern or method of production. It is reasonable to conclude that both local party and state organs and the actual farm management have been much freer to respond to local circumstances and needs.

However, this does not mean that plans are made only for procurements, and that there is no longer any interference with the farms' own plans. Evidence to the contrary can be readily assembled. Thus V. Demidenko, chairman of the "Sibir'" kolkhoz of the Novosibirsk Oblast, complained that he is not allowed to sow half of his land to grain, while leaving a quarter fallow:

> We may be asked: If this is evidently advantageous, why not adopt this structure of sowings? After all, you have the right to decide what and how much to sow. Well, yes and no. If we were to propose such a structure to the raion agricultural administration, they will at once make an appropriate "correction." . . . They happen to follow the principle "the larger the area, the more secure the procurements plan," and they have no interest either in profitability or in yields per hectare. Not only does the local agricultural administration interfere in deciding what and how much to sow, but it also continues arbitrarily to vary procurement quotas: the plan of sales to the state is distributed [among farms] on the principle "the stronger the farm, the bigger the quota; the weaker—the smaller."

Is this exceptional? There is no reason to suppose that it is. One has only to look at *Pravda* editorials on the subject of procurements (for instance, that of September 20, 1969) or the praise still publicly given to party secretaries for overfulfilling procurement plans ahead of time, to be sure that interference and orders do in fact persist.[10] Indeed they must do so, because prices remain irrational, as will be shown in detail in a moment. What is needed and what is profitable do not coincide. Nonetheless, the absence of central campaigns, other than those relating to procurements, has led to correspondingly reduced

---

[10] See also *Pravda*, Dec. 27, 1969, where it was reported that the secretary of the Gomel *obkom* was dismissed for not ensuring fulfillment of plans.

pressure on local officials, and this in turn must have had a beneficial effect.

If kolkhoz chairmen complain of interference, the situation of sovkhoz managers is undoubtedly worse. They are, to begin with, in a much weaker position: unlike kolkhoz chairmen, they are formally accountable to the ministerial organs that appoint them. Repeatedly the managers complain that they are given precise sown-area plans, even when they contradict their crop rotation scheme or when some of the produce in question cannot be disposed of because the procurement organizations refuse to take it. Plans for output and deliveries are often unfulfillable, yet managerial and employee bonuses depend on such plans. There was also much criticism of the overdependence of sovkhozes on the state budget for investment finance. This not only undermined financial autonomy but also led frequently to the acquisition (or unwanted deliveries) of unsuitable equipment.

For all these reasons there arose a move to put sovkhozes on what came to be called "full *khozraschet*," which placed them in many ways on an equal footing with kolkhozes. Prices paid to sovkhozes were lower as a rule, because, unlike kolkhozes, they did not have to meet their investment expenditure out of revenue. A sovkhoz on full *khozraschet*, however, would be paid the same price as kolkhozes and would have to finance its own investments, therefore enjoying greater powers over what to invest in. This move was part of an attempt to provide greater managerial autonomy, the agricultural counterpart of the reform in industry. At the time of writing, approximately one third of all sovkhozes are operated under this new system.

The new system raised several questions. One is related to prices. As with kolkhozes, profitability varied far too widely between different products. Genuinely full *khozraschet* was therefore bound to be limited; orders from above about what to produce and deliver will therefore continue. Another question concerns the relationship between sovkhozes and kolkhozes in the same area. Under Khrushchev, the Territorial Production Administrations were set up to control both categories of farms, and *Sel'khoztekhnika* supplied both, at the same prices in most instances. This arrangement has been retained. However, a potentially contradictory principle was proclaimed: the association of kolkhozes into local and even all-union organizations, which could undertake joint activities (additional to interkolkhoz industrial units, which have existed for many years) and represent the interests of kolkhozes to higher authority. The "kolkhoz union" (*kolkhozsoiuz*) idea was not a new one: it was put forward by Matskevich when he was still minister under Khrushchev. The proposal was revived in the most recent years. The idea, in turn, was linked with a discussion concerning the desirability of continuing the distinction between kolkhozes and sovkhozes. After all, once kolkhoz peasants are paid wages and sovkhozes finance their own investments, and both pay and receive the same prices, why maintain the separate categories of agricultural producers?

The basic differences between kolkhozes and sovkhozes are now two: cooperative as opposed to state ownership, and elected as opposed to appointed management. How important are those distinctions? There is evidence of argument over this, in which some of the protagonists see great importance in the principle of elected management. (One wonders if some of these arguments are intended to provide indirect support for the ideas of workers' self-management à la Belgrade.) The efficiency of the two kinds of farms does not differ greatly. Sovkhozes have the high output per man-day, but they have a proportionately higher amount of capital per head, so that one analyst considers them to be less efficient than kolkhozes. Be that as it may, the kolkhoz union principle has been conceded by the much-delayed kolkhoz congress, held in November 1969. Elected kolkhoz councils (*sovety kolkhozov*) were set up at raion, oblast, and all-union levels, the raion council being elected by representatives of the local kolkhozes, each of the others by the representatives of the council at the level below it. The all-union council was elected at the congress itself, and it is significant that its chairman became none other than the minister, Matskevich. The council of 125 members includes also a deputy-chairman of Gosplan and several republican ministers of agriculture. If this sets the pattern, then clearly this "representative" body will be under firm official control, and will in no way replace existing organs of party and state.[11]

However, that does not mean that this is an insignificant development. The experience of the USSR, and indeed of any other bureaucratic structure, teaches us that organizations provide opportunities to act as pressure groups, or at the very least to give expression to feelings, grievances, and problems that otherwise would not obtain a hearing. The mere existence of bodies with the function of representing the common interests of kolkhozes may ensure that they do get represented, even if Matskevich and other official personages act as controllers and censors.

Another major organizational question relates partly to the size of farms and partly to incentives. There is a widespread view in the West that Soviet farms have become unmanageably big. Certainly kolkhozes have been enlarged through successive amalgamations; the sovkhozes are even larger, though the average size has been decreasing slowly in recent years. Matters have been complicated by the pressure exerted to ensure that kolkhozes and sovkhozes produce a wide range of crops and keep a variety of animals.[12] Thus we do not have any analogy

---

[11] Indeed, the first meeting of the council was attended by the party officials responsible for agriculture, D. Poliansky and F. Kunakov, neither of whom are members of it.

[12] Thus, to take one example, the average "sheep raising" sovkhoz also had 1,968 head of cattle, and the average cotton sovkhoz 2,196 head of sheep.

for the huge farms or ranches found in Texas and Australia. The labor force often lives in scattered villages, and the lack of roads impedes intrafarm communications. Under all these circumstances, efficiency depends greatly on the subunits of which the farms are composed—in the first instance the brigades. In kolkhozes these brigades are often equal in size and area to one of the preamalgamation kolkhozes.

Because brigades are also big, smaller subunits—that is, the *zveno* or "link"—composed of five to ten persons, might be the answer. The *zveno* controversy has been widely misunderstood. The *zveno* has existed all along, and still exists, as a work gang to perform specified tasks. In this form it is not controversial. The real issue is a different one: Should there be a semipermanent *zveno* which has a long-term attachment to a specified area of land, along with the necessary equipment, and which is left to perform broadly agreed upon tasks as it sees fit, with its income depending on the results? This has been called the *beznariadnoe zveno*, in the sense that no work duty schedule (*nariad*) is imposed upon it from above. It could operate in either a sovkhoz or a kolkhoz. Its advantages are clear: a small group would share responsibility; it would recover that "love of the land" which, according to another supporter of this kind of *zveno*, has been lost within the large impersonal units; since it would be interested only in results, it would not waste resources fulfilling quantitative plans; it would use the minimum amount of equipment and would have every incentive to keep it in good repair. These are important factors, as was pointed out in *Novyi mir* by Streliany: in sovkhozes and kolkhozes the "mechanizers" are paid on a piecework basis, which means quantity, or "hectares." Obviously it is easier to fulfill a plan expressed in hectares of plowing and to gain overfulfillment bonuses by plowing as shallowly as possible, and so inspectors strive (often in vain) to ensure that plowing is efficiently done; the actual tractormen are uninterested in the harvest. None of this would happen in the free *zveno*. Its members would be free to arrange their own work and free time, and would work very long hours at peak periods. Output would rise, productivity would rise, costs would fall—or so the advocates of this species of *zveno* loudly claim.

Arguments against this *zveno* idea are seldom stated, but in one of the articles referred to above, Rebrin has attempted an analysis. One argument has it that norms and discipline are necessary; another stresses the fear that the farm will break up or its labor force will become so subdivided that separate groups would not be able to help each other out ("Why not?" counters Streliany). Yet another argument points out that many peasants might be repelled by the long hours and pressures of the fully autonomous *zveno*; peasants want fixed hours of work or they will move to town. Uncertain, and possibly excessive, earnings is seen as another drawback. Should this not be regulated by some authority? Finally, Streliany alleges that many officials instinctively dislike the new idea because by providing effective incentives it would deprive the petty supervisors of their raison d'être.

The kolkhoz congress failed to pronounce on this whole question, and presumably we shall be witnessing further cautious experiments with the *zveno* on a small minority of the farms.

Finally it is necessary also to mention the growth of interkolkhoz and other subsidiary enterprises. There were in 1967 in the whole USSR 3,884 interkolkhoz organs of every type, of which 1,622 were specialist construction enterprises and 589 were concerned with poultry and eggs. Many made building materials, some were artificial insemination centers, others sanatoria for peasants. Some oblasts and republics possessed control organs to supervise these various organizations, and some of them also operated industrial and construction enterprises. They were all small scale, and there were frequent complaints about shortage of supplies, especially of building materials, for these nonpriority units whose requirements were incorporated in no allocation plans. At the same time, the reluctance of state building organizations to undertake work in rural areas was and is notorious.

Thus far the problem is only one of priority and organization, not of principle. But there is evidently some friction over the question of auxiliary industrial enterprises in kolkhozes. No one objects to the processing or canning of farm produce. But an indignant *Pravda* correspondent denounced those who set up printing shops, make ball-point pens, paper clips, springs, electrical components, nuts and bolts, and sell these things at higher prices. It is legal for kolkhozes to run auxiliary enterprises, but the author complained that the kolkhoz serves as a cover for a species of private enterprise by nonmembers, and also that energies are diverted from more directly relevant tasks. *Pravda* also seems particularly to have been hurt by the tendency to produce "goods in deficit," through to an ordinary economist this might even seem a virtue.

The new kolkhoz statute, adopted by the congress, contained little that was new, in the sense that it incorporated changes already made, with the single exception of the kolkhoz councils. The congress must have been preceded by some arguments and disagreements, possibly over the questions discussed above, since one had been promised by Khrushchev, and Brezhnev undertook at the March 1965 plenum to call one "already next year." No major changes appear to be contemplated at present.

Prices

We have seen that under Khrushchev state procurement prices had been raised several times and then somewhat lowered in real terms in

1958.[13] In the period 1961–64 there were already some increases in prices of livestock products, cotton, and sugar beets. The 1965 changes affected livestock products again, and also grain, although comparability is complicated by the existence of an over-quota bonus price for some grains and an increase in regional differentiation. A further complication is that if free-market prices are much higher than state procurement prices, an increase in the latter may be of no help to kolkhoz finance if at the same time state procurements take a larger share of the product (as is the case with livestock products).

Local variations around the averages were allowed, indeed encouraged. In more recent years the 50 percent bonus was extended also to millet, barley, oats, corn, and peas; a 100 percent bonus is now paid for sunflower seed deliveries in excess of those made in the previous year, 50 percent for cotton sales above the average of the previous three years. Prices paid to sovkhozes were also increased; in most cases they were below kolkhoz prices (e.g., 45 rubles as against 76 rubles per ton for wheat in the Ukraine), but sometimes equal to them (e.g., in the north and west of the RSFSR, and the Central Asian and Baltic republics, for both wheat and rye).[14] It must also be recalled that prices charged to kolkhozes, and also taxes, were reduced. Consequently, *net* revenues increased sharply, making possible large increases in peasant pay, which will be documented below. The increases were particularly large in the relatively infertile and high-cost areas of the north and west.

One Soviet writer has calculated the relationship between costs and prices for particular products for the USSR as a whole. The method of calculation may be questionable, but at least it is consistent between products. ("Profit" and "loss" are hard to compute where there are no clearly defined labor costs.) He demonstrates strikingly that there are still very great differences. Despite price increases, the livestock sector remains hardly profitable at all—for some products and areas positively unprofitable—whereas crops as a rule are sold at a considerable profit, including grain and potatoes that could otherwise be fed to livestock. Clearly this is not a rational price structure, a situation that may help to explain the lag in livestock products, which will be analyzed in subsequent pages. Furthermore, the bonus price offered for over-quota deliveries of most grain does not apply to livestock products, though several delegates to the 1965 plenum asked that it should. Even in 1967, a year of average harvest, 13.4 million tons of grain out of the total of 57.2 million procured by the state was paid for at a rate 50 percent above the quota price.

Why has such a situation been tolerated? The answer is all too clear.

---

[13] "Real terms" in the sense that the increases were less than the extra expenses incurred by taking over the MTS.

[14] It will be recalled that sovkhozes on full *khozraschet* are paid the same prices as kolkhozes.

After the unpopularity of the 1962 retail price increases in livestock products, it was decided not to change food prices in 1965. The effect was to impose a large burden of subsidy upon the budget. Thus "in 1966 the expenses incurred in purchasing beef from kolkhozes exceeded the [retail] price by 60 percent, or by 43 percent allowing for proceeds from sales of by-products." Taking into account also purchases from sovkhozes and from individuals, the total expenses of the state exceeded retail prices of beef by 55.2 percent, of pork by 12.1 percent, of mutton by 10.7 percent. There are then strong financial grounds for resisting further increases in purchase prices. In fact, the 1965 increases for livestock products were described as *nadbavki* (premiums or addenda) to existing prices, as it was and is presumably hoped to reduce them when the high costs of production fall, thereby eliminating or reducing the subsidy burden. It is evident that the contradictions of the price system have not been eliminated by the 1965 price changes. We shall be looking into costs again below.

The issue of regional price and cost differences deserves much more space than it can receive here. It is intimately connected with three other vital questions: specialization, farm autonomy, and land rent. Let us briefly explain what the connection is.

Supposing that the cost of growing wheat is 100 percent higher in Belorussia than in either the Ukraine or the black-earth areas of the RSFSR, should the price also be 100 percent higher? Or do these facts constitute a reason for not growing wheat at all in Belorussia, but concentrating instead on a crop that is profitable with local soil and climate, such as flax, or on raising livestock with locally grown or purchased fodder? Why should high-cost producers be "rewarded" by higher prices? Should not prices in principle be the same, and natural differences be taken care of via differential rent, levied in the form of a highly differentiated tax? Such a rent should not eliminate all cost differences, because price-and-profit ought to have the effect of encouraging specialization.

There has been widespread discussion for many years about the need for land valuation, which has a bearing also on payment of compensation (or a price) for the use of agricultural land for industrial, residential, or hydroelectric purposes. There are evident difficulties. A full cadaster would require years of work. There would be the danger of basing the rent or tax on actual yields achieved instead of on the potential, thereby "taxing the intelligence of the cultivator" and penalizing past hard work. Experiments have been conducted by the University of Tartu in Estonia. Regional price differences, assert the critics, are a poor and clumsy way of obtaining results which require highly differential valuations and rents (taxes). But no decision to act on an all-union scale has yet been taken.

To return to the relationship between prices and rational costs, one's attitude inevitably depends on the extent of desired autonomy of farm management. If kolkhoz chairmen and sovkhoz managers are to be ordered what to grow and especially what to sell to the state, it is obviously unfair that they and their farm hands should suffer from the fact that costs happen to be high. It might then be possible to instruct state procurement organizations to buy where possible from low-cost areas. But if the farms choose, prices should surely be such as to encourage specialization on lower-cost products in appropriate areas. Of course, agricultural prices have odd features in "capitalist" countries too, and so we ought at no time to assume that we have much to teach the Soviet Union in "rational" pricing in this sector of the economy.

However, higher prices for over-quota deliveries of various crops do raise a peculiar problem. Such prices existed before 1958, and they were abandoned because they rewarded the successful disproportionately and because the average price paid in a good year exceeded that paid in a bad one (i.e., the greater the abundance the higher the average price, since more is sold at the over-quota rate). These arguments are just as valid today.

Have the new prices finally eliminated the "exploitation" of Soviet agriculture for the benefit of the urban-industrial sectors of the economy? Before this question is answered, two other matters require consideration: peasant incomes and agricultural investments.

Peasant Income, Consumption, Private Plots

What has been happening to peasant pay in the last ten years or so? Systematic data are unpublished, and the scattered figures which exist may not be all on the same basis (the problem is one of valuing peasant income in kind; mostly this seems to be at retail price for statistical purposes). It is clear that the dip in incomes in 1959–60 was only temporary and was followed by a sharp upswing.

The "labor pay fund"—that is, the total amount paid out to kolkhoz peasants—rose from the low point of 1959–60 to 1965 by 88 percent. It is thus quite clear that a large rise had taken place before Khrushchev's fall. It was also Khrushchev who announced old-age pensions for kolkhozniks, jointly financed by kolkhozes and the state, though this system did not come into operation until after his political demise.

The rise in incomes has continued since. Payment is now predominantly in cash; whereas in 1965 a quarter was in kind, by the end of 1968 cash accounted for 92 percent.[15] It should be noted that increases in cash per man-day may or may not imply an equivalent increase in total earnings, depending upon the number of days worked. There is no guaranteed pay per week or month.

---

[15] But if the peasants have to buy bread grains at retail prices, they may still prefer payment in kind!

A change of great importance dates from July 1966. There was finally introduced a guaranteed minimum payment per job done, based in principle on rates applicable to sovkhozes. A trend toward guaranteed pay, and toward ending the unsatisfactory *trudodni* (work-day units) and the residuary nature of kolkhoznik pay, was clearly visible under Khrushchev. Indeed, recommendations were made to this effect, and by July 1966 about 50 percent of all kolkhozes already paid a fixed cash rate of some kind. Two key decisions were required to make a reality of a minimum based on sovkhoz rates (apart, of course, from higher prices and revenues in general). One was a formal decision to make payment of peasants a priority charge on revenue instead of the residual, which in effect meant abandoning the requirement that a given percentage of gross revenue be paid into the so-called indivisible fund (i.e., devoted to investments). The other was to allow farms to borrow from the bank to pay their members, which was not permitted until 1966.

Obviously, an assured income for work done is a great, if belated, step forward. The change was not by any means carried through smoothly. As late as January 1969 it was reported that 92.2 percent of the farms were paying guaranteed rates, so the practice was at this date still not universal, and the system of *trudodni* survived in some places, indeed being still predominant in Armenia and Azerbaijan. Furthermore, the actual rates varied widely between farms and regions, as the following figures demonstrate: in 1963 Estonia paid 146 percent of the all-union average to its kolkhoz peasants and Belorussia only 62 percent—that is, Estonia was 1.35 times higher (Belorussia was the lowest, the highest being Kirghizia and Turkmenia with 168 percent). In 1968—that is, two years after the "guaranteed pay" decree— Belorussia was still far behind. It can be calculated that Estonians received over 2.5 times what Belorussians did (i.e., the disparity had risen). Both republics had gained in absolute terms. But the Belorussian average must be far below sovkhoz rates of pay, these being similar in the two republics. This remains the case even though in some of the more prosperous areas many kolkhozes pay a good deal more than sovkhozes. Clearly, then, large numbers of kolkhozes cannot afford to pay sovkhoz rates. Credits are of little help to them: in 1968 only 1.5 percent of total peasant pay was financed by credits.

Nonetheless, though we must allow for local variations, it is clear that pay has risen greatly, and there has also been some reduction in differentials: thus in 1965–67 the lowest-paid group, the "horse and manual" field worker, gained an average 28 percent, the "mechanizers" 20 percent, milkmaids 14 percent, and chairmen 8 percent.

The pay increases since 1958 have greatly exceeded the increases in productivity, thereby adding significantly to labor cost. Thus "from 1958 to 1965 labor productivity rose by 35 percent, total pay of labor by 81 percent," while the Seven-Year Plan had envisaged 100 percent and "at least 40 percent," respectively. We will be discussing costs later. There was at the same period a substantial rise in pay of sovkhoz workers, though kolkhoz pay increased faster. It is clear, therefore, that incomes in rural areas showed a very sharp upswing; and this change has contributed significantly to inflationary pressures, since there has been hardly any rise in official retail prices, at least in theory. It has also meant a change in relative incomes of town and country.

It is true that kolkhoz peasant incomes are still well below the average earnings of workers, particularly if it is borne in mind that they are paid only for work done, not for slack periods. However, the total income of a kolkhoz peasant—and to a lesser extent also of a sovkhoz worker—includes the proceeds in cash and produce of his private plot and livestock. It is therefore necessary to turn to this and see what has happened to peasants' private enterprise since 1965. The figures for private livestock holdings present little change on balance, but it must be recalled that numbers had been falling in Khrushchev's last years and that after his fall various restrictions on livestock were eliminated. Consequently one might have expected something better. Apart from sales in the market, the private sector remains of vital importance as a source of food for the family. Even today the bulk of the peasant family's consumption of meat, milk, eggs, and potatoes comes from their private plot. According to the Soviet economist Suslov, who quoted family budget surveys, of the total income in cash and kind of kolkhoz families in 1964 the private plot provided 43.9 percent and the kolkhoz 43.3 percent. The rest presumably came from other activities (including work for the state).

There is no index of private incomes, so we can only note that total peasant consumption increased less rapidly than did their incomes for collective work. (The production of potatoes, vegetables, fruit, and other crops in private plots seems to have altered little.) Free-market prices were and are well above state prices, and have risen faster. In 1968 the former were 28 percent above 1960, though the official index for state retail prices of foodstuffs had risen by only 3 percent during the period.

What has been holding back the private sector? Two explanations suggest themselves. First, more time is required for collective work, leaving less for the plot; furthermore this work is now better paid, so that there is less incentive to work hard on one's allotment and to lose pay by taking time off to take goods to market. (We have no means of telling how much of this is a voluntary reaction to incentives, how much a consequence of tighter discipline.) Second, a general shortage of fodder has adversely affected supply for private livestock. No less a person than Shelest, First Secretary of the Ukraine, made this point, as well as a critic writing about Belorussia. Both urged that adequate supplies of fodder be provided.

It is interesting to note that the peasants' labor inputs on private plots went up after 1958. Yet numbers of private livestock fell somewhat in the years 1958–63. One explanation is that more time had to be devoted to procuring fodder. No doubt the percentage has fallen again since 1963, especially as collective work is now better paid, but I cannot find more recent figures. Suslov believes that labor on private plots produced roughly as much per head as collective labor (but of course it did so with far less capital).

The level of housing, culture, amenities, and conditions of work has often been deplorably low, and the authorities know this and have attempted to improve matters. If they do not, the migration of young and energetic villagers to town will continue. The restrictions on such movement—by the denial of passports—is resented, and is also circumvented. Ample evidence exists of unplanned drift to town, and many statements show consciousness of the need to attract and hold labor by improving conditions. A big drive has been launched to increase the range of services available. There is talk of regular hours and holidays with pay, though neither have yet become normal. At the 1965 plenum S. Pavlov spoke of a milkmaid who worked from morning to night without a day off for up to fifteen years, and incredibly some delegates found this a subject for humor (shouts of "how old is she?"). Even now regular shift work is not the rule. Bitter complaints about working conditions are common. The heaviest work is done by women. Few livestock farms have anything like adequate mechanical aids. Water has to be fetched in buckets, the cleaning of cowsheds and the milking are still mostly done by hand, and so on.

Much depends, as far as the peasant is concerned, on the good will of his brigadier, who may or may not allow him to borrow a horse for a trip, enter up correct particulars on the work sheet, or allocate fuel or hay. In fact, "the kolkhoznik does not always [!] have the feeling that he is the master in the kolkhoz."

There are many criticisms of existing incentive and wage structures, particularly in sovkhozes. They all agree on one point: payment is related not to the quality of work or to its net effectiveness but to quantity and plan fulfillment: "Rewards go to those who can get a modest plan adopted." Hence the arguments in favor of the *beznariadnoe zveno*. However, the system has yet to be altered.

The Soviet Union is, of course, far from alone in facing the problem of migration of village youth to town. The gap between rural and urban standards in the USSR is so wide that even the impressive relative increase in pay for collective workers has not slowed the rate of migration. Indeed, they can now more easily afford a rail ticket to the city (and perhaps even a bribe to the passport officer).

It may be said: But surely, relative to other industrial countries, the USSR has a large population on the land. Is not large-scale migration to town both desirable and expected? To this question there are two answers. First, given existing levels of mechanization there is frequently a labor shortage, which at peak periods requires the annual mobilization of millions of townsmen to get the harvest in. Second, much of the rural labor force consists of older and unskilled women who are of little use in industry and cannot operate modern agricultural equipment, while those who are skilled move into urban occupations in alarming numbers. Therefore, although the total agricultural labor force is declining only slowly, its composition inhibits technical progress and helps to explain low productivity.

This situation may be illustrated by quoting a report on a social survey of peasants in Siberia: "Migration has an extremely unfavorable effect on the quality of kolkhoz and sovkhoz labor. The proportion of young people who are the most intelligent and qualified is declining." Many "mechanizers" leave. "Rural youth have an extremely strong psychological urge to go to town." The only way to halt this process is "to improve housing, communications, water supply, cultural amenities, schooling, trade. . . ." One Soviet contributor to the discussion also said: "It is necessary to abolish all remaining civil-law distinctions between the rural and urban population, so as gradually to modify the negative attitude of youth toward agriculture and the village." Thus a passport, the *right* to travel, and the means to do so are among the necessary preconditions for youth to stay and work in agriculture.

Investments and Material Supplies

A full statistical study of these matters would occupy too much space. We will confine ourselves to a brief look at promise and fulfillment, and at the difficulties and achievements since Khrushchev's fall.

We have already noted that Brezhnev's investment plans were much above Khrushchev's promises, but that the latter had not been kept. Nor have Brezhnev's. Deliveries of equipment to agriculture fell far behind schedule. One reason, it is said, was "the international situation." In other words, heavy military spending has eaten into the agricultural investment allocations. To take one example in the machinery sector, deliveries of tractors to agriculture are expected to reach roughly 1,470,000 over the five years, whereas the plan for 1966–70 specified 1,790,000, and most other equipment is below plan to an even greater extent. Housing construction fell in absolute terms: in kolkhozes the figure was 26.8 million square meters in 1960, 18.3 in 1965, 20.3 in 1966, 18.6 in 1968—hardly an impressive beginning to the much-needed effort to transform the village.

Nonetheless, productive investments did go up. The 1968 total was 110 percent above 1961, 31 percent above 1965. Deliveries of tractors in 1970 are expected to be 312,000, compared to 239,500 in 1965 and 157,000 in 1960. The 1969 figure was 303,000.

There are various difficulties in getting building done in rural areas, and also in obtaining building materials for agricultural construction. Demands are frequently heard for the creation of some effective rural building organization. Widespread dissatisfaction also exists over the weakness of the link between farms and the agricultural machinery industry. The wrong equipment is often made, and the demands of the users are not taken into account. *Sel'khoztekhnika* is not doing this job properly, and a resolution on the subject was adopted by the October 1968 plenum of the Central Committee. Frustrated demand for capital goods is given as one reason for the practice, condemned by the party leadership, of distributing to peasant members much of the money which should be devoted to investment: it may be impossible to get the equipment and materials needed for the investment project.

Failure to fulfill plans has in fact led to considerable shortfalls and imbalances. Thus "in Poltava Oblast in 1968 the purchase requests [*zaiavki*] of kolkhozes and sovkhozes were met to the following extent: tractors 58.4 percent, grain combines 61 percent, silage combines 32 percent, tractor trailers 24.5 percent, truck trailers 10.8 percent, trucks 27.6 percent, five-unit plows 9.7 percent, milking machines ("A.D. 200") 18.4 percent, nitrogenous fertilizer 75.3 percent, potash 44.8 percent. . . . Approximately the same situation exists in other areas and throughout the country." These, be it noted, were items which the farms had the financial means to buy.

Soviet critics have had much to say concerning the continuing undercapitalization of agriculture, lack of electric power, and poor quality of much of the equipment, though of course investments and power supplies have greatly increased. In regard to total power (in tractors, electricity used, etc.), not only was the Soviet Union far behind the United States in 1960, but also she was *further* behind in 1967 (see Table 1).

TABLE 1
Comparison of Power Used for Agriculture in USSR and USA

	USSR		USA	
	1960	1967	1960	1966
Power per agricultural worker (h.p.)	5.4	8.8	39.0	77.8
Power per hectare (h.p.)	74	116	215.8	418.2

Source: I. Karliuk, "Tekhnicheskii progress i ukreplenie material'notekhnicheskoi bazy sel'skogo khoziaistva," *Voprosy ekonomiki*, 1969, No. 12, p. 62.

The same author points—as Brezhnev did—to the old age and obsolescence of many tractors and trucks in agriculture. Even most of the newly built cowsheds and pigsties lack equipment; of 1,020 cowsheds in the Kursk Oblast in 1967 only 46 were fully mechanized. Many of the available machines are inefficient or lack proper maintenance. Thus "at the beginning of 1969, 28 percent of all milking machines were out of action. In West Siberia and Altai only 15 percent of the milking machines work normally. . . . In some farms the milking apparatus goes wrong 60 to 100 times per month." Prices of machines used on livestock farms are exceedingly high, although they are "far from perfect, they are unreliable, many of them do not last long." It was pointed out at the October 1968 plenum that livestock-farm equipment is made in 150 enterprises of which only 30 are under the Ministry of Tractors and Agricultural Machinery. The rest are scattered among 13 other ministries, which means high-cost production and irresponsibility. The author documents increases in prices in recent years: the SL-44 sower, which used to be sold for 230 rubles, has been replaced by the SUL-48 sower, of similar quality but priced at 350 rubles. Tractor production and prices have been more satisfactory, but their utilization has become less efficient. Poor maintenance and repair and lack of skilled labor and supervision have led to a 25 percent increase in costs of tractor work, while tractor utilization per day declined by 20 percent in the period 1960–67. Their utilization is also adversely affected by shortages of plows, trailers, and other tractor-hauled equipment. These and other circumstances have reduced the effectiveness of investments.

Fertilizer production has gone ahead impressively, even if the extremely ambitious plans have not been fulfilled. There have been complaints about the quality, assortment, prices, packaging, and transporting of the fertilizer, but substantial progress has been made, and fertilizer is now available for an increasing range of crops. On the podzol soils of the north and west it is essential, along with liming, if tolerable yields are to be attained. Liming, since 1965, has been undertaken at government expense. Another urgent need in rural areas is roads. Progress is being made, but it will require many years before an adequate network can be built.

Production and Costs

Have yields risen? What has been the net effect of the policies described on production? Table 2 gives the official statistics of production and also the plan, which is available only as an annual average. It should be noted that the quinquennium 1961–65 includes two poor harvest years. Table 3 gives livestock numbers.

Before analyzing the figures, we shall briefly comment on their reliability. Suspicion is justified by the past record of agricultural statistics, not only in the bad old days of "biological yield" but also in Khrushchev's time. There were cases of statistical redefinition, such as the (temporary) inclusion of unripe corn as grain, and also of simulation under the pressure to fulfill impossible plans. There was also some sus-

TABLE 2
Soviet Agricultural Production, 1961–65 Annual Average, 1966–69, and 1966–70 Plan Annual Average

	1961-65 Annual Average	*1966*	*1967*	*1968*	*1969*	*1966-70 Plan Annual Average*
Gross agricultural output index (1960 = 100). . . .	105.0	122.0	124.0	128.0	124.0	130.0
Grain (million tons).	130.3	171.2	147.9	169.5	160.5	167.0
Grain yield (quintals per hectare)	10.2	13.7	12.1	13.9	n.a.*	n.a.
Potatoes (million tons). . .	81.6	87.9	95.5	102.2	91.7	100.0
Sugar beets (million tons) .	59.2	74.0	87.1	94.3	71.0	80.0
Sunflower seeds (million tons)	5.07	6.15	6.61	6.70	6.30	n.a.
Cotton (million tons). . . .	5.0	5.98	5.97	5.95	5.71	5.6–6.0
Meat (dead weight, million tons)	10.0†	10.7	11.5	11.6	11.6	11.0
Milk (million tons)	72.6†	76.0	79.9	82.3	81.6	78.0
Milk yield per cow (kgs.). .	1,987†	2,021	2,128	2,232	n.a.	n.a.
Eggs (billions)	29.1†	31.7	33.9	35.7	37.0	34.0
Wool (thousand tons). . . .	356.9†	371.0	395.0	415.0	390.0	n.a.

*Not available.
†1965 only.
Source: Soviet official statistics.

picion of a downward revision of figures relating to the past in order to make the present look better.

These things may still be happening. Grain harvest figures can be in terms of "bunker weight" or after winnowing and cleaning. The former appear in statistics, and are also the basis for piece-rate pay, and so everyone concerned is happy to use such figures, even though harm is done when the weight "includes dirt." But no evidence exists that such practices are more prevalent today than they were in 1965 or 1960, and so the relative figures should not be affected. Figures on livestock products used to be treated with great suspicion by Western critics, and I was once severely criticized for suggesting that we have no alternative but to use them. But by now there is general agreement that they

TABLE 3
Soviet Livestock Numbers, 1965–70
(million head on January 1)

	1965	*1966*	*1967*	*1968*	*1969*	*1970*
Cattle (including cows).	87.2	93.4	97.1	97.2	95.7	95.0
Cows	38.8	40.1	41.2	41.6	41.2	40.6
Pigs	52.8	59.6	58.0	50.9	49.0	56.1
Sheep and goats	130.7	135.3	141.0	144.0	146.1	136.3

Source: Soviet official statistics.

are not greatly inflated. They often show an unfavorable trend, and so it is very unlikely that they are doctored or more unreliable today than yesterday. In general, because so many of the products are used or consumed on the farm, agricultural statistics are always less reliable than those of other sectors, where a cross check can be made via sales (within agriculture, this can be done with cotton, for instance, but not with grain, milk, or potatoes). So a degree of skepticism would be quite proper.

This said, what do the figures tell us? First, there is marked progress in crop yields. The weather in 1969 was unfavorable, and so the results of that year in no way imply a change in the underlying general trend. Better incentives and more fertilizer, and less "campaigning" interference, would seem to be the explanation. Performance compares well with plan because it was a modest and feasible one, the first such plan in the history of Soviet agriculture.

Much less satisfactory is the livestock situation. Numbers are not rising; there are many complaints about shortage of fodder. True, Brezhnev was able to report a 35 percent increase in the use of grain for fodder since 1965, which has contributed to higher livestock productivity. However, hay supplies have gone up very little, and silage showed a marked decline, from 166.7 to 147.1 million tons, already by 1967. The inadequacies of mechanization in the livestock sector have already been amply discussed, and so has the fact that the livestock sector is the least profitable of any activities undertaken by kolkhozes and sovkhozes. There is also supposed to have been an epidemic of swine fever, though animal diseases, like train crashes, are not reported in the Soviet press. When it is considered that meat prices have been kept at unchanged levels since 1962, despite a sharp increase in demand and the necessity of a budgetary subsidy which reached no less than 5.3 billion rubles in 1968, then it should occasion no surprise to learn that there are long queues for meat, and also that free-market prices often rise to double the official price. Only political fears can explain the refusal of the government to raise the retail price of meat. The 1966–70 production plan for livestock was in fact so modest that its overfulfillment was, so to speak, planned.

Difficulties in food supplies are often due to causes outside agriculture: innumerable sources speak of lack of roads, specialized transport and storage space, insufficiency of packaging materials, shortage of refrigeration, and also lack of interest on the part of the distributive trades in handling perishables such as green vegetables and fruit, so that farms complain about being unable to dispose of their produce.

Have the achievements involved a disproportionate cost? It may well be so. Over the years 1960–68 total agricultural investments doubled, and mineral fertilizer deliveries more than trebled. Meanwhile labor inputs have fallen only slowly. In kolkhozes and sovkhozes the numbers engaged in collective and state agriculture (on an annual basis) were 27.9 million in 1950, 26.1 million in 1960, and 24.7 million in 1967.[16] The net effect has been a rise in gross agricultural output by 28 percent between 1960 and 1968, or 24 percent between 1960 and the less favorable 1969. The high prices of state procurements of meat still leave livestock farming relatively unprofitable because of the high labor cost involved. The prices paid for grain, especially for over-quota deliveries and in the higher-cost areas, are substantially above word-price levels at any reasonable exchange rate. No wonder the party leadership is anxious not only to increase production but to reduce costs substantially. Statistics do show a decline in labor inputs per unit of product, but this has been partly or wholly offset by the rise in pay in kolkhozes and sovkhozes. Statistical compendia are likely to quote figures of costs which assume unchanged incomes of peasants, but one Soviet source at least has computed kolkhoz costs using actual pay. The results show increases, from 1964 to 1968, ranging from 3 percent for grain and 6 percent for milk to 32 percent for potatoes and 53 percent for sunflower seeds; eggs and pork show reduced costs. On the average, according to the author, costs in 1958 were 11 percent higher than in 1964.

The size of the farms may be a source of diseconomies. Suslov wrote: "Whereas in a small unit the whole process could be observed by all the kolkhozniks . . . , in a big kolkhoz containing dozens of villages and several thousand hectares of land the sense of seeing the results of one's labor disappeared. The peasant can see what is happening in his own brigade, but the rest is unknown to him. But since his pay is depersonalized, . . . being determined by the work of all peasants and brigades in the given kolkhoz, he begins to lose interest also in the results of the work in his own brigade." Hence the case made out for smaller units of the *zveno* type.

Then the question arises: Has the exploitation of the peasantry ended? It is by no means easy to answer this question. Some Soviet writers can readily be quoted as saying that agricultural prices are still below their true "value," or that the net profits of kolkhozes ought to be higher than they in fact are. Thus it is argued that a margin over costs of 12–15 percent is essential to pay taxes, insurance, and interest on credits and social security, to which must be added depreciation and obsolescence, so that 15–20 percent is the minimum "profit" margin even if there is no net investment. This leads to the conclusion that, allowing for the necessary investments, the profit margin over costs should be 40–50 percent, and this under conditions in which kolkhoz peasants earn as much as sovkhoz workers. Prices paid to sovkhozes, when allowance is made for various budgetary grants, in fact exceed costs by this sum.

---

[16] It seems certain that on the average each devoted more hours to collective agriculture in 1967 than in 1960.

When the problem is viewed in this way, the 1965 price increases are still insufficient. In 1963, according to Suslov, the profit rate averaged only 8.3 percent for all kolkhozes, and this figure is confirmed by another source too; but there has been a sharp rise since then. All such calculations depend on the level of pay of kolkhozniks, real or assumed. So another way of looking at the problem is to see whether their pay has reached reasonable levels. In doing so one must bear in mind that rural incomes tend generally to be below urban ones in most countries, and also that part of peasant family incomes comes from private plots plus casual labor outside agriculture.

The average pay per day of kolkhozniks in 1964 was 74 percent of sovkhoz pay, with wide regional variations (for instance, 101 percent in Central Asia, 49 percent in the Volga-Viatka region). The source considers sovkhoz rates to be adequate approximations to the full "necessary reward" of kolkhoz labor. By 1969 kolkhoz pay must have averaged 90 percent of sovkhoz pay (of course earnings per *year* are much less, as are social benefits, but kolkhoz peasants devote more of their time to the private plot). The very large regional variations are much criticized by many Soviet analysts.

Still another way of looking at the question is by comparing farm selling prices with what Zaslavskaia called "net retail prices" (i.e., net of handling and transport costs). Average prices paid to kolkhozes were only 62 percent of net retail prices in 1964 and on the same basis must by now be around 70 to 75 percent, but the computation can only be indirect, for lack of published data, and it would all look quite different if comparison were made with free-market prices. Of course, kolkhozes can reasonably be expected to contribute a share to the state budget, and there is no very clear criterion of what the "proper" share should be. In another computation the same author calculated that in 1962–63 a full-time kolkhoz laborer contributed 674 rubles to the state budget on the average in a year, while a sovkhoz laborer only provided 120 rubles.[17] The figures today would be a good deal lower.

It seems reasonable to conclude that the scale of "exploitation" is not now significant, and that it is best measured by the extent (if any) to which rural labor is underpaid in relation to an incalculable free-labor-market rate, and perhaps also by the undersupply of goods and amenities in rural areas.

To obtain historical perspective, another dimension should be added. In the thirties the kolkhozes delivered grain to the government at nominal prices and sold industrial crops at better prices. The bulk of foodstuffs other than grain was produced by peasants and sold in the free market. Therefore the compulsory delivery quota was in a sense a tax in kind, and its relationship to costs did not matter (costs were not

---

[17] The "contribution" was by underpayment, and also via high profits of state enterprises using agricultural produce or supplying goods to farms.

even computed); no one expected peasants to live on their collective pay. Collective work was a kind of *barshchina**; most peasants lived on their private produce. The situation gradually changed, so that now a much higher proportion of peasant time is devoted to, and peasant income derived from, collective work. State procurements are the main source of marketed produce in nearly all categories. So prices, costs, and incentives in the collective and state sectors matter a great deal and are more directly relevant to the issue of "peasant exploitation" than they ever were in the thirties.

CONCLUSION

We have seen that the Soviet government is prepared to pay a very high price in terms of material and financial resources to improve and increase agricultural production, even though in almost every year the actual investments made were less than had been planned. There has been a marked improvement in crop production, and a spectacular increase in deliveries of mineral fertilizer. Peasant incomes for collective work have risen to a level that amounts to a genuine wage, instead of the derisory sums of the not-so-distant past. But lack of labor-saving equipment, excessive size of farms, irrational incentives, and loss of skilled and young labor have adversely affected efficiency and productivity, so that costs have been high. "With 5 percent of their total labor force the Americans produce more than we can with 30 percent of ours," said a Soviet university teacher at a lecture I attended. So, apart from shortages due to wrong prices or bad distribution, it remains true that Soviet agriculture is, compared to the West, the least efficient sector of the economy. The production gains of recent years have been achieved at high cost.

The future? The leadership well knows that massive investments will be necessary in farm equipment, roads, trucks, electric power, amenities, irrigation, drainage, and the distribution trades. Plans do provide for this, but progress will be necessarily slow and expensive. One wonders what could be achieved by harnessing peasant initiative, through the *zveno* and similar small joint enterprises (one critic has proposed giving the autonomous *zveno* the time-honored designation of artel). More autonomy in farm management, and a less irrational price system, would also cost little. However, in its present mood the leadership seems unwilling to launch major experiments. It knows that higher yields—"intensification"—are indispensable. The system is not necessarily inconsistent with increased efficiency. Estonia has done well in recent years, and great gains would follow if Estonian standards could be achieved in the northern and western areas of European Russia. We

---

* Editors' note: Corvée, i.e., fully or partly unpaid labor exacted by public authorities for building roads or other purposes.

must expect that present policies will continue, and therefore that higher inputs of capital and of fertilizer will provide a continued gradual improvement in food supplies. Meanwhile, there could well be outbursts of impatience among the citizens. Fifty-three years after the revolution, they can be forgiven for expecting the shops to have meat, vegetables, and flour available on demand. This is certainly not the case today, even in Moscow, and the situation in provincial towns may be a good deal worse.

10. RECENT DEVELOPMENTS IN SOVIET AGRICULTURE

Douglas B. Diamond and Constance B. Krueger

The Brezhnev agricultural program entered a new phase in the Ninth Five-Year Plan (1971–75). It seeks to expand agricultural output chiefly through larger supplies of farm equipment, agricultural chemicals, and construction materials, as well as land reclamation—rather than by higher prices and greater incentives to peasants. The main components of the new agricultural program are analyzed and evaluated in this selection by Douglas B. Diamond and Constance B. Krueger, economists in the Office of Economic Research of the Central Intelligence Agency. They consider the new agricultural targets ambitious, but they find evidence—in the implementation of the plan during its first years—of the regime's commitment to achieving them.

This selection is excerpted from pp. 316–25 of a longer article by the authors, "Recent Developments in Output and Productivity in Soviet Agriculture," in *Soviet Economic Prospects for the Seventies* (A Compendium of Papers Submitted to the Joint Economic Committee, 93rd Cong., 1st sess.) (Washington, D.C.: U.S. Government Printing Office, 1973), pp. 316–39. The derivation of their estimates of Soviet agricultural inputs and outputs, which often differ from the Soviet official figures (used by Nove in the preceding selection), is explained in detail in the original article.

I. INTRODUCTION

SINCE ASSUMING POWER in 1965, the Brezhnev regime has committed itself increasingly to a policy of raising consumer welfare, especially through improvements in the Soviet diet. The extent to which these commitments could be met has depended, until recently, on the regime's ability to stimulate farm production. While considerable progress was made in increasing farm output during 1966–70, agricultural production has stagnated since 1970. The lack of progress in Soviet agriculture

225

in 1971, followed by a decline in 1972, has brought agricultural production back to about the level of 1968.

A major part of the decline since 1970 can be attributed to less favorable growing conditions; the very favorable weather conditions of 1968 and 1970 have been replaced by normal (1971) or worse-than-normal conditions (1972). Other important reasons include the failure of the farm sector to improve its productivity performance in the use of resources.

Even before the production shortfall of 1972, however, it had become apparent that the rate of progress achieved by the farm sector was not keeping up with the demands stemming from new consumer programs. Although agricultural production in 1971 remained at the record level achieved in 1970, the USSR imported a record-high volume of farm products in fiscal year 1972 in an effort to maintain the forward momentum in improving the quality of the Soviet diet. The regime apparently is no longer willing to permit food consumption to follow the whims of Soviet weather but rather requires a steady increase in the availability of meat and other quality foods.

This paper reviews the production achieved by the Soviet farm sector and the resources provided under successive programs of the Brezhnev regime. Section II discusses trends in output and productivity in the 1960s.[1] In section III the implementation of the latest Brezhnev Program for 1971–75 is evaluated.

II. TRENDS IN OUTPUT AND PRODUCTIVITY, 1961–70

Soviet farm output grew more rapidly in the last half of the 1960s compared to the first half of the decade (see Table 1), despite a decline in the rate of increase of resources committed to the agricultural sector. Aggregate inputs in 1970 were 6.5 percent above 1965, one third of the rise slated under the Brezhnev Program for 1966–70[2] and even below the 9 percent growth posted for the period 1960–64.

More significant for the present leadership, output grew substantially faster than inputs during 1966–70, thus reversing the declining trend

---

[1] In an earlier paper for the Joint Economic Committee, one of the authors reported on trends in farm output and productivity for the period 1950–64. See Douglas B. Diamond, "Trends in Output, Inputs, and Factor Productivity in Soviet Agriculture," *New Directions in the Soviet Economy*. (Studies Prepared for the Subcommittee on Foreign Economic Policy, Joint Economic Committee, 89th Cong., 2d sess.) (Washington, D.C.: U.S. Goverment Printing Office, 1966), Part II-B, pp. 339–81. These series are revised and extended in the present article.

[2] The program for improving the state of Soviet agriculture—popularly termed the Brezhnev Program—following the political demise of Khrushchev in October 1964 was first announced at a Plenum of the CPSU in March 1965. The plan for additions to total inputs entailed a boost of 18.5 percent over the five years 1966–70, or 3.5 percent per year.

TABLE 1
Average Annual Rates of Growth of Soviet Net Agricultural Output, Selected Periods, 1951–72, and Plan 1971–75*

	Straight Annual	3-Year Moving Average†
1951–71	3.9	3.8
1951–60	4.4	4.9
1960–64	2.3	1.2
1961–65	2.8	2.8
1966–68	4.7	3.0
1966–70	4.7	3.4
1971	0.1	1.5
1972	−7.8	−5.3‡
1971–75 plan	3.6	4.5‡

*The base year for the calculations shown in each line is the year before the stated initial year of period; that is, the average annual rate of increase for 1951–60 is computed by relating production in 1960 to base year 1950.

†Average annual rates of growth were computed by relating the three year average for the terminal year (for example, output in 1960 as the average for 1959, 1960, and 1961) to a similar three year average for the base year (1950).

‡Output for the terminal year only over the three year average for the base year.

in the growth of productivity[3] registered during 1960–64. In part, the gain in productivity of 2 percent annually in 1966–70, compared with —0.5 percent in 1960–64, was attributable to more favorable weather at the end of the 1960s. The terminal year 1964 in the Khrushchevian era includes the impact of the disastrous years 1963 and 1965 for which there are no counterparts at the end of the decade.

Whatever the underlying causes of the relatively rapid productivity gain in 1966–70, the striking success in increasing farm output by nearly one fifth was achieved with the use of a level of resources far short of the original intention for the five-year period. The evidence would suggest that most of the shortfall in implementing the first Brezhnev Program came in the period 1967–69. The three years 1966–68 were favorable and output averaged nearly one fourth above the last three years of Khrushchev's regime, 1962–64, permitting moderate improvement in the quality of the consumer's diet, the replenishment of grain reserves, and the elimination of large net imports of farm products. Apparently as a result of these successes, there were major cutbacks in original plans for 1967–69 to allocate large additional resources to farms, particularly those that depended primarily on industrially produced goods. The decline in farm output in 1969, taken together with evidence of a marked increase in the population's dissatisfaction with the slow pace

[3] That is, growth of output not explained by inputs. These are comparative rates when output is centered on a three-year average. However, use of actual output in the base and terminal years in the two five-year comparisons would not change the overall finding.

of improvements in the diet, apparently persuaded the leadership that a step-up in resource flows to agriculture was required in 1970 and beyond.[4] In 1970, the last year of the first Brezhnev program, inputs increased by nearly 2.5 percent, or as much as the total aggregate increase had been for the period 1967–69. This increase in the resource base in 1970, coupled with generally favorable weather conditions for crops, boosted net farm output to a record level.

III.   PLAN 1971–75: BREZHNEV PROGRAM II AND ITS IMPLEMENTATION

In addition to the decision to step up markedly the flow of inputs in 1970, further evidence of the regime's concern over the lag in farm output came even before the results of the 1970 harvest were known. The second five-year program for improving the state of Soviet agriculture was first spelled out at a Plenum of the CPSU in July 1970, nearly a year before the balance of the overall economic plan was considered at the Twenty-Fourth Party Congress and at another Plenum in the spring of 1971. Again, as in the launching of the 1966–70 plan for agriculture, Secretary General Brezhnev acted as spokesman for the regime's second major program.[5]

At first glance, the farm output targets for 1971–75 appear only moderately ambitious. Net agricultural output would have to increase by about 3.5 percent per year above the 1970 level to achieve the official goal for the new plan period. However, when the impact of favorable weather on production in the base year 1970 is dampened by averaging output for three years (1969–71) the required average annual rate of growth would have to rise to 4.5 percent.

The estimated plan for additions to total inputs to farms entails a boost of 10 percent between 1970 and 1975, with marked emphasis on industrially produced inputs. As a result, capacity in selected branches of industry is to be expanded to provide the flow of producer durables, construction materials, agricultural chemicals, and other producer goods necessary to support the higher levels of direct investment in agriculture.

The highlights of the new plan are as follows:

> Investment directly into agriculture is scheduled to be nearly 129 billion rubles (about $172 billion) during 1971–75.[6] Meeting this goal will require agricultural investments to grow an average of 9.5 percent a year

---

[4] This increased dissatisfaction was focused in large part on meeting consumer demand for meat. Following impressive increases in per capita availabilities of meat in 1965–67, consumption levelled off in 1968 and 1969. Moreover, the continued rise in personal money incomes added to the already existing and substantial unsatisfied demand for meat.

[5] Because of his continuing close association with plans for agriculture, the 1971–75 plan will be referred to as Brezhnev Program II.

[6] The nominal value of the ruble is 0.75 rubles to U.S. $1. Conversion at this value gives a rough idea of the magnitude of economic quantities involved in the second Brezhnev program for Soviet agriculture.

and to rise as a share of all investments from 23.5 percent in 1970 to 27.5 percent in 1975.

Total investment in machinery and equipment (producer durables) for farms during 1971–75 is planned to be 35.5 billion rubles, a 54 percent increase over the value of such deliveries to farms in the last half of the 1960s.

About one fifth of total investment in agriculture is to be expended on land amelioration, mostly reclamation by irrigation and drainage. The boost in investment in land reclamation is to result in an expansion of about 30 percent in the stock of irrigated and drained land. In support of the reclamation effort, Soviet industry is to deliver new construction equipment into agriculture in an amount equal to nearly 90 percent of the total inventory of such equipment in the overall construction sector at the end of 1970.

In addition to a step-up in the flow of investment goods to agriculture, the flows of other types of industrially produced goods to farms are to be expanded. Overall deliveries of major types of producer goods used in current productive activity in agriculture are to rise at an average annual rate of 6.5 percent during 1971–75.[7] Especially noteworthy are a scheduled rise of two thirds in the use of fertilizer and a significant growth in use of plant protection materials (pesticides and herbicides). The required increase in production of these goods will necessitate further large investments in the chemical industry.

All of the 19.5 percent increase in output for the period 1971–75 is to come from the country's collective and state farms. Production from individual holdings which contributed 30 percent of total output in 1970 is implicitly slated to decline slowly in the 1971–75 period. As a result, if the initial plans for output in the private sector are carried out, the above measures for achieving a rapid advance in output in the socialized sector may be partially offset.

Although some parts are slightly behind schedule, important steps were taken in 1971 and 1972 to implement the 1971–75 plan for agriculture. Overall, total inputs increased at an average annual rate of 2 percent, slightly above the growth required to meet the 1975 goal. Hence, despite the surge in output in 1970—up 13.5 percent over 1969—followed by a repeat of the record level of output in 1971, the regime apparently remained firm in its resolve to sustain the resource commitments embraced in Brezhnev Program II.

Investment

Investment growth in 1971–72 averaged 11 percent—slightly above target and considerably above the rate achieved in 1966–70. As a result,

---

[7] The major types of producer goods included here are fertilizer, electric power, fuels and lubricants, current repair services, rubber products, industrially produced feeds, and lime.

the growth of the stock of fixed assets (buildings, machinery, and equipment) rose to the rate called for in the 1971–75 plan, and substantially above the preceding five years. The marked slowdown in growth of investment—especially the construction component—in 1972 compared to 1971 is thought to reflect the disrupting influence of the farm situation in 1972 rather than a shift in priority away from agriculture.[8]

Farm Machinery

Although deliveries of tractors and combines are somewhat behind schedule, shipments to farms of trucks and other types of agricultural machinery are at or above the original targets. The spurt in deliveries of trucks to farms in 1972—up 44 thousand over 1971—may, in part, reflect the special measures taken last year to cope with the bumper crop in the East and the drought-stricken areas in European Russia.[9]

Despite the impressive record in 1971–72 in sustaining high levels of deliveries of principal types of machinery to farms, the net growth in inventories has been declining. In 1971, parks of major types of machinery increased at a rate of 3 percent compared to an average annual rate of 4 percent in 1966–70 and 5 percent in 1961–65. If this tempo continues, the increase in total inventories of machinery in 1971–75 will be about 80 percent of that planned. The problem lies in the deficiencies in machine quality and durability which, taken together with poor maintenance and high rates of usage, result in very high retirement rates. For example, the discard rate for tractors in 1970 and 1971 averaged 12.5 percent, more than three times the rate of retirement from U.S. parks. Moreover, the recent Soviet rates of retirement for tractors and trucks are above the high levels of the 1960s. The Soviet press continues to be rife with complaints about the abysmal quality and unsuitability of machinery delivered to agriculture, about the shortage of spare parts, and about the lack of satisfactory facilities for repair and maintenance.

---

[8] The above-normal manpower and transportation requirements of the 1972 planting and harvest periods probably held down investment activity in rural areas. More construction workers than usual were detailed to support farm work, and the supply of construction materials and delivery of producer durables must have been interrupted by the round-up of trucks for agricultural work. The unusual demands leading to a major diversion of resources included a record-high spring sowing (due to a severe winterkill of fall sown crops) and an all-out effort to garner the record-high grain crop in the New Lands of Siberia and Kazakhstan, following the officially expressed anxiety over a harvest failure in European Russia.

[9] The share of total truck production delivered to farms rose from 25 percent in 1971 to 31 percent in 1972. In addition to the logistical problem of moving a record crop in the area east of the Urals before the onset of winter, the Soviets were required to carry out a massive transport effort in a 33 oblast area of European Russia affected by drought. The farms in the area, which includes more than one third of the livestock in the country, required either supplemental livestock feed supplies from other parts of the country to sustain herds or temporary transfer of livestock to areas outside of the drought zone.

Land Reclamation

In the USSR irrigation has long been an important means of increasing production of crops, particularly high-value crops such as cotton, fruits, and vegetables. Drainage,[10] a less expensive method of reclamation, has had considerably less emphasis during the course of the five-year plans. But both irrigation and drainage are now being brought to the fore because of lack of alternative opportunities for a major expansion of cropland.

During 1971–75, more than 6.5 million additional hectares are scheduled to be added to the stock of irrigated and drained land, compared with a slight decline of a half million hectares in 1966–70.[11] This is only about 3 percent of the total cultivated acreage (sown and fallowed) in 1970. But because of higher productivity per hectare, especially on the irrigated land, such an addition of reclaimed land would add the equivalent of about 10.5 million hectares to the present stock of tilled acreage.

While the step-up in annual gross additions of drained land in 1971–72 lagged somewhat behind the level required to meet the five-year plan goals, the cumulative increases for drained and irrigated land taken together were impressive—nearly two fifths of the overall target for 1971–75. However, accomplishment of the 1975 acreage targets for properly drained and irrigated land will not be easy. The USSR has had a poor record in maintaining drainage and irrigation systems in operating conditions. For example, in the past the covered and tiled drainage systems, which are scheduled to expand rapidly, and to account for more than half of total drained acreage in 1975, have been built with inferior tile that collapsed under the weight of heavy Soviet farm machinery. In irrigated areas about two fifths of the land is subject to salinization to some degree. Annual washings carried out in rotation to lower the salinity remain partially ineffective because of disrepaired and uncleaned collection and drainage networks.

As a result of these and other problems, the rate of retirement of reclaimed land from production has been high enough in the past to nullify the sizable annual gross additions. During 1966–70, for example, 5.5 million hectares of newly reclaimed land were not enough to offset the discarding of 6 million hectares because of low productivity. In order to meet the target for the net additions to the stock of reclaimed land by 1975, the rate of retirement for irrigated land will have to be reduced by more than one half and for drained land by three fourths.

Under Brezhnev Program II, irrigated and drained land is to provide nearly one third of the 32 million ton increase in grain output between

---

[10] The removal by artificial means of excess water from the soil to enhance crop production.

[11] Net additions.

the annual average output for 1966–70 and that planned for 1975. The use of irrigated land for growing grain is relatively inefficient under Soviet conditions—under the assumption of normal weather conditions. Given the risk of future sharp fluctuations in nonirrigated grain yields, the regime apparently feels that high-cost grain from irrigated acreage is preferable to relying on emergency imports.

Agricultural Chemicals

The availabilities of agricultural chemicals will be decisive factors both in the expansion of farm output and in achievement of improved stability. The new plan calls for a large expansion in the use of these chemicals—fertilizer and lime as soil additives, herbicides and pesticides as plant protection materials. Indeed Soviet planners expect that nearly two fifths of the gain in total gross farm output in 1971–75 will be attributable to the increased use of fertilizer alone.

Annual deliveries of fertilizer are to reach 75 million tons by 1975, nearly two thirds above the 1970 level. Of this amount, about 32 million tons of fertilizer are scheduled to be applied to grain in 1975, thereby raising the share of fertilizer allocated to grain crops from 36 percent in 1970 to 43 percent in 1975. Even if deliveries of fertilizer to agriculture fall short of the planned 75 million tons, the priority of grain crops may be maintained because of the anxiety of the regime over the grain supply.[12]

Periodic application of lime to neutralize acid soils is essential for efficient use of mineral fertilizers. The new plan calls for the liming of nearly 30 million hectares—an area equal to 14 percent of total Soviet sown acreage in 1970. This is significantly more than the 22.5 million hectares treated in the last half of the 1960s which was a major factor in rapidly raising grain yields in the "non-black soil zone" of European Russia. Indeed, a large part of the country's additional grain output in the latter years of the 1966–70 period in comparison to the first half of the decade was attributable to expanded use of fertilizer and lime in this area, where, because of the usually adequate moisture in the region, application of fertilizer on well-limed soil provides high and stable yields. In this area production of grain in 1969 and 1970 averaged 25.5 million tons, or more than 80 percent above the annual average level of output attained in 1961–65. As a result, this area, which accounted for only 13 percent of the country's total production in 1961–65, provided more than one third of the country's total increase in grain production

---

[12] There are indications that a similar anxiety over the lagging production of sugar beets in 1971–72 will lead to a temporary shift of fertilizer from cotton to sugar beets in 1973. Sugar beet production in the past two years has averaged 9.5 percent below the average for 1966–70. The shortfall in domestic output, coupled with a decline in available supplies from the Cuban crop, has led to Soviet hard currency outlays of nearly $300 million in 1971–72 for imports from third countries.

between the two time periods (that is, the annual average production in 1961–65 and 1969–70).

The soil additive programs for 1971–72 are generally on schedule. Nearly ten million tons (or one fifth) more fertilizer were delivered to farms in 1972 than in 1970, and an additional 10 million hectares of acid soil received a periodic application of lime.

On the other hand, the record in the first two years in providing farms with additional amounts of plant protection materials has not been impressive. While production of these materials in 1972 was 3 percent above 1970, net imports—a major source of supply for the farms— fell in both 1970 and 1971.

Although the 1973 plan for fertilizer calls for only a modest boost of 7.5 percent in production, recent and planned developments in adding new production capacity are a harbinger of high rates of growth in 1974 and 1975. Gross additions to new production capacity more than doubled in 1972—up to 7 million tons compared to 3 million tons in 1971—and are scheduled to rise to 9.5 million tons in 1973. In order to offset failures in the first two years, investment in 1973 in the fertilizer industry is to rise by a whopping 80 percent.

Policy toward Private Agricultural Activity

Private agriculture in the USSR today is almost exclusively composed of individual holdings—"victory garden" size up to 0.5 hectare—frequently combined with the ownership of one or two head of livestock and a small flock of poultry. Although the share of total farm output produced in the private sector has declined during the decade, the sector has provided nearly one third of production in recent years. The private sector has specialized in potatoes, of which it contributes about 65 percent of total output; other vegetables, 40 percent of total output; meat and milk, 35 percent of total output; and eggs, 50 percent of total output. Although long-run official policy toward private activity can be characterized as one of repression, in the past, campaigns to suppress private activity have alternated with periods of relaxation. An important element in the stagnation of overall agricultural growth in the latter years of the Khrushchev era was a small decline in output from the private sector between 1958 and 1964, reflecting a policy of official discouragement. Since 1964, policy under the Brezhnev regime has fluctuated between encouragement, indifference, and outright antagonism. Overall, however, policy during 1965–70 was tolerant enough to bring about a 10 percent increase in output originating from individual holdings, an important contributing factor to total farm output.

The original 1971–75 output goals imply a less lenient policy for the five-year period. By 1975, output from the private sector is to be nearly a tenth below 1970. Under such circumstances all of the burden for realizing the planned increase in overall net agricultural output will fall on the socialized sector; output from collective and state farms would have to increase at an average annual rate of about 6 percent in contrast with the 3.5 percent rate targeted for overall (socialized plus private) net production.

In 1971, output from individual holdings remained unchanged from 1970. While official figures have not yet been released for 1972, the effects of the drought impinged more on the private than the socialized sector.[13] As a result, output in the private sector may have declined by as much as 10 percent. However, since official policy toward private activity is tactically flexible when necessary, the sharp setback in output in 1972 in both the private and socialized sectors may be followed by an active policy of encouragement to the private sector in 1973 and 1974.

---

[13] In the drought-affected area of European Russia, individual holdings play a relatively more important role in total output than for the country as a whole. This distribution effect, taken together with a probable official policy of favoring the socialized sector in allocating the extremely limited feed supplies, led to a relatively larger reduction in private herds. Compared to a slight increase in livestock inventories in the socialized sector, individual livestock holdings decreased about 4 percent between the beginning and the end of 1972.

III

SOVIET ECONOMIC GROWTH

Although the Soviet economy has achieved a striking record of economic growth, it is fair to say that growth has now become an important problem for the economy. Growth rates have slowed down in the last 15 years, a changing economy and society have altered the direction of growth, and the sources of growth are likely to be different in the future.

Because of the increasing demand for high-quality consumption goods, planners find it more difficult to concentrate resources on the development of heavy industry for the output of producer goods. Population increases—and thus increments to the labor force—will be smaller. Much of the readily available supply of natural resources has already been exploited, and future resource development will be more costly. The large amount of fixed capital already in operation means that a greater proportion of capital accumulation must be used for replacement and a smaller share will be available for expansion. In the future, high rates of growth will require more emphasis on efficient use of existing resources and improved productivity. Investment in human capital, in high-efficiency energy sources such as natural gas, and in computers and other advanced technology will be of great importance.

Part III examines these and related issues. It includes a brief evaluation of Soviet statistics; an analysis of the sources of Soviet growth; studies of changing consumption patterns and the new place of the automobile; a group of papers dealing with criteria for investment allocation, technical progress, and computers; and a review of ecological problems related to growth.

11. A NOTE ON THE AVAILABILITY AND RELIABILITY OF SOVIET STATISTICS

Alec Nove

To what extent can we rely on Soviet statistics published in Soviet sources? To some extent we are in the position of the gambler who knew the roulette wheel was crooked but had to play it anyway: it was the only one in town. We are also hampered by the fact that statistics are often gathered for one purpose and used for another, with resultant difficulties in coverage, validity, and so forth. Finally, we are hampered by the natural wish of bureaucrats to make themselves look good by fudging their reports to statistical agencies of government.

Through all of the discussions of Soviet statistics three general conclusions emerge:

1. Soviet index numbers are tricky. They tend to inflate the levels of output and the growth they are designed to measure. Use them with care.

2. Figures on units of output are much more reliable. The Soviet Union does not keep a double set of books. Production statistics reported by Soviet sources are generally the ones used by the planners themselves and are usually as accurate as the statistical agencies can make them.

3. When the Soviet Government wants to conceal something, it doesn't publish false figures; it just refrains from publishing anything on the matter.

There are exceptions to these general rules, but you won't go far wrong by keeping these three points in mind. The following article presents an evaluation of Soviet statistics by an eminent British scholar, which gives the reasoning behind these conclusions.

Alec Nove is Professor of International Economic Studies at the University of Glasgow. His article is reprinted with permission from his book *The Soviet Economy: An Introduction* (2d rev. ed.; London: George Allen & Unwin Ltd., 1968; New York: Frederick A. Praeger, Inc., 1969), pp. 346–54. References to Russian-language publications have been omitted.

AVAILABILITY

A FEW YEARS AGO, it would have been easiest to make a quite short list of the few figures which were available. The fact that the contrary procedure is now the most convenient one is a measure of the "liberalization" achieved since the death of Stalin, or rather since 1956, when the systematic publication of economic statistics gradually began again after a long interval. However, there are still some conspicuous gaps, of which the following are the most important.

(a)   Output figures for some *industrial products* are missing, among them non-ferrous metals, ships, aircraft, many chemicals, some machines, as well as military weapons.

(b)   While more is now appearing about the breakdown of the *labor force,* including agriculture and the military services,[1] numbers in particular industries are not given in any detail.

(c)   While since 1964 we have had some average wage statistics, there is nothing about average pay in different industries or as between different categories of workers, and hardly anything at all about actual earnings of peasants.*

(d)   There is no information given on the composition of turnover tax revenue, and only a few actual rates of tax are published.

However, let us give credit where credit is due. Gone indeed is the day when one had to search for statistics in leaders' speeches and make do with percentages of an unknown base. The statistical compendia on the economy as a whole, on agriculture, on various republics and localities, on transport, and so forth, together with the reports on the 1959 census, do give us a sizeable stock of statistics to work on, despite the remaining gaps. One difficulty is that many of the figures given are ill-defined; there is an unfortunate lack of explanatory notes; though minor attempts are being made to remedy this, we badly need longer explanations, and a new edition of a handbook on economic statistics is much overdue.[2] The lack of clarity about definitions, and especially changes in definitions, is a constant danger; it affects budget data, and also a number of the output figures and indices.

CREDIBILITY: PHYSICAL OUTPUT FIGURES

Industry

Whatever the vagueness of definitions, the first question to ask is: are the figures true, or are they invented? Very few persons now believe

---

[1] Until it was decided to publish the numbers in the armed forces (1960), the number of peasants and the age and sex distribution of the population were unpublished, no doubt to prevent calculation by residual.

* Editors' note: Publication of such data began in 1968.

[2] There used to be such an explanatory handbook, but this was last published in 1948. Some notes do now appear at the back of the annual statistical volume.

that they are invented. The evidence against such a view is very strong. Despite captured documents,[3] despite the presence in the West of various Soviet officials who had defected, no evidence exists that the central Soviet statisticians invent figures to order, to produce propaganda effect. By this is meant that no issues orders to print a figure of 400 knowing that the correct one is 350. Further support for this view comes from the fact that, when certain figures were discreditable, they were on occasion simply suppressed; many years later, they were published and showed that there was a fall in production in the "suppressed" year. If it were possible simply to invent, then such behavior would be pointless. Of course, we must note that selective suppression is a means of distorting a statistical table, but it is not invention. Not to tell the whole truth is not the same as telling a lie. Therefore we can legitimately conclude that when, for example, the Soviet authorities announce that 60 million tons of steel or 300 million pairs of shoes have been produced in a given year, this accords with the records of the central statistical office in Moscow.[4] However, there are several qualifications to be made. One of these relates, not for the last time, to ambiguities of definition. Footwear sometimes includes only leather footwear, sometimes all footwear; the definition of leather footwear can and does alter; handicraft production can be omitted from the base-year without this being stated. Furthermore, most commodities for which statistics are published are not homogeneous, are in reality many different kinds of goods aggregated under a single head for statistical convenience. The methodology of aggregation is often unspecified. Of course, this is often true of similar statistics in all countries. But the point is that rewards for growth are so important in Soviet industry that the definitional changes, and the adjustment to definitions at local level, can aim deliberately at whatever result looks best from the standpoint of statistical publicity. This point is also relevant to the reliability of aggregate indices, and we shall return to it.

The figures may correctly reflect the data available in Moscow, yet this data could be wrong by reason of statistical "padding" by the reporting agencies, especially the enterprises. They are interested in claiming plan fulfillment, and this could lead them to exaggerate. Scattered reports of measures against directors who indulge in such practices confirm that such dangers exist, but measures are taken to minimize them. The close link between production and disposals (*sbyt*) puts a limit on the amount of likely cheating; to report nonexistent production which one would be called upon to deliver is asking for trouble. There are also some tempta-

---

[3] Especially the *1941 Plan*, published in America by the American Council of Learned Societies, after it had been taken from the Germans.

[4] This is also the broad conclusion of Gregory Grossman in his searching examination of *Soviet Statistics of Physical Output of Industrial Commodities* (Princeton: Princeton University Press, 1960).

tions to conceal output in order to keep extra stocks in hand or to cover up pilfering or some semilegal deal. Defective goods, on the other hand, seem frequently to be foisted on customers in the guise of standard products, the quality inspectors being overruled. On balance, one should expect some exaggeration in reporting, and no doubt the possibilities of getting away with it vary in different sectors and at different periods. Unless it can be shown that the *extent* of exaggeration changes, the rate of growth remains unaffected, for obvious reasons; this is the "law of equal cheating," which the author of these lines "invented" in 1956.[5] There seems no evidence one way or the other, in industry at least, to suggest that the rate of growth since, say, 1937 or 1950 has been affected by falsification from below.[6] However, it is maneuvering within the system of success indicators—without actually cheating—which seems much the most serious source of distortion.

Clearly then, care is needed in interpreting the various figures; exaggeration is possible. But an excess of scepticism can lead to unfortunate results. Thus a certain American commentator noticed that cotton and wool cloth output figures were below the previous year in physical terms while the official statistical report claimed an increase, and jumped to the conclusion that this was evidence of cheating. It was not; there had been a shift of statistical reporting from linear meters to square meters, the object of which was in fact to stop cheating by those who sought to fulfill plans by making cloth narrower. This illustrates the danger of using the "cheating" hypothesis. Far better is it to assume that the figures represent some aspect of reality, and proceed, on that assumption, to examine with care the coverage and definition of the figures cited.

Agriculture

For many years, until 1953, crop data were published in terms of "biological yield," for reasons which cannot be gone into here.[7] It is very much to the credit of N. Jasny to have been the first to have documented and calculated with great ingenuity and surprising accuracy the extent of the consequent exaggeration.[8] This was due partly to the nature of the "biological" statistics, which purported to represent the on-the-root crop, and were therefore gross of the considerable harvest losses, and partly to the tendency of the inspectors to exaggerate the

---

[5] In *Lloyd's Bank Review*, No. 40 (April 1956), p. 3.

[6] This is also the conclusion of Grossman, *Soviet Statistics of Physical Output of Industrial Commodities*, p. 133.

[7] See A. Nove, "Some Problems in Agricultural Statistics," *Soviet Studies*, Vol. VII, No. 3 (January 1956), pp. 248–68.

[8] See his *Socialized Agriculture in the USSR* (Stanford, Calif.: Stanford University Press, 1949), and other works.

on-the-root crop estimates, since certain delivery obligations of *kolkhozy* (payment to the MTS)* were dependent upon them. In 1952, the grain harvest was said to have been 130 million tons. This has officially been revised downwards to 92 million tons, an exaggeration greater than many of the fiercest Western critics thought possible.

Biological yield figures were dropped in 1953, and for several years no physical output data were published at all. Then they reappeared, and are now available in abundance, for every major farm product, down even to non-cow milk and non-sheep wool. However, there are several reasons for supposing that the "law of equal cheating" may fail to operate in agriculture. First, the large volume of unsold products makes it harder to keep track of reality. Second, a series of agricultural campaigns (grain, maize, meat, milk, and so on) have placed great pressures upon local officialdom, and we have Khrushchev's own word for it, at the January 1961 plenum of the Central Committee, that it drove them into various kinds of simulation and exaggerated reporting (including the purchase of butter in the shops and its re-delivery to the state as new produce). Third, the much better prices now paid for produce probably led to a discouragement of various forms of evasion by which production remained unreported.[9] Finally, the very large proportion of meat and milk originating in the private sector is very inadequately counted, through a sample survey, and seems to be unreliable and possibly overstated. For all these reasons, there are grounds for supposing that both the absolute level of and the rate of increase in the output of some farm products are overstated, though we cannot tell by how much.

It is also noteworthy that the definition of meat includes offal, lard, rabbits, poultry, and so is wider than that usually adopted in the West. Maize figures included the grain equivalent of ensilaged cobs in the period 1955–64, but this has been abandoned. American analysts have claimed that milk sucked by calves is included in the Soviet milk statistics, but this has been denied.[10]

Foreign Trade

Very full data are published, but with some irritating omissions and one yawning gap in the figures. Two items which did appear before

---

* Editors' note: The kolkhozy (collective farms) made payments in kind to the MTS (machine tractor stations) for services performed.

[9] An interesting parallel may be found in Great Britain, where an increase in the official buying price for eggs shortly after World War II led to a spectacular rise in the *reported* number of eggs laid.

[10] See *Comparisons of the United States and Soviet Economies,* Papers Submitted by Panelists Appearing before the Subcommittee on Economic Statistics, Joint Economic Committee, 86th Cong., 1st sess. (Washington, D.C.: U.S. Government Printing Office, 1959), p. 236.

World War II are not there. These are, using the trade classification numbers which are entered in the prewar figures and which do not now appear at all:

> 28 . . . . "Objects of gold and precious stones"
> 31 . . . . "Pyrotechnical materials"

Does this mean that these items are no longer traded in, or rather that exports of arms and of some gold are kept out of statistical sight?

The gap mentioned above has become apparent since the USSR has divided its current trade statistics into three country categories: socialist, capitalist-developed, and capitalist-underdeveloped. The first two present no problems at all: the figures for the obvious countries add up exactly to the import and export totals. The figures for the "underdeveloped" do not, as the following figures (in millions of rubles) show:

	1962		1966	
	Import	Export	Import	Export
Total "underdeveloped capitalist countries". . . .	525.9	889.5	783.5	1090.6
Total of all countries given	522.8	484.4	779.7	758.3
Difference	3.1	405.1	3.8	332.3

The difference for imports is consistent with the fact that some minor trading partners are omitted from the returns. The export figures are clearly incredible. Obviously, some sales of something to someone have been statistically "dumped" into this category. No explanation has been forthcoming. But logically this entitles one to query the other figures, too, in which these not inconsiderable sums ought (somewhere) to belong.

INDICES: ARE THEY CREDIBLE?

According to the official statistics, gross industrial output rose almost twenty-one times between 1928 and 1955. The highest Western estimate, by F. Seton, allows for a twelve-fold rise. The lowest, by W. Nutter, supports a much lower figure, a five-and-a-half-fold increase. There are some others in between. There is not the space here to comment in detail on the many Western attempts to reconstruct an index of industrial production based on Soviet physical output series. The point is that all are unanimous in completely rejecting the official index, even while at odds with each other about the "correct" figure. My own view tends to favor the Seton index, because the much lower figures of Nutter and some other analysts seem to me inconsistent that what is known and accepted about Soviet fuel utilization and freight transportation. However, this still leaves the official index way up above the realms of possiblity.

It is not that this index is deliberately "cooked." But all indices are conventional aggregations, necessarily lacking in accuracy. So much depends on price weights and on the treatment of new products, especially where, as in the machinery sector, these are extremely numerous. Anyone who wishes to make any such calculations should take an awful warning from A. Gerschenkron's calculations, in which he showed that, from 1899 to 1939, American production of machinery increased more than fifteen-fold with 1899 price weights, but less than doubled with 1939 price weights, and he emphasized the enormous difficulties due to changes in type and design. What is "truth" when such divergences are possible?[11] This is why the care and refinements of some attempts to aggregate all available physical output data for the USSR seem to me to lead to such uncertain results, which would remain uncertain even if there were none of the sizeable statistical gaps in the output series.

The official series suffers from the following defects:

(1) Until 1950, the weights used were those of 1926–27. Apart from giving "preindustrialization" weights to the fastest growing sectors of industry, the introduction of new products gave an opportunity (for directors) to maneuver so as to adopt for them high "1926–27" prices. Despite occasional efforts to check this practice, the big rise in costs in the thirties meant that the prices at which new products were introduced into the index were higher than they would have cost in 1926–27. There was then a tendency to concentrate on the production of items bearing high "1926–27" prices, even at the cost of underfulfilling plans for the less highly valued items, because plan fulfillment was measured in 1926–27 prices. All this led to a creeping inflation of the index, made easier by the fact that it was genuinely difficult to determine what is a new product and what it would have cost to produce in 1926–27.[12]

(2) It is a "gross" index. Therefore, it is affected by vertical disintegration.*

Several Soviet writers have claimed that the behavior of the authorities is affected by the knowledge that by dividing up production processes between enterprises they can artificially increase the growth rate, and

---

[11] *A Dollar Index of Soviet Machinery Output* (Santa Monica, Calif.: Rand Corporation, 1951).

[12] See A. Nove, "1926–27 and All That," *Soviet Studies,* Vol. IX, No. 2 (October 1957), pp. 117–30. Soviet journals have denied these exaggerations, but contemporary evidence, cited in the above-named article, is against them.

* Editors' note: The Soviet index is calculated by adding up the total output of all industrial enterprises. Therefore, if an enterprise is broken up into two enterprises, one producing component parts and the other assembling the final product, the index of production will show an increase even though output of the finished product may not have changed at all.

thereby inflate the output of intermediate goods in relation to the final product.

(3)   While since 1950 the index is no longer based on 1926–27 prices (it was calculated first in 1952 and then in 1955 prices), the growth rates prior to 1950 were simply chained on to the new index and were not recalculated; or, if they were, the results have not been published. Much remains unclear about how the index is compiled. For instance, suppose that machinery output is expressed in 1955 prices; the problem of valuing new models remains, and, since in all countries such valuations are somewhat artificial, this makes possible the systematic selection of the highest of a range of possible figures, which can lead to distortion. It is only right to add that all analysts agree that the post 1950 indices are markedly less unreliable than those for earlier years. However, whatever the price base and whatever the regulations, the directors and local officials tend so to choose between possible alternatives as to be able to report a large increase in output. Because of the unavoidable imprecision of the regulations and of the definitions, the index can be affected by such choices in ways which are unlikely to arise in the West (where there is also a degree of imprecision and of arbitrary comparison), because increases in production as such are not vital "success indicators" in a Western firm.

With so much room for more or less legitimate maneuver, Soviet statisticians can select the base and the weights which help them to show very large increases and omit to publish calculations which reflect less credit on the system. For instance, base-year weights give a larger increase in output than end-year weights, so, in discussing industrial production indices, one Soviet statistician went so far as to proclaim that end-year weights were contrary to science, a remarkable doctrine indeed. Yet, when Soviet statisticians calculate a cost of living index, they are careful to use end-year weights, which minimize the increase in prices and so represent real wages in a more favorable light.

NATIONAL INCOME

The official index is at all times to be treated with a degree of suspicion. The official claim to a seventeen-fold increase in the period 1913–55, for instance, is utterly incredible. Thus it seems very widely agreed, by Soviet economists among others, that the national income of the Russian empire in 1913 was approximately a fifth of that of the United States. If the official claim were even remotely correct, the Soviet national income would now be well ahead of that of the United States, which, even allowing for the familiar vagaries of index numbers, just is not acceptable. Then it is decidedly odd that the national income can increase by seventeen-fold when one of its principal components, agriculture, showed a rise (in gross output) of only 70 percent. The computational methods are not properly explained. There seems to have been a substantial overstatement of the growth of the net product of trade and construction, at least during the period of "1926–27" prices.[13] But even in more recent years strange things happen to national income data. Thus an increase of 5 percent in 1964, given by several reliable Soviet sources, including Kosygin, was suddenly transformed into an increase of 7 percent in the statistical report published in *Pravda* on January 30, 1965, and then coverted into an increase of well over 9 percent in the statistical handbook for 1964, without (so far) a word of explanation. One can but show reserve in using official claims, and seek explanations where possible to clear up doubtful points.

SOME OTHER ITEMS

Housing data (in square meters) may be given in *living* space (excluding kitchens, corridors, etc,) or in *total* space (*obshchaya ploshchyad'*). The former is roughly two thirds of the latter, and the unwary are sometimes confused between them.

Real wage and other such figures are sometimes given by reference to the year 1940, or to some early post-war year. It should be noted that these were not good years for the consumer, and that a fairer picture of progress achieved requires a calculation based on some better year, say 1937 or 1928. This is never done by the official statisticians. It is important to distinguish data on real wages, which, allowing for the chosen base year, check well against other figures, from vague and barely credible claims about "real income per head"; these include estimates of the value of social services and such indirect "income" as the length of vacations with pay, and the methods used are never explained.

CONCLUSION

Despite some justifiable scepticism about certain Soviet data, it should be clearly stated that the published physical output series and many other figures must be taken seriously, that they generally represent an expression (though sometimes an ambiguous or distorted expression) of reality. Much greater doubt attaches to some of the index number series, which are in some instances just not credible. Yet these comments are by no means intended to deny that the Soviet system has achieved rapid growth. Undoubtedly it has, though not at the tremendous pace which the official indices allege. Its achievements have, indeed, been such that it is surely about time that some of the wilder claims were quietly buried.

---

[13] See A. Nove, "1926–27 and All That," already cited.

12. ANALYSIS OF THE SOVIET GROWTH MODEL

Stanley H. Cohn

What are the sources of rapid economic growth in the USSR? How does Soviet growth compare with economic growth in other advanced nations? These basic questions are answered in the following selection. Cohn examines the inputs into the Soviet economy since 1928, shows how they were directed into growth-producing uses, and points out which sectors of the Soviet economy tended to lag behind. Comparisons with other economies at comparable stages of their development reveal both Soviet accomplishments and Soviet deficiencies.

This selection is revised and updated from Cohn's *Economic Development in the Soviet Union* (Lexington, Mass.: D.C. Heath and Company, 1970), pp. 57–85. Reprinted by permission. Stanley H. Cohn is Professor of Economics at the State University of New York at Binghamton.

THE RECORD

Inputs and Efficiency—The Production Function

OUR TECHNIQUE will be to examine the Soviet growth trend in terms of the economys' potential, i.e., the sum total of productive resources available for economic utilization. Since the Soviet system has been under chronic overstrain, the question of inadequate demand is hypothetical. The critical question has been the regime's ability to affect the supply of productive inputs; that is, the growth of inputs has determined the growth of output.

In the technical language of economists, the relationship between factor inputs and gross national product (GNP) is termed the production function.[1] Since it is not feasible to measure some of the more intangible

---

[1] For those who have some background in economic theory, the production function used in my estimates is the conventional Cobb-Douglas function with the two inputs weighted according to their income shares as calculated by the author, plus

inputs, such as management, or to obtain unambiguous data on others such as technology or scale of output, the explicit inputs are limited to the two most important—labor and physical capital. When data is available, education (human capital), land, and livestock may be included. Since not all inputs are included in empirical studies, the trend in GNP will always be larger than the trend in the inputs measured. If only one input is used, the difference will, of course, be even larger. The difference between the growth of inputs and the growth of GNP is termed growth in *productivity*, i.e., in the output per unit of a specific input or combination of inputs.

Productivity

The most common productivity measures are those for capital and labor (Table 1).[2] Productivity measures are often used as indicators of efficiency in the use of resources. The more rapid the rate of increase in labor productivity, the more efficient is the economy in its use of a limited supply of manpower. In our analysis of the Soviet growth record, we will distinguish between the system's success in infusing productive resources and in efficiently utilizing those resources. To provide perspective, the record of the USSR will be contrasted with that of other leading industrial powers at similar stages of development.

Table 1 provides the key to our understanding about trends in factor productivity or economic efficiency in the USSR since 1928. For pertinent periods since 1928, average annual rates of change have been computed for GNP in the aggregate and for GNP in terms of output per labor unit and per capital unit. Not shown in the table are rates of changes in employment and in capital stock. They may be found in Table 8. The productivity estimates are the quotients of average annual rates of change in aggregate GNP (expressed as index numbers) divided by the same rates of increase or decrease in employment and capital stock obtained from Table 8. The trends in GNP per employed person have

---

trends in unmeasured inputs.

$$P = L^{.7}K^{.3}Z$$

where P = trend in GNP,
   L = flow of employment (man-hours) raised to its power of .7,
   K = flow of physical capital raised to its power of .3,
   Z = flow of unmeasured factors.

The coefficients represent the marginal productivities of the two inputs and in a two-factor model add up to one, since they are assumed to exhaust the product. In the symbols used above, labor productivity = P/L and capital productivity = P/K.

For derivation of coefficients see my study, *Derivation of 1959 Value-added Weights for Originating Sectors of Soviet Gross National Product* (TP-210) (McLean, Va.: Research Analysis Corporation, 1966), p. 21.

[2] The difference between the two main magnitudes measures our degree of ignorance as to other inputs, particularly technology, which influence the production function. However, the concept of productivity is widely used as an expedient explanation of these unmeasured influences.

TABLE 1
Average Annual Growth Rates of Soviet Gross National Product for Selected Periods
(in percent)

Period	Gross National Product		
	Aggregate	Per Employed Person*	Per Capital Unit
1928–1937†.	4.8–11.9	1.8–8.0	–0.7–+1.0
1937–1940	3.6	–0.4	5.8
1940–1950‡.	1.8–2.2	1.3–2.4	0
1950–1955	6.9	4.9	–2.6
1955–1960	6.0	6.3	–3.5
1960–1965	5.0	2.4	–3.3
1965–1972	5.1	3.3	–1.6

*Adjusted to account for less than full-time employment and changes in the length of the work year.
†Lower limit based on valuation of ruble factor cost in 1937 prices; upper limit on valuation in 1928 prices.
‡Lower limit based on valuation of ruble factor cost in 1950 prices; upper limit on valuation in 1937 prices.

been adjusted to represent the full time annual equivalent of persons employed corrected for changes in man-hours of annual employment.

A minus sign does not denote negative productivity, but declining marginal productivity. For most of the periods since 1928, additional units of capital have not meant a decline in GNP, but a reduced increment to GNP. More frequently the measure favored by economists is the inverse of the one shown in the right-hand column of Table 1 and measures the amount of capital required to obtain an additional unit of GNP. This ratio is termed the incremental capital-output ratio. The negative trends in the right-hand column indicate that the capital-output ratio has been rising almost continuously since 1928.

Comparative Growth Performance

By any international standard, the aggregate growth record of the USSR since 1928 is outstanding, although at similar or lower per capita levels the United States approached the lower 1928–1937 Soviet limit in 1870–1890[3] and Japan equalled it in 1890–1900 and surpassed it between 1920 and 1930.[4] In the postwar years the Soviet growth spurt in the early and middle fifties was high, but not unique, as more developed economies, such as West Germany, almost matched it. These comparisons are shown in Table 2. Since 1958 the USSR growth rate has

---

[3] Angus Maddison, *Economic Growth in the West* (New York: Twentieth Century Fund, 1964), pp. 201–2.

[4] Michael C. Kaser, "Education and Economic Progress," in *The Economics of Education,* ed. E. A. G. Robinson and J. E. Vaizey (London: Macmillan; New York: St. Martin's Press, 1966), p. 169.

TABLE 2
Comparative Trends in GNP, Employment, and Productivity
(average annual rates in percent)

Country	1950–58			1958–65			1965–70*		
	GNP	Employment	Productivity	GNP	Employment	Productivity	GNP	Employment	Productivity
USSR.	7.1	1.7	5.3	5.3	1.7	3.5	5.1	1.8	3.3
France	4.4	0.4	3.9	5.4	0.2	5.0	5.8	0.9	4.8
Germany.	7.6	2.4	5.1	5.8	1.1	4.6	4.6	0.1	4.5
Italy	5.6	1.6	3.9	6.1	-0.9	6.5	5.7	-0.3	6.0
United Kingdom	2.4	0.4	2.0	3.9	0.8	2.9	2.1	-0.5	2.7
Japan.	6.1	2.1	3.8	12.0	1.4	9.2	12.0	1.5	10.4
United States	2.9	1.0	1.9	4.4	2.0	2.6	3.2	2.0	1.1

*1965–72 for USSR.

only been average among nations with relatively high levels of per capita GNP. The Japanese record has been much superior. The postwar growth position of the USSR testifies not only to the inability of the system to maintain growth superiority but also to the success of the market economies in maintaining high levels of employment and demand.

When the comparative basis for growth performance is cast in productivity terms relating GNP to some factor input or combination of inputs, the Soviet record is less noteworthy. As to its efficiency in utilization of the most important input, manpower, Soviet advances in GNP per man-hour in the first two five-year plans were exceeded at the lower limit by all of the major continental European economies and the United States in pertinent decades of the 19th century, as shown in Table 3.

TABLE 3
Comparative Historical Trends in Growth of
GNP per Man-Hour
(annual average rates in percent)

Country	Period	Rate
USSR.	1928–37	1.8–8.0
	1937–40	–0.4
France	1880–90	2.5
	1890–1900	2.2
Germany.	1871–80	2.5
	1880–90	2.4
	1890–1900	1.9
United Kingdom	1880–90	3.8
	1890–1900	1.2
United States	1871–90	2.7
	1890–1900	2.2
Italy	1900–13	2.6

In the early postwar years through the mid-fifties, the Soviet record of growth of man-hour labor productivity was the highest of any of the major powers, but since 1958 it has fallen behind Japan and the major continental economies (Table 2).

In its utilization of fixed capital the Soviet system has been glaringly inefficient, especially in the postwar years. The trend in marginal capital productivity (additions to GNP per unit of capital investment) has been steadily falling (Table 1). In perhaps more familiar language, the marginal capital-output ratio has been rising continually. Historical estimates for the United States[5] and postwar estimates for Western Europe[6]

---

[5] Simon Kuznets, *Capital in the American Economy* (Princeton, N.J.: Princeton University Press, 1961), p. 80, and John Kendrick, *Productivity Trends in the United States* (Princeton, N.J.: Princeton University Press, 1961), p. 167.

[6] Edward Denison, *Why Growth Rates Differ* (Washington, D.C.: Brookings Institution, 1967), pp. 189–95, and United Nations Economic Commission for Europe, *Incomes in Postwar Europe* (Geneva: 1967), chap. 3, p. 2.

indicate that such a persistent negative trend is probably unique. One would intuitively expect that in an economy like the Soviet, with its extensive technological borrowing activities and the presence of a large corps of trained engineers, scientists, and managers, the capital-output ratio would decline, or at least remain relatively constant. Since new capital would be more productive than older capital, the rise in the capital-output ratio would be offset. The postwar experience of Western Europe and Japan, where unlike the USSR capital-output ratios have tended to remain low and below historic trends, supports this hypothesis.[7]

It would seem from these two tests that efficiency in resource use has not been a strength of the Soviet system. Rather the key to Soviet success lay in the ability of the system to infuse vast inputs into the production process. A comprehensive test is to expand the production function described at the beginning of this section to include two additional inputs, farm land and productive livestock. In this way the unexplained residual factors in growth are reduced. In Table 4 the historical experi-

TABLE 4
Comparative Growth Contributions of Factor Inputs* and Combined Factor Productivity
(annual average rates in percent)

USSR			United States		
Period	*Inputs*	*Productivity*	*Period*	*Inputs*	*Productivity*
1928–37	3.7	1.0–7.9	1869–78 to		
1937–40	3.8	−0.2	1899–1908	3.0	1.5
1940–50	0.6	1.2–1.6	1899–1908 to		
1950–60	3.1	2.9	1929	1.5	1.8
1960–65	4.3	0.7	1929–48	0.4	2.2
1965–72	3.3	1.8	1950–57	1.2	2.4
			1957–63	0.8	2.4

*Weighted inputs for man-hours, fixed capital, farm land, and productive livestock. Productivity = index of GNP ÷ index of inputs.

ence of the USSR is compared with that of the United States, from 1928 to the present for the USSR and since 1869 for the United States. The historical comparison is divided into pertinent developmental periods for each country.

For a comparison of postwar non-residential, fixed capital-output ratios, see Stanley Cohn, "Soviet Growth Retardation," in *New Directions in the Soviet Economy* (Studies Prepared for the Subcommittee on Foreign Economic Policy, Joint Economic Committee, 89th Cong., 2d sess.) (Washington, D.C.: U.S. Government Printing Office, 1966), Part II-A, p. 120. If historical ratios of investment to output, as computed by Simon Kuznets, are compared with my postwar ratios, those for Germany and Italy prove to have been at historic lows after World War II and those for Japan at the lowest level in this century.

For the USSR the infusion of productive inputs has been more important than their utilization in explaining growth. By contrast, for the United States, except for the last two decades of the 19th century, the utilization of inputs has played a greater role. Since the Soviet productivity growth rate is no higher than that of the United States for most of the years covered, the superior Soviet growth margin is almost entirely explained by higher trends in the employment of productive factors. Other things being equal, the usual developmental pattern is for the lesser developed country to show higher productivity growth rates because of its advantage in assimilating the accumulated technology of older industrial economies.

The extent to which Soviet growth has mainly been a result of the regime's ability to increase the quantity of resources can be graphically illustrated by contrasting Soviet experience in increasing employment and in accretions to fixed capital stock with that of other major economies. By any international standard the rates of growth in the Soviet labor force have been prodigious. No other economy has remotely matched the Soviet labor influx rate at comparable stages of development, especially during the period of the first three five-year plans (Table 5). In these years employment was increasing by over 3 percent

TABLE 5
Comparative Historic Rates of Increase in Employment
(annual average rates in percent)

Country	Period	Rate
USSR.	1928–37	3.7
	1937–40	3.0
United Kingdom	1821–31 to 1851–61	0.9
	1851–61 to 1871–81	0.7
Germany	1851–55 to 1871–75	0.7
	1871 to 1886–95	1.4
	1886–95 to 1907	1.7
United States	1874–89	2.8
	1889–1914	2.4
Japan	1883–87 to 1903–07	1.0
	1893–97 to 1913–17	0.6
	1918–22 to 1938–42	0.9
Italy	1861–81	0.2
	1881–1901	0.2
	1901–21	0.3
	1921–36	0.3

per year, while even in the years of heavy immigration before 1914 U.S. employment was rising by about 2.5 percent on an annual average. At comparable stages of growth with presumably similar demographic and structural advantages, the major Western European economies and Japan had much lower employment growth rates.

During the postwar years demographic disasters stemming from the war and agricultural stagnation have prevented continuation of so high a rate of labor influx, but given the more limited untapped manpower reservoir, additions to employment have been unusually large.

This accomplishment during the years 1928–40 was made possible by ability of an authoritarian state to move labor rapidly from the countryside to the city through the drastic reduction in agricultural real incomes under collectivization and through a policy of conscripting rural school graduates for employment in burgeoning industrial plants. Since most labor was provided only seasonal employment in agriculture, while activities continued throughout the year at capacity pace in industry, the transfer of labor, in effect, greatly increased the average number of hours worked per year. If we compare employment (in full-time equivalents) with the labor pool of the prime working age groups, we find that the ratio, termed the labor force participation ratio, rose sharply between 1928 and 1937—from 57 to 70 percent (Table 6). So

TABLE 6
Trends in the Labor Participation Ratio in the USSR

Year	Work-Age Population (thousands)	Employed Population (thousands)	Participation Ratio (percent)
1928	87,000	49,400	56.8
1937	98,000	68,700	70.1
1950	111,530	84,700	75.9
1960	132,290	98,100	74.6
1965	138,370	110,100	79.7
1970	149,230	121,870	81.7

rapid an increase in a comparatively short time span is historically unique. In fact, since 1913 the participation ratio has tended to fall in most West European economies.[8]

After the mid-fifties, when the natural increments to the labor force were drastically reduced by demographic factors, the regime managed to maintain the incremental employment rate at relatively high levels by again increasing the participation ratio from 76 percent in 1950 to 82 percent in 1970 (Table 6). Since the potentialities for transfers from agriculture were greatly diminished, the source of active manpower had to come from the remaining reservoirs of women and youths. By 1950 the Soviet participation ratio was the highest among the major industrial powers.[9] It probably cannot be increased much further, thus restricting the economy in its principal traditional growth approach.

[8] Maddison, *Economic Growth in the West*, p. 31.

[9] Cohn, "Soviet Growth Retardation," p. 114.

The extent to which the USSR has maximized the economic participation of its manpower resources is illustrated by the unusually large role played by the female population in productive life. The high general labor participation ratio is explained by this feature. The female proportion of total employment is not only much higher than in the economies of the West, but is higher in all of the principal economic sectors. Particularly striking is the large role of women in industry, agriculture, construction, and transportation. Even in the sectors in which heavy female employment is traditional in the West, such as commerce and the services, the Soviet proportions are still the highest (Table 7).

TABLE 7
Comparative Female Labor Participation, 1970
(in percent of total civilian employment)

Country	Agriculture	Industry	Construction	Transport	Commerce	Services	Total
USSR.	62.5	48.0	29.0	31.0	75.0	67.0	53.7
West Germany.	52.9	28.6	5.6	16.8	55.6	48.0	36.2
Italy.	30.7	20.4			32.8		27.0
United Kingdom . . .	14.4	29.3	5.5	17.3	53.0	53.1	36.9
Japan	50.9	36.8	13.5	12.9	45.9	44.5	39.9

Striking as has been the tendency for the Soviets to infuse labor massively into the production process, even more so has been the case with capital. As noted earlier there has been a steady upward trend in the capital-output ratio. Furthermore, such a persistent upward trend appears to be unique in international developmental experience. Normally rates of increase in capital stock exceed those in the labor force, since trends in the latter magnitude are constrained by population growth. Under the law of diminishing returns, such disparate growth rates should lead to declining marginal productivity of capital, but such a tendency has been offset by technological progress. Technology has enabled the quality of capital to rise sufficiently to keep its marginal productivity rather constant, or inversely to keep the capital-output ratio largely unchanged. Even though the USSR has been able to assimilate rapidly foreign technological developments, the expected productivity benefits have apparently been overwhelmed by the rapid rates of increase in capital stock. Prior to 1965, except for the disrupted decade of the forties, increments to capital stock, exclusive of retirements, had been above an annual rate of 8 percent (Table 8). During the mid- and late 19th century, the comparable rates for the United States ranged between 4.5 and 4.8 percent.[10] Even in the boom conditions of the postwar

[10] Kuznets, *Capital in the American Economy*, p. 64.

TABLE 8
Annual Average Rates of Growth of Employment, Fixed Capital, and
GNP in the USSR
(in percent)

	Employment			
Period	*Persons Employed*	*Man-Hours Worked*	*Fixed Capital*	*GNP*
1928–37	3.7	3.6	8.2–10.8	4.8–11.9
1937–40	3.0	3.8	10.3	3.6
1940–50	0.3	0.6	–1.7–2.2	1.8–2.2
1950–55	2.5	1.9	9.8	6.9
1955–60	1.5	–0.3	9.8	6.0
1961–65	2.2	2.2	8.5	5.0
1965–72	1.8	1.8	6.8	5.1

period neither the United States nor any Western European economy has approached the Soviet rate,[11] and Japan did so only after 1958.[12]

The rise in the capital-output ratio (declining marginal productivity of capital) occurred not only because the expected technological offset was nullified by the high rate of capital formation, but also because the infusion of this input was disproportionately large compared with that of manpower. Even if the rate of capital formation had been relatively lower, the law of diminishing returns would apply if the growth rate for capital stock were greatly in excess of that of the labor force. Disparity in the Soviet case is evidenced in the high incremental capital-labor ratios[13] shown in Table 9, as compared with U.S. experience at similar growth stages. With their strong fixation for rapid growth, Soviet leaders have indiscriminately channeled immense resources into capital investment, even though rapidly diminishing returns were the result of such a policy. Substitution of capital for labor was especially prominent after 1958 as the demographic pinch on manpower became acute. During the 19th century U.S. incremental fixed capital-labor ratios were far lower than anything experienced by the Soviets, except for the atypical war and recovery decade. Postwar computations for Western Europe indicate no ratio higher than the 5.5 for Germany between 1955 and 1962 with ratios for most countries in the 3.0 to 4.5 range.[14]

Undoubtedly the peculiar nature of the Soviet system of pricing played a role in the disproportionate infusions of capital because of

---

[11] Denison, *Why Growth Rates Differ*, p. 190.

[12] Shuntaro Shishido, "Japanese Experience with Long-term Planning," in *Quantitative Planning of Economic Policy*, ed. Bert G. Hickman (Washington, D.C.: Brookings Institution, 1965), p. 214.

[13] Defined as the rate of increase in capital stock divided by the rate of increase in man-hours of employment.

[14] Denison, *Why Growth Rates Differ*, p. 193.

TABLE 9
Incremental Capital-Labor Ratios*

USSR		United States	
Period	*Ratio*	*Period*	*Ratio*
1929–37	2.4–3.0	1869–79	1.9
1937–40	2.7	1879–89	1.5
1940–50	2.8–3.7	1889–99	2.2
1950–60	6.4	1899–09	1.7
1960–65	4.3	1909–19	2.1
1965–72	3.8	1919–29	2.9

*Increase in fixed capital, net of retirements, divided by increase in man-hours of employment.

the absence of an interest charge. In a market economy the imposition of interest charges would have led to low returns to capital investment long before attaining the investment rate reached in the Soviet economy. Determined as it was to foster rapid industrialization, the regime might have ignored the rising cost of investment, but at least it would have possessed an adequate criterion for reaching a judgment.

THE EXPLANATION

Resource Allocation Policies

We have noted thus far that a major explanation of rapid Soviet growth was the intensive exploitation of the nation's bountiful endowment of human resources through unusually rapid rates of increase in employment and high rates of capital formation. Productivity considerations were subordinated to the aim of industrialization at a maximum pace. What policies enabled the state to sequester resources for this all-compelling purpose?

In general terms, rapid growth occurred because the regime could channel a large share of current output into investment. This policy, of course, meant that a relatively small share could be used to satisfy consumer needs, a share further reduced as defense claims burgeoned after 1937 and continued at a high proportion all through the postwar years (see Table 10).

Even in 1928 before the progressive squeezing of the consumer to direct resources into investment commenced, the share of GNP devoted to private consumption purposes was low by the historical standards of other major economies at similar levels of per capita GNP. Bergson's estimate of 64.7 percent for 1928 compares with 83.0 percent for the

TABLE 10
Trends in Allocation of Soviet GNP*
(in percent of total)

End Use	1928	1937	1940	1950	1955	1965	1969	1972
Private consumption	64.7	52.5	51.0	54.7	54.5	51.3	50.9	50.1
Communal consumption† . . .	5.1	10.5	9.9	5.5	5.3	6.6	7.1	7.5
Investment‡	25.0	25.9	19.2	23.9	25.1	30.8	29.5	31.2
Defense§	2.5	7.9	16.1	10.8	12.3	9.1	10.1	9.2
Other‖	2.7	3.2	3.8	5.1	2.8	2.2	2.4	2.0
Total	100.0	100.0	100.0	100.0	100.0	100.0	100.0	100.0

*The estimates are in terms of factor cost; i.e., they exclude indirect taxes and subsidies. For an explanation of the differences between the prewar and postwar estimates, see Stanley H. Cohn, "The Soviet Economy: Performance and Growth," in *The Development of the Soviet Economy: Plan and Performance,* ed. Vladimir G. Treml and Robert Farrell (New York: Frederick A. Praeger, Inc., 1968), p. 40, table 11.
†Outlays for public education, health, and science.
‡Fixed investment and inventories.
§Budgetary category of defense, 1928–40; budgetary plus estimates of defense expenditures under other portions of state budget, 1950–65.
‖ Largely composed of governmental administrative expenditures.

United Kingdom in 1860–69, 82.6 percent for Germany in 1851–61, 79.7 percent for the United States in 1867–78, 84.1 percent for Italy in 1891–1900, and 82.0 percent for Japan in 1931–40.[15] Equally without historical precedent is the rapidity with which the proportionate claim of private consumption on GNP declined, reaching a share in 1937 of only 52.5 percent. No other major economy approached this low proportion in peacetime circumstances until Japan in the late 1950s. In the nine years following 1928, the USSR achieved a proportionate reduction in the share of private consumption in GNP by 12 points, an accomplishment which required 40 years in Germany, 50 in the United Kingdom and Italy, 30 in the United States, and over a half century in Japan.[16]

Another way of casting perspective on Soviet consumption policy is to compare rates of change in per capita private consumption levels in other major economies at similar levels of per capita income (Table 11). Depending on the base year prices used, Soviet per capita private consumption either declined from 1928 through 1941, or showed a moderate increase between 1928 and 1937 and then declined for the next four years.[17] If there were an increase, it was more nominal than real, as much of it reflects the costs of urbanization, i.e., the commercial purchase of commodities and services formerly supplied by the consumer himself in a rural environment. In no other historical instance did con-

[15] Simon Kuznets, "The Share and Structure of Consumption," *Economic Development and Cultural Change,* Vol. X, No. 2 (January 1962), Part II, pp. 72–74.

[16] Ibid.

[17] In either case per capita consumption declined from 1928 to 1937.

TABLE 11
Comparative Trends in per Capita Private Consumption
(annual average rates in percent)

Country	Period	Rate of Growth
USSR	1928–37	– 1.0–+2.6
	1937–40	–1.0
	1940–44	–8.1– –8.8
	1944–50	9.5
	1950–58	5.0
	1958–65	2.8
	1965–70	6.1
United Kingdom	1880–89 to 1890–99	1.7
	1890–99 to 1900–09	0.6
	1950–58	1.6
	1958–65	2.6
	1965–70	1.4
Germany.	1851–60 to 1861–70	1.9
	1861–70 to 1871–80	1.4
	1871–80 to 1881–90	0.8
	1881–90 to 1891–1900	1.8
	1950–58	6.3
	1958–65	4.8
	1965–70	3.7
Italy	1861–70 to 1871–80	0.1
	1871–80 to 1881–90	nil
	1881–90 to 1891–1900	1.2
	1950–58	3.1
	1958–65	4.5
	1965–70	5.9
United States	1869–79	4.2
	1879–89	2.0
	1889–98 to 1899–1908	2.9
	1950–58	1.1
	1958–65	3.2
	1965–70	2.6

sumption decline in other economies under peacetime conditions, nor were increases so largely reflective of urbanization costs, as shifts out of agriculture were more gradual.[18]

With Stalin's demise, the policy of treating the consumer as a residual claimant ceased. Thanks in good part to the rehabilitation of agriculture in the mid- and late fifties, per capita consumption increased by 5.0 percent per year through 1958, but after that date with stagnation again prevailing in agriculture the rate of increase was cut almost in half. The resurgence of agriculture under Brezhnev-Kosygin, combined with good weather, led to a 6.0 percent annual average increase between 1965 and 1970.

----

[18] There is divided opinion on whether or not per capita consumption levels fell in the United Kingdom during the early part of the Industrial Revolution, years prior to those shown in Table 11.

Investment Emphasis

The rapid rate of industrialization of the USSR after 1928 was ultimately a function of the high rate of investment, supported by a rapid increase in the urban labor force. As the ratio of private consumption to GNP was unusually low, so the ratio of investment was unusually high. Low income, underdeveloped economies customarily cannot invest a large portion of their national product, as consumption cannot be easily diverted from a population living close to the margin of subsistence. Through close control over resources, especially in agriculture, the Soviet state was able to sequester the saving which enabled the economy to enjoy a high rate of investment.

No other major economy similar to the Soviet Union of 1928–37 was able to invest anything like the quarter of GNP the USSR attained in these years. In the mid-19th century the British proportion was only about an eighth, the German ranging from a seventh up to a fifth toward the end of the century, the Italian a seventh early in the 20th century, the Japanese only as high as a sixth in the 1920s and 1930s, and the U.S. a fifth in the 1870s and 1880s, but at a higher per capita income level than the USSR in 1928.[19] It was only in the 1950s that some large market economies began to approach the high Soviet investment ratios, and none of these had relative defense burdens comparable to that of the USSR.

The ability of the Soviet economy to devote so large a share of product to investment at low per capita income levels appears all the more unique when it is realized that the entire burden of saving occurred within national boundaries. By contrast, other economies at the stage of development of the USSR in 1928–40 were able to draw on capital inflows from more highly developed nations. The United States was partially dependent upon European sources of financing until the 1890s, with foreign sources providing about 11 percent of net capital formation in the 1870s, and probably considerably more earlier.[20] Japan was heavily dependent on foreign investment until World War I, as was Italy for most of the period under review. This dependence was particularly sharp for such countries as Canada, Australia, and Argentina.[21]

In addition to its large magnitude, Soviet investment has also been distinguished by its concentration in growth supporting sectors. The most graphic illustration of this propensity has been the unusually small portion of fixed investment devoted to housing. Between 1928 and 1940 this proportion was only 15.5 percent compared with around 25 percent

---

[19] Simon Kuznets, "Long Term Trends in Capital Formation Proportions," *Economic Development and Cultural Change*, Vol. IX, No. 4 (July 1961), Part II, pp. 10–11.

[20] Kuznets, *Capital in the American Economy*, p. 133.

[21] Kuznets, "Long Term Trends in Capital Formation Proportions," pp. 52 and 53.

for the United States in the 1870s and 1880s, a third for Germany from 1851 to 1890, a quarter to a third for Italy from 1861 to 1915, and a quarter for Japan from 1887 to 1906.[22] The small Soviet proportion is even more significant, given the rapid rate of urbanization in these years. The combination of circumstances led to a drastic decline in housing standards with per capita availabilities falling from 5.8 square meters in 1928 to 4.6 in 1937[23] and rising only to 6.4 in 1964.[24]

During the period of relaxation following Stalin's passing, the share of housing in fixed investment increased to around 21 percent, just under the proportions for the United Kingdom, Germany, and Italy. However, with the resource and productivity constraints that developed after 1958, the regime chose to sacrifice housing in favor of maintaining the rate of productive investment. As a result, the housing share fell back below 20 percent, considerably below the proportions for all major economies other than the United Kingdom. In fact, there was an absolute decline in the annual volume of housing investment from 1959 through 1964. The Brezhnev-Kosygin regime, with its renewed concern for the interests of the consumer, has renewed the growth in housing investment, but the proportion is only a sixth of the total.

Investment has been directed not only to productive sectors of the economy, but also toward those with the heaviest growth orientation. In the 1928–40 period Soviet investment was concentrated much more in industry and agriculture, and less in commerce and services, than was the case in mid-19th century United States. Within industry it has been more directed to the growth-inducing metallurgical and machinery branches.[25] In the postwar years Soviet investment has continued its orientation toward industry and agriculture and its neglect of the service sectors and transportation.

Defense Burden

The Soviet development model has been characterized not only by a high rate of investment and slow increases, and even declines, in consumption, but also by a large defense burden since the Third Five-Year Plan. Whatever the considerations which have prompted the regime to pursue policies of heavy defense expenditures, their continued prevalence (between 9 and 12 percent of GNP since 1950) alongside high shares

[22] Ibid., pp. 65, 73, 97, 116.

[23] Janet G. Chapman, "Consumption," in *Economic Trends in the Soviet Union,* ed. Abram Bergson and Simon Kuznets (Cambridge, Mass.: Harvard University Press, 1963), p. 238.

[24] Timothy Sosnovy, "Housing Conditions and Urban Development in the USSR," *New Directions in the Soviet Economy* (cited in fn. 7), Part II-B, p. 533.

[25] Norman M. Kaplan, "Capital Formation and Allocation," in *Soviet Economic Growth,* ed. Abram Bergson (Evanston, Ill.: Row, Peterson, 1953), pp. 59, 63.

of investment in GNP has further worsened the position of the Soviet consumer. In the postwar period only the United States has devoted as large a share of its resources to military purposes, but with a much lower investment ratio. By contrast, countries with investment ratios as high as the USSR, such as Germany and Japan, have had small or minuscule defense programs. Defense ratios amounted to 10.1 percent of GNP in the USSR and 8.6 percent in the United States in 1969, compared with 5 to 7 percent in the United Kingdom, France, and Germany. Investment ratios were 29.5 in the USSR, 34.8 in Japan, 28.2 in Germany, 20.5 in Italy, 25.2 in France, 18.0 in the United Kingdom, and 16.8 in the United States. Only an economy with the strong, centralized controls of the Soviet Union could tolerate so small a claim for the consumer out of available resources.

Not only the consumer bears the sacrifice of heavy defense spending, for the growth potential of the economy is also restrained. Those periods in Soviet history which have seen sharp increases in defense spending, such as 1937–40, 1951–52, and 1960–63, have also been periods in which rates of increase in investment have sharply declined. Furthermore, as defense expenditures are composed more and more of research and developmental outlays for aerospace and nuclear weapons, the greater becomes the demand for the scarce services of highly trained scientists, engineers, and managers. The absorption of a significant share of such personnel into military-oriented activities means that civilian-oriented investment is deprived of vital inputs. Part of the explanation for the sharp rise in capital-output ratios may be slower technological progress because of the drain of so many skilled personnel into defense production. If these personnel could be released into the civilian economy, they could devote their energies to research, development, and adaptation of civilian-oriented technology. If the pace of technological development and assimilation into the production process could be accelerated, there would be increased cost savings which would serve to retard the inexorable rise in the capital-output ratio.

Education—Human Capital Investment

Concomitant with and of equal importance to the heavy emphasis on fixed capital investment has been the high priority which the Soviet leadership has placed on education, i.e., investment in human capital. At an early stage Soviet leaders were aware that their strenuous physical investment efforts would be for nought if not accompanied by provision for training a skilled labor force. In the prewar years the main objective of educational policy was mass literacy through universal elementary education and an extensive program of adult education. Since the war the emphasis has been on universal secondary education and rapid expansion of higher and technical education.

The USSR is the one country in Europe to have emulated the U.S. in goals of mass secondary and higher education. As of about 1960 the enrollment ratio, i.e., the proportion of a given age group enrolled in school, was just under half for the age group 15–19 compared with two thirds in the United States and only about a sixth in the major West European countries. In the age group 20–24 years, the Soviet ratio was about a twelfth, compared to an eighth in the United States and only a twenty-fifth in Western Europe. Since Soviet per capita income is considerably below that of the principal countries of Northwestern Europe, its educational effort is disproportionately large. Furthermore, the present high ratio has been attained in a much shorter time period than in Western Europe.

While the increase in the ratio for most other economies was slow until after World War II, the Soviet ratio rose steadily during the years of comprehensive planning, reaching 3.3 by 1937, 4.7 by 1950, 6.7 by 1964, and 19.0 by 1969 (Table 12).[26] Since 1932 the Soviet university enrollment ratio has been second only to that of the United States, even though its relative per capita income level would warrant a much lower ranking. The comparison in terms of university enrollments may somewhat understate the relative Soviet educational effort, as that country's program of training high-level technicians is much more advanced than those of the principal West European economies.

As in the case of physical capital, Soviet investment in human capital has also been narrowly channeled toward growth-supporting activities. At the elementary and secondary levels, Soviet students on the average are exposed to more instruction in science and mathematics than their American equivalents. In higher education, liberal arts curricula are unknown in the USSR, where students specialize narrowly in their major disciplines. In universities, graduates in engineering and the sciences comprise a much larger share of the total than in the United States. In 1960, for example, 38 percent of all Soviet graduates were in these fields, compared to only around 15 percent in the United States. By contrast, 31 percent of U.S. graduates majored in the humanities and social sciences other than economics, compared with only 3 percent in the USSR.[27]

Structural Transformation

The rapid industrialization of the Soviet economy after 1928, as previously emphasized, was accomplished by heavy infusions of manpower

---

[26] The 1969 estimate includes part-time students, whereas earlier estimates cover only full-time equivalents. The full-time equivalent ratio is 9.3 percent.

[27] Nicholas DeWitt, "Education and the Development of Human Resources: Soviet and American Effort," in *Dimensions of Soviet Economic Power* (Studies Prepared for the Joint Economic Committee, 87th Cong. 2d sess.) (Washington, D.C.: U.S. Government Printing Office, 1962), p. 259.

TABLE 12
Comparative University Enrollments

Country	Year	Full-Time Students per 1000 Population*
USSR.	1914	0.8
	1928	1.2
	1932	3.2
	1937	3.3
	1950	4.7
	1958	6.4
	1964	6.7
	1969	19.0
United Kingdom	1901	0.9
	1911	1.1
	1921	0.9
	1931	1.1
	1937	1.1
	1951	1.9
	1958	2.2
	1969	7.5
Germany.	1901	0.9
	1911	1.1
	1922	1.8
	1932	1.9
	1937	1.1
	1951	2.5
	1959	3.7
	1969	7.5
France	1921	1.1
	1931	1.5
	1954	3.3
	1959	3.7
	1969	12.0
Italy.	1881	0.4
	1901	0.8
	1921	1.3
	1941	3.2
	1951	3.1
	1958	3.4
Japan	1890	0.3
	1910	0.9
	1920	1.3
	1930	2.5
	1940	3.2
	1950	2.9
	1958	7.1
	1969	15.9
United States	1870	1.3
	1890	2.5
	1910	3.8
	1920	5.6
	1930	8.9
	1940	11.3
	1950	17.6
	1960	20.0
	1969	39.0

*Estimates for 1969 include part-time students but exclude correspondence programs.

and capital into productive industrial enterprises. This process was accompanied by rapid transformation in the structure of the system. In terms of the proportion of the labor force employed in agriculture, the Soviet economy of 1928 was far less industrialized than were the other major economies at comparable levels of per capita income (Table 13).

TABLE 13
Agricultural Employment as Proportion of Total Employment
(in percent of total)

Country	Year	Proportion
USSR.	1928	71
	1937	54
	1940	51
	1950	46
	1958	41
	1964	34
	1970	32
France	1788	75
	1845	62
	1866	52
	1886	48
	1906	43
	1926	39
Italy.	1861	62
	1881	57
	1901	59
	1921	56
	1936	48
Japan.	1877–82	83
	1887–92	76
	1897–1902	70
	1907–12	63
	1920	54
	1940	42
Germany.	1882	42
	1895	36
	1907	34
	1925	30
	1939	27
England and Wales	1841	23
	1861	19
	1881	12
	1901	9
United States	1870	50
	1890	42
	1900	37
	1920	27
	1940	17

Within 12 years the transfer of labor from farm to urban occupations through collectivization and organized recruitment reduced the agricultural proportion by 20 percentage points. The shift was far more rapid than in the other major economies, with shifts of comparable proportions requiring 60 years in France, 65 in Italy, 40 in the United States, and 30 to 35 in Japan (Table 13). Yet, because of the huge initial size of the farm population and the rapid increase in population as a whole, agricultural employment actually increased by 2.4 million between 1928 and 1937 and by another 4 million between 1937 and 1940. The latter increase is largely explained by the territorial acquisitions of 1939–40.

The unbalanced nature of Soviet growth under the first three five-year plans is reflected in divergent productivity trends in the various sectors of the economy. In terms of man-hours, industrial labor productivity increased at an average annual rate (depending on the prices used to value output) of between 3.1 and 10.4 percent from 1928 to 1937 and at a rate of 2.7 percent from 1937 to 1940.[28] By contrast, in agriculture the rise of employment was coupled with a decline in production,[29] implying, of course, a fall in productivity. Historically, in other economics the transfer of labor out of agriculture has been accompanied by rising labor productivity trends at rates not too different from industry, especially since World War I.[30] In no instance has agricultural productivity declined. While the rapid reduction in the agricultural share of employment and the decline in production are not functionally related, both stemmed from the drastic collectivization campaign, with its emasculation of incentives and wholesale destruction of livestock.

The imbalance between industrial and agricultural development is the corollary of the policy of suppression of consumption in favor of investment and defense. Within the aggregate of industrial production, output of industrial raw materials and producer durables rose much more rapidly than that of consumer goods, inclusive of home-processed food and clothing. Within the broad category of services, production- and investment-oriented services increased more swiftly than did consumer services. This dichotomy makes generalizations as to output and productivity trends in the services sector meaningless as a guide to development policy.

In the years following Stalin's passing, the formerly unbalanced sectoral growth pattern was considerably rectified by rapid progress in agriculture through 1958. Since the rapid rise in output was extensive in nature, being partially based on an 18 percent increase in cultivated acreage,[30] farm employment actually increased by a million from 1950 to 1958.[32] Though the proportion of manpower on the farm continued

---

[28] Raymond Powell, "Industrial Production," in *Economic Trends in the Soviet Union,* ed. Bergson and Kuznets (cited in fn. 23), p. 178.

[29] Gale Johnson, "Agricultural Production," ibid., p. 218.

[30] Deborah Paige, "Economic Growth: The Last Hundred Years," *National Institute Economic Review,* No. 16 (July 1961), p. 39.

[31] Douglas Diamond, "Trends in Outputs, Inputs, and Factor Productivity in Soviet Agriculture," in *New Directions in the Soviet Economy,* Part II-B, p. 353.

[32] Murray Feshbach, "Manpower in the USSR," ibid., Part III, p. 786.

to fall, the relative decline was far slower than the breakneck pace of 1928 to 1940. After 1958, with the cessation of acreage expansion, agricultural employment resumed its secular decline, but at a much more deliberate pace than in the prewar Stalinist years or in the major market economies.

Role of Foreign Trade in Soviet Economic Development

The foregoing analysis of Soviet growth has assumed the existence of a closed economy. Compared with most other nations in the course of development, foreign trade played a minor role in the USSR, but nevertheless it was important at certain stages of Soviet development and should be evaluated, even in summary fashion.

Foreign investment and technology played a vital role in Tsarist economic development.[33] Russian grain and other raw material exports financed the imports of machinery and of capital which were essential to industrial development in an agricultural economy. In 1913, about 12 percent of the grain crop, 25 percent of lumber, and 12 percent of petroleum produced were exported. Over a third of imports were comprised of machinery and textile raw materials. Exports amounted to about 10 percent of national product in 1913.

In the Soviet period the importance of foreign trade has been considerably less, though of considerable weight in particular periods. After falling to the vanishing point in the years immediately after the Revolution, foreign trade volume recovered slowly during the NEP period, but by 1927 attained only about 35 percent of the 1913 level of exports and 39 percent of the level of imports. Export volume was limited by the great reduction in the marketed share of the grain crop arising from the establishment of small, private farms in agriculture. Imports were, of course, limited by the economy's export capabilities, but by the late twenties their composition was already being shifted in the direction of growth- and reconstruction-supporting products.

With the onset of the First Five-Year Plan with its greatly increased requirements for industrial imports, foreign trade volume rose sharply, particularly through 1931. By 1930 the ratio of exports to national product had risen to 3.5 percent, a proportion not to be attained again since that date. What is of greater developmental significance is the composition of trade during these early plan years. Even though these were years of great privation in agriculture with sharply reduced grain and livestock product output, nearly half of total exports consisted of these agricultural products. The creation of such exporting capability may have been one of the purposes of the collectivization program. The com-

---

[33] Data in this and the following four paragraphs are from Franklyn Holzman, "Foreign Trade," in *Economic Trends in the Soviet Union,* ed. Bergson and Kuznets, pp. 284–95.

position of imports was closely geared to the frenetic industrialization effort. In the early 1930s machinery and ferrous metals comprised nearly 75 percent of total imports.

During the Second Five-Year Plan, with the fruition of domestic productive capabilities in machinery and in metals, foreign trade volume fell not only relative to national product, but absolutely. By 1938, exports were down to 62 percent of the 1929 level and the ratio of exports to national product to only 0.5 percent. During World War II exports declined drastically, but imports increased in the form of Allied military assistance. Since World War II, the role of foreign trade has again increased, reflecting first extensive trading relations within the Soviet Bloc and more recently wider economic relations with the industrialized market economies and the less developed nations. In recent years the ratio of foreign trade to national product has been approaching the 3.0 to 3.5 percent peak of the early plan years. For the most part, Soviet imports have been keyed in recent years to imports of prototype industrial plants from the industrialized market economies and specialized industrial machinery from the planned economies of Eastern Europe. Exports still heavily emphasize raw materials—oil, lumber, and metals to the industrial market economies, and industrial raw materials to the Eastern European economies.

If foreign trade has played a positive role in furthering economic development, the question arises as to why the Soviet leadership, commencing with the Second Five-Year Plan, pursued a policy of autarky. Politically this policy was consistent with the aim of the leadership to secure and maintain military and economic independence from the capitalist world. The experience of World War II in which the Soviet Union had to rely largely on its own resources confirmed the defense argument. The economic rationale for autarky is the desire of economic planners to control as many of the economic variables as possible. A large foreign trade sector would have considerably reduced the planners' independence in decision-making.

One of the costly legacies of the policy of minimization of foreign trade has been the perpetuation of an uneconomic agricultural sector. The nearly total dependence of the economy on domestic sources of supply of farm products has been a limiting factor on economic development. Perhaps if foreign trade were liberalized, the Soviets would find it to their comparative advantage to import a considerable portion of their agricultural requirements, such as feed grains, and to concentrate their exports on industrial products, the production of which has been the beneficiary of their tremendous technological efforts. Such a change would have to overcome the fixation of an adequate domestic grain supply as the cornerstone of defensive logistical capability.

While the constraints on foreign trade have been largely political in nature, they undoubtedly have had the effect of increasing the cost

268 *The Soviet Economy*

of economic development and thereby constraining growth. The new post-Khrushchev leadership with its enhanced economic perception is aware of this limitation. In his general assessment of economic affairs in 1965, Kosygin berated Soviet planners for turning their backs on an efficiency-conscious outside world distinguished by an incredibly fast tempo of technological change. The new Ninth Five-Year Plan urges in several passages an enhanced Soviet interest in the potentialities of foreign trade. Among other statements, the Plan Directives decree "improvements in the commodity structure of Soviet trade, on both the import and export side of the exchange, that would in fact make it possible for the USSR to take part in a rational division of labor on an international scale." The Directives presage a sharp reversal of the policy of economic isolationism by urging that the structure of domestic production be guided by comparative costs in the world market and that the Soviet economy no longer produce but import "articles whose production inside the country entails greater costs and capital investment." Should these Directives be implemented, the Soviet economy will be taking belated advantage of efficiency gains it has long denied to itself in its development policies.

SUMMARY

We have briefly surveyed the techniques and policies which enabled the Soviet Union to achieve its rapid rise to second position among the world's economies. This success stemmed from the determination of the regime to channel the country's prodigious resource endowment into economic growth and the building of the nation's international power position. The abundance of resources and the regime's ability to suppress consumer demands brought success, so long as these favorable conditions held. Meanwhile the economy was incurring deferred obligations in the form of housing, transportation facilities, consumer services, and consumer durables production. As the day of deferred payment drew closer, some sweeping modification in the traditional Soviet development model was becoming ever more compelling. The increasing recognition of the need for change on the part of the leadership has led to a permissive atmosphere, reminiscent of the twenties, in which Soviet economists have again engaged in intellectual controversies as to the future shape of the Soviet economic system. At the same time, the traditional Stalinist and post-Stalinist development model is evolving in directions which more closely resemble those which the advanced market economies of the West have followed.

13. CONSUMPTION IN THE USSR: A SURVEY

Gertrude E. Schroeder

When the Soviet leadership decided to push for rapid economic growth through massive industrialization, it had to keep living standards from rising. Every man-hour devoted to production of consumer goods was one man-hour that could not be used to produce investment goods. Every ton of steel used in automobiles or refrigerators was a ton that could not be used to produce turbines or tractors. The trade-off between living standards and economic growth was clearly understood, and Soviet policymakers have not masked their preference for the latter. The Soviet population had to work and produce more now, in order that future generations might benefit.

There is a more subtle trade-off between growth and living standards, however. People cannot be expected to work hard indefinitely without some rewards in the form of improved living conditions. As Soviet economic growth proceeded, it became necessary to provide those rewards in order to continue economic expansion, particularly since the ordinary person in the USSR could perceive how much the production potential of the economy had expanded. Why not more now? Even before the death of Stalin, these new forces had begun to appear. After his death the regime had added reason to provide higher living standards, in order to improve its political position.

The result was a shift in emphasis in economic policy, toward a higher priority for private consumption. The regime had always sought to develop "collective consumption," especially in health care and education, and had gone further in those areas than many other nations. In the last 20 years, however, household consumption of food, clothing, durables, and housing has grown significantly.

Gertrude E. Schroeder, Professor of Economics at the University of Virginia, provides a comprehensive survey of these developments. She analyzes the USSR's consumption policies in relation to larger economic issues in a planned economy, and gives a balanced account of both achievements and difficulties. This chapter combines material from her "Consumption in the USSR: A Survey," *Studies on the Soviet Union,* Vol. X (1970), No. 4, pp. 1–18, 26–29, and 33–38, and from her "Consumer Problems and Prospects," *Problems of Communism,* Vol. XXII, No. 2 (March–April 1973), pp. 14–24. Reprinted by permission. Some footnotes to the text and tables have been omitted.

THE PURPOSE of this essay is to review and evaluate the advance in the level of living of the Russian people during their half century under Communist rule. Comparisons will also be made with the progress by other peoples during the same period, and during comparable initial stages of economic development. As a measure of levels of living use will be made mainly of estimates of total consumption per capita, including communal consumption, with subdivision into major components wherever possible. The data underlying the text discussion are shown in Appendix Tables 1 and 2.

Judging by the promises of communist ideology the Russian people might have expected the improvement in their lot to be unprecedented and spectacular. The Bolshevik Revolution itself was to have brought with it a veritable paradise compared with the people's plight under the Tsars. Communism promises nothing if not abundance for all. And in the early days of planning for rapid industrialization, claims were made that the level of living of the Soviet people would be three times that of even the wealthiest capitalist country—the United States—in 10 to 15 years. Those years passed with little or no progress toward that grandiose goal. The ebullient Khrushchev took up the theme three decades later, promising to catch up with the U.S. in meat and milk production in 3–4 years and to eliminate the housing shortage by 1970. But even more spectacular—the USSR was to achieve the highest standard of living in the world by 1980!

Clearly, achievement of these goals, if it occurs at all, is still far away. But people, especially those carefully protected by their government from contaminating foreign influences, tend to judge their lot by looking back to where they were yesterday. And the Russian people have moved up appreciably from the levels of living of their fathers and grandfathers, albeit by fits and starts, as have their conterparts in the West who live under a radically different economic and political system.

CONSUMPTION TRENDS, 1913–1968

Overall Trends

Pre-Revolutionary Levels of Living.   Precise measurements of the level of per capita consumption attained in the final years of Tsarist

Russia are impossible to make. One must make do with generalizations from various relevant statistics and from impressions based on what is known about the general level of economic development of the country. There is general agreement that during the half-century before World War I economic growth in Russia was proceeding at about the average rate of the rest of Europe, although much more slowly than in the U.S.[1] Evidently consumption per capita also was rising somewhat during that period. Economic growth was somewhat faster after 1900, as was the gain in consumption. In 1913, however, Russia was still an underdeveloped country by any of the usual measures, with more than three fourths of its population dependent on agriculture for a livelihood. The vast bulk of the peasantry lived at a near-subsistence level, and a bad harvest threatened even that level. Consumption consisted mainly of food, mostly bread and potatoes. Urban levels of living, while better than in rural areas by perhaps one third to two thirds, were reminiscent of those in English cities during a comparable stage of industrialization in the early 1800s. City dwellers' consumption also consisted mostly of food, with a somewhat greater proportion of meat and vegetables. Housing was poor and costly, and State-provided health and education services were minimal, although rising.

Perhaps the best general impression of where the Russian consumer stood before the Revolution can be had from a look at relative levels of national income per capita in Russia and in other countries. While total national income includes more than consumption, the latter formed the vast bulk of the total in all countries at that time. Again, precision is impossible because of the sorry state of the statistics available. The conclusion of one researcher is that per capita national income in Russia in 1913 was perhaps about one third that of the U.S. and Great Britain and about the same as that of Italy.[2] Another author asserts, without giving the evidence, that the Russian level was much lower—about one seventh of the U.S. and one quarter of Great Britain.[3] Still other compilations of data suggest results somewhere in between these positions.[4] These are controversial matters still unresolved and probably unresolvable. Perhaps one should conclude merely that the Russian level of living before the advent of the Communists was far below that of the U.S. and Western Europe, clearly much less than one half and perhaps less than one quarter.

[1] Raymond W. Goldsmith, "The Economic Growth of Tsarist Russia," *Economic Development and Cultural Change,* Vol. IX, No. 3 (April 1961), pp. 441–43.

[2] Ibid., p. 443.

[3] Maurice Dobb, *Soviet Economic Development Since 1917* (New York: International Publishers, 1966), p. 59.

[4] Stanley H. Cohn, "The Soviet Economy: Performance and Growth" in *The Development of the Soviet Economy: Plan and Performance,* ed. Vladimir G. Treml (New York: Praeger, for the Institute for the Study of the USSR, 1968), pp. 28, 52.

From Tsardom to Full-Scale Soviet Planning (1913–1928). The events of the 15 years between the last peace-time year of the Tsarist regime and the first year of the Soviet First Five-Year Plan were cataclysmic, and most were also catastrophic. They included a foreign war, an internal revolution, a civil war, 4 years of "War Communism" with its total state regimentation of the economy, and 6–7 years of a "New Economic Policy" (NEP) involving the partial restoration of a market economy. The impact of these events on consumption was profound. Although the statistical record is almost non-existent, the general outlines of what happened are clear. Changes in the level of living must have roughly mirrored the changes in agricultural and industrial output that took place during this chaotic period. According to statistical data officially reported by the USSR, agricultural output (crops) dropped moderately during 1913–17 and then fell drastically during 1918–21 to reach less than half the 1909–13 average in 1921.[5] The number of sheep and cattle also dropped sharply. Data from the same source show that industrial output was 75 percent of the 1913 level in 1917 and 20 percent in 1920.[6] A Western calculation of industrial output indicates similar results.[7] All of these sources show a rapid recovery during 1921–27, with the pre-war levels of output having been regained in both industry and agriculture by 1927–28.[8] Grain output had not completely recovered however. This general pattern of change in domestic output means that levels of living in Russia must have declined drastically during World War I and War Communism, culminating in the disastrous famine of 1921. Thereafter, there evidently was a rapid recovery, spurred by the economic freedom permitted during the NEP.

To what extent did per capita consumption recover? Evidently not to the 1913 level, if we are to judge by an analysis of Soviet statistics, even though the Soviets themselves assert elsewhere that the pre-war consumption levels had been regained by 1928.[9] Firstly, total population in 1928 was higher than in 1913 by some 10 million, with the rural areas accounting for most of the growth. Moreover, per capita output of grain—so crucial to relative consumption levels in that early stage

---

[5] *Collection of Statistical Figures of the USSR, 1918–23*, pp. 123, 131, 137, 146. Cited in Alexander Baykov, *The Development of the Soviet Economic System* (New York: Macmillan, 1948), p. 23.

[6] Ibid., p. 8.

[7] G. Warren Nutter, *The Growth of Industrial Production in the Soviet Union* (Princeton: Princeton University Press, 1962), pp. 522–23.

[8] The official Soviet index of industrial production, which for this period seems to pertain only to large-scale industry, shows a growth of 32 percent during 1913–28. Nutter's index (all industrial products) gives a growth of only 2 percent for the period. Nutter, *The Growth of Industrial Production in the Soviet Union*, p. 155.

[9] For a careful review of the scattered and often conflicting evidence on this point see Philip Hanson, *The Consumer in the Soviet Economy* (Evanston, Ill.: Northwestern University Press, 1968), p. 25–31.

of economic development—was about 10 percent below pre-war levels; perhaps total farm output per capita was also slightly less. Although by 1928 the domestic per capita output of a number of manufactured consumer goods was somewhat above the 1913 levels, per capita stocks of many consumer durables may have been below pre-war levels. But food availabilities are the most critical variable in consumption for a population still 80 percent rural, and per capita domestic supplies clearly were lower than in 1913.

The patchy and conflicting data on incomes and employment also suggest that the pre-war levels of living may not have been fully restored on the eve of the all-out drive toward industrialization.[10] But this may be splitting hairs. It is surely correct to conclude that the first decade of Bolshevik rule left Russian consumers no better off in material welfare than they were in 1913, and perhaps a little worse off. In terms of communal consumption—mainly public-provided health and education services—they evidently were better off, however, although communal consumption was a tiny fraction of the total at the time. Total state budget expenditures on social and cultural measures in 1927–28 were triple those of 1913; local budget expenditures for these purposes apparently had also risen considerably.[11] The data on this element of consumer welfare during this early period still await compilation and analysis.

Trends in Per Capita Consumption, 1928–1950.   (See Appendix Table 1.) With the termination of the NEP and the advent of central economic planning and administration the fairly rapid improvement in the level of living of the Soviet people during the 1920s came to an abrupt halt. The outcome of the historic debate over the path and rate of industrialization was settled in favor of forced, rapid industrial growth and of the overriding priority of investment and producer goods over consumption and consumer goods. These momentous decisions were followed by the historic resolve to collectivize agriculture at all costs. And the costs turned out to be very great indeed. The impact of these decisions on overall consumption can best be understood through a look at what happened during the Five-Year Plans, prosaic though this approach may seem.

The First Five-Year Plan (1928–32) promised a large gain in consumption but ended instead with a substantial loss. The decline cannot be quantified with much precision, as Soviet statistics are notably silent on this sensitive subject. For the rural population these were the years of the mass collectivization and its aftermath—the severe famine of 1932–33. For the urban dweller they brought rationing, an increase in

---

[10] This is the conclusion of Hanson, *The Consumer in the Soviet Economy*, pp. 30–31.

[11] R. W. Davies, *The Development of the Soviet Budgetary System* (Cambridge: Cambridge University Press, 1958), pp. 65, 83.

state retail prices officially admitted to be 255 percent, a 5–10 times greater rise in free market prices, and a rise of 226 per cent in money wages. As a result, real wages dropped significantly. Some notion of the dimensions of the decline in consumption that occurred in these years can be gained from an inspection of available data on per capita output of various foods and other consumer goods.[12] Per capita output of the critical food product, grain, was lower by perhaps 10 percent or more and per capita output of meat, milk, and eggs was lower by 47 percent, 37 percent, and 61 percent, respectively. On the other hand, per capita output of potatoes, vegetables, and fish rose, while that of various fabrics and shoes either fell somewhat or remained as in 1928. In contrast, communal consumption as indicated by school enrollments and hospital beds per 10,000 persons showed substantial gains. These diverse indicators add up to a clear impression of a substantial fall in overall per capita consumption for the years 1928–32; real wages may have dropped by as much as two fifths.[13] Whether the drop was greater for peasants or for urban dwellers is a moot question; the intrepid Naum Jasny has calculated measures of "real per capita incomes" for both groups in this period which suggest that there may have been little difference.[14]

The period of the Second Five-Year Plan (1933–37) brought a measure of relaxation in the frantic tempo of the race to industrialize and collectivize, and the population's level of living was permitted to regain lost ground. For the statistical record of the measurable changes between 1928 and 1937 we are indebted to the definitive studies by Abram Bergson and Janet Chapman,[15] whose findings are the principal basis for the discussion to follow. According to these calculations, per capita consumption rose from the depressed levels of 1932–33 to a level in 1937 that was 10 percent above that in 1928. All the improvement made over the period 1928–37 as a whole was the result of a more than tripling of government expenditures for education and health and similar communal benefits, for per capita household expenditures actually declined a little. By 1937 per capita output of all major foods except meat, milk, and eggs were above 1928 levels, but in the case of the three quality

---

[12] The figure for grain is derived from Naum Jasny, *Socialized Agriculture of the USSR* (Stanford, Cal.: Stanford University Press, 1949), p. 792. All other data, compiled from a variety of sources, are derived from citations in Janet G. Chapman, "Consumption," in *Economic Trends in the Soviet Union,* ed. Abram Bergson and Simon Kuznets (Cambridge, Mass.: Harvard University Press, 1963), pp. 238–39.

[13] This order of magnitude is suggested by Hanson, who carefully reviews and summarizes the diverse evidence on this question. *The Consumer in the Soviet Economy,* pp. 33–37.

[14] Naum Jasny, *Soviet Industrialization, 1928–1952* (Chicago: University of Chicago Press, 1961), p. 447.

[15] Abram Bergson, *The Real National Income of Soviet Russia Since 1928* (Cambridge, Mass.: Harvard University Press, 1961). Janet G. Chapman, "Consumption," in *Economic Trends in the Soviet Union,* ed. Bergson and Kuznets, pp. 235–82.

foods was still about a third lower. Food was rationed throughout most of this period. Per capita outputs of nearly all important non-food goods were significantly higher in 1937 than in 1928. In contrast to overall per capita consumption, real wages of nonagricultural wage and salary workers in 1937 were still only some 60 percent of the 1928 level. The main explanation for the lag in real wages is to be found in the large and continued influx of unskilled workers into the cities; their relatively low wages and large share of the total slowed the rate of growth of average urban wages.

The traumatic events of the period of the purges, along with a rapid military buildup, brought another setback in the population's level of living during 1938–40. Almost without exception the various indicators of consumption declined. Overall per capita consumption in 1940 was 4 percent below 1937, and real wages were 6 percent lower. The only improvement in a major aggregate was in communal services, but by a mere 1 percent. With the advent of full-scale mobilization and war, levels of living fell precipitously, reaching perhaps about two thirds of the 1928 level in 1944. The low levels apparently continued for several years after the end of the war.[16] In summary, one may conclude that thirty years of war, revolution, and radical economic transformation had left the Russian people far worse off in material welfare than they were before World War I. Beginning in about 1948 things began to improve rapidly, as the period of reconstruction neared completion.

Consumption Trends Since 1950. (See Appendix Table 1.) The two decades since 1950 have brought a radical improvement in the lot of Russian consumers. The rise in both per capita consumption and real wages was steady and fast;[17] by 1967 per capita consumption had doubled compared with 1950, and had risen somewhat more than that, when compared with 1928 or 1913. Significant improvement occurred in all major areas of consumption. In contrast to the previous two decades, however, private household consumption increased a little more rapidly during the past two decades than did communal services, and

[16] Jasny, *Soviet Industrialization, 1928–1952*, p. 447. His index for real per capita personal income in 1948 is 67 with 1928 as a base of 100.

[17] The basic data for the period since 1950 are those presented in the several publications of the Joint Economic Committee, in particular: David W. Bronson and Barbara S. Severin, "Recent Trends in Consumption and Disposable Money Income in the USSR," in *New Directions in the Soviet Economy* (Studies Prepared for the Subcommittee on Foreign Economic Policy of the Joint Economic Committee, 89th Cong., 2d sess.) (Washington, D.C.: U.S. Government Printing Office, 1966), Part II-B, pp. 495–529; *Soviet Economic Performance, 1966–67* (Materials Prepared for the Subcommittee on Foreign Economic Policy of the Joint Economic Committee, 90th Cong., 2d sess.) (Washington, D.C.: U.S. Government Printing Office, 1968), pp. 89–96; and David W. Bronson and Barbara S. Severin, "Consumer Welfare," in *Economic Performance and the Military Burden in the Soviet Union* (A Compendium of Papers Submitted to the Subcommittee on Foreign Economic Policy of the Joint Economic Committee, 91st Cong., 2d sess.) (Washington, D.C.: U.S. Government Printing Office, 1970), pp. 93–99.

in contrast to the pre-war period, real wages grew more rapidly in the post-war period than did per capita consumption: in 1968 the respective indexes were 228 and 215 (1950 = 100). Another notable feature of this period is the far more rapid improvement in real incomes of the peasants than in those of urban dwellers,[18] although progress was not even throughout the period. During 1950–55 per capita consumption rose at an average annual rate of 6 percent, but the rate fell to 3.5 percent in 1956–60 and to 2.7 percent in 1961–65, standing at an average annual rate of about 5 percent during 1966–69. During the 1950s per capita household consumption grew much more rapidly than communal consumption, but during the 1960s the relationship was reversed.

This pattern in consumption reflected the rapid rate of overall growth in GNP during the early 1950s, the subsequent sharp slowdown in the early 1960s and the moderate recovery in the late 1960s. Above all, however, the pattern reflected major events in agriculture—the large gains following the initial success of Khrushchev's Virgin Lands program, the crop failures of 1963 and 1965, and the above-average crops of 1966–68. Also, the steady though erratic improvement in the consumer's material welfare is the result of a clear upgrading of the regime's investment priorities in favor of consumer-oriented activities. Consumer-oriented investment (agriculture, consumer goods industry, housing, services) actually grew faster than producer-oriented investment during the 1950s and again in 1966–68. The post-Stalin leadership seemed willing at long last to make a start toward redressing the extreme imbalances in the economy that were the legacy of 25 years of Stalinist priorities.

Trends in Major Components of Private Consumption

A clearer understanding of how the material lot of the Soviet people has changed under Communism can be obtained by looking at the major components of household consumption—food, non-food goods, and services including housing—than is possible by contemplating a statistical aggregate such as real per capita consumption. These three categories make up the sub-aggregate "private household consumption," which at present comprises about nine tenths of the value of total consumption. Expenditure on food now makes up nearly three fifths of household consumption; outlays on non-food goods represent about one quarter of the total and for services nearly one sixth. As would be expected, in the USSR, as elsewhere, rising levels of consumption have been accompanied by a heavy fall in the share of food in the total; in the case of the USSR the share of non-food goods has risen more rapidly than

---

[18] According to official Soviet statistics, "real incomes" of wage and salary workers doubled during 1950–67, whereas those of collective farmers tripled. Although these indexes may be somewhat overstated, there is no reason to think that the general picture is not correct.

the laggard services, mainly because of failure by the government to invest adequately in housing and other service facilities. Selected categories of private consumption are discussed in detail in the following sections. (See also Appendix Table 1.)

Food. Clearly, the Soviet people are eating more and better foods than they did in 1913 or in 1928, but the improvement has not been spectacular. Their diet is still heavily loaded with bread and potatoes, and deficient in quality foods such as meat, milk, fruits, and vegetables. The quality of the diet evidently deteriorated during the 1930s and 1940s, with no steady improvement until the post-war period. The greatest gains apparently have come in the consumption of fish, eggs, vegetable oils, sugar, and beer. Per capita consumption of meat, poultry, and lard evidently did not regain the 1928 level until around 1960 and even in 1968 may have been only about one third above 1928. Important gains have been made in consumption of milk and vegetables. Although per capita output of industrially processed foods has nearly quadrupled since 1928, some of this gain represents a shift of processing activities from homes to factories. Again, practically all the advance in this area has come since 1950. These generalizations are based on estimates of agricultural output adjusted to allow for feed and seed where relevant. No allowance has been made in any of the production measures for foreign trade, which would not alter the overall picture significantly in any event.

The Soviet government has also published data on per capita consumption of selected foods in physical units for selected years during 1913–68, but conspicuously absent are data for the intervening years between 1913 and 1950. According to these official statistics, per capita consumption in 1950 was significantly above the 1913 level in all categories except "meat, poultry and lard" and grain products. Since 1950 per capita consumption of grain products and potatoes has fallen steadily, reflecting an improvement in the quality of the diet. Per capita consumption of meats, fish, and milk products nearly doubled, per capita consumption of vegetables rose by half, and kilograms of sugar consumed per capita more than tripled.

Although precise checks cannot readily be made, the data on per capita outputs previously cited tend roughly to support the general validity (or at least the consistency) of the official data on the trends in food consumption, which may, however, exaggerate the trend to some degree. The results of a careful Western estimate show that the official index of food consumption for the period 1959–63 exceeded an independently constructed measure by 8 percentage points.[19]

Clothing. As indicated by output data corroborated by official statistics on consumption, the Soviet people were clothed far better by the end of the 1960s than they were in 1913 or 1928. Per capita output

---

[19] Bronson and Severin, "Recent Trends in Consumption and Disposable Money Income in the USSR," p. 523.

of fabrics more than doubled over the period, with most of the improvement again having come after 1950. The increase was about one quarter during 1928–50, compared with some two thirds during 1950–68. Judging from observations reported by Western visitors to the Soviet Union, the variety, color, and assortment of fabrics underwent something of a revolution during the latter period. Gray was the predominant hue of clothing in the early 1950s, whereas in the late 1960s a wide range of colors and designs was to be seen. In 1928 less than half a pair of hosiery and only half a pair of shoes per person were produced (at least in factories); by 1950 these items were produced at the rate of 2.6 and 1.1 pairs per capita, respectively; and by 1968 these figures had reached 6.2 and 2.5. After 1955 clothing availability and varieties were considerably improved by the government's willingness to import soft goods, albeit almost entirely from other Communist countries. During the 1950s, imports of clothing and footwear amounted to a mere 25 million rubles in most years, but these imports increased rapidly in the 1960s, to reach a total of nearly a billion rubles in 1968. Particularly noteworthy was the five-fold increase in the number of pairs of shoes imported during 1956–68. Despite the great improvement in overall availability, the quality, design, and durability of shoes and clothing are still generally poor, the variety and assortment are extremely narrow, and the prices are relatively high by Western standards. Specific availabilities of a given item, a particular size or color, a given brand, are still a large question mark, as the Soviet press itself points out almost daily.

Consumer Durables.   For all practical purposes, consumer durables were absent from the Soviet consumption pattern prior to World War II. Only clocks, watches, radios, gramophones, sewing machines, bicycles, and motorcycles were produced in any significant quantities before 1950. During 1950–68, however, the output of most consumer durables expanded very rapidly. Particularly noteworthy was the development of a large-scale television industry and of capacities to produce refrigerators, vacuum cleaners, and washing machines. Passenger automobiles also began to be produced in significant quantity around 1955, and the growth in output of bicycles and motorcycles continued apace. But a five-fold increase during the 1950s in the number of sewing machines produced per 1,000 persons evidently brought a satiation of demand, and production was subsequently cut back sharply. Cameras experienced a similar fate.

In appraising progress in the availability of consumer durables, however, data on stocks are much more revealing than production data. Official Soviet statistics on stocks of durables are available for 1960-68; the data for 1968 are given in Appendix Table 2. These data show a steady and rapid increase in per capita stocks of all major consumer durables except automobiles, with television sets, refrigerators, and washing machines far outpacing the others. To put the matter more graphically, about one household out of 10 owned a television set in 1960, whereas about one out of 2 will have a set by the end of the decade if 1970 plans are fulfilled. Comparable figures for washing machines are one out of 20 and one out of 2 and for refrigerators, one out of 25–30 and one out of 3. This is rapid progress indeed. But no such gains were achieved in the other major symbol (or curse?) of modern high-consumption levels—the passenger automobile. Roughly, one Soviet family out of 125 had a car in 1968, the lion's share of the annual output of automobiles being reserved for government use and for export.

Housing. In no major area of consumption has the Soviet citizen made less progress than in the critically important area of housing. In 1913 over four fifths of the population was rural, and therefore the vast bulk of the populace lived in the tiny, one-storey wooden huts typical of the countryside in that period. In terms of housing space per capita, the small urban population was housed little better: according to Soviet official statistics, per capita urban (useful) housing space amounted to 6.3 square meters in 1913, a figure that indicates great overcrowding. Some urban housing was destroyed during World War I and the Civil War. As a result of the widespread urban food shortages accompanying the chaos of World War I, the Civil War and War Communism, city dwellers fled en masse to the countryside, where food was easier to obtain. With the economic freedom that characterized the period of the NEP there was a considerable amount of housing construction, and the net effect of these developments, again according to official statistics based on the 1926 census, was to increase per capita urban housing availability as measured by useful space to about 8 square meters in 1926. Conditions in rural areas may well have worsened, not only because of the increased population, but also because of the destruction resulting from the Civil War.

During the 1920s urban housing construction did not keep pace with the large growth of urban population that accompanied the forced industrialization drive during the years of the First and Second Five-Year Plans. As a consequence, per capita urban housing space dropped sharply, and in 1940 was well below the level in 1926 and only a little above the level of 1913. Rural dwellers perhaps fared better during this chaotic period, in view of the decrease of some 6 million in the rural population. After World War II the pace of housing construction was stepped up, but not until 1960 did the amount of per capita housing space in cities regain the level attained in 1926. Housing construction continued to outpace the growth of urban population, but at a snail's pace. In 1968 the per capita stock of urban housing measured in *living* space rather than in total *floor* space ("useful" space in Soviet terminology) was still only 7 square meters, well below the norm of 9 square meters that the Soviet government has established as the minimum standard for health and decency. "Useful" (or floor) space includes kitchens, bathrooms, closets, and halls, whereas the measure "living space" excludes them.

Judging from official statistics, the per capita supply of rural housing is at present about the same as in urban areas, and therefore also well below the government's sanitary norm. However, the nature of housing in the two areas differs radically. While the typical home for a majority of city residents in pre-revolutionary Russia was a small wooden one-family dwelling "completely lacking in utilities and differing but little from rural huts in respect to design and conditions of sanitation and hygiene,[20] housing in Russian cities at present consists largely of multi-family dwellings with many modern utilities. The typical urban family lives in a one- or two-room apartment built by the state, and a sizeable proportion of families still share kitchens and baths. In rural areas the tiny, one-room wooden house is still the typical dwelling unit, and even the new ones being built on the collective farms are "just like grandfather's hut but with electricity." Virtually all urban dwelling units now have electricity, as do about nine tenths of rural ones, according to Soviet claims. In 1968, 71 percent of urban floor space was in units equipped with running water, and 68 percent in units equipped with plumbing.

The typical Soviet town-dweller is dependent on the government (or on his state enterprise employer) for the quantity, quality and upkeep of his housing. The state owns and directly allocates some two thirds of the total urban housing stock, and is also the principal builder of new housing, accounting for about four fifths of the total in 1968. The average size of apartments in even the newest of such buildings is quite small—about 45 square meters per unit. In addition to its direct role as home-builder the government has permitted and encouraged, to a greater or lesser degree, the construction of houses and apartment buildings by individuals and cooperatives. Although state policy toward private home-building has fluctuated over the years for reasons of expediency, the activity is regarded as ideologically offensive. For a brief period under Khrushchev the state actively encouraged the building of private housing, which spurted sharply during 1957–60, only to recede again following renewed official restrictions. In 1968 private building accounted for 13 percent of the total of newly constructed urban housing, with the cooperatives providing about 6 percent. In rural areas most new housing is privately built.

Although frequent promises have been made to "eliminate the housing shortage" and "to give every single person his own room and every family its own apartment," the plans for housing construction have been regularly underfulfilled in recent years. Only a very large increase in investment and resource allocations can make any substantial dent in the

[20] Timothy Sosnovy, "Housing Conditions and Urban Development in the USSR," *New Directions in the Soviet Economy* (cited in fn. 17), Part II-B, p. 535.

present acute housing shortage, which is the accumulated result of decades of neglect.[21] During 1918–28 some 22 percent of total state investment went to housing; Stalin quickly cut this rate in half during the 1930s and even in the period of post-war reconstruction (1946–50) the rate was only 12 percent. The upgrading of the priority of the sector under Stalin's successors has resulted in the allocation of 15–20 percent of total state investment to housing, but even this larger share has been inadequate to satisfy the population's demand for more and better housing.

Conditions in the cities are slowly improving, nonetheless, notably with regard to provision of more privacy. Most new apartments have private baths and kitchens, but in 1964 in Moscow alone, the tenants in two fifths of the housing units still had to share these facilities with others. Although electricity is nearly universal in cities, other amenities are lacking. For example, in the RSFSR at the beginning of 1969 over one fifth of the urban housing units had no water supply or central sewage, over one quarter did not have central heating and two fifths did not have bath or shower. Worse still, the quality of both new and old housing is poor, a fact which the Soviet press itself frequently laments. And finally, despite recent gains, the waiting lists for new apartments are still long; 18 months to 3 years seems to be typical in most cities. Summing up the situation as of 1958, Janet Chapman concluded that the housing conditions for the average Soviet urban resident probably were similar to those of the city tenement dweller in the U.S. in the 1890's.[22] This same statement may also apply to the situation a decade later, at least insofar as the occupancy rate is concerned; it certainly is above 2 persons per room (excluding kitchens), a rate regarded in the U.S. and Western Europe as representing extreme overcrowding.[23]

Urban housing in the USSR is heavily subsidized by the state, the subsidy amounting to perhaps as much as 80 percent of total housing costs. Rents are nominal and do not cover even the costs of current maintenance. As a result of this huge subsidy, Soviet families spend only about 3.5 percent of their money income on rent, with perhaps a like percentage spent on utilities.[24] As a result, however, the inadequate

[21] Timothy Sosnovy, "The Soviet City (Planning, Housing, Public Utilities)," in *Dimensions of Soviet Economic Power* (Studies Prepared for the Joint Economic Committee, 87th Cong., 2d sess.) (Washington, D.C.: U.S. Government Printing Office, 1962), p. 329.

[22] Chapman, "Consumption," p. 257.

[23] Sosnovy estimated the occupancy rate at 2.33 persons per room in 1965, in his "Housing Conditions and Urban Development in the USSR," p. 545.

[24] Leon M. Herman, "Urbanization and New Housing Construction in the USSR," in *Industrialized Housing* (Prepared for the Subcommittee on Urban Affairs of the Joint Economic Committee, 91st Cong., 1st sess.) (Washington, D.C.: U.S. Government Printing Office, 1969), p. 38.

stock of urban housing is poorly maintained, and a sizeable portion usually is in need of major repairs.[25] Probably in no area of consumption is the gap between the wishes of the people and the priorities of the regime so wide, and no other market in the USSR is in so massive a state of disequilibrium as that for housing.

Personal Services.   The Soviet Union has yet to enter the age of the "service economy." Until 1964 the statistical handbooks contained almost no data on supply of facilities and expenditure on personal services, such as barbering, dry cleaning, hairdressing, laundry and repair of clothing, automobiles and household equipment. Data are now regularly published on "everyday services" and cover the years since 1960. According to these data, some 1.6 million workers were employed in 1968 in 226,000 such service establishments, with a total revenue of 3.1 billion rubles. This amounts to a mere 2 percent of total personal consumption, according to Soviet national income estimates. It should be noted, however, that these services evidently are not wholly included in the "personal consumption" component of these national income estimates which cover only "material production." Personal services are also provided privately, but their extent cannot be measured.

Both the number of establishments and total revenues have increased rapidly since 1960. During 1960–68 the number of enterprises rose by nearly three fifths and revenues tripled. The volume of such services grew far faster than average earnings of wage and salary workers, which increased by about 40 percent. With rising money incomes Soviet consumers, like those elsewhere in the world, are demanding more and better personal services. Part of the growth in expenditure on services in the USSR is a reflection of the greater availability of consumer durables, expenditure on repair of which increased over 5-fold during 1960–68.

Judging by the perennial press complaints, both the quality and the quantity of personal service facilities are grossly inadequate. This sector, like retail trade, has been the victim of decades of investment neglect and a low social status generally. Some idea of the backwardness of the sector in 1968, after a decade of rapid improvement, is shown by the following data on number of service enterprises per 10,000 urban residents: shoe repair, 2.45; dry-cleaners, 0.07; laundries, 0.23; repair of consumer durables, 1.82; barber-shops and hairdressers, 3.08. The backlog of needs in the personal service sector clearly is enormous. By way of contrast, the U.S. in 1963 had the following amenities available per 10,000 population: shoe repair establishments, 1.13 (reflecting both larger quantities of shoes and much better quality than in the USSR);

---

[25] One Soviet source estimates that 24 percent of the residential buildings under control of local Soviets in the RSFSR in 1968 were in a state of "technical disrepair."

dry cleaning shops, 1.8; laundries, 2.28; shops for repair of household appliances, 7.74; and barber and beauty shops, 13.58.[26]

Trends in Communal Consumption

Soviet policy and ideology favor the development of communal consumption at the expense of private consumption, and Soviet consumers have fared relatively better in the favored area as a consequence. Almost from the outset the Soviet government has fostered large-scale programs to develop health services and to educate its people. This heavy state expenditure is reflected in the rapid growth of the index of communal services per capita (expenditure on education, health and physical culture). This index more than tripled during the period of the First and Second Five-Year Plans, rose by nearly one third during 1937–50, and doubled during 1950–68. (See Appendix Table 1.)

These aggregative measures reflect diverse and notable accomplishments. According to Soviet data, literacy is now almost universal among the population aged 9–49, whereas the literacy rate in this group was only 28.4 percent in 1897 and 56.6 percent in 1926. Schooling through the eighth grade is now free, compulsory, and nearly universal, and a program for universal secondary education is being actively pursued. The average educational attainment of the population aged 16 years and older is now a little over 7 years, compared with 5 years in 1950 and perhaps about 4 years in 1926.

Another measure of educational progress is the proportion of the relevant population age groups enrolled in school. In 1926 only 31.6 percent of children aged 8–17 were in school, but by 1958 the proportion had risen to 87.1 percent.[27] Notable gains also have been made in college education: in 1914–15 a mere 127,000 persons were attending higher educational institutions, compared with 4,123,000 in 1966–67. The Soviet government also operates an extensive system of schools for semiprofessional and technical training, mainly at the secondary level; these schools had nearly 6 million students in 1966–67. Finally, the government has provided a rapidly growing network of nurseries, kindergartens, and day-care facilities, a critically important communal service in a country where most urban women of working age are employed. Extensive provisions have been made for physical culture and sports.

A variety of indicators reflect the government's considerable efforts to provide health care for the population. The number of doctors and dentists per 1,000 population increased from 2 in 1913 to 4 in 1928

---

[26] *Statistical Abstract of the United States, 1969*, p. 768.

[27] Nicholas De Witt, *Education and Professional Employment in the USSR* (Washington, D.C.: National Science Foundation, 1961), p. 138.

and to 25.9 in 1968. The number of hospital beds per 10,000 people rose from 12 in 1913 to 16 in 1928 and to 105 in 1968. The average length of life rose from 44 years in 1926–27 to 70 years in 1966–67, while the infant mortality rate dropped from 182 per 1,000 births in 1928 to 26 in 1968. The last two measures are a reflection not merely of the large government expenditures on public health, but also of the widespread improvement in living conditions in general.

These are impressive gains. Health care, as well as education, is provided to the people without direct charge, except for prescriptions, drugs, books, and a few similar items. While the quality of both education and health services may leave something to be desired, the fact that they are "free" undoubtedly impresses Soviet citizens when they assess and compare the achievements of the economic system. Also important is the steady and rapid improvement in the accessibility of at least a secondary education to everyone and of a higher education to the carefully selected few, whose number, however, continues to grow faster than the relevant population age group. Thus, the opportunities for upward social mobility continue to be numerous, growing, and evident.

In addition to these material aspects of communal consumption, the Soviet government redistributes resources via substantial transfer payments under an extensive social security scheme. Pensions and allowances of all kinds have comprised a growing share of total household incomes; according to one estimate they amounted to 3.2 percent of household outlays for consumption in 1928, 2.8 percent in 1940, 6.5 percent in 1950 and 10.4 percent in 1958.[28] While this calculation has not been extended, the share must have continued to rise during the following decade, since total pensions and grants have increased considerably faster than total household consumption expenditures. The bulk of these transfer payments takes the form of pensions for old age and disability. Other major components are sickness benefits and maternity grants of various kinds. By the end of 1937 all these programs had been extended to all wage and salary workers. Notably absent were provisions for unemployment compensation (abolished in 1930 along with the "abolition" of unemployment itself.) Also missing was a provision for state pensions to collective farmers. The value of all state social benefits, moreover, declined steadily relative to average wages until 1957, when a new pension law took effect, sharply raising benefits and extending coverage. Since then, social insurance payments have risen only a little more slowly than average wages. In 1968 the minimum wage was increased from 40 rubles per month to 60 rubles per month, although the minimum old age pension remains at 30 rubles per month—the same as in 1957. Collective farmers were finally brought under a state pension and social insurance system by major reforms adopted in 1964 and 1968. While the farmers' benefits are not yet on a par with those for wage and

---

[28] Chapman, "Consumption," p. 244.

salary workers, these measures represent a giant step toward removing the second-class citizenship status long accorded to collective farmers.

A Sketch of Urban-Rural Differences in Consumption

A thorough investigation of long-term trends in relative levels of consumption by the rural and urban population of the USSR has yet to be made. The data with which to do so are not very satisfactory. In the preceding sections diverse evidence has been adduced on this question. The few pertinent official Soviet statistics indicate that the lot of the peasant has improved more than that of the urban worker since 1913. The Soviet authorities publish summary indexes of "real incomes" of wage workers in industry and construction and of "real incomes" of peasants for the period of Soviet power, and according to these official claims the real income of the peasants rose 11-fold during 1913–68, compared with a 7-fold increase for workers. "Real incomes" include a variety of state-provided benefits and services. The method of constructing these indexes is only dimly understood, and they clearly are greatly inflated, particularly for the years before 1950.[29] Neverthe-less, it may well be true that the peasants are now better off relative to urban wage earners than they were in 1913, and nearly all this relative improvement must have occurred since 1950, when the post-Stalin rulers took numerous measures to reduce the differential. According to Soviet data "real incomes" of collective farmers more than tripled during 1950–67, whereas "real incomes" of wage and salary workers doubled.

Nevertheless, the present gap in levels of living in rural and urban areas in still large, even if one accepts the Soviets' own claims about the relative levels in 1913 and their rates of improvement since then. A variety of official Soviet statistics reveal the differences unequivocally. The data on per capita consumption of various foods indicate a substan-tially better diet in urban areas than in rural areas. According to these data the average collective farmer consumed nearly 25 percent less meat and vegetables, nearly 10 percent less milk, about 40 percent less fish, and more than 10 percent less sugar and vegetable oil in 1968 than did the average wage and salary worker. On the other hand, collective farmers ate much more bread and potatoes. Manufactured consumer goods also were far less available in rural areas than in urban areas. In 1968, per capita sales of watches, radios, television sets, and several other major consumer durables in rural areas were only half or less of those in urban areas. Per capita sales of non-food goods in state

[29] For a discussion of these Soviet measures of real income see Gertrude E. Schroeder, "An Appraisal of Soviet Wage and Income Statistics," in *Soviet Economic Statistics,* ed. Vladimir G. Treml and John P. Hardt (Durham, N.C.: Duke University Press, 1972), pp. 287–314. For an indication of the gross inflation of the index pertaining to wage workers, see Janet G. Chapman, *Real Wages in Soviet Russia Since 1928* (Cambridge, Mass.: Harvard University Press, 1963), pp. 155–64.

and cooperative trade outlets in rural areas in 1968 were only a little over one third of those in urban areas. Similar large differences are shown by data on total sales of a wide variety of manufactured consumer goods by state stores compared with those by consumers' cooperatives, which operate almost entirely in rural areas. Fortunately for the rural inhabitant the long-existing discriminatory price surcharges on a wide variety of everyday household items were finally removed in 1966. In contrast to the clearly lower level of per capita consumption of consumer goods, however, the average rural resident now has a slight edge over the average town-dweller in housing—7.5 compared with 7.2 square meters of living space. The social and cultural amenities available in rural areas are far fewer than those in urban areas, and the communist goal of eliminating the difference between city and village is still far in the future.

CONSUMER PROBLEMS AND PROSPECTS

Changing Policies and Problems

For Stalin the policies to be pursued in relation to the consumer were clear and simple to put into effect. A bare minimum of the essentials of life—food, clothing, and shelter—and little else must be provided in order to maintain the ability of the labor force to produce. Substantial investment would have to be made in human capital—health and education—in order to raise productivity, while the surplus above subsistence would have to be mobilized and overwhelmingly directed toward producer-oriented investment in order to achieve rapid growth and military potential and "eventually" to provide a greater flow of consumer goods. To maintain incentives, money incomes would need to be permitted to rise, and, moreover, to rise more rapidly than the supply of consumer goods. This latter policy was elevated by Stalin himself to the status of a "law of socialism," namely, that demand must always exceed supply. This "law" was most convenient, for the chronic sellers' market meant that any product could find an eager buyer, thus greatly facilitating the management of the consumer sector. Under these policies, per capita consumption at the time of Stalin's death in 1953 was little higher than at the outset of the industrialization drive in 1928. Within the period, moreover, consumption was sharply reduced at times by exogenous crises—the collectivization disasters of the early 1930s, the purges, and the events of World War II.

The result of the single-minded pursuit of these policies for 25 years produced an economy with the dubious distinction of being the most unbalanced in the world among industrialized countries. Stalin's legacy was a population ill-housed, ill-clothed and ill-fed and a set of problems of vast dimensions—an acute housing shortage, a primitive retail trade network, a technologically backward and inefficient consumer goods industry, and a stagnant and unproductive agriculture. Small wonder that his successors felt constrained to resort to shock tactics in an attempt to begin redressing the balance. During his brief tenure as Premier, Malenkov took the unprecedented and ideologically suspect step of scheduling a faster rate of growth of consumer goods (group B) than for producer goods (group A). Khrushchev quickly corrected this heresy, but himself proceeded to give consumption a boost by means of a great leap forward in agriculture—the colossal Virgin Lands venture. The impact was quickly noted in rapid gains in both food supplies and light industry output. Machinery plants were given the go-ahead to turn out consumer durables in quantity, and the claim of housing on investment resources was sharply raised. During the 1950s consumer oriented investment grew much faster than producer-oriented investment.[30] With this notable reorientation of policy, per capita consumption took a great leap forward, rising by 50 percent in 8 years (1950–58). This was indeed a remarkable achievement.

But suddenly and without warning Khrushchev reasserted the old priorities, and in each of the years 1959–64 consumer-oriented investment grew much more slowly than producer-oriented investment. Housing investment in each year declined absolutely, and the previous policy of state encouragement of private home building was reversed. A similar fate befell the private sector in agriculture. Unfortunately, these policy reversals were accompanied by a series of poorer than average crop years, and a severe crop failure in 1963. Although the regime hastened to import wheat in large quantities, it also took steps to conserve grain (and foreign exchange) by raising the extraction rate in milling grain into flour, thus degrading the quality of bread and bakery products. This blow to consumers followed upon one a year earlier that entailed sharply increased prices for meat and butter, a measure resulting in open civil disturbances. In statistical terms all this produced a halving of the rate of growth of per capita consumption during 1959–64.

Yet one more problem—new to the Soviet scene—arose to plague the hard-pressed Khrushchev. The period of relative affluence for Soviet consumers in real terms was accompanied by a rapid increase in money incomes of both urban workers and collective farmers (about 10 percent annually during 1950–58). The most urgent consumer wants were met, and the urban consumer became choosy and no longer willing to buy anything and everything that was put before him. Stocks of unsaleable goods accumulated in retail stores, and during 1959–64 inventories of textiles, clothing, and shoes increased nearly twice as fast as retail sales. Although the rate of growth of personal disposable incomes was cut

---

[30] *Soviet Economic Performance, 1966–67* (cited in fn. 17), p. 43, and *Economic Performance and the Military Burden in the Soviet Union* (cited in fn. 17), p. 52.

in half during 1959–64, it still exceeded the rate of growth of retail sales. The growth of savings bank deposits accelerated rapidly, and repressed inflation became evident in the steady rise in the ratio of food prices on collective farm markets relative to those in state retail stores (from 1.31 in 1959 to 1.63 in 1964).[31] Clearly, all was not well in the consumer sector.

Following Khrushchev's ouster in late 1964 the new leadership abruptly reversed some of his latter-day policies. In each of the years 1965–69 the rate of growth of consumer-oriented investment exceeded that of producer-oriented investment, and was scheduled to do so again in the plan for 1970.[32] "Group B" industrial output grew faster than "Group A" in 1968 and 1969. Khrushchev's restrictions on the private sector in agriculture were lifted, but not in housing. A poor harvest in 1965 was met by importing wheat, not by degrading the quality of flour. Then, three above-average crop years in a row gave a big boost to consumption. The quality and variety of clothing and footwear benefited greatly from a near-doubling of imports of these items during 1965–68. The jubilee year of 1967 saw the import of 100 million dollars' worth of goods from the West.[33] In the aggregate these developments produced a new spurt in per capita consumption during 1965–69, with an average annual growth of nearly 5 percent.

Some of the problems inherited from the 1950s and early 1960s have eased somewhat, but others have become worse. The piling up of unsaleable stocks of consumer goods was reversed by a combination of selective price cuts, installment credit and allocation of larger supplies to rural areas, where incomes have been rising faster than in ruban areas, but where the still relatively low incomes and still pervasive shortages make consumers less fussy. However, press complaints about erratic shortages and poor quality of goods and services are as rife as ever. Repressed inflation is becoming even more evident. The growth of money incomes during 1965–68 considerably outpaced the growth of real consumption, and savings bank deposits grew nearly 20 percent annually in each year. In 1968 the average savings deposit equalled 4 months' wages for the average urban worker and even more for the average rural worker. In 1969 almost 70 percent of each additional ruble of income was saved.[34] A level and rate of saving of this magnitude is a remarkable phenomenon for a relatively low-income country. On the one hand, it attests to the gross failure of the regime to provide the kind and quality of goods and services that the people want to buy and doubtless would buy at their income level. On the other hand, it testifies to the faith

---

[31] Bronson and Severin, "Recent Trends in Consumption and Disposable Money Income in the USSR," p. 514.

[32] *Economic Performance and the Military Burden in the Soviet Union,* p. 52.

[33] *Soviet Economic Performance, 1966–67,* p. 90.

[34] *Economic Performance and the Military Burden in the Soviet Union,* p. 99.

of the people that one day what they want will become available and that their savings will not be confiscated by a monetary revaluation or other device in the meantime.

Recent Leadership Response

Although the difficulties in the consumer sector are not new, the scope of the government's recent efforts to deal with them has been unusually great, suggesting a serious if still conditional commitment to a more consumer-oriented economic policy. The principal initiatives that have been taken have involved allocation of additional resources to the consumer sector, reform of incentives and administrative arrangements in the production and distribution of consumer goods, and a variety of *ad hoc* measures adopted to cope with specific problems.

Resource Allocation. Reflecting a shift in recent years to be a more balanced and moderate pattern of economic growth, the Soviet government has been allocating an increasing share of annual increments in output to consumption. Western calculations indicate that the average annual rate of growth in the Soviet gross national product decelerated from 6.0 percent in the 1950s to 5.4 percent during 1961–70, while the growth rate of consumption slowed only 0.3 percentage points, from 4.7 to 4.4 percent. In the years 1966 to 1970, consumption actually increased at a slightly faster rate than the gross national product. In the last three years of that period, the growth rate for the output of industrially produced consumer goods was greater than that for the output of producer goods, a phenomenon which once would have been regarded as a heretical violation of ideological prescriptions. In addition, the consumer sector was allocated a larger share of total investment than in the past. For the first three years of the 1966–70 plan period, consumer-oriented investment (including that in agriculture) actually increased somewhat faster than producer-oriented investment, although the latter reasserted a small lead thereafter. Partly as a result, the consumption goals of a five-year plan were fulfilled in 1966–70 for the first time in Soviet history. In the same period, the government began to use more of its scarce hard currency to import considerable amounts of consumer goods from the West. Annual imports of nonfood goods increased steadily during 1966–70—from $123 million in 1966 to over $290 million in 1970.[35]

The allocation of resources in the newest five-year plan (for 1971–75) will be discussed shortly in the context of the overall objectives of the plan and its record of performance to date.

Reforms in the Consumer Sector. Radical improvements in the efficiency of the consumer sector, in the quality and assortment of consumer products, and in retail services were among the main objectives of the general economic reforms that were adopted in 1965 and are

---

[35] Based on data compiled by the author from Soviet sources.

still being implemented. Indeed, experimental reforms were first tried out in a number of consumer-goods plants, before a revised variant was adopted for application to the general economy. The major provisions of the 1965 reforms seemed tailor-made for solving the chronic problems in the production of consumer goods. Replacement of "value of output" with "sales" as a success indicator for enterprises seemed to provide an inducement for managers to produce only goods that could be sold and thus to pay more attention to the quality and the assortment of output. Extension and enforcement of direct contracts between producers and retail stores again seemed aimed at orienting production plans toward meeting consumer demand. Adoption of profits as a second success indicator appeared to offer a prod to managers to economize on resources. Finally, new pricing arrangements seemed to encourage managers to produce new and higher-quality products.

The adoption of the economic reforms proceeded more slowly in the two major branches producing consumer goods (food and light industries) than elsewhere, allegedly because of the large number of small and low-profit enterprises in those branches. As of mid-1970, when all enterprises of most industrial ministries were operating under the new arrangements, 30 percent of the enterprises under the USSR Ministry of Light Industry and 6 percent of those under the USSR Ministry of the Food Industry still operated according to pre-reform rules. The experience of those consumer-goods plants to which the reform was applied was similar to that of enterprises in general.[36] In practice, the sales-oriented performance indicators merely supplemented rather than supplanted gross-value-of-output assignments and specific quantitative targets; ministerial tutelage and proliferating regulations circumscribed the managers' freedom of action; direct contracting turned out to be largely a formality, and penalties for contract violations were largely ineffective; pursuit of profits led managers to turn out the products that an arbitrary pricing system made "profitable," irrespective of what customers wanted or contracts provided; the new success criteria, coupled with new pricing rules, led managers to "upgrade" and "renovate" product assortments in ways that in reality amounted to hidden price increases.

The continuation of consumer complaints about quality and assortment in 1971–72 testified to the ineffectiveness of the reforms in ameliorating, let alone solving, these longstanding problems. The failure of the economic reform to improve matters in the consumer sector is graphically illustrated by a recent article in *Izvestia*, which details the woes of the clothing firm "Bolshevichka." This firm's experience under the experimental reforms in 1964–65 was a great success story. But in 1972, nobody seemed to want to buy Bolshevichka's suits any more; they began to

---

[36] For details of the experience under the reform in general, see Gertrude E. Schroeder, "Soviet Economic Reform at an Impasse," *Problems of Communism,* Vol. XX, No. 4 (July–August 1971), pp. 36–46.

pile up in warehouses, and even the firm's own retail stores pleaded for a halt in deliveries. Nonetheless, superior organs increased the production plan, which the plant could not fulfill because it could not obtain the higher-priced fabric required. As a result, the plant's workers were penalized by loss of bonuses, and more unsalable goods were produced.

The much-touted introduction of direct commercial ties between producers and retail stores has also failed to rationalize the manufacture and delivery of consumer goods to any significant degree. In the first place, only the relatively few retail stores that operate independently on a system of profit-and-loss accounting (*khozraschet*) and large firms like Bolshevichka are allowed to contract directly with producer enterprises and suppliers; the rest continue to be supported through wholesale outlets which in turn place orders with industrial producers. Even where direct ties have been established, a host of problems have developed: contracts are frequently violated by one or the other or both parties; financial sanctions have proved ineffective in preventing contract breaches; goods delivered according to contracts concluded at trade fairs turn out to be different from the original samples; and so on. Producing enterprises fail to deliver promised consignments because production plans have been arbitrarily changed by higher authorities, because needed inputs do not arrive on time, because shipment of goods other than those specified in contracts is more profitable, or because there are transport failures. Retail units, in turn, refuse to accept goods because they find they have overestimated demand or because the goods do not meet specifications as to quality or mix. On the other hand, stores sometimes accept unordered goods because the alternative is not to receive anything and not to fulfill the plans for turnover. A kind of vicious circle thus prevails, where there are failures all along the line and everybody can blame somebody else. Nobody (or everybody) is at fault, and foul-ups are epidemic. A lengthy government decree (of early 1969) prescribing the rules and regulations governing the delivery of consumer goods apparently has been of little help.

The government has also attempted to introduce various managerial reforms in the area of retail trade. In this sector the reforms have been adopted in two stages. The first stage, completed in 1969, essentially involved a simplification of planning procedures and was ostensibly designed to increase the leeway for managerial initiative. Instead of a long list of specific targets, only the volume of trade turnover and of profits for a given year were to be set in central agencies. However, in exercising their right to set all other plan indicators, managers of retail trade enterprises were required to remain within a host of centrally determined parameters for such items as wage rates and prices.

The second stage entailed the adoption of a new system of incentives stressing sales and profits and resembling that in industry. Although this phase was started experimentally in 1966, only in 1971, following the issuance of a detailed set of instructions governing the new arrangements, did the system begin to be broadly applied. By early 1972, this phase of the reform encompassed some 18,000 retail enterprises, accounting for about 28 percent of the total trade turnover in the USSR Ministry of Trade. The extention of the incentive features of the reform to retail trade is severely handicapped by the low rate of profitability of the sector. In 1970 only 4 percent of retail trade enterprises were on profit-and-loss accounting, and even some of those units worked at a loss. Retail trade markups are widely regarded as being too low. Also, the pricing system makes some goods very "profitable" to sell (e.g., vodka), while others (e.g., potatoes and vegetables) result in losses to the stores. Although spectacular successes have been reported for some trade enterprises put under the new incentive arrangements, the problems in this sector appear to be unusually complicated. A major concern, for example, is how to devise a bonus system that will induce employees to cater to customers' wants with courtesy and efficiency.

Resort to Decrees and Campaigns.   Mounting evidence of continuing malaise in the consumer sector, due in part to the inadequacy of the reform program, has led the government to try once again to cure its economic problems by administrative fiat, an approach used often in the past but with little effect. A decree adopted in late 1969 called for a broad range of actions to increase and upgrade consumer everyday services. In late 1969 and 1970, two decrees were issued dealing with the intractable problem of product quality; they applied to industry in general and provided various penalties for laxity. The press uproar in 1970 over shortages of dishes produced a resolution "On Increasing the Production, Widening the Assortment, and Improving the Quality of High-grade Dishware."

Continuing signs of consumer frustration—given added impact, perhaps, by the eruption of discontent in Poland in December 1970—resulted in at least four more major decrees. Two of them were aimed at increasing output and facilities during 1971–75 in two consumer-related industries—chemical fibers and meat-and-dairy products. These measures were issued in September and December 1971 respectively and were typical of similar action-demanding documents issued in the past.

A third decree, published on January 30, 1972, outlined measures to improve retail trade. Like numerous predecessors, it relied mainly on an exhortation to the ministries and agencies concerned to ensure the solution of all the problems in retail trade. It also specified targets and investment allocations for 1971–75. One innovation provided for the establishment of an Interdepartmental Council under the Ministry of Trade to study the demand for consumer goods. The membership of this Council was to comprise representatives of the Ministry of Trade, the ministries producing consumer goods, the trade unions, and the Central Union of Consumer Cooperatives—the agency responsible for retail trade in rural areas.

The fourth decree, entitled "On Measures for the Further Development of the Production of Goods in Mass Demand," was published under joint party-government imprimatur on October 29, 1971. By far the strongest of the recent directives, this measure reflected the leadership's extreme frustration at the continuing shortages of a wide variety of ordinary household items, especially "odds and ends" ranging from meat grinders to wood screws, which the press refers to as "a thousand trifles." The decree specified output targets for 1971–75 for a long list of such goods, many of which (at least 67) had not previously been centrally planned. Among other provisions was a demand for the full utilization of existing capacities for production of such goods and the expeditious creation of new ones. In a departure from past practice, the decree also provided that consumer goods output was to count toward plan fulfillment at plants in the heavy industrial sector manufacturing such goods as a secondary line of output. Enterprise performance in this regard was to affect the size of incentive funds, and bonuses for managerial and office employees were to depend on fulfillment of plans and contracts for delivery of consumer goods. "Personal responsibility" was assigned to the heads of ministries and departments for fulfilling the provisions of the decree and for "ensuring the production of high-quality goods in mass demand in accordance with the orders placed by trade organizations"; "personal responsibility" was also assigned to the all-union and union-republic ministers of trade for the "correctness of their stated needs for goods." The councils of ministers of the 15 union republics were instructed to "ensure systematic checkups on the state of affairs with respect to the production of consumer goods in every industrial enterprise, regardless of its departmental subordination, and to take steps for the utilization of emerging possibilities for increasing the production of goods in popular demand." These were unusual assignments of responsibility. In addition, party organs at all levels were instructed to "exercise daily supervision" over fulfillment of the tasks spelled out in the decree.

There has been an unusually large amount of follow-up on this edict and also on the decree concerning retail trade, suggesting that strong party pressure is being brought to bear to insure their implementation. As might be expected, the various bureaucracies concerned soon published detailed instructions on the new planning and incentive arrangements for ordering and producing consumer goods. The new council to study demand was quickly set up, complete with republic and lower level subcouncils, and has begun publication of an information bulletin. The injunction to produce more consumer goods has assumed the status of a major "campaign," with heavy emphasis placed on publicity, pledges, socialist competition, and checkups on performance by party and control bodies at all levels. Producer-goods plants are being pressured to climb on the band wagon *en masse;* the leadership evidently is convinced that large "hidden reserves" exist in heavy industry that can be tapped for consumer-goods production. Short of direct imports, the mobilization of such reserves may appear to be the fastest way to meet the needs of impatient consumers.

Although there have been a number of "success" stories in the press concerning plants that have fulfilled consumer-goods pledges, increased the proportion of their consumption output, introduced new consumer products, and so forth, the problems created by this latest and most energetic campaign appear to be legion. The overall impression is one of utter confusion. Nobody seems to know how much of what is needed where, so plants, under severe pressure to produce something, make whatever they can produce most easily. Usually they also have to make their own designs and parts. Long delays and red tape are involved in getting designs and prices approved by appropriate agencies. Several plants in a given city may begin making the same articles—say, trays or candlesticks—thus producing a glut on the local market. Nobody knows if the surplus products are needed in other areas of how to organize their sale. Numerous local agencies are now involved in the endeavor to "force" greater consumer-goods output on enterprises of heavy industry, and conflicts arise between these agencies and the producer ministries. Meanwhile, press complaints of sporadic surpluses and shortages and of the poor quality of goods have continued at the same level of intensity as in the past.

The Ninth Five-Year Plan

Evidence bearing on the seriousness of the regime's stated intent to give priority to the consumer sector may be gleaned by a detailed examination of the goals set in the Five-Year Plan for 1971–75. At the time the plan was announced, much publicity was focused on the scheduling—for the first time in a Soviet five-year blueprint—of a faster growth rate for industrially produced consumer goods than for producer goods and of a rise in the share of consumption in national income. The plan in fact provided for substantial increases in the production of consumer goods and services and for a broad range of increases in money incomes and social benefits. A close look at the numerous published targets reveals, however, that the rate of improvement in per capita consumption was actually scheduled to be somewhat lower than that achieved during the preceding plan period, although considerably above the low rate recorded in 1961–65. The slowdown was particularly evident in such areas of state-provided communal (or social) consumption as health and education. On the other hand, a notable exception was a large planned increase in the provision of passenger automobiles for sale to the public. Table 1 offers some comparisons of the rates of growth achieved in 1966–70 with those planned for 1971–75.

With reference to the first category, i.e., "Indicators," planned in-

TABLE 1
Deceleration of Consumer Gains, 1966–70 and 1971–75
(in percent)

	Growth, Plan	
	1966–70	*1971–75*
Indicators*		
Real income per capita.	33	31
Average wages.	26	22
Real income of collective farmers.	54	40
Social consumption funds per capita.	44	34
Retail trade per capita	37	35
Per capita consumption of food		
Meat and meat products	17	23
Milk and milk products	22	11
Eggs	28	21
Fish	22	43
Vegetables.	14	33
Per capita consumption of non-food goods		
Cloth.	15	15
Knitwear.	26	43
Leather shoes	25	20
Household stocks of consumer durables†		
Television sets.	112	41
Refrigerators	191	100
Washing machines	148	29
Radios	22	30
Sewing machines	8	9
Housing		
Urban living space per capita	10	8

*Calculated from Soviet data and based on Soviet definitions of these indicators.
†Derived from Soviet statistics on stocks per 100 families.

creases in wages and welfare benefits for 1971–75, although less than the rates of growth achieved in 1960–70, implied a rise in per capita disposable income that should significantly exceed the planned increase in per capita household consumption (consisting largely of purchases of goods and services by the population). Thus the problem of repressed inflation will persist. According to a Western estimate, per capita disposable money income should rise by 5.8 percent annually from 1971 to 1975, whereas total private and communal consumption will increase only 4.8 percent annually in the same period.[37] Various wage adjustments

[37] Douglas B. Diamond, "Principal Targets and Central Themes of the Ninth Five-Year Plan," in *Analysis of the USSR's 24th Party Congress and Ninth Five-Year Plan,* ed. Norton T. Dodge (Mechanicsville, Md.: Cremona Foundation, 1971), p. 52.

were scheduled to raise average wages in the state sector by 22.4 percent, while the pay of collective farmers was to increase by 30.6 percent. Reduction in income taxes and resumption of repayments of state loans (halted in 1958 but now slated to be resumed in 1974) should further augment disposable income. Furthermore, the plan called for a total of some 8.7 billion rubles in new pension benefits to be disbursed during 1971–75 and for a program of family allowances to be inaugurated in 1974.

With respect to per capita food consumption (the second grouping in the table), while the overall rate of increase was slowed down, the plan called for significant improvements in the quality of the Soviet citizen's diet. Notably, per capita consumption of meat, fish, and vegetables was scheduled to grow much faster than during the 1960s, while the share of bread and potatoes in the diet was to continue to fall. Unhappily, the achievement of these projected gains was seriously jeopardized by the poor harvests in 1971–72.

In the category of soft goods, the plan provided for accelerated growth in the output of cloth, knitwear, and stockings, and for decreased rates of growth but better quality and assortment of shoes and clothing. The latter decisions were probably related to the recent buildup of inventories of these items and to the fact that, with respect to leather footwear, per capita consumption by 1975 should exceed the "scientific consumption norm" (a Soviet index that estimates "reasonable need").

For most consumer durables, the rates of increase in output were scheduled to slow down; actual decreases in output were planned for television sets and washing machines, likely as a response to mounting retail stocks. In part as a result of the difficulties experienced in selling many models of these and other household appliances, the plan called for sharp curtailments in the number of models and concentration on the production of more modern ones. For example, six models of refrigerators were to be produced instead of the former 26, and six models of washing machines were to be made instead of 32. Stocks of most durables in the possession of households were to continue to rise rapidly, although somewhat more slowly than in the past. (Even if the plan is met, however, the supply of such items will remain far below those now available in the Western industrial countries.)

The most grandiose plans for consumer production in 1971–75 concerned implementation of the decision to produce more passenger automobiles for sale to the ordinary citizen. The output of passenger cars was scheduled to increase by more than 300 percent during 1971–75, compared with a rise of about 75 percent in 1966–70; the number of cars sold to the general public was to rise from 124,000 in 1970 to 800,000 in 1975, putting a total of about 3.7 million cars in private hands, compared with 1.2 million in 1970. The key manufacturing facility is the huge new Togliatti plant, which makes Fiat-designed small cars; as of this writing, it is behind in its production schedule. Plans also called for development of a network of large service centers and for close to a sixfold increase in employment in auto service and repairs. Again, however, the implementation of these decisions has already fallen behind schedule, despite a government decree dealing with the subject. Acute shortcomings in this area were illustrated by a press complaint at the end of 1971, when there were only 688 service stations and repair shops in the entire USSR, that repair facilities could fill only about 20 percent of their orders and that as of the previous spring, "about 25 percent of the private cars in Moscow were unable to move." Moreover, as of 1970 the USSR had a mere 128,663 miles of paved roads (compared with 1.66 million in the U.S.).

In the sectors of personal services, retail facilities and housing, the projected rates of improvement were substantial but again somewhat below the rates achieved during the preceding five-year period. The ruble value of a wide variety of personal services was scheduled to double, total retail floor space was to increase by one fifth, and the number of seats in restaurants was to grow by two fifths. The plan provided for the construction of 580 million square meters of new housing; fulfillment of this goal would raise living space per urban resident from about 7.5 square meters to about 8.1 square meters. This projection represented a slower rate of improvement in living space per capita than in the last plan period and reflected a reduced investment priority for housing, whose scheduled share in total capital investment was to drop from 17.1 percent in 1966–70 to 14.7 percent in 1971–75. Even if the plan for housing were met (and if so, it would be the first time that the Soviet government achieved its stated goals in this sector), per capita urban living space would still be well below the minimum standard for health and decency accepted by the government (9.0 square meters per capita). Clearly, only a token installment has been made toward fulfilling Khrushchev's promise to eliminate the housing shortage, and by 1975 the Soviet people should still have poorer housing by far than any major Western country.

Finally, government expenditures on health and education were scheduled to increase only 3.5 percent annually on a per capita basis, the slowest rate of increase in the postwar period.

As already mentioned, the Ninth Five-Year Plan got off to an unauspicious start, largely because of poor weather in agriculture and also because of unexpected difficulties encountered in getting new industrial plants into operation. According to Western estimates, the annual growth of GNP averaged considerably less than 3 percent during 1971–72, agricultural production declined in both years, and the rate of industrial growth was the lowest in the post-war period.[38] Consumer gains slowed significantly, with both per capita consumption and money incomes rising

[38] Based on data in *Soviet Economic Prospects for the Seventies* (A Compendium of Papers Submitted to the Joint Economic Committee, 93d Cong., 1st sess.) (Washington, D.C.: U.S. Government Printing Office, 1973).

by less than 4 percent annually. The output of most consumer goods in 1972 was below the targets set in the Five-Year Plan, as was the number of square meters of housing completed.

As a result of the economic difficulties experienced in 1971–72, the government has approved a plan for 1973 that reduces the original goals for national income, industrial production and investment by substantial amounts. The goals for most consumer-related targets have been cut back, especially for the output of processed food and clothing. Goals for the growth of money incomes and of the money value of state-provided benefits have also been reduced. On the other hand, housing construction in 1973 is scheduled to increase faster than originally planned, and the plan's original priorities for investment in agriculture and in consumer goods industries have been retained. With these large investments, the government hopes to regain some of the setback in the rate of improvement in consumer welfare that has occurred thus far in the plan period.

Systemic Dilemmas

The mix of consumer-related problems urgently in need of solution in the Soviet economy presents the system's administrators with their greatest challenge since the advent of central planning. These problems must be viewed in the context of the gradual ongoing shift to a balanced growth model that accords consumption equal status with investment as a claim on increments of output. With labor reserves largely utilized, future growth depends much more on productivity gains. Moreover, the current stage of development requires that production be oriented to the provision of quality goods and services instead of mere quantities and that the system of distribution be radically improved. Within limits, the present leadership has acknowledged these economic facts; indeed, it has little choice, but the inherent dilemma is painful. On the one hand, consumer wants must be heeded in order to provide the incentives for increased productivity and earnings. But, on the other hand, the system's present institutional arrangements are uniquely unsuited to managing the production and distribution of consumer goods and services for a populace whose basic subsistence needs have been more than met.

Clearly, the leadership is aware of the risks of widespread alienation of the work force, a social disease that could manifest itself in general lassitude and unwillingness to put forth effort, be it physical or mental, routine or creative. Signs of a low-grade current crisis in incentives include the high rate of savings out of current income, the apparently widespread indifference to doing a job well, high rates of absenteeism and labor turnover, and pervasive drunkenness. Up to now, the regime has responded in largely traditional ways—by emphasizing moral incentives, socialist competitions and emulations; by increasing the social pressures exerted by party and control bodies; and by taking measures to combat "parasites" and alcoholism. Such approaches have not been notably effective in the past.

The targets of the Ninth Five-Year Plan indicate that the regime is now seriously concerned about heeding consumer wishes but only partially ready to take the steps necessary to achieve a genuine measure of success. There is no great push to redress the legacies of past imbalances, and the traditional investment priorities have not, on the whole, been greatly altered, although agriculture and the consumer goods industries have been allocated larger shares. A number of measures to increase the quantities of consumer goods and services have been launched with great fanfare, the most spectacular being the effort to make more passenger automobiles available for purchase by the general public. An intensive effort is also being made to alleviate perennial shortages of consumer goods of the "odds and ends" variety by increased centralization of planning and by a campaign to force their production in enterprises of heavy industry. So far, however, the results of these efforts have been disappointing. With respect to the "odds and ends" drive, the regime's approach is palpably short-run and stop-gap in nature; in view of the implicit cost and open confusion generated by this campaign, there is a fair chance it may simply peter out, leaving matters little improved.

Meantime the regime has resorted to increased imports from the West to alleviate shortages of consumer goods. As noted earlier, there is reason to suppose that the Polish riots at the end of 1970 were a sensitizing factor in this respect. Thus, in 1971 imports of non-food consumer goods from the West jumped sharply (by nearly $90 million in just one year). Over the same period, consumption rose significantly faster than the GNP. Again, in response to the crop failure of 1972, the decision was made to import large quantities of grain rather than permit domestic food consumption to deteriorate. It will be interesting to see whether, and to what extent, consumer-oriented rather than producer-oriented imports are curtailed as a consequence of the need to finance these grain purchases.

Obviously, such stop-gap efforts do nothing to eradicate the underlying causes of the consumption crisis. The problem confronting the regime is not simply to provide more or better consumer goods, but to modernize the consumer sector all across the board—and to do so with reasonable dispatch. With by far the most unbalanced economy of any modern nation, the planners face a truly staggering task. In order to redress this imbalance in the short run, massive investments would be needed to provide more housing, retail and service facilities, and machinery for agriculture. Consequences for the rate of economic growth aside, a reorientation of traditional investment priorities on the scale required would meet with formidable resistance from the powerful bureaucracies in defense and heavy industry. Perhaps a really determined leadership with a sense of mission could accomplish the task. Its political prestige with the populace would be enhanced thereby, and the basic essentials of the existing *modus operandi*—of the centrally administered economy—could be preserved. But there are as yet no signs of any such radical change in investment priorities.

Aside from the need for a major reallocation of resources to the consumer sector, the most critical task confronting the Soviet regime is to forge the economic organizations and design the incentives that would assure the matching of supply and demand in fine detail, and with efficiency and dispatch, over the whole range of consumer goods and services. The essence of this problem is to achieve micro-efficiency in a system in which the organizational structure and producer incentives are geared to producing gross quantities that do not necessarily reflect consumer demand.

A key aspect of this task is the radical upgrading of quality—not only of final products, but of the entire chain of material inputs into them. In market systems, competition and the profit motive do the job. Soviet planners are attacking this perennial problem with renewed vigor by imposing a host of norms and standards, by establishing mandatory quotas of "highest grade" products in output plans, and by tying bonuses to a variety of quality indicators. These latest attempts to substitute multiple and complex administrative rules and penalties for the discipline afforded by competition in other economic systems are not likely to be any more successful in the future than in the past.

Another major facet of the problem is to devise means of accurately forecasting current and shifting demand for consumer goods in fine detail—size, style, color, material, models, etc. This is no easy task in any system; for a centrally administered economy, it is herculean. In market economies the tricky task of estimating demand and reacting to it is performed in a highly decentralized process involving numerous independent units, each looking after its own products and spurred to act speedily by competition. In the Soviet economy the forecasting of consumer demand is in its infancy. Market surveys are little used. The function is highly centralized, based on primitive methodologies and poor data, and obviously ineffective.[39] Forecasts are supplemented by the use of "scientific (rational) consumption norms"—calculations of "all that a reasonable man could want," to quote Khrushchev—but these are of little use in short-term planning. Currently, under the impetus of two party-government decrees, a mass assault is being made on the problem of forecasting consumer demand. Everybody is being enjoined

---

[39] The underlying data on surveys of family budgets have been severely criticized in Soviet journals. For a general discussion of the quality of Soviet statistics on consumption and their utility for planning, see Marshall I. Goldman, "Consumption Statistics," in *Soviet Economic Statistics*, ed. Treml and Hardt (cited in fn. 29), pp. 318–46.

to get into the act—individual stores, the Ministry of Trade, its research institutes and its regional subordinates, producer enterprises and their supervisory ministries, and local executive bodies. Party organs at all levels have been directed to assist in and monitor forecasting endeavors. A super-coordinator for all this effort—complete with counterparts at the regional level—has recently been set up.

Meanwhile, the agency created seven years ago with the explicit charter to study market demand is now engaged in coordinating a massive—and seemingly ineffective—demand-forecasting project involving 40 separate research institutes. Bureaucracy seems to be running wild! Granted that the task of forecasting consumer demand without markets is nightmarish, the present approach can scarcely generate much more than frenetic activity and reams of reports by the multiple bureaus involved.

Even if demand could somehow be accurately forecast with the requisite detail and timeliness, there would remain the problem of how to generate incentives ensuring a rapid and precise response to forecasts on the part of producers and the distribution system. The leadership still seems to believe that, given more time, the ongoing economic reform will accomplish this tricky task. The reform's incentive rules are to be extended throughout the economy by the end of 1975. The experience thus far gives no ground for optimism. The reform's new incentive and administrative arrangements have not changed the essentials of the old system, but they have added greatly to the bureaucratization of economic life.

To sum up, the leadership seems committed to the gradual orientation of the economy to better satisfy consumer needs—a policy that is required, in any event, to provide work incentives and political stability. But up to now, the efforts to deal with the manifold problems in the consumer sector have been largely of the traditional variety—campaigns, moral suasion, tinkering with bureaucratic rules, and reorganizations and minor alterations in incentive arrangements. In short, a policy of acquiescing to a slower rate of economic growth and of muddling through seems to have been tacitly adopted. The present ways of tackling the malaise in the consumer sector hardly seem likely to bring about noticeable improvement. If popular unrest becomes widespread, the leadership may be forced to make more radical changes—possibly to permit more private activity and to introduce some degree of decentralization and marketization, at least in parts of the consumer sector. Such a reintroduction of markets and private activity, reminiscent of Lenin's "New Economic Policy" of the early 1920s, would modify the present system in major degree. It would probably take a bold leadership—or a really frightened one—and a real economic crisis to effect a major reform of this nature; but at least the authorities could cite the historical precedent of NEP, and Leninist scriptures could be invoked to lend such a course ideological legitimacy.

APPENDIX

TABLE 1
Selected Indicators of Consumption in the Soviet Union, 1928–68

	1928	1937	1940	1950	1955	1960	1965	1968
1. Total per capita consumption (indexes)								
(1937 = 100)	91	100	96	116				
(1950 = 100)				100	131	158	183	215
2. Per capita consumption excluding communal services (indexes)								
(1937 = 100)	103	100	96	114				
(1950 = 100)				100	130	156	177	207
3. Per capita consumption of communal services (indexes)								
(1937 = 100)	29	100	101	131				
(1950 = 100)				100	119	143	186	211
4. Per capita purchases of goods (indexes)								
(1937 = 100)	91	100	95	120				
(1950 = 100)				100	166	231	281	351
5. Wages (indexes)								
a. Real net average annual wage (excluding non-industrial agriculture)								
(1937 = 100)	175	100	94	101				
b. Real average annual earnings of wage and salary workers								
(1950 = 100)				100	146	165	193	228
6. Hours								
a. Hours actually worked per week in industry	37.3	36.1	39.3	42	42			
b. Hours per calendar week.	46.8	40.8	44.4	48	48			
c. Average scheduled hours of work per week					47.8	40.7	40.7	40.7
7. Per capita industrial output of consumer goods (indexes)								
a. Foods (1937 = 100)	70	100	88	87				
(1950 = 100)				100	146	189	245	271
b. Non-foods (1937 = 100)	64	100	97	114				
c. Soft goods (light industry)								
(1950 = 100)				100	149	190	206	243
d. Consumer durables (1950 = 100)				100	317	574	881	1,364
e. All consumer goods								
(1937 = 100)	68	100	92	97	156			
f. Non-durable consumer goods								
(1950 = 100)				100	147	189	223	255
8. Per capita consumption of selected foods (Official Soviet data in kilograms, except eggs) (Data in column 1 pertain to 1913, not 1928)								
a. Meat, poultry, and lard.	29			26		40	41	48
b. Milk and milk products in terms of milk	154			172		240	251	285
c. Eggs (number).	48			60		118	124	144
d. Fish and fish products	6.7			7.0		9.9	12.6	14.3
e. Sugar.	8.1			11.6		28.0	34.2	37.4
f. Vegetable oil	–			2.7		5.3	7.1	6.5
g. Potatoes	114			241		143	142	131
h. Vegetables and melons.	40			51		70	72	79
i. Grain products (bread in terms of flour, flour, groats, pulses, macaroni products).	200			172		164	156	149
9. Per capita output of selected foods								
a. Flour (kilograms).	158	169	149	121	163	163	160	164
b. Potatoes (kilograms)	110	200	191	259	186	182	180	204
c. Meat, poultry, and lard (kilograms)	32	18	24	24	29	34	38	43
d. Milk (kilograms)	178	141	141	168	187	233	266	292
e. Eggs (number)	65	45	56	65	94	128	126	149
f. Fish (catch) (kilograms)	5.5	9.7	7.2	9.7	14.0	16.5	25.0	28.5
g. Sugar (kilograms).	8.5	14.7	11.1	14.0	17.4	29.7	47.9	45.3

TABLE 1 *(continued)*

	1928	1937	1940	1950	1955	1960	1965	1968
9. Per capita output of selected foods (continued)								
h. Vegetable oil (kilograms)	3.0	3.3	4.1	4.5	6.0	7.4	12.0	13.2
i. Vegetables (kilograms)	53	66	53	52	72	77	76	80
j. Vodka (liters)	3.7	5.4	4.7	3.5	6.0	6.4	–	–
k. Beer (liters)	2.6	5.4	6.2	7.3	9.4	11.7	13.7	16.1
10. Per capita output of selected non-foods								
a. Cotton fabric (linear meters) . .	17.7	20.9	20.3	21.6	30.1	29.8	30.7	31.8
b. Wool fabric (linear meters). . . .	0.6	0.6	0.6	0.9	1.3	1.6	1.6	1.9
c. Silk and synthetic fabric (linear meters)	0.1	0.4	0.4	0.7	2.7	3.8	4.1	4.5
d. Linear fabric (linear meters). . .	1.2	1.7	1.5	1.6	1.6	2.6	2.5	2.9
e. Hosiery (pairs)	0.4	2.5	2.5	2.6	3.9	4.5	5.9	6.2
f. Shoes (pairs).	0.5	1.1	1.1	1.1	1.4	2.0	2.1	2.5
g. Soap (kilograms)	2.0	3.0	3.6	4.5	5.5	6.8	7.7	7.0
h. Cigarettes (number)	327	540	515	695	1,011	1,143	1,318	1,215
11. Consumer durables (output per 1,000 population, except furniture)								
a. Radios	–	1.2	0.8	6.0	18.1	19.4	22.4	29.4
b. Television sets.	–	–	.002	.07	2.5	8.1	15.8	24.1
c. Refrigerators.	–	–	.02	.007	0.8	2.5	7.3	13.3
d. Washing machines.	–	–	–	.002	0.4	4.2	14.9	19.8
e. Vacuum cleaners	–	–	–	.03	0.7	2.3	3.5	5.2
f. Sewing machines	1.9	3.1	0.9	2.8	8.2	14.5	3.5	5.5
g. Electric hot plates	–	–	3.7	9.4	23.4	32.1	26.3	33.2
h. Clocks and watches.	5.9	20.6	12.8	42.0	100.5	121.6	132.6	152.5
i. Cameras	–	2.1	1.8	1.4	5.2	8.2	4.6	7.7
j. Bicycles	0.2	3.0	1.0	3.6	14.7	13.0	16.8	18.1
k. Motorcycles	–	.08	.03	0.7	1.2	2.6	3.1	3.4
l. Automobiles.	.0003	0.1	.03	0.4	0.5	0.6	0.9	1.2
m. Furniture (rubles per 1,000 population)	–	–	–	–	2.5	5.2	7.9	10.2
12. Urban housing space (Per capita living space) (1926 instead of 1928).	5.8	–	4.1	4.7	4.8	5.8	6.8	7.2
13. Publications per capita per year and movies attended per capita								
a. Newspapers	13	–	41	39	51	70	100	117
b. Periodicals	–	1.5	1.3	1.0	1.8	3.6	6.7	9.7
c. Books and pamphlets	1.8	4.1	2.4	4.6	5.2	5.8	5.5	5.8
d. Movies attended	–	–	4.5	6.4	12.8	16.9	18.6	19.8
14. School enrollment per 1,000 population								
a. Grades 1–4	65	128	110	111	70	88	88	90
b. Grades 5 through university . . .	15	64	85	101	110	107	161	164
15. Medical care and health								
a. Doctors per 10,000 population .	4.0	6.0	7.9	14.0	16	20.0	23.9	25.9
b. Hospitals beds per 10,000 population.	16	36	40	56	66	81	97	105
c. Crude death rate per 10,000 population.	23.3	18.9	18.0	9.7	8.2	7.1	7.3	7.7
d. Infant mortality, deaths under one year per 1,000 births	182	170	182	81	60	35	27	26

TABLE 2
USSR and US: Comparison of Selected Indicators of Consumption: USSR, 1968; US, 1890 and 1968

	USSR 1968	UNITED STATES		US 1968 As Percent of USSR 1968
		1890	1968	
1. Per capita consumer income and communal services				
In 1966 Dollars	863*	518	2,362*	274†
2. Average wage, non-farm employees				
a. Annual gross.	1,233*	1,986	6,055*	491†
b. Hourly gross.	0.62*	0.71	2.56*	413†
3. Per capita consumption of major foods (calories per day)				
a. Flour.	1,474	922	647	44
b. Potatoes	255	163	91	36
c. Meat and poultry	204	530‡	634	311
d. Milk	353	575	380	108
e. Fish	20	16	26	130
f. Sugar	354	229	530	150
g. Fats and oils including water . . .	346	408‡	562	162
4. Clothing, output per capita				
a. Cotton fabrics (linear meters). . .	31.8	42.9	37.1	117
b. Wool fabrics (linear meters)	1.9	6.4	1.2	63
c. Other fabrics (linear meters). . . .	7.5	–	26.1	348
d. Hosiery (pairs)	6.2	–	13.1	211
e. Shoes (pairs).	2.5	2.7	2.7	108
5. Consumer durables, sales per 1,000 population (units)				
a. Radios	22	–	59	268
b. Television sets.	21	–	59	281
c. Refrigerators	12	–	26	217
d. Washing machines	18	–	22	122
e. Vacuum cleaners	4	–	32	800
f. Bicycles	17	–	117	688
g. Automobiles.	0.4	–	44	11,000
6. Consumer durables, stocks per 1,000 (units)				
a. Radios	186	–	1,450	780
b. Television sets.	112	–	420	375
c. Washing machines	106	–	207	195
d. Refrigerators	58	–	244	421
e. Automobiles.	5	–	412	8,240
7. Urban housing space				
a. Stock (square meters per capita) .	6.8	–	18.6	271§
b. Rooms per capita	0.4	1.0	1.2	300§
8. Utilities				
a. Percentage of housing with electricity				
Urban	98–100	–	99–100	100–101
Rural.	91	–	99–100	109–110
b. Telephones per 1,000 population.	45	3.7	540	1,200
9. Newspapers per capita				
Per year	117	42	110	94

TABLE 2 (continued)

	USSR 1968	UNITED STATES		US 1968 as Percent of USSR 1968
		1890	1968	
10. Higher education				
a. Enrollment in college, percent of college age population	34.6	3	47.3	137
b. College graduates, percent of population over 24	5.0	–	8.8‖	176§
11. Medical care and health				
a. Doctors per 10,000 population . .	22.5	16	15.5	70
b. Dentists per 10,000 population . .	2.1	2.8	5.6	267
c. Hospital beds per 10,000 population.	105	47	83	79
d. Crude death rate per 1,000 population.	7.7	19.4	9.6	125
e. Infant mortality, deaths under one year per 1,000 births	26	163	21.7	84

*1966.
† US 1966 as percent of USSR 1966.
‡ 1909–13 average.
§ US 1965 as percent of USSR 1965.
‖ 1965.

14. AUTOMOTIVE TRENDS IN THE USSR

Imogene Edwards

The classic symbol of a high-consumption economy is the private automobile. As the Soviet economy shifts toward greater emphasis on individual consumption in a more affluent economy, it is moving toward a large expansion of automobile production. The output of trucks for freight transportation is being increased as well, but the big push is in automobiles.

The Soviet Union is only in the early stages of the automotive era, however. Much of the advanced automotive technology must be imported, service facilities are meager, and the road network is backward. But the USSR has now committed itself to the automobile as part of its pattern of economic growth and increased emphasis on private consumption. The current stages of this transformation are described in this selection.

Imogene Edwards is an economist in the Office of Economic Research of the Central Intelligence Agency. Her paper is reprinted from *Soviet Economic Prospects for the Seventies* (A Compendium of Papers Submitted to the Joint Economic Committee, 93rd Cong., 1st sess.) (Washington, D.C.: U.S. Government Printing Office, 1973), pp. 291–307 and 311–13, with the omission of some source references.

SINCE 1966 the USSR has been engaged in a major effort to modernize its small and underdeveloped automotive industry, and to boost sharply the production of passenger cars and heavy trucks. The modernization and expansion program, vigorously pushed by Soviet leadership at the highest level, marks a radical change in official policy. Soviet leaders from Stalin through Khrushchev had purposely kept output at a low level in order to maintain high growth rates in other sectors of industry. Thus, by 1965, total output of motor vehicles amounted to only 616,000 units and of passenger cars only 201,000, far below that of any other industrialized country. Moreover, Soviet motor vehicle production facilities were antiquated, and the design and quality of both passenger cars and trucks were far below world standards.

The decision to expand motor vehicle production, once made, rapidly assumed the proportions of a crash program. Construction of a new passenger car plant at Tol'yatti during 1966–70 and a new heavy truck plant at Naberezhnyye Chelny during 1971–75 were the largest single industrial investment programs of the Eighth and Ninth Five-Year Plans respectively. The entire modernization program, which will continue at least until 1980 and involve the construction of at least one more truck facility and expansion of the Tol'yatti plant, represents an enormous investment in plant and equipment of up to $5 billion. Secondary and tertiary expenditures for service stations and automotive repair facilities could push total program costs well above the $5 billion mark by 1980. Outfitted mostly with Western (including U.S.) machinery and equipment, the program represents the largest investment in Western technology ever made by a Communist country.

OVERALL GOALS FOR THE NINTH FIVE-YEAR PLAN (1971–75)

The USSR has set ambitious goals for its automotive industry during the current (Ninth) Five-Year Plan (see Figure 1). In 1975, output

FIGURE 1
Soviet Production of Motor Vehicles in Recent Years and Plans for 1975
(thousands of units)

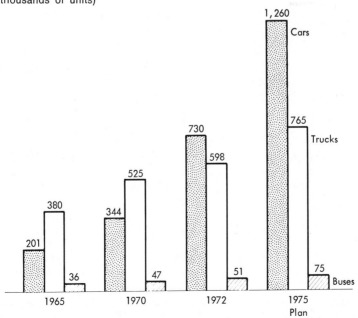

of all motor vehicles—passenger cars, trucks and buses—is planned to reach 2,100,000 units compared to 916,000 units in 1970, an increase of 129 percent. Such an increase in motor vehicle production is unprecedented in Soviet experience and rarely matched in non-Communist countries. In recent years only Japan has achieved a higher rate.[1] Output of passenger cars in the USSR is planned to grow at an especially rapid rate of 30 percent a year as shown in the tabulation below:

	Goal for 1975 (thousands of units)	Increase Over 1970 (percent)	Average Annual Rate of Increase (percent)
Passenger cars	1,260	266	30
Trucks	765	46	8
Buses	75	60	10
Total	2,100	129	18

If output goals are achieved, the USSR will join the United States, Japan, the United Kingdom, West Germany, France, and Italy as a major producer of motor vehicles. Soviet output of motor vehicles will rise from 11 percent of U.S. production in 1970 to about 20 percent in 1975. Output of cars, trucks, and buses for the years 1960 through 1972 is given in Table 1.

TABLE 1
Soviet Production of Motor Vehicles, 1960, 1965, 1970–72 and 1975 Plan
(thousands of units)

	Passenger Cars	Trucks	Buses	Total*
1960	139	362	23	524
1965	201	380	36	616
1970	344	525	47	916
1971	529	564	49	1,143
1972	730	598	51	1,379
1975 (plan)	1,260	765	75	2,100

*Individual figures and totals may not agree because of rounding.

THE PASSENGER CAR PROGRAM

The expansion of the Soviet passenger car industry is a dramatic example of a program whose time had come. Increased availability of

---

[1] Output of motor vehicles in Japan during the past decade grew at an average annual rate of 36 percent.

large consumer durables such as passenger cars is needed to abate the inflationary pressures generated by steady growth in spendable personal income and to increase worker incentives. Moreover, a small and backward passenger car industry is inconsistent with the status of the USSR as the world's second most powerful industrial nation. In 1970 the USSR had only 7 cars for each 1,000 of the population compared to 439 in the United States, 85 in Japan, and 200 to 300 in the car producing countries of Western Europe (see Table 2). Moreover, less than one half of the total Soviet inventory of passenger cars in 1970 was owned by private citizens.

TABLE 2
Motor Vehicles in Use per 1,000 Persons in the USSR and Selected Non-Communist Countries, 1970

		Registrations (thousands)			Vehicles per 1,000 Persons	
	Population (millions)	Cars	Trucks and Buses	Total	Cars	Total
USSR.	241.7	1,650	4,600	6,250	7	26
France	50.8	12,290	2,115	14,405	242	284
Italy	53.7	10,209	929	11,138	190	207
Japan.	103.5	8,779	8,803	17,581	85	170
United Kingdom	55.7	11,792	1,910	13,702	212	246
United States	203.2	89,280	19,127	108,407	439	533
West Germany.	59.6	14,376	1,228	15,604	241	262

Source: Derived from official statistics of the U.S. Department of Commerce and *1972 Automotive Facts and Figures* (Washington, D.C.: Motor Vehicle Manufacturers Association of the United States, Inc., 1972), pp. 28–29.

During 1971–75, a total of 4.7 million cars will be produced, and about 55 percent of these will be sold to private owners. However, sales to consumers as a share of total output are increasing each year and by 1975 will be about three fifths. Most of the remainder will be used by the government for official purposes and to expand the taxi fleet, although a sizeable number of cars also will be exported to Eastern Europe in payment for automotive parts supplied to the Tol'yatti plant. After 1975 the USSR plans to sell large numbers of cars in non-Communist countries, particularly in Western Europe. These sales will constitute a new source of hard currency earnings and, equally important from the Soviet point of view, enhance the image of the USSR as a modern industrialized economy.

Expansion of Plant Capacity

Large increases in passenger car output are possible during 1971–75 because the Tol'yatti plant has come on-stream and is rapidly moving toward capacity output, and because new production capacity was added during 1966–70 to the Moscow and Izhevsk passenger car plants. About $700 million was spent in the West for equipment and technology for these plants. Together these three plants will produce one million cars a year by 1975 and account for about 95 percent of the total increase in output during 1971–75 (see Tables 3 and 4). Major Soviet producers of passenger cars are discussed below.

TABLE 3
Soviet Passenger Car Production by Plant and Model, 1965, 1970–72 and Estimates for 1975
(thousands of units)

Plant Location	Plant Name	Model Produced	1965	1970	1971	1972	1975
Tol'yatti	Volga (VAZ)	Zhiguli	0	22	172	320	600
Moscow	Moscow (AZLK)	Moskvich	72	98	85	110	200
Zaporozh'ye	Zaporozh'ye (ZAZ)	Zaporozhets	41	87	92	96	135
Izhevsk	Izhevsk (ZIMA)	Moskvich	0	20	70	94	200
Gor'kiy	Gor'kiy (GAZ)	Volga	54	70	65	65	75

Source: Derived from official Soviet statements.

TABLE 4
Soviet Passenger Car Production by Model, 1972 and Estimates for 1975

Model	Production (thousands of units)		Percent of Total	
	1972	1975	1972	1975
Zhiguli	320	600	44	48
Moskvich	204	400	28	32
Zaporozhets	96	135	13	11
Volga	65	75	9	6
Other*	45	50	6	4

*Mostly jeep-type vehicles and limousines.
   Editors' note: In the U.S. economy the most efficient size for an automobile assembly plant, as of 1972, was about 640,000 units' annual output, up from about 420,000 ten years before.

Tol'yatti. The Volga Motor Vehicle Plant (VAZ) at Tol'yatti is by far the largest and most modern passenger car plant in the USSR. Built under a 1966 agreement with Fiat of Italy, it is also the largest cooperative project ever undertaken by a Western firm and a Communist country. Designed by Fiat and built at a cost of $1.5 billion (1965 dollars), the plant employs up-to-date machinery and technology purchased in the West for about $550 million. Most of the machinery, which was specified by Fiat, was purchased in Italy and in other countries in Western Europe under credits provided by an Italian State Bank, Istituto Mobiliare Italiano. About 10 percent of foreign expenditure was made in the United States for technology, licenses, and equipment. The Tol'yatti plant has been designed to produce 600,000 cars a year on two shifts. However, the Soviets are pushing hard to produce 660,000 cars a year by 1975 or at a level 10 percent above the plant's designed capacity, probably by running extra shifts or speeding up the assembly lines. The USSR plans to expand the Tol'yatti plant to perhaps twice its present size at some time in the future. Some of this work may be accomplished during 1976–80, probably with further assistance from Fiat.

Tol'yatti is a highly integrated production facility that combines all basic production processes at one site: casting (foundry), forging, stamping and pressing, engine production, assembly, and tooling. In addition, a large spare parts storage and distribution center is in operation at the site to provide spare parts to repair stations and outlets across the country.

Components and parts not produced at Tol'yatti are supplied to it by a system of vendor plants, most of which also have been newly constructed, many with assistance from Western firms. These include: a rubber fittings plant at Balakovo built with the technical assistance of Pirelli of Italy; plants for making oil and air filters and upholstery materials, purchased from Japan; a plant for car seats from West Germany; a plant for oil seals at Kursk; and an anti-friction bearing plant at Vologda. In addition, countries in Eastern Europe are supplying a large array of parts and components under five-year cooperative agreements and are receiving payments mainly in finished cars. Poland and Yugoslavia, which also build Fiat cars, are supplying dozens of different small parts. Hungary is supplying car radios, dashboards, and electrical fittings; Bulgaria is supplying batteries.

The industry is training workers on a massive scale to operate the production lines at VAZ. At capacity (two shifts) the plant will employ between 50,000 and 60,000 workers. Scores of engineers and technicians have been trained by Fiat in Italian plants, and hundreds of line workers have trained at other Soviet plants, mainly in the Gor'kiy area. A large training facility at VAZ is staffed with personnel from technical schools in the area and with specialists from the VAZ cadre.

Moscow. The Moskvich Motor Vehicle Plant (AZLK) in Moscow was for many years the largest producer of passenger cars in the USSR until superseded by Tol'yatti in 1971. The plant recently was redesigned and expanded to a capacity of 200,000 a year—more than twice its former size—under a technical assistance contract with Renault of France. Full operation of the new facilities, scheduled initially for 1970, was not achieved until 1972, partly because the project had to compete with Tol'yatti for construction materials and labor. Now principally an assembly facility, the plant is dependent upon a large number of specialized supplier plants for components and parts, including the Ufa Engine Plant for motors and a new plant in Kineshma for castings and other parts and materials. The remodeled plant now builds the recently redesigned Moskvich-412 and its station wagon version, the Moskvich-427. Further expansion, to 300,000 cars a year, is planned for the future.

Izhevsk. The city of Izhevsk in the Urals, long noted as a center of Soviet motorcycle production, now has become an important car building center as well. A large new passenger car facility, the Izhevsk Motor Vehicle Plant (ZIMA), was completed in 1972. Built with capacity for the production of 220,000 cars a year, the plant is to be further expanded to produce 300,000 cars a year at some time in the future. Like the Moscow plant, Izhevsk also was designed and equipped by Renault of France to produce Moskvich cars and station wagons. The plant is equipped with Renault-built stamping presses for making body parts, U.S.-built machine tools for making differential gears, and with other Western equipment.

Zaporozh'ye. The Zaporozh'ye Motor Vehicle Plant (ZAZ), which builds the smallest and least expensive of the Soviet cars—the Zaporozhets—is the least efficient and most neglected car producer in the USSR. Converted from an agricultural machinery plant in the 1950s, it is to be expanded to produce 135,000 cars a year by 1975. This goal is 10 percent below that originally planned for 1970 (150,000). Because investment funds were insufficient and skilled labor was scarce, the plant during the Eighth Five-Year plan failed to meet both construction and output goals. Unlike most of the other plants in the industry, Zaporozh'ye has not received technical assistance and equipment from the West. Moreover, its domestic supplier system works poorly. The Melitopol Engine Plant that supplies the ZAZ air cooled engines often fails to meet delivery schedules and supplies an inadequate quantity of spare parts for engine repairs. Because of other delivery failures, ZAZ has been forced to build some parts in crowded shops ill-suited for that purpose. In 1972 the plant produced 96,000 cars, an increase of only 10 percent over 1970. ZAZ will have to more than double that production rate to achieve even the reduced goals for 1975.

Gor'kiy. The Gor'kiy Motor Vehicle Plant (GAZ), primarily a builder of trucks, also produces the Volga car (GAZ-24), the most expensive of the passenger cars in mass production. Unlike the other car plants, the Volga facilities are not being expanded. GAZ is focusing instead on improvements in quality and design. Production lines for the Volga recently were modernized and newly equipped using some machine tools and a new conveyor system from the West.

Car Models

Only four types of cars are in mass production in the USSR: the Volga, produced by the Gor'kiy plant; the Moskvich, produced by the Moskvich and Izhevsk plants; the Zhiguli,[2] produced at Tol'yatti; and the Zaporozhets, produced by the Zaporozh'ye plant. Most of the cars in production are standard sedans, although some station wagons are produced by all but the Zaporozh'ye plant. Only the Zhiguli is built in three models: the VAZ-2101 standard sedan and VAZ-2102 station wagon (copies of the Fiat-124) and the VAZ-2103 deluxe sedan (copy of the Fiat-125). In 1972 total output of all makes amounted to 685,000 units as follows:

Make and Model	Description	Output
Volga		65,000
Moskvich		204,000
Zaporozhets		96,000
Zhiguli:		
VAZ–2101	Standard sedan	300,000
VAZ–2102	Station wagon	10,000
VAZ–2103	Deluxe sedan	10,000

All cars in mass production in the USSR have 4-cylinder engines and are smaller than U.S. cars except for the subcompact class. The Zhiguli (60-horsepower) resembles the Chevrolet Vega in size but has less engine power. The Volga is slightly larger in size and engine power and is more luxurious but very expensive. The tiny Zaporozhets with a 40-horsepower engine is about the size of the Fiat 850. Until recently Soviet-made passenger cars were underpowered because engines were designed with low compression ratios in order to use inexpensive low octane gasolines (ratings in the 70s and 80s were standard). Now that higher octane fuels are more plentiful, the industry is using higher compression engines (8.2 to 1 or above) in all passenger cars except the Zaporozhets to provide more power and better engine performance. Most models now use 93 octane gasline. The Zaporozhets uses 76 octane gasoline and ZIL limousines, 98 octane. Table 5 shows the principle characteristics of cars built in the USSR.

All Soviet cars now in production are relatively new models that incorporate modern Western styling. In external appearance they are vastly improved over earlier models. The Volga and Zaporozhets, though copied after Western models, were wholly designed by the Soviets. Renault helped with the design of the Moskvich, and the Zhiguli, designed in Italy, is virtually a replica of the Fiat-124. All cars, with the exception

---

[2] The export model is called Lada.

TABLE 5
Principal Characteristics of Passenger Cars Built in the USSR

Model	Number of pas- sengers	Weight (pounds)	Horse- power	Top Speed (miles/ hour)	Engine Displace- ment (cubic inches)	Com- pression Ratio	Cylin- ders	Gasoline Type (octane rating)
Cars in mass pro- duction:								
Volga (GAZ–24) . .	5–6	3,080	98	90	149.2	8.2	4	93
Moskvich (412) . . .	4	2,200	75	87	90.2	8.8	4	93
Zhiguli (VAZ–2101)	5	2,079	60	87	73.0	8.8	4	93
Zaporozhets (968) .	4	2,376	40	74	73.0	7.2	4	76
Limousines:								
Chaika (GAZ–13). .	7	4,620	195	100	336.8	8.5	8	93
ZIL–114	7	6,787	300	118	424.6	9.5	8	98

perhaps of the Zaporozhets which is not highly esteemed in the USSR, also are of somewhat higher quality than previous models. The Zhiguli, in addition, has been modified and strengthened to stand up under rougher Soviet road conditions and has been adapted for colder winters. However, Soviet-made cars generally do not meet the high standards for quality and dependability of Western cars. Metal surfaces are not as even,[3] paints and other finishes are not as long-lasting, and engines have to be repaired more frequently.

Prices and Sales

Prices for current model Soviet cars in rubles and in dollars are as follows:

		Price	
Car Name and Model		Rubles	U.S. Dollars*
Volga, GAZ–24		9,000	12,000
Zhiguli, VAZ–2101		5,500	7,400†
Moskvich, Moskvich–412		4,936	6,600
Zaporozhets, ZAZ–968.		3,510	4,700

*Rounded, converted at the rate of 1 ruble equals $1.34.
†This model is sold in Western Europe for about $2,000.

Prices of these new model cars are very nigh relative to domestic consumer purchasing power. For example, wages of Soviet workers in

---

[3] The stamping of body parts such as fenders and roofs requires the use of high grade flat rolled steel of good deep drawing quality. Soviet-made steel often does not meet these standards, and defects (wrinkles and roughness) in the surfaces result.

1972 averaged 130 rubles per month or about 1,600 rubles per year. Thus, the price of a Zhiguli is equivalent to nearly two years' total earnings for an average family with two incomes. By comparison, a moderately priced car in the U.S. in 1972 was equivalent to about six months' earnings for an average industrial worker. The price of the Volga is particularly exorbitant and out of reach of the average Soviet citizen. The price also appears to bear little relation to the cost of production—it is about 60 percent higher than the price of the model it replaced. Possession of a Volga at this extraordinary price serves to differentiate high-income earners in a society in which individual status is otherwise obscured.

Soviet passenger cars must be purchased in cash; no cars are sold on credit. Buyers may pay in one lump sum or make periodic downpayments up to the time of delivery. Whatever the arrangement, the car must be fully paid-up at delivery.

Used cars also command high prices on the Soviet market, although they are priced well below new models. For example, a used Moskvich in 1972 cost about 3,700 rubles compared to nearly 5,000 rubles for a new model. In addition to the lower prices, buyers are attracted to the used car market by the prospect of relatively quick delivery. Whereas buyers must wait from two to three years for delivery of new cars, used cars are delivered within six months to one year.

Under a recent regulation designed to reduce black market sales, car owners now are allowed to sell their cars privately. However, the transaction must be registered and the seller must pay the government a fee equal to 7 percent of the sale price. In private sales, the buyer pays a price somewhat higher than that in the government-regulated used car market, but possession is immediate—a feature that is particularly attractive to the long-denied Soviet citizen.

During 1971–75, the USSR plans to supply 2.6 million cars for sale at retail. By 1972 the annual level of sales already had climbed to 377,000, nearly six times as many as were sold in 1965 (64,000). In 1975 retail sales are planned to rise to 750,000 units, nearly double the 1972 level (see Figure 2).

Growth in Private Ownership

As a result of the burgeoning growth in retail sales, private ownership of cars in the USSR now exceeds government ownership. In 1970 about 800 thousand cars, less than 50 percent of all the cars in use, were privately owned. By 1975 three million cars, or about two thirds of all cars in use, will be in private hands. According to official Soviet statistics, the number of cars "in private use" was 1.5 million in 1970. However, official statistics are misleading because the rubric "in private use" includes a very large number of cars (700,000 in 1971) that are

FIGURE 2
Soviet Passenger Cars: Retail Sales as a Share of Output, Selected Years, 1965–72 and 1975 Plan

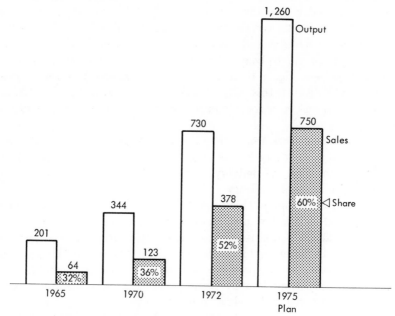

Note: Output and sales in thousands of units.

state-owned but are assigned to officials for both public and private use. Estimated distribution of ownership in thousands for 1970–72 and 1975 is shown in the tabulation below.

| Year | Inventory* | Private† | State | | | Total |
			Assigned to Officials‡	Taxis	Other State Use§	
1970	1,700	800	700	90	110	900
1971	2,000	900	850	100	150	1,100
1972	2,400	1,250	850	110	190	1,150
1975	4,700	3,000	1,000	180	520	1,700

* Estimates based on output adjusted for exports and retirement.
† Estimates based on retail sales adjusted for retirement.
‡ Derived from Soviet data on cars in private use minus figures in second column (estimated for 1972 and 1975). Official data on number of cars in private use has been given as follows: 1970—1,500,000; 1971—1,800,000.
§ Residual.

Although figures for private car ownership in the USSR are impressive in view of the historic neglect of the consumer, they also are misleading. As long as prices remain high compared with income levels and time payments are not allowed, the "average" Soviet citizen will share un-equally in the new affluence. Only the professional and managerial elite who have accumulated sufficient savings to pay the high price in cash can likely afford a new car in the foreseeable future.

Soviet Cars and Foreign Markets

The USSR is exporting an increasing share of its passenger car produc-tion and no longer imports any passenger cars. Exports represented 24 percent of output in 1965 but 28 percent in 1971. More than four fifths of all car exports at present go to the Communist countries of Eastern Europe. Increasingly, cars are being exported to Eastern Europe in pay-ment for automotive components and parts supplied to the Tol'yatti plant. In 1971 Bulgaria, Czechoslovakia, East Germany, and Hungary each received 20,000 to 30,000 cars from the USSR; Poland, Rumania, and Yugoslavia, 1,000 to 6,000 each (see Figure 3 and Table 6).

FIGURE 3
Soviet Exports of Passenger Cars in 1965 and 1971

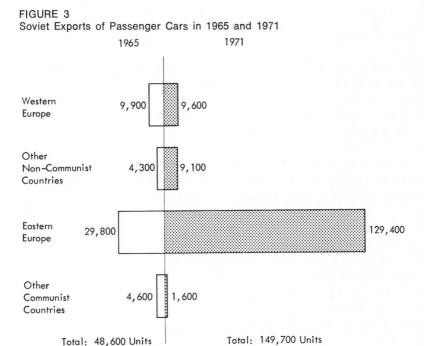

The USSR also is interested in expanding sales in Western Europe. In 1971, 9,600 cars were exported to Western Europe; 4,400 to Finland, 1,100 to the Netherlands, and amounts ranging from 200 to 800 to other countries. Shipments to Western Europe in 1971 represented only 6 per-cent of total Soviet passenger car exports. The USSR operates two mar-keting firms in Western Europe: Scaldia-Volga in Brussels (since 1964),

TABLE 6
Soviet Exports of Motor Vehicles by Geographical Area, Selected Years, 1965–71
(units)

Motor Vehicles and Year	Total	Eastern Europe	Other Communist Countries	Western Europe	Other Non-Communist Countries
Cars:					
1965	48,600	29,800	4,600	9,900	4,300
1968	82,300	64,200	1,700	8,300	8,100
1970	84,300	65,000	1,400	8,300	9,600
1971	149,700	129,400	1,600	9,600	9,100
Trucks:					
1965	15,100	5,200	4,300	200	5,400
1968	29,100	13,200	7,000	600	8,300
1970	34,400	16,000	7,600	1,000	9,800
1971	31,700	13,000	6,100	1,500	11,100
Buses:					
1965	597	302	66	113	116
1968	1,158	364	199	222	373
1970	1,400	247	193	510	450
1971	2,200	280	223	426	1,271

and Konela in Helsinki (since 1967). Because the Soviet Moskvich and Volga models being marketed have had little attraction to Western European buyers, neither firm has been very successful. Sales through Scaldia-Volga have been particularly slow and, in fact, have declined from 1,700 units in 1966 to 535 in 1971.

The USSR now is attempting to develop markets for its new Zhiguli (Lada) through Scaldia-Volga and Konela. Moreover, in 1972 the Ministry of Foreign Trade hired a market research firm in Austria (with branches in Paris and Munich) to assess market prospects for Soviet cars in Western Europe for the period 1975 to 1980. The Lada should be better able to compete in Western markets than other Soviet cars because of its better quality and popular Italian design. Moreover, because it is a Fiat-designed product, it can be serviced by Fiat dealers throughout Western Europe. Adequate maintenance and servicing for Soviet-made cars has always been a bottleneck to the Soviet export program. Furthermore, the Lada is priced to compete with Western built cars including the Italian-made Fiats.

Service Facilities

The existing network of automotive service facilities in the USSR, including both filling stations and repair garages, has been described by *Izvestia* as "primitive," serving less than one-third the country's needs. For example, Moscow's 100,000 privately owned cars presently are serviced by only 12 filling stations and three repair garages. The country's entire inventory of 800,000 privately owned cars in 1970 was served by only 370 repair garages, or one garage for each 2,200 cars. Many cities have few, if any, repair facilities. Under the current program of expanded output and sales to private individuals, about one million new cars a year will be added to the passenger car inventory by 1975, swelling the demand for service facilities to overwhelming proportions.

During 1971–75, the network of repair facilities is being expanded. Most stations will be larger and provide a wider range of services than those now operating. According to the Ninth Five-Year Plan Directives, 33 sales and service centers are planned for Zhiguli cars alone to provide new car warranty service and repair. These stations, scheduled for completion in 1973, will be among the largest stations to be built in the USSR with a capacity for handling about 50 cars per station at any one time. Overall, 600 repair centers (including the Zhiguli centers) are to be built, providing a total work space for 8,500 cars, an average of 14 work spaces per station. In 1972 nearly half the repair garages in operation had work space for less than five cars. Stations are being designed in six basic configurations and sizes; those with 25 to 50 work spaces will operate in conjunction with sales offices. Repair facilities are to be built at a cost of 580–600 million rubles. Several thousand filling stations also will be built during 1971–75.

The number of repair centers and filling stations in existence and planned is as follows:

Type of Facility	Total in 1970	Planned for 1971-75	Planned Total in 1975
Repair centers	370	600	970
Filling stations.	2,000	4,000*	6,000

*Estimate.

Construction of repair facilities is progressing very slowly and only about half of the construction funds allocated to the program were used during 1971 and 1972. Ministry officials claim that 670 repair stations were servicing private cars in 1972, but many of these are temporary shops hastily set up to meet pressing needs. Only a few of the 33 VAZ centers are likely to be in operation by the end of 1973 as scheduled. Hence, the VAZ management has made special *ad hoc* arrangements in many areas to provide warranty service for Zhiguli cars. In fact, VAZ is permitting Zhigulis to be sold only in areas where factory authorized servicing can be carried out.

The USSR has made a special effort to publicize its new program for automotive service by building gigantic showplace centers in several locations for sales and service of all makes of Soviet cars. The largest, Moscow's 3 million ruble automotive center located on the Warsaw Highway near the city's beltway, was about half finished in early 1973. Other centers, on the Minsk Highway in Moscow and at Yakhroma to the north, also are partially built but are far behind schedule. In Tbilisi, in southern Georgia, a new sales and service center began partial operation in 1973, the only large center known to be open thus far.

When present plans for the service network are realized, motorists in the USSR will find service available on main highways and in the large cities, but still almost non-existent in smaller cities, towns, and rural areas. By 1975 there is to be one filling station for every 24 miles of main highway on the average, compared with 36 in 1970, and one repair station for every 37 miles, compared with 121 in 1970.

THE TRUCK PROGRAM

Modernization of the Soviet truck industry, under way since about 1968, is long overdue. Since the Soviet truck industry was established more than 40 years ago with U.S. technical assistance,[4] all Soviet truck models have incorporated U.S. design, and production technology has been patterned after U.S. practice. However, during the past two decades Soviet truck design and technology have undergone few changes and still compare in general with that of the U.S. in about 1950. For example, the GAZ-51 cargo truck has been in continuous production without major modification at the Gor'kiy plant for 24 years. Although scheduled to be replaced by an improved model in 1963, it continues to be produced in greater quantity than any other Soviet medium-sized truck.

Unlike U.S. and Western practice where truck models number in the hundreds, the USSR produces trucks in only eight basic models. Most are medium-sized types with cargo-carrying capacities of 2.5–5 tons, too large for a wide range of intracity commercial and institutional uses and too small for intercity hauling. Soviet trucks also are built with almost no optional equipment, whereas U.S. truck builders offer a wide variety of options including a choice of gasoline or diesel engines in various sizes and makes and a dozen or more different transmissions. Moreover, most Soviet-made trucks are underpowered, are heavy relative to their cargo-carrying capacity, and hence are relatively inefficient in use and costly to operate. Soviet truck manufacturing techniques also are outdated. Computer-assisted control systems for management and production, which typify U.S. practice, still are rare in Soviet truck plants. Automated equipment is in wide use, but much of it is out of date by Western standards.

---

[4] The first major Soviet truck plant was established at Gor'kiy in 1932 using the architectural drawings of the Ford River Rouge Plant, technical advice of Ford engineers, and machinery and equipment for producing the Ford Model-A truck, which, by then, was obsolete.

Goals

In 1970, the USSR produced 525,000 trucks in eight assembly plants. Output from these facilities is planned to rise to 765,000 units in 1975, an increase of about 46 percent. In particular: output of light utility type vehicles of one-ton capacity is being rapidly expanded from 10,000 units in 1970 to a planned level of 60,000 units in 1975, a five-fold increase, and output of medium-size trucks—2.5 to 5 tons—is to increase 40 percent. Production of heavy-duty 3-axle trucks of 8–11 ton cargo capacity is to begin in 1975 and reach 150,000 units a year at capacity, probably in the late 1970s. To carry out this program, production capacity is being expanded at Ul'yanovsk (for light trucks) and at the Gor'kiy and Moscow Likachev plants (for medium trucks) using both process technology and equipment imported from the West. Firms in the U.S. already have supplied sizable amounts of automated transfer machinery; machine tools for making differential gears, wheel hubs, and brake drums; overhead conveyor systems; and computer control systems.

The Kama Complex

To produce heavy-duty transport trucks, the USSR is building the world's largest heavy truck plant at Naberezhnyye Chelny on the Kama River 600 miles east of Moscow. At capacity, this plant will produce 150,000 three-axle trucks a year and 250,000 diesel engines. By comparison, the United States in 1971 built 93,000 trucks with three or more axles. The Kama complex comprises six major production plants, extensive support facilities, and housing for an eventual labor force of 80,000. Although slated for completion in 1974, construction work is at least one year behind schedule. At the end of 1972, only about half of the construction work had been completed.

The Kama plant is being built at a cost of 3 billion rubles or more than $3.3 billion at the official rate of exchange.[6] Of this amount, about $1 billion will be spent on machinery and equipment for the six major facilities.

The plant is being built with extensive foreign assistance, though the foreign input is somewhat less than the Soviets had originally planned. About three fourths of all the machinery, equipment, and technology for Kama—about $750 million—will come from Western suppliers. Major portions of the engineering and design work for the two largest facilities—the engine plant and the foundry—have been subcontracted to Renault of France, and to a large U.S. engineering firm, respectively. In both cases, the subcontractor is specifying equipment suppliers and providing much of the equipment. The foundry, in particular, will represent a major technological gain for the USSR. Designed and built

---

[6] 1970 dollars at the exchange rate of 1 ruble = $1.11.

for a major U.S. automotive firm around 1970, the foundry embodies advanced processing technology and equipment that is not available in this form outside the United States. In particular, it includes a highly automated casting process that has been of interest to the USSR for several years.

The Free World countries supplying equipment for Kama and types of equipment being supplied are summarized below:

Country	Type of Equipment
United States	Foundry design and equipment (electric arc furnaces, holding vats and molding lines); gearmaking machines.
West Germany	Machinery for making transmissions; forging presses.
France	Engine plant design and part of the equipment; plant lines; welding lines.
Italy	Conveyor systems.
Japan	Press lines; transfer presses.

The Production Base

Two large truck building plants, in Gor'kiy and Moscow, which specialize in medium cargo trucks (2.5 to 5 tons), build 80 percent of the trucks produced in the USSR. The Kutaisi plant in the Georgian SSR also builds trucks in this class. All other truck plants are relatively small (less than 30,000 units a year), and specialize in building light service trucks, heavy transport trucks, or large off-highway dump trucks. Light trucks, of one-ton capacity or less, are made at Ul'yanovsk; heavy transport trucks, of 7.5 to 14-ton capacity, at plants in Minsk, Kremenchug, and Miass; and off-highway or quarry vehicles, 27-ton capacity and above, at the Belorussia plant (BelAZ) in Zhodino. Modernization and expansion programs are being carried out or planned in most Soviet truck plants. Table 7 shows Soviet truck production by major plant.

IMPLICATION OF AUTOMOTIVE TRENDS FOR THE SOVIET ROAD SYSTEM

Although the number of motor vehicles in use in the USSR is still quite small by U.S. standards, Soviet cities are already experiencing some of the unhappy side-effects of automobilization: congestion on city thoroughfares and on highways connecting major cities, air pollution, and accidents. These problems have mounted with extraordinary rapidity because of a relatively backward and underdeveloped road system. Although twice the size of the United States, the USSR has a road system about one fourth as long—847,500 miles—excluding urban streets and roadways (see Figure 4). Moreover, only 16 percent is paved with as-

TABLE 7
Soviet Truck Production by Major Plant, 1970–72 and 1975 Plan
(thousands of units)

Producer	Cargo Capacity (metric tons)	Estimated Output*			Plan, 1975
		1970	1971	1972	
Light: Ul'yanovsk (UAZ) 1		10	15	23	60
Medium:					
Gor'kiy (GAZ) 2.5, 4		272	297	310	380
Moscow (ZIL). 5		144	150	155	200
Kutaisi (KAZ). 4.5		14	15	18	22
Heavy:					
Minsk (MAZ) 7.5		26	28	29	30
Kremenchug (KAZ). 12, 14		20	20	24	24
Miass (Ural) 7.5		16	16	16	16
Off-highway:					
Zhodino (BelAZ) 27, 40		3	3	3	3
Other.		20	20	20	30
Total.		525	564	598	765

*Estimates derived from annual production statistics of the individual Soviet Republics and from information on the individual plants.

phalt or cement and 24 percent with gravel, making the total hard surface roads only about 40 percent of the system. Thus, 60 percent of the system is made up of dirt roads, impassible to ordinary traffic in wet weather. Most of the paved roads are asphalt highways that link the major population centers of the European USSR. Roadways adjacent to many of the larger cities are wide and well built. The Moscow beltway, opened in 1962, was the first limited access highway to be built. The design of this 68-mile stretch of two-lane divided highway is equal to U.S. road design of about 1940. Much of the outlying area—the frozen wasteland, desert, and mountainous area—is roadless. The Far North (which includes about half the land area but only 2 percent of the population) has less than 5,000 miles of surfaced roads. The USSR has yet to build a highway linking Moscow with the Pacific coast, although sections of such a route do exist. In size and structure, the Soviet road network resembles the U.S. road system of about 1920.

Soviet passenger cars and trucks, by and large, are limited to the use of hard surfaced roads. In bad weather, unsurfaced roads often can be travelled only by all-wheel-drive trucks and jeep type vehicles. Heavy-duty cargo trucks are further limited in use by low load–bearing roads and bridge structures; unsurfaced roads have load limits of 5–7 tons whereas on paved roads the maximum allowable weight per axle ranges from 6 to 10 tons.

Because the USSR is a planned society, it has an opportunity histori-cally denied Western societies to plan and build roads consistent with

FIGURE 4
Road Systems of the USSR and the United States, 1971
(thousand miles)

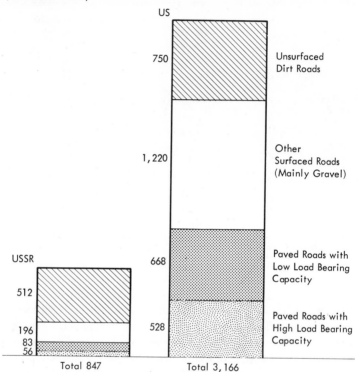

the growth in motor vehicles and thereby facilitate the free flow of traffic and efficient movement of goods. In fact, the development of the road system is not keeping pace with the accretion of motor vehicles. During 1971–75, the USSR plans to build about 68,000 miles of hard-surfaced road, less than was built during the preceding five-year period. Much of the new construction is designed to ease traffic congestion on two-lane highways leading into the larger cities. Elsewhere roads are being improved to accommodate increasing traffic flows.

OUTLOOK

The USSR has made giant strides in automotive production, design, and technology since 1965, and has established a solid base for future growth and development. Prospects for meeting 1975 planned output goals of 1.26 million cars a year are good, and capacity output of about 1.35 million cars could be reached by 1976. Construction of the Kama plant for heavy transport trucks is one to two years behind schedule, but construction is now in full swing. Most importantly, detente with the United States has produced a striking new trading relationship, by virtue of which the USSR no longer is denied access to highly productive U.S. machine tools and other automotive production equipment and technology. Ability to purchase up-to-date U.S. technological advances, has fundamental long-range significance for the modernization of the Soviet automotive industry. Moreover, the growing exchange of information and visitors between the USSR and the U.S. on both policy and working levels will facilitate the transfer of U.S. managerial and organizational techniques to the USSR.

By 1975 the USSR will have about 4.7 million cars in use—18 cars for every 1,000 of the population, or about one car for every 54 persons. About 3 million cars will be in private hands. After 1975 the sale of cars on the domestic market is planned to increase by about 10 percent a year. Thus, by 1980, some 8 million cars out of a total inventory of 10 to 11 million could be privately owned. According to long-range forecasts by Soviet planners, 40 million cars will be in use in the USSR by the year 2000, and the family car will be common. Obviously, this goal is achievable only if personal incomes of workers are raised greatly, prices lowered, or extended-term financing is made available.

The use of private cars in the USSR for some years ahead will be greatly restricted by the scarcity of automotive service and repair facilities and by the poorly developed road system. Because the service program is poorly administered and lacks the high priority granted motor vehicle plants, construction of service stations and repair centers is far behind schedule, trained auto-mechanics are in critically short supply, and garage repair and servicing equipment practically non-existent. Many car owners will have to perform service and repair work themselves, a not uncommon practice in the USSR. The road system, already inadequate for present traffic conditions, is not being improved or expanded fast enough to accommodate the flood of new cars and trucks being turned out, and motorists in and around major cities will encounter massive traffic congestion until road improvements are made.

On the world market, and particularly in Western Europe, the USSR can expect stiff competition for its exported cars. The export model Lada is well designed for sale in the West, can be priced below the Fiat cars built in Italy, and can be serviced by existing Fiat dealerships. However, quality and durability *vis à vis* Western models will have to be proven. Soviet plants may not be able to meet the consistently high standards of Western producers for quality and workmanship, and defects in finished cars that result from inferior materials or poor quality control probably will not be acceptable to buyers in most Western markets.

Despite notable improvements in the truck industry, short-run prospects are that the USSR can meet no more than its most urgent needs for trucks. During 1971–75 the traditional truck mix is not being significantly altered and a wide range of trucks, especially small service and heavy cargo types, will continue to be in critically short supply. The Ul'yanovsk plant, major center for the production of light vehicles, is having difficulty completing its construction program, and producers of heavy trucks (Minsk, Kremenchug, and Miass), already operating at or near capacity, are not being enlarged.

For the longer run, 1976–80, prospects are somewhat better. Completion of the new construction at the Ul'yanovsk facility will increase output of light trucks to 150,000 units a year, two and one-half times the number planned for 1975. In addition, the Kama complex during 1976–77 should be building heavy diesel trucks at a rate of 115,000 per year and during 1977–1980 at the rate of 150,000 per year.

15. STANDARD METHODOLOGY FOR INVESTMENT ALLOCATION

Several types of investment decisions must be made in any economy: (1) the total amount or share of investment in GNP; (2) the distribution of investment among buildings, equipment, and inventories; (3) the allocation of investment by sector, branch, and enterprise; and (4) the relative proportions of capital and labor in a specific production process (sometimes called the choice of "techniques" or "variants").

In capitalist regulated market economies, these decisions are made by business firms and financial institutions in the light of relative prices and interest rates, under the influence of monetary, fiscal, and other types of government intervention. Capital markets channel funds into the most profitable uses, as investors compare the rate of return on alternative investments.

In the Soviet economy, the central planning apparatus makes the major decision on the size, composition, and allocation of investment, while lower-level agencies and in some cases enterprises determine the choice of techniques. The Standard Methodology for Investment Allocation is intended to provide an efficiency criterion for use in these decisions, although other considerations—such as political factors, growth strategy, and regional development policies—also affect and often dominate investment decisions. However, the importance of efficiency measures in investment allocation appears to have increased with the adoption of a new and more sophisticated Standard Methodology in 1969.

Selection A presents the complete text of the new Methodology. An evaluation of it then follows in Selection B.

A. STANDARD METHODOLOGY FOR DETERMINING THE ECONOMIC EFFECTIVENESS OF CAPITAL INVESTMENTS

This translation from the Soviet economic weekly newspaper *Ekonomicheskaia Gazeta,* No. 39, 1969, pp. 11–12, was prepared by Michael Melancon, a student at Indiana University, under the supervision of Robert W. Campbell, Professor of Economics at Indiana University. It is reprinted, by permission of the Association for Comparative Economic Studies, from *The ASTE Bulletin,* Vol. XIII, No. 3 (Fall 1971), pp. 26–36.

I. GENERAL PRINCIPLES

1. THE TASK OF THE standard methodology is to establish basic methods for calculating and substantiating the economic effectiveness of capital investments for the purpose of raising the efficiency of social production in working out plans for capital construction and analyzing their fulfillment, in planning the construction and introduction of new technology, in working out and substantiating organizational-technical measures for the development and improvement of production in existing enterprises, as well as in determining how economic projects outside the sphere of production are.

The standard methodology is designed in the light of the tasks of improving planning and strengthening the economic stimulation of production, and is intended for use by planning organs, ministries, departments, associations, enterprises, and scientific-research and project-making organizations. It contains basic principles which are obligatory for all branches of the national economy.

On the basis of the standard methodology, branch instructions are to be worked out and approved by ministries and departments, with the approval of Gosplan USSR, which take into account the peculiarities of calculating the effectiveness of capital investments in various branches of the national economy and industry, and also methods for determining the effectiveness of capital investments in solving individual economic problems (the location of production, economic evaluation of the quality of output, etc.).

2. An obligatory condition for calculating and validating the effectiveness of capital investments is adherence to a national economic approach. This means that the variant of capital investments chosen not only must be the most effective in an individual branch or sub-branch of social production, but also must contribute to raising efficiency in the national economy as a whole.

In this connection, the effectiveness of capital investments must be considered both in that branch of the economy where they will be made, and in related (associated) branches of production or with respect to the consumer.

3. In project-making, determination of the effectiveness of capital investments has as its aim the selection and economic justification of the very best variants for constructing new enterprises and expanding and reconstructing existing enterprises and structures singly and in complexes, and best variants for developing new technical processes, equipment, machines, materials, and other types of technology which support technical progress in the national economy.

4. In determining the economic effectiveness of capital investments connected with the solution of long-range problems in the development of the economy, with the introduction into social production of important scientific discoveries and inventions and new forms of modern technology, with the development of important new natural resources (unique mineral deposits, new economic regions which are difficult to develop, and so on) an evaluation and validation of the economic effectiveness of capital investments must be made with long-range factors in mind; that is, in the light of the full accomplishment of corresponding construction programs, changes in the location of raw material sources and consuming regions, the creation of necessary conditions for realizing new scientific-technical achievements, and, where necessary, in the light of possible changes in the norms of effectiveness and in prices.

5. The effectiveness of capital investments is determined by comparing effects with expenditures. In planning and project-making, a general (absolute) effectiveness is determined as the ratio of the effect to the total investment. In the choice of variants for solving economic or technical tasks, a relative economic effectiveness is determined, showing to what extent one variant is more effective than another.

6. The criterion of economic effectiveness of capital investments in the national economy is the increase in national income (in comparable prices) in relation to the capital investments causing the increase.

7. The total of capital investments taken for calculating effectiveness includes investments, whatever their source of financing, in the sphere

of material production—in the construction of new enterprises; in the expansion, reconstruction, technical re-equipment, and maintenance of capacity of existing enterprises; and in the construction of structures and other objects of production significance. When determining the economic effectiveness of all expenditures in the creation or expansion of production assets, it is also necessary to include in the calculation expenditures for acquiring or replenishing working capital or reducing its amount.

8. In determining the effectiveness of capital investments, when the necessity arises for capital expenditures for developing related branches of production, one should take into account the full capital investment including the associated expenditures. These related capital investments are counted only with respect to those elements of working and fixed assets subject to significant increases in the related branches. In this case, also to be considered is the gain obtained for the associated group of branches, this group being determined by branch instructions.

9. In evaluating the effectiveness of capital investments, depending on the location of enterprises, also to be considered are the rise (or fall) in construction costs and changes in current expenditures on production and transport of output, under the influence of changes in the location of newly created capacity. At the same time, the tasks of complex development of the economies of the union republics and economic regions are to be considered.

This means that all calculations of the economic effectiveness of capital investments must include the associated expenditures for the development of related facilities of production significance, in particular:

a. the development of construction capacity;
b. road construction required to make connection to the existing road network;
c. the development of an energy base, construction of water supply facilities, etc.;
d. losses caused by construction, such as the inundation of land, for example.

Depending on the specific line of production, the following should also be considered:

a. labor supply: in cases where the location involves a considerable movement of the labor force, capital investments in housing, municipal, cultural, trade, and other facilities and expenditures for relocating workers and their families must be considered in the total capital investment requirements for the intended construction;
b. proximity and cheapness of raw material sources;
c. proximity to concentrations of consumers of the output of the branch.

10. In calculating and analyzing the effectiveness of capital investments, it is recommended that the time lag between the outlay and the effect be considered. The procedure for determining the lag and for using it in the calculation is established in branch instructions on the basis of the length of the construction period and the corresponding distribution of capital investments by years, and on the attainment of projected capacity and other technical-economic indices.

11. In the absence of official prices for new materials, machines, and equipment, calculations of economic effectiveness are made on the basis of their production cost, including capital charges, calculated by existing methods of price formation.

II. GENERAL (ABSOLUTE) ECONOMIC EFFECTIVENESS OF CAPITAL INVESTMENTS

12. Calculations of overall economic effectiveness of capital investments are made at all stages of working out annual and five-year plans, and also plans of longer time horizon, for the national economy as a whole; for the economies of the union republics; for sectors of the national economy and branches of industry, agriculture, transport, and construction; for ministries, departments, economic associations, individual enterprises, and construction projects; and in working out individual technical-economic problems of development and location in the national economy and its branches, and also in the evaluation of plan fulfillment for capital construction.

Calculations of absolute effectiveness of capital investments afford the possibility of measuring the general magnitude of their economic impact, and are used for the more precise measurement of the resources of national income and net income of society for the purpose of estimating the possible rate of growth of the national economy and the rate of growth of the material welfare of the population, and also in determining the results of the activities of enterprises, associations, and production ministries.

13. In the process of working out the plans of capital investments, the computed indices of economic effectiveness are compared with planning norms and with analogous indices for a preceding period of the same length as the plan period, and also with effectiveness indices in progressive enterprises of the corresponding branches and sub-branches.

14. The contemplated direction of capital investments can be considered economically effective if the coefficients of general effectiveness arrived at are not below the planning norms and analogous indices for the preceding planning period.

In making capital investments in existing enterprises and associations which have been transferred to the new conditions of planning and economic stimulation, the economic effectiveness of these investments, and accordingly the additional profit achieved as a result of them, must be high enough to provide for payment of the corresponding capital charges, interest payments for bank credits, and other obligatory payments, and also for the formation of the corresponding incentive funds in the enterprises and associations.

15.   In the calculation of general economic effectiveness of capital investments the following indices are used:

a.   for the national economy as a whole, the economies of the union republics and the branches of the national economy (industry, agriculture, transport, construction)—the ratio of the increase in annual volume of national income (net product) in the planned composition in comparable prices (ΔD) to the capital investments in the sphere of material production causing the increase (K);

$$E_{kpn} = \frac{\Delta D}{K} \qquad (1)$$

b.   for individual branches and sub-branches of industry, agriculture, transport and construction, for ministries, departments, economic associations (if net product is not calculated for them)—the ratio of the increase in profit to the capital investments causing the increase, expressed as

$$E_{kpp} = \frac{\Delta P}{K} \qquad (2)$$

where ΔP is the increase in annual profit for the planning period (year, or five years), and K is capital investments in the construction of objects of production significance;

c.   for individual enterprises and construction projects, individual measures, and technical-economic problems—the ratio of profit to capital investments, expressed as

$$K_{kp} = \frac{Ts - C}{K} \qquad (3)$$

where K is the estimated cost of the facility being built (capital expenditures for realization of the measure or the technical-economic problem); Ts is the value of the projected annual output at enterprise wholesale prices (excluding turnover tax); and C is the cost of the annual output of the product;

d.   in branches and enterprises, where settlement prices are used, and also for enterprises planned to operate at a loss, the index of general economic effectiveness is characterized by the ratio of the savings from cost reduction to the capital investments which brought about the reduction.

In computing the general economic effectiveness under points (b), (c), and (d), the recoupment periods of the total volume of capital investments are determined as the reciprocal of the above ratios.[1]

16. In determining the general effectiveness of capital investments, an analysis is made of factors that would influence it upwards or downwards. Included in these factors are:

a. changes in the labor intensity of the product, which would open the possibility of reducing the labor force as a result of the capital investments or would require an increase in the labor force;

b. a change in the material intensity of the product, which would free additional means of production in the national economy or would increase expenditure of these resources;

c. changes in the capital intensity of the product, which would provide investment economies or would cause an excess outlay;

d. a shortening of the period of construction and a reduction in its estimated cost.

17. In order to take account of the influence of the most important factors on the economic effectiveness of capital investments and to take account of the interaction of this effectiveness with other divisions of the plan, the following additional indices are used: productivity of labor, capital-output ratio (for marketed output, gross output, and output in physical units), captial investment per unit of output (for capacity commissioned and for output increases), physical indices, and others.

18. Indices of the general economic effectiveness of utilization of existing production assets are determined as follows:

a. for the national economy as a whole, its branches, and the economies of the union republics—as the ratio of the annual volume of national income (net product) to the total average annual production assets (fixed and working);

b. for branches (sub-branches) of industry, agriculture, transport, construction, for production associations and individual enterprises

---

[1] Calculations of the recoupment period of the total volume of capital investments under points (b), (c), and (d) are made by the following formulas:

$$T_{kpp} = \frac{K}{\Delta P} \tag{4}$$

$$T_{kp} = \frac{K}{Ts - C} \tag{5}$$

$$T_{ks} = \frac{K}{C_1 - C_2} \tag{6}$$

where C_1 and C_2 are the cost of production before and after the capital investments. The other symbols are the same as under points (b) and (c).

and objects—as the ratio of profit to the total average annual production assets (fixed and working) expressed as:

$$E_{rf} = \frac{P}{F} \qquad (7)$$

where P is the annual profit and F is the average annual value of production fixed assets and normed working capital.

19. Calculation of the general effectiveness of capital investments for enterprises and establishments outside the sphere of production which operate on *khozraschet* (urban transport, tourist establishments, etc.) is made on the basis of the same principles as for the production enterprises.

III. COMPARATIVE ECONOMIC EFFECTIVENESS OF CAPITAL INVESTMENTS

20. Calculations of comparative economic effectiveness of capital investments are used in comparing variants of economic or technical decisions, location of enterprises and complexes; in choices between mutually interchangeable products; in the introduction of new types of technology; in the construction of new or the reconstruction of existing enterprises; etc.

21. The index of comparative economic effectiveness of capital investments is the minimum cost, including capital costs (*privedennye zatraty*). Capital costs for each variant represent the sum of current outlays (i.e., *sebestoimost'*) and capital investments, reduced to a common denominator, according to the normative coefficient of effectiveness.

$$C_i + E_n K_i = \text{minimum}^2 \qquad (8)$$

where K_i is the capital investments for each variant; C_i is current expenditures (i.e., *sebestoimost'*) for each of these variants, and E_n is the normative coefficient of effectiveness of capital investments.

The indices C_i and K_i can be used either as aggregates or per unit magnitudes.

22. The normative coefficient of effectiveness for the national economy as a whole is set at a level not less than 0.12. Where necessary, to stimulate technical progress, to allow for different wage levels (between zones or branches) or price levels, and differences in the length of time for completion of construction programs and regional differences, departures from the established normative coefficients of effectiveness

---

[2] Capital costs can also be calculated by the following equivalent formula:

$$K_i + (T_n \cdot C_i) = \text{minimum} \qquad (9)$$

where T_n is the normative recoupment period of capital investments, which is the reciprocal of E_n.

will be permitted in branch instructions, with the agreement of Gosplan USSR.

Normatives of economic effectiveness are subject to review, which it will be appropriate to schedule at times when five-year plans are drawn up.

23. In determining the economic efficiency of measures, the indices of the best available solution of given economic problems are used as a basis of comparison; and in the introduction of new technology, indices of the best technology already introduced (or developed to the project stage), either domestic or foreign.

Indices of variants of capital investments under consideration are compared with normatives and indices of economic effectiveness achieved in preceding periods.

In determining the magnitude of the economic effect of introducing measures, in concrete cases indices of the most widespread methods of solving given problems are used as a basis of comparison; and in the introduction of new technology, indices of the technology replaced.

24. In calculating the economic effectiveness of capital investments, it is necessary to assure comparability of expenditure and effect for the variants being compared in terms of:

a. the enterprises and branches of production covered;
b. the timing of expenditures and attainment of the effect;
c. the prices used in valuing the expenditures and the effect;
d. the character of the expenditures and the effect in terms of their impact on simple and expanded reproduction;
e. the various expenditures included in the total of capital investments;
f. methods of calculating the value indices used in the effectiveness calculation, and other factors.

All the variants of capital investments under comparison must be brought to a comparable form with respect to all features (volume of production, its composition and quality, length of the production period, etc.) except for the feature the effectiveness of which is being determined.

The procedure for bringing the variants into comparable form with respect to volume of production and quality is indicated in the branch instructions.

25. In comparing variants of capital investments differing in length of construction period, in distribution of capital investments over the construction period, or by the possibility of construction by stages without interfering with fulfillment of production tasks, a calculation of the influence of the difference in the timing of investments on the effectiveness of the variants is made.

If the capital investments in the variants being compared are made at different periods, and the current expenditures change over time, then comparison of the variants should be made by bringing expenditures of the later years to the present moment by applying a discount coefficient calculated by the following formula:

$$V = \frac{1}{(1 + E_{np})^t} \qquad (10)$$

where V is the discount coefficient, t is the period of time of discount in years, and E_{np} is the normative for discounting expenditures at different times.

Given the existing procedure for charging depreciation on fixed assets, the normative for discounting expenditures in different years is set at a figure of 0.08.

The discounting of expenditures made in different years is used only in calculating economic effectiveness of variants and cannot serve as a basis for changes in the estimated costs of construction.

26. In comparing variants differing from each other in length of construction period, a real, once-for-all effect in the form of the extra profit received during the period of early completion of the project is determined.

27. Determination of the comparative economic effectiveness of capital investments for the reconstruction of existing enterprises is made by comparing indices of the reconstruction variants with the indices of the enterprise before reconstruction and with new construction variants.

Along with this, it is necessary to consider losses of production and profit, and increases in current expenditures during the reconstruction period.

28. Economic effectiveness of variants of capital investments involving regional differences is determined by comparing indices of cost including capital charges, taking into account the associated capital investments in transport and transport expenditures for the delivery of output to the consuming region.

29. In the introduction of new technology, in changing the quality and use characteristics of the output, it is necessary to consider changes in expenditures and effects in the sphere of production as well as in the sphere of use of the product.

The economic effectiveness of capital investments in the creation of new types of raw materials and other materials, and in the improvement of the character and quality of raw materials and other materials, is determined by considering capital investments and current expenditures during production, transport, and use of these materials. The calculation must be made with reference to the annual volume of use of the material envisaged in the project.

30. The economic effectiveness of capital investments in the creation of new types of machinery and in the improvement of already function-

ing types of machinery, equipment, mechanisms and other instruments of production which are part of the user's fixed assets is achieved at the places of their use. Therefore, the extent of this economic effectiveness is determined by comparing the user's capital outlays on the indicated equipment with the lowering of the cost of his product or work achieved with the help of the given piece of equipment. In this connection, it is also necessary to consider changes in the labor intensity, material intensity, and capital intensity, the length of the construction period, and other factors.

31. In comparing technical-economic indices of projects to develop new enterprises and new technology with the economic indices of already functioning production, it is necessary to make corrections of the latter, to take into account changes from better utilization of existing production assets by the time the new project is completed.

32. The comparative economic effectiveness of capital investment variants in existing enterprises financed from the fund for the development of production and from bank credits for carrying out measures for the introduction of new technology, mechanization, automation and modernization of equipment, renewal of fixed assets, the acquisition of means of transportation, improvement of the organization of production and labor, and other measures is determined by comparing the profit increase with the investments, so that the profit received as a result of the measures introduced assures the payment of the corresponding capital charges, charges for bank credit and other obligatory payments, and also for the creation of enterprise incentive funds.

In carrying out measures which affect related enterprises and have an interbranch impact, the calculation of economic effectiveness takes into account the effect achieved in the enterprises affected.

33. If the new capital investments are connected with the scrapping of existing assets (or if their further use is unknown), the unamortized value of these funds (less any scrappage value realized) is added to the corresponding capital investments.

The unamortized value is determined as the difference between the replacement value and the total depreciation already charged. If in introducing a new technology into an existing line of production (automatic lines, new systems of equipment, and others) a part of the existing equipment is utilized, but part is transferred to other industries for more efficient use, then in the calculation of effectiveness what is compared is the fixed assets after introduction of the new technology (including the assets of existing production) and the fixed assets of existing production before the introduction of new technology, for a comparable volume of production.

34. The economic effectiveness of capital investments for maintaining the capacity of existing enterprises in the branches (sub-branches) of industry is determined by direct comparison of the effectiveness of capi-

tal investments for that purpose with the effectiveness of existing production and the effectiveness of capital investments for the construction of new enterprises.

35. The selection of project solutions and variants of capital investments for enterprises and establishments outside the production sphere functioning on the basis of *khozraschet* (urban transport, tourist establishments, etc.) are made on the basis of the same principles as are used for production enterprises.

The choice of project solutions for facilities outside the sphere of production which are supported from social consumption funds (health, education, and others) is made by comparing capital investments for their construction and current operating expenditures for their maintenance. In this connection, comparability of the variants in regard to the level of service and other project-making norms for such facilities must be assured.

B. THE NEW SOVIET STANDARD METHODOLOGY FOR INVESTMENT ALLOCATION

Alan Abouchar

This article compares the 1969 Standard Methodology with its predecessor issued in 1959. The major changes include a measure of the overall efficiency of investment, an explicit normative capital charge, and a discount rate to compare streams of investments and costs over different time periods. However, the Standard Methodology does not cover some important investment decisions, and there is some uncertainty about how widely the new Methodology will actually be used in those investment choices to which it is addressed.

Alan Abouchar is Associate Professor of Economics at the University of Toronto. The article is reprinted by permission from *Soviet Studies,* Vol. XXIV, No. 3 (January 1973), pp. 402–10, with the omission of some footnotes.

I. INTRODUCTION

IN 1969 THE STATE Planning Commission, in conjunction with the Academy of Sciences and the Construction Ministry Institute of Economics, introduced a new "Standard Methodology for Determining the Economic Effectiveness of Capital Investments" (SM–69) to replace the earlier methodology which had been introduced in 1959 (SM–59). The new rules are intended to serve as the basis for elaboration of individual sectoral methodologies.

The new methodology remedies some of the deficiencies in SM–59, and makes some of its procedures more explicit; it is especially striking for the greater faith that it shows in the ability of economic criteria to guide investment, for its clearer and reasonably consistent statement of sectoral and regional investment criteria, and in its willingness to rely on a single value for the coefficient of relative effectiveness, other than in special situations. In this article we shall review the changes between the old and new methodologies (Section II) and assess the new rules (Section III). Section IV contains a brief summary.

II. CHANGES IN THE STANDARD METHODOLOGY

Description of SM–59

The essential contribution of SM–59 was to present a way to choose between two methods of doing the same thing. The annual operating cost difference of two variants was compared to the capital cost difference, through the ratio $E = (C_2 - C_1)/(I_1 - I_2)$, called the coefficient of relative effectiveness. Its reciprocal $(1/E) = T$ was designated the recoupment period and denoted the number of years necessary for the investment to be recovered. In the simplest case of invariant annual operating cost and instantaneous investment, this was the end of it. Where operating costs of either or both alternatives were to vary, or if the investments themselves had different time patterns, it was necessary to make all investment and operating cost streams commensurable by means of a discount coefficient, K_{pr}. This coefficient was a function of the normative coefficient of effectiveness for the sector ($\bar{E}_i$), viz. $K_{pr} = (1 + \bar{E}_i)^t$.

$\bar{E}_i$ and $\bar{T}_i$ were not uniform. Rather, each industry had a peculiar value, with a decision rule to choose technology 1 rather than 2 if the coefficient of effectiveness of the first technology exceeded the industry norm $\bar{E}_i$, and technology 2 otherwise. The coefficient would be used, for example, in trying to choose between the wet and dry processes for cement production in some region. Suppose capital costs of the wet and dry methods are 50 and 30 rubles per ton of annual output respectively and annual operating costs are 6 and 10 rubles for the same volume. In this case the calculated coefficient of the project with the greater investment cost (wet process) is $(10 - 6)/(50 - 30)$, or 0.2, and the recoupment period is five years. If the cement industry norm is 0.14, which allows seven years to recover the investment, the more capital-intensive project should be chosen. With a norm of 0.25, the less capital-intensive process should be selected. Typically, the consumer goods industries had higher normative coefficients. This served to impose more stringent requirements on their investments.

The main contribution of SM–59 was to codify practice for final enterprise-level technological decision-making that had been developing gradually since the start of national planning.[1] SM–59 did also propose, albeit casually, some investment guidelines for higher levels: (*a*) it described in broad terms the coefficient of general or absolute effectiveness as the incremental net output/capital ratio for the nation as a whole,

---

[1] A good discussion is contained in Gregory Grossman, "Scarce Capital and Soviet Doctrine," *Quarterly Journal of Economics,* Vol. LXVII, No. 3 (August 1953), pp. 311–43.

without specifically calling for its use; and (*b*) it proposed as a criterion for investment in enterprises the incremental output/capital ratio associated with the investment ($E_p = Q(P - C)/I$), where output QP was defined to be net of turnover taxes on the selling price of the final product. These criteria—especially the first for which a symbolic representation was not even given—were treated almost incidentally as a prelude to the discussion of the coefficient of relative effectiveness. No clear indication was given whether they were intended as obligatory considerations in allocating investment funds.

Since SM–59 was adopted, the focus of dispute has been the question of variable industry norms, with attention also directed to the failure of the methodology to provide clear-cut guidance for inter-industry investment allocation. Summaries of the debate are readily available,[2] and will not be detailed here. The variable norm was defended as necessary to ensure that consumer goods industries did not receive too great investment funds. Since even in the wake of SM–59 intersectoral investment continued to be made by political rather than economic decision (i.e., no attempt was made to orient basic investment plans according to the coefficient of absolute effectiveness proposed in SM–59), there could be no certainty that the final ruble of annual investment allocated to each industry or sector would have the same return in each industry, and each industry would have to have its own interest rate to apportion its allocation. On the other hand, since the relative coefficient was only to apply to technological choice, there should have been no fear that the variations in this coefficient would influence the basic investment allocation in the first place.

Main Features of SM–69

There are four major differences between the old and new methodologies. First, SM–69 gives an explicit expression for the coefficient of absolute effectiveness $E_{KPI} = \Delta ND/I$ which is to serve as the basic sectoral or regional investment distribution criterion. In this expression, ND is national income. Now, this national income measure is a net criterion, unlike most of the Soviet macro-economic indicators, such as gross social product or gross output, and is calculated in market prices which include turnover taxes. Therefore, it is a reasonably efficient criterion, in the sense that it can guide investment to those areas with the biggest social payoff (market prices representing consumer valuations), while the large social surplus generated thereby, through the turnover taxes, will then provide an investment fund which will serve to leave control over further investment in centralized hands for amendment if necessary (political or strategic investments). However, one important qualification, to which we shall return below, which may undo the application of

---

[2] For example, Alec Nove, *The Soviet Economy* (2d. rev. ed.: London: George Allen & Unwin Ltd., 1968; New York: Frederick A. Praeger, Inc., 1969), ch. 7.

the criterion, is the addition at this point in the text of a qualifying phrase that the ratio be calculated "under a given output structure" of national income.

The second change is the introduction of an intrasectoral criterion for distributing investment. This is the incremental output/capital ratio, where output is a value-added rather than a gross concept. This is given by $E_{KPP} = \Delta\pi/I$, where π is defined as profit. It is presumably calculated in terms of enterprise wholesale prices, which do not contain turnover taxes, although the document is not clear on this. On the other hand, the enterprise allocation coefficient $E_p = (Q(P - C)/I)$, measured in terms of enterprise wholesale prices, is retained from SM–59. These two criteria have essentially similar areas of application, although the latter is explicitly tied to enterprises. This suggests, either that they amount to the same thing (i.e., both use enterprise wholesale prices), in which case one must wonder why two have been decreed, or that a mistake has been made.

The third change—and the one which appears to have been viewed as most significant by Russian observers—is the introduction of a uniform value for the coefficient of relative effectiveness. However, exceptions are permitted to "stimulate technological progress, and to take account of industry or regional wage variations, differences in price levels, length of construction periods and regional differences." A value of 0.12 is proposed for the coefficient.

Finally, the discount rate to be used to make differential capital and operating cost time streams commensurable is now taken to be uniform throughout the economy and independent of the coefficient of relative effectiveness. A value of 0.08 is proposed as the discount coefficient.

III. EVALUATION OF THE NEW METHODOLOGY

The new methodology contains several pioneering ideas which may be too radical for early implementation so that any predictions concerning its application are hazardous at this time. We shall therefore evaluate it primarily in terms of its internal consistency and the implications which its use would have for investment.

It leaves several issues unresolved, the two most notable of which are (a) specification of the amounts to be allotted to different sectors and (b) the reconciliation of the areas of application of the relative and absolute coefficients. These flaws can be best appreciated against the background of the positive contributions of SM–69. We start accordingly.

Improvements in the New Methodology

In using the sectoral coefficient of absolute effectiveness ($\Delta ND/I$) along with the enterprise investment indicator expressed in enterprise wholesale prices, the methodology confronts the spectre of overinvestment in highly profitable consumer goods industries with new-found maturity. To recall, this was a central concern in the earlier discussion surrounding the uniform rate, and it is indicative of the new attitude that Khachaturov, one of the leading proponents of the variable coefficient of relative effectiveness in the late fifties,[3] is the chief author of the new methodology. Planners can now be guided by national income optimality considerations, and need not fear an overinvestment in consumer goods production.

The new methodology stipulates allocation criteria quite clearly in terms of national income, in the first place, and of industry or enterprise profits, in the second. As noted above, these were alluded to but not spelled out in the first methodology; now they are sharply defined.[4] Where a sector has a high incremental net national income/investment ratio, it will receive a high priority. This ratio reflects final selling price, retail or wholesale, so that an investment in a consumer goods production or marketing scheme (which includes high turnover taxes) may count for more than, say, an investment in jet engines, and greater attention should be accorded the former.

At the same time, it does not follow that every enterprise will redirect its effort towards consumer goods output. For the enterprise, investment is determined by a different incremental net output/investment ratio, viz., incremental profitability. But profitability is the difference between enterprise wholesale price (selling price less turnover tax), and production cost. Suppose that an electrical equipment enterprise can produce large motors or kitchen mixers; for national income calculations, the latter may be valued higher per unit of input (in view of the turnover tax), but at the enterprise wholesale level they are, in principle, the same per unit of input, on a cost-plus mark-up basis (in actual fact, this will vary from plant to plant depending on the capital stock mix and vintage, not to speak of random factors). Therefore, the new measures give no great impetus to consumer goods production at existing enterprises, either those whose primary function is capital goods production or those producing consumer goods exclusively. That is to say, there need be no great fear that enterprises will redirect their existing capital or expand for the purpose of producing goods which the higher planning levels do not really want them to do. And where a larger investment is allocated to consumer goods output by centralized decision, a large budget revenue will be generated through the turnover tax, mitigating the inflationary impact of rapidly increasing consumer goods production and permitting relatively more of the nation's investment to be made by centralized decision rather than through the enterprise.

[3] T. S. Khachaturov, "The Economic Effectiveness of Capital Investments in the USSR," *American Economic Review,* Vol. XLVIII, No. 2 (May 1958), pp. 368–84.

[4] The new title probably indicates something about the authors' hopes for the more general application of the new rules. The complete title of the old methodology was "Standard Methodology for Determining the Economic Effectiveness of Capital Investments and New Technology." The new title stops after "Investments."

The question naturally arises of the administrative consistency of the investment allocation if investment is distributed among sectors by the national income criterion, and among enterprises according to a profit indicator. What happens if enterprises have low profits in an industry which has a high absolute coefficient of effectiveness? The answer is that no inconsistency need arise, and in fact this is one example of the harmony of the new methodology. In this case the industry will, in the first place, be allocated a large investment; then that allocation should be distributed according to enterprise profit potential until it is exhausted. Profits will be low because they are calculated net of turnover taxes, even though investment in the industry has a high payoff evaluated in market prices, which include turnover taxes. The hypothesized administrative inconsistency would arise only if allocation were being made through the two criteria simultaneously—ordering all enterprises across industry or sectoral bounds, on the one hand, and all sectors or industries on the other. In this case the textile industry, for example, would get a small allotment on the basis of plant profitability and a large allotment on the basis of the national income sectoral criterion. But there is no suggestion in SM–69 that the criteria operate simultaneously, and we would expect the more reasonable two-stage operation.

Problems in the New Methodology

No one can tell, of course, the extent to which Gosplan will insist on implementation of the new scheme of absolute coefficients. There is in any event the contradictory instruction that the national income criterion is to be applied subject to a given output mix. If this last clause is interpreted literally, of course, the methodology is useless, since a fixed output mix is incompatible with the notion of sectoral investment choice. The qualifying phrase may turn out to be simply a relic of antiquated politically oriented thinking . . . . However, there are other problems which, for the present, do limit the applicability of the absolute criteria.

First, there is no way to indicate how much investment should go to any sector. Suppose that the sectors have been ranked according to the net incremental national income criterion. This would not tell Gosplan how much to allocate to each sector, and, indeed, it would not even follow that the industry rankings calculated for a one-billion ruble investment allocation would be the same when calculated for five billion rubles. Therefore, the amounts actually allotted will be somewhat arbitrary, even if the planners are committed to economic calculation.

The other outstanding issue is the relationship between the area of application of the relative coefficient and the enterprise absolute coefficient. In principle, the relative coefficient is to be used to evaluate alternative technologies, with output fixed. Sometimes, of course, it might be more rational to produce at a completely new plant; for example, it might be cheaper to choose a more capital-intensive process at a single new plant and produce 200 units annually, than to expand two existing plants and produce 100 units at each of them by means of a less capital-intensive method. But as long as each plant thinks in terms of investment for a specified output mix, each will choose the more labour-intensive method, which has lower unit costs at low output levels than the big plant, even though the cost of the latter at the level of production of the two plants combined is cheaper.

In practice, it will very probably turn out that use of own-generated investment funds will be based on the relative coefficient, while investment funds allocated out of central budget through ministries is to be assigned according to the absolute coefficient. This seems reasonable, although the notion of applying different criteria to investments depending on their source has been objected to ("no matter what the source of financing of the project under review, its economic effect for the national economy, one would think, should not change"[5]). While one can sympathize in principle with this view, it is probably best for the moment to recognize that economic planning is the art of the possible, and accept the trade-off between the inefficiencies implicit in the application of two criteria for the administrative flexibility which it involves, since it obviates the need for additional channels to redirect the own-investment funds to centralized decision-making, encouraging local technological evaluation skills, which itself enriches the economy. To put this in perspective, and disabuse us of condescension here, we might consider the similar problem of multiple criteria as it is encountered in the West. Road project evaluation, for example, customarily relies on a consumer surplus-type criterion for situations in which there is some large existing traffic (a large road improvement project, for example) while for penetration roads with no existing traffic a net incremental national income criterion is applied.[6] If criteria are diverse within sectors, they are even more so across sectors,[7] and there is little basis to hope for early reconciliation of the diverse criteria.[8]

---

[5] A. L. Lur'e, "On Certain Recommendations of the Standard Methodology for Determining the Economic Effectiveness of Capital Investments," *Matekon*, Vol. VIII, No. 1 (Fall 1971), pp. 53–64.

[6] See chapters by Bergman and Hirsch in George W. Wilson and others, *The Impact of Highway Investment on Development* (Washington, D.C.: Brookings Institution, 1966).

[7] An extended and illuminating discussion of this issue is contained in C. D. Foster, "The Economics of Roads: Surplus Criteria for Investment," *Bulletin of the Oxford University Institute of Statistics*, Vol. 22, No. 4 (November 1960), pp. 327–57.

[8] A rather different issue of multiple criteria was raised by Lur'e. He points out that Sections 21 and 32 of SM-69 imply use of two different selection criteria within an enterprise, the first being cost minimization for technological variants,

There remains to be discussed one aspect of the relative coefficient of effectiveness, the escape clause in Section 22 previously mentioned, which permits exceptions from the uniform coefficient in special circumstances. If the methodology does actually come to be used as we have outlined, variation of the coefficient will have little effect, since the scope of its application will be very limited—the major sectoral and intrasectoral investment distributions will be made by the absolute coefficient. The retention of an escape clause may simply reflect traditional thought habits, which we suggested above was the case for the escape clause in incremental national income calculations. The greatest danger is that it will be used to support variation in the absolute coefficient, which at present is supposed to be evaluated on a uniform basis. But, since the new methodology represents a step forward in expunging irrationality, it seems reasonable that the next version of the methodology will go further in this direction.

Miscellany

A few minor points should be mentioned. Lur'e is quite right in pointing to the double-counting of capital cost (as the investment and through depreciation) in formula (8) in the new methodology, which probably arose as an oversight.

The treatment of residual book value of capital (SM–69, Section 33) is open to question, but there are probably offsetting compensations. The methodology recommends that it be added to the cost of the new technology. Adding it in goes against the grain of sunk-cost rationality, as Lur'e argues. But in this case depreciation charges should also be subtracted from the prime cost of the old technology if it continues in use. This would reduce the calculated operating cost saving of the new technological variant. Since nothing is said about excluding this charge, it may be as well to add it into the cost of the investment as recommended by the methodology.

Finally, in discussing the new methodology, Kantorovich, Bogachev and Makarov have proposed a completely different approach for the basic criterion, a consumer's surplus measure,[9] without coming to grips with the difficult conceptual and practical difficulties it would involve.

---

and the second cost reduction in comparison with the existing technology. The main reason for the discrepancy, however, seems to be that the two criteria were not properly formulated. To be compatible with the cost minimization criterion of Section 21 of the methodology, his numerical example (Lur'e, "On Certain Recommendations," pp. 833–34) should include, in the numerator of the cost reduction criterion, the interest cost (the coefficient of effectiveness) of the two investments. In this case, as may easily be verified, the criteria give the same answer.

[9] L. V. Kantorovich, V. N. Bogachev, and V. L. Makarov, "Estimating the Effectiveness of Capital Expenditures," *Matekon*, Vol. VIII, No. 1 (Fall 1971), pp. 25–53.

IV. CONCLUSION

The new Standard Methodology is an important step in the direction of economic rationality, representing a consistent framework within which investment can be allocated and projects chosen. It is not without problems, including the major defect that it is at present unable to specify the intersectoral investment quantities, although this may be overcome through an iterative process as more information becomes available each year on the potential investment alternatives in each sector. What we feel very much warrants emphasis is the consistency of the criteria as conceived, although the new methodology has been faulted by others on this score. It remains to be seen whether or not they will come to be applied as envisaged.

Other difficulties will inevitably arise, perhaps most of all in pricing (e.g., treatment of turnover taxes in calculating input cost). These appear to be of less consequence at this time. They will become more important if the basic investment distribution starts to be based on the economic criteria presented in the new Standard Methodology, and it becomes possible to refine investment selection further.

16. PROBLEMS OF TECHNICAL PROGRESS IN THE USSR

Robert W. Campbell

Soviet economic growth after 1928 relied primarily on an "extensive" strategy of development involving increases in factor inputs of labor and capital. Labor inputs were enlarged by drawing women into the labor force, channeling new workers into the industrial sector, and reducing labor turnover and unemployment. Saving was mobilized through the state budget, and the output of consumer goods was held down in order to release resources for investment to build up the capital stock. Fixed investment was directed particularly to heavy industry, and human capital was developed through education and health programs.

By the late 1950s, however, the growth rates produced by this strategy began to decline. In the last decade a new approach has emerged, stressing such "intensive" factors as more efficient allocation of available resources, improved work incentives (including more attention to consumer wants), and the contribution of technological progress in increasing productivity and modernizing the economy.

Despite such highly publicized accomplishments as the Soviet space program, the USSR has lagged behind leading industrial nations of the West in developing and introducing new technology. Reasons for the Soviet technological lag are analyzed in this selection by Robert W. Campbell, Professor of Economics at Indiana University. He finds that the basic cause in the Soviet system of planning and management, which creates problems of incentives and organization hampers industrial research and development in the USSR.

This paper was originally presented at a Symposium on Recent Reforms in Eastern Europe at the University of Missouri–Kansas City in 1970, and has not been previously published. It has been revised and updated by Dr. Campbell especially for this book. Reprinted by permission.

I. INTRODUCTION

SOVIET LEADERS HAVE always had a great faith in science and technical progress as forces ensuring the historic victory of socialism. The socialist system is alleged to have a special advantage in unleashing this productive force, harnessing it to the task of raising the productivity of labor, and creating socialist abundance.

One consequence of this faith is that the Soviet system has long treated "science" (which will be more or less equated with research and development in this paper) with greater care than market-organized societies generally have. The leaders have deliberately accepted it as a function worthy of attention at the highest level of decision-making, and meriting generous support and appropriate administrative machinery to ensure that it is properly organized and directed to make the maximum possible contribution to the growth of the economy. Such an attitude toward science and research does not seem distinctive today, since most advanced countries now have high level science policy and machinery and generous government support, but the Russians showed this concern much earlier.

In the Soviet Union research and development is a favored and burgeoning enterprise. With a total GNP probably no more than half as big as that of the United States, the Soviet economy supports an R and D establishment which, in terms of manpower at least, is larger than ours. This is one of the fastest growing sectors of the Soviet economy. Both before and after the second World War, employment in research and development organizations has grown at an average rate of about 12 percent per year, though in the last decade this growth has begun to decelerate somewhat. Expenditures on "science" have grown at a similarly rapid rate, having roughly tripled in the 1960–1970 decade.

In recent years there has been an intense concern on the part of Soviet scientists and officials about the effectiveness with which these resources, so lavishly provided, are being used to achieve the goals of technical progress and economic growth. The general suspicion was well summed up by the Soviet physicist Peter Kapitsa in his often-cited comment that although the Russians have about as many scientists as the United States, Soviet scientific output (measured by publications) is only about half what the Americans produce. The suspicion of low productivity in research and development has been extensively reiterated and documented in the literature of the last several years, which is full of reference to scientists who don't publish, research organizations that expand each year but have never made an invention or discovery, and lines of inquiry that have been pursued for 30 years without results. The situation is alleged to be the same across the spectrum from basic to applied and developmental research. One class of horror stories concerns design institutes which design new machines that are less productive and more costly than the old machines, that have to be completely redesigned by the enterprise that is to produce them, or that are badly obsolete by the time they are put into production. The biggest worry of all is a conviction that new knowledge is not applied, that the "achievements of Soviet science and technology" are not translated into technical progress in production.

II. THE R AND D FUNCTION IN THE SOVIET ECONOMY

The centralized approach characteristic of the Soviet system fits some of the elements of the R and D enterprise much better than others. The R and D function, and its goal of technological progress, involve a range of disparate activities, some of which benefit from attention and strategic direction from the center, and some of which do not. There are many possible subdivisions of R and D, but for present purposes it will be most useful to distinguish two broad categories of the overall endeavor. The first is primarily concerned with establishment and support of a research and development establishment, and the formulation and execution of strategic missions and projects. This is the area where centralization has its strongest rationale. The second category is what we have in mind when we talk about innovation, diffusion, and application. This is the part of the job that has no effective champion in the Soviet system. It requires the participation of the enterprise in a significant way, but in the Soviet Union technological progress has never been conceived as an enterprise function. That the enterprise must play a role is accepted, but the designers of the Soviet system have never succeeded in lodging with the enterprise responsibility and authority for this function. Each of these areas has its special problems. The problem of getting the two effectively co-ordinated and integrated in the planned economy context is the central issue today in the Soviet administration of their R and D establishment.

The basic problem of the first sphere might be formulated as follows: High level, centralized science planning can be seen from two quite different points of view. The first, which I will call the "science" view, is in terms of scientific fields and problems, creation of a backlog of scientific knowledge, and mobilization of resources for and organization of a research establishment. This activity can be defined in terms of its basic goal, i.e., to understand the underlying principles by which the world works. It is not much concerned to show how some specific goal can be accomplished. Its purpose is concept formation, discovering and making sense of new phenomena, formulating and validating theories—it also seeks a more applied kind of knowledge that involves accumulation of data, experimental results, and engineering validation of these basic principles. This is what Soviet writers on research and development mean when, as they so often do, they speak of the necessity to create a *nauchno-tekhnicheskii zadel*—an inventory of scientific knowledge on which technical improvements can be based. The focus of this view is by field, discipline and scientific problem area, because that is the way theories, training, research, and profiles of research institutions are organized. This view of research provides one important rationale for centralization. Just because science is seen as oriented toward expanding abstract knowledge, the directions of which are not foreseeable, rather than toward the creation of new technology, it must be appreciated and justified more as an end in itself than as an instrument of some other goal.

At the same time the other half of the mind knows that this search is not an end in itself. The Soviet attitude is quite clear on this, and has always rejected the idea that science might be a self-sufficient game or quest driven solely by its own internal dynamics. The Soviet philosophers of science explicitly stipulate that the reason for a socialist society to support science is that it will have a payoff, even though it may be pursued by its practitioners in a frame of mind that does not focus primarily on the payoff.

This concern with the payoff, however, is conceptualized in forms quite different from the science view. It means conceiving projects and goals for new things or ways of doing things that are desirable, but as far as our knowledge of natural phenomena is concerned not impossible, and organizing to get them done. This "mission" view, as it is sometimes described, offers a second argument for centralization on the grounds that only from the center can one discern the most vital needs to be served by new technology.

These missions may be more or less self-sufficient goals such as landing a man on the moon, or the creation of a new fighter plane, but more commonly they are thought of as strategic breakthroughs that will have a widespread applicability and stimulative effects in many areas, as might be expected of better computers, for example. And even when missions are more or less self-sufficient they are justified in part because they will involve breakthroughs that will affect many other technologies as is commonly argued for the space program. But just because they are often envisaged at this kind of strategic level of generality, the missions the central planners set themselves do not extend to the application—innovation—diffusion aspects. This central process is more likely to end with the creation of a prototype, the demonstration of technical feasibility, or satisfactory application in a particular context.

Both elements in this rationale for a centralized approach to R and D are internally complex, and both views are equally vital. The choice of missions involves a creative process in their formulation, the collection of a great deal of information to assess their technical feasibility, and a need to evaluate them economically by forecasting costs and payoffs. In addition, for the big projects with which this central process concerns itself, the job of organizing and executing fulfillment is an administrative task of high order. But if science planners held only to this view there would be little in the way of new knowledge created. So they must pursue in parallel a complicated process of allocating a research budget among fields, organizations, and lines of inquiry following criteria based on "scientific" payoff only.

There are serious deficiencies in the way the Russian approach R and D from either of these points of view, but the really thorny problem for them is to find ways to reconcile them.

Problems in the Central Management of "Science"

There is a well known proposition that it is impossible to plan science, that the most one can aim for is to plan *for* science. The argument is that uncertainty and the speculative character of scientific advance make it impossible for outsiders to guide this part of the enterprise effectively. All the planners can do is to provide the funds, and let the scientists go their own way. Science is purposeful, and does have goals describable in terms of science itself, but it is impossible to evaluate these *ex ante* in terms of the ultimate payoffs which are the rationale for supporting science in the first place. On the whole the Soviet planners seem to have accepted this view of the matter. They have had the faith to encourage basic research and have contented themselves with supporting it rather than trying too hard to direct it in detail. When there has been interference, it has more often been motivated by ideology, as in cybernetics or genetics, than by a central prejudice for practical work. In recent years there has been a growing attempt to impose a set of priorities in terms of fields and problem areas. The procedures for setting these priorities are complex, but it seems fairly clear that the priority structure is largely determined by scientists rather than by outside fiat.[1]

Reasonable choice of priorities depends on scientific judgment, which really means forecasting and information. From the literature, one gathers that Soviet science planners are rather dissatisfied with the information and forecasting institutions and procedures they now have, but at the same time it is obvious they are putting improvement of them at the center of attention.

Even when the screening and decision-making process is in the hands of scientists themselves, institutional biases still operate. There seems to be passion for eliminating duplication, and therefore instituting monopoly, that is misplaced in this kind of endeavor. Also, the Soviet scientific institutions find the rigid environment of Soviet planning un-

[1] See Eugène Zaleski and others, *Science Policy in the USSR* (Paris: Organization for Economic Cooperation and Development, 1969), and Linda Greenberg, *Soviet Science Policy and the Scientific Establishment, 1955–1965* (unpublished Ph.D. dissertation, Indiana University, 1969).

responsive to some of the distinctive needs of scientific work—flexibility in supply, for example. There also seem to be some systemic biases that make it difficult to get the proper number of assistants, secretaries, equipment, and capital facilities.

The most serious difficulties in the science planning area, however, lie in a different direction. A corollary to the rejection of outside control is that control has to be internalized. If the research choices are going to be made by the researchers, the standards, objectives, and other criteria have to be internalized in individuals, and controlled like any other professional conduct by the peer group. More than most professionals, Soviet scientists have been able to establish professional independence, but one gets a strong feeling that the Soviet science establishment lacks professional responsibility. It seems to be full of dead wood. In the rapidly expanding Soviet literature on concrete sociological studies one of the favorite subjects is scientists and research organizations. There is much concern with how scientists entered the field, what career motives they hold, how they get along with their colleagues, problems of advancement and the relationship between young and old. The research is probably motivated by and also confirms the suspicion that a lot of people in science are there not because they are suited for such a career by talent or temperament, but for careerist motives—the high pay, prestige, chances of advancement, and so on. There is also a lot of complaint to this effect on the part of scientists about their colleagues. Some of the bitterest complaints are that these people make advancement and administration rather than science their career, so that the establishment comes to be directed at all levels by people who do not have any understanding or appreciation of research, who are incapable of recognizing a good idea when it is handed to them (or when they are, will steal it) and whose main accomplishment as directors of institutes is to get themselves nominated for prizes and honors. We get a very vivid indication of how thoroughly this diagnosis has been accepted in the emphasis the decree of October 23, 1968, placed on purging unsuited and untalented people from their scientific positions.[2] The decree requires that research positions be filled only through open competitions, and that holders of these positions be subject to review and reappointment at least once every three years. Further discussion in the press suggests that this is going to be a drastic pruning, and that many people feel themselves quite vulnerable.

Another way of expressing this weakness would be to say that the whole R and D establishment aspires to, and has achieved in excess, a freedom to formulate its tasks that is appropriate only for the best scientists at the more fundamental end of the spectrum. There is a strong

---

[2] This decree, following years of criticism, diagnosis, and experiment, is a long delayed program of decisions and actions for improving the effectiveness of research and development and the introduction of new technology into the economy.

theme expressed in Soviet writings about R and D that a lot of the work with which Soviet research concerns itself is utterly useless. In the early sixties when an effort was being made to regain some central control over the science establishment, an extensive review of what the science establishment was really doing led to conclusions of this kind. An especially interesting article by the head of the State Committee for the Co-ordination of Research Work of the Armenian SSR concluded that about half the research work in the Armenian SSR was out of control and without scientific justifications. Much work was criticized as useless in the sense that it was scientifically misconceived—not properly posed, designed, or conducted to advance knowledge. This was not just the biased viewpoint of planners who think that all research should have some practical payoff.

As a corollary, some Soviet commentators see a kind of Gresham's Law at work. Those scientists who do good research are most likely to be drawn into mission-oriented activities, leaving those least capable of self-direction to be the ones that have the greatest freedom to choose their own directions.

Problems in the Definition of Missions

A desire to exploit central vision and to impose central priorities on technical advance was the original rationale for treating technical progress as a central function rather than as an enterprise function. In the early stages of their growth drive, the Russians thought of technical progress primarily in terms of borrowing certain crucial elements of technology from abroad where they were already developed, and introducing them into the economy in new production facilities, the latter being a job which was itself a central function.[3] This "strategic" approach was characteristic of the whole program, which was conceived in terms of leading links, crucial technical innovations, and "keys" to the solution of any problem. The situation has changed in the sense that technical progress is today less a matter of copying, and more a matter of making independent technical gains. But the old habit of strategic thought still holds sway, so that Soviet planners believe that there are certain crucial innovations, which properly chosen and achieved, will be decisive for the general level of technology in the economy as a whole. Typical examples would be the computer, unconventional power generation, achievement of space capability, and automation of planning and management.

---

[3] This point is well developed by Marvin Jackson in *Soviet Project and Design Organizations: A Case Study of Technological Decisionmaking in a Command System* (unpublished Ph.D. dissertation, University of California, Berkeley, 1967), which shows how the whole structure of planning, institutions, and incentives was oriented to the goal of borrowing and mastering key innovations.

The big successes of Soviet science and technology have been achieved through this approach. This method has made it possible to challenge and match other countries in such areas as space and military technology at the same time the general level of technology is backward by the standards of the advanced countries. This approach has serious limitations, however.

1. One difficulty is that only a limited number of missions can be pursued in this way. It stretches logic a bit to say that you can give "first priority" to even a reasonably short list of missions. This, incidentally, is one of the lessons recent experience has taught the Russians. In the 1950s they listed a very large number of missions in the annual R and D plan—on the order of thousands—most of which never got completed. In later years they have cut down drastically the number of tasks listed in the central plan to something of the order of a few hundred.

2. A second difficulty is that these big missions usually take a long period of years to achieve but have been prosecuted in the framework of an annual plan. Even more than other economic activity, R and D will be distorted by being subjected to too short a time horizon. This, too, the Soviet planners learned from experience, and it is said that beginning with the 1966–1970 Five-Year Plan, broad missions are no longer being expressed in terms of annual plans, but only in the five-year perspective. There then arises the problem, however, of getting them actually tied into the annual planning processes which control resource use.

3. The problem of choosing missions to concentrate on is very difficult. There are always more projects than can successfully be pursued at a given time, and Soviet planners seem to have done a poor job of economic evaluation in their formulation and choice of strategic missions. One can find totally wrongheaded examples, as in the great emphasis once put on gasification of coal as a way of raising the productivity of the energy economy. That particular incident is perhaps attributable to the technical isolationism of the Stalin era, and may not be indicative for today. The undoubted success which was achieved in oil drilling technology through the turbodrill was badly marred by errors in economic calculation in its design, and by exclusive concentration on it as the great maneuver to bypass the very great difficulties of improving rotary drilling technology in the Soviet situation.[4] In the process the R and D decision-makers in the oil industry simply abandoned any effort to try to improve rotary drilling technology. An interesting proposition advanced by some U.S. military planners is that the real function of R and D is to buy options. A decision on some new weapons system as the "best" and a commitment to its development and deployment by one side will prompt the optimum countermove, nullifying much of

---

[4] See Robert W. Campbell, *The Economics of Soviet Oil and Gas* (Baltimore: Johns Hopkins Press, 1969).

the gain expected from the innovation. Hence it is necessary to develop alternatives parallel with the original commitment, as a basis for a counter-countermove. The principle applies whenever there is uncertainty. The Soviet drilling industry also experienced a dynamic change in environment—increases in well depth, changes in type of rock drilled, and the economizing possibilities of slim-hole well design—which robbed the turbodrill of much of the advantage it had conferred. But, having made so precise a choice and so firm a commitment to the turbodrill technology (which after all is the whole point of centralization in the "mission" view), the R and D planners neglected to buy the options they now so sorely miss.

Research on the civilian applications of space technology in the USSR makes one wonder whether the Soviet space officials have not made analogous errors in their concepts and calculations for a communications satellite system. The Soviet system is based on a quite different concept and serves quite different purposes from the Western Intelsat system. The Soviet system was originally designed as basically a TV distribution system and the satellites are placed in twelve-hour elliptical orbits so that it takes three satellites to achieve continuous coverage. The satellite design is also quite different from that used in the West, and the upshot is that the Russians have had to orbit a much larger cumulative weight to obtain a system with a much smaller capacity than the synchronous-satellite Intelsat system. The centralized approach worked well in the sense that it was possible to take a decision, make a commitment, and put into operation a TV distribution system in a very short time and well ahead of anyone else. On the other hand, though numbers are hard to come by, the benefit-cost ratio in this endeavor must be very low. The space officials seem to have committed themselves to their distinctive concept before it was very clear how the technology was going to develop, and now that it seems ever clearer that the synchronous system is the optimal one, they have an expensive commitment and little defensive R and D backlog, which makes a switch difficult.

The meteorological satellite program also suggests something along these lines. An early decision was taken, apparently, to develop a system using heavy, complicated, and expensive satellites, reminiscent of the U.S. Nimbus satellites, rather than some simple type, like the Tiros. It took a long time for the Russians to get their system properly established to make the contribution it should to practical forecasting problems. In the United States, on the other hand, there were alternative programs. The Tiros concept, cheap and simple but limited in capacity, became operational quite early and has been a great success, though it generates less information than might be obtained from a more complicated system. The Nimbus program aimed at a satellite with a higher output, but there turned out to be many difficulties with the Nimbus concept. Nevertheless, we have been able to win great practical benefits within the limitations of the Tiros system, while waiting for decisions and breakthroughs on the more advanced and complicated alternatives. This the Russians missed.

The turbodrill and space examples are especially important because they reflect the novelties of the situation in which Soviet R and D will more and more find itself during the coming years. Technical and economic evaluation of alternatives is a great deal simpler when a country is catching up than when it is on the frontier. The Russians place great hope on technological forecasting to show them the areas where breakthroughs are likely and when such breakthrough can be expected, and anyone who reads Soviet science literature is surely impressed with the fascination this idea has for them. But their work in this field seems to be derivative, and they have not yet discovered the "secrets" of successful forecasting. It is quite possible, of course, that much more careful and advanced work is being done in secret sectors than what we see published in open sources.

These choices also depend heavily on economic evaluation, and on this subject, too, their practice as reflected in the literature[5] seems weak. For example they seem strongly oriented toward evaluating effectiveness by stages, i.e., allocating the benefits from some innovation, a new machine, for example, among the enterprise that produces it, the bureau that did the design work, and the institute that did the theoretical work, in order to calculate separate benefit-cost ratios for each. This seems to be a thoroughly misguided idea. Also, there are enough fuzzy variables in the standard effectiveness calculation (such as the scale of application) to permit large biases toward over-optimistic evaluations.

Coordination of the "Science" View and the Mission View

The melding of the two perspectives on R and D by the science planners is a difficult problem. *Resarch*, especially at the more basic end, is carried out by institutes specialized according to particular classes of phenomena. *Missions*, however, generally cut across fields and disciplines, drawing on knowledge generated in several areas of science.

Presumably there are payoff coefficients relating "science" activity to "mission" achievements. But in the nature of things these coefficients are not known, so that it is difficult to optimize the allocation of effort among fields to achieve the maximum accomplishment of missions. Because of the uncertainties involved there has to be a continuous process of reallocation among fields and problems, and between basic and applied

---

[5] I. G. Kurakov, *Science, Technology, and Communism* (New York: Pergamon, 1966). Since at the time he wrote the book Kurakov was head of the economics division of the State Committee for the Co-Ordination of Scientific Research Work, what he says should be a good indication of thought and practice of those who actually make these evaluations.

research on the science side, and continuous redefinition of the internal structure of the means for implementing the broad missions, as experience reveals more about the problem and its solution.

There is one way to allow for this flexibility and make the process work, and indeed this is how the Russians do make it work. In may sound paradoxical, but their approach really works by decentralization. Full authority over some mission is given to a project boss, who is permitted great flexibility in choosing the alternative means of implementation, in drawing on the resources of different parts of the R and D establishment and in defining what he wants from them to achieve results. This is the secret of Soviet success in those areas where they have been most successful—designing airplanes, producing hydrogen bombs, conducting a space program. One of the prerequisites for the boss to be able to do this, of course, is that his field of responsibility be small enough in the total situation so that flexibility for him is consistent with overall fixity. This kind of approach can be implemented for only a limited number of missions. Some people can be permitted this flexibility, initiative, and priority status only if such freedom is denied to others.

III. LOWER-LEVEL INITIATIVE AND COOPERATION

Whatever criticism we may make of the central processes just described, the greatest obstacles to technical progress in the Soviet economy lie in the second of the two big subdivisions of the R and D effort described earlier, that is, small-scale formulation and execution of missions, innovation at lower levels, and diffusion of new technology. This function has ultimately to be carried out at the level of the producing and using enterprise. As a minimum the co-operation of the enterprise, and more frequently active initiative on its part, are essential in this phase. The failure of Soviet enterprises to act in this way is the biggest obstacle to technical progress in the economy. Nearly everything that anyone has said on this matter can fit nicely under two main headings—incentives and organization.

Incentives

Put in the most simple terms, the incentive problem is that, for the enterprise, incentives for innovating are very weak while incentives to avoid it are very powerful. The gains that come from an innovation are usually won at the expense of some temporary dislocation and learning costs, and the success indicator system of the Soviet economy has traditionally done little to allow for either. For one thing, the success indicator system works on a very short time horizon, far shorter than the cycle that innovations of any size are likely to involve. The costs of innovation to the innovator are unlikely to be allowed for, or the gains to the economy acknowledged, in measuring the success of enterprise performance. The prototypical illustration is the truck factory that turned out a certain truck model for 15 years without improving its deficient engine. The engine block castings were machined without having been fully cured, with small subsequent changes in dimensions leading to violations of the tolerances to which they had been machined. The result was rapid wear and high repair costs for the users of the trucks. The design department in the plant had suggested several relatively simple solutions to the problem, but these were always rejected by management, because the extra costs, though small in relation to the savings for the users of the trucks, would have worsened the cost performance indicators of the plant. Variations on this principle are the standard stuff of Soviet diagnoses of failures to innovate.

The point also applies to diffusion of technological spinoffs from the strategic advances generated at the center. Research on spillovers from the space program has identified several managerial innovations that originated in space and military programs, and the histories of diffusion or nondiffusion of these innovations to other branches of the economy is instructive.[6]

One of these is the quality control program which the Russians call the Saratov system, very similar to the "zero-defects" system used in the United States. In both countries these systems were first worked out in the aerospace industry. It is unnecessary to describe the Saratov system in detail, but basically it works by making quality control a real objective, allows for it in the internal structure of the firm, embodies it in the success indicator system, and provides significant bonuses for performance. The system is claimed to have radically raised quality in the plants where it was developed. There seems to have been no spontaneous diffusion of this method, or any transfer effort on the part of economic agencies. It was the Party that provided the push, first on the regional level, then throughout the RSFSR, and finally on the all-Union level. It took something like 10 years for the Party at the central level to become aware of the innovation and initiate a campaign to get it widely adopted. Enterprises must go through the motions of compliance when such campaigns are waged, but apparently the Saratov system was diffused only slightly compared to what happened with zero defects in the United States. The explanation is that quality control was just not something Soviet enterprises were interested in. In was the great bargaining power of the military customers which had stimulated the development of the system in the first place, but this situation is largely absent in the rest of the economy so there is little incentive for enterprises to take this function seriously.

---

[6] See Robert Campbell, "Management Spillovers from Soviet Space and Military Programmes," *Soviet Studies,* Vol. XXIII, No. 4 (April 1972), pp. 586–607.

There is an interesting article by one of the advocates of the system, voicing two complaints. The author is bothered by the Americans' failure to acknowledge Soviet priority in the invention of the system, but he is especially and acutely distressed that is has not been widely adopted in the Soviet economy. "What is vexing, bitter and inspires amazement and alarm is something else. Why do no more than 10 percent of Soviet enterprises so far work on the basis of the principles of the [Saratov] system?"

Another of these innovations was PERT-type methods for control of big investment projects and R and D efforts. The Russians call it SPU (*setevoe planirovanie i upravlenie*), or network methods of planning and control. The transfer mechanism here was State and Party initiative, through special training programs for management, and through decrees requiring the establishment of SPU offices for certain kinds of projects. In this case there was fairly widespread and effective diffusion of the technique, especially in construction and R and D, though as usual in such cases, with quite a bit of formalism, caused by the need to accomodate to a campaign despite the absence of an inherent interest on the part of the adopters. As one author says:

> Evaluating in general terms the practical status of the adoption of SPU in our country, it is difficult to draw comforting conclusions. If the number of mastered network systems seems on the surface rather large, and they are distributed in almost all branches of the national economy, still many of these systems have not been brought to the level of real management systems based on networks. A situation is frequently observed in which a network system which is considered to be fully mastered operates, but without exerting any real influence on the progress of the project. Still less satisfactory is the situation when system is equated with a network *model*, that is, when it is limited to the drawing up of a network, which is never used and never corrected during the carrying out of the project.

Reliability theory and engineering also arose as byproducts of meeting goals in military and space programs, but with big spillover potential for other sectors, such as television, computers, and the civilian communications system. In this area the Russians seem to have been content to let diffusion take place through the medium of professional experts, which is an approach strongly reminiscent of what seems to have happened in this country. In the United States the reliability engineers have a strong professional organization and esprit, and active professional communications and interchange. A firm that wants to deal with a reliability problem hires the right kind of people and relies on them to keep it up to date in the application of the latest ideas and experience proved elsewhere in the economy. This is largely what also happened in the USSR. But this form of diffusion seems not to have worked very well for the Russians, presumably because enterprises feel little need to improve reliability, and so do not draw on the experience available through the contacts of their professional employees. One group of people has recommended that there ought to be a more active governmental program to get reliability engineering experience diffused—persuasive testimony that the other approach does not work very effectively.

The shift under the economic reform to fewer and more general success indicators doesn't really make much contribution to the problem of incentives for innovation. The difficulty is that the pricing system is not flexible enough to make innovation "profitable" in the new sense. There is an interesting literature on how pricing should be handled to encourage innovation, and the State Committee on Prices has been instructed to improve pricing wherever possible to encourage technical progress. For a long time Soviet economists were perplexed by the difficulty that what would encourage the producer of new technology, say a high price for an improved machine, would discourage the user. That confusion was finally cleared up, and the present approach is said to be one of splitting gains between the producer and the user. There is also much discussion, and apparently some action, in the price changes that were adopted in 1967, to introduce into the price system bonuses for innovative features, especially quality improvement, and financial penalties for failure to innovate. A recent article by V. K. Sitnin (head of the State Committee on Prices) recommends the introduction of a dual price system involving scheduled price reductions after an innovation comes into use, so as to discourage production of obsolete goods. To avoid the attraction for the old which this would offer the user, however, the user would continue to pay the original price, with the difference going to the budget. This would penalize the obsolete producer, but would fail to benefit the innovator. The Sitnin proposal is interesting as an effort to introduce a substitute for the competition that forces a firm in the competitive market to keep innovating. The price differential is a tax on the non-innovator. In a competitive market, however, the innovator gains through the protection afforded by patents, while the burdens on non-innovators are levied by the market. The competitive market's encouragement approach is in principle probably better than the discouragement approach.

The Russians occasionally use subsidies, as in the case of the fund for the mastering of production. This is a ministry-level fund, formed by charges against all firms in the jurisdiction of a ministry, and against which some enterprise-level development costs can be charged. The main problem is that these funds are not large enough to absorb much of the cost of innovation, especially since the ministry is likely to assume control over them and use them for its own purposes. There are complicated rules about what development costs can be charged to these funds, and one of the rules seems to be that they can be used only in the first instance of serial production of a new item. One Soviet commentator complained that production of new items was frequently shifted among producers, each of whom had to bear the learning costs, but only one of whom got recompensed. This is but one example of a more fundamental difficulty, i.e., that there seems to be little in the way of property rights in the results of innovative behavior. There are a few, as in the recently established system of state certification of quality, which gives the innovator some competitive edge and some pecuniary advantages. But in general, there is little indication in Soviet statements that they perceive the possible usefulness of property rights in innovation in solving the problem.

Organization

The problem of lower-level innovation can also be interpreted in terms of organizational deficiencies. Obviously there need to be nodes in the lower levels of the administrative hierarchy at which a process like that already described for the center can be carried out, but on a more applied and specific level and on a smaller scale. Many failures in the innovation process can be laid to the fact that the system lacks centers of initiative where all the ingredients—motivation, information, and access to or authority over resources—coincide neatly to provide the push for innovation. The enterprise is ineffective as such a node. Its independence is severely restricted in setting many of the economic variables connected with an innovation, such as investment, what to produce, and price. The enterprise not only lacks motivation, as already indicated, but in the USSR is often far too small to have the technical and market information needed to conceive and evaluate innovations. This is basically why the system designers have not made innovation an enterprise function.

The responsibility for innovation is placed primarily on the ministry, which then discharges it through its subordinate specialized research institutes and design bureaus. But it has often proved difficult to give these agents the proper motivations and make them work in the proper directions. No attempt will be made here to survey even briefly how the general ills we know from the rest of the economy manifest themselves in research and design organizations—distortions in measuring performance, peculiarities of the bonus system, price and wage anomalies, supply uncertainties, etc. The central point is that these pressures are likely to wall off the branch institute or design organization from contact with production enterprises or other participants in the process, and make it unresponsive to their needs.

The design organizations aren't commercially oriented, do not make correct economic evaluations, are not in close enough contact with the client plants that will use the process or produce the new machine. A design institute can usually deliver the blueprints, good or bad, and wash its hands of any further concern. An institute which develops a new technique may be unable to get any enterprise interested in testing or using it. This may be because the institute can't carry the work far enough, say through prototype production or pilot plant operations, to show that the idea is sound. On the basis of an order and specifications from the ministry, the institute designs new equipment that fails to take account of the production peculiarities of the enterprise which is to produce it, so that the enterprise has to redesign the equipment before it can actually produce it. The enterprise may find it impossible to get any institute to interest itself in finding solutions to important problems the enterprise faces. When R and D organizations work on contract rather than ministry directives, they may be able to finance themselves only by accepting routine and overdefined work from enterprises which fails to exploit the institute's capabilities.

These difficulties relate primarily to the problem of integrating the activities of the design organizations and the producer of a new item, but most innovations really require the co-operation of still more parties as well, and the general point about the weakness of the lateral ties applies to all of them.

There are several possible techniques for integrating these fragmented roles. One is through contracts between institutes and enterprises. In the early sixties an effort was made to get a large share or the lower level institutes and design bureaus off budget financing and onto a system of financing through contracts with enterprises, though apparently this shift was never carried as far as originally intended. A second possibility would be to combine all functions under a single organization, either by making the R and D organization subordinate to the production enterprise, or giving R and D organizations the production and testing capacity they need to carry an innovation through the experimental and pilot production stage. Extreme versions of this idea suggest something like the venture capital–new technology firms that exist in capitalist countries, or analogues of the university-industrial complexes symbolized by Route 128 in Boston.

One of the main themes of the 1968 decree is the need to expand the use of all these devices. There are allegedly successful precedents in Soviet experience for all of them. In the aircraft industry the R and D directors have an extremely powerful position in the whole structure, with enough resources and powers to develop a new aircraft to the point where it can be turned over for production to a series plant. The large electrical engineering firm Elektrosila in Leningrad is supposed to have internalized effectively the R and D activities underlying its production mission. The Siberian Department of the USSR Academy of Sciences is supposed to have been very successful both in the integrated combine approach and with the contract method.

On the other hand, there are numerous illustrations in Soviet experience of pitfalls associated with each of these methods. When R and D organizations, test facilities, and pilot production capacity are made subordinate to the production enterprise, they may be used in an un-imaginative and production-oriented rather than an innovative way. Giving greater power to the designers may indeed be effective where speed and assurance in fulfilling a mission take precedence over economy, as in a fighter plane. But Soviet airplane designers have yet to produce a "commercial" plane that is commercially competitive. The contract method seems to suffer from numerous technical crudities. For a long time there was no contract law for this sphere that would allow for subleties in incentive measures, protect the interests of both parties, and adjudicate the conflicts. A new statute for these contracts was adopted in 1969 which may improve matters, although early discussions by Soviet economists suggest that the new statute may be rather biased against the interests of the R and D organization.

This simply underlines what one ought to know anyway—that in creating nodes of initiative for innovation it will be important to avoid a stereotyped approach, and the arrangements must be adapted to the distinctive features of specific cases.

IV. CONCLUSION

It is probably better at this stage in our study of Soviet research and development not to offer general conclusions about the Soviet approach to achieving technical progress. We can probably agree with the Russians' own evaluation that they are not achieving what they might expect from the resources devoted to this effort, but that does little to explain what they are doing wrong, or what they need to do to get better results. Indeed, if this paper has a main point, it is to remind us that technical progress is a many-sided, but integral, venture, each part of which poses a different problem and a different perspective, so that success depends on differentiation and integration. The paper has not done justice to the number of these different aspects—having completely ignored such problems as scientific and technical information, individual incentives, international co-operation and transfer of technology, and having oversimplified the global-local issue by presenting it primarily as a central planner–enterprise distinction. Indeed this is probably one of the main points we can make about the Soviet experience so far. As a problem of differentiation and integration, of reconciling tactical and strategical aspects, balancing long-run and short-run considerations, the problem of getting technical progress on their own exceeds in complexity any problems the planners have dealt with before, and is far less susceptible of solution by methods previously used.

17. THE CASE OF COMPUTER TECHNOLOGY

Richard W. Judy

One of the most striking instances of lagging technology in the Soviet Union is computer technology. Computers have obvious and important advantages in solving complex problems with many variables, such as arise in large-scale planning and management decisions. Yet it was not until 1972 that the USSR produced its first series of third-generation computers with miniature integrated circuits like those developed seven years earlier in the United States, where these circuits are now used to make inexpensive electronic pocket calculators. The USSR has also been slow to introduce computers into widespread use in the economy.

In the following selection, Richard W. Judy, Professor of Economics at the University of Toronto, analyzes the reasons for the lag in the development and use of computers in the USSR. The selection is reprinted by permission from a larger article with this title in *East-West Trade and the Technology Gap: A Political and Economic Appraisal,* ed. Stanislaw Wasowski (New York: Praeger Publishers, Inc., 1970), pp. 66–71. The footnotes have been omitted.

SOVIET COMPUTER TECHNOLOGY lags badly behind its counterpart in the West and particularly in the United States. This lag was most apparent to the 1959 U.S. Technical Delegation in Computers to the Soviet Union. But the delegation was impressed with the intelligence, vigor, and dedication of Soviet computer specialists, and many felt that the gap would be closed in a few years. After the passage of nearly a decade, however, the lag persists and has perhaps increased. In this section, we examine some possible explanations for the existence and persistence of the lag.

SCIENTIFIC COMPETENCE

It is not difficult to dispose of the argument that the Soviet computer lag results from theoretical or scientific incompetence. Westerners who

365

know Soviet computer scientists can testify to their competence and their thorough knowledge of the field. Soviet excellence in basic science and mathematics is no secret, and the enthusiasm and ability of computer scientists contrasts with the mediocre machines with which they must work.

Translations of Western scientific and technical publications in the fields of computer science and cybernetics are widely available in the USSR. Many Soviet scientists and engineers have at least a reading knowledge of English and can make their way through technical publications. The bibliographies of Soviet works in this field are scattered with references to an amazing variety of Western, mainly American, technical literature.

If additional evidence of the competence and ingenuity of Soviet computer scientists is required, we have but to examine the bold experimental applications being carried on in various institutes of the Academy of Sciences. Soviet experiments in the fields of artificial intelligence, machine translations, control systems, and character recognition are in many cases very good. The excellence of Soviet work in numerical analysis is well known. It should be noted, however, that the quality of Soviet experimental (not theoretical) work may have suffered somewhat in recent years from the unavailability and deficiencies of the computing machines with which scientists have to work.

Confronting the evidence, we have no alternative but to reject the hypothesis that a lack of theoretical and basic scientific and technical knowledge is responsible for the lag in Soviet computer technology. We must look elsewhere for the problems.

IMPROPER ORGANIZATION

Although part of a supposedly centralized and planned economy, the Soviet computer industry displays an amazing degree of fragmentation and lack of coordination. Responsibilities for design, manufacture, installation, maintenance, operations, and software development are distributed among a multitude of organizations. The result is that no single organization has overall responsibility for satisfactory research, development, and operation of computing systems.

The first computers in the USSR were designed by institutes of the Academy of Sciences. To some extent, this has remained the case; all of the BESM computers have been designed by groups under the leadership of S. A. Lebedev in the Institute of Precision Mechanics and Computing Equipment, Academy of Science, Moscow. Academic institutes in Kiev, Erevan, and other republic capitals have produced one-of-a-kind machines. The early Ural computers were designed by teams headed by B. I. Rameev at the Ministry of Radio Industry high-speed electronic machine plant in Penza. More recent Ural computers have also originated in Penza. The Minsk computers are designed at the Minsk calculating machines plant, which is part of the Ministry of Radio Industry. Some design work for process control computers is done by the institutes of the Ministry of Instrument-Making, Automation Devices, and Control Systems.

The manufacture of computers is carried on both in the Ministry of Radio Industry and in the Ministry of Instrument-Making, Automation Devices, and Control Systems. The BESM and M-20 have been made at the Moscow calculating machines plant. The Ural machines have been manufactured in Penza; and the Minsk machines, naturally enough, are made in Minsk. All of these plants belong to the Ministry of Radio Industry. The Dnepr-2 is manufactured at the Kiev plant of computers and control equipment that belongs to the Ministry of Instrument-Making, Automation Devices, and Control Systems. Both ministries have given hints that third-generation computers are on the drawing boards.

The responsibility of the computer manufacturer, at least until recently, has ended with the manufacture of the central processing unit. The responsibility for gathering together the required peripheral devices, such as magnetic tapes, magnetic drums, and high-speed line printers, has often rested with the purchaser of the systems. Assembly of these diverse subsystems, installation, and maintenance have also been the responsibilities of users. On numerous occasions the central processor and other expensive equipment have remained idle or underused at the customer's location because of a lack of vital peripheral devices, such as printers, tape units, and so forth.

Until recently the manufacturing ministry bore no responsibility for the provision of programming languages, executive systems, or other software. These were developed by users, usually in the Academy of Sciences. Typically the development of languages did not begin until the user had a machine available to use in the development process. User agencies, even in the Academy of Sciences, rarely have had sufficient resources to mount crash software development programs. The result has been that the appearance of languages, utility programs, and such has lagged far behind the physical availability of the machines themselves.

Systems help, that is, helping the unsophisticated user to develop programs and other software for his application, is no one's responsibility in the Soviet Union. The result is that the job is not done. Every user is basically alone in his battle to tame the electronic monster that he has acquired. Even such large enterprises as the Moscow Likachev automobile plant, the Gorky automobile plant, and the Leningrad optical-mechanical combine have spent five to seven years on the creation of systems and then did not complete them.

An attempt was made by the Communist Party and the Soviet Government in April 1966 to redefine the responsibilities of various ministries and scientific institutes in the field of computer technology. The Ministry of Radio Industry was given greater powers and responsibility in the field of design and manufacture of hardware and development of basic software. Recent evidence suggests that this reorganization has not had the desired effect. Proposals have recently been put forth to create a special Ministry of Computer and Organizational Technology, which would assume full responsibility for the development of this field. Such a ministry, its advocates argue, could unite all the factories, scientific research institutes, and design bureaus in the field of computer technology, thereby eliminating parallelism and overlap. It would also direct specialization and coordination of production. Such proposals are opposed on the grounds that such a specialized ministry would infringe on the jurisdictional interests of other ministries. The problem remains unresolved.

INCENTIVES AND MOTIVATION

It is hard to avoid the conclusion that something more fundamental than faulty organization is responsible for the lag in Soviet computer technology. If organizational untidiness were a major inhibiting influence on the development of computer technology, one would expect to find little progress in the United States, where a great many large and small companies and other institutions are frantically competing. Decentralization should not inhibit progress, so long as the decentralized organizations have strong incentive for seeking improvements. In the Soviet Union, it is in no one's personal or organizational interest to aggressively seek improvements in hardware, develop software that makes computers more accessible to more users, or furnish systems help.

Until 1965, the criterion by which enterprises in the Ministry of Radio Industry were judged was the gross value of output. The annual plan was stated in terms of this criterion, and bonuses were linked to the fulfillment of the plan as stated.

Computer technology is a new and very dynamic field, in which success comes as a reward for a mixture of technical competence in design, efficiency and quality control in manufacturing, aggressive financial planning, and a high degree of entrepreneurship in marketing and product innovation. The technology is developing so rapidly that only the most adaptive organizations are able to thrive or, indeed, to survive.

The Soviet system of "success indicators," both before and after the reform of 1965, has encouraged patterns of behavior that are inconsistent with the dynamic responsiveness that is required to stay abreast of the computer revolution. The system has encouraged the production of obsolete machines (e.g., Ural-1 and -2) long past the point when greatly superior technologies were available. The great pressure on Soviet managers to minimize the probability of being unable to meet the planned targets has helped to guarantee the modesty of those targets and impose strong deterrents to risk taking. Every new machine that is developed means that design and production "bugs" must be worked out. There is always some probability that the difficulties of innovation will jeopardize fulfillment of the plan. This seems to be the case particularly in the Soviet Union, where the manufacture of a new product means that new components must be ordered from suppliers who in turn must reorganize their operations.

The rigidities of the Soviet system increase the risks that inevitably attend the design and manufacture of a new computing system. The desire to avoid accepting additional risk has led the Ministry of Radio Industry to resist acceptance of the responsibility for software development and maintenance.

The computer industry in the United States is extremely volatile. Repeatedly, individuals or groups of people employed by established computer manufacturers have left their salaried positions and gone into business for themselves in new companies. Veterans of IBM and Sperry-Rand (UNIVAC) are working diligently in such organizations as Computer Sciences Organization, Control Data Corporation, Digital Equipment Corporation, Computer Machinery Corporation, and many others. These firms typically start with a handful of bright people and a few good ideas. They manage to obtain financing from one or another source and launch themselves into the competitive struggle. Some of them succeed brilliantly (e.g., Control Data Corporation); others fail miserably,

The U.S. computer scene is dominated by one giant whose management has been aggressive in research and development, finance, and marketing and has been relentless in its pursuit of profit. Several other large companies (RCA, Philco-Ford, General Electric, Westinghouse, and others) wait eagerly for Number One to slip. Many small new firms with bright ideas keep the major companies alert.

Nothing that has been said above should be taken as a denial of the important role played by the U.S. Federal Government in the development of computer technology. Many, if not most, of the major strides in the development of this technology have come about as a direct result of government research and development funding. The agencies primarily responsible for this have been the Department of Defense, the National Aeronautics and Space Administration, and the Atomic Energy Commission. ENIAC was a government-sponsored effort to develop better machines for trajectory calculations. Whirlwind was developed at the Lincoln Laboratories of MIT and provided much of the computer technology for the semiautomatic ground environment (SAGE) air defense system. Work on transistors and integrated circuitry was sponsored by government contracts in order to develop smaller and more robust computers for military and space systems. The COBOL language came about as a direct result of Department of Defense pressure. The highly sophisticated and powerful Control Data computers were created to meet AEC specifications.

The point to be made is that the American computer industry has been characterized by aggressive competition. There have been major rewards for the men and the companies that could figure out what the customer needed and then design, manufacture, and deliver that product and help him use it. This has made it possible to translate the fruits of government-sponsored research and development into commercially available technology.

The computer industry in the Soviet Union is a startling contrast to the competitive and responsive American industry. New ideas must run a gauntlet within the bureaucratic structure. A "customer is usually wrong" attitude characterizes the Ministry of Radio Industry and other suppliers. Computers are but one of many products and responsibilities of the Ministry. Few administrators in the Ministry have any direct experience or competence in the field of computer technology, and they lack a dedication to it. But young men with bright ideas, aggressiveness, and enthusiasm have no alternative but to work within the jurisdictional and administrative structure. The result is that innovation and entrepreneurship are frustrated.

LOW PRIORITY

The bureaucratic and incentive structure of the Soviet computer industry may discourage innovation and hinder progress. We know, however, from Soviet achievements in the military and space fields that, if a problem area is accorded sufficiently high priority by the Soviet leadership, progress will be made.

It seems incredible that computer technology should not occupy a prominent place in the Soviet list of priorities. The rhetoric of party and government pronouncements about the importance of automation and cybernetics would lead one to think that nothing had a higher priority.

When we look at the slow pace of development in the computer field and observe the same user complaints year after year, however, these statements of high priority lose their credibility. Doubts increase when we hear Soviet sources say that the BESM-6 will be produced at a rate of five per year and that the Minsk-22 rolls off the production lines at the rate of seven per month. It is difficult to believe that software development would be entrusted to small groups of workers in various institutes of the Academy of Science if the computer program had high priority.

The lack of input of high quality men and materials into the computer field must surely signify a fairly low priority. There would appear to be some lack of conviction on the part of the Soviet leadership that computers are really as important as their enthusiasts claim.

WEAK USER DEMAND

The demand of scientists and mathematicians for computing machinery adequate to their needs has been moderately met. Soviet computers, for the most part, have been designed for scientific computing and they have served that purpose reasonably well.

The demand from Soviet industrial enterprises and other economic organizations for computers has been rather weak. This has been noticeably true with respect to "business data" processors. It has been much less true for process control machines. The reason for this may be that automatic data processing equipment often cannot be justified under Soviet conditions on labor-saving grounds alone. Much of the clerical work of Soviet enterprises is done by workers who would have low productivity in any other occupation. Because the enterprises cannot easily discharge superfluous employees, they are unable to realize payroll savings by the introduction of computing machinery in their data processing applications. In process control, the computer is often used to provide a kind of on-line control that would be difficult or impossible for a human being to match.

Whatever validity there may be to the idea of weak demand for computers in the Soviet Union should be balanced with an awareness of Soviet eargerness to import foreign computer equipment. Sluggishness of demand would seem to be only one minor reason for the lag in the development of Soviet computer technology.

18. THE SOCIAL COSTS OF MODERNIZATION: ECOLOGICAL PROBLEMS IN THE USSR

David E. Powell

Like the United States, the USSR has serious problems of air, water, and land pollution. The main causes of environmental disruption in the USSR are the achieved level of industrialization, the strategy of economic development, the dominant performance indicators and the scheme of cost accounting, and the weakness of official and unofficial anti-pollution forces. Only recently has the Soviet regime begun to consider seriously the ecological aspects of economic development. This article examines the scope of the problem, analyzes the causes, and evaluates anti-pollution efforts in the USSR.

David E. Powell is Associate Professor of Government and Foreign Affairs at the University of Virginia. The selection is from *World Politics,* Vol. XXIII, No. 4 (July 1971), pp. 618–34, with the omission of footnote references to foreign-language sources. Copyright © 1971 by Princeton University Press. Reprinted by permission of Princeton University Press.

Let us not be too proud of our victories over nature. For every such victory nature takes revenge on us. True, each of these victories, the first time, has the consequences we calculate, but the second and third times, the consequences are altogether different and unforeseen and very often destroy the significance of the first ones.

—Friedrich Engels[1]

---

[1] *The Dialectics of Nature,* as cited in *Literaturnaya gazeta,* December 20, 1967. [Written by Engels in 1876. A slightly different translation appears in Friedrich Engels, *Dialectics of Nature,* trans. by Clemens Dutt (Moscow: Foreign Languages Publishing House, 1954), p. 241.—The Editors.]

VIRTUALLY ALL of the existing literature on modernization is concerned with the virtues of modernity. It focuses on the gains to be derived from modernization—industrialization, material progress, social welfare, political rationality, etc. But experience suggests that gains are usually achieved at some cost: the drive toward modernity seems invariably to produce new social and personal problems. In the USSR—perhaps the world's most developed underdeveloped country—the modernization process has been accompanied by massive social costs.

To be sure, the Soviet regime has been responsible for a number of significant achievements, and has fashioned a central authority capable of mobilizing the nation's resources toward social, political, economic, and scientific-technical change as effective as that of any country. But Soviet modernization has been achieved at a heavy cost. Traditional patterns of family life, religion, personal freedom, and community organization have been disrupted. The USSR is presently faced with a growing drinking problem, crime and juvenile delinquency, the beginnings of a drug problem, and alienation and emotional tension among substantial numbers of citizens. These difficulties have accompanied the Soviet Union's rapid social and economic change.

In an assessment of the Soviet experience, then, achievements must be weighed against failures, and gains must be balanced against perceptible costs. Perhaps this cost/benefit dualism can be seen most clearly in the realm of ecology: the ambitious Soviet effort to transform the environment, despite (or rather because of) its many successes, has at the same time resulted in much harm. Recent years have witnessed growing evidence of pollution and misuse of the land throughout the Communist world. States as different as Czechoslovakia, Poland, Rumania, and the USSR have shown signs of profound ecological damage. The Soviet Union seems to have "progressed" furthest in this direction: Soviet sources admit to the full range of symptoms, from littering, an excess of pesticides, and despoliation of the land to noise, air, and water pollution of sometimes immense magnitudes.

Soviet industrialization, no less than American industrialization, has given rise to vast damage to the environment. I will spell out below how the Soviets perceive this problem and what they are doing and intend to do about it. As we shall see, the USSR confronts many of the same problems as the United States does, and for many of the same reasons. A strong urge toward industrial production, a weak and divided anti-pollution lobby, and official ignorance of, or indifference toward, damage to the environment—all these facts are clearly visible both in the USSR and the United States. Industrial development has, by and large, taken priority over the care of nature; environmentalists are not heard until the damage has been done. Only now is the Soviet government beginning to heed the warnings uttered as long ago as the 1950s. And, though it is too late to save certain communities and bodies of water, it may not be too late to protect and preserve the rest.

The official response to the growing menace of pollution has been piecemeal and unsystematic. Local government agencies have experimented with a number of approaches, but, until recently, the central authorities have simply avoided the problem. In the past two years, however, the Party has begun to mobilize its resources for a broad-scale attack on pollution and polluters. The official policy of focusing attention on one area, which for many years had allowed the Party to remain indifferent to ecological damage, may now be working to the benefit of the environment. New principles of land legislation (1968), public health (1969), and water legislation (1970) suggest a concern and resolve that had long been absent. Whether these measures are enforced, whether these general principles are transformed into public policy, remains to be seen.

THE SCOPE OF THE PROBLEM

Air and water pollution in the USSR represent formidable problems. Soviet industry, geared for rapid economic growth, has, over the course of half a century, dumped untold millions of tons of sewage into the nation's waters and millions of tons of particles of dirt into the air. Until very recently, the authorities have paid little heed to the environmental costs incurred. Pollution of Soviet waters has now assumed crisis proportions, and air pollution, too, represents a considerable threat to the well-being of citizens. Although the problem of clean air is not nearly so manifest as the problem of clean water, it is much more than a minor nuisance, and there is every reason to expect the situation to deteriorate further. At present, concerned citizens and officials are devoting their primary attention to the nation's rivers, lakes, and streams. Nonetheless, aware that the problem of dirty air has assumed the proportions of a national disaster in other countries, and aware that the USSR is entering the automobile era, central and local authorities are devoting increasing attention to air pollution. They are determined to deal with the situation before it gets out of hand.

Pollution in some regions of the USSR has reached formidable levels. Millions of tons of acid, petroleum products, metal, fiber, and salts are discharged each year into Soviet rivers. Only a small part of the more than seventy million cubic meters of waste water that flow into them annually has been decontaminated.[2] As a result, hundreds of major rivers are polluted, and thousands of lesser rivers and streams have

---

[2] Perhaps one tenth of this effluent undergoes biochemical purification (thus removing 80–95 percent of the impurities). Another third of the waste water is subjected to less thorough purification, removing perhaps 40 percent of the impurities, and the remaining waste water empties into other bodies of water without undergoing any decontamination whatsoever.

suffered the same fate. Industrial enterprises, power plants, mines, agricultural fields all contribute to the problem. In addition, many forests have been "timbered out"; the resulting soil erosion damages the land and adds to the dirt flowing into bodies of water.

Pollution is noticeable even to the casual tourist. Visitors to Moscow and other large urban centers can see smog and haze in the air, as well as filth in local rivers. Only a decade ago these were not present. In some parts of the country, pollutants in the atmosphere have reached appalling concentrations. Scientific studies indicate that in many major industrial cities the concentration of harmful substances in the air greatly exceeds the norm set for people's health. The city of Mayevka, for example, the site of a steel mill, has been described as "literally covered with soot." In Siberia, "a dense cloud of smoke and dust constantly hangs over" the city of Irkutsk. And, as the Soviet automobile and truck population increases, the problem is getting worse. In 1966, a *Pravda* editorial observed that "the poisonous haze of exhaust gases over cities is becoming thicker and thicker," and a year later the same newspaper charged that exhaust gases from automobiles "thoroughly pollute the atmosphere of our cities." As the date approaches when Togliatti's Fiat plant begins adding dramatically to the number of cars in the Soviet Union, the problem can only get worse. And, as Soviet industry continues its rapid rate of economic growth, industrial enterprises add more and more dirt to the air. Air pollution thus threatens to become as significant a problem as water pollution.

Pollution in the USSR, like pollution elsewhere, involves two major costs: (1) to the health of citizens, and (2) to the national economy. Human physiology knows no ideological boundaries; excessive concentrations of certain gases and solids suspended in the air or dissolved in water can do serious damage to people's well-being anywhere. Soviet scientists know this as well as their counterparts in the West do. But although the Soviet authorities are familiar with the implications of pollution for public health, they seem far more concerned with its economic consequences. Following Soviet practice, we will focus our attention on these.

Pollution caused by an individual enterprise is likely to raise the costs of production of other factories located downwind or downstream from the guilty enterprise. As the air becomes filled with soot, for example, the use of electric power for artificial lighting increases. Thus, in the city of Leningrad, a sharp rise in power consumption has been attributed chiefly to dirty air. Moreover, ash carried through the air accelerates wear and tear on the friction parts of machinery with which it comes into contact. Sulphuric and sulphurous anhydrides, coming into contact with moisture in the air, help to corrode metal.

Though pollution inflicts harm on virtually all sectors of the economy, its economic costs are seen most vividly in the fishing industry. Spokesmen for the fishing industry, scientists, and environmentalists have published numerous articles describing the damage done to spawning grounds or to adult fish by effluents from chemical enterprises, oil refineries, pulp and paper mills, sugar refineries, and other polluters. Sulfates, chlorides, and suspended particles oxidize, thus using up oxygen from river water without which fish cannot live. Hundreds of rivers and other bodies of water that used to contain large fish have completely lost their importance for the fishing industry. In the USSR as a whole, the fishing industry is said to lose between 120 to 300 million rubles a year because of river pollution.

Although industrial wastes exact their toll on fish gradually, there have also been instances of mass destruction of fish due to the sudden emission of large quantities of effluent. In July, 1965, one such incident occurrred near Volgograd; millions of fish were poisoned by the discharge of unpurified waste water by the Kirov Chemical Plant in Volgograd. Losses were estimated at ten to twenty million rubles. The year before, the Iset River caught fire near Sverdlovsk. Many of the city's enterprises had been dumping their sewage, filled with fats and oil by-products, into the river. The concentration of combustible materials in the river grew so dense that a lighted cigarette thrown into the water one day was enough to ignite it. Countless numbers of fish perished. "Once a transparent stream abounding in fish," a Soviet citizen lamented, "the Iset lies dead for hundreds of kilometers below Sverdlovsk, turning into a collection of sewage."

Pollution of fishing waters has reached such vast proportions that a procedure was adopted in 1969 whereby the Chief Administration for Fish Breeding and Protection of Fish must agree to sites where enterprises are to be constructed near commercial fishing waters. Proof that there will be adequate devices for decontamination must be submitted to the fish-protection agencies for their approval before the site-selection process can be completed.

CAUSES OF POLLUTION

Numerous factors are involved in any explanation of why pollution has reached such an alarming level. The explanation involves political, economic, and scientific components. As we shall see, the most important factor contributing to pollution is the ignorance, indifference, or outright hostility that Soviet officials traditionally have manifested toward efforts to curb pollution.

Some pollution is an inevitable correlative of industrial civilization. Production involves the creation of by-products and waste; even the best-intentioned technological society has yet to devise means capable of preventing waste entirely. As industry develops, it produces a greater volume and variety of substances, and methods for extracting these new substances from waste water or the atmosphere are either unknown or difficult to carry out. Though some substances can be extracted from waste, others invariably remain. For the foreseeable future, then, some part of industrial or agricultural waste will inevitably be carried into the sea or the atmosphere.

Although some pollution is inescapable, certain aspects of the problem in the USSR are attributable to the operation of the Soviet system. We can identify four causal factors.

1. Technological Backwardness. Anti-pollution technology is rather backward in the USSR. Methods for utilizing waste products and purifying effluents have not been studied very carefully, in part because few people have been encouraged to study these processes. Higher educational institutions have not expressed interest in stimulating such study, and those who are already in the field are treated badly and have little incentive to combat pollution. The specialized institutes that train students for work in the petroleum industry, for example, do not prepare specialists for the water-supply and water-disposal shops of oil refineries or chemical enterprises. There simply is no opportunity available for those who would specialize in water purification. Indeed, even basic courses in conservation or ecology are rarely offered, and when they are, they are available only to certain students. As long ago as 1947, Moscow University introduced a course in conservation, and similar courses were soon set up at other institutions of higher learning. However, none of the courses is open to all students—not even to all students in technical fields. The course at Moscow University is offered only to zoologists and biogeographers; Rostov University's course is open only to botanists; and only geographers may register for the course at Perm University.

The level of scientific work done in universities, specialized institutes, and technical schools is also rather low. Little time is spent devising instruments and techniques for purifying wastes. According to a 1965 decree of the RSFSR Supreme Soviet, "The designs of installations for purifying industrial wastes are often based on methods that have not been tested even in laboratory conditions, let alone in production conditions; this lowers the effectiveness of the funds expended. Research and higher educational institutions are doing an extremely poor job of working out and introducing progressive methods of purifying sewage water and the wastes released into the atmosphere and of rationally using and reproducing natural resources." Most of the installations that are designed and put to use are inefficient; moreover, they are not given proper care and often break down. Inferior designs, poor workmanship, delays in building, and excessively low capacities all contribute to the problem. Pollution equipment is not large enough to handle the job in most enterprises, and much of the equipment is poorly managed. Repairs are carried out infrequently, and by ill-trained technicians.

The same problem inhibits efforts to curb air pollution. Existing gas-purification machinery often fails to function, and the process of replacing equipment with new, improved designs is slow. Many devices are too small for the task assigned to them; others suffer from inadequate maintenance and repair. Unproved systems of gas removal and pollution control are employed, and as a result they frequently break down or operate inefficiently. Little attention is paid to the design and construction of new installations, and existing ones deteriorate rapidly.

2. The Low Status of Anti-Pollution Work. If few students are provided with an intellectual appreciation of conservation when they are in school, fewer still develop an incentive to deal with such matters once they are at work. Water-disposal shops and personnel are considered auxiliary. Salary levels are lower than in other sections of plants, the opportunities to earn bonuses are fewer, and, even in the matter of retirement pensions, employees of water-disposal or purification shops are subjected to discrimination. As a result, few choose a career in anti-pollution work, and the rate of turnover in this sphere of industry is very high. For example, large numbers of anti-pollution specialists at the Baikalsk Pulp Plant near Lake Baikal give up their jobs every year and move to Bratsk, where they receive higher wages at the lumber industry complex.[3] In view of the inadequate training available and the low level of financial incentives, it is understandable that anti-pollution technology has stagnated and that not many have chosen this line of work. The system provides few incentives to potential environmentalists.

3. Appropriations and Incentives. A third major factor influencing pollution hinges on the question of money. Two components are involved here: (a) the authorization for and actual levels of expenditure, and (b) the incentive system, which stimulates a drive toward production rather than toward conservation of the environment. We will deal with each of these in turn.

State agencies invariably allocate insufficient funds to industrial enterprises for anti-pollution purposes. In addition, plant managers often choose not to spend all the funds allocated to them, diverting resources to production shops instead. Economic units strive to achieve high production indices per ruble of capital invested; they often succeed by delaying construction work on purification installations. Thus, during the period 1960–64, more than 25 percent of the funds allocated for the construction of purification installations in all industries was not put to use. The directors of individual plants have their own priorities, and they prefer not to invest "their" funds in ways they regard as nonproductive.

Production and profit, not social purposes or care of the environment, motivate both the central authorities and the managers of industrial

---

[3] During the summer of 1967, for example, more than 100 persons (out of a total of 230–240) left their jobs at the Baikalsk purification installation.

plants. They are rewarded for economic output, not for maintaining, purifying, or enhancing the beauty of the environment. "Produce the plant product—that is the main thing," managers are said to reason. "The purification installations can wait." Plants are permitted to begin operation before work is completed on their purification facilities—sometimes even before it is begun. The sluggishness with which commissions of experts (who must pass on purification installations) work is striking in comparison with the drive to begin production operations. According to B. Voltovskii, Chairman of the Ukrainian Council of Ministers' State Committee on Conservation: "It has become a common bad practice to plan the construction of decontamination installations as a second or even a third stage, after the main shops have already worked full blast for years." Moreover, he goes on, "In the construction of new industrial units, serious attention has been directed to only one aspect, the purely production aspect. Almost no calculation was made, for example, of the losses we would suffer if the industry discharged every year so much poisonous wastes into the air, or dumped so much water polluted with harmful substances, the effect it will have on the health and longevity of the people, how much it will decrease the available amounts of drinking water, irrigation water, etc."

There appears to be widespread indifference—even outright hostility—to the arguments of conservationists. An article in *Izvestia* several years ago told of the director of an enterprise who began "to fuss about to have himself relieved of all these unnecessary headaches, the installation of all kinds of filters and sediment traps." Officials, mindful of their production assignments, devote little attention to anti-pollution measures because of their involvement in production; they consider the protection of nature minor in comparison with their "more urgent" production tasks. One critic of this order of priorities has complained: "If . . . an enterprise does not fulfill its production plan, its executives have to make a strict accounting to the party organization, the trust and the ministry. But when this same enterprise pollutes the air and releases dirty water into a river, poisoning all the life in it, it is hardly likely that anyone will demand an accounting from the guilty parties." Other commentators are equally indignant. One has recalled the example of an official who, in a discussion of Russia's polluted rivers, declared that "first we have to build communism and only afterward raise fish." But protests against such attitudes have been to little avail. Official public policy is that increased outputs of goods compensates for damage to the environment. "Victors are not judged," as the saying goes. When the time comes to receive a bonus, no one reminds the managers of a plant about the pollution they have caused.[4]

---

[4] A 1965 conference of conservationists and fishing industry representatives adopted a resolution requesting the Ministry of the Fishing Industry "to prohibit the awarding of bonuses to officials of enterprises that have failed to take steps to eliminate and prevent the pollution of fishing waters."

4. *Organizational Weakness of Anti-Pollution Forces.* No single individual or organization has been assigned overall responsibility for dealing with pollution and polluters. The two agencies with the greatest influence here, the USSR Ministry of Public Health's Sanitary Protection Service and the USSR Council of Ministers' Chief Administration for the Hydrometeorological Service, have neither the power nor the will to combat pollution effectively. Their responsibility is "the protection of the natural environment against pollution by sewage, harmful discharges into the atmosphere, and toxic chemicals," but they share this responsibility with a dozen other state, Party, and public bodies. The problem is not simply one of variety; there are overlapping jurisdictions and rivalries, with no single agency competent to coordinate the efforts of all. "With such a large number of 'masters,'" two scientists have noted, "it is rather difficult to speak of the integrated utilization of water resources. Various kinds of lack of coordination are frequently encountered. . . ."

A third agency, the All-Union Gas Purification and Dust Removal Association, attached to the Ministry of the Petroleum-Refining and Petrochemical Industry, is the major source of research and design work in the field of air pollution. But its powers are limited. The Association has always been attached to a single ministry, and thus it lacks a broad perspective. Many industries cause air pollution, but the Association is concerned only with "its own" problems; it refuses to assist in solving pollution problems in other branches of the economy. The Association has been described as "a second-class appendage of a branch ministry," which cannot and will not adopt a national perspective. Its resources are modest, and its point of view is restricted. Indeed, the Association has only one plant, which cannot possibly fulfill industry's needs for gas-purification equipment.

The fact that there is no single center to coordinate research and development efforts in the area of air pollution involves considerable costs. Construction and testing of experimental installations proceed at a lethargic pace, and previously approved methods for trapping harmful fumes and dust are introduced even more slowly. As a result, "primitivism, amateurishness, and the crudest design errors" occur, and the pace of scientific progress is extremely slow. Moreover, because of the confusing and uncoordinated bureaucratic picture, managers of individual plants tend to see matters from a limited point of view, and individual plants and ministries continue to pour pollutants into Soviet rivers and lakes.

WHAT IS TO BE DONE?

Given the nature and magnitude of the problem, what remedies are available to those who wish to combat pollution? Some see the problem as purely technical; their response is to call for more and better purification installations, the design of electric vehicles, etc. Others' see it as an expression of the wrong attitudes; they suggest a propaganda campaign to persuade citizens of the merits of conservation and the evils of pollution. One of the traditional approaches has involved the establishment of "health-protection belts" between factories and residential areas, which protect urban residents from the harmful effects of industrial wastes. The major thrust of the official response to pollution, however, involves two elements: (1) the use of legal sanctions, and (2) the use of financial incentives. Both approaches seek to persuade polluters and potential polluters that marring the environment is bad business.

The most widespread response has been to reprimand and/or to fine polluters. In addition to serving to punish the guilty, this approach is designed to deter others from further pollution. Until very recently, however, the maximum fine was set so low that the system failed to exert any influence whatsoever on the industrial community. Errant managers usually escaped with a reprimand and/or a nominal fine. With such lax controls, industrial executives simply ignore the instructions of sanitation inspectors. Instead, they follow the lead of local Party and Soviet officials, who are more concerned about industrial output than they are about the purity of the air and water. In the words of an *Izvestia* editorial, "The harm wrought by all this [polluting of rivers] is enormous, but the local soviets and the various inspection teams vested with considerable powers in the struggle against the destroyers of nature display timidity and excessive delicacy 'in the showdowns.' Indulgence and protection from consequences cover up the affliction." The system of fines has not acted as a brake on pollution. Many enterprises pay millions of rubles in pollution fines but continue to pour filth into the nation's waters and air. In fact, the system of fines is said to have been turned into an insidious device. The funds are turned over to the local soviets, which use the money to pave streets, build clubhouses, and lay water mains. "This becomes a peculiar kind of redistribution of state funds," it turns out. "The local soviets begin to regard pollution indulgently, if not favorably." To provide local government authorities with a vested interest in pollution is a very inadequate way of protecting the environment.

In the past few years—interestingly enough, since the fall of Nikita Khrushchev—the Soviets have resorted to a much stronger weapon, i.e., criminal law. After the mass destruction of fish near Volgograd in July 1965 was traced to poisoning by unpurified waste water discharged by the Kirov Chemical Plant in Volgograd, the legal authorities moved against the plant's director, chief engineer, assistant chief engineer, shop chiefs, and chief of the plant's purification installations. All were charged with "an attitude of criminal negligence toward the performance of their duties, leading to the pollution of the river with waste water." Similar episodes elsewhere have brought criminal punishment, and it appears that resort to criminal sanctions will be one of the principal weapons in the Brezhnev-Kosygin struggle against pollution.

The new Principles of Public Health and Draft Principles of Water Legislation prohibit the putting into operation of industrial facilities unless they are provided with anti-pollution devices. Moreover, most of the union republics have adopted conservation laws. Typically, they prohibit "any action leading to the pollution of water resources or the air," or industrial activity that "adversely affects the health and sanitary conditions of the population's everyday life." Penalties include the closing down of enterprises whose pollution endangers people's health, and deprivation of freedom for up to three years for the guilty officials. The government's position was further strengthened in the spring of 1970, when the new Article 223 was added to the RSFSR Criminal Code. According to this law, pollution of bodies of water or the air that is harmful to human beings is punishable by corrective labor for up to one year or by a fine of up to 300 rubles. Pollution that causes "substantial harm" to the health of human beings or agricultural production, or that results in the mass destruction of fish, is punishable by deprivation of freedom for a period of up to five years. Though it is too early to say what effect these new laws will have, experience with conservation legislation in general suggests cause for considerable skepticism. Managers may continue to ignore the law's clear mandate unless prosecution officials take the offensive. Experience indicates that fines are likely to be fairly light, and the possibility of criminal punishment or the closing down of an enterprise is remote.

Because of this, some Soviet commentators have begun to argue that only by appealing to the economic self-interest of plant managers can the battle be won. This approach has been pursued along two lines: (1) demanding a charge for the use of water, and (2) persuading managers to extract valuable by-products from wastes emitted by their plants.

In Soviet industry, water is a free good: enterprises use it free of charge. No one has a material interest in economizing on its use, and, as a consequence, industrial plants make no effort to reduce the volume of water they pollute. If, however, they were charged for polluting it, they would have an incentive to purify and re-use it. At present, there is no reason—except the moral one, which is not enough—to be concerned about purification. Although the technical means for saving water exist, the incentive system does not stimulate water conservation. It has been suggested, therefore, that economic responsibility for dirtying water be borne by the guilty enterprise. In Czechoslovakia, a plant must deduct charges from its own budget for each cubic meter of water it contaminates. Managers quickly learn that when the overall sum of these deductions is large enough, it will be more profitable to construct purification installations than to pay these sums. The system involves a kind of tax or fine—but one that, at least in Czechoslovakia, promotes environmentalism. Although the suggestion promises much, it has yet to win the endorsement of top Soviet officials.

The second approach has been tested, though not on a very broad scale. The logic is simple. Industrial sewage contains valuable substances whose discharge into water sources represents a considerable economic loss. Petroleum refineries typically lose up to 3 percent of their total output in this way; artificial fiber plants lose up to 4 percent of certain products, and cellulose-paper combines lose up to 8 percent of wood fiber. Great quantities of acids, alkalis, dyes, and oils are lost, even though these substances can be easily separated from the waste waters. Phenols, too, which even in miniscule concentrations give water a medicinal taste, can easily be extracted from sewage. Furfuraldehyde and methyl alcohol (which serve as the raw material for the production of plastic) can also be obtained from sewage water, and waste liquid from soda plants can be converted into fertilizer. Efforts to save some of these valuable substances have proven successful. In Irkutsk, for example, organic substances are extracted from the sewage of a number of plants and are used to obtain fodder yeast. A cable plant in Perm, which for a long time dumped etching solutions into the Kama River, built a simple recovery installation and now produces copper foil from the former wastes. Oil, too, can be saved. Special oil traps for multistaged sewage purification have decreased the oil content in sewage waters at certain plants by up to 80 percent and organic pollution by up to 95 percent.

But although there are successes, there still is much room for improvement. Despite the fact that the USSR organized a broad campaign during the mid-sixties to save ferrous metals, tremendous amounts of these substances were simply washed away with waste water. Cadmium, for example, was simply dumped into the water, although by adding a small amount of alkali to the sewage waters, the cadmium could be made to settle and could then be recovered. Soviet enterprises sustain an annual loss of dozens of tons of lead, copper, nickel, chromium, cobalt, zinc, and other metals in sewage waters, although modern technology is capable of extracting these metals from waste water with the help of ion-exchange resins. This loss of metals has led at least one water-conservation authority to call for the elimination of the so-called "discard norms," maximum possible amounts of matter in waste water, for substances that can be completely extracted from sewage. The idea is still new, and the outlook for adopting such a measure is far from bright.

Central and local authorities have recently adopted a more vigorous stance with respect to two of the most significant sources of pollution, the lumber industry and the automobile. Activitiy here would seem to indicate that Brezhnev and Kosygin are serious about preserving or restoring the natural environment.

The lumber industry's practice of sending "log floats" downstream to pulp mills for processing results in considerable river pollution. Whole logs, bark, sawdust, shavings, and other wood scrap sink to the bottoms of rivers. An *Izvestia* correspondent, investigating the result of log-floating on the Volga, described the picture as "an ugly one." "Sunken trunks stuck out of the water like artillery for many kilometers along the shore. You see shapeless giant heaps of logs. Waves wash off logs, and chips ·. . . float with the current. . . ." The bottoms of many rivers "are lined with a thick layer of logs." Perhaps five to ten percent of floated timber goes to the bottom. These "drowned logs," as they are called, consume the oxygen dissolved in the water and form an anaerobic, or dead, zone. Deposits of wood and rotten bark remain on the river bottoms, and food sources for fish are damaged or ruined. As the wood scraps dissolve in the water, they absorb the oxygen the fish need, and give off acids, phenol, and other poisonous substances. As a result, some rivers have lost their value as spawning grounds and are no longer useful to the fishing industry.

The authorities have begun to remedy this situation. In some areas, government agencies have prohibited the loose floating of logs down rivers used for fishing. The lumber industry in these areas now must ask permission every time it wishes to float logs. The Draft Principles of Water Legislation have added further controls, banning the loose floating of timber on navigable waterways and certain other bodies of water.

To minimize the harm done by motor vehicles, the Soviets have adopted a number of tactics, the most important of which is to limit the number of privately owned vehicles. Other steps have been taken as well. Moscow claims to be the only capital in the world in which the use of ethylated gasoline is banned. (Ethylated gasoline pollutes the air with lead compounds, which are among the most highly dangerous products of exhaust.) Moreover, Soviet scientists have begun to develop and produce neutralizers that render exhaust virtually harmless. An automobile engine that emits virtually no pollutive exhaust gases (special chambers at the head of each cylinder insure the complete combustion of the gasoline) has passed state tests and is currently being tested on vehicles in Central Asia.

More imaginative steps have been taken in several cities in the Ukraine and elsewhere. Municipal authorities in Kharkov, for example, have switched to electrically powered vehicles for public transportation. The city's central districts are served by trolley-busses, and the outlying districts are served by streetcars. Kiev, Riga, and a number of smaller cities are planting greenery, which absorbs carbon dioxide while giving out oxygen. By replacing noxious fumes with oxygen, they help to combat air pollution. This is a promising approach to the problem that probably will be emulated by other Soviet cities.

CONCLUSION

Where man lives and works, it would seem, filth appears. Man everywhere threatens to upset natural ecological balances. No state, regardless of its social, political, or economic system, has been able to escape the consequences of man's callous treatment of the environment. We might have expected the Soviet Union to be preeminently suited to preserve and enhance nature's gifts. It is less advanced than the West and thus can profit from our mistakes. The Soviet political elite claims to be guided by the lofty ideals of socialist humanism. The Communist Party, the "leading core" of all organizations, is capable of enforcing its will on any problem facing the country. The State owns the land and the means of production. The regime is committed to a rational course of modernization. In view of these facts, we might have expected tht USSR to be safe from the depredations of "robber-baron" industrialists and other despoilers of nature. We might also have expected the Party to create an environment of genuine beauty, which would serve man's aesthetic, social, and economic needs.

However, as the Soviet experience shows, centralized decision-making and the capacity to mobilize the energies of the entire nation have not always led to socially desirable ends. Socialist industrialists, no less than their capitalist counterparts, have shown themselves capable of despoliation on a massive scale. Indeed, centrally determined priorities, allocations, rewards, and punishments have long meant an excessive fixation on production, at the expense of all else. Recent efforts to introduce reforms in the economic system illustrate only one dimension of the problem of overcentralization. Production for production's sake has led not only to economic distortions, but to social and ecological blunders as well.

In the political realm, the absence of autonomous groups in the community—the very essence of pluralist systems—has meant that over the years no one "represented" the environmentalists. The political elite, virtually unanimous in its desire to industrialize rapidly, and insulated from the masses, effectively denied a hearing to those more concerned with the beauty of nature. This monopoly of public opinion prevented others—with a different conception of the public good—from presenting their views. The lack of access to decision-makers experienced by conservationists, when added to the politicians' focus on rapid industrialization, meant that there was no one to lobby for nature. Only when the social and economic costs of pollution and misuse of land had assumed menacing proportions did the Party respond.

At present, the Soviet leadership, like its counterparts in the West, is faced with a pollution problem of considerable proportions. Decades of indifference to the environment have exacted their toll, and the authorities must now deal with matters that their predecessors simply ignored. They have given little indication of a desire to meet the problem head on; until recently, they resorted to makeshift measures that were uncoordinated, superficial, and quite inadequate. Recent legislation in the fields of land use, water use, and public health suggest more concern and better organization and may indicate the beginning of a broadly based, comprehensive policy of pollution control.

To cope with the problem, however, will require the expenditure of massive sums of money. More important, it will require a fundamental re-ordering of priorities, from the almost pathological fixation on production to a more balanced attitude, showing as much concern for ecology as for production indices. Communism in the USSR and elsewhere has been basically oriented toward *transforming*, not preserving, nature. Now this transformation must proceed in a more balanced manner. As a Soviet conservation official has argued: "Man transforms nature. This relationship to nature should always be one of mutual benefit. That is the main thing. In other words, in using nature, protect it; in protecting nature, use it—sensibly." It may well be that the policy-makers have now turned their full attention to ecology, interpreting their modernizing mission somewhat more broadly. If this is so, their monopoly of power should enable them to mobilize the nation's resources effectively and deal with the problem. If Soviet socialism is to manifest the profound humanism its leaders claim for it, steps will have to be taken very soon, for the social costs of modernization thus far have been substantial. Whether or not the regime takes the necessary steps remains to be seen.

IV
SOVIET FOREIGN
ECONOMIC RELATIONS

Although Soviet foreign economic policy has been shifting away from its former emphasis on self-sufficiency for some time, that trend has speeded up in recent years for a variety of reasons. Domestic economic problems can be eased by trade and imports of capital; for example, large imports of grain from the United States after the crop failure of 1972, and Italian participation in the construction of a new major automobile plant. But political objectives are also involved, as shown in efforts to tie the East European countries more closely to the USSR, to improve Soviet relations with the West, and to increase Soviet influence among the less developed countries.

Part IV is devoted to these important issues. The four selections deal with economic integration of the East European countries with the USSR, trade and investment relations between the USSR and the United States, Soviet interest in obtaining Western technology, and Soviet foreign aid.

19. COMECON INTEGRATION

Z. M. Fallenbuchl

The Soviet-East European trade bloc known as Comecon originated in 1949 as a response to the economic recovery of Western
Europe under the United States–sponsored Marshall Plan. The
group's formal name is the Council for Mutual Economic Assistance
(CMEA). Membership includes the USSR, Bulgaria, Czechoslovakia,
the German Democratic Republic (East Germany), Hungary, Poland,
Romania, Mongolia (since 1962), and Cuba (since 1972).

The bulk of Soviet trade is with its Comecon neighbors, and
a central feature of Soviet foreign economic policy has been
to link the East European economies with its own through trade
flows. Within this general framework, Comecon has passed through
several stages. Initially, it stressed trade agreements between the
USSR and the East European countries which were highly favorable
to the former. After the death of Stalin in 1953, the East European
countries were able to adopt a more independent policy, and most
of them moved toward greater economic self-sufficiency through industrialization. But by the late 1960s, the autarkic approach was increasingly seen to be uneconomic, and steps have recently been
taken to develop greater specialization and trade among the Comecon countries. At the same time, however, they have been turning
more to the West for the technology and products needed to modernize and expand their economies.

The recent changes and conflicting forces in Comecon are analyzed in the following article by Z. M. Fallenbuchl, Professor of Economics at the University of Windsor, in Canada. It is reprinted from
Problems of Communism, Vol. XXII, No. 2 (March–April 1973), pp.
25–39. Footnotes referring to foreign-language sources, and some
tables, have been omitted.

NEARLY TWO YEARS have passed since the Council for Mutual Economic
Assistance (Comecon or CMEA) adopted a "Comprehensive Program for
the Extension and Improvement of Collaboration and the Development
of Socialist Economic Integration of the CMEA Countries." It is perhaps
appropriate at this juncture to examine the economic forces at work

in Eastern Europe which led to the adoption of this program in Bucharest in July 1971, to describe its salient features and their prospects for resolving exisiting problems in the East European economies, and to assess the likely trend of future development within Comecon.

The Comprehensive Program has been grandiosely depicted in Eastern Europe as an important step toward Lenin's vision of "a single world economy which as a whole is regulated by the proletariat of all nations in accordance with one overall plan." In somewhat more restrained terms, it is viewed as the beginning of a new stage in the development of Comecon, a period lasting 15–20 years in which there will be "a gradual switch from relatively simple forms of cooperation to socialist economic integration" of the Comecon member states. It is also represented as "a logical consequence of the past economic development of the member countries and the achievement by them of a high level of economic activity, as well as the result of a series of measures which have been taken over a period of time in order to increase the effectiveness of cooperation." While one may question whether this process has been as logical or "scientific" as these statements seem to imply, the Program is clearly an outgrowth of, as well as response to, the post-war patterns of economic development in the socialist countries of Eastern Europe and of economic relations among themselves and with other parts of the world. It is to that history that we now turn.

POSTWAR ECONOMIC DEVELOPMENT

The Era of "Extensive" Development

For a brief period after World War II, the countries of Eastern Europe pursued diverse economic courses. But once the USSR had firmly established its dominance over the region (signified in the economic realm by the imposition of the Soviet system of planning and management and the Soviet development strategy on each of the East European states, with only minor variations), these countries adopted a more or less uniform "Communist pattern of industrialization."[1] This pattern was characterized by two related principal features: (1) reliance on what is known in Communist economic parlance as an "extensive pattern of development," and (2) strong autarkic elements in the economies of the individual states.

Under the "extensive" strategy, high rates of growth in national income were indeed attained in these economies during the 1950s by mobilizing huge amounts of manpower and investment and allocating them

---

[1] Z. M. Fallenbuchl, "The Communist Pattern of Industrialization," *Soviet Studies,* Vol. XXI, No. 4 (April 1970), pp. 458–84.

according to a system of rigid priorities to branches of industry producing capital equipment—a process for which the centralized Soviet-type administrative system was well geared.[2] At the outset, growth was generated by channeling excess rural manpower into nonagricultural sectors, particularly heavy industry, and by investing heavily in the construction or enlargement of industrial plants. What increases there were in labor productivity resulted primarily from increases in the ratio of capital to labor. When sources of new manpower began to grow scarce, even larger volumes of investment were needed to maintain high rates of growth. Examining the time span from 1951 through 1970, one notes that the officially reported rates of growth of national income (as defined in the East European states) were lower than the rates of growth of investment for all Comecon countries in each five-year period, with the exception of Hungary in 1951-55 and the USSR in 1966-70.

The pattern of "extensive" development resulted in "growth for its own sake" or "barren growth," as a well-known Polish economist described it. Even when working relatively smoothly to effect rapid growth of national income and of industrial production, the "extensive" strategy was unable to satisfy the aspirations of the respective populations. It required a high proportion of producer goods in the total output and hence a restricted production of consumer goods. Because the strategy relied on large-scale transfers of unskilled labor from agricultural to other occupations, growth in productivity, and thus of real wages, could not be high. Faced with a declining efficiency of capital and unable to borrow abroad, the East European economies were forced to increase the share of accumulation (i.e., savings) in national income in order to sustain burgeoning investment programs. It is, however, impossible to increase the share of accumulation beyond a certain point without reducing work incentives and creating politically dangerous situations.[3] In some drastic cases this policy resulted in riots, as happened twice in postwar Poland.

The second striking feature of the Communist pattern of industrialization was the tendency toward autarky. The East European countries pursued what has come to be called a strategy of "import substitution," i.e., the effort to develop domestic capacity to produce virtually everything which a given country previously imported. This quest for self-sufficiency even encompassed the "domestic raw materials base," which was to be expanded in every Comecon country whatever the cost. International trade performed only a supplementary role, serving to finance imports of investment goods and raw materials only where they were

---

[2] Z. M. Fallenbuchl, "Some Structural Aspects of the Soviet-Type Investment Policy," ibid., Vol. XVI, No. 4 (April 1965), pp. 432–47.

[3] See Z. M. Fallenbuchl, "Investment Policy for Economic Development: Some Lessons of the Communist Experience," *Canadian Journal of Economics and Political Science,* Vol. XXIX, No. 1 (February 1963), pp. 26–39.

not available domestically at any price. Exports—mainly of temporary surpluses achieved at the expense of domestic consumption—were generated merely to finance such unavoidable imports.

Such autarkic policies created very similar industrial structures in all the Comecon countries, and there was consequently little basis for trade among them. They all competed for the same raw material supplies and external export markets. Moreover, the industries created at such enormous sacrifice on the part of the population proved to be highly inefficient, and their output enjoyed little demand on world markets.

Faced with these intractable realities, Marxist economists gradually "rediscovered" the principle of comparative advantage. But even when Comecon attempted to create a more rational international division of labor in the late 1950s and early 1960s, the measures taken had a strong autarkic flavor—the emphasis was on *intra*branch rather than *inter*branch specialization, because each member country still wished to develop its own comprehensive industrial structure comprising all branches of production.[4]

The disadvantages of the socialist pattern of industrialization and its autarkic tendencies manifested themselves in the late 1950s and early 1960s in a slowing of the rate of economic growth throughout the East European bloc. This occurred in spite of the fact that the share of accumulation in national income increased during the 1950s in every country except the USSR (which nevertheless continued to show the highest proportion of accumulation relative to national income). The problem was that investment proved to be of diminishing productivity (see Table 1). Furthermore, the rate of growth of labor productivity likewise proved lower in 1961–65 than in 1951–55 for every country except Hungary.

Pressures for Change

By the middle of the 1960s, it was clear that important steps would have to be taken not only to prevent further declines in the rates of growth of national income, industrial production and labor productivity, but also to reverse the accelerating demands which growth in national income were placing on capital investment and hence on accumulation or savings. Two essential measures were needed: (1) a shift from the "extensive" to an "intensive" pattern of growth, and (2) a considerable increase in the role of international trade in the development process. Yet these two changes in turn required modification both of the traditional Communist system of economic administration and planning and of the existing industrial structure. The nature of the struc-

---

[4] See Z. M. Fallenbuchl, "International Economic Relations in the Communist Policy of Economic Development," in *East-West Trade*, ed. Philip E. Uren (Toronto: Canadian Institute of International Affairs, 1966), pp. 67–86.

TABLE 1
Ratio of Increase in National Income to Gross "Productive Investment"
in Previous Year, Selected Periods, 1950–55 to 1966–69*

	1950-55	1956-60	1961-65	1966-69
Bulgaria	0.62	0.61	0.29	0.24
Czechoslovakia	0.54	0.44	0.10	0.31
East Germany†	0.78	0.37	0.17	0.24
Hungary	0.31	0.45	0.22	0.22
Poland	0.48	0.38	0.29	0.24
USSR	0.83	0.62	0.41	0.31

*Figures for national income and gross "productive investment" are in constant prices.
†Total investment.

tural change required in the shift to "intensive" growth has been described by Polish economist M. Gluzek as follows:

> A shift to the intensive phase of development requires a far-reaching modernization of productive capacity, including the necessity to effect considerable structural changes within the national economy. The changes consist of starting new lines of production, the expansion of the most effective production and restriction or complete elimination of inefficient lines of production which are based on obsolete technology or operate on an insufficient scale.

Yet the countries of Eastern Europe faced a serious dilemma in attempting simultaneously to reform their economic system and to restructure the patterns of output of their industry. As Polish economist J. Kleer pointed out, these two changes make incompatible demands on the economies involved. On the one hand, the combined retooling of existing productive facilities and development of new leading sectors in order to increase the productivity of the economy and its competitiveness in foreign trade necessarily place heavy demands on investment. On the other hand, economic reforms—involving some decentralization of management, expanding the role of market forces in the allocation of resources, and relying increasingly on material incentives—require a certain "slack" in the economy. Reserves of foreign exchange, consumer goods, raw materials, and human resources needed for successful reform are incompatible with an investment drive, with its high degree of mobilization of resources and the attendant shortages and bottlenecks. Consequently, although there was some measure of economic reform in each of the Comecon countries in the second half of the 1960s, the degree of reform has tended to vary inversely to the scope of action to modify the structure of industrial production.

With the exception of Hungary and (for a brief period) Czechoslovakia, the East European states eschewed major reforms in favor of a rapid restructuring of industrial production. In the absence of any significant increase in the role of market forces, this reconstruction was introduced "from above," i.e., the central planners singled out certain branches of industry and certain products as "progressive" and likely to modernize the economy and find good export markets, and assigned them high priority in the allocation of resources. Thus, in the German Democratic Republic, the New Economic System was associated with "structural planning" aimed at developing "the most modern industries," which, interestingly, remained highly centralized despite decentralization occurring in the rest of the economy. Likewise, the Fifth Congress of the Polish United Workers' Party (held in 1968) stressed "selective development," particularly of some 100 enterprises specializing in production for export.

There is an implicit danger in this approach to restructuring an economy. Lacking a realistic mechanism for setting prices and determining costs, and operating with fictitious exchange rates and with foreign trade activities virtually isolated from the rest of the domestic economy, the central planners can have no assurance that the new structure will prove more efficient that its predecessor. An alternative approach to the problem has been tried—to a certain extent—in Hungary, where it has been recognized that the industrial structure should be created "from below" in response to existing demand and that "the starting point for actual development priorities should be found in the micro-structure and not in the macro-structure."

ECONOMIC COOPERATION

While the individual CMEA countries were grappling with the problems of economic reform and the restructuring of industry, they were also pursuing a complementary effort to increase the degree of specialization and cooperation within the bloc. In 1962, at a "Conference of Communist and Workers' Parties of the Socialist Countries," the CMEA states approved a set of "Basic Principles of the International Socialist Division of Labor," which were to set the main objectives and methods of economic cooperation among the member countries. This document envisaged an expansion in mutual trade based largely on coordination of the five-year economic plans of the member states, particularly the sections of such plans dealing with investment priorities.

To facilitate economic cooperation, Comecon also expanded its institutional structure. The 1962 conference created a Comecon Executive Committee, a Bureau on General Problems of Economic Plans, and Institute of Standardization, a Chartering Coordination Bureau, and a Central Administration of the Joint Power System, in addition to increasing the number of Comecon standing committees (dealing with such matters as statistics, scientific and technological research, and standardization).

In 1963, a Joint Railway Rolling Stock System was also established. In the same year, Comecon accepted the principles of multilateral clearing of trade accounts within the bloc on the basis of a so-called "transfer ruble," and in 1964 it established an International Bank for Economic Cooperation to handle such transactions.

Trailing Trade Growth

However, the extension of the activities of the Council failed to generate any dramatic increase in the role of international trade in the process of economic growth in the member countries. In the years 1964–69, the average annual rate of growth of exports was lower than the 1958–63 rate in all the East European countries except the German Democratic Republic.[5] An East European economist documented the unsatisfactory growth of exports during the late 1960s by comparing the share of Comecon's exports in total world exports to the share of its industrial production in total world industrial production. The ratio of the two declined from 0.37 in 1950 to 0.35 in 1968 and 0.33 in 1970 for Comecon as a whole; and from 0.81 to 0.72 and 0.71 in the same years for Comecon exclusive of the USSR. The ratios for individual countries in 1970 are also illuminating: Bulgaria, 1.00; Czechoslovakia, 0.75; the GDR, 0.63; Hungary, 1.33; Poland, 0.55; and Romania, 0.60. These ratios contrast to 1.23 for all developed non-socialist countries and 2.18 for members of the European Economic Community (Common Market). In the period 1965–70, only Poland—of the CMEA states—was able to increase its share in total world imports and exports, and that increase was from a very low level. Comecon's share in exports dropped from 10.6 to 10.2 percent; and in imports, from 10.0 to 9.5 percent.

Most significant in terms of Comecon's announced goal of increasing cooperation among the CMEA states was the actual decline in the share of intrabloc trade in total trade of the member states (from 63.09 percent in 1965 to 60.69 percent in 1970). Only in Bulgaria and Poland did the share of dealings with fellow CMEA states in the individual country's total foreign trade increase during this period.

The failure of Comecon trade exchanges to grow as planned spurred a second great debate on the future of the organization during 1968–71, culminating in the adoption of the Comprehensive Program with its ambitious integrative targets. Clearly the 1962 "Basic Principles" and institutional measures had been insufficient to create a satisfactory division of labor among the CMEA countries. Co-operation was blocked by a number of "barriers": e.g., administrative protectionism, failure to develop direct links between economic units located in different countries, the practice of basing trade on rigid quotas, the persistence of bilateral-

---

[5] These data were derived from the statistical yearbooks of the respective countries.

ism in trade arrangements and the clearing of international accounts, the lack of a true international currency within Comecon, unrealistic exchange rates, distorted domestic prices and their separation from world prices, and a lack of mobility of capital and labor.[6] These barriers, moreover, were grounded in the reality of the East European economies, particularly in the difficulties encountered in the quest for so-called "intensive" economic growth and in the deep-rooted penchant for autarky. Let us examine these factors before turning to the Comprehensive Program itself.

One can get a clear picture of the achievements and failings of the 1966–70 economic plans in Eastern Europe. Every country was able to accelerate its rate of growth during this period except Poland (which maintained its 1961–65 pace) and Romania (which slowed to a still impressive 7.6-percent average annual growth rate). However, everywhere growth continued to be associated with heavy increases in investment—in fact investment grew faster than planned in all countries except Bulgaria and Romania. The share of accumulation in national income reached new highs in 1967 in all the East European countries and continued to grow thereafter in Czechoslovakia, Poland, Romania, and the USSR. The efficiency of capital improved only in Czechoslovakia and East Germany—two countries which had shown exceptionally low levels of efficiency during 1961–65—and despite heavy investment outlays, the targeted average rates of growth of labor productivity were realized only in Czechoslovakia, Poland, and Romania.

From this evidence, it is clear that economic growth in Eastern Europe during the second half of the 1960s continued to be of the "extensive" rather than of the desired "intensive" variety. Consequently, the need to modernize and restructure the respective economies remained urgent. Furthermore, in attempting to restructure their industrial production, the countries tended to turn *en masse* to the manufacture of the same new commodities, viewed as "progressive"—e.g., automobiles, trucks, tractors, metal-working machines, textile machines, equipment for the chemical industry and power generation, and railway engines. Little attention was paid to specialization and coordination in these areas. As noted by two observers, ". . . independent decisions of individual CMEA countries as to the starting of new production leads to uneconomic dispersion of resources and increasing disintegration. . . "

In light of this continued autarkic tendency, specialization within Comecon made slow progress. Comecon directives concerning mutual supplying of specialized products covered at most 30 percent and as little as 2 percent of total imports of various groups of machinery and equipment. Furthermore, in the absence of any sanctions, the rate of nonfulfill-

[6] J. M. Montias, "Obstacles to the Economic Integration of Eastern Europe," *Studies in Comparative Communism*, Vol. 2, Nos. 3–4 (July–October 1969), pp. 38–60.

ment of specialization tasks was very high. For example, Poland exported 22 out of 29 items subject to the directives in 1963; 24 out of 40 in 1964; 15 out of 34 in 1966; 48 out of 68 in 1967; and none out of 79 in 1969. This reflected a combination of neglect by the exporters or their inability to meet obligations because of dispersion of resources to other sectors of the given economy and of changes in demand on the part of importing countries because of delays in plant implementation or rejection of goods because of late delivery or low quality.

Forces for Integration

There were, however, important economic forces pushing toward integration within Comecon, including the need to overcome the technological gap between CMEA states and the advanced non-socialist countries, the machinery bias in industrial output and the resulting export priorities, and the need to solve major problems concerning the supply of fuels and raw materials.

Eastern Europe apparently became fully aware of its technological backwardness relative to the West only in the late 1960s. As the CMEA states groped for means to overcome this handicap, they discovered that self-sufficiency would no longer work. No individual country could hope to incorporate the most recent technology into its production processes on a wide front through its own efforts. The purchase of advanced machinery or of licenses from the West was one possible solution, but there was precious little foreign exchange available to permit such an approach. Consequently, there was a need for the socialist economies to participate in international exchange of scientific and technological knowledge, at least within Comecon, if not on a broader, world-wide scale.

Another compulsion which has ultimately led toward integration within Comecon has been what Professor Peter Wiles terms structural "snobbery" in East European foreign trade—that is, a predilection to limit the import of consumer goods and the export of raw materials while emphasizing the expansion of both imports and exports of machines and equipment.[7] This perspective was an outgrowth of the switch from stressing basic heavy industries to a very rapid expansion of machine-building industries. Unfortunately, with the exception of the USSR, the countries of Eastern Europe have insufficient domestic markets for such products and must therefore find export markets or produce at a suboptimum scale.

Indeed, the share of machines and equipment in the total exports of all CMEA countries has increased rapidly (see Table 2), and this level is considerably higher than the share of such items in exports

[7] P. J. D. Wiles, *Communist International Economics* (New York: Praeger Publishers, Inc., 1968), pp. 19 and 185.

TABLE 2
Share of Machines and Equipment in Total Exports and Imports,
Comecon Countries, 1950 and 1970
(percent)

	Exports		Imports	
	1950	*1970*	*1950*	*1970*
Bulgaria	0.0	28.1	37.2	40.1
Czechoslovakia	26.4	50.2	11.2	33.4
East Germany	28.0	49.9	5.5	32.8
Hungary	23.0	32.4	22.0	31.0
Poland	7.8	38.5	32.4	36.4
Romania	4.2	21.7*	37.1	44.3
USSR	11.8	21.5	21.5	35.0

*1969.

of non-socialist economies with similar levels of development. This comparison excludes the USSR, which, as noted above, has a sufficient internal market for its own output. The share of other industrial products in CMEA exports is lower than the corresponding figure for all developed non-socialist economies except Denmark—and then only East Germany and Hungary exceed Denmark's low level of 20.3 percent.

The CMEA countries, however, have experienced serious difficulties in attempting to export their machines and equipment to markets outside of Comecon, particularly to the advanced non-socialist countries. The quality and level of technological sophistication of products have proven to be low, and even the products of some brand-new factories have proven obsolete as soon as production commenced. This may happen even when production is based on licenses or produced on machines purchased from the West, because of inordinate delays in the completion of investment projects. Ineffective marketing, shortages of spare parts, inadequate packaging and servicing, as well as the creation of various tariff barriers of discrimination against CMEA products, aggravate the situation.

Consequently, during the 1960s, trade with the West in these categories never attained as much as 10 percent of the total export of this group of commodities by any CMEA country. Comecon has been somewhat more successful in marketing its machines and equipment in the less developed non-socialist countries. However, expansion of trade in this sector requires the ability to offer credit, and the markets are scattered geographically and difficult to service.

As a consequence, a very high proportion of the CMEA countries' exports of machinery and equipment is traded within Comecon, and this commodity class accounts for high proportions of total exports to other CMEA states except in the cases of the USSR, Romania, and Bulgaria

TABLE 3
Share of Machines and Equipment in Intrabloc CMEA
Exports, 1957, 1965, and 1971
(percent)

	1957	*1965*	*1971*
Bulgaria	8.8	29.9	36.8
Czechoslovakia	42.4	56.3	60.8
East Germany	48.6	58.6	60.7
Hungary	45.8	42.8	46.8
Poland	28.6	48.6	52.4
Romania	11.0	24.5	31.9
USSR.	8.6	18.0	23.8

(see Table 3). Yet, in the second half of the 1960s, it became increasingly more difficult for these countries to export such products even to their CMEA partners, because there was a strong preference for obtaining technologically superior machines from the West.

This interest in Western machinery was partly based on the belief that the relatively inefficient and obsolete machinery used in CMEA countries was an important factor in deceleration of growth throughout the region. Imports of machines from Western sources were growing at an annual rate of 15 percent, contrasted to an 11-percent rate for imports from other socialist countries. Intra-bloc trade in machinery in the 1960s grew at almost the same rate as in 1956–60—a situation interpreted by some as a sign of "saturation" in this trade.

Such a situation is especially serious, because it involves precisely the products of newly established or newly modernized industries which have consistently received high priority in the allocation of managerial skills, manpower, and investment funds. In light of the limited possibilities of increasing exports of this commodity group to non-socialist countries, the CMEA market remains the most important outlet; yet expansion in this direction cannot take place unless that market is reorganized and unless the products are improved and made comparable to those available from other sources.

The Position of the USSR

In this connection, the Soviet market is of decisive significance. In the years 1966–70, the USSR purchased about half the total exports of machines and equipment of the other CMEA countries. This included 85 percent of ships, boats, and marine equipment; 60 percent of railway equipment; 60 percent of equipment for the chemical and food industries; and over 50 percent of machinery for light industries (textiles, leather goods, etc.). As one East European expressed it, this means that ". . . to a considerable extent, the structure of the Soviet Union's demand for machines and equipment determines the directions of specialization of the CMEA countries." Furthermore, Soviet imports of machines and equipment from other CMEA countries are expected to increase from the 12 billion rubles imported in 1966–70 to over 18 billion rubles during 1971–75.

Thus, in attempting to utilize their industrial potential, the other countries of Comecon must adjust production to the needs of their largest customer, even when—it is alleged—the profitability of this trade is not high.[8] From Moscow's viewpoint, moreover, it is essential that the machinery imported from its East European partners be of the right types, of high quality, and of the most advanced technological design, if it is to contribute to the "intensive" growth of the Soviet economy. Under such circumstances one can understand the interest in far-reaching integration of East European and Soviet industries—both to solve the problems encountered by exporters of machinery and equipment and to satisfy the standards set by the users of such goods within the bloc.

Equally important for the economies of Comecon is the question of fuel and raw material supply. These economies have continued their emphasis on heavy industry—particularly on the production of steel, which requires large inputs of fuel and raw materials—in the face of inadequate local supplies of these commodities. Despite heavy investments to develop domestic raw material bases, the East European states have experienced sharply rising deficits in these commodities, particularly since the beginning of the 1960s. Moreover, the serious imbalance between demand and supply in this sector has been aggravated by a continued "leakage" of raw materials from Comecon trade to countries outside the bloc. The extent of this leakage can be gauged by examining the destination of increases in exports of Comecon countries in the years 1955–67. For foodstuffs, 59.7 percent of increases in exports were directed outside the bloc; for fuels and minerals, 50.8 percent; and for other raw materials, 71.3 percent. If one looks—for purposes of comparison—at the trends in exports for the same categories of goods by European Common Market countries for the same time frame, it turns out that the corresponding figures for shares of increases in exports of these three categories of raw materials which were directed outside of the EEC were 29.5, 34.2 and 32.2 percent, respectively.

The tendency of Comecon countries to export raw materials outside of the bloc is caused, in part, by balance-of-payments difficulties experienced by CMEA countries in their attempts to purchase specialized machinery from the West for new investment projects. Having lost traditional consumer-goods markets during the industrialization drive and

---

[8] In the absence of realistic prices, exchange rates, and methods of cost calculation, it is almost impossible to judge when exports are profitable.

experiencing difficulties in marketing the output of newly established industries, the East European countries can earn essential "hard currencies" only by exporting raw materials and foodstuffs—what Professor J. M. Montias has termed "hard goods"[9]—to the advanced non-socialist countries. Export of fuels and raw materials to countries outside of Comecon has also been fostered by the practice of using world prices for transactions in these commodities within the bloc. These prices do not reflect the relative degree of scarcity of raw materials which exists within the bloc and therefore cannot make the Comecon market more attractive than other markets.[10]

On the other side of the coin, the CMEA countries rely on sources within the bloc for between 54 and 72 percent of total national imports of raw materials and fuels. Here, as in the trade in machinery, the role of the Soviet Union is decisive. It supplied 41 percent of total intrabloc imports of this group of commodities in 1955, 56 percent in 1965, and above 60 percent in 1970; and it has agreed to increase considerably its annual exports of some basic fuels and raw materials to other CMEA countries during 1971–75: i.e., oil from 138 million tons in 1970 to 243 million in 1975, natural gas from 8 to 33 million cubic meters, electric power from 14 to 42 billion kwh, and iron ore from 72 million to 94 million tons. It is on the basis of these figures that the five-year plans of the recipient countries for 1971–75 have been built.

Despite the enormous Soviet potential in this field, maintenance of an adequate and continuing supply of raw materials and fuels from the USSR to the other CMEA countries is regarded by Soviet and East European economists alike as a very difficult problem, and a considerable deficit is expected to appear in the CMEA countries other than the Soviet Union by 1980.

Part of the problem lies in the costliness of the Soviet extractive industries. Already at the time when the five-year plans were coordinated for 1966–70, Soviet economists pointed out that the average capital-intensity of the basic raw materials and fuels exported to other CMEA countries by the USSR was from 3 to 3.5 times higher than that for the machinery supplied to the USSR by those countries in exchange. Moreover, the gestation period for investment in extractive operations in the USSR is long (10–12 years); worsening conditions of exploitation and unfavorable contract prices have decreased the "effectiveness" (profit-

---

[9] See his *Economic Development in Communist Rumania,* (Cambridge, Mass.: MIT Press, 1967), and "Socialist Industrialization and Trade in Machinery Products: An Analysis Based on the Experience of Bulgaria, Poland and Rumania," in *International Trade and Central Planning,* ed. Alan A. Brown and Egon Neuberger (Berkeley: University of California Press, 1968), pp. 130–59.

[10] An analysis of the foreign trade prices of the CMEA countries can be found in Paul Marer, *Postwar Pricing and Price Patterns in Socialist Foreign Trade (1946–1971)* (Bloomington, Ind.: Indiana University International Development Research Center, 1972).

ability) of fuel exports; and it is increasingly difficult to meet export needs from resources in European Russia, while exploitation of deposits in Siberia and the Far East requires larger outlays of capital and of manpower. Consequently, the USSR is seeking to foster increased integration in the fuel and power industries of Comecon, to be accomplished principally through investment in these Soviet industries by other CMEA countries. Indeed, the Comprehensive Program of 1971 envisaged a large number of such mutually financed projects to produce fuel and raw materials, most of them to be located in the USSR and Mongolia. The investors are to be repaid with the raw materials produced.

In light of all the factors examined above, it was recognized by the outset of the 1970s that the degree of cooperation within Comecon was not commensurate with either the needs or the potentialities of the CMEA countries. Soviet leader Leonid Brezhnev highlighted this view in his speech to the 24th Congress of the Communist Party of the Soviet Union:

> [The] possibilities of the socialist location of economic activity and division of labor are not yet fully utilized. . . . It is necessary to deepen specialization and cooperation in production, to establish closer links among national economic plans, in short, to advance along the road of economic integration of the socialist states.

While discussion favoring integration tended to stress the economic factors (presented as "the outcome of objective development tendencies"), there also were various political factors militating both for and against such a course. Advocates of integration saw it as a means of forging closer relations among the socialist states and strengthening them against the alleged divisive policies of capitalist countries aimed at "softening socialism" in Eastern Europe.

Resistance to Integration

However, the national interests and aspirations of individual member states loomed as a potential obstacle to comprehensive integration. In the early 1960s, Romania was the most vociferous in defending member-state sovereignty against Khrushchev's proposal to make CMEA supranational.[11] Such concerns are very real, particularly in light of the dominating political, military, and economic power of the Soviet partner and the very high degree of economic dependence of the other partners on the USSR as a supplier of raw materials and as a market.

The less developed CMEA states, again Romania in particular, feared that closer integration within Comecon would benefit the most developed countries while petrifying the less developed economies at their present

---

[11] For a discussion of diverging interests with CMEA in the years 1961–66, see Michael Kaser, *Comecon: Integration Problems of the Planned Economies,* 2nd ed. (London: Oxford University Press, 1967), pp. 92–129.

level of industrialization—fears similar to those which had earlier defeated efforts to develop interbranch international division of labor involving the division of countries into suppliers of foodstuffs and raw materials, on the one hand, and those specializing in industrial production, on the other. It was only after obtaining various concessions and guarantees on this issue that Romania signed a joint document expressing the need for integration at the 23rd CMEA Session in April 1969.

The more advanced countries of the bloc also had their fears. Czechoslovakia did not want excessive integration to hinder its growing trade with Western markets—its main source of advanced technology and a highly useful medium for "verifying" the technological standards and quality of Czechoslovak exports. For its part, East Germany wished to safeguard its special relations with West Germany—a member of the EEC. To satisfy these reservations, it was agreed at the 23rd CMEA session that integration should not hamper the development of member states' economic relations with the rest of the world.

The Comprehensive Program

The "Comprehensive Program" finally adopted at the 25th session of the Council for Mutual Economic Assistance at Bucharest in July 1971 reflected the various compromises hammered out on these complex issues over a period of several years. The Program stated:

> . . . further intensification and improvement and the development of the socialist economic integration of CMEA member nations will be carried out in accordance with the principles of socialist internationalism and on the basis of respect for national sovereignty, independence, and national interests, of nonintervention in the internal affairs of nations, and of total equality, mutual advantage, and comradely reciprocal aid.

It further noted that:

> . . . socialist economic integration is carried out on an entirely voluntary basis and is not accompanied by the creation of supranational organs, nor does it affect matters pertaining to internal planning or the financial and cost-calculating activities of organizations.[12]

In other words, each country decides whether to participate in a given integration project on the basis of calculations of the benefits of the project to its own economy and of the profits which participating production and trade organizations would gain.

Furthermore, one whole section of the Program was devoted to provisions for eliminating differences in levels of development between member countries—a task specified as one of the objectives of integration.

---

[12] An English translation of the full text of the Program appeared in *Soviet and Eastern European Foreign Trade*, Vol. VII, No. 3-4 (Fall–Winter 1971–72), pp. 187–305.

Less developed members would be allowed to select certain new lines of production for specialization in order to spur individual growth as long as the products were of sufficiently high quality and technological sophistication. More advanced members were to extend assistance in this regard, as well as to help less advanced members participate fully in research and development activities. To coordinate efforts in this latter area, the July 1971 session of Comecon created a Committee for Scientific and Technical Cooperation to direct the establishment of various joint research institutes, the allocation of tasks among national institutes, the exchange of scientific personnel and of research findings, and the joint production of scientific instruments and equipment.

Since the Comprehensive Program created no supranational planning authorities, other measures had to be devised to coordinate efforts toward cooperation and integration. The Bucharest session created a' Committee for Cooperation in Planning to promote closer coordination of national five-year and long-term economic plans and exchanges of information on economic policies and planning experience. With regard to national five-year plans, preliminary joint discussions are to be held concerning ways of coordinating economic activities within the bloc, and decisions reached are to be formalized in bilateral or, where feasible, in multilateral agreements prior to formal adoption of the plans by the respective state authorities—a procedure designed to guarantee full incorporation of such coordinating decisions into the individual national plans.

The most important concrete tasks of the new Committee for Cooperation in Planning appear to be (1) to solve "in a comprehensive manner" problems such as the assurance of adequate supplies of raw materials and power throughout the bloc, introduction of the most advanced technological processes in the manufacture of new machines and equipment, and expansion of the transportation system within Comecon; (2) to prepare proposals for international cooperation in the construction of important investment projects; and (3) to further joint planning among interested members for individual branches of industry and types of production. Such joint planning will encompass all stages, including forecasting of demand, preparatory activities, the production process, and the distribution of output among various markets over an agreed period of time. The stress will be on specialization in the production of parts rather than finished products. There will be very close direct links among cooperating units with a system of severe penalties for nonfulfillment of contracts.

In addition to introducing some mobility of capital within the bloc through joint investment by exporting and importing countries in the development of natural resources, the Program also introduced an element of labor mobility. Building on the experience of joint Czechoslovak-Polish construction work and of the use of Bulgarian workers to help exploit forest resources in Northern Russia to produce timber for both the USSR and Bulgaria, the Program provides that construction companies fulfilling a contract in another country may be asked to provide line workers in addition to technical personnel. In this manner Poland, with a surplus of labor, may be of assistance to East Germany and Czechoslovakia, which have labor shortages. In addition, movement of labor-intensive industries across international frontiers to regions with surplus labor is expected to result from coordination of plans and from specialization agreements.

Intra-Comecon trade will continue to be based on multiyear commercial agreements with annual joint decisions concerning implementation, but these agreements are supposed to be more closely connected with the five-year plans. In order to increase flexibility in trade, there will be three types of exchange. Trade in the most important raw materials, fuels, machines and equipment, and even some foodstuffs and manufactured consumer goods, will be governed by rigidly defined quotas specifying quantities, delivery dates, and other matters. For a second group, composed of less essential commodities, the only quota established will be a figure for the total value of goods exchanged. A third group will not be subject to any quota and will not have to be bilaterally balanced. In order to facilitate integration, a new ruble—freely convertible within the bloc—is to be introduced, and the rates of exchange of all CMEA currencies are to be revised to make them more reflective of economic realities. A CMEA Investment Bank has been established to facilitate long-term investments, and the International Bank of Economic Cooperation will be reorganized in order to stimulate credit transactions and multilateral clearing.

CONCLUSION

What concrete results does Comecon expect from these measures, and how likely are they to materialize? During the 1971–75 plan periods in each of the Comecon countries, international trade—and particularly intrabloc trade—is expected to play an important part in national growth and the shift to "intensive" patterns of development. Every East European member of Comecon (excluding the USSR) anticipates that international trade will grow more rapidly than national income, even though in all countries the rate of growth is to be more moderate than in 1966–70, in keeping with more modest targets for growth of investment and of national income. More significantly, trade with socialist countries is generally expected to grow more rapidly than total trade during 1971–75, in contrast to the pattern witnessed in 1966–70 (see Table 4). One may assume that the major part of this "intersocialist" trade will take place among Comecon member states.

But while trade within Comecon will doubtless increase during the current five-year period, one cannot predict with any certainty to what

TABLE 4
Growth of Comecon Foreign Trade: 1966–70 Results and Plans for 1971–75
(percent)

	Total Trade		*Trade with Socialist Countries*	
	1966–70	*1971–75*	*1966–70*	*1971–75*
Bulgaria	70	60–65	62	84
Czechoslovakia	40	36–38	34	43–45
East Germany	60	n.a.*	55	75
Hungary	50	40–50	52	75
Poland	55	46–57	60	50
Romania	75	70	n.a.	n.a.
USSR	52	33–35	43	50

* Not available.

extent it will be along the multilateral lines envisaged in the Comprehensive Program and to what extent it will flow through traditional bilateral channels. Nor can one foresee just how extensively the Comprehensive Program's integrative measures will be implemented. Nevertheless, one can anticipate the development of closer integration within Comecon in some fields, particularly fuel extraction, power generation, metallurgy, and the engineering and chemical industries. Most industrial organizations in these categories are likely to be bloc-wide units rather than smaller regional units. Although the recent opening of the frontier between Poland and East Germany and the formation of various specialization agreements between two or three of the smaller CMEA states does raise the possibility of a regional type of development, one suspects that the USSR would not allow this tendency to become widespread.

If the plans for creating numerous Comecon-wide integrated industries materialize, there will be little need to establish any supranational Comecon planning authorities. All essential decisions in major industrial sectors would then be made within the corresponding integrated industries and be incorporated in the national plans of the member states through the process of preliminary coordination described above. This would not, however, indicate the absence of a broader coordination; for this function would, in effect, be performed by the State Planning Commission of the Soviet Union, which will effectively control these industries through its own decisions to purchase industrial output and to provide essential raw material inputs.

The integration envisaged in the Comprehensive Program is thus quite different from the integrated CMEA market which many East European economists had hoped might serve to increase the role of market forces and to permit decentralization of decision-making. To the contrary, one might expect the integrated industries to become more centralized—although the degree of centralization or decentralization will presumably be decided individually within each integrated industry.

Of course, it will take considerable time for the new Comecon machinery even to begin coping with the complex problems of such a gigantic venture. Moreover, the decision to do without supranational authorities, coupled with the existence of various provisions for safeguarding the autonomy of member states in economic planning and management and allowing them the right to decide whether or not to participate in particular integration measures, seems likely to place serious constraints on the Program. Such limitations may, indeed, perpetuate the gradualist approach of the past described by Egon Neuberger as a "limited regret strategy."[13]

Nevertheless, one must not discount the possibility that Comecon will achieve a significant measure of integration, both economically and hence politically and militarily as well. This, indeed, appears to be the main objective of the Soviet Union even while it finds it necessary to expand its own economic relations with the advanced capitalist states in order to modernize its own industrial structure and introduce the intensive pattern of growth.

For their part, the East European members of Comecon—faced with the prospect of intensified economic pressures resulting from an enlarged Common Market—have very little choice but to go along with integration. They need larger markets in order to support efforts to modernize their industrial production, and they must readjust the structure of that production to take account of existing export possibilities. They also must secure for themselves essential supplies of raw materials, which—because of shortages of convertible currencies—they can only acquire from the USSR. They will certainly find it increasingly difficult to find any domestic surpluses of foodstuffs or raw materials to export to the advanced capitalist countries to finance imports of modern technology. Unless they can increase the number of specialization agreements with Western firms and expand exports of industrial goods to nonsocialist countries, their only alternative would appear to be integration within Comecon, and integration within Comecon means integration with the Soviet Union.

[13] Egon Neuberger, "International Division of Labor in CMEA: Limited Regret Strategy," *American Economic Review*, Vol. LIV, No. 3 (May 1964), pp. 506–15.

20. EAST-WEST TRADE AND INVESTMENT POLICY ISSUES: PAST AND FUTURE

Franklyn D. Holzman

The recent (1972) detente between the United States and the USSR marks the end of the Cold War era, and new patterns of economic relations are beginning to emerge. This paper by Franklyn D. Holzman, Professor of Economics at Tufts University, examines the economic issues involved. The first three sections were written before the 1972 detente. Holzman argues against the Cold War type of trade and investment restrictions applied by the United States against the USSR, pointing out that they failed to achieve their goals, probably benefited rather than hurt the Soviet Union, and probably injured the United States both economically and politically. The final section, written after the 1972 agreements, discusses the trade and investment problems likely to characterize the new era of liberalized trade and investment relations between the United States and the USSR.

This article is reprinted from *Soviet Economic Prospects for the Seventies* (A Compendium of Papers Submitted to the Joint Economic Committee, 93rd Cong., 1st sess.) (Washington, D.C.: U.S. Government Printing Office, 1973), pp. 660–89. The first three sections were originally published in *United States International Economic Policy in an Interdependent World* (A Compendium of Papers Submitted to the Commission on International Trade and Investment Policy and Published in Conjunction with the Commission's Report to the President) (Washington, D.C.: U.S. Government Printing Office, 1971), Vol. II, pp. 363–95.

HARDLY A YEAR goes by without an investigation by some branch of the United States Government into our East-West trade policies. How much impact these investigations have had on U.S. policies is difficult to say. On the one hand, our official Government policies have changed little. This is evidenced by continued existence of the Johnson Act of

1934, embargoes on China and Cuba, Export Control Act and Battle Act, unwillingness to grant most-favored-nation (MFN) status to most Eastern nations, and so forth. On the other hand, there has been considerable, though gradual, relaxation over the past 20 years at the administrative level as evidenced by less restrictive enforcement of the Export Control and Battle Acts, and the Johnson Act of 1934. This trend is, in my opinion, a sensible adaptation to changing objective conditions; primarily (but not exclusively) the lessening of Cold War tensions; belated recognition of the important fact that the "enemy" is not united and (to use a hackneyed phrase) monolithic; and increasing difficulties in obtaining Western European cooperation in our policies, without which these policies are largely ineffective in achieving their purposes. Even if conditions hadn't changed, serious questions could be raised regarding the conception of our legislation on East-West trade and investment and whether this legislation was properly designed to achieve American objectives.

The various Acts mentioned above will be reviewed below for their appropriateness in light of present conditions and for their effectiveness. The time has come, it seems to me, to bring our legislation into harmony with our national interests as well as with the individual interests of our citizens as consumers and businessmen. In the final section of the paper, we consider future East-West trade problems, particularly those relating to the currency inconvertibility and balance of payments difficulties of the Soviet Bloc nations.

I. POLICY ISSUES

Direct Physical Controls over Exports to the USSR and Eastern Europe

Since the end of World War II, probably the single greatest deterrent to an enlargement of East-West trade imposed by the West has been in the form of export controls. As time has passed, these controls have been progressively relaxed so that the statement applies with greater force to the early postwar periods. These controls have been embodied primarily in two pieces of Congressional legislation, the Export Control Act of 1949 and the Mutual Defense Assistance Control Act of 1951, better known as the Battle Act.

The Export Control and Battle Acts. The Export Control Act was passed originally as a substitute for various ad hoc measures used right after the War to prevent the export of goods deemed to be important to our national security. The goods listed under the Act as "strategic" presumably were selected because of their possible contributions to the military-industrial potential of recipient nations as well as, at the time (1949), to prevent export of goods which were in short supply in the United States. While the Act applied in theory to exports to all countries, in fact licenses for exports of listed commodities were usually easily obtained when the recipient was from a Western nation, but not often granted when the importing nation was in the Soviet Bloc. In an amendment to the Act in 1962, the basis for including commodities on the proscribed list and denying export license was substantially broadened from what had been primarily a military criterion to one which could encompass almost any commodity desired by another country. Congress found that "unrestricted export of materials without regard to their military and economic significance may adversely affect the national security of the United States" and provided for the denial of a license for the export of any commodity "to any nation or combination of nations threatening the national security of the United States if the President shall determine that such export makes a significant contribution to the military or economic potential of such nation or nations which would prove detrimental to the national security and welfare of the United States."[1] Since no nation is likely to seek trade which does not provide it with military or economic benefits, this amendment gives the President the power to ban the export of any—or all—commodity to the Soviet Bloc if he sees fit. While the spirit of the amendment is drastic, in practice it means little or no change but simply justified, ex post facto, the denial of export licenses in the past for many commodities which had been hard to justify under a "military" criterion.

In the Export Administration Act of 1969, the "economic" criterion was deleted and the only goods proscribed from export were once again those contributing to military potential. Further, as noted above, the trend has been toward progressive relaxation of export controls. In fact, from 1966 to 1968, approximately 450 additional items were removed from the Commodity Control List of "strategic" commodities administered by the Department of Commerce; this still left, however, some 1,800 commodities which require a validated license for export to the USSR and East Europe.[2]

The Battle Act, passed under the influence of the Korean War, essentially was an attempt by the United States to enlist the cooperation of the NATO nations and Japan in achieving the goals of our Export Control Act. Lists (called Cocom lists) of "war materials" and "other materials" which should not be exported to "nations threatening the security of the United States, including the USSR and the countries under its domination"[3] are drawn up under mutual agreement. In the event that one of the NATO nations or Japan knowingly allows the

---

[1] Both citations taken from *East-West Trade* (Hearings before the Subcommittee on International Finance of the Committee on Banking and Currency, U.S. Senate, 90th Cong., 2d sess.) (Washington, D.C.: U.S. Government Printing Office, 1968), Part 3, pp. 1194–95.

[2] Leon Herman, *East-West Trade: An Overview of Legislation, Policy Trends, and Issues Involved* (Washington, D.C.: Legislative Reference Service, Library of Congress, June 17, 1968).

[3] Cited by Herman, p. 5.

shipment of a proscribed item to the Communist Bloc, the Act provides that the United States terminate all military, economic, and financial aid to that nation. The President is empowered, however, to direct continuance of aid if it is in the interests of U.S. security. At the time the Act was passed, the potential penalty was severe since Europe was receiving Marshall Plan aid. Penalties were rarely, if ever, applied in the 1950s, however, despite the fact that the Act was frequently breached. In the past decade, the flow of aid to Western Europe has been so slight (or non-existent to many nations) that the penalty provision has become inoperative vis-á-vis most of these nations.[4]

A Digression on Economic Warfare. These are the basic provisions of the two Acts. They were basically conceived as temporary extensions of wartime measures. As such, there may have been some justification for their continuation until, say, the mid-1950s. Their continuation after that time is, in my opinion, completely misguided and has resulted in more harm than good to the interests of this nation. By the mid-fifties, the two Acts should have been allowed to lapse except for the maintenance of controls over the export of classified military goods and perhaps a few commodities embodying very advanced military-industrial technology in which the United States has a monopoly.

I have said that our export control policy may have been justified before the mid-fifties. I think it is worth pointing out, however, that it was highly optimistic to believe that it could have had, even at that time, a significant effect on the military capabilities of the Soviet Bloc. The most dramatic evidence that our embargo policy was not likely to have much effect was contained in the experts' assessments of the impact of our World War II embargo and strategic bombing efforts vis-á-vis Germany, which were carried out with infinitely greater intensity than our present policies directed at the Soviet Bloc. I quote one of many similar judgments based on the evidence:

> During World War II the Allied bombing of Germany was based on the so-called "bottleneck theory." It was thought that the military-supporting base would collapse if industries producing certain strategic components, such as antifriction bearings, were destroyed. The futility of that denial was demonstrated in surveys carried out after the war. They showed that even under blockaded wartime conditions, substitutes for materials denied or destroyed were rapidly developed and factories were quickly reconstructed by transfers of machinery from other less essential industries. It was concluded that denials, whether by bombing or embargoes, to be really effective must be very broadly based or near-complete.[5]

---

[4] Control over exports is by no means confined to the two Acts under discussion in this section. Controls are also exercised through the Trading with the Enemy Act of 1917, Agricultural Act of 1961, and others.

[5] Jozef Wilczynski, *The Economics and Politics of East-West Trade* (New York: Frederick A. Praeger, 1969), p. 286.

Another piece of evidence that weighs heavily against the possible success of an embargo policy is that provided by Soviet foreign trade behavior in the 1930s.[6] The first two Five Year Plans (1928–1937) placed very heavy dependence on imports of machinery, equipment, and other such commodities scarce to a nation just launching a forced industrialization program. The commercial conditions under which the USSR was forced to trade, partly because of Western hostility but also because of the great depression, were so adverse that, despite well-laid plans, it practically withdrew from foreign trade. By 1937, imports had declined to 30 percent of the 1931 level and had fallen from more than 3 percent of GNP to about 0.5 percent of GNP. What this little bit of history points up is that the USSR (and today the Soviet Bloc), like the United States, imports from choice, not necessity. At present, in peacetime, even a very tight embargo may be a cause of passing inconvenience and delay, and perhaps a small cost—but no more than that. Small costs like these are especially easy for a centrally planned economy to bear. This is because, for the most part, their economies are growing rapidly; and because it is easier for them to shift such costs to the consumer sector. Look how difficult (so far impossible) it is even in a democracy like the United States to remove resources from the inflated military machine into the battle for less pollution, less poverty, more medical care, better cities, and so forth!

A final point to be made regarding the optimism of our efforts to hurt the Soviet Bloc militarily, and this point is more relevant now than it was before 1955, is the relative divorce of military power from industrial power. With the advent of nuclear weapons and of rockets to deliver them, preparation for war and the fighting of war no longer involve total economic and industrial commitment as it had in the past. A policy there, designed to do anything more than deny the enemy crucial military know-how or materials, is misguided.[7]

Having presented evidence that our policies were "optimistic" as implemented in the early postwar period when the Cold War was intense, indeed, and some possibility of open hostilities may have existed, let me now turn to two fundamental misconceptions behind these policies as implemented over the past 15 to 20 years. In discussing these misconceptions, it is assumed that an embargo policy might succeed in its objectives, an assumption which I have already attempted to show has little basis in reality.

The first misconception amounts to a confusion between the short-run and the long-run. If the short-run probability of war is high, proper

---

[6] Cf. this writer's "Foreign Trade," in *Economic Trends in the Soviet Union,* ed. Abram Bergson and Simon Kuznets (Cambridge, Mass.: Harvard University Press, 1963), pp. 282–332.

[7] This must be qualified for "limited wars"; but "limited wars" were not the target of the Acts under review.

strategy dictates a policy similar to that followed by the United States: deny the potential enemy strategic commodities. If, on the other hand, the probabilities of war are low in the short-run, as they have been over the past 15 years, then a different strategy is called for. The better long-run strategy against a potential enemy is to make him as dependent upon you as possible. For the more the opponent is dependent upon you, the more vulnerable he is to damage from economic warfare at the time when it really counts. It is well known, for example, that the rapid development of Polish and Russian aluminum capacity owes a debt to our postwar embargo policy. Furthermore, that necessity is the mother of invention is evident here also. It has been pointed out[8] that (1) the embargo of natural rubber to the USSR led to technological developments by that nation in the production of synthetic rubber and to the growth of a large synthetic rubber industry; (2) the embargo of industrial diamonds was responsible for both a research effort in which an electric arcing device was developed and used as a substitute for the diamonds in some uses, and for an intensive prospecting effort which culminated in the discovery of vast diamond ore reserves in Eastern Siberia. Many other examples could be cited. It seems clear that our policy of the last 15 years, rather than weakening the Soviet Bloc, has undoubtedly put it in a better position to fight a war today should a war suddenly break out.

The second major misconception behind our policies is the idea that an embargo should concentrate on military or so-called strategic commodities as opposed to non-military non-strategic goods.[9] Once it is agreed that war is not imminent, two strategies appear possible. The first, just discussed, is to trade freely (with minor exceptions) with the potential enemy in the hopes of making him as dependent as possible on you. If this policy is rejected, then the appropriate economic warfare strategy would seem to be to concentrate the embargo on commodities where the gains from trade to the enemy are likely to be very large.[10] That economic as well as military gain should be a criterion of embargo policy seems to have been recognized in the 1962 amendment to the Export Control Act cited above. However, implementation has been deficient. Defense-related items still predominate on the lists of controlled

---

[8] By Robert Loring Allen in *East-West Trade: A Compilation of Views of Businessmen, Bankers, and Academic Experts* (Committee on Foreign Relations, U.S. Senate, 88th Cong., 2d sess.) (Washington, D.C.: U.S. Government Printing Office, 1964), p. 215.

[9] It is interesting to note that the USSR allows us to import on a regular basis, a sizeable list of strategic commodities despite the Vietnam War: platinum, iridium, palladium, rhodium, nickel, magnesium, titanium, cadmium, chrome ore, molybdenum, and aluminum scrap (cf. Herman, *East-West Trade*, p. 19).

[10] Losses from denying trade to the opponent would have to be balanced, of course, against the losses to the nation imposing the embargo. This point never seems to weigh in U.S. calculations. See below.

exports. Further, those who have been administering the control lists do not seem fully aware of the fact that the gains to the enemy from imports are not necessarily larger when the commodities in question are products of defense-related industries. A better assumption in the case of the USSR is that the gains from imports are larger the further removed the products are from the defense area. This has been clear to specialists for a long time from information of diverse sorts about the Soviet economy. Fifteen years ago it was generally thought among Sovietologists that if the United States and the USSR were to trade freely with each other on the basis of comparative advantage, the USSR would import agricultural products and consumers' goods from the United States and the United States would import industrial products from the USSR. These "informed guesses" were substantiated by a series of unclassified studies of product-by-product dollar-ruble ratios carried out by the RAND Corporation and the Central Intelligence Agency. These studies clearly demonstrated that the ruble was worth relatively more in the industrial sector relative to the dollar than in the agricultural and light industry sectors. Early this year, attention was called to these studies, particularly to that of Abraham Becker of RAND published in 1959, by Michael Boretsky in his Joint Economic Committee study "The Technological Base of Soviet Military Power."[11] The following are selected dollar-ruble ratios for 1955 as calculated by Becker, Boretsky, and the C.I.A.:

	1955 Dollar-Ruble Ratios
Electrical control apparatus	9.09
Power boilers and steam turbines	8.33
Metal-cutting machine tools	5.56
Electro-technical products, excl. control instruments and electronic equipment	3.52
Railroad equipment	2.70
Farm machinery and tractors	1.54
Motor vehicles	1.23
Food and non-food consumers' goods	1.00*

*In a C.I.A. study, the ruble was shown to be worth approximately $0.63 in food and $0.56 in non-food consumers goods. For comparability, the turnover tax should be removed and this would bring these ratios up to about $1.00. Cf. U.S. Central Intelligence Agency, *A Comparison of Consumption in the USSR and the US* (Washington, D.C., 1964).

What these ratios say is that a ruble was worth $9.09 in the production and purchase of electrical control apparatus but only $1.54 in farm machinery and tractors, $1.23 in motor vehicles, and somewhere around $1.00 in consumer goods. Why should this be so? Boretsky theorizes

---

[11] Michael Boretsky, "The Technological Base of Soviet Military Power," in *Economic Performance and the Military Burden in the Soviet Union* (A Compendium of Papers Submitted to the Subcommittee on Foreign Economic Policy, Joint Economic Committee, 91st Cong., 2d sess.) (Washington, D.C.: U.S. Government Printing Office, 1970), pp. 189–231.

(p. 203) that ". . . the decisive factor is the relative priority for investment, research funds and other resources which a particular Soviet product line has enjoyed in Gosplan and/or the party over the years . . ." Since defense-related industries receive priority in investment and research effort whereas consumer-oriented industries and agriculture do not, the latter tend to be relatively inefficient and high cost, the former relatively efficient and low cost. An embargo policy designed to prevent the USSR from reaping large gains from trade would do well to concentrate on low dollar-ruble ratio commodities.

For those who are still not convinced, let me quote a statement by Thomas Schelling of Harvard University before the Senate Committee on Foreign Relations in 1964:

"Wheat shipments may have the same effect on military programs as jet engine sales. Wheat shipments may permit the Soviets to keep chemical industries oriented toward munitions rather than fertilizers; jet engine sales may permit the Soviets to allocate engineering resources to consumer goods rather than jet engines."[12] What Schelling doesn't say is that the relative gain to the Russians in this resource reallocation process is much greater in the case of grain imports than jet engine imports because they are relatively more efficient in production of the latter.

Before turning to the case of commodities such as computers which embody very high technology and know-how, let me first point out briefly a number of other deficiencies in the conception of the Export Control and Battle Acts. First, as already footnoted above, there is a tendency in establishing control lists to ignore the fact that trade benefits not just the importer, but the exporter as well. The gains from exporting accrue (1) to the exporter in the form of profits, (2) to the exporting nation in the form of foreign exchange reserves, (3) or if the reserves are spent on imports to the importing enterprise in the form of profits, and (4) to the ultimate user of imports in the form of cheaper or better products. In this connection, it is important to note that the gains from trade which are sacrificed by the United States as a result of the Export Control Act are of relatively much less consequence to this country than are the gains foregone by Western Europe in the implementation of the Battle Act. This is because exports and imports amount, on the average, to perhaps 20 or 25 percent of the GNPs of the nations of Western Europe in comparison with the 4 or 5 percent of U.S. GNP.[13] It may well be that implementation of the Battle Act hurts our allies

---

[12] In *East-West Trade* (cited in fn. 8), p. 290.

[13] Comparable figures for the smaller countries of Eastern Europe and the USSR, respectively, explain Eastern Europe's greater interest in East-West trade than is true of the Soviet Union. It is also worth pointing out that the Soviet Union's very small ratios of exports and imports to GNP, of around three percent each, suggest the futility of trying to seriously hurt their economic or military efforts via economic warfare.

as much or almost as much as the smaller nations of Eastern Europe and more than it hurts the Soviet Union.

Second, for at least a decade it has been stressed over and over by critics of our East-West trade policies that the Communist nations are not a monolithic group but encompass considerable political diversity. Further, it is clear that each nation puts its own national interest above that of the group, an important factor in the failure of the Comecon nations to "integrate" their economies to any significant degree. While some cognizance has been taken of this situation, we certainly have not in our trade policies exploited it as fully as we might have.

Third, to a considerable extent our control lists are ineffectual in preventing the sale of embargoed commodities. This is because (1) the list observed by the United States is longer than that observed by Western Europe, and (2) implementation of Western European controls appears to be considerably less stringent than implementation of U.S. controls. In either case, commodities which this nation feels should not be shipped to Communist countries nevertheless find their way eastward. This is deplorable on two counts. First, it needlessly deprives American enterprise of markets. Second, it creates an image of impotency and ineffectualness.

High-Technology Commodities.   So far the discussion has centered on commodities in general. Consider now the policy toward the export of goods, whether military[14] or civilian, which embody advanced technology. Computers are probably a classic case of a high-technology commodity which has both civilian and military uses, and in which the U.S. has the technological lead. The case against exporting computers, advanced weaponry, and the like to the Eastern Bloc is probably made more cogently than for any other group of commodities. Recent developments are taken by some scholars to suggest that the Soviet Bloc may be particularly vulnerable at this time to export controls over commodities embodying advanced technology. The developments I am referring to are the retardation in growth rates experienced by all of the European Communist nations. Further, analysis of the causes of the slowdown in the Soviet growth rate by both Soviet and Western economists suggests that a decline in the contributions of technological progress may have been primarily responsible.[15] Those who believe in economic warfare therefore find the present situation an ideal one for employment of export controls.

In my opinion, the case for controls is not so irresistible. With the exception perhaps of the most highly strategic commodities embodying

---

[14] It seems highly dubious that the USSR would want to buy weapons from us which did not embody advanced technology; they are probably as efficient at producing them and as overstocked as we are.

[15] Alfred Zauberman, "Pushing the Technological Frontier Through Trade," in *East-West Trade and the Technology Gap*, ed. Stanislaw Wasowski (New York: Frederick A. Praeger, 1970), pp. 139–47.

new technology, the case for export controls here is subject to most of the criticisms presented above. For example, it remains true that many products, the export of which we would like to ban, will be available from Western Europe. Further, even if the Bloc nations cannot import prototypes, they can derive considerable information from the technical journals which are freely available. According to an authoritative study, Soviet computer experts are fully abreast of developments in this field through the literature even though the Soviet computer industry lags way behind.[16] Also, in the area of technology, the possibility of differentiating our control policies to favor some Communist nations but not others is virtually negligible because of the present relatively free dissemination of "know-how" in the Bloc and the fact that dissemination is almost costless. It also remains true that while there may be short-run losses from not being able to import technology, there may be long-run gains and development of greater independence. This point was put another way by the so-called Miller Committee,[17] which concluded: "In today's world no country can continue to rely heavily on the . . . importation of technology to improve its relative industrial position. To do so may appear to be cheap in the short run, but could turn out to be a sure way of perpetuating second-class industrial status." The fact is that by the time a prototype is exploited by an importer, it is out of date; reliance on importation of technology leads to a systematic lag in technology.[18]

One may also question the interpretation to be placed upon studies cited above which show a declining role for technology in the growth performance of the USSR. Several recent studies[19] suggest that the problem with technology arises not so much from lack of know-how, although this may contribute, but rather from problems of organization.[20] That problems of economic organization in the centrally planned economies are serious is well-known. Further, they are largely responsible for the

---

[16] Richard W. Judy, "The Case of Computer Technology," in *East-West Trade and the Technology Gap*, pp. 43–72.

[17] *Report to the President of the Special Committee on U.S. Trade Relations with East European Countries and the Soviet Union* (Commercial Policy Series No. 201) (Washington, D.C.: U.S. Department of State, 1966), pp. 14–15.

[18] Cf. Leon Herman, "Economic Content of Soviet Trade with the West," in *East-West Trade—A Symposium*, ed. Philip E. Uren (Toronto: Canadian Institute of International Affairs, 1966), p. 34.

[19] See articles by Judy, Woroniak, and Wasowski in *East-West Trade and the Technology Gap*.

[20] Let me add a skeptical note on quantitative measurements of the contributions of technology to growth. Technology itself cannot be measured, of course. It must either be approximated by proxy variables of dubious validity (consider that there are even serious problems in getting good measures of changes in labor and capital inputs) or be viewed as part of the "residual"—that part of the growth in output not explained by identifiable inputs. As part of the residual, it shares the honors with other unmeasurable inputs like "organization"—certainly a factor of significance in the centrally planned economies today.

recent attempts at reform. Difficulties in the development and introduction of new technology into industry appear to be one of the major consequences of the organizational crisis. The Soviet computer industry is one such victim of organization dysfunction, according to Judy. The lag behind the West, he argues, is not due to lack of information or lack of competent personnel but rather to the poor incentive-motivational system which discourages risk-taking and encourages the production as well as use of obsolete equipment.[21] What is true of the computer industry is true to a greater or lesser degree of most of the industries in Eastern Europe and the USSR.

There would seem then to be no special economic reason why commodities embodying advanced technology should be treated differently from other commodities. The failure, if any, of technology to contribute to the growth of the Communist nations does not appear to be due primarily to an inability to import, and continued restrictions along these lines are unlikely to have a significant economic effect. There may, of course, be military reasons why products like our most advanced computers should not be exported to the USSR. Judgments on matters of this sort are beyond the competence of the economist. My hunch is, however, that those who make judgments on these matters usually err several orders of magnitude on the conservative side.

If technology is to be treated like any other commodity, then it should also be paid for like any other commodity and properly protected according to Western conventions. That this has not always been the case in the past is well-known. The reasons are that under Communist convention, inventions and technology are in the realm of public goods; further, as large-scale net borrowers, no motivation to adopt Western conventions has existed. This situation is changing. As their technology has caught up, they have technology to sell. Even the Soviet Union finally joined the Paris Convention for the Protection of Industrial Property in 1965. Within the Soviet Bloc, there are pressures to end the free distribution of know-how and put technological exchange on a commercial basis. American firms which want to export technology should bargain for proper price (as they probably do) and secure appropriate guarantees. There is no reason for them to settle for less—and under present changing conditions, they probably will not have to.

The Total Embargoes on China and Cuba.   In 1950, the United States applied a total embargo on trade with Mainland China under the Trading with the Enemy Act of 1917 because of China's participation in the Korean War.[22] With minor exceptions, a similar embargo was

---

[21] He also argues that the Soviet authorities have not accorded the industry high priority in terms of personnel and investment, suggesting that if they did so their lag could be substantially cut.

[22] North Korea was similarly embargoed at that time and North Vietnam was also subject to total embargo.

placed on trade with Cuba in 1961. In 1952, the NATO powers and Japan agreed, as a result of U.S. pressure, to apply more severe controls over exports to China than were in operation against the European Communist nations. Our allies were unwilling to maintain this so-called "China differential" and it was abolished in 1957 leaving China on the same footing as other Communist nations. The Cuban embargo is participated in by the other nations of Latin America.

At the time the embargo on China was applied, there was, under the circumstances, almost no alternative open to the United States. The embargo at that time may even have had an economic and military impact on China and North Korea since, so soon after World War II, the nations of Western Europe were not able, and after 1952 willing, to supply China with commodities denied to them by the United States. Over the past decade, however, the economic and military effects of our embargo must be judged to be close to zero. Certainly, China can get most of the things she needs and probably at not much greater cost, from the USSR or Eastern Europe, if not from Japan and Western Europe. Furthermore, like the USSR and the United States, China is a big country with a small trade participation ratio (exports and imports each no more than 3–4 percent of GNP), and therefore with a naturally limited vulnerability to the effects of economic warfare. The really bizarre feature of this affair is that some 17 years after hostilities with North Korea have ceased, the embargo was maintained with virtual wartime completeness. Continuation of the wartime embargo appeared even more bizarre when one considers China's relatively unagressive military behavior since Korea and her serious political split with the USSR. In fact, there would seem to have been absolutely no reason not to immediately reduce controls over exports to China to the level enjoyed by the USSR and Eastern Europe.[23]

While China was never very vulnerable to embargo, Cuba was. A small country, Cuba's trade participation ratio is high, in the neighborhood of 30 percent; and Cuba depended heavily upon the United States as a market for sugar and other products and for supplies of machinery and equipment. The embargo certainly hurt Cuba: she lost her sugar market and the source of supply of spare parts to keep her machinery and equipment running smoothly. The Soviet Union was forced to step in and bear a large part of the costs of adjustment. According to Dean Rusk in 1964,[24] the purposes of the embargo were fourfold: to reduce Castro's will and capacity to export subversion to Latin America, to

---

[23] Lest someone should contend that by our embargo we might have influenced China's behavior, recall that China broke with the Soviet Union on political and ideological matters, although at the time this meant disrupting economic relations with the nation which took half of her foreign trade and from whom she had received long-term credits.

[24] Cited by Wilczynski, *The Economics and Politics of East-West Trade,* pp. 376–77.

disenchant the Cubans with Castro, to show other Latin American nations that Communism has no future in the Western Hemisphere, and to raise the cost of Cuba to the USSR. With the exception of the fourth purpose, the embargo would seem to bear little relation to the achievement of these goals.[25] And to a nation willing to spend 10 percent of its GNP on defense, the fraction of one percent required of the USSR to assist Cuba must appear to be a small price to pay for a base in the Western Hemisphere. This is not to deny that the Soviet Union undoubtedly makes her contribution to Cuba with reluctance and would like to devote these resources to other ends. Given Soviet priorities, the Soviet consumer undoubtedly is fractionally (of one percent) poorer for the Cuban affair.

Our embargo strategy does not appear to have had its desired effect in Cuba.[26] In retrospect, there is cause to wonder whether Cuba would not have become another Yugoslavia had the United States treated her revolution with sympathy or even with neutrality rather than with an act of total economic warfare. Had we not severed trade relationships, Castro would have had to think twice before allowing Soviet missile emplacements in Cuba. The threat, at that time, of severed trade relationships with the United States would have constituted a substantial deterrent. Our embargo no longer has deterrent power. In my opinion there is no percentage in treating Cuba differently from other Communist nations.

Extension of Medium- and Long-Term Credits to the USSR and Eastern Europe

Control of credits extended by private businesses or banks to Communist nations lodges in the Johnson Debt Default Act of 1934. This Act prohibited the extension of credits or of financial assistance in any form to any foreign government which is in default on its obligations to the United States. It has since been modified to exclude all nations which are members of the IMF or IBRD. Further, in 1963, in connection with the proposed sale of wheat to the USSR, the Justice Department stated that the Act was not intended to rule out the granting of ordinary commercial credit by exporters—presumably 90-day credits.

With the exceptions of Albania and Bulgaria, all of the European Communist nations are considered to be in default under the Johnson Act. The major items of default, in most instances, are on World War I debts and on Lend-Lease. The Soviet Union's World War I indebted-

---

[25] Witness the recent coup in Peru and the Allende victory in Chile.

[26] Not only was the embargo vitiated by an increase in Soviet Bloc trade and aid, but the nations of Western Europe continued to trade with Cuba despite the imposition of sanctions by the United States. Cf. Gunnar Adler-Karlsson, *Western Economic Warfare, 1947–1967* (Stockholm: Almqvist & Wicksell, 1968), ch. 17.

ness is now considered to be in the neighborhood of $700 million, of which $192.6 million is principal and the remainder accrued interest. The major unsettled item in connection with Lend-Lease refers to deliveries made before V-J Day. Negotiations on the roughly $11 billion worth of wartime shipments bogged down in the early postwar period with the United States asking for an $800 million settlement on the estimated $2.6 billion worth of civilian-type supplies in Soviet custody at the end of hostilities and the USSR offering $300 million.

It is difficult for an economist qua economist to discuss the Johnson Act soberly: its major (and only) purpose at present would appear to be the political one of denying the Communist nations medium- and long-term non-governmental credits. Consider that some 20 nations still owe the United States more than $23 billion in World War I debts[27] (of which roughly half is accrued interest) and that only the Soviet Bloc nations with less than $1 billion of this debt are denied credit; consider also that the nations of Western Europe and Yugoslavia are exempt from the Johnson Act by virtue of having become members of the Bretton Woods organizations, a fact quite unrelated to their debt defaults and to the original concept of the Johnson Act; consider finally that the World War I debt for which the USSR is held responsible was incurred by a hostile government subsequently overthrown by the present government, after which the present government was blockaded by the allies; and that the debts were for a war which the Bolshevik leaders did not believe was in Russia's interest and which they denounced.[28]

It is now 52 years since World War I ended. Many of the nations which owe us money no longer exist. To the extent that there is validity to the concept of "statute of limitations," it would seem to apply to World War I debts. We should wipe the slate clean of these "bad debts." Some day they will have to be forgiven or written off, for they will never be repaid. Or is it possible that in the year 2071 we shall still claim that some 20 nations owe us (with constantly accruing interest) more than $100 billion?

The case against Lend-Lease is somewhat different. The present government of the USSR can be held responsible for Lend-Lease. Further, payment has been within their means and the requested settlement is in fact only a fraction of the original value of the equipment delivered. Nevertheless, Soviet reluctance to pay is not difficult to understand. For while they profited enormously from the lend-lease shipments, by any measure which can be constructed, they incurred greater losses and underwent more suffering during World War II than any other allied

---

[27] Margaret Myers, *A Financial History of the United States* (New York: Columbia University Press, 1970), p. 407.

[28] It is perhaps worth noting that the credit-worthiness of the USSR has been unquestioned in its post-World War II dealings.

nation. Their losses include about 25 million lives, the destruction of most of their major cities, and much of their industrial capital.[29]

On the other side of the picture, Lend-Lease to the USSR certainly saved large numbers of American and Allied lives and resources. In fact, ignoring repayment, Lend-Lease to the USSR was probably the single most profitable investment made by this nation in World War II with the possible exception of the atom bomb. Furthermore—and this applies to the World War I debt also—to ask repayment is in basic conflict with international economic mores as they have evolved in the postwar period. Now, even in peacetime, large grants are made to other nations to assist them to develop and reconstruct. If World War II were to be fought all over again, resources would be shared, not loaned. In fact, a hint of misgivings over the fact that any repayment might be expected is contained in President Roosevelt's Letter of Transmittal to the *Eleventh Report to Congress on Lend-Lease Operations* for the period ending July 31, 1943:

> The United Nations are growing stronger because each of them is contributing to the common struggle in full measure—whether in men, in weapons, or in materials. Each is contributing in accordance with its ability and its resources. Everything that all of us have is dedicated to victory over the Axis powers. The Congress in passing and extending the Lend-Lease Act made it plain that the United States wants no new war debts to jeopardize the coming peace. Victory and a secure peace are the only coin in which we can be repaid. . . .

Like the World War I debt, the Lend-Lease debt would seem to be a purely "political" and in my opinion somewhat hypocritical basis upon which to deny non-governmental credits to the USSR under the Johnson Act. Also, like the World War I debt, the Lend-Lease debt is an anachronism. If recommendations regarding a Lend-Lease settlement were in order, my own would be the following. A recommendation based on purely moral considerations would hardly fail to involve, it seems to me, outright cancellation of the debt. Such a step would be based entirely on the situation during World War II under which the debt was incurred and would not imply approval of Soviet policies and actions since that time. Since moral considerations of this purity are not likely to gain many adherents,[30] however, I would offer a second, more pragmatic course of action. It is unlikely that the USSR will improve on their offer of $240 million. Since under the Lend-Lease Agreement, all

---

[29] In 1924, Louis Marin expressed similar views in the French Chamber of Deputies: "While war still raged, statesmen in every country appealed to the common cause. Some gave their ships, some munitions, some the lives of their sons, some money, and today only those who gave money come saying to us: 'Give back what we loaned'." Herbert Feis, *The Diplomacy of the Dollar, 1919–1932* (New York: Norton, 1966), p. 22.

[30] Such a proposal faces the additional problem that Lend-Lease settlements were collected from other allied nations.

debts are interest-free, it behooves us to accept this offer without undue delay. By accepting the offer, we stand to gain $240 million which might otherwise never be collected. Acceptance of this offer could, of course, be used as part of a package deal in which concessions are made by the USSR on some other policy issue.[31]

The major economic consequence of invoking the Johnson Act with regard to non-governmental credits is to place our businessmen at a disadvantage in Soviet Bloc markets. It is noteworthy that the Western European nations apply no such restrictions to their own nations. It is well-worth devoting a few lines to Western European credit policies. Since 1963, in particular, Western European and Japanese attitudes on this matter have been particularly liberal. Before 1963, credits were usually for less than five years in accordance with Berne Union rules and interest rates were higher than charged non-Bloc customers. Since 1963, long-term credits of 10 to 15 years have commonly been granted on large contracts such as those calling for the construction of large (e.g., chemical and fertilizer) plants and interest rates have fallen in many instances to the 4–6 percent range. These credits have usually been guaranteed by governments or by government corporations; direct government loans have also been extended by a number of nations.[32] Even more dramatic than the extension of credits and loans on favorable terms have been the large number of business ventures which, over the past seven or eight years, have been undertaken jointly by private corporations in Western Europe and nationalized enterprises in Eastern Europe, particularly Bulgaria, Hungary, Czechoslovakia, and Poland. Some of these undertakings are located in the West, others in the East. With the exception of Yugoslavia, Western firms do not have an equity in joint ventures located in the East but do, of course, share in the profits. These ventures have assumed many forms from joint production to joint marketing activities. A major impetus to Western enterprises has been the lower cost and availability of labor in the East plus entrance to protected markets; the socialist nations are interested in the technological, organizational and marketing know-how which is made available as well as the import of capital which is involved in most agreements.[33] Joint ventures have not been concluded with the USSR although Western firms have contracted to construct plants within that nation's borders.[34]

---

[31] The USSR is not likely to be willing to make concessions at this point to get a $240 million as opposed to an $800 million settlement since they are probably satisfied with the *status quo* in which settlement remains in abeyance. However, if at some future date another issue is on the table, a $240 million settlement might be used by the United States for bargaining purposes.

[32] Cf. for example, Wilczynski, *The Economics and Politics of East-West Trade,* ch. 10.

[33] Wilczynski, *The Economics and Politics of East-West Trade,* ch. 15.

[34] An outstanding case in point is the Fiat Auto plant. In contrast, our Government advised the Ford Motor Company in 1970 not to enter negotiations for a similar undertaking.

So, to sum up: U.S. policy on credits to and direct investments in Eastern Europe, like our export control policy, suffers the serious defects of being ineffective in achieving its goal as well as in delivering potential markets to others.[35] However, aside from the ineffectiveness of our policy, a question remains as to whether an absolute denial of credit to Communist nations makes good economic sense on any grounds. This question is discussed directly below and can be taken to apply to governmental as well as non-governmental credits.

The question of credits to the USSR and to Eastern Europe is usually discussed in terms which are not very satisfactory ones to the economist. The question is usually posed in "yes or no" terms rather than in terms of: how much? for how long a period? and at what interest rate? Further, extension of long-term credits, as opposed to commodity trade, is often mistakenly viewed as a form of aid. To quote Dean Rusk:

> While short-term credits are a normal facility in connection with international trade transactions, long-term credits raise different problems. They amount to an extended advance of resources to the purchasing country and, in that sense, they have some of the characteristics of foreign aid.[36]

Let me deal with this latter issue by means of a simple hypothetical numerical example. Suppose a nation borrows $1 million at 4 percent interest which is to be fully repaid in 10 years in a single payment which will amount to $1,480,000. Suppose that the $1 million is invested instantaneously and that the marginal productivity of capital in the borrowing nation is 6 percent. In this case, at the end of 10 years, the borrower will have accumulated an additional $791,000. After repayment, the borrower will have a profit on the transaction of $311,000 over the 10-year period. If the rate of return on capital were 8 percent, the 10-year gain would have been $678,000.

For purposes of comparison, suppose now that a nation is able to export abroad at a 5 percent higher price than at home, and import at a price which is 5 percent below the cost of producing an import substitute. This amounts to a 10 percent profit on balanced trade. Balanced trade in one year of $10 million would generate savings, then, of $1 million which could be invested as above but without the necessity of repayment. The gains over 10 years from this investment would amount to $1,629,000 at a 5 percent marginal productivity of capital;

---

[35] This statement and the analysis of this section apply not only to Johnson Act restrictions but also to the 1968 Fino Amendment to the Export-Import Bank Act. This Amendment prohibits the Bank from providing export credit facilities for trade with nations which are aiding North Vietnam while hostilities with that nation continue. All the Eastern European nations, excluding Yugoslavia, and the USSR fall under this prohibition.

[36] *East-West Trade* (Hearings Before the Committee on Foreign Relations, U.S. Senate, 88th Cong., 2d sess.) (Washington, D.C.: U.S. Government Printing Office, 1964), Part I, p. 15.

$1,791,000 at 6 percent; and $2,158,000 at 8 percent.[37] Or to put it another way, under our assumption, balanced trade of $1,734,000 in one year would provide as large benefits over a 10-year period as would a $1 million loan which has to be repaid in 10 years when the marginal productivity of capital is 6 percent; balanced trade of $3,139,000 is required if the marginal productivity is 8 percent.

What do these figures tell us? The first lesson is that the gains to a borrower from a loan are not necessarily different from trading commodities with him at prices which yield a profit. As a first approximation, it could then be argued that if we are prepared to engage in peaceful trade with a nation, it is inconsistent to not also be willing to extend loans.

In rebuttal, it will be argued that a loan enables the borrower to invest more in the current period than would otherwise be possible. This may well be true, particularly given the "over-full employment" which characterizes the centrally planned economies (CPE's), although usually more savings can be made available, when necessary, by squeezing the consumer a little harder.[38] Granting that it is true, it is nevertheless misleading. First, at the end of the 10-year period the borrower has to repay principal and interest to lender, a transaction typically viewed as a hardship by borrowers. At that point in time, there is a net transfer of resources available for investment from borrower to lender. Secondly, not only are the resources for investment made available at that time to the lender, but unless the lender has been extending credit at a rate of interest which is below the marginal productivity of capital at home, then the lender as well as the borrower is richer than would have been the case had the transaction not taken place.[39]

To sum up: given a time horizon which encompasses a longer period than the immediate present—and except in times of acute international crisis one would expect that our national policies would be framed with such a perspective in mind—then there would not appear, in principle, to be much economic difference between trade with an the extension of credit to another nation. Instead of applying absolute prohibitions on the extension of credits, we should be concerned rather with specifying terms under which the gains from the transaction are properly shared and the risks not undue. So, for example, an intergovernmental $10 billion–4 percent–20 year loan to the USSR would probably be viewed as risky (in terms of repayment), unprofitable, and with potentialities for changing the balance of power. On the other hand, a $500 million–8

---

[37] If the marginal profit on balanced trade were 10 percent, investment would be directed into exports, of course.

[38] Poland in December 1970 constituted an important exception to this statement.

[39] In further rebuttal it might be argued that before the loan is repaid, war may break out. If such a contingency is viewed as probable, of course, one can only admit that it would be imprudent to extend credit.

percent-6 year loan might well be viewed as contributing to our national interest. As far as extension of credit to the Soviet Bloc by private business is concerned, it is hardly likely to be on sufficient scale to matter one way or another. I would favor repealing the Johnson Act and the Fino Amendment to the Export-Import Bank Act, thereby harmonizing our credit and investment policies toward the Soviet Bloc with those of Western Europe.

Restrictions on Imports from Communist Nations: The Most-Favored-Nation Problem

A major purpose of GATT and the use of MFN clauses is to foster non-discrimination in trade and to encourage a lowering of trade barriers[40] and an increase in trade on the basis of reciprocal advantage. The Soviet Bloc nations have been very desirous of being accorded MFN status since, without it, they must sell their products in Western markets at a disadvantage—subject to higher tariffs (and other impediments) than the exports of other nations. The difficulty which arises in admitting these nations to the MFN community is that they cannot reciprocate MFN treatment in the conventional way. They either do not have tariffs to lower or, where two-level tariffs have been introduced by some Communist nations in recent years, application of the lower set of rates has no automatic effect either on domestic prices or on total quantities imported, since prices and quantities are both directly determined by the planners.

Before World War II, the USSR developed an *ad hoc* solution to this problem in bilateral negotiations with individual Western nations by agreeing to increase imports (thereby simulating the effect of a tariff reduction) from any nation in return for MFN tariff treatment from that nation. Since World War II, this arrangement has been employed widely by the nations of Western Europe to extend MFN tariff treatment to the nations of Eastern Europe and the USSR. The United States is a striking exception to this practice. MFN status was withdrawn from all of the Communist Bloc nations in 1951 and restored in 1962 only to Yugoslavia and Poland. Without MFN status, imports into the United States from the remaining Communist nations must pole vault over the very high Smoot-Hawley Tariff of 1930, an almost impossible barrier.[41]

---

[40] This applies to all trade barriers. The discussion here will be confined to tariffs. Other forms of discrimination against Soviet Bloc nations are in the administration of quantitative controls over imports, and in the unwillingness of some Western nations to allow unrestricted transferability of Soviet Bloc holdings of their currencies.

[41] This statement is relevant only to commodities subject to that tariff. Many commodities are not, of course, and on these the Communist nations can compete on an even footing.

Bilaterally negotiated MFN relationships of the kind just described are very far from an ideal approximation of how MFN is supposed to work. For one thing, it is usually not easy to identify the increase in imports which corresponds to a given reduction in tariff rates. This is a minor point, however; presumably the negotiating nations can and do reach agreement. More important, the device fosters bilateralism and is contrary to the "equal treatment" and "anti-discriminatory" spirit of MFN as it has developed under GATT. This is because under bilateral negotiations there is no attempt to ascertain, and perhaps no way to ascertain, whether the increase in imports by the Communist partner truly represents a specific increase in its overall imports or simply a diversion of imports from other Western nations. Furthermore, and related to this point, any Western nation which is a member of GATT would normally expect that if a nation lowers its trade barriers to one GATT member, it will lower them by the same amount to all GATT members. This multilateralization of trade barrier reductions is not involved, of course, in the bilateral negotiations between capitalist and Communist nations.

One way around some of these difficulties was suggested by Alexander Gerschenkron many years ago.[42] He argued that the USSR should enter into negotiations not just with one Western nation but with a large group of them simultaneously. In return for MFN status, the USSR should agree to a global increase in its imports, which increase would be distributed among these nations on a basis of strictly commercial considerations. Apparently this suggestion has been adopted, for it is reported ". . . that Poland was admitted as a full contracting party to GATT upon pledging an annual increment in imports from GATT members of at least 7 percent annually without a time limit . . ."[43] It is well worth noting that under present and foreseeable conditions, a Soviet Bloc nation which is granted MFN status is more likely than not to increase its imports as though it had agreed to an annual global increase—even if it had not. These nations with the exception of the USSR, hold almost no foreign exchange reserves, spending them as they earn them. Since intra-bloc trade is almost always perfectly balanced on a bilateral basis, foreign exchange earnings are spent in the West and presumably on the basis of commercial considerations except when discrimination is enforced by Western trading partners.

Poland's admission to GATT brought to three the number of Eastern European nations which belong. Czechoslovakia and Yugoslavia already were members; Rumania and Hungary are currently negotiating for

---

[42] Alexander Gerschenkron, *Economic Relations with the USSR* (New York: Carnegie Endowment for International Peace, 1945), pp. 37ff.

[43] Michael Kaser and C. F. G. Ransom, "Relations with Eastern Europe," in *Economic Integration in Europe*, ed. G. R. Denton (London: Weidenfeld and Nicolson, 1969), p. 93.

membership. The Polish case does represent something of a breakthrough, however, for the "global quota" principle. Czechoslovakia was a member of GATT before it became a Communist nation and holds its position through "heredity." Yugoslavia is a member by virtue of having converted to market socialism, thereby placing itself in a position to conform to MFN status by conventional means. Presumably, Hungary, with its advanced economic reforms, will attempt to follow the Yugoslav road. Rumania and other Soviet Bloc nations will be admitted, if at all, by the Polish formula. It is worth noting that the United States, presumably obligated as a member of GATT to grant MFN status to Czechoslovakia, does not do so.

The nations of the Soviet Bloc have argued that they are entitled to MFN status. They claim that they do, in fact, grant equal treatment to all nations in trade. In their way of thinking, the long-term trade commitments which characterize intra-Bloc trade and which lead to greater intra-Bloc than East-West trade constitute an advantage to a centrally planned economy of a commercial nature. Hence, the apparent preference of CPEs for intra-Bloc trade cannot be designated discrimination, they argue, since it has a "commercial" base. Further, MFN and equal treatment are not absolutes. Customs unions like the EEC receive exceptional treatment. The less developed nations are allowed to discriminate when in balance-of-payments difficulties. Exceptions are made by advanced nations for protection of domestic agriculture. The U.S. and NATO nations discriminate against the Communist nations under the Export Control and Battle Acts and this is sanctioned by GATT. And so on.

There is certainly some substance to this position. However, there are at least two major difficulties with it. First, when one considers the absolutely gigantic shift in trade patterns which occurred at the time Communist governments were established in Eastern Europe, it is hard to escape the conclusion that this shift was politically motivated and could not be rationalized in terms of commercial considerations. Consider that intra-Bloc trade, which constituted less than 15 percent of the total trade of those nations in 1938, has been between 60 and 75 percent of the total since 1950! Second, it is impossible to verify the importance of commercial considerations in determining the direction of Bloc trade both because these considerations are by and large not quantifiable and because the trade barriers used by the Bloc nations are implicit, not explicit.

Clearly, there will be no easy solutions to the MFN problem unless market socialism comes to predominate among the Communist nations. Institutional differences between systems can only be imperfectly reconciled. Even the "global quota" technique, for example, probably results in some approximation to equal treatment in connection with increments to trade each year but does nothing in the short-run about the discrimination implicit in previously existing trade. Hopefully, as time passes, larger and larger percentages of Polish trade will come to be non-discriminatory. Unfortunately, there do not seem to be any superior solutions on deck at the moment. Given the differences in economic systems, one cannot expect the CPE's to multilateralize all of their trade, to give up their mutual trade agreements, or to institute drastic shifts over a short-time period in trade patterns. The dead hand of the past lies too heavily on their shoulders. At the moment, if Western nations wish to use MFN to expand trade with the East, they can probably do no better than to adopt the bilateral and global quota devices described above.

The United State's unwillingness to negotiate MFN status with the Communist nations (excluding Poland and Yugoslavia) can be analyzed very much in the same frame of reference that we have used to analyze control over exports and capital flows. I think it is fair to say that U.S. policy is basically an act of economic warfare, although from the preceding discussion it is clear that it could be rationalized on technical grounds relating to equal treatment and non-discrimination. In effect, we attempt to hurt the Communist nations, economically, by depriving them of export markets. From this point of view, it is largely equivalent to our export and credit controls. Like these other policies, it is largely ineffective since we pursue the policy without the support of other nations. Further, while the case of Poland is exceptional, the policy generally does not take cognizance of political differences among countries in the Bloc. Thus it would certainly be an act of gross stupidity if this country, after its recent overtures of friendship toward Rumania, and in light of Rumania's independent posture in the Bloc, were unwilling to enter into negotiations toward an MFN agreement with that nation! Finally, of course, our policy does involve an economic loss to ourselves in the form of foregone cheaper or more desirable imports and, in return, foregone exports. While in the short-run these do not appear to amount to much, over the longer-run they might be not inconsiderable.

Dumping

The question of dumping by CPEs is a real one to Western nations for one major reason. Because of planning difficulties, the CPEs often go to the world market to purchase commodities which they happen to run short of because of production failures or sudden changes in plan. To finance these extra purchases, attempts are made to export items which may be in temporary surplus supply or which are allocated to low priority use at home.[44] Additional exports are usually necessary because convertible foreign exchange reserves are very scarce. Because

---

[44] Oleg Hoeffding has written a fascinating account of how the Soviet Union financed emergency imports of wheat in the early 1960s. See his "Recent Structural Changes and Balance-of-Payments Adjustments in Soviet Foreign Trade," in *International Trade and Central Planning*, ed. Alan A. Brown and Egon Neuberger (Berkeley: University of California Press, 1968), pp. 312–36.

exporting is urgent, and because the returns from imports are so great under these bottleneck conditions, exporting becomes profitable even at prices which involve a nominal loss. Under these circumstances, Western markets may suffer disruption. Disruption is worth tolerating of course, where it leads to the long-run supply of a product at lower prices to the purchaser; it is not worth tolerating where it is a one-shot deal—a possibility under the circumstances outlined.

It is almost impossible to tell when a CPE is exporting at below costs of production. It is easy enough, however, to judge when the CPE export price is below the market price of either domestic or other foreign suppliers. This is the comparison which must be relied upon, as a first approximation, to determine whether or not dumping is taking place. This is not sufficient evidence, however. For in order to enter Western markets, even with products which they are prepared to supply on a long-run basis, the CPE nations have often been forced to sell at below Western prices. They do this not out of choice but out of necessity. Fundamentally, the foreign trade combines are profit-maximizers and their orders are to sell at as high a price as possible. They are not interested in market disruption for its own sake.

The problem, then, is to determine whether or not products which are being sold by CPEs at below normal market prices are a normal export or a crisis export. In the latter case, of course, the products should be subjected to a countervailing tariff under our anti-dumping laws. Generally speaking, however, where suspected dumping has been protested by injured enterprises in Western European countries, counter-vailing tariffs have not had to be resorted to—the problems have been ironed out through consultations. This has been particularly true of those Western European nations which have trade agreements with the CPEs. While we should be prepared to use our anti-dumping laws if necessary, it does not seem likely that such drastic action will often be necessary.

II. POTENTIAL ECONOMIC GAINS FROM TRADE LIBERALIZATION

There is a tendency to understate the possible gains to the United States from liberalizing trade with Eastern Europe and the USSR because our trade with them has been so minute. In 1967, for example, our trade with these nations amounted to roughly $200 million each way (of which about 25 percent was with the USSR, just a fraction of one percent of our total trade. In fact, if trade had not been so severely restricted over the past 20 years, the picture would undoubtedly be substantially different. In comparison, for example, Western Europe's exports and imports with the European Communist nations in 1967 amounted to $4.4 and $6.4 billion respectively. It is impossible to say just what part of this trade would have fallen to American enterprise had it not been for the differential between ours and Western Europe's trade and credit controls, but it is not improbable that our exports might by now have reached close to $1 billion annually, our imports somewhat less. John Michael Montias recently pointed out that ". . . if this country could direct the same fraction of its machinery and equipment exports to the area as it did in 1928 these exports would rise from the present $64 million to $606 million . . ."[45] Using a technique which measured our general competitiveness with Western Europe in markets for machinery, equipment, and metals and metal manufacturers in 1962, Mose Harvey came to comparable conclusions.[46] To these can be added, of course, hundreds of millions of dollars of exports of other products, including our agricultural surpluses which could well compete with the very large Canadian and Australian exports to Eastern Europe, the USSR and China. Liberalization of our trade policies toward the Communist nations would enable us to gradually reassert our position in trade with them although it is unlikely that we would ever again recapture the total markets projected above.

Two other possible sources of increased exports exist. The extension of loans on acceptable terms would certainly lead to a roughly comparable expansion of exports. The second possibility is greater trade with the Soviet Bloc at the expense of intra-Bloc trade. As we have already noted, intra-Bloc trade presently amounts to more than 60 percent of their total trade. This is excessive by any measure. Any weakening of political ties within the Bloc or rationalization of foreign trade decisions is bound to increase East-West trade at the expense of intra-Bloc trade. In fact, over the past 10 years, intra-Bloc trade, as a percentage of the total, has declined by about 10 percent. Rumania's trade with the Bloc has fallen by an even larger percentage. The extent of possible gains to the United States at the expense of intra-Bloc trade must not be exaggerated, however. First, we will have to compete with Western Europe for any diversion which develops. Second, any net increase in imports from the West by Bloc nations depends completely on additional sources of convertible currency obtained either through increased exports to the West or loans. The Bloc nations have not been notoriously successful in shifting their exports from East to West. Their competitive abilities have been blunted by the nature of their systems and their 20 years adaptation to meeting each other's needs under long-term trade agreements and in protected markets.

A substantial liberalization of trade controls could provide this nation with a special set of benefits which might be viewed as defense-related.

[45] *A Foreign Economic Policy for the 1970s—Part 6: East-West Economic Relations* (Hearings Before the Subcommittee on Foreign Economic Policy, Joint Economic Committee, 91st Cong., 2d sess.) (Washington, D.C.: U.S. Government Printing Office, 1971), p. 1235.

[46] Mose Harvey, *East-West Trade and United States Policy* (New York: National Association of Manufacturers, 1966), pp. 49–50.

Recall that after World War II, tariffs on imports of watches were presumably designed to protect that industry in order to maintain intact a labor force with specialized skills useful in defense industries in case of war. At present, there is a very high level of unemployment among engineers and scientists who typically are employed in high-technology and defense-related industries. This nation has many peaceful needs to which the talents of these people could be applied. Unfortunately, very little effort is being made along these lines and the situation is apt to get worse rather than better in the forseeable future. Liberalization of trade controls followed by appropriate marketing efforts could provide a subtantial amount of employment for highly skilled workers in these categories and thereby prevent the deterioration of an important American defense-related resources, not to mention the gains to the individuals concerned as they are spared a serious psycho-social as well as economic adjustment.

So far, we have concentrated on the gains to be had from increased exports to the Soviet Bloc. The counterparts of these gains are to be had in two forms: more and cheaper imports and/or an improvement in our balance of payments position. Potential gains from both of these sources are obvious enough not to need elaboration here. It is perhaps worth noting that the nation in the Soviet Bloc from whom we import (as well as export) the most is Poland, the one nation in the group which enjoys MFN status with the United States.

III. SUMMARY OF PROPOSALS

Basically, I am in favor of virtually ending the state of economic warfare which has existed between the United States and the Communist nations since 1945. It is a negative policy which has, in my opinion, not added significantly to the security of this nation. We have little to lose and, possibly, much to gain from adopting positive policies. In fact, because other Western nations refuse to cooperate with us on restricting East-West trade, the major consequence of our policies is to inflict economic losses on ourselves—our business and consumers.

At least two changes should be made in our export control setup. First, Mainland China and Cuba should be put on the same footing as the other Communist nations. The total embargoes on these nations are not achieving desired ends and are politically anachronistic—particularly the embargo on China. Second, I feel that as a minimum we should eliminate the "Cocom differential," that is to say, we should reduce our controls on exports to all Communist nations at least to the same level of stringency as applied by Western Europe and Japan. More stringent controls than those enforced by other nations are ineffective and constitute, in effect, economic warfare by the United States Government against its own enterprises and labor force. Beyond this, I would favor removing export restrictions from all commodities except perhaps those embodying important new military technology and those embodying new technology for which it would be impossible to recover adequate compensation.

I am in favor of not using World War I or Lend-Lease debts as a basis for invoking the Johnson Act of 1934. World War I debts should be stricken from the books as bad debts. We should attempt to reach a settlement with the USSR on Lend-Lease by either accepting her offer of $240 million or offering a settlement which is comparable with terms of settlement offered other allied nations, taking some account of the relative war losses suffered by the different nations. As with export controls, and for the same reasons, our credit and investment policies should be harmonized with those of Western Europe. U.S. private enterprise should be allowed to compete on even footing with enterprises of other nations in the extension of credits to facilitate exports and the construction of industrial plants in Eastern Europe and the USSR. This government should not close the door to extension of credits to Communist nations but should include the extension of loans in its arsenal of diplomatic tools. Loans could be granted to some Communist countries and not to others or, preferably, on more favorable terms to some countries than to others. Adopting an open loan policy does not mean giving away something for nothing; we are after all always free to and should set terms which benefit ourselves economically as well as politically.

We should be prepared to negotiate mutual MFN status with some or all of the Communist nations. This will harmonize our policies with the nations of Western Europe and will also put us in a position to honor our obligations under GATT as more Eastern European nations are admitted, which seems probable in the near future.

The above measures make the most sense for this country when viewed as a package. For example, removal of export controls will probably not increase our exports significantly—but only redistribute them—if our exporters cannot compete on even credit terms with foreign exporters and if the Communist nations are prevented by discriminatory tariffs from earning more dollars.

Since I am an economist rather than a lawyer, political scientist, or politician, my proposals are very general and should be viewed as judgments and sentiments based on economic analysis rather than as specific legislative prescriptions. Further, while my paper as a whole as well as my proposals concentrate on "our" policies rather than "their" policies, I do not mean to imply that we should necessarily take action unilaterally and without an attempt to obtain concessions from the other side. In fact, the most fruitful approach, it seems to me, would be for this nation to enter into commercial agreements with the various Communist nations as envisaged in the proposed East-West Trade Relations Act of 1969 in order to:

. . . promote constructive relations with Communist countries, to contribute to international stability, and to provide a framework helpful to private United States firms conducting business relations with Communist state trading agencies by instituting regular government-to-government negotiations with individual Communist countries concerning commercial and other matters of mutual interest . . .

Under such agreements, this country could provide for: increased markets for the products of both nations; ". . . satisfactory arrangements for the protection of industrial rights and processes; . . . the settlement of commercial differences and disputes; . . . facilitation of entry and travel of commercial representatives . . .";[47] procedures to handle dumping charges; and so forth. Agreements of this sort have long facilitated trade between Eastern and Western Europe. I would hope that we would soon regularize our own economic relationships with the Communist nations in a similar fashion.

IV. POSTSCRIPT: SOME FUTURE EAST-WEST TRADE PROBLEMS

A lot of water has passed over the dam since the first three sections of this paper were first published in July 1971. Political and economic relations with China are rapidly becoming normalized and will no doubt be on roughly the same footing as those with other Communist nations in the very near future. While hard to believe, it is nevertheless a fact that American businessmen are negotiating with Chinese planners in Peking and American tourists are free, as far as our government is concerned, to travel in China and eat Peking duck at its breeding grounds. No less significant, a trade agreement between the USSR and the United States has been hammered out and, if approved by the Congress (in the form of supporting legislation), will mark a significant break with the past. The agreement settles many outstanding issues and problems. Among other things, the Russians have agreed to third-country arbitration of trade disputes and to provide American traders with business facilities in Moscow at least as good as those of other foreign traders and the American Government with an official "U.S. Commercial Office." They have also agreed not to try to export to us commodities which might distress domestic American firms—a way of avoiding the dumping problem. We, in return, have agreed to extend MFN treatment to the USSR, to allow the credit facilities of the Export-Import Bank to be used in trade with the USSR and to otherwise help facilitate a trebling of U.S.-USSR trade over the next few years. The Ex-Im Bank provision was dependent on a settlement of the Lend-Lease account, which settlement was certainly one of the major accomplishments of the trade agreement. From all accounts, Lend-Lease was the toughest nut in the package

---

[47] All quotes excerpted from provisions of East-West Trade Relations Act of 1969.

to crack, with the Russians apparently objecting to U.S. terms (as I did above) on grounds of equity and morality.

They finally agreed to a total payment of interest plus principal of $722 million with the final installment coming due on July 1, 2001.[48] Since the settlement of Lend-Lease was an essential condition to receiving MFN status and large U.S. long-term investments, it could be viewed, economically, as costing the Russians nothing over the short run (while American capital is flowing in) and possibly nothing over the long run, depending on the value to them of MFN and gains from increased trade with the United States. This is undoubtedly one important reason why they finally agreed to settle despite reservations regarding equity and morality.

Although some of the more immediate obstacles to increased U.S.-USSR economic relations have been reduced or eliminated, East-West problems remain. The remainder of this section will be devoted, therefore, to a brief look into some of these problems of the future. The topics to be discussed are: international monetary problems, joint investment projects and inconvertibility, comparative advantage and balance of payments problems, and commercial policies.

International Monetary Problems

If present trends toward economic and political detente continue, there will undoubtedly be interest and impetus, on the part of both Eastern and Western nations, to do something about Bloc currency inconvertibility. Just as the GATT has attempted to adapt its rules to the institutional peculiarities of Communist trade, so it is likely that some attempt will be made to include the Eastern nations in the International Monetary Fund (IMF).[49] Further, mini-moves toward monetary integration are represented by the joint credit operations engaged in by Soviet overseas banks with Western banks and by the admission to the USSR of branches of capitalist banks.

The real question is, however, whether the IMF can admit as full members (or, if admitted, does membership have real significance in the case of) a group of nations which conducts about two thirds of its trade (intra-Bloc trade) on what amounts to a barter basis, whose currencies are as inconvertible as any currency in history, and whose exchange rates are accounting units but not true prices and serve no

---

[48] A White House "Fact Sheet" on the Trade Agreement suggests that the USSR received harsher terms than the U.K. with regard to interest rate, period of repayment and percent of Lend-Lease deliveries which had to be repaid. These harsher terms may be explained by the fact that the British settlement was made 25 years ago when prices were much lower. U.S. Office of the White House Press Secretary, "Fact Sheet: Trade Agreement, Lend-Lease Settlement, Reciprocal Credit Arrangements, Joint U.S.-USSR Commercial Commission," October 16, 1972.

[49] Since this was written, Rumania was admitted to the IMF (December 1972).

function in regular international trade. East-West trade itself is not a really serious problem since the Communist nations are willing to trade at world prices and to use foreign exchange earned in trade with one Western nation to finance deficits with others, i.e., trade is relatively multilateral. In this regard, the Communist nations are not too much different from most small Western nations which conduct the bulk of their trade in key currencies rather than in their own. But East-West trade is strictly bilateral and there appears to be little reason to believe that things are going to change in the near future. Certainly, the establishment in 1964 of a Bank for International Economic Cooperation (IBEC) with its so-called "transferable" ruble had no impact whatsoever on the problem, as could have been predicted.[50] The Comecon "Comprehensive Program" of 1971 says little about problems of inconvertibility and bilateralism and what it does say smacks of wishful thinking rather than effective therapy. As noted earlier, the distinctive feature of the Communist problem is not currency inconvertibility but what has been called commodity inconvertibility. Currency inconvertibility is the garden variety capitalist-type disease and can be cured (temporarily at least) by devaluation. This is not the case with commodity inconvertibility. As we noted, the exchange rate is not a real price in the case of countries which suffer from commodity inconvertibility—hence devaluation is meaningless and has no effect on trade; trade is conducted at world prices regardless of domestic prices and official exchange rates.

The one sure solution to commodity inconvertibility which comes to mind[51] is the drastic one of economic reforms which involve decentralized planning, including the opening up of domestic markets to foreign buyers and sellers and concomitantly, of course, the establishment of rational internal prices organically linked to world prices via a real exchange rate. Such a decentralization would solve the commodity inconvertibility problem fundamentally—by removing its causes. The Hungarian economic reform has involved considerable decentralization of internal transactions, and some rationalization of domestic prices. As yet, however, it has not gone far enough to meet the conditions necessary to eliminate commodity inconvertibility. The reforms of the other Communist nations, particularly that of the USSR, involve even less of a substitution of market mechanisms for direct controls. At this point, it seems highly unlikely that the USSR will adopt far-reaching reforms in the foreseeable future. Their relatively small involvement in international trade (exports/GNP and imports/GNP each less than 4 percent) reduces the impetus from a sector which has loomed large in the reform plans of the smaller Communist nations.

---

[50] Franklyn D. Holzman, "Foreign Trade Behavior of Centrally Planned Economies," in *Industrialization in Two Systems: Essays in Honor of Alexander Gerschenkron*, ed. Henry Rosovsky (New York: John Wiley & Sons, 1966), pp. 237–65.

[51] Other possible solutions were proposed and rejected in the study cited in fn. 50.

The important question which comes to mind is whether it would be possible for any or all of the Eastern European nations to decentralize sufficiently over the next decade to eliminate commodity inconvertibility at the same time that the USSR (and some of the others) did not. My feeling is that it would be impossible unless the USSR were willing to stand by and see the cohesiveness of the Soviet Bloc as a trading group rapidly eroded. Any nation which adopts drastic enough reforms to eliminate commodity inconvertibility is going to be in a position in which its trade decisions will be made by thousands of enterprise managers and on the basis of market criteria. This will automatically lead over time to a substantial diversion of this nation's trade from East to West as the managers find that for the most part they can make much better deals (especially in imports) in capitalist than socialist markets. This result is to be expected since the high level of intra-Bloc trade is due, in the first instance, to state controls over trade, controls which discriminate heavily in favor of other Bloc nations. It might be averted by levying very high discriminatory tariffs against Western suppliers or by the introduction of quotas on Western goods. However, the levy of high discriminatory tariffs or quotas would put the Bloc nations in trouble with GATT; and the introduction of stringent quotas, furthermore, would essentially reverse or substantially weaken the impact of the economic reform on the nation's trade problems. Since the Bloc nations conduct about two thirds of their trade with each other, an economic reform in the foreign trade area only makes sense if this figure is substantially whittled down so that most of the reforming nation's trade is conducted on competitive markets and guided by market criteria. I do not believe that the USSR is ready at present to allow the dissolution of their trading bloc and I feel, therefore, that internal economic reform is not a politically feasible solution to commodity inconvertibility in the foreseeable future. Further thought will have to be devoted to this problem if the Communist nations are to be admitted to the IMF in the near future and are to function as regular members.

Joint Investment Projects and Inconvertibility

There is one other international monetary issue which deserves to be raised, particularly in light of the recent increase in Western capital investments in the USSR and Eastern Europe. It is worthy of note that while East-West (as opposed in intra-Bloc) commodity trade is largely "monetary" and multilateral, East-West joint investment relations are expressed "in kind." That is to say, Western investors typically take their interest, profits, and repayments in the commodities which result from the investment rather than in convertible currencies or gold. While this is simple to arrange in cases in which foreign investment leads to easily exportable stable-valued products (natural gas, petroleum), it is certainly not appropriate to the broad spectrum of possible investments and therefore must be viewed as sub-optimal.

Why is it that while East-West trade is "monetary," East-West investments are not? The major reason would appear to be what amounts in Western trade relations to an exchange rate risk. While the exchange rate risk is a serious one to those who hold the currency and bonds of another Western country, it is minimized for direct investors. The direct investors are largely protected against this risk by the fact that if a devaluation is necessitated by inflation, the probability is good that the value of the investor's holdings will have risen along with the value of everything else. The Western investor in a Communist country receives no such protection and faces problems more similar to those of the Western currency holder. If an investment arrangement with a Communist government were to be stated in monetary rather than real terms, it would have to be denominated in a Western currency (usually the investor's own currency or a "key" currency) since, as noted above, Communist currencies are inconvertible and internal prices are irrational and unrelated to world prices. If prices rise in the country whose currency is being used as medium of exchange and standard of deferred payment, then the investor suffers an equivalent loss (and regardless of whether the exchange rate regime is fixed or flexible) since the value of his investment in the Communist country does not automatically rise commensurately.

In absence of other safeguards (see below), this analysis suggests that the more stable a nation's price level and currency, the more likely would its businessmen be willing to undertake investments in Communist countries with repayment in currency. This hypothesis parallels that of Robert Aliber who argues that a major factor determining the country origin of capitalist direct foreign investment is the relative premium on various currencies: the higher the premium on a currency, the more acceptable and profitable is direct capital investment from the country in question.[52] This parallel should not be stretched too far, however, because the investor in a Communist country is much more vulnerable to loss as a result of chronic inflation in all Western industrial nations. In fact, it is unlikely that Western investors would often accept repayment in Western currency without protection against the exchange (price) risk.

How can such protection be achieved? One possibility is to denominate contracts in gold with payment to be made in an equivalent value of any convertible currency. For this system to provide a proper hedge against inflation, the price of gold would have to fluctuate reciprocally with the values of the various national currencies. This has not been the case. Until recently, at least, par values in gold have changed infre-

---

[52] Robert Aliber, "A Theory of Direct Investment," in *The International Corporation,* ed. Charles P. Kindleberger (Cambridge, Mass.: MIT Press, 1970), pp. 17–34.

quently despite substantial over- and undervaluation of different currencies. Further the relation between the price of gold and various major currencies has been erratic and has, in any case, not reflected movements of internal national prices. For example, the German mark was recently revalued upward against the dollar, which was perfectly proper in terms of the balance of payments positions of the two nations and of the more rapid inflation in the United States. On the other hand the revaluation raised the value of the mark in terms of gold—despite internal price increases in Germany![53]

One other solution to the exchange risk problem is to include in contracts a provision which escalates the value of interest and repayments for price level increases in the nation whose currency is to serve as medium of exchange. This type of inflation hedge device has a long and respectable history.[54] It clearly provides the investor with adequate protection. And the debtor nation is not unfairly disadvantaged by this arrangement since presumably its export earnings in the currency in question will be appropriately increased. There is one caveat to this latter statement, however, and that is that the currency in question must not be substantially overvalued. If it is overvalued, its exchange rate not reflecting the full extent of its price inflation, then the debtor nation will find that its exports to third Western nations will not have risen sufficiently in value to compensate for the price rise in the creditor nation. This problem would not arise, of course, under a floating exchange rate regime.

To sum up, some technique will have to be devised to circumvent the barter-over-time problem if East-West investment relations are to reach a high level of fulfillment.

Comparative Advantage and Balance of Payments Problems

With the signing of the U.S.–USSR trade agreement and the opening up of relations with China again, American businessmen are extremely optimistic over the future of East-West trade. Certainly, the relaxation of trade restrictions by all parties concerned will lead to some increase in mutual trade.

Many observers are concerned, however, by the fact that the Eastern nations seem to want much more from the Western than vice versa. Specifically, they want grain, technologically advanced machinery and

---

[53] Exchange rates reflect capital flows, unilateral transfers, and other factors not directly reflected in commodity prices and this destroys the purchasing power parity relationship between gold and exchange rates of currencies. Even more important, until a few years ago the price of gold in terms of most currencies rose much more slowly than internal price levels.

[54] Cf. this writer's "Escalation and Its Use to Mitigate the Inequities of Inflation," in Joseph Conard and others, *Inflation, Growth, and Employment* (Englewood Cliffs, N.J.: Prentice-Hall for the Commission on Money and Credit, 1964), pp. 177–230.

equipment, and capital (that is they want to buy on medium- and long-term credits). The Western nations are willing to buy light industrial products and over the long-run will be interested in purchasing raw materials, most of which will have to come from the USSR. Without going into greater detail here, it seems clear that Western exports will substantially exceed Western imports over the next few decades (if credits are forthcoming) unless the Eastern nations curb their appetites with import controls. Many economists despair that an East-West trade "equilibrium" will ever be possible and even question the future ability of the Eastern nations to repay any substantial amount of credit.

Like the arguments of the "dollar shortage" school of two decades ago, it is hard to square these conclusions with a foreign trade theory which tells us that every country has a comparative advantage in some products and disadvantage in others. Perhaps the law of comparative advantage has been repealed for non-market economies! Apparently not for the USSR, at least. The two Leontief-paradox type studies done for that nation[55] both show that its trade, in aggregate as well as in particular markets, has factor proportions which make sense in terms of a Heckscher-Ohlin model.

The comparative advantage model is, of course, fairly abstract and, to be useful in interpreting actual phenomena, must be modified for many real world conditions including such obstacles to trade as costs of transport, tariffs, and so forth. There is a major obstacle to Soviet Bloc exports and that is their inability to "sell the product" because of difficulties in adapting to the special requirements of Western buyers, low quality, poor packaging, poor servicing of equipment, inadequate advertising, and so forth. This is not the place to go into these problems in detail. Let it suffice to say here that they are deeply rooted in central planning and have to do with the existence in these nations of perennial seller's markets as well as, in the foreign trade area, with the fact that foreign trade combines rather than producers of exportable products are the ones who are in contact with Western buyers. The result of all this is an asymmetrical frustration of comparative advantage in East-West trade similar to that which would be created if the West levied high tariffs or quotas on Eastern products whereas the East placed no barriers at all on imports of Western products. This is certainly part of the explanation of the poor balance of payments position of the East in East-West trade.

The argument is reinforced by a second related consideration. In the days of the "dollar shortage," it was argued that the problem was partly a result of the great innovative capacity of the United States

---

[55] Carl McMillan, *Aspects of Soviet Participation in International Trade* (unpublished doctoral dissertation, Johns Hopkins University, 1972), and Stephen Rosefielde, *Factor Proportions and the Commodity Structure of Soviet International Trade, 1955–68* (unpublished doctoral dissertation, Harvard University, 1972).

which served to improve its competitive advantage in world markets vis-à-vis Western Europe. In effect, dynamic factors constantly intervened to prevent comparative advantage from asserting its stabilizing influence. More recently, Raymond Vernon, in his product cycle paper,[56] has argued that the innovators quickly lose their markets to lower cost (i.e., lower wage) imitators and, after a few years, find themselves importing products they formerly exported and from the same nations. In terms of our argument, the balance between innovator and imitator is maintained, at least in part, by the innovators' coming forth with new products as fast as they lose old ones. Now the Communist Bloc nations are not notorious innovators. While they do innovate, they have more commonly played the role of imitator. As imitators, they have not been particularly efficient, as have, for example, the Japanese. One does not find Bloc nations firing products embodying a four-year-old technology back to the West as exports. This statement is reinforced by factors mentioned in the previous paragraph. What this suggests is that the Bloc nations are in a constantly moving disequilibrium in terms of dynamic comparative advantage such as was envisaged for Western Europe vis-à-vis the United States some twenty years ago.

A "net comparative disadvantage" could not be the whole explanation in the capitalist market model of trade because, once money and exchange rates are superimposed, it becomes impossible to achieve equilibrium regardless of comparative advantage, via balance of payments adjustment mechanisms. Unfortunately, these mechanisms are not all available to the centrally planned economies, a factor to which must be assigned major responsibility for the balance of payments problems of these nations. Put quite simply, a nation with commodity inconvertibility cannot devalue its currency by altering its exchange rate and thereby improve its balance of payments. As noted above, the Communist nations trade at world prices which are not related to internal prices through their official exchange rates. The official exchange rates are not real prices and changes in these rates have absolutely no effect on trade. A nation which has balance of payments problems and cannot effectively devalue its currency has lost an important instrument variable.

Inability to devalue is not particularly important in the case of imports since a planned economy can always limit imports by imposing quotas. The real problem is with exports—which are a problem in their own right as noted above. At first glance it might seem reasonable to argue that if it is not possible to expand exports by lowering prices through devaluation, why not just simply price exports at below world prices as they would be if devaluation were possible? Unfortunately this recourse is not available either to the Communist nations since they

[56] Raymond Vernon, "International Investment and International Trade in the Product Cycle," *Quarterly Journal of Economics* VoL. XXX, No. 2 (May 1966), pp. 190–207.

would find themselves running afoul of Western anti-dumping laws. Given their irrational prices, it would be very difficult to refute dumping charges even when the commodities in question were not being sold at true loss.

Another factor which in the absence of effective balance of payments adjustment mechanisms creates chronic balance of payments pressures is the fact that the Communist Bloc of nations constitutes, in effect, a relatively high-cost economic region or customs union in comparison with the rest of the world community. This is largely due to their relatively small size, isolation from the world market and policy of concentrating their trade among themselves. Before World War II, the nations of Eastern Europe and the USSR conducted about 15 percent of their trade with each other. In comparison, the comparable percentage in recent years has been between 65 and 75 percent. These figures imply that Comecon is the Communist counterpart of a trade-diverting customs union which leaves its members producing for each other at higher costs than would have been the case had the customs union not been formed. This conclusion is probably deducible also from the fact that the trade and output of these nations are a relatively small part of the world totals and that they therefore produce a smaller variety of products and at a higher cost. If one views Comecon as a small and high-cost enclave in the world economy, it follows that any relaxation of controls or mutual lowering of barriers to trade between East and West will lead to more imports by East than by West. This process will continue so long as the East-West barriers exceed East-East and West-West barriers.

There is still one further explanation of the balance of payments problems of the Eastern nations, namely the chronic practice of "taut" or overfull employment planning. Overfull employment planning means that planned demand exceeds available supplies. Under these circumstances domestic producers and consumers will fight for exportables and more imports and thereby create pressures which, if at all successful, will cause deterioration in the balance of payments. The "absorption" approach suggests that even a devaluation is unlikely to improve the balance of payments under these conditions. Balance of payments "equilibrium" is unlikely to be achieved so long as plans remain so taut.

What is the solution, if any, to the chronic balance of payments pressures? To this observer, it would seem that the only way to eliminate the balance of payments effects of the first four difficulties mentioned above is to institute drastic economic reforms—although some ameliorative action may be possible short of such reforms. In principle, it should be possible to eliminate the fifth—overfull employment planning—even under central planning with direct controls. Nevertheless, it should be noted that although Soviet and East European economists have been aware for at least 15 years of the dysfunctional aspects of "taut" planning, the problem has never been remedied.[57] It should also be noted that the case of Yugoslavia demonstrates that drastic socialist economic reform, while perhaps removing some of the causes of chronic payments disequilibrium, is nevertheless no panacea.

State Trading

As noted above, the next 20 years are likely to see a substantial expansion of East-West trade and investment. Such a development would have been hard to envision 20 years ago not only because of the political climate but because a central concern of the Western nations at that time was to achieve the goal of universal, free, multilateral trade. "Rules of the game" were established by GATT and the IMF and some progress toward the utlimate goal was made.

The great expansion of East-West trade in the past decade and the prospects for future expansion are all to the good. This is especially true of that expansion which has occurred as the result of the dismantling of discriminatory controls. On the other hand, it should be recognized that extension of MFN to the Communist nations does not guarantee non-discrimination. Further, expansion of East-West trade has depended, and will continue to depend, on trade agreements and state trading as a device for bridging the institutional gaps between the two Blocs. These agreements usually involve large package deals including many purchases and sales which are not based on commercial considerations. As Alec Nove has put it, there are Italian but no British cars in Budapest because ". . . the Italians demanded a quota for cars in their bilateral agreement and the British did not."[58] This is not to say that intra-Western trade is simon-pure. Thus, when President Nixon met with the Premier of Japan in September, 1972, he was able to return home with guarantees that the Japanese would buy certain American products and would limit competition in our market of other products! Nevertheless, since Communist Bloc trade is conducted exclusively by state trading bodies, the presumption is that deviations from the "rules of the game" are much more prevalent in East-West trade.

At present the seriousness of this problem is minimized by the fact the East-West trade amounts to less than 5 percent of Western trade.

---

[57] For some possible reasons why, see this writer's "Some Notes on Over-Full Employment Planning, Short-Run Balance, and the Soviet Economic Reforms," *Soviet Studies,* Vol. XXII, No. 2 (October 1970), pp. 255–61. For evidence that the present (Ninth) Soviet Five-Year Plan is too taut, see Gregory Grossman, "From the Eighth to the Ninth Five-Year Plan," in *Analysis of the USSR's 24th Party Congress and 9th Five-Year Plan,* ed. Norton Dodge (Mechanicsville, Md.: Cremona Foundation, 1971), pp. 54–66.

[58] Alec Nove, "East-West Trade," in *International Economic Relations* (Proceedings of the Third Congress of the International Economic Association, Montreal, 2–8 September 1968), ed. Paul A. Samuelson (London: Macmillan; New York: St. Martin's Press, 1969), p. 111.

Should this trade expand rapidly over the next decade, its impact on liberal trading practices and goals could be significant. Clearly some work needs to be done on how to achieve non-discrimination in the context of government trade agreements. And the Western industrial powers should take some time out from competing for Eastern markets in order to develop and agree to adopt a common code of operation in trade with the Eastern nations which conforms as much as possible with the trading principles that have served to guide Western trade conduct in the past.

21. USSR-WESTERN INDUSTRIAL COOPERATION

Kenneth Yalowitz

As the Soviet Union has moved toward a growth policy emphasizing technological change and productivity gains, it has sought increased access to the advanced technology of the West. In exchange for Soviet raw materials such as lumber, oil, and gas, the USSR wishes to obtain the latest Western equipment and production processes. Perhaps the most spectacular example of the import of Western technology in recent years was the construction by Fiat of a complete automobile plant, using largely Western equipment, to produce the Russian Zhiguli car, already described by Imogene Edwards in Selection 14.

In the following article, Kenneth Yalowitz examines the present pattern and future prospects of Soviet industrial cooperation with the West, and its relationship to larger issues of Soviet economic growth. The author is a Foreign Service Officer assigned to the Bureau of East-West Trade in the U.S. Department of Commerce. The selection is reprinted from *Soviet Economic Prospects for the Seventies* (A Compendium of Papers Submitted to the Joint Economic Committee, 93rd Cong., 1st sess.) (Washington, D.C.: U.S. Government Printing Office, 1973), pp. 712–18, with the omission of some source references.

I. INTRODUCTION

THE USSR IN RECENT years has encouraged the conclusion of industrial cooperation agreements with Western countries and firms as a primary means of promoting the larger goal of increased trade and technological exchange. A variety of undertakings is included in the Soviet connotation of the term, ranging from scientific and technical exchange agreements to barter-type industrial and natural resource development ventures.[1]

---

[1] Factual information cited below regarding specific industrial cooperative agreements and projects has been obtained from the following newsletter sources:

Despite the relatively small scale of USSR trade with the industrial Western countries ($5.6 billion turnover in 1971), industrial cooperation could prove the catalyst for a qualitatively significant degree of technological and industrial interdependence.

The USSR's interest in increased economic and scientific interchange with Western countries stems from a combination of political and economic considerations. East-West trade is a building block in the USSR's strategy of peaceful coexistence and probably is viewed as another reinforcement for the political and territorial status quo in Europe. The economic incentives for increased cooperation may be even more compelling for the USSR. Foremost are the twin needs to obtain advanced Western equipment and technology while limiting hard currency expenditures, and to increase exports to convertible currency markets.

Faced with declining economic growth rates over the past decade and difficulties in developing and emplacing advanced technology in other than the military-space sector, the USSR is now looking to the West for the means to modernize key economic sectors, including motor vehicles, chemicals and petro-chemicals, mining and metallurgy, agricultural equipment, computers, and telecommunications. Of particular interest is the specialized Western, especially U.S., equipment and technology suitable for the development of Siberian natural resources, natural gas, oil, and various minerals. These resources are needed, not only to meet growing demand at home and in East Europe, but also as potential hard currency exports. The Soviet leadership's commitment to improve consumer welfare has also led to interest in importing whole plants or processes for the means of consumer goods production.

To sustain the desired level of imports, however, the USSR must increase its exports to the West. As USSR-Western trade has increased, the Soviet Union has incurred persistent annual convertible currency trade imbalances which averaged $240 million in the period 1960–69.[2] Since the mid-1960s, these deficits have been financed mainly by Western medium- and long-term credits. The resultant indebtedness has meant an increasing debt service/export ratio, a factor which industrial cooperation is meant to ameliorate. In fact, a key feature of many industrial cooperation agreements is the commitment of the Western side to market the end product instead of simply providing equipment or a license.

The success of industrial cooperation as a strategy was, of course, contingent on the calculations of many Western countries that increased trade would serve their bilateral interests, vis-à-vis the USSR. In fact,

---

Reuters "East-West Trade News," Moscow Narodny Bank "Press Bulletin," and "Soviet Business and Economic Report."

[2] Robert S. Kovach and John T. Farrell, "Foreign Trade of the USSR," in *Economic Performance and the Military Burden in the Soviet Union* (A Compendium of Papers Submitted to the Subcommittee on Foreign Economic Policy, Joint Economic Committee, 91st Cong., 2d sess.) (Washington, D.C.: U.S. Government Printing Office, 1970), p. 106.

most of the West European countries and Japan eased strategic export controls directed at the USSR in the mid-1960s and, perhaps most significantly, extended the necessary credits to finance Soviet purchases. Only now is the United States adopting a similar approach.

Within this overall framework of mutual willingness to pursue increased economic cooperation, there remained, however, practical constraints largely rooted in Soviet institutional habits. These include the USSR's restriction on foreign equity and management participation and the reluctance to permit foreign onsite project surveys and free movement and access for foreign businessmen and technicians. These factors, combined with the USSR's persistent convertible currency shortages, necessitated novel approaches to secure the desired flow of Western goods and services and to develop new and more diverse Soviet exports. It is within these parameters that the USSR has sought to conclude industrial cooperation agreements.[3] Four general types of agreement appear to be included.

II. FORMS OF INDUSTRIAL COOPERATION

(1) The USSR, first, has sought the conclusion of intergovernmental agreements on economic, scientific, and technological cooperation with Western countries to create an overall framework within which to increase collaboration and set the stage for detailed project agreements. Since 1966, eight such agreements have been concluded by the USSR with West European countries, including France, West Germany, and Great Britain. These generally provide for the establishment of a mixed consultative commission and a number of subsidiary joint working groups which explore possible common ventures. In May 1972 the United States and the USSR signed an agreement which establishes a U.S.-USSR Joint Commission on Scientific and Technological Cooperation and provides for broad scientific and technological exchanges and for possible joint projects.

A variant to this approach is the conclusion of cooperation agreements between major Western firms and the USSR State Committee for Science and Technology, which supervises and coordinates research and development in the USSR. Typically, such an agreement calls for exchanges

---

[3] One point of clarification must be made. Industrial cooperation projects within the USSR (or co-production enterprises, as they are sometimes called) are not joint ventures in the usual Western sense of the term. Neither foreign ownership nor foreign management participation is presently allowed in the USSR. Other East European countries (Romania, Hungary, and Yugoslavia) now have laws which permit minority foreign ownership. Even should the USSR eventually move in this direction, the question would still remain whether the Soviet Union would allow foreign management to exercise decision-making powers over an enterprise which is part of a centrally planned economy. Soviet officials have recently stated that for now Soviet policy will remain intact. (See interview with Dzherman Gvishiani, Deputy Chairman, USSR State Committee for Science and Technology, *Der Spiegel,* May 1, 1972).

of specialists and information, joint research programs, purchases of equipment and technology and licenses for production processes, and specialized consultations. Japanese and European firms have taken the lead in this area, but in recent months several U.S. firms, including General Electric, American Can and Occidental Petroleum, have concluded cooperation agreements with the USSR. Soviet officials apparently hope that such joint research endeavors will lead to joint patenting and sales of licenses and perhaps to joint projects in third countries.

(2) The second type of cooperation is the more conventional process of licensing agreements and importing whole factories or processes. Probably the most celebrated example is the 1966 agreement between the USSR and the Italian firm, Fiat, to build a large automobile plant at Togliatti. Presently, the USSR is also encouraging Western concerns to take on a continuing role in marketing the end product rather than simply selling licenses and equipment.

(3) The third form of industrial cooperation is specifically designed to facilitate exports to Western markets as well as enhance the USSR's industrial capacity.

One method to achieve this goal is the formation of joint or wholly owned companies outside the USSR. Many of these concerns, which now number more than 30, are, in effect, foreign distributorships for Soviet products. Nafta-B, the oldest such operation, was established as a joint stock company in 1967 in Belgium to handle the export of Soviet petroleum products. Russebois is a firm engaged in the purchase and sale of timber and timber products in France. Joint companies have also been established in developing countries, including Ethiopia and Morocco, to promote sales of Soviet machinery and equipment.

A variation in this approach could be termed production-sharing. On a limited basis to date, agreements have been reached which involve partial manufacturing or assembly within the USSR, with the product usually then being marketed by the Western partner. A similar technique has been employed outside the USSR. In Belgium and Nigeria, the USSR has established joint firms which operate facilities to assemble and market Soviet-produced automobiles.

The USSR has also proposed creation of industrial joint ventures with Western firms in developing countries where the question of joint ownership would not present ideological obstacles.

Finally, the USSR is proposing a form of cooperation in which the Western side would provide equipment and technology on credit for an industrial plant in the USSR, but would not receive any equity or supervisory rights as under a joint venture. Repayment of principal and interest would be in product from the new installation at prearranged prices which guarantee a "profit" on the original investment. Long-term contracts, also on favorable terms, to supply product to the Western concern following credit repayment may also be concluded. In short, the USSR would simply allocate a set percentage of the new plant's production for sale to the Western partner at a price which guaranteed an acceptable return on its investment.

The USSR has already negotiated some agreements along these lines and is discussing others, including some with U.S. firms. In late 1972, the USSR and two West German steel firms reached preliminary agreement regarding construction of a steel mill in the USSR. The German equipment, financed by bank credit, would be repaid with deliveries of iron pellets over a 10-year period.

The USSR, conversely, is seeking to export whole plants and equipment to Western countries as part of the industrial cooperative interchange. At the present time, the USSR is supplying equipment for a metallurgical complex being constructed in southern France.

(4) The best-known and potentially most significant form of industrial cooperation relates to natural resource development projects in the USSR, mainly in Siberia and the Far East. Typically the Western firm supplies equipment and technology on credit with repayment, usually deferred until the project is well on stream, in product at prearranged prices. Supply contracts following credit repayment may also be concluded. The immensity of some of these arrangements combined with their potential impact on East-West trade has resulted in their being monitored by top-level Soviet trade officials.

In this category is the series of agreements concluded since 1968 calling for provision to the USSR of more than $1.2 billion of large-diameter steel pipe on credit by West European countries (Austria, West Germany, Italy, Finland, and France) in return for long-term natural gas deliveries; and two USSR-Japanese deals to develop timber resources in the Soviet Far East and Siberia. Japan agreed to provide some $190 million in timber-production equipment in return for timber and wood chips.[4]

Under the various natural gas deals, the USSR will supply West Europe with approximately 18 billion cubic meters of natural gas annually after 1975. Some of the deals amount to a simple barter of gas for pipe, but at least two, those with Italy and Austria, will earn an estimated combined total of about $90 million annually once the original credits are repaid. The USSR is using the imported steel pipe, mainly of 48 and 56 inch diameter, to construct a pipeline from the gas source in West Siberia to West Europe, a distance in excess of 5,000 kilometers.

Negotiations for these deals have generally been prolonged. The USSR, in effect, seeks to turn its position as a raw material exporter and machinery importer to advantage by demanding high product prices and credit terms of about 6 percent interest at a minimum of five to eight years. Some of the deals, reflecting Soviet sensitivities on the matter, have involved concessionary interest rates which, however, have

---

[4] For an analysis of USSR-Japanese cooperation in Siberia, see Kiichi Saeki, "Toward Japanese Cooperation in Siberian Development," *Problems of Communism*, Vol. XXI, No. 3 (May–June 1972), pp. 1–11.

usually been recouped in the form of higher equipment prices. The deals have all been sizeable, ranging from $100 million to in excess of $1.5 billion turnover for the USSR-West German gas-pipe agreements of which there are now two.

The major Soviet contribution to such projects, in addition to local costs, is the natural resources which might otherwise not get to market for years for want of Soviet capital and technology. Indeed the Soviet negotiating position has generally been that the Western side must provide financed equipment if it expects to receive the natural resources. Only then could the requisite Soviet investment be factored into future plans. Any other arrangement, it is held, would disturb present investment plans and priorities. Viewed from this perspective, the USSR's desire to encourage Western governments to take a role in financing these projects not only reflects its preferred way of doing business but also the desire to obtain an added guarantee for the successful implementation of the project.[5]

The Soviet bargaining stance, however, does not fully take into account the USSR's intrinsic interest in Siberian development, principally for strategic purposes. A priority development project, the construction of a pipeline from the Tyumen oilfields in West Siberia to the Port of Nakhodka in the Soviet Far East, would facilitate servicing military as well as civilian installations in the Eastern USSR.

United States firms recently have been involved in discussing possible resource development projects, including the multibillion dollar development of natural gas and oil resources in the Tyumen province of Siberia and natural gas development in the Yakutsk region.

III. THE USSR'S PERSPECTIVE

Industrial cooperation is a strategy designed to limit some of the financial and political ramifications resulting from increased trade with Western countries. It aims at reducing the USSR's convertible currency trade imbalances and winning access to specialized technological and scientific equipment and information while at the same time husbanding Soviet investment resources. Indeed, some of the large-scale industrial and natural resource "barter"-type projects could produce a short-term negative balance of payments effect for the Western country partner since the initial capital outflow would not be repaid for several years under the usual extended repayment terms. The USSR, however, is cognizant of this problem and appears willing to spend returns derived from sales after repayment is completed for goods produced by its trading partner country, thereby reducing this concern.

---

[5] In fact the financial requirements for some of the natural resource projects may be so large that even though the matter is expected to be handled primarily by Western private capital, government involvement would also seem to be warranted.

Politically, industrial cooperation appears acceptable to a broad range of Soviet interest groups. For Party bureaucrats, it represents the means to modernize the economy without the necessity for major systematic modifications. In fact, until now the attraction for Western countries of political returns and of the "untapped" Soviet market, combined with the growing Western natural resource import needs, have allowed the USSR to deal basically on its terms. For Soviet technocrats and managerial groups, industrial cooperation offers increased economic and scientific exchange with the West and the prospects of introducing more efficient techniques into the Soviet economy.

IV. POSSIBLE OBSTACLES?

Notwithstanding the USSR's relative success to date in concluding industrial cooperation agreements, several practical problems could impinge on the future outcome of the strategy.

Conclusion of the cooperative industrial and natural resource development deals depends on the Western concern's willingness to forego formal ownership or management rights, to rely on sometimes incomplete or inaccurate Soviet technical data, and to accept repayment in the particular product (at a set price) over an extended period. These arrangements have sufficed in the past. Still upcoming, however, are the negotiations, primarily by U.S. and Japanese firms, on large-scale participation in Siberian development. The USSR is apparently calculating that Western resource needs and the competition for new markets, combined with its own official guarantee of the terms of such projects, will enable it to sustain its bargaining terms. Ultimately, the Western firms' decisions will be made essentially on economic criteria, but with an eye toward the prevailing political situation. Negotiations will likely be extended and complex. Should the Soviet terms prove unacceptable, the USSR could be faced with the choice of making some modifications in favor of potential investors or of risking a possible lower level of Western involvement.[6]

Should the large-scale cooperation agreements be concluded, the USSR must still mobilize the financial, administrative, construction, and logistical resources needed to complete its share of the undertakings. Undoubtedly these projects would receive top priority in view of their hard currency earnings potential, but the necessary coordination on schedule of the inputs of several ministries is a potential problem.

---

[6] Recent developments indicate that such problems can be resolved to the satisfaction of the Western partner. On April 12, 1973, an agreement was concluded between the USSR Ministry of Foreign Trade and the Occidental Petroleum Co. This agreement provides for cooperation in the establishment in the USSR of a manufacturing, storage and transportation complex for chemical products, and for mutual supply of superphosphoric acid from the U.S. in exchange for ammonia, urea, and potash from the USSR.

If industrial cooperation proceeds on a broad scale, it will inevitably mean an expanded Western technical and commercial presence in the USSR. Increased opposition from ideological conservative elements is thus also possible.

Finally, in the area of scientific and technological cooperation and exchanges, both sides must continue to perceive tangible benefits if a long-term fruitful relationship is to evolve.

V. CONCLUSION

Industrial cooperation is the USSR's primary method of expanding on a long-term basis trade and technological cooperation with the West. As Premier Kosygin stated in his report on the Ninth Five-Year Plan (1971–75) to the Supreme Soviet on November 24, 1971:

> New possibilities are being opened up in our relations with the countries of the West as we undertake the conclusion of long-term agreements that ensure regular orders for industry. Consideration can be given to mutually beneficial cooperation with foreign firms and banks in working out a number of very important economic questions associated with use of the Soviet Union's natural resources, construction of industrial enterprises, and exploration for new technical solutions. We are convinced that diverse forms that are in the interest of all participants can be found for carrying out this cooperation.

Implicit in the Soviet strategy of industrial cooperation is not only a commitment to the international division of labor but also a growing recognition that in the future the base of national power will be determined more by economic and technological criteria than by military hardware computations. In this sense, industrial cooperation represents the USSR's tacit acknowledgment that a strategy of economic autarky is impossible in an era of rapid technological change.[7] More specifically, it reflects a growing interest in producing for the export market and in mastering, or at least better utilizing, Western marketing techniques.

The prerequisites exist for a substantial expansion of East-West trade based on Soviet machinery and equipment import needs and the USSR's natural resources for potential export to Western markets. Unless the USSR can increase its exports to the West, however, it may not be able to sustain its desired level of imports. Its success in this matter may well be linked to imports of Western equipment and technology. Ultimately, then, the decisions of Western firms and countries on industrial cooperation with the USSR could hold a vital key to the development of East-West trade.

---

[7] Already at the 23rd CPSU Congress in 1966 Premier Kosygin had stated: "In our time it is becoming more and more evident that the scientific and technical revolution under way in the modern world calls for freer international contacts and creates conditions for broad economic exchanges between socialist and capitalist countries."

22. SOVIET FOREIGN AID: SCOPE, DIRECTION, AND TRENDS

Leo Tansky

Like the United States, the Soviet Union uses foreign aid to enhance its political, military, and economic position. The bulk of Soviet aid to the non-Communist less developed countries of the "Third World" has gone to the Middle East, South Asia, and Africa, in pursuit of these goals. In recent years, however, the USSR has made increasing use of foreign aid agreements to create markets for Soviet machinery and equipment and to secure imports of fuel, raw materials, and consumer goods. This change in the aid program is part of the reorientation of Soviet economic policy toward greater efficiency in resource allocation and greater involvement in international trade.

The following selection analyzes the size and nature of the Soviet economic and military aid programs in the Third World. For comparison, it also includes statistics on Soviet economic aid to other Communist countries. Leo Tansky is an economist in the Office of Economic Research of the Central Intelligence Agency. The article is reprinted from *Soviet Economic Prospects for the Seventies* (A Compendium of Papers Submitted to the Joint Economic Committee, 93rd Cong., 1st sess.) (Washington, D.C.: U.S. Government Printing Office, 1973), pp. 766–76, with the omission of a table and some footnotes.

I. INTRODUCTION

THE USSR HAS EMPLOYED foreign aid as the primary instrument for promoting its interests in the Third World for almost 20 years.[1] Throughout these years, Moscow's basic objectives have remained largely unchanged—to erode Western influence and substitute its own; to counter the Chinese challenge to Soviet "leadership" of the national liberation movements; and to convince Third World countries that socialism (i.e.,

---

[1] The terms Third World and less developed countries (LDCs) are used interchangeably in this paper and include the non-Communist countries of Asia, except Japan; Africa, except the Republic of South Africa; and Latin America.

453

Communism) offers the only solution to their economic problems. The Soviet Union has made available some $16.7 billion of economic and military aid since 1954 in pursuit of these goals.

Tactically, Moscow's program also has not changed much throughout the two decades. Economic and/or military aid continues to be used where appropriate to establish, maintain, and expand the Soviet presence in aid-receiving countries. In the initial years of the program, economic aid was used to gain entry to such South and East Asian countries as Afghanistan, Burma, Cambodia, India, Indonesia, and Sri Lanka (Ceylon). Military aid was used in the Middle East, and not until Egypt, Iraq, Syria, and Yemen (San'a) signed arms accords with Moscow did they receive economic aid.

II.   IDEOLOGICAL FOUNDATIONS

Although military aid usually has the greater immediate political impact, Moscow considers the economic aid program more important in forging long-run ties with Third World countries. The economic aid mechanism is a conduit through which flow the materials, personnel, and ideas that Moscow hopes will encourage the growth of socialist institutions in aid-receiving countries and their ultimate "transition to socialism."

During Khrushchev's regime, Soviet theoreticians held that Moscow's aid was encouraging its aid recipients to pursue a "non-capitalist path of development" and to achieve the status of a "national democratic state." The concept emerged during one of Moscow's early ideological gyrations to justify its aid to military dictatorships and other "non-progressive" regimes. To achieve the status of a national democracy a country had to nationalize private investment and generally expand the state sector; pursue an anti-imperialist (i.e. anti-Western) foreign policy; establish extensive economic and cultural relations with socialist countries at the expense of the capitalist nations; and permit the "working class in alliance with the peasantry and progressive elements" to participate in the country's political and economic activities. Egypt (also Algeria, Iraq, and Syria to varying degrees) was held up as a prime example of a former colonial country which, with the aid of the "socialist camp," was proceeding along the proper path.

Khrushchev's euphoria has not been shared by his followers. They have been less sanguine about such achievements in the near future, particularly after the demise of such "revolutionary democrats" as Ben Bella, Keita, Nkrumah, and Sukarno, the massacre of Sudanese Communists by a leftist regime in Khartoum, and the ouster of Soviet military personnel from Egypt—Moscow's favored aid client. Nevertheless, Soviet literature still expounds on the use of aid to achieve Khrushchev's goals. One no longer sees the emphasis on the national democratic state, but theoreticians still claim to judge progress in terms of nationalization, expansion of relations with the "socialist camp," and the domestic roles played by "progressive elements."

III. THE ECONOMIC AID PROGRAM

Magnitude and Direction

Since 1954, the Soviet Union has extended about $8.2 billion of economic aid to 44 less developed countries (LDCs). Nearly 75 percent of the total aid committed has gone to Middle Eastern and South Asian countries (see Table 1). Afghanistan, Egypt, India, Iran, Iraq, and Turkey have been allocated about 65 percent.

TABLE 1
Extensions of Soviet Economic Aid to Less Developed Countries, by Area, 1954–72 (millions of U.S. dollars)

	1954–72	1954–60	1961–64	1965	1966	1967	1968	1969	1970	1971	1972
Africa.	1,236	209	535	28	77	9	–	135	51	192	–
East Asia	154	124	23	3	4	–	–	–	–	–	–
Latin America	445	30	–	15	85	55	2	20	56	38	144
Middle East	3,336	880	549	84	422	200	178	287	76	418	242
South Asia	3,025	969	475	286	656	5	194	20	11	214	195
Total	8,196	2,212	1,582	416	1,244	269	374	462	194	862	581

The Khrushchev Years, 1954–64

As the Soviet economic aid program has grown, it has experienced severe annual fluctuations and periodically undergone structural changes. Largely Khrushchev's creation, the program during its first decade reflected his flamboyant style. He offered aid to any willing country and generally extended umbrella type credits before agreeing on specific projects. The early years were largely ones of initial penetration—years in which Moscow sought to manipulate the "neutralist spirit" of the Bandung Conference of 1955. Aggregate economic aid commitments were not large and went mainly to Asia.

The program underwent its most rapid expansion during 1958–61 and assumed the basic character that still prevails. More than $2 billion were extended, about $855 million in 1959 alone—still one of the largest years for new Soviet commitments. More significant was Moscow's willingness to commit funds for national economic development plans. About $1.8 billion were provided for the development of Afghanistan, Egypt, India, Indonesia, and Iraq. India alone received pledges of about $550 million; Egypt, $500 million. Soviet-African relations also developed rapidly in these years with the first aid extensions to Ethiopia, Ghana, Guinea, Mali, Somalia, Sudan, and Tunisia.

The level of commitments dropped sharply in 1962–63, to an annual level of about $150 million. This decline was almost wholly the result of the huge backlog of commitments built up in previous years. Extensions bounced back to $825 million in 1964, the last year of Khrushchev's rule. Moscow responded quickly to opportunities for further participation in Egyptian and Indian development programs and, to a lesser extent, to the Chinese challenge to Soviet influence among Afro-Asian countries.

The Post-Khrushchev Era

After Khrushchev's fall from power in 1964, his successors adopted a more conservative style in foreign aid. Moscow became more cautious in announcing specific credits before cost surveys were completed, more selective in its recipients, and more inclined toward countries that could absorb economic aid at a satisfactory pace. Since 1964, about 80 percent of Soviet aid has been concentrated in countries which form an arc running from the eastern Mediterranean, through the Red Sea, to the Arabian Sea. The conclusion of large economic aid agreements with Iran and Turkey was particularly gratifying to Moscow because it marked Soviet entry into countries belonging to Western military alliances.

Africa became secondary in Soviet policy considerations. Whereas Khrushchev committed about 20 percent of Soviet economic aid to Africa, his successors have extended only 10 percent. And about half of that has gone to Algeria and Morocco. Some aid resources have been allocated to Latin America in recent years as opportunities have opened in Chile and Peru.

Sectoral Distribution

Soviet aid always has had a large industrial content. The emphasis on this sector has become even more pronounced in recent years. Perhaps as much as 65 percent is being channeled into industrial projects compared with half during the mid-1960s. About $1.7 billion, or more than 20 percent of total Soviet aid, has been committed for the construction of steel plants. Moscow has extended about $420 million for the construction of the Iskenderun steel mill in Turkey, which now outstrips in aid costs China's $400 million for the Tan-Zam Railroad and Moscow's $325 million for the Aswan High Dam.[2] More than 15 percent of Soviet aid has gone for agricultural and multipurpose projects, 10 percent for mineral development, and 10 percent for transportation facilities. Less than 5 percent has been provided in commodities and foreign exchange.

---

[2] In March 1973 Moscow extended nearly $190 million to expand Iran's Isfahan steel plant. This commitment raises to $500 million the amount allocated for the plant, making it the costliest Communist aid undertaking.

Drawings on Soviet Aid

Although the annual level of Soviet extensions has fluctuated, aid expenditures have risen almost constantly. More than $4 billion—or half of total aid commitments—had been drawn by the end of 1972. About $1.2 billion were spent during 1969–71 with a peak of $420 million reached in 1971. Aid outlays during 1972 fell to around $400 million because of lower levels of project construction in Egypt, India, and Iran. The fact that Afghanistan, Egypt, India, and Iran account for nearly two thirds of total drawings but about half of total extensions indicates the slow overall progress of Soviet programs.

The difficulties Moscow encounters in most LDCs are common to all aid donors. Most cannot absorb project type aid rapidly because they lack adequate skilled and professional personnel, possess primitive infrastructures, and fail to acquire sufficient funds to finance the local costs of these projects. However, the character of the Soviet program compounds these problems because it makes no provision for local cost financing. Although the aid-receiving countries' share of project expenditures often is as high as 50 percent, the USSR had provided only about 5 percent of its total aid in the form of commodities to be sold locally for local currency to cover those costs.

The success Moscow has achieved in pushing forward its programs in Egypt, India, and Iran reflects their greater absorptive capacity in terms of available financial and human resources. The rapid rate of project construction in Afghanistan stems from Soviet willingness to provide large numbers of professional, administrative, and technical personnel in conjunction with a commodity aid program to raise the local currency for Soviet projects.

Terms and Repayment of Economic Aid

The terms of repayment for Soviet economic aid generally fall into two categories. The largest consists of development project credits which call for repayment over 12 years at 2.5 percent interest, usually beginning one year after the project is completed. Occasionally, a longer repayment period is allowed, such as 19–24 years and 6–8 years grace for some credits to Afghanistan. The second category covers trade credits with 8–10 years to repay at slightly higher interest rates. Only 5 percent of Soviet aid has been provided as grants.

As deliveries of goods and services under credits have expanded, aid repayments by the LDCs also have increased. By the end of 1972, an estimated $1.4 billion had been repaid on the more than $4 billion in economic aid obligations incurred by LDCs. Most of these repayments have taken place during the past six years. Such payments totaled an estimated $10 million in 1959, jumped to more than $100 million in 1967, and reached a peak of $260 million in 1972.

The rising volume of repayments in the face of slower rising aid deliveries has narrowed the net Soviet aid outflow. It dropped from $225 million in 1970 to $140 million in 1972, lessening the already light aid burden on the Soviet economy. The net aid outflow in 1972 represented less than 0.03 percent of Soviet GNP.

IV. TECHNICAL ASSISTANCE

Economic Technicians

An important part of Moscow's aid activities is the provision of technicians to compensate for shortages of technical, administrative, and managerial personnel needed to implement its aid projects. Such personnel generally supervise construction, assemble machinery and equipment, and train local counterpart technicians. There also are large numbers of nonproject technicians working as doctors, teachers, and advisors to official organizations.

As the pace of early Soviet aid activities quickened, the numbers of personnel sent to the LDCs grew rapidly. In 1955, an estimated 400 technicians were located in LDCs; in 1958, more than 1,600; and in 1962, about 8,700. Since 1965, the number employed has fluctuated between 10,000 and 12,000.

The services of project-type technicians generally are dispensed within the framework of specific project credits, thus resembling the technical services made available by Western contractors. Expenditures for the services of Soviet technicians consume some 15–20 percent of the project credit.

The foreign exchange costs of Soviet technical services usually include salaries, round-trip plane fare, leave accumulated at a rate of about three days per month, round-trip fare to spend leave in the USSR, and life insurance premiums. If a technician brings his family, the recipient country must pay their round trip fares and a family transfer allowance. The host country also is responsible for such local expenditures as medical care, hospitalization, office space, local transportation, and furnished quarters.[3] These services are costly, especially in contrast to Chinese and most Western technical assistance, which is largely grant aid.

Technical and Academic Training in the USSR

In addition to on-the-job training provided at construction sites and technical training in Soviet-built centers in the host country, Moscow also accepts local personnel for training in the USSR. This type of train-

---

[3] For sample agreements with such detail see Klaus Billerbeck, *Soviet Bloc Foreign Aid to the Underdeveloped Countries* (Hamburg: Hamburg Archives of World Economy, 1960). Although the publication is somewhat dated, the contract requirements have not changed.

ing consists mainly of six to twelve month programs at industrial facilities and partly of specialized training of up to three years at Soviet technical institutes. Perhaps 15,000 LDC personnel have received such training. Some 31,000 Third World students also have gone to the USSR for academic training since 1955—about half from Africa—under Soviet scholarships.

V. MILITARY ASSISTANCE

In the short run, military assistance continues to be the more dynamic of the two main elements comprising Moscow's foreign aid program. Because of the political framework within which such accords are concluded, Moscow becomes associated with the recipient's security needs and national aspirations. Current agreements, however, no longer create the shock waves in Western capitals that they once did. Soviet military sales flow into the lucrative Third World arms market which currently runs at $2.5–3 billion annually from all sources.[4]

Since 1955, the USSR has made available about $8.5 billion of arms aid (see Table 2). Some 95 percent has gone to eight countries—about 70 percent to Egypt, India, Indonesia, and Iraq.

TABLE 2
Extensions of Soviet Military Aid to Less Developed Countries, by Country, 1955–72
(millions of U.S. dollars)

Egypt	2,685
India	1,220
Indonesia	1,100
Iraq	1,000
Syria	715
Iran	480
Afghanistan	455
Algeria	395
Other	425
Total	8,475

Because the Soviet military aid program responds to opportunities presented by regional conflicts and LDC internal security needs, its flow is highly erratic. Nearly 30 percent of total commitments occurred in 1970–71, reflecting the large Egyptian air defense build up, Indian preparations for war with Pakistan, Syrian and Iraqi tensions with Israel, and Iraqi concern over Iran's arms acquisitions. These four Soviet arms clients acquired some $2 billion of arms during those two years.

---

[4] U.S. Arms Control Disarmament Agency, *The International Transfer of Conventional Arms, an Interim Report to the Congress, January 1973* (Washington, D.C.: U.S. Government Printing Office, 1973). The $2.5–3 billion does not include arms aid to Indochina.

Another feature of the program which keeps its annual level high is the constant upgrading of weapons systems and replacement of worn out equipment. The less complex MIG–15 and –17 fighter aircraft are being replaced or supplemented with various versions of the MIG–21 and the SU–7 fighter bomber; T–34 tanks with T–54 and T–62 tanks; conventional antiaircraft artillery with SA–2, SA–3, and SA–6 surface-to-air missile systems. Such cycles are likely to continue since Moscow is prepared to provide most types of arms except nuclear and strategic weapons.

These new generations of weapons are not only expensive but also highly complex. Consequently, Moscow must maintain a large number of advisers and technicians in the LDCs to train indigenous personnel in the use and maintenance of those arms. For the past several years, an estimated 10,000 Soviet military personnel have been stationed abroad to perform these functions. In addition, as many as 2,000 LDC personnel have been going to the USSR annually for training not available at home.

VI. MOSCOW'S ECONOMIC BENEFITS

While political and ideological considerations continue as the dominant motivations for Soviet aid, in recent years there has been a surge in agreements generated by Moscow's economic requirements. All indications point to a rapid growth of these accords, e.g., joint projects and beneficial aid and trade arrangements.

The dam built on the Aras River between Iran and the USSR is providing electric power and water irrigation to both countries. Soviet assistance for the Kindia bauxite deposits in Guinea will be repaid in bauxite. Soviet-built pipelines in Afghanistan and Iran are carrying natural gas to the USSR as aid repayments; gas which Moscow is purchasing at the low prices of $5.70 to $6.60 per 1,000 cubic meters.[5] The gas is supplementing dwindling supplies in the Azerbaijan and Turkmen Republics and saving Moscow the distribution costs of piping it in from distant fields in Central Asia. A second pipeline is being built in Afghanistan and another is planned in Iran.

The Soviets also profit from the assistance they provide for building port facilities and developing fishing industries. The Soviet-built shipyard at Alexandria provides repair facilities for Soviet vessels and is building merchant ships for the Soviet Union as payment. Soviet aid to fisheries is repaid in storage and repair facilities, food and fuel supplies, and shore privileges for Soviet crews. These services enable Soviet vessels to operate for longer periods before returning to their home ports.

---

[5] The price for Soviet gas to be delivered to Western Europe is about $12 per 1,000 cubic meters.

Moscow has such access to ports in Chile, Peru, Senegal, Guinea, Algeria, Egypt, Sri Lanka, and Bangladesh.

Of particular significance is Moscow's assistance to Middle Eastern oil development, for which the Soviets are providing nearly $450 million of aid. The USSR supports the establishment of national oil companies in these countries, and hopes to develop additional sources of supply to meet its own expanding export requirements. By 1980, Soviet oil production may not be adequate to meet domestic needs and still (*a*) fill most of Eastern Europe's requirements and (*b*) maintain exports of oil to Western Europe.[6] Imports of Soviet crude by East European countries have doubled since 1965, and Moscow already has advised these countries to find supplemental sources of oil in the Middle East.

The recently opened North Rumaylah oil fields in Iraq are being developed with some $200 million of Soviet aid. This aid will be repaid in crude oil that probably will be reexported to other Communist countries. East European countries have provided an additional $100 million for Iraq's petroleum development, also to be repaid in oil. They also will receive Iranian oil as repayment for economic aid.

In addition to aid repayments in oil, the USSR and Eastern Europe are purchasing Middle Eastern crude commercially. By 1975, shipments on Soviet and East European account will reach 35 million metric tons annually under both arrangements. Although these shipments represent only a small part of Soviet requirements, they will equal about one third of East European consumption in 1975.

Aid repayments and trade in other goods also are becoming significant. Soviet imports of manufactured goods, largely from newly created industries, have grown from almost nothing to about 20 percent of Moscow's imports from LDCs. These imports—much of them from Soviet-built plants and not marketable in the West—include tractors, industrial machinery, aluminum products, rolled steel, wire, automobile stampings, clothing, fabrics, footwear, furniture, and other consumer goods. About 45 percent of the Soviet imports from India in 1971 were manufactures, as were 40 percent of its imports from Egypt and 25 percent of its imports from Iran. Moscow is willing to import large amounts of these goods because they help LDCs repay their aid debts, use much of the unused capacities of Soviet-built plants, and help the USSR meet some of its domestic demand for such goods. As one Soviet author points out:

> Soviet purchases of their traditional exports and of products of their young national industries are of great importance for this group of countries. Our economic ties with these countries have also begun to play a greater role in solving the Soviet Union's national economic tasks. Our

---

[6] The USSR already has run into production difficulties. Output in 1972 was well below the planned goals. This could lead Soviet planners to look for supplementary sources outside the USSR much sooner.

increased purchases in these countries, and the delivery of their products in repayment of Soviet credits, enable the USSR to organize a better supply of many types of raw materials for foodstuffs and consumer goods for its population.

Along the same lines, another states:

> The resources received in redemption of the credits and in payment of interest are utilized by Soviet foreign trade organizations for the purchase in India of tea, wool, jute, coffee, tobacco, as well as rolled ferrous metal, products of engineering plants, and manufactured consumer goods. The Arab Republic of Egypt redeems Soviet credits with such traditional Egyptian exports as cotton, yarn, fabrics, and rice as well as the products of enterprises built with Soviet assistance—ferrous metals, stampings, parts for automobiles and tractors, and other goods.

VII. PROSPECTS

The aid program will remain a major element in Soviet policy toward the Third World. The program remains the only effective tool for expanding Soviet influence in these countries and for countering the influence of other major powers. New extensions of economic aid will rise and fall in response to new opportunities and Soviet short-run economic capabilities. Large sums probably will be made available to Egypt and India over the next few years as these countries move into their next development programs.

Heavy emphasis also will continue to be placed on military aid because of its greater political impact and the immediate dependence it creates. The political setback in Egypt did not result from Moscow overplaying its hand but from its unwillingness to become more involved. The Moscow-Cairo arms relationship has shown that the Kremlin's primary interests are in Western Europe, China, and the United States and that it will not permit the secondary concerns to determine its relations with the major powers. It is likely that, on balance, Moscow was relieved with the end of what it probably considered an overcommitment in Egypt and the return to a normal aid relationship.

Economic returns are not likely to be a major concern in Moscow's policy considerations over the near term. Nor is it likely that the Soviets will permit economic dependency to develop. And yet, Soviet literature frequently refers to the developing international specialization of labor of socialist countries with the Third World, a policy that appears to be emerging in the increasing volume of Soviet imports of goods produced in Soviet-built plants. The development represents a significant trend in Soviet policy in the LDCs, a trend that is more likely to establish long range abiding Soviet-LDC ties than any of Moscow's other foreign policy tools.

VIII.   CONCLUSIONS

Since 1954, the Soviet Union has made available $16.7 billion of economic and military aid to Third World countries. More than $11 billion have been spent. About 70 percent of the aid committed has gone to six countries; 40 percent to Egypt and India.

The basic objectives of the USSR in dispensing aid have remained stable over this period—to expand its influence at the expense of the other major powers and to offer itself as a model for economic development for the recipient countries. Although these political and ideological motivations remain the major determinants for Soviet aid programs, economic considerations also are becoming important. Many recent aid agreements have been designed largely to increase imports of fuels, raw materials, and consumer goods and to create markets for Soviet machinery and equipment.

The cost of foreign aid—as measured by the net outflow of economic resources—is now less than 0.03 percent of GNP. In recent years, Soviet aid outlays have leveled off while LDC aid repayments have risen rapidly, reducing even further Moscow's foreign aid burden. As long as the economic costs remain low and the political and economic returns high, Moscow will continue to employ foreign aid as the primary instrument for expanding its influence in the Third World.

APPENDIX: SOVIET ECONOMIC AID TO OTHER COMMUNIST COUNTRIES

This paper is concerned only with Soviet aid to non-Communist less developed countries. However, for comparative purposes, data on Soviet economic aid to other Communist countries is presented below in Table 3.

TABLE 3
Extensions of Soviet Economic Aid to Other Communist Countries, by Country, 1954–72
(millions of U.S. dollars)

	1954–72	1954–64	1965	1966	1967	1968	1969	1970	1971	1972
Total	16,175	5,500	1,115	695	1,240	1,305	1,360	750	2,125	2,085
Eastern Europe	5,105	2,900*	30	—	10	500	555	—	1,110	—
Bulgaria	—	—	—	—	—	335	555	—	—	—
Czechoslovakia	—	—	—	—	—	—	—	—	—	—
East Germany	—	—	—	—	—	—	—	—	—	—
Hungary	—	—	—	—	10	165	—	—	—	—
Poland	—	—	—	—	—	—	—	—	1,110	—
Romania	—	—	30	—	—	—	—	—	—	—
Far East	3,280	1,000†	85	150	200	270	325	440	410	400
People's Republic of China	—	—	—	—	—	—	—	—	—	—
North Korea	—	—	—	—	—	30	75	95	95	150
North Vietnam	—	—	85	150	200	240	250	345	315	250
Other	7,790	1,600‡	1,000	545	1,030	535	480	310	605	1,685
Albania	—	—	—	—	—	—	—	—	—	—
Cuba	—	—	390	415	480	535	480	310	505	1,025
Mongolia	—	—	570	—	550	—	—	—	100	120
Yugoslavia	—	—	40	130	—	—	—	—	—	540

* Estimates not available by country by year during 1954–64, but most of it went to Bulgaria and East Germany.
† Estimates not available by country by year during 1954–64, but the largest part probably went to China.
‡ Estimates not available by country by year during 1954–64, but most of it went to Cuba and Mongolia.

V
ECONOMIC REFORM

The basic system of Soviet planning emphasizing quantity of output, adopted in the early 1930s, has not been significantly altered, despite successive administrative reorganizations, changes of personnel, and the introduction of new planning tools. This system was successful in expanding total output rapidly, building military strength, and maintaining the centralization of political power in the hands of the leadership of the Communist Party. However, by the late 1950s flaws in the system of planning and economic administration were clearly evident. Shortages were widespread, and low quality of goods was common. More significantly for the Soviet leadership, technological change lagged, and the rate of economic growth started to slow down.

In the early 1960s, Soviet economists began to discuss these problems more openly, following an article in *Pravda* in 1962 by E. G. Liberman which proposed changes in central planning, enterprise management, and incentives. In 1965 Premier Kosygin announced an economic "reform" incorporating some of Liberman's ideas. Yet in subsequent implementation the reform proved to be modest, without fundamental changes. However, the search for ways to improve the operation of the economy while maintaining centralized control continues, with the latest effort through a reorganization of industrial administration.

In the first article in this section, Liberman evaluates the 1965 reform measures and their subsequent implementation. The second article analyzes recent developments in planning and incentives. The last selection appraises the newest attempt to improve industrial performance by reorganizing firms into multiplant "associations" similar in some respects to Western corporations.

23. THE ECONOMIC REFORM IN THE USSR

E. G. Liberman

On September 27, 1965, Premier Kosygin announced an economic reform in a long report to the Plenary Meeting of the Central Committee of the CPSU entitled "On Improving Management of Industry, Perfecting Planning, and Enhancing Economic Incentives in Industrial Production." The main features of the reform included the following: (1) The territorial scheme of economic administration by regional economic councils adopted in 1957 was abolished and the former system of ministries for individual branches of the economy was restored. (2) The number of targets ("indices") fixed for the enterprise by ministries and intermediate agencies was reduced somewhat. (3) Sales and profitability (profits in relation to capital) were to become the chief enterprise performance indicators, instead of the value of total ("gross") output. (4) Enterprises were to retain a larger share of profit, for use in paying bonuses (the "Material Incentives Fund"), investment in productive facilities (the "Production Development Fund"), and housing and recreational facilities for their employees (the "Fund for Socio-Cultural Measures and Housing Construction"). (5) New investments were to be financed to a greater extent from retained profits, amortization allowances, and long-term credits, and less from nonrepayable budget grants. (6) Enterprises were to pay a tax ("payment for assets") on the balance sheet value of fixed and working capital.

However, as shown by the subsequent implementation, the reform has proved to be a modest one, without fundamental changes in the Soviet system of planning, enterprise management, and incentives. A relatively sympathetic Soviet evaluation of the reform is provided in this selection by E. G. Liberman, a Soviet economist whose advocacy of reform in the early 1960s drew considerable attention both in the USSR and abroad. He discusses both positive results of the reform and the many problems it has failed to solve—such as excessive administrative interference in enterprise operations, the persistence of supposedly abolished targets, unsound performance indicators, and improper incentives.

E. G. Liberman is Professor of Political Economy at Kharkov University. This selection is reprinted by permission from *Economic*

Methods and the Effectiveness of Production, trans. by Arlo Schultz (White Plains, N.Y.: International Arts and Sciences Press, 1971), pp. 10–41. The original Russian edition was published in 1970. Footnote references to Russian-language sources have been omitted.

I. MOST IMPORTANT FEATURES OF THE REFORM

THE SEPTEMBER (1965) Plenum of the Central Committee of the CPSU made a detailed examination of the state of affairs in USSR industry. It was noted that the organizational structure of management existing at that time and the methods of planning and of economic incentive in industry were not in keeping with present conditions and with the level of development of productive forces.

Improvements in the system of management were outlined in the following basic directions: (1) raising the scientific level of planning, the optimization of planning, and the intensification of the role of long-term plans and norms; (2) eliminating excessive regulation of the economic activity of enterprises and allocating the necessary means to develop their production; (3) strengthening and developing cost-accounting* and intensifying economic production incentives with the aid of prices, profits, bonuses, and credit; (4) converting to the branch principle of industrial management.

As we know, the economic reform was elaborated in a rather extensive, specific form. First, there was a substantial reduction in the range of obligatory plan indices communicated to enterprises on a centralized basis, a number of indices were replaced, and the new profitability index was introduced.

Plan targets for the volume of output to be sold are being established for enterprises instead of the gross output index. This substitution is very substantial: it places production under the economic control of purchasers and creates prerequisites for the establishment of organic unity between planning and cost-accounting. The basic product-mix (*nomenklatura*) is also confirmed from above.

In addition to other indices, profit and profitability calculated as the ratio of profit to fixed productive capital and to normed working capital have been established as indices for evaluating the effectiveness of the work of enterprises. Thus, yardsticks of effectiveness which, although they have existed in our country for a long time, have not played a part in planning—to say nothing of the evaluation of the work of enterprises—have been brought into economic circulation.

---

* Editors' note: Although the Soviet term *khozraschet* is often translated as "cost-accounting," the concept refers to a broad framework of "business calculation," which includes keeping books, purchasing and selling goods on the basis of contracts, remaining solvent, and maximizing profits (or minimizing losses) within the limits of the enterprise plan.

In our opinion, the plan should confront production with ultimate goals but should not directly regulate the means of their attainment within the enterprise, which would deprive the enterprise of the necessary maneuverability in finding optimal solutions for the fulfillment of plan targets.

Although they retain their importance as accounting indices within the branch, such indices as the number of personnel, the average wage, labor productivity, and enterprise cost of production are not included in the number of obligatory indices that are confirmed for each enterprise.

Even now, certain economists cannot see how such a very important index as labor productivity can be left outside the realm of obligatory centralized planning. But the reform in no way denies the fact that labor productivity is a most important index to the effectiveness of production. The task consists in monitoring the correspondence between the growth of wages (including bonuses from profits) and increases in labor productivity. Difficulties arise in this area because we still have not elaborated a fully satisfactory method for measuring labor productivity at enterprises.

Payments to the budget and allocations from the budget are established as obligatory plan targets. The volume of centralized capital investment is also confirmed, since this is absolutely necessary for securing the required proportions in the development of branches of production in keeping with centralized national economic plans. The basic targets pertaining to the installation of new equipment as well as the indices of material and technical supply are also planned. In discussing the indices of material and technical supply, it must be borne in mind that, in keeping with the decisions of the September (1965) Plenum of the Central Committee and the Twenty-Third Congress of the CPSU, there will be a gradual transition to the planned distribution of equipment, supplies, and semimanufactures through the wholesale trade system.

Naturally, the restriction of the number of plan indices confirmed by higher-echelon organizations considerably expands the economic autonomy of enterprises. In no small measure, this autonomy is also promoted by the statute on the Socialist State Production Enterprise, which extends and legislatively confirms many rights to enterprise heads.

The September (1965) Plenum of the Central Committee of the CPSU outlined such a structure of the incentive system in order to arouse the enterprises' interest in elaborating and fulfilling higher plan targets and in making fullest use of internal reserves and resources. This goal is realized through the unity of the system of planning and economic incentives for enterprise collectives, which serves to increase the country's national income. In this instance, the interests of society and of enterprises are combined more harmoniously.

The development of production is financed by centralized sources as well as by the enterprises' own resources. It is important to emphasize that provision is made for the broader utilization of the internal resources of enterprises and economic organizations as well as of bank loans, instead of nonreturnable budget financing of capital investment.

As a rule, the financing of capital investment and the augmentation of working capital at existing enterprises are done through the enterprise's own financial resources and through Gosbank loans. This essentially alters the attitude of enterprises toward the reconstruction and expansion of production, requires the more thrifty and economically substantiated utilization of new equipment and production areas, and obliges management to give greater attention to increasing the effectiveness of capital investment.

In order to increase the effectiveness of production, payments for fixed and working productive capital have been introduced. In the future, this type of payment may become an important source of national centralized net income and may, to a certain degree, replace other types of payments, including the turnover tax. This is specifically the method of exerting economic influence on production which basically must counteract the squandering and mismanagement of social productive capital.

It is also important to note that normative payments for capital are established for a number of years so that a properly functioning enterprise will have a profit for offering incentives as well as for covering planned outlays. The more effective an enterprise's operation, the more profit it receives and the larger the share of this profit (after fixed payments to the budget, payments for the use of capital, and loan interest payments) is left at the disposal of the enterprise.

There are also a number of other important innovations that promote the strengthening of cost-accounting and the imparting to it of the nature of a real rather than a formal method of exerting economic influence on production. The role of the economic contract and the material liability of parties for its fulfillment are being strengthened, even to the point of providing for the complete compensation of losses to the injured party by the injuring party.

Liability is being established both horizontally, i.e., between enterprises, and vertically. We allude here to the establishment of guarantees of material liability not only of enterprises to ministries and agencies but also the liability of these organs if they are responsible for losses incurred by the enterprises. The first step in this direction is the conversion of economic and production associations as well as main administrations of industrial ministries to cost-accounting.

The strengthening of the cost-accounting of enterprises is also promoted by the better formulated system of using internal working capital. In the event that this capital is in short supply due to unsatisfactory management, the shortage should not be made up by the budget. An enterprise should apply for a bank loan, and the interest on this loan should be higher. The interest payment diminishes that part of the profit which is used to form the enterprise's economic incentive fund. This means the realization of the urgent demand that sanctions affect the personal incomes of those responsible for the losses and that these losses not be automatically transferred to the government, as frequently was the case in earlier times. This kind of undefined responsibility was specifically one of the chief features in the formal nature of cost-accounting.

Contractual relations between suppliers and purchasers play a basic part in strengthening cost-accounting and, simultaneously, in improving the planning process. At the same time, direct contractual relations are a way of making product-mix planning more specific. Naturally, direct relations make sense if they are backed up by sufficient legal and economic guarantees.

The system of economic incentives makes provision for the formation of a special source of incentive payments above and beyond centrally established wage rates. The profit created at an enterprise is this source. It has been recognized that the amount of deductions paid from profits into the incentive fund depends on the fulfillment of the plan for increased sales or profits and on the profitability level contemplated in the annual plan (provided that the prescribed mix of key products stipulated in the plan is observed). In those instances when an increase in sales volume is not advisable, the size of the material incentive fund is determined as a function of increased profit.

Three economic incentive funds are formed on this basis: the production development fund, the material incentive fund, and the fund for sociocultural measures and housing construction.

(1) The production development fund serves as a supplement to centralized sources of capital investment. It is formed through deductions from profits as well as through the use of a certain amount of the amortization deductions earmarked for the total renovation of fixed capital.

(2) The material incentive fund is created solely from profit. The size of the deductions from profits paid into the material incentive fund is determined according to norms depending on the increase in the sales volume (or the amount of profit) and the profitability level stipulated in the annual plan. Norms are established as percentages of the wage fund: for every percentage point of increase in sales volume in comparable prices (or amount of profit) stipulated in the plan for a given year as compared with the previous year; for each percentage point of profitability stipulated in the annual plan.

Norms are envisaged as stable for a number of years and are differentiated by branch (and, where necessary, by groups of enterprises within a branch). Limits on deductions paid into the material incentive fund are not established.

Payments of an established amount are made to the material incentive fund when the enterprise fulfills the profit and sales plan for the product-mix stipulated in the plan. When an enterprise overfulfills the profit and sales plan, additional payments are made to the material incentive fund. When an enterprise fails to fulfill the profit and sales plan for the established product-mix, payments are made to the material incentive fund at a lower rate. The product-mix is assigned to enterprises by higher-echelon organs in the process of confirming the indices of the yearly plan, and, if it is not fulfilled, payments to the material incentive fund are reduced. Other restrictions on deductions to the material incentive fund are not established.

The formation of the incentive fund is connected with the quality of planning at the enterprise. In order to eliminate, or at least diminish, the striving to conceal reserves in the elaboration of plans at enterprises so as to make these plans easier to fulfill, resources are paid in full into the incentive fund only if the production growth plan is fulfilled. But in the event the plan is overfulfilled, the rates are reduced by approximately 30 percent for that part of the increase in output which represents overfulfillment. The idea is to make the deliberate lowering of plans disadvantageous, since the enterprise will thereby lose one third of the incentive it would otherwise receive for the increase in sales which is overfulfillment.

On the other hand, the plan should not be unduly high. Therefore, if the plan is not fulfilled, the incentive payment is also reduced by the same amount compared with the established normative rates. The procedure for reducing rates of payment for the overfulfilled and unfulfilled part of the plan concerns not only the increase in sales (or profits) but also incentives for the profitability level, and such incentive is established without discounts for the level of profitability actually attained on the basis of normative rates solely within the framework of the plan.

(3)   The same methods have also been adopted for the formation of the third incentive fund, which is earmarked for sociocultural measures and housing construction.

Of basic importance is the fact that enterprises are not regulated by strictly centralized instructions in the matter of distributing the incentive fund among production participants. Enterprises may elaborate one or another provision on the procedure for awarding incentives on the basis of standard recommended methods in accordance with the specifics of their production. The only point that has been established is that bonuses to workers under presently existing statutes will be awarded from the wage funds in the future as well. But in addition to this, workers may also be paid bonuses from the material incentive fund formed from profit. Furthermore, these bonuses may be paid under special provisions, for example, for improving the quality of production, for economizing on materials, for mastering new products or processes, as well as on a one-time basis for individual attainments on the job.

The awarding of bonuses to managerial, engineering, and technical personnel and employees is also regulated by special provisions. In addition, certain sums in the incentive fund are reserved for one-time assistance. An important feature is that part of the material incentive fund is earmarked for rewards to personnel based on their performance for the year, depending on their length of service at a given enterprise.

The September (1965) Plenum of the Central Committee of the CPSU emphasized that the price formation system must be improved if the reform is to be successful. Price must more completely reflect socially necessary labor outlays and must assure the compensation of production costs and the accumulation of profit by every normally functioning enterprise. At the same time, prices must also stimulate an improvement in the quality of production and in the expedient service life and reliability of products. Therefore, prices must take into account additional outlays by the producer for the improvement of the quality of goods as well as the effect of such improvement on productive or personal consumption. It has been emphasized that, as a rule, retail prices on consumer goods may be revised only in a downward direction. The reform of wholesale prices was carried out in 1967. The new prices reflect socially necessary outlays much more closely and completely. Nonetheless, in the future as well, it will be necessary to conduct work to improve prices.

The reform of the system of planning and economic incentive in industry is inseparable from the simultaneous restructuring of industrial management. The regional economic councils did a certain amount of useful work, especially in production cooperation locally, i.e., on a territorial level. But at the same time, administration based on the territorial principle has also carried negative effects: it has hindered the implementation of a single-branch technological policy; it has weakened intra-branch specialization and cooperation, which are no less important than territorial cooperation; it has led to a certain irresponsibility due to the lack of strict distribution of functions among regional economic councils and branch committees; etc. After all the advantages and shortcomings of the branch and territorial systems of management were carefully weighted, a branch system of management was adopted and appropriate branch industrial ministries were created.

The September (1965) Plenum of the Central Committee of the CPSU emphasized the great importance of measures proposed to improve the organization of management and to intensify economic methods for industrial management. The importance of these measures is that they combine unified government planning with total cost-accounting operation of enterprises, centralized branch management with broad republic and local economic initiative, and the principle of one-man control with the enlargement of the role of production collectives. Moreover, democratic principles of management are further expanded and economic prerequisites are created for broader mass participation in production management and for mass influence on the results of the economic work of enterprises. As stated in the Decree of the September (1965) Plenum of the Central Committee of the CPSU, such a system of economic management more closely conforms to modern requirements and permits the better use of the advantages of the socialist system.

The extensive training and retraining of managerial personnel are required for the successful implementation of the economic reform.

Of great importance is the organizational and educational work of the party organizations, whose role is substantially increasing. At the September (1965) Plenum of the Central Committee of the CPSU, A. N. Kosygin stated: "While not supplanting the economic organs, and by abandoning petty tutelage over them, from the bottom to the top, party committees are called upon to use their inherent means and methods, especially in working with people, with cadres, with workers, and with the production intelligentsia. Most important is the ability to mobilize the initiative and activity of toilers in our industry, to accumulate their experience and their creative energy."

II. FIRST SUCCESSES IN THE IMPLEMENTATION OF THE REFORM

The introduction of the new system at enterprises has been carried out on the basis of careful preparations under the leadership of ministries and of a special Joint Commission created under USSR Gosplan.

Initially, certain of the best prepared enterprises in various branches of production were converted to the new system. The Joint Commission under USSR Gosplan elaborated guidelines for the conversion of individual industrial enterprises to the new system and, on this basis, a great deal of preparatory work was carried out at many enterprises. This work began with a careful analysis of production potential. In the process, new and higher plans—compared with those previously confirmed—were determined with respect to both sales volume and profit and profitability of enterprises.

The most important prerequisite for converting enterprises to the new system was that the financial relationships with the budget for each ministry not be violated. All additional resources required by the enterprises for the formation of incentive funds had to be sought in additional profit resulting from the use of reserves on the basis of the enterprises' own initiative. The allocation of between 60 and 90 percent of the additional profit to the formation of enterprise economic incentive funds was authorized, and this served as a powerful stimulus for disclosing and utilizing reserves for increasing profitability through increased sales volume as well as through lower enterprise cost of production.

By early 1967, 704 enterprises employing more than 2 million persons had been converted to the new system. Of these enterprises, 43 had operated under the new system since January 1, 1966; 200 enterprises, since April 1; and the remaining number, since July 1, 1966. On their own initiative, the enterprises raised the sales plans initially established for them by more than 300 million rubles and their profit plans by 130 million rubles. In connection with this, planned payments to the budget also increased by 34 million rubles. At the same time, there was a considerable increase in the amount of net income that was left at the disposal of enterprise collectives as the creators of this income: the material incentive fund increased by 80 percent as compared with 1965, the fund for sociocultural measures and housing construction increased by 60 percent, and the production development fund increased by 210 percent. At the overwhelming majority of enterprises operating under the new system, all plan targets were successfully fulfilled and overfulfilled. By the fall of 1967, 5,500 enterprises, which produced approximately one third of all industrial output and which at the same time accounted for approximately 45 percent of all profit, were operating under the new system.

In 1966, enterprises operating under the new system sold 600 million rubles' worth of output in excess of the plan and realized 250 million rubles in profits in excess of the plan. In the first half of 1967, these indices improved and amounted to 1,200 million and 300 million rubles, respectively.

The fact that the sale of one third of the output yielded approximately 45 percent of the profit shows that enterprises which had converted to the new system worked more profitably than the others.

By December 1, 1967, the reform already encompassed approximately 7,000 industrial enterprises producing 40 percent of the output and accounting for more than half of all profit. To a large extent, these enterprises were responsible for the high indices for industry during 1966–67. At these enterprises, sales increased by approximately 11 percent in 1966 and by 12 percent in 1967; profit increased by 23.5 percent and 25 percent, respectively.

Enterprises belonging to the USSR Ministry of Instrument-Building, Means of Automation, and Control Systems functioned especially well, since all enterprises and a number of main administrations (associations) belonging to this ministry were entirely converted to the new system in 1967. Under the plan adopted by this ministry in 1967, the sales volume increased by 3.9 percent over the initially established plan while profit increased by 4.8 percent. Economic incentive funds rose to 72.5 million rubles. Is this a large or a small amount? K. N. Rudnev, USSR Minister of Instrument-Building, Means of Automation, and Control Systems, cited interesting calculations on this matter in an article. If the enterprises had not been converted to the new conditions at all, then the fulfillment of the initially established plan would have placed 23.8 million rubles at thier disposal under the old statutes, or only 33 percent of the amount they received under the reformed system. But even if the initial plans were overfulfilled precisely to the amount that the enterprises raised their plans in keeping with their conversion to the new system, then the enterprises would have received only 41.4 million rubles, or a mere 57 percent of the sum that was left at their disposal after their conversion to the new system.

The average yearly increase in production for 1966–1968 amounted to 16.5 percent for enterprises belonging to this ministry. The average annual increase in profit was from 19.3 to 29 percent. The average annual increase in labor productivity was 10 percent. The number of small plants diminished by one third, while the number of large plants increased by 50 percent. In 1968, the conversion of all main administrations to cost-accounting was complete. This was a record-breaking year for production growth rates—which reached 18 percent—and for growth of labor productivity—which reached 11 percent. By the end of 1968, the reform fully encompassed enterprises belonging to eight union and union-republic ministries as well as many enterprises and main administrations of other ministries.

By January 1, 1969, all railroad administrations, seagoing steamship lines, civil aviation administrations, river steamship lines, and automotive common carriers had been converted to the new system of planning and economic incentives. Experiments connected with the conversion to the new system are in progress in trade, in construction, and at communications enterprises. By April 1969, 3,743 state farms had been converted to complete cost-accounting.

In the first quarter of 1969, more than 5,000 additional enterprises were converted to the new system of planning and economic incentives. Thus, in April 1969, more than 32,000 enterprises producing more than 77 percent of all industrial output were operating under the new conditions.

In most cases, those indices which are now generally planned by the enterprises themselves have improved following conversion to the new system. Thus, in the case of enterprises that were converted to the new system from the beginning of 1966, labor productivity increased by 8 percent in a half-year, whereas the industrywide average increase was 5.2 percent. The number of personnel was lower than planned, and the growth rate of labor productivity surpassed the growth of wages on the whole.

In the case of the first two groups of enterprises (converted prior to June 1, 1966), profit increased by 23.3 percent in 1966 as compared with the corresponding period in 1965, which was more than twice as high as the average growth in profit throughout industry as a whole (10.6 percent). More than half of the total increase in profit was due to the reduction in the enterprise cost of production. This attests to the unquestionable success of the first steps of the reform.

The new economic system not only has had an impact directly on production but also has affected the circulation sphere. The turnover rate has been accelerated in the "commodity-money" phase and this has meant considerable additional commodity resources for the national economy without special investment. Of course, this is a one-time reserve which chiefly takes effect only upon conversion to the new system, but it can have very substantial consequences.

As yet there are no generalized data on the acceleration of turnover of capital in production and in circulation at those enterprises that have been converted to the new system. But individual facts are a good illustration of this beneficial process. Prior to its conversion to the new system of operation, the Kirov Turbine Plant in Kharkov required an average of about 60 days for such operations as the dismounting of turbines after the experimental assembly and testing of finished machines, the mothballing and packing of parts, shipping, billing, and collecting amounts due from its purchasers. After the reform, all these operations require only 25 days. Approximately the same thing occurred at the Leningrad Twenty-Second Party Congress Plant: the period between finished production of turbines with a capacity of 200–300 mv. and billing was cut in half.

Furthermore, it is not enough to manufacture parts and submit them to the technical control section. Today, they must be delivered on time and in a uniform fashion. The prerequisites for the elimination of rush work have been created on a firm economic basis—the interest of collectives in the ultimate effect, specifically, in product sales.

Following the price revision in 1967, the Erevan Chemical Combine began operating at a loss. But with the assistance of its ministry, its equipment was quickly renovated, and as early as 1968 the combine was rhythmically operating at a profit. In the fourth quarter of 1968, its monthly plans were fulfilled, on the average, by 32.2 percent during the first 10 days of the month, by 33.9 percent during the second, and by 32.9 percent during the last 10 days of the month.

In order to ensure rhythmic operations, many plants have converted to shipping on a 24-hour schedule. The Tbilisi Machine-Tool-Building Plant has regularized its shipping documentation and has accelerated the process of submitting payment documents to the bank. One-time purchasers have been completely converted to letters of credit, and in the case of regular purchasers, shipments are made at the beginning of each month so that money for products will be transferred to the plant's current account by the end of the month. While before, overdue indebtedness of purchasers at the end of every month used to amount to 400,000 rubles, in 1969 this amount did not exceed 50,000 rubles. In addition, in 1968, the plant's operation was profitable, and profit increased by 20 percent over 1967.

The considerable improvement in the use of fixed capital is no less important a consequence of the new system than is the accelerated turnover of capital and the increased measure of rhythmic production. Most important, enterprises have begun to divest themselves of unneeded capital. During 1966, the Kirov Turbine Plant in Kharkov discovered 1,600,000 rubles' worth of superfluous fixed capital and reduced its working capital by 1 million rubles. At the Norilsk Mining and Metallurgical Combine, the value of released equipment, including equipment in very short supply, amounted to 1.3 million rubles.

At the Mozdokskii Tulle Mill, the workers thought of ways of fulfilling the program on one machine instead of two in order to increase the profitability of production and thereby increase the enterprise's incentive fund; they left two machines instead of five in one of the shops and offered the remaining three to another enterprise.

First and foremost, the economic methods of influencing production result in a changed attitude of people toward production. A. Biriukov, Hero of Socialist Labor and senior rolling-press operator in the rolling shop of the Taganrog Metallurgical Plant, wrote: "The conversion of the plant to the new system of planning and economic incentive has had an extremely favorable impact on our work. We closely watch every sheet [of metal—E.L.], and we see to it that it goes directly to delivery, to a freight car and the purchaser, and that all output is more quickly sold. . . During this time, labor productivity has increased by 30 percent. . . . The secret of success lies in the friendship and solidarity of the collective, in a conscientious attitude toward the cause."

The reform has also had a favorable impact on improving the quality of output. At the Volgograd Red October Metallurgical Plant, shops "sell" products to one another on the basis of accounting prices that take the gradings and quality of the products into account.

Using their right to choose various types of incentives for different shops, many enterprises have achieved good results in improving product quality specifically with the aid of well-planned material incentive systems. At the Voronezh Excavator Plant, bonuses have been established for many workers for the manufacture of flaw-free goods and for acceptance of goods the first time they are submitted. Shop cost-accounting is also used skillfully for the same purpose.

The Khmelnitskii Forge and Press Equipment Plant offers an interesting example. In order to test the machine tools it produced, the plant used much plastic, stamping various plastic parts that no one needed. This expenditure was entirely within the "base" for the enterprise cost-of-production plan and, prior to the conversion to the new system, the plant gave no thought to the use of these "legal" waste materials. But now the workers are trying to use them. The plant has begun receiving press forms and orders for parts and has begun stamping the required items in the course of testing the machine tools. The expenditure of several dozen tons of metal is replaced by the utilization of 2.5–3 tons of plastic which were previously wasted in the form of scrap. Such are the unexpected resources for increasing sales and profits.

The struggle for output quality at enterprises operating under the new conditions has become a permanent process. At the First Watchmaking Plant in Moscow, the terms of material incentive are differentiated by shop. Furthermore, the assembly workers are rewarded when their timepieces are accepted the first time they are submitted, and the inspectors in the Technical Control Section are rewarded for the absence of claims, as is done at the Voronezh Excavator Plant and at other plants.

In the sewn goods industry, there has been an important change that was observed as far back as the experiment conducted at the Gorky "Maiak" Production Association. The factories began producing items from inexpensive but fashionable material, using the technology for sewing high-quality items.

In view of the particular importance of the problem of improving the quality of output, a number of indices characterizing the quality of the means of production are presently proposed: service life, reliability, repairability, etc. Moreover, the question of including such indices as evaluation indices in enterprise plans is being raised. Proposals have been made to adjust the volume of output against quality coefficients, to introduce special incentive systems for increasing the quality of output, etc.

Of course, such indices may play a positive part. However, in our view it would be irrational to again increase the number of obligatory evaluation indices. Coefficients of quality are needed to substantiate plans for the introduction of new equipment. They are also necessary to certify the quality of output and hence to establish price markups for high-quality products, as well as price discounts on obsolescent products. This factor itself affects the volume of sales and the amount of profits, i.e., the ultimate indices upon which output quality should exert a decisive influence.

No matter how important they might be, economic incentive measures for individual attainments at enterprises are not sufficiently complete. Incentives must be provided for final, aggregate production results. This is why it is difficult to communicate to the enterprises special plan indices pertaining to the quality of output. Quality must have a powerful impact on the ultimate and most important results of production: profit and sales. And it is the business of the enterprise proper to reward those workers who are responsible for product quality from incentive funds formed from profit. In practice, this is what is done. The sewn goods industry rewards workers for the quality of work performed in finishing operations. At clock, excavator, and other plants, rewards to assembly workers for the quality of their output play an especially important part. At many enterprises, the quality index is taken into account, although perhaps as yet to an insufficient degree, in rewarding the workers and executive personnel in those sectors of production where such rewards are called forth by technological requirements.

The flexibility of methods for stimulating workers is an important attainment of the reform. Plants elaborate and apply specifically those systems of incentives which serve to prod the laggards or to stimulate workers in the decisive sectors of production. At the specialized automotive plant in Gorky, workers in the assembly shop are given additional bonuses for rhythmic output during the month. And this promotes the more successful fulfillment of sales plans.

No less substantial are successes in the utilization of material and moral incentives at light-industry enterprises. At the Rigas-Aditais Knitwear Factory, managerial personnel are rewarded for fulfilling the plan with respect to product-mix, product grades, and profit. In addition, supplementary bonuses are awarded for specific performance indices for each service. For example, personnel in the production planning department are also rewarded fof the fulfillment of cooperative delivery schedules; personnel in the engineering department are rewarded for the implementation of planned measures relating to new equipment; and personnel in the sales department are rewarded for the fulfillment of contractual deliveries of basic products and for observing the norms for inventories of finished goods.

Light industry has conducted an interesting experiment which places at the disposition of shop chiefs a certain incentive fund as a percentage of the actual shop profits to be used for additional bonuses to individual workers achieving the best results in intrashop socialist competition (the Voroshilovgrad "Severokhod" Fiftieth Anniversary of the Great October Revolution Combine). In the pattern-cutting shop of this combine, the leading shift receives a monthly bonus of 300 rubles and the leading brigade receives a monthly bonus of 150 rubles (in 1969). Thus, moral incentive in the form of awarding the titles of leading shift and leading brigade is reinforced by material incentive.

One of the most notable results manifested in the work of enterprises in 1966–68 was the disclosure of reserves and their inclusion in counterplans initiated by enterprises, even though individual enterprise directors initially accepted this task with a certain amount of conservatism.

In this connection, N. E. Drogichinskii, Chief of the Department for the Introduction of New Methods of Planning and Economic Incentive of USSR Gosplan, wrote:

> The habit of striving for an easy plan and of maintaining a reserve for the overfulfillment of the plan virtually became the norm, and for this reason the present striving to obtain a higher target, observed on the part of all plants, factories, and firms converted to the new system of planning and economic incentive, seems rather strange to some people. But all of us must surmount this psychological barrier. Indeed, such is the impact of economic methods: you cannot argue with them as you previously argued with higher-echelon organizations in an attempt to prove that the targets assigned to you were unrealistic.

This is a characteristic confession by a specialist who has himself long worked in the system of planning organs.

Less resources—more output! This slogan is being implemented in practice by the collective of the Shchekino Chemical Combine. The Central Committee of the CPSU has heard a report on the work of the party committee of this combine. As a result of work carried out at the combine, there has been a substantial increase in output and a simultaneous decrease in the number of personnel through improvements in the organization of production, labor, and wages. In the space of two years, labor productivity has increased by 87 percent and output by more than 80 percent, while the number employed has decreased by 870 persons. This work is of great national economic importance, and it is recommended that the experience of the Shchekino Chemical Combine be broadly disseminated.

Ability rather than number! This important slogan has been advanced and implemented at many enterprises that have been converted to the new conditions of planning and economic incentive.

At one time, an article published in *Pravda* in 1966 correctly emphasized that prior to the reform, enterprise heads recognized a very important stage—"the defense of the plan"—when the directors spared neither energy, time, nor eloquence in arguing that the proposed plans for production and labor productivity were intolerably high, while the capital investments, wage fund, number of personnel, and amount of material resources were absurdly small. In principle, the new system changes not only this procedure but the very psychology of managers as well. The "defense" of the plan gradually is losing its former nature, and, instead of "defending themselves," enterprises are beginning to go on the "offensive." To be sure, they are still timid (and, as we shall see later, there are unfortunately serious reasons for timidity). As a result of their timidity, even the higher plans of 1966 and of the first half of 1967 were overfulfilled to a considerable degree, with respect to the volume of both sales and profits.

In spite of the significance of material incentives, they will not be fully effective unless they are combined with moral incentives. Our leading workers realize this fully. K. Fomin, a machine-tool operator in Rostov-on-the-Don, wrote to *Pravda* that during 20 years on the job, he had received bonuses, commendations, and certificates many times. But what did he remember most? An instance when, at the end of the shift, the brigade leader took a short break and shook the then young Fomin's hand in the presence of all, saying: "Fomin, you did a good job today. The entire brigade thanks you."

K. Fomin correctly observes that such a good thing as the awarding of bonuses should not be bureaucratized. Unquestionably, bonuses "have become a perceptible addition to wages but nothing more. And yet the meaning of the bonus also includes something else. A bonus should carry an educational thrust and should produce in others the striving to follow leading workers." Bonuses should not be awarded in the conventional way: "A thick document is shoved through a narrow window. You sign opposite your name and the cashier quickly counts out the proper sum—take it and leave."

Bonuses "with a garnish of indifference" that offends the actual recipients must everywhere become a thing of the past. Those who reduce our reform to "the power of the ruble or ready cash" are mistaken. *Social recognition of labor services and skill—this is the most important thing that every ruble of bonuses carries with it.*

As we see, changes in psychology have affected not only the managers—heads of shops and enterprises—but the workers as well. In his letter to *Pravda*, A. Pozdniakov, a steel founder at the "Red October" plant, told how the reform genuinely aroused the interest of workers in the result of the work of the entire collective of open-hearth shop No. 1. Pozdniakov wrote: "It is no secret that not every worker previously thought seriously about the fulfillment of the plan. They knew that in one way or another the program would be fulfilled. And since there was a plan, there would also be a bonus. For this very reason, the meetings were sluggish, boring, and without particular activity."

Now the picture has changed entirely. Every worker at the plant knows how much a given material costs and how much the overexpenditure of each ton of fuel or ferroalloy amounts to. Questions of how to improve the quality of output and reduce defects are very actively discussed.

This is one of the most important results of the economic reform: the increase in the effectiveness of production is genuinely becoming the common goal for one and all. And this must be developed in every way by improving the methods of evaluating and stimulating every working collective through the combination of material and moral incentives.

The production development fund is also being skillfully used. The "Conditioner" Communist Labor Plant in Kharkov has used this fund to implement measures to raise standards of production and industrial design, and to improve working conditions. These measures enabled shop No. 5 to increase labor productivity by 20–25 percent and enabled the foundry shop to raise labor productivity by 10 percent. The share of manual labor has been reduced to 19 percent, and manpower turnover has been sharply reduced. In the space of three years, the average annual increase in the production of central air conditioners was 21 percent, balance-sheet profit increased by 18.3 percent, production profitability increased by 14 percent, and profit per ruble of fixed capital increased by 15.9 percent. It is noteworthy that the entire increase in the volume of production was realized exclusively through higher labor productivity without an increase in the number of personnel.

The successes of the reform by no means indicate that everything has been perfectly smooth and that there are no difficulties in the implementation of the reform. Against the background of the existing possibilities, many shortcomings in various aspects of the implementation of the reform have been revealed. The economic reform has taken only its first successful steps on the complex road to bringing our production relations into correspondence with the level of development of the productive forces, and the methods of planning and management into line with the demands of the objective laws of socialism.

III. SHORTCOMINGS IN THE IMPLEMENTATION OF THE REFORM

Certain shortcomings in the implementation of the reform are objectively due to the complexity and novelty of the tasks involved in the profound reorganization of management methods. Some of the difficulties are connected with the vitality of conventional methods of management and with the striving to preserve former indices, calculation methods, and methods of evaluating the work of enterprises.

Noting the difficulties and shortcomings in the first stage of the economic reform, N. K. Baibakov, Chairman of USSR Gosplan and Deputy Chairman of the USSR Council of Ministers, wrote: ". . . The introduction of the new system requires a change in the methods of production management and necessitates learning how to work under the new system. And this does not come immediately." He noted that many shortcomings are also due to the "habits of individual personnel. These shortcomings cannot be eliminated all at once, by an order. The more complete and consistent introduction of the economic methods of management will result in the disappearance of voluntaristic administrating." Painstaking and extended work is required to overcome these difficulties. There are problems stemming from the fact that not all organizational-technical and methodological questions were elaborated with sufficient completeness. And under the influence of the new economic conditions, they require additional work.

It is most advisable to consider shortcomings in the implementation of the reform in terms of the basic directions of improving the methods of planning and economic incentive, beginning with the communication to enterprises of targets concerning the volume of sales and the product-mix for the most important items.

In planning the indices for 1968, some ministries did something that did not comform at all to the reform. Z. Belozerova, Director of the Rosa Luxemburg Knitwear Factory (Kiev), told participants in the *Ekonomicheskaia gazeta* "Business Affairs Club" that the Ministry of Light Industry—both republic and all-union—was planning production in terms of 15 (!) indices, including enterprise cost of production as well as the number employed, even by groups.

In practice, since the wage fund is planned, ministries must control the correspondence between the actually expended wage fund and the volume of gross output. V. Firsov, Director of the Nevskii Machine-Building Plant, wrote in this connection:

> A strange situation is created whereby an index planned from above (wage fund) will be controlled in terms of its correspondence to a calculated index planned by the enterprise itself (gross or commodity production). And since there can be no control without a plan, clearly the wage fund will be planned on the basis of the volume of gross output, and the latter can be restored to its rights through this roundabout but "reliable" way. Moreover, if the plant tries to work on the basis of minus tolerances and to decrease the weight of items, this is bad for the "gross." It is specifically according to the volume of gross output that the planning calculation of the directive index—the wage fund—is made, and this places the plant in a difficult position, since it has to abandon economic items in the name of gross output.

The wage fund for the Voronezhsel'mash [Agricultural Machinery] Plant is planned in the old way—based on output per worker and gross output. But since the plant has a special design office, four fifths of whose activity is not connected with the needs of the plant, the wage fund was slashed by 190–200 thousand rubles.

The restriction on the number of indices planned from above would seem to be a question already resolved in documents on the economic reform. Attempts to increase the number of obligatory indices planned for the enterprises were still explicable in the early period of the reform, for example in 1966. But here we have before us a publication of a talk between L. Kulichenko, First Secretary of the Volgograd Regional Committee of the CPSU, and A. Karpov, Chief Economist at the "Red October" Metallurgical Plant. This plant is one of the 43 enterprises first converted to the new operating conditions in January 1966. And it would seem that everything should be in exemplary order at this plant. But it turns out that the Ministry of Ferrous Metallurgy decided (with reference to the early part of 1969) to confirm even repair schedules for all open-hearth furnaces, rolling mills, and all metallurgical equipment. A. Karpov states: "For some reason, they take care of us as if we were little children. If we spend 1,000 rubles on capital repair, we have to write a certificate. . . . We write reports on the work of each unit, with respect to every index. And the number of planning indices is already approaching 20."

Basic shortcomings are also manifested in the striving of ministries to impose higher sales volume on the enterprises. This is an expression of uncertainty that, independently, the enterprises will sufficiently utilize their production capacities and disclose reserves. This aspect of planning requires further improvement.

The question of what the "product-mix of most important items" is must be clarified. At present, its definition is chiefly left to the ministries. But the ministries tend to expand rather than restrict this product-mix, and this expresses a tendency to retain the old methods—to provide a greater degree of regulation, since otherwise they supposedly cannot be responsible for the results.

The following curious example can be cited. Among a number of indices, the Republic Ministry of Light Industry also plans the quantity of most important products for the R. Luxemburg Knitwear Factory in Kiev. Trade organizations have been demanding such items as open-work stockings. Such hosiery is more labor-intensive, and the productivity of the equipment declines somewhat in their production. In terms of cost, such hosiery is a profitable product, and the factory could realize 10 million rubles in profit, though the number of items would naturally be somewhat smaller—3.9 million pairs as opposed to 4.5 million pairs. But the ministry officials say: "No, you are not entitled to do so. You can produce stockings and socks in any assortment, but you must turn out 4.5 million pairs in keeping with the plan." It can be guessed that the knitwear branch, like many others, also reports to Gosplan, to the Central Statistical Administration, and to the ministry on the quantity of items as well as on other indices. Hence, here we observe a tendency to retain the old methods of evaluating work.

Let us now turn to the indices of profit and profitability. The Ust'-Kamenogorsk Lead and Zinc Combine put into operation a shop for processing slag. The shop employed a mere 200 persons. In order to produce the same amount of raw zinc that is produced by this shop, it would have been necessary to open a new mine employing 800 persons. However, the combine is reproached for having excessive manpower. But the result is that the combine increases its profits by reducing waste while its work is evaluated in the old way: according to "gross output." The extraction of raw materials from waste is a more labor-intensive operation than the extraction of raw materials from ore. Therefore, average output per person declines while wages per ton of raw material may rise somewhat. In return, society obtains an additional amount of valuable raw materials without considerable capital investment and virtually without material expenditures.

This example illustrates with sufficient clarity the possible consequences of evaluating and stimulating production according to the gross output index instead of basing the evaluation on the volume of sales and profitability.

Profit and profitability still do not occupy their proper place in the system of planning and evaluating the work of enterprises. In many cases, payments for assets comprise an insignificant share of payments into the budget. For example, at the Kosinskii Knitwear Factory, payment for productive assets comprised only 3.8 percent of the profit, while payments of the free remainder into the budget amounted to 80 percent of the profits (following the formation of incentive funds). This is also the case at many profitable enterprises.

Enterprises have used their right to reward increased sales volume and profitability in such a way that the reward for increases in sales was dominant. Therefore, the importance of profit and profitability would seem to be relegated to a lesser place. In accordance with the Standard Recommendations of the State Committee on Labor and Wages of the USSR Council of Ministers, principal attention should be focused on rewarding increased output or, more correctly, fulfillment of the plan for such growth, while profit, irrespective of its volume, serves only as a source for awarding bonuses. But since the shops almost always fulfill the plans for increased output, even after the reform it is rather frequently the case that engineers and technicians do not feel the connection between their activities and the amount of profit or the level of profitability of production. The only thing they truly feel is the necessity to divest themselves of superfluous productive capital and to make better use of available capital in order to "fit into" planned profitability, and even then this is true only when the index of profitability has been brought down to the shop level. However, in other respects everything has remained virtually the same at certain plants: there is still the striving to lower the shop plan for output volume and to "fit into" the wage fund. The realization of a large increase in the planned volume of output or profit vis-à-vis the preceding year is important only for the formation of the incentive fund for the plant as a whole. In the shops, the impact of these increases is not felt, since frequently no direct quantitative relationship exists between shop incentives and such a criterion as the increase in plantwide profit or the profitability level. This shortcoming in method is being overcome in the course of improving the methods and norms of economic incentives.

Interruptions in the supply of materials and component parts continue to be a major difficulty in the work of enterprises. It is to be assumed that these difficulties are temporary. They are due to the fact that material-and-technical supply organs have still not been converted to the new work methods, and the system of contractual relations and increased sanctions for the violation of delivery schedules is still not fully in operation. On the whole, the supply system is going through a period of reorganization, and the demarcation of duties between planning organs, branch supply and sales organizations, and territorial material-and-technical supply administrations is still not complete.

Instability of supply also frequently leads to instability of production plans. At the Petrovskii Plant in Dnepropetrovsk, product delivery targets have been changed repeatedly. The same complaints have come from other Dnepropetrovsk enterprises as well. The Raichikhinskii Meat Combine was converted to the new system in July 1968. And already during the period of operation under the new system, its plan has been changed three times, and on January 15, 1969, on the basis of a telegram from Rosglavmiaso,* its plan indices for the already elapsed 1968 were changed with respect to the production of meat and sausage. As a result, notwithstanding the rather high indices actually attained, the plan proved to be unfulfilled and it was impossible to reward personnel for the fourth quarter of 1968. And this is because plans are sometimes even "corrected" retroactively.

In 1969, the Kharkov Petrovskii Bicycle Plant's profit plan was revised upward four times.

The insufficient stability not only of deliveries but also of plans as a whole stems from the existing procedure whereby only a ministry can alter a plan, while main administrations can transfer the plan target from one quarter to another. When the targets are unrealistic and unfulfillable, they are initially transferred from one quarter to another with the idea of requesting the ministry to correct the plan retroactively only once at the end of the year, when it is already evident that the plan cannot be fulfilled.

The product-mix of the most important items for bearing plants is determined by the sales organization, which does not always have the proper picture of the plants' production resources. On the other hand, the plan for the development of capacities is determined by the main administration, which does not have a sufficient knowledge of the demand for items produced by the plants. This is why, for example, immediately after the Kuibyshev Bearing Plant was converted to the new system and the yearly product-mix plan had been confirmed, in the first quarter of 1966 the plan was changed with respect to 361 types of bearings for a total of 769,000 rubles, and in the second quarter the plan was changed for 801 types in the amount of 2,064,000 rubles.

This is a complicated and fundamental question. In our opinion, changes in orders for bearings are inevitable. In their aggregate, these orders constitute the product-mix plan. And the initial planned product-mix is only a guideline. Orders for metal for bearings produced in small batches need not be determined in advance. Metal should be purchased on the basis of the probable demand for bearings of various types, and, in addition, there should be a certain surplus in the supply of metal in warehouses of Metallosbyt† bases or of the plants. Similarly, standard bearings in small batches should be sold from the warehouse, while major purchasers of bearings should be assigned directly to the producing plants.

Unfortunately, discrepancies in metal supply which were permissible

---

* Editors' note: Main Administration of the Meat Industry of the RSFSR.

† Editors' note: Administration for Sale of Metals.

in the initial stage of the reform are also found today. Deliveries under the product-mix plan are made with great interruptions and losses. Some metal profiles are replaced by others, and, according to estimates that are far from complete, this results in a loss of 450–500 thousand tons of metal a year. The reader may say, what of it? That is approximately 0.5 percent of the rolled metal that is supplied. But how many times are the delivery terms not met? Such disruptions concern not only special but ordinary rolled metal as well.

The reason is that the production of metal is planned by USSR Gosplan and the Ministry of Ferrous Metallurgy, whereas the orders are distributed by Glavmetallosbyt of USSR Gossnab.* Not one of these agencies is responsible for unsatisfactory supply to the purchaser. The Ministry of Ferrous Metallurgy can alter the production plans for one mill or another without considering orders already issued. Metallosbyt can issue orders for mills for which the given assortment has not yet been mastered. As a result, in 1968 Soiuzglavmetall† received 37,000 letters and telegrams concerning disrupted delivery schedules. These "shortcomings in metal supply are felt especially keenly under the conditions of the new system of planning and economic incentive." Deliveries are frequently disrupted because of the violation of government discipline at enterprises and in ministries.

In order to eliminate these and other similar shortcomings, in addition to strengthening cost-accounting relations and increasing the role of material sanctions, it is essential to educate cadres in the spirit of observing government discipline in all elements of our economic system. This is a very essential prerequisite to the success of the economic reform.

Let us now examine the question of difficulties that have been discovered in the realm of economic incentives. As already indicated, in 1966 the rewarding of shops at plants and factories was aimed chiefly at heightening their interest in fulfilling the plan for increased sales. But at the same time, increased output volume is not required in many branches. After all, commodity lists are not confirmed by chance, and overfulfilling a government plan confirmed for these commodities is forbidden.

At many enterprises it is found that the existing system of economic incentives does not sufficiently resolve the key task of making full use of reserves and of increasing interest in the elaboration of intensive plans. Intensive plans are adopted very timidly, as can be seen in the considerable overfulfillment of plans by many enterprises. This is because a "fine" (i.e., reduced incentive norms) has been established not only for the overfulfillment of plans but also for the underfulfillment of them.

---

* Editors' note: Main Administration for Sale of Metal of USSR State Committee for Material and Technical Supply.

† Editors' note: Main Administration for Interrepublic Deliveries of Metal Products.

One must consider which is more advantageous from the standpoint of the formation of the enterprise's incentive fund: to lower the plan and overfulfill it or to adopt a high plan and risk its nonfulfillment. On the basis of existing experience, it can be stated that for the enterprise—in the person of its general plant services—the nonfulfillment of the plan is extremely disadvantageous, since the case of nonfulfillment, even if there is an incentive fund, the heads of plant services lose their bonus either entirely or to a considerable degree. And this is a powerful hindrance to the adoption of sufficiently high plans.

Many believe that the procedure for forming incentive funds is too complex. This point was also discussed at the All-Union Economic Conference in May 1968.

Enterprises justifiably complain that they do not have a sufficient economic interest in adopting an ambitious sales plan and that the incentive norms are revised each year "based on the level attained." At the Omsk Instrument-Building Plant, the personnel themselves have elaborated and proposed the use of profit-per-ruble-of-wages rather than increased profit or profitability as the fund-forming index. They correctly believe that labor productivity will grow more rapidly than the average wage.

Tire workers in Dnepropetrovsk believe that the point in the statute on material incentive funds which stipulates that bonuses based on the results for the year not be paid out with the nonfulfillment of sales or profits plans retards the adoption of maximally possible plans. They believe that the nonfulfillment of plans is a punishment in itself, since the size of the incentive fund is diminished. Thus, in the given instance the complete deprivation of bonuses is unnecessary and hinders the implementation of the principle of the reform: all-around stimulation of the use of all potential in the actual planning process.

Difficulties also arise with the use of incentive funds. It is difficult to buy or build anything using the fund for sociocultural measures and housing construction. Even though allotments of material were already made in 1968–69, the ministries did not always make these allotments available to the enterprises. We have many enterprises, some of whose development funds are relatively small. And if every small enterprise builds or manufactures everything it needs in a primitive way, this proves very costly to society. Therefore, the enlargement of enterprises must play an important role here.

The enterprises themselves do not always make able use of the incentive fund. The greater part of the bonuses is not paid monthly for the fulfillment of plans but instead is paid as rewards for "the fulfillment of especially important assignments." But frequently additional payment for work on days off and holidays is concealed in such cases. For example, at the Minsk Meat Combine, during 1968 and three quarters of 1969, 55 days off were declared working days in individual shops, and 14 days off were declared working days throughout the combine as a whole. In addition, 4,548 overtime man-hours were worked at that combine. Because of the incorrect use of incentive funds in ways not connected with increased labor productivity and in order to legitimatize rush work, the average wage outstrips labor productivity in some places.

Concerning the strengthening of cost-accounting, numerous complaints about the billing and crediting procedure should be noted. The billing procedures do not ensure the prompt payment of money to a conscientious supplier.

Government arbitration boards are supposed to examine claims involving illegal refusal to make payments within ten days, but in actual practice when a favorable decision is made, as a rule no order for compulsory payment is issued. The respondent is simply obligated to pay off his indebtedness within a month. And only after nonpayment during this period is an executive order issued for the compulsory issuance of payment. Thus, the receiver can make free use of products for two or three months and thereby disrupt the fulfillment of the sales plan on the part of the conscientious supplier.

Frequently, enterprises refuse loans solely because of the great amount of work involved in drawing up operational information on worthiness for credit. Therefore, in January 1966, authorization was granted for issuing credit on the basis of credit worthiness as determined from the enterprise's balance sheet, but this right was qualified with such terms that it is still purely formal. A new approach is needed to the organization of credit and accounts as a whole in the spirit of the reform.

The new Statute on the Socialist State Production Enterprise, ratified in October 1965, is frequently violated. Point 104 of the statute stipulates which organs perform total audits of the work of enterprises and at what times. But in 1966, the Suchanskii Branch of Gosbank did not recognize this point and organized numerous checks on the work of coal enterprises. Similar things are also being done by many other organizations.

The rights of enterprises are not uniformly interpreted by various agencies. Should a higher-echelon organization confirm administrative expenditures for an enterprise operating under the new system? In response to a question by A. Iufit, Director of the Leningrad Electrotechnical Plant of the Ministry of Railways, N. E. Drogichinskii, chief of a department of USSR Gosplan, replied that a higher-echelon organization should not do so and referred to a protocol of the Joint Commission under USSR Gosplan dated January 17, 1967, according to which this is a gross violation of the rights of enterprises and undermines the reform. At the same time, in response to a similar question, M. Kuzin, Chief of Personnel Administration and member of the Collegium of the USSR Ministry of Finance, replied that, according to existing data, ministries, in keeping with Point 79 of the Statute on Enterprises, confirm allocations for administrative costs for enterprises converted to the new conditions of work, and stated that the Central Personnel Administration believes that ministries are operating in accordance with the law in this process.

Also deserving of attention is the action taken by certain finance organs locally vis-à-vis enterprises that have been converted to the new conditions of work. Upon being converted to the new system, the Volgograd "Red October" Metallurgical Plant adopted a higher plan and pledged itself to reduce spending on production, including spending on wages to administrative personnel, by 815,000 rubles. This sum was written into the plan for 1966. Then the plant received a belated directive from the ministry to reduce expenditures by only 205,000 rubles as opposed to the initial plan. The plant paid no attention to this document on the assumption that, since the plant's pledges to economize on spending were higher than this sum, the matter was taken care of. But far from it! The local finance organs interpret the matter in their own way. They regard the sum of 215,000 [sic] rubles as an additional target in excess of the plant's pledges and immediately exact the money from the plant. And even though all authoritative bodies—USSR Gosplan, USSR Ministry of Finance, USSR Ministry of Ferrous Metallurgy—believed that an error had been committed, it was not corrected for a period of four months.

If an enterprise sustains a loss due to violation of the established planning procedure, the plant must have the right to exact compensation for its loss. A procedure must be elaborated for compensating for losses which are not the fault of the enterprise from the special reserve fund of the ministry that has now been created. The recommendations of the All-Union Scientific-Technical Conference on the Organization of Industrial Management (Moscow, 1966) state that higher-echelon economic and planning organs must be made liable when they are responsible for the enterprises' nonfulfillment of plans.

24. RECENT DEVELOPMENTS IN SOVIET PLANNING AND INCENTIVES

Gertrude E. Schroeder

Although the economic reform announced in 1965 appeared to presage some relaxation in central administrative control and greater autonomy for the firm, the subsequent implementation of the reform in fact brought little decentralization of decision-making power to the enterprise. The phrase "economic reform" is now used in the Soviet press instead to describe any change in economic management procedures intended to improve the existing system, including those which attempt to tighten central control over the economy.

Recent developments in planning and incentives are analyzed in this article by Gertrude E. Schroeder, Professor of Economics at the University of Virginia. The Soviet leadership is emphasizing more detailed and more "scientific" planning using mathematical models and computerized information systems, although their introduction has met various difficulties. Planners are seeking better measures of efficiency in resource use, especially the allocation of investment, and more effective ways of achieving different aspects of technological progress. Enterprise incentive schemes have been revised again in the continuing effort to get managers to adopt taut plans, improve product quality, introduce new technology and products, and reduce costs. However, although these measures expand the administrative bureaucracy and increase central control, they leave the essential features of the Soviet economic system unchanged and fail to solve the basic problems of the economy.

This selection is reprinted from *Soviet Economic Prospects for the Seventies* (A Compendium of Papers Submitted to the Joint Economic Committee, 93rd Cong., 1st sess.) (Washington, D.C.: U.S. Government Printing Office, 1973), pp. 11–38, with the omission of references to foreign-language sources.

I. INTRODUCTION

UNDER FREQUENT PRODDING from an increasingly impatient political leadership to raise economic efficiency and solve some chronic problems, Soviet planners have introduced in the past few years numerous changes in the traditional methods of planning and in the system of incentives for enterprises. These changes stem from the so-called economic reforms announced by Premier Kosygin in September 1965. In the ensuing seven years the search for "improved" methods of planning has seemed frenetic, and changes in the formal rules governing enterprise incentives have followed one another in rapid succession. Since an extensive literature already exists on the early experience with the economic reform,[1] this paper focuses on two recent developments: (1) the changes in planning methods and approaches that affected the preparation of the Ninth Five-Year Plan and are slated to affect future plans, and (2) the changes in incentive arrangements introduced in connection with the current five-year plan. Although the discussion refers mainly to the particulars of the industrial sector, much of it has relevance for the economy in general.

As background for assessing the most recent developments, it is instructive to review the general philosophy that seemed to underlie the Kosygin reforms at the outset and to consider their specific objectives. As originally announced, the reforms involved the idea that some relaxation of rigid central planning and management of enterprises would be good for the economy. Fewer targets would be handed down to enterprises, whose freedom of action was broadened by statute, notably in the areas of the management of labor and investment. Economic "levers"—sales, prices, profits, a capital charge and enterprise incentive funds—were to predominate over administrative methods in orienting enterprises to produce saleable products at minimum cost. Thus, sales, profits and return on capital (profitability) replaced gross value of output as success criteria and the basis for bonuses. Enterprises were given their own incentive and investment funds to manage as they pleased. Some "spontaneity" thus would be engendered in the economy. Reacting spontaneously to these levers, enterprises would cease to "produce for the warehouse," skimp on product quality, conceal real production possibilities, ignore costs, resist innovation, "storm," and waste capital. Fewer detailed controls would be needed, and a long list of chronic economic ills would be eliminated, or at least ameliorated.

In the course of implementing the reform during 1966–70, an element of spontaneity did indeed develop. Enterprises allowed to operate under the new procedures started to exercise their new freedoms and to respond

---

[1] The most recent account of the experience with the economic reform during 1966–70 is given in Gertrude E. Schroeder. "Soviet Economic Reform at an Impasse." *Problems of Communism*, Vol. XX, No. 4 (July–August 1971), pp. 36–46.

to the new economic parameters. Economic levers began to take hold, and in many cases things started to happen. But the planners did not always like the results. At the same time, the newly created bureaucracies continued to exercise petty tutelage over enterprises in the traditional ways, in violation of the rules of the reform and the new statutory rights granted to enterprises. To cope with these "problems," i.e., undesired, spontaneous enterprise actions, the planners successively amended the rules of the reform to restrict enterprise managers' leeway for action. The economic "levers" were administered in ever greater detail, and the size of the administrative bureaucracy steadily increased. Spokesmen for the reform began describing it as a long process, involving two phases: an "extensive" phase essentially comprising the years 1966–70, during which most industrial enterprise were gradually shifted to the new system, and an "intensive" phase during which the reform would be "deepened," and its real potentials would be realized. As the Soviet press made abundantly clear, the first phase witnessed little, if any, progress toward removing the chronic malfunctioning of the industrial sector. Industrial growth did not increase, and factor productivity improved only moderately over 1961–65.[2] At the beginning of 1971 the new system encompassed 83 percent of all industrial enterprises, most of transport and communications and substantial numbers of enterprises in other sectors.

The Ninth Five-Year Plan included, for the first time, a major section on planning and management. The Plan states that the reform is to be extended throughout the economy by 1975. It specifies a number of ways in which planning and incentives are to be "improved" over the course of the Plan. Some of these approaches were reflected in the Plan itself, and others were on-going developments given emphasis by the Plan. All of them are aimed at raising economic efficiency in general, and solving persistent problems of the system that bear especially on consumer welfare and technological progress.

II. MODIFICATIONS IN PLANNING APPROACHES
     AND TECHNIQUES

In addition to reorganizations of the administrative bureaucracy, Soviet planners typically have seen the solutions to malfunctionings of the economy to lie in "improving planning." Bad performance can be traced to bad plans; good plans, therefore, will result in good performance, provided only that enterprise managers' incentives are tied to fulfilling these good plans. In this vein, the "extensive" phase of the

---

[2] James H. Noren and F. Douglas Whitehouse, "Soviet Industry in the 1971–75 Plan," in *Soviet Economic Prospects for the Seventies* (A Compendium of Papers Submitted to the Joint Economic Committee, 93d Cong., 1st sess.) (Washington, D.C.: U.S. Government Printing Office, 1973), pp. 206–45.

reform witnessed a wide-ranging search for planning approaches that would produce these elusive, "optimal" plans. The resulting approaches, emphases and methodologies affected the preparation of the Ninth Five-Year Plan for 1971–75, now in mid-course and behind schedule; they are also now slated to influence future plans. The principal developments in planning since 1965 will be considered under four themes: (1) the larger role assigned to five-year and longer-range plans; (2) the efforts to devise more "scientific" plans, of whatever kind and duration; (3) the attempt to plan in much more detail technological progress, improved product quality, and economic efficiency; and (4) the use of mathematical models and computers, including input-output techniques.

The Larger Role of Five-Year and Long-Range Plans

In his original speech announcing the reforms, Premier Kosygin noted that contemporary developments in science and technology require that enterprise guidance have a time-horizon longer than is provided by annual plans. "Proper importance has not been attached to long-range plans," he said. He called for "as a basic form of planning, a five-year plan with breakdowns of the more important assignments by years." The recommendations of the All-Union Conference on Improving Planning and Economic Management, held in May 1968, included this proposal, along with the stricture that the five-year plans be worked out within the framework of a system of long-range plans. The emphasis on long-range plans was reinforced in the Party-Government decree on science and technology adopted in October 1968. The decree instructed Gosplan, the State Committee for Science and Technology, and other agencies concerned to work out 10–15 year forecasts of scientific and technical developments to be used in planning. Speaking at the 24th Party Congress in the Spring of 1971, both Brezhnev and Kosygin stressed the importance of long-range plans.

The Ninth Five-Year Plan embodies the approach called for by Kosygin in 1965. It includes, for the first time in Soviet planning experience, specific detailed targets for individual years in the plan period. Also, this Plan was published, the first time such detail has been given for a five-year plan since the 1930s. Moreover, in contrast to past plans, the Plan for 1971–75 was formally enacted into law by the Supreme Soviet, thus giving it directive force. Responsible agencies were instructed to ensure that a five-year plan was worked out for each individual enterprise. In anticipation of this task, Gosplan had published lengthy instructions to industrial enterprises for drafting these plans. Judging from these instructions, it appears that enterprise five-year plans are supposed to be worked out with annual breakdowns in a level of detail corresponding to that of a typical annual plan. The enterprise five-year plan contains 11 basic parts, the key indices for which are set by superior organs as sub-components of the aggregates in the national plan. If "life dictates," however, the plans for individual years within the quinquennium may be changed; indeed, numerous changes already were made in the plan for 1973, in response to the poor performance in agriculture and in the completion of new capacities during 1971–72.

In accord with a frequently cited Leninist dictum that "one cannot work without a plan designed for the long run," Soviet planners have been doing preparatory work on the formulation of several sub-plans for 1976–80 and on a 15-year plan for 1976–90. In late 1971 the Collegium of the USSR Gosplan approved a "General Plan for the Development of USSR Power Systems to 1980," which is mandatory for use by subordinate Gosplans in formulating annual and five-year plans in that period. Gosplan also has set up a number of special task forces to do the preparatory work for drafting the various major sections of the long-range plan. Based on the work of these task forces, Gosplan, together with the State Committee on Science and Technology and the USSR Academy of Sciences, has adopted a decree establishing a list of the most important problems to be considered and the kinds of scientific and technical forecasts and economic projections required for developing the plan for 1976–90. The objective is, evidently, to provide the basis for simultaneous preparation of a 15-year plan with five-year breakdowns and the Tenth Five-Year Plan for 1976–80.

Providing a More "Scientific" Basis for Plans: The Role of Forecasts

In connection with the genesis of the 1965 economic reform proposals, Soviet planners became convinced that the key to improved economic performance lay in developing much more "scientific" bases and methodologies for centralized planning. The call for more "scientifically-based" plans involved two major ideas. First, long-term forecasts of scientific and technological developments should be made in some detail, and second, all parts of the plan should be based on projections (forecasts) of economic and social variables made with the use of modern mathematical and economic models. The planners perceived that the Soviet economy was not participating in the ongoing, world technological revolution and evidently believed that if accurate forecasts of technology were made, the plans could take them into account, and the USSR's track record in this area would be improved. The current forecasting craze that has resulted apparently had its genesis in a speech that Premier Kosygin made to Gosplan officials in 1965. Stressing the importance of scientific and technical progress, he said, "Can we, in projections of the national economy, ignore substantiated forecasts relating to the future? No, we cannot."

Forecasting was institutionalized by providing as part of the Eighth Five-Year Plan a "State Plan for Highly Important Scientific Research" that included a comprehensive plan for working out socio-economic forecasts and forecasts of technological developments for 1971–75 and beyond. Dozens of institutes launched forecasting programs, the effort being greatly facilitated by the increasing availability of more and better computers. In December 1966, the first Scientific Conference on Economic Forecasting was held under the auspices of Gosplan and the Academy of Sciences. The high-level, active support for forecasting also touched off a lively, theoretical debate over the role of such forecasts in Socialist planning; this subject was sensitive, since it revived methodological-ideological issues in planning that had lain dormant since the 1920s. The pragmatists have overcome the ideological scruples with the dictum "A plan without a forecast is just as impossible under socialism as a forecast without a plan." They take pains to emphasize, however, that forecasting is a part of pre-plan work. First, the past is analyzed, and forecasts are made of likely developments in science and technology and likely trends and relationships of socio-economic variables; then with this information the specific social aims and purposes are selected for the plan period by the political leadership; finally an "efficient" plan for achieving these goals is formulated.

With the added impetus provided by the 1968 Party-Government decree on scientific research, the forecasting effort has burgeoned. Everyone and his research institute have got into the act. The numerous scientific research institutes under the USSR Academy of Science and the economic ministries were charged with forecasting developments in science and technology. Economic research institutes took on the task of forecasting a variety of social and economic variables. An Economic Forcasting Section was created in the Institute of Economics of the Academy of Sciences and in Gosplan's Economic Research Institute, and 56 temporary commissions were set up to make various kinds of forecasts. In April 1970 a Conference on Economic Planning and Forecasting Methodology was held under the aegis of Gosplan's Economic Research Institute. Another conference was held on the same subject in 1971, and a conference on forecasting prices was held in 1972. As forecasting became the thing to do, complaints were voiced about lack of coordination, overlap and duplication of effort, inconsistent and incompatible methodologies, and use of different basic assumptions. Indeed, the 1970 Conference on forecasting had noted these phenomena and recommended that a national center be established to oversee a unified forecasting effort and to allocate tasks. There should be developed (1) a list of required forecasts and indicators to be projected, (2) a single system of forecasting models to be worked out on computers, and (3) a standard set of reliable statistics.

The pleas for a coordinator for the disparate forecasting efforts produced an awe-inspiring decree issued in late 1972 under the imprimatur of Gosplan, the State Committee for Science and Technology, and the USSR Academy of Sciences. This document, an appendage to the already approved plan for research in the natural and social sciences in 1971–75, parcels out forecasting assignments to the various research institutes in connection with the preparation of the new 15-year plan and its sub-plans. But the decree does much more than make research assignments, for it is accompanied by an equally awe-inspiring decree with the impressive title "Main Methodological Principles and Mandatory Requirements for the Compilation of Scientific and Technical Forecasts." It aims to cover all kinds of forecasts—both technological and social. This very epitome of a bureaucratic document defies adequate summarizing. Perhaps a bit of its flavor can be had from the following sketch. Each separate forecast: (1) must contain both technical indicators and indicators of the economic effectiveness of various ways "to implement domestic and world achievements" in the field involved; (2) should include an evaluation of the "social consequences" of each forecast development; (3) should include an analysis of relevant past and present developments in the USSR and the world and a prediction of developments in the period concerned; and (4) must be submitted to five separate agencies, with mandatory coverage of a large number of specified items. How the recipients will manage the mountain of paper that will surely result from this massive forecasting project is an interesting question.

Precisely what influence the forecasting work of research institutes had on the final draft of the Ninth Five-Year Plan cannot be determined by anyone outside Gosplan. On the one hand, Gosplan Chairman Baibakov states in a preface to the published plan that such research played a "significant" role. On the other hand, the head of Gosplan's Economic Research Institute stated at the beginning of 1971 that "forecasts are still little used in planning and managing the national economy." Although price forecasts were made for branches of industry and groups of commodities, the projections were not used in the plan. It is clear, however, that, largely because of the availability of computers, many more computations and disaggregations were made for this plan than for previous ones. Thus, for the first time in planning history balances were worked out for 5,500 different kinds of equipment in natural units and in value. Material balances with annual breakdowns were computed for 235 basic products, and investment requirements for materials were determined on the basis of technical norms, thus dispensing with the specific ministerial order documents that used to be required.

Probably the most influential of the "scientific" forecasts were projections of a variety of technical indicators (norms) of projected savings in resources per unit of product. The norms for savings in materials were very bullish, especially those that underlay the plan for machinery and the plans for introduction of new capacities.[3] Goals for labor productivity and for completion of new capacities also are very ambitious. Soviet planners seem to have been carried away in particular by the results that could be achieved, on paper, at least, through reduction of material expenditures per unit of product. In his report to the 24th Party Congress Premier Kosygin called such reduction "an enormous reserve" in the economy. The Soviet press frequently cited calculations of savings that could be achieved. For example, planners calculated that a reduction of 1 percent in use of ferrous metals in machinery production is equivalent to 260,000 tons of rolled metal, enough to make 100,000 T–74 excavators and over 60,000 SK–4 grain combines. Gosplan's Scientific Research Institute for Planning and Norms prepared methodological materials to guide the ministries in recomputing norms and, based on ministerial submissions, worked out final proposals for reduction in materials expenditure norms during 1971–75 that were "used by Gosplan" in drafting the Plan. It is clear that planning norms of all kinds were calculated and recalculated in a level of detail much greater than heretofore. Although expenditure norms have been developed for only about 70 percent of all industrial materials, work is underway to expand the list. Moreover, as a recent book on planning points out, "Planning norms must be higher than the average attained and near to those attained by the best enterprises." Finally, the planned reductions in material expenditures during 1971–75 were handed down to ministries and to enterprises as mandatory indices in their plans.

Gosplan clearly was under strong pressure to make the plan for 1971–75 as taut as possible. In a rare description of the formulation process, a Deputy Chief of Gosplan stated, "On several occasions the CPSU Central Committee and the Council of Ministers reviewed the basic problems involved in the draft Five-Year Plan and directed attention of Gosplan, the ministries, and the union-republics to increasing the role of efficiency in the economy and finding additional resources for strengthening agriculture and raising living standards." From his description, it appears that Gosplan at several points in the drafting process tightened up plans submitted from below. In preparing the taut plan demanded by the leadership, Gosplan could defend its realism by reference to the "scientific basis" for its underpinnings—the projected gains in efficiency. As indicated, this Plan, more than its predecessors, was formulated using detailed forecasts of technical possibilities for resource savings that were worked out by engineers in the numerous industrial and scientific research institutes. Such people well might forecast as generally achievable efficiency gains that were technically possible with existing know-how and that may, indeed, have been realized in some

---

[3] Ibid., pp. 215–20.

plants. Under great pressure to "uncover hidden reserves" in the economy, Gosplan could only welcome such "scientifically substantiated" forecasts. Could it be that attempts to "improve" planning by making it more "scientifically based" may render it more unrealistic instead?

Planning Technological Progress

A principal concern of planners and economists in the past few years has been the search for ways to boost the rate of technological progress within a framework of socialist central planning. This search has involved, first of all, the attempt to devise satisfactory measures of the rate of progress, frequently considered to mean the efficiency of resource use in general. A second facet is the effort to devise specific technical parameters for planning and achieving particular aspects of technological progress.

1. Measures of Efficiency. Mindful of Kosygin's criticism in 1965, "It must be said that our economic scholars have not busied themselves greatly with analysis of the effectiveness of social production and the elaboration of proposals for increasing it," economists have filled the economic press with discussions of how best to measure economic efficiency at various levels—economy, ministry and enterprise. One objective of the discussion was to devise a set of specific indices of efficiency that could be included in plans and that could serve both to force greater efficiency on producing units and to measure and compare the results achieved. The vigorous debates on the issue, still continuing, culminated in the publication by Gosplan in early 1972 of a draft set of "uniform and inter-related indices" for measuring the efficiency of economic activity. For the economy as a whole and the republics, the indices are national income and consumption per capita, national income per ruble of capital invested, and per ruble of wages. For ministries, associations and enterprises a long list of indicators is provided. Essentially, they amount to calculating ratios of both net output and gross output per ruble of capital, labor and materials expenditures, along with a number of subsidiary indices. The draft list of indicators has been sent to ministries and some large enterprises, with instructions to compute the indicated measures for the period 1971–75. Presumably, the next step will be to incorporate the finally agreed upon set of indices into the formal plan documents and to make fulfillment of the plans for some or all of them mandatory. These steps have already been taken with respect to two of the indicators, profitability and labor productivity.

According to Gosplan Chief Baibakov, a wide variety of indicators of efficiency in the use of capital, labor and material resources were used in preparing the Ninth Five-Year Plan—many more than in previous plans.

An important recently adopted document is a "Standard Methodology for Calculating the Efficiency of Capital Investment," published in 1969. Because the new Methodology represents a revision of an earlier (1959) Methodology to which Western specialists on the Soviet economy have paid considerable attention, it is worthy of extended treatment. Unlike the earlier document, the new Methodology was formally approved by Gosplan, the State Committee on Construction (Gosstroy) and the Presidium of the Academy of Sciences and is described as "mandatory" for all sectors of the economy. On the basis of it the ministries are to work out specific branch methodologies. The revised General Methodology is at once broader and more explicit than its predecessor. The revision was intended basically to serve two purposes: (1) to establish a uniform definitional and methodological basis for calculating the efficiency of investment throughout the economy and at key administrative levels, and (2) to bring this facet of planning in line with the concepts and terminology of the on-going economic reform. Both purposes are in furtherance of the greatly increased emphasis of the current leadership on the critical importance of raising the return on investment, following its dramatic, sharp decline during Khrushchev's latter years.

The new Methodology represents an advance over its predecessor in the direction of greater economic rationality. What its actual impact will be in practice is another question. The principal differences between the old and the new Methodologies are the following:

(1) Unlike its predecessor the new Methodology specifies formulae for calculating the overall efficiency of capital investment termed "coefficients of absolute effectiveness." For the whole economy, the republics and the major sectors, this measure is the incremental output/captial ratio, with output defined as national income (Soviet concept). For sectoral sub-branches and for ministries and their subordinate organizations, the measure is the incremental profits/capital ratio. The first formula includes the proviso that the ratio is to be calculated "under a given output structure," a phrase whose intent is obscure, perhaps deliberately so.

(2) Like its predecessor, the new Methodology provides a formula for the so-called "Coefficient of Relative Effectiveness" or CRE. This measure is supposed to be used in choosing between two technical solutions for a given problem such as the location of new enterprises. Although the conceptual basis is the same, the revised Methodology provides a different formula for calculation, namely: $C_i + E_a K_i =$ Minimum, where C_i is the current operating cost for each variant, E_a is the Standard CRE, and K_i is the capital investment for each variant. The reciprocal of the CRE is the recoupment period.

(3) Unlike its precessor, the new Methodology fixes a Standard CRE of 0.12 and a standard discount rate of 0.08, the latter to be used in calculations involving streams of investments and costs over different time periods. With the approval of Gosplan, the ministries may set lower

CRE's for their sub-branches "when necessary to stimulate technological progress and to take account of dissimilar wage levels (zonal and branch), differences in price levels, the lengths of construction programs and regional differences."

(4) The new Methodology provides more guidance than did the old one on the kinds of items to be taken into account in the various computations, and it also allows for lags.

The revised Methodology has occasioned much comment in the economic press. From this discussion it is evident that many ambiguities exist in the document, particularly over the precise uses to which the two coefficients (absolute and relative) are to be put. While the document specifies the standard CRE in the section that discusses the choice between technical variants, the press comment suggests that it is being regarded as a guideline for the minimum return on investment in general.[4] The figure itself apparently was derived as the actual average return (profits/capital) on investment in the economy as a whole in 1967–68. The establishment of a standard CRE culminated a decade or more of academic debate over whether a uniform or differentiated coefficients should be fixed. The provision of a clause in the new Methodology allowing for deviation below the standard CRE has produced cries of outrage from the advocates of uniformity. Fedorenko, for example, says that the escape clause "in essence opens the door to the greatest arbitrariness in calculating the efficiency of project variants and reduces the scientific significance of the Methodology to naught." The branch methodologies thus far adopted do indeed allow for considerable deviation. While the distress of economists like Fedorenko is understandable, deviations probably are essential in practice, and perhaps even "rational," given the arbitrariness of Soviet prices.

2.   Technical Parameters.   On a less aggregated level, the planners have been trying to devise specific technical parameters for inclusion in plans, in order to force various aspects of technological advance in a narrower sense. The plans have long included targets for the number of new machines and new products to be produced. The current effort is focused on the upgrading of product quality and concerns not only

---

[4] To avoid misunderstanding on this point, it should be said that specification of standard calculation rules and a standard CRE does not mean that inter-sectoral, inter-industry or enterprise investment allocations are actually being made on the basis of relative rates of return or even that planners believe that they should be. Both average and marginal rates of return differ widely among sectors and branches and enterprise profitability varies enormously for reasons that have little to do with relative efficiency. As allocations in the Ninth Five-Year Plan indicate, investment continues to be allotted mainly on the basis of political policy rather than on economic calculation. For a somewhat different interpretation of the purposes and uses of the new Methodology, see Alan Abouchar, "The New Soviet Standard Methodology for Investment Allocation," *Soviet Studies,* Vol. XXIV, No. 3 (January 1973), pp. 402–10. [The new Standard Methodology and the Abouchar commentary are reprinted above as Selections 15–A and 15–B, respectively.—The Editors.]

the inclusion of more indicators in plans, but also measures to enforce them. In 1965 Kosygin said. "It is necessary to provide in the plans for the most important indices of the technical level and quality of output. . . . It is necessary to raise the role of the State standards as an effective means of improving the quality of output. State certificates of the quality of output should be introduced." Besides a voluminous press discussion on these topics, a number of government actions have been taken to implement these facets of the economic reform. The Standard Methodology for formulating enterprise five-year plans includes "indicators of the quality of output" in the list of targets that are set by higher-level organs. An elaborate procedure has been worked out for specifying these plan indicators. The government has instructed the ministries, beginning in 1972, to classify all of their products into three categories—"highest," or those that meet the best domestic and foreign achievements; "first," or those of lower quality but which are in demand; and "second," or those that are of inferior quality or obsolete and whose production should be phased out. A standard procedure for such quality certification has been published under the imprimatur of Gosplan and several other agencies. Enterprise plans are to include centrally set percentages of total output that are to comprise products of the highest category; targets for raising this share are to be established, and the products involved are to be included in the plant's obligatory nomenclature list in physical units.

Another approach concerns a highly publicized program to award a "State Seal of Quality" to superior products, particularly consumer goods. The Ninth Five-Year Plan includes the goal of raising the number of products with the Seal from 4,000 to about 15,000. Despite a vigorous press campaign pushing the program, the amount of red-tape involved has been a considerable deterrent to progress. Moreover, it was reported in late 1972 that of the 1,900 items produced by the Ministry of Light Industry that have been awarded the Seal of Quality, only 1,200 are actually being produced; for clothing only 347 of the 821 products certified are being produced.

Still another approach is a vigorous effort to establish and upgrade State standards. Although standards have long been a feature of Soviet industrial practice, their use is being greatly expanded, as vehicles for promoting technological progress. The State Committee on Standards, elevated in status in 1970, is in charge of this program. In 1969 its research institute published a "Standard Methodology for Determining the Effectiveness of Standards," and the importance of standards in the technical sections of the plans has evidently been raised considerably. A Party-Government Decree of December 5, 1970, ordered a review and updating of all standards during 1971–75 and instructed Gosplan and the ministries to include in enterprise plans beginning in 1972 specific assignments for raising the level of product standardization, particularly in machinery production. The Standards Committee was to issue in 1971–72 a series of uniform procedures relating to technical upgrading of output, viz., procedures for "the confirmation of technical assignments, for the conduct of expert examination of designs, for testing of experimental models, for the issuance of permits for putting new types of output into production, and the conduct of control tests of series output." The bureaucracy leaves nothing to chance! The Decree gives the Standards Committee powers of inspection and checking up on observance of standards. If enterprises sell products that deviate from state standards or technical specifications, such sales are not counted for purposes of plan fulfillment, and the attendant profits must be paid into the state budget. Finally, on a note of desperation, the Decree states, "The USSR Ministry of Justice, in conjunction with the USSR Prosecutor's Office and the USSR Supreme Court, has been charged with studying and generalizing the practice of the application of legislation on responsibility for the production of poor-quality, nonstandard and incomplete output and with elaborating measures for increasing the effectiveness with which this legislation is applied, so that officials who permit the systematic production of poor-quality output do not go unpunished." In furtherance of this mass assault on the intractable problem of product quality, the State Standards Committee is drafting a mammoth set of procedural regulations for a uniform system of quality control for all industry, parts of which are to be introduced during 1971–75. In the meantime, in the real world, as opposed to the paper-creating bureaucratic world, the beleaguered ministries are already behind schedule on standardization tasks, and quality problems are rife.

Role of Mathematical Models and Computers in Planning

After some withering away of ideological shackles, Soviet economists have turned their attention to the use of mathematical models for economic analysis and prescriptions for plans. Also, with the increased availability of computers of sizeable capacity, Soviet planners have begun to fit them into the planning routine. It is also evident that some persons in high places, some economists, and some planners view these models and machines as a great "reserve" for raising efficiency in the economy, while preserving both central planning and central administration. Despite some initial foot-dragging, the planning bureaucracy has now accepted, and even embraced, the new techniques. Like the economic reform, which has already been successfully assimilated and bureaucratized into impotence,[5] the planners now seem to have discovered that planning for the use of mathematical models provides an enormous scope for bureaucratic activity. The amount of such computer-related activity

---

[5] For a defense of this thesis see Schroeder, "Soviet Economic Reform at an Impasse."

has burgeoned in the past several years, and the amount already set *en train* is awesome to behold. The aim of this section is to try to reduce this enormously complex subject to intelligible proportions. It will (1) outline the highlights of the drive for computerization of planning and management since 1965; (2) describe two key computer-managed planning systems that have been launched—ASPR and ASN; and (3) assess the present state of the use of input-output (I-O) in actual planning practice. The focus throughout will be on what the government agencies have done or are actually doing. Thus, we abstract from the comprehensive, cybernetic models of an "optimally functioning socialist economy" that some academic economists are writing about.[6] What the planning bureaucracy has launched, however, is also labelled as steps toward a system of optimal planning and administration. It will help the reader to keep reminding himself that none of the projects described below is actually operational. They are preliminary plans for systems or plans for planning systems, or systems analysis of current planning with a view to planning new systems.

1. The Drive for Computerization of Planning. The amount of information required and generated in a centrally administered economy is enormous. Electronic data processing appeared to be the obvious answer to the Soviet statistical and planning problems. In the early 1960s, Soviet cyberneticists developed models for a nationwide system of computer centers for information collection, processing and use. At that time, the work on this project and the related mathematical models for economic management was coordinated by the Main Administration for the introduction of Computers into the Economy, under the State Committee for Coordination of Scientific Research. In 1966, a government decree provided for establishing "a state network of computer centers for the collection and processing of information and the solution of problems of planning and control in the economy." As then envisioned, the network was to be based on the existing facilities of the Central Statistical Administration. Sectoral and branch computer systems for "planning, accounting, control and information processing" also would be created subsequently, and their facilities would be connected with the state network. It appears that for several years a bureaucratic tug of war ensued between Gosplan and the Central Statistical Administration over which agency was to be in charge of this vast project. In the interim, both agencies acquired more computers and put them to work in their respective bailiwicks. Gosplan had also created a Department for the Introduction of Economic-Mathematical Methods into Planning.

Although little, if anything, was actually being accomplished, the idea of a statewide computer network continued to receive support—notably

---

[6] These models are described in some detail in Michael Ellman, *Soviet Planning Today: Proposals for an Optimally Functioning Economic System* (Cambridge, Eng.: Cambridge University Press, 1971).

in the recommendations of the 1968 Conference on Improving Planning and in the Directives for the Ninth Five-Year Plan. A prestigious All-Union Conference on Using Computers in Economic Management was held in January 1972. The bureaucratic jurisdictional quarrel was settled, at least for the moment, when the task of coordinating plans for the network was given to the Institute for Problems of Organization and Management set up in late 1971 or early 1972 under the State Committee for Science and Technology. Its Director, D. G. Zhimerin, revealed the present embryonic status of this project, when he stated in mid-1972 that his institute has been entrusted with the task of developing the principles of organizing a "Statewide Automated System for Collecting and Processing Information for Planning and Administration (OGAS)," and that as a part of this project the Institute is drawing up a plan for the location of a statewide network of computer centers and a general plan for the construction of a statewide data transmission system.

In addition to the computer network and the data transmission system, OGAS is conceived as having a number of key functional subsystems, which are in various initial stages of development. These are: an automated system of plan calculations (ASPR), an automated system of norms (ASN), an automated system of state statistics (ASGS), an automated system for managing supply (ASU MTS), an automated system of standards and metrology (AIUS), an automated system for processing price information (ASOI tsen), and an automated system for management of scientific-technical progress (ASUNT). In addition to these nationwide subsystems, there are to be subordinate "line" automated systems of management (ASUs) for republics and ministries (OASUs) and also for enterprises (ASUPs). The ultimate aim is to link the computers in all of these systems with one another, via the state data transmission system. Thus, a single, unified, automated system of management—"the state's unified cybernetic brain"—will be created for the entire economy. This grandiose scheme is being taken very seriously by the Soviet government, generating voluminous press reporting, and a large amount of bureaucratic activity in the form of conferences and a flood of documents. To provide some notion of what is involved and what has already been done, we report below on the plans for one subsystem—ASPR—and its auxiliary subsystem—ASN.

2. ASPR and ASN. The objective of ASPR is to provide an integrated, computerized and uniform system for working out national economic plans and monitoring their fulfillment. In its simplest aspect, it is initially a project to link all of the planning bodies—USSR Gosplan, the Gosplans in the republics, local Planning Departments, and planning departments in the ministries and their main administrations—with computers and with the mandatory use of a common set of information and procedures. In this least ambitious form, the system's successful introduction presumably would speed up plan calculation and the exchange of information in plan formulation and also would provide faster information feedback and exchange during plan implementation. ASPR would then represent essentially merely the mechanization of the existing planning system. Ultimately, ASPR may amount to no more than this, for even this limited task is an enormous undertaking. It appears that in late 1972 functioning computer centers were in operation only in the Gosplans of the Ukraine, Kazakhstan, Belorussia, Uzbekistan, and Lithuania, while in the other republics "the effort to employ mathematical methods and computers in planning is just beginning." Apparently, USSR Gosplan's Main Computer Center has not yet been linked operationally with any of these centers or with those in the ministries.

ASN, ASPR's auxiliary system, is intended to computerize the system of planning norms for labor, materials and financial expenditures that are a fundamental part of the present planning methodology. Thus, ASN would transfer to computers the laborious task of storing, aggregating and updating the ubiquitous planning norms and would facilitate the calculation and use of such norms in much greater detail. The planning for this practical project seems to be well underway, with Gosplan's Research Institute for Planning and Norms having been designated to coordinate the work. A number of methodological documents for the system have been approved, and many more types of norms are already being calculated and used in planning. Creation of ASN may even have been accorded priority, given its intimate connection with current planning practices.

As described in the literature, however, ASPR is intended ultimately to be much more than a mere computerization of existing planning practices. It is supposed to represent an entirely new system of planning, "scientifically based," and making large use of consistent economic-mathematical models of all kinds and at all levels to calculate plan variants and to optimize planning decisions. It is supposed to be based on a unified and improved information system, the inputs into which are being separately developed in the other nationwide systems noted above.[7] In the words of a planner, "Thus, the quality of the plans for economic development will be substantially improved." Academic mathematical economists view ASPR as a vital unit in the actual application in practice of their overall models for the "optimally functioning socialist economy."

Th first work toward the creation of ASPR was begun in Gosplan in November 1966. A draft statement of the basic approaches to developing the system was formally approved in 1969 at a meeting of the various Gosplans and a unit of the Academy of Sciences. In 1970, a coordinator, Gosplan's Main Computer Center, was designated for the task, and in May 1972 a detailed coordination plan and a series of procedural documents were approved by Gosplan. Thus, the work of designing the projected system has been formally launched.

---

[7] For example, the Automated Systems for state statistics and for prices.

ASPR is supposed to consist of some 300 sectoral and support subsystems. The sectoral components parallel the basic substantive parts of the national economic plan—summary balances, level of living of the population, labor, etc.—and the major geographic and economic sector breakdowns. The support components concern procedures; information; mathematical, technical and organizational support; and personnel. Task forces have been set up to devise each of the subsystems. Present scheduling calls for the full introduction of the system in 1977, with five stages of implementation being envisioned as follows: development of technical specifications—six months; preliminary designing—one year; technical designing—one year; working designing—18 months; introduction—18 months. Apparently, the system is now being designed for the capabilities of the second generation Minsk–32 computer, but is supposed to be modified when more powerful ones become available. The problem of planning the coordination of all these task forces and their subsystem designs has yet to be faced.

3. Use of Input-Output (I-O) Techniques in Planning Practice. The contrast between the planned future planning and the present procedures is extreme. While planning a comprehensive, integrated computer network drags on from year to year, the actual installation of computers throughout the economy proceeds haltingly and at random at various levels, including some enterprises. Problems of deficient hardware, inadequate software, and insufficient trained programmers continue to plague the users. The owner of each computer procedes to program his machine to his problems as best he can, thus adapting the machines and programs not to the ASPR of the future, but to the present organization and procedures. This lag is most clearly seen in the use of input-output techniques.

Despite much writing about the use of mathematical models and extolling of their virtues, their advent seems not to have changed traditional planning practices in any significant way. Rather, these models, including I–O, appear to serve merely as adjuncts to the traditional approach. This seems to be the present situation, despite high-level political support for mathematical approaches to economic problem-solving and frequently expressed laments of academic model-builders that their models are not being used. Thus, Academician Fedorenko writes,

> . . . I regret to say that so far the use of economic and mathematical models has not been of a consistently systematic nature and has served, as it were, as an extraneous addition to the economic planning and management system. However, to insert models directly into the planning process is impossible, for this very process is unadapted in terms of its methods, technology, organization, and information base to systematic model use. These are the same reasons why electronic computers in national economic planning have also been used thus far basically for mechanizing separate, comparatively homogeneous calculations.

Another mathematical economist, S. S. Shatalin, states, "Hitherto, mathematical-economic models and computers have been used mainly for the solution of one-time only, individual plan tasks, often ones that are scarcely inter-connected. Calculations on the basis of models have been a sort of 'extension' to the existing system of planning and control." But, significantly, he continues, "One of the weakest points in the use of mathematical-economic models is the absence of the necessary statistical, technical, and economic-planning information. This situation has inevitably made models over-simplified and crude, which has watered down the conclusions and results obtained from them." Both of these economists pin their hopes for change on the fundamentally new approach and information base that is supposed to be generated by OGAS and its component, ASPR.

Soviet economists regard input-output models as the most developed of their planning models and potentially of great utility in improving the quality of plans. It seems useful, therefore, to try to discern from the literature the present state of affairs with respect to the actual use of I–O techniques in planning practice. Despite the compilation of two ex post I–O tables (for 1959 and 1966) and a considerable amount of work on developing planning I–O tables,[8] an economist could write in early 1968, "It would be no exaggeration to say that not a single important decision in current or long-range plans has been taken on the basis of contruction of I–O balances either in physical units or in value form." Probably, the same statement could be made by someone writing in 1973. The author of a descriptive book on Soviet planning published in 1971 merely states with respect to I–O, "At present, measures are being taken to speed up the introduction of I–O into planning practice." Descriptions in the planning literature indicate clearly that the advent of I–O data has not altered traditional planning approaches in the least; rather, the availability of sets of I–O data and of computers has made possible the addition to the planning process of a large number of new kinds of calculations and a type of analytical work that was not possible before. It is also evident, however, that there is considerable political and academic pressure to use I–O techniques as a means for making the plans more "scientifically based" and the Gosplan is now carrying out a large amount of work in an attempt to build bridges between I–O and the traditional techniques.

What specific actions have been taken since 1965? First, the whole effort was given strong impetus by a Council of Ministers' Instruction requiring the use of the 1966 ex post I–O table in compiling the Ninth Five-Year Plan. A chapter on the methodology to be used in calculating

---

[8] For a description of Soviet work on I–O, see Vladimir G. Treml, Dimitri M. Gallik, Barry T. Kostinsky and Kurt W. Kruger, *The Structure of the Soviet Economy: Analysis and Reconstruction of the 1966 Soviet Input-Output Table* (New York: Praeger Publishers, 1972), pp. 11–32.

planning I–O tables was included for the first time in Gosplan's volume of Methodological Instructions for compiling the national economic plan, published in 1969. Planning I–O balances were calculated for 1970 in physical and also in value form. As described in the methodology, these balances seem to be calculated by working backward from preliminary plan targets already developed in the usual way, namely, from general overall policy goals; sets of planned coefficients for direct expenditures of materials, fuels, and labor per unit of product; and calculations of total sectoral outputs that are deemed to be in accord with planned availabilities of investment and labor. The resulting I–O tables are used to check on the consistency and feasibility of the preliminary set of plan targets.

A commonly cited reason for the delay in using I–O in planning has been that the former is worked out as a commodity-commodity matrix, whereas material balances and plan indexes are worked out primarily on a branch-of-industry basis, with the results ultimately becoming mandatory plan targets addressed to economic ministries. Moreover, even for physical products the systems of product classification are not uniform. Gosplan economists apparently have perceived the problem of utilizing I–O as involving its adaptation to conform to traditional planning approaches. As early at 1968, it was recommended that Gosplan should draw all of its departments into the work of developing I–O in usable form. Gosplan apparently has now begun to tackle this problem with vigor, using the basic approach of "connecting" I–O with plan indexes. A sub-department for I–O has been created in Gosplan's Department of Summary Balances. Extensive experimental work has been done by Gosplan's Economics Institute and its Main Computer Center, and a program has been underway to familiarize all Gosplan Departments with I–O work. This effort resulted in the preparation of a planning I–O table for each of the years 1971–75 in physical and value units and a consolidated table in value terms for the period as a whole. It appears that the former is a 260-sector model and the latter an 18-sector model and that work on an 800-sector physical table is in process. The annual planning tables for 1971–75 were worked out "in Gosplan terms," i.e., the list of products, industries and ministries included in the I–O tables correspond to those used in the national economic plan. The list included 257 products, 25 industrial ministries, and 20 sectors of the economy. The basic information for calculating the I–O tables was obtained from the Gosplan departments for the various balances and for sectors of the economy. The data consisted of calculations of gross output of industrial ministries and agriculture, requirements for basic kinds of industrial and agricultural products, material balances for basic products, and calculations of labor productivity and capital requirements by ministries and branches.

Gosplan economists describe the development of these planning tables for 1971–75 as "a decisive step" in adopting I–O for application in planning practices. With the use of the tables, a number of analytical calculations were made in connection with preparation of the Ninth Five-Year Plan. They reportedly revealed, among other things, that some planned outputs (many kinds of machinery, chemicals, and agricultural products) were not matched with demands, and that there were inconsistencies between physical and value indices in some machinery branches. Information deficiencies of various kinds also came to light, including the interesting finding that various Gosplan departments were using different methodologies to calculate similar plan indices.

In summary, I–O tables are now being used to (1) calculate plan variants: 15 variants were calculated using the planning I–O table for 1970; (2) perform a variety of analyses relating to the feasibility and consistency of the plans; (3) ascertain detailed, structural interrelationships among sectors of the economy; (4) improve the planning norms used in calculating material balances; (5) provide full input coefficients, not previously obtainable; and (6) forecast long-term developments, aggregated dynamic models being used for this purpose. Thus, it seems that the plan is being formulated in the traditional ways, but the new I–O adjunct is making useful contributions by providing analytical results and types of information not previously available to the planners.

Writers on the use of I–O and other types of models in planning agree that their present and potential usefulness is seriously limited by the lack of a sufficiently complete and reliable information base. The same lament is made in regard to planning by the traditional method of balances. With respect to both, the complaint usually takes the form of assertions about the poor bases for calculating the innumerable technical and value norms that are part and parcel of these methods. The creation of ASN is supposed to yield great improvements in this area. The quality of the present information basis for Soviet planning and for model-building by economists is described most graphically by S. S. Shatalin, Deputy Director of the Academy of Sciences' Central Economic-Mathematical Institute (TSEMI):

> Information is one of the biggest bottlenecks in the practical use of mathematical-economic methods in planning and management and in raising the scientific level of planning and management. At the present time, statistical and economic planning information is clearly insufficient, not sufficiently unified, and of a poor time sequence. Internally coordinated information on expenditures of material, man-power, and natural resources for the production of output is also insufficient and poorly systematized. Yet, whereas without the use of mathematical-economic models the defects in information in planning calculations do not result in shortcomings that are clearly visible in the plan (but are clearly felt in reality), for the developers of models, who have to convert their mathematical symbols

into figures, they result literally in "natural calamities," to which unfortunately we are gradually becoming accustomed. This is one of the basic reasons for the conversion of mathematical-economic modeling into abstract academic exercises in the bad sense of this word.

Other Approaches to Improving Planning

The chronic shortcomings in planning that were pointed out and severely criticized at the 24th Party Congress produced a *mea culpa* editorial in Gosplans house organ and vows to put matters right along the lines indicated in the Plan Directives. Besides the specific measures being taken in areas noted above, Gosplan has launched two major efforts to solve the intractable and all-pervasive planning problems. Following complaints that planning was becoming fouled up by lack of uniformity in methodological approach—because subordinate agencies, institutes, and ministries were ignoring Gosplan's published Methodological Instructions and issuing their own—Gosplan dispatched an order forbidding this practice and requiring Gosplan clearance for all planning instructions.

Subsequently, Gosplan launched a project to enlist all Gosplan departments and research institutes, along with the ministries and other agencies concerned, in developing proposals for revising the volume of official Methodological Instructions published in 1969. Specific drafting assignments were made, with a deadline of February 15, 1973, for submission of the final draft to the Gosplan leadership. At the end of 1971, Gosplan launched still another project—this one to get ideas on how to improve planning and management in general. It set up a high-level Committee of Gosplan officials charged with the task of preparing recommendations on a specified list of problems. In a subsequent order, issued in April 1972, Gosplan assigned its various departments specific responsibilities for preparing recommendations. The Councils of Ministers in the republics and the economic ministries are also being required by government directive to submit recommendations. Gosplan's order appends a detailed list, consisting of eight major sections and 51 subsections, covering the areas on which proposals are to be submitted. Another mountain of paper will result from this project.

Meanwhile, academic economists continue to criticize the present methods and approaches used by Gosplan in developing the plans. This critical literature has begun to advocate, among other things, the application of systems analysis to planning. One economist argues, for example, that the present ministerial-branch approach should be replaced by systems of plans based on major sectors and all of their inputs, e.g., agriculture. The implied allegations that Gosplan planning is not systematic produced a long article by Gosplan's Deputy Chairman, maintaining that the USSR has now, and always has had, a "systems" and "program" approach to planning.

III. RECENT DEVELOPMENTS IN THE SYSTEM OF INCENTIVES FOR ENTERPRISES

Under the rules of the economic reform as announced by Kosygin in 1965, the success criteria for enterprises were to be fulfillment of plans for sales (or profits) and profitability. Bonuses for managerial personnel were to depend on fulfillment of these plans, along with fulfillment of the plan for production of key products in physical units, and the Ministries were permitted to add other conditions for receipt of bonuses. Enterprises were to form three types of incentive funds—a bonus fund, a fund for social-cultural measures, and an enterprise investment fund. Monies for the funds were to come out of profits, in accordance with complicated formulae relating profit deductions to enterprise performance with respect to the new success criteria, via sets of ministry-set norms that were then taken as percentages of the enterprise wage fund (for the bonus and social-cultural funds) and of the value of capital stock (for the investment fund).

As extension of the reform proceeded during 1966–70, these complicated incentive arrangements were made more so by a series of amendments to the original rules. The experience of enterprises operating under the new procedures disclosed a number of inconsistencies and perversities in the rules and produced types of behavior that the planners did not like. The most frequently cited shortcomings were: enterprises did not pay sufficient attention to raising labor productivity; white collar workers received an unduly large share of rewards from the new bonus funds; tying the norms for forming the incentive funds to the size of the wage fund and to the capital stock did not induce managers to economize on labor and capital costs; the size of incentive funds differed widely among enterprises and branches of industry; ministries frequently changed both enterprise plans and the fund-forming norms; contrary to expectations, the new incentives did not strongly motivate enterprise managers to adopt tight plans, improve product quality, be eager to introduce new technology and make new products, or economize on costs. These criticisms amount to a tacit admission that the reforms were not really accomplishing their objectives, notwithstanding the repeated assertions by Soviet planners about the numerous "positive" effects of the reform.

With the expressed purpose of remedying these deficiencies, the Soviet government, mainly in a Council of Ministers' Decree of June 21, 1971, has made a number of changes in the incentive system in Soviet industry. The changes relate to (1) the methods of determining the size of the incentive funds for enterprises, (2) the establishment of incentive funds in the ministries and intermediate bodies, and (3) the management of the incentive funds and the criteria for bonus payments. The following sections will describe the present basic incentive arrangements of the economic reform in the industrial sector, as modified by the new approaches. The reader is warned that the journey through this labyrinth will be tedious and wearing; hopefully, he will be rewarded by additional insight into the ways of a bureau-administered economy.

Formation of Incentive Funds

The new methods for establishing the bonus and social-cultural funds are spelled out in two official documents issued in April 1971 and May 1972. In contrast to past procedures, the amount of the basic bonus fund for each year in the five-year plan period is now determined for an enterprise by its supervisory ministry. Enterprise funds are set within the limits of the total funds allocated to the ministry as a whole by Gosplan, which sets them for the final year of the plan period, in accord with planned changes in employment by major occupational categories and the planned average wage. Enterprise bonus funds for the intervening years increase in accord with the planned growth of output (marketable or total), a target that the ministry also establishes for enterprises. Thus, the "planned" size of the incentive fund is fixed for each year. If an enterprise exactly fulfills the originally planned, annual tasks for output, level of profitability, and labor productivity as specified in the five-year plan, its incentive fund for that year will also be as originally planned. If enterprise performance with respect to any of those original targets deviates from plan, the size of the incentive fund increases or decreases in accordance with fixed, "stable" norms for each of the three targets. For the plan period 1971–75, the norms are calculated in stages as follows: (1) in planning the original bonus funds for enterprises, the ministry also determines the percentage of the total that is to come from the growth of output, usually 40 percent, and from profitability, usually 60 percent; (2) the norm for annual deductions into incentive funds with respect to output is then calculated by multiplying its planned share of the bonus fund by the planned average annual growth of output for the five-year period; (3) similarly, the norm with respect to profitability is calculated by multiplying its planned share of the bonus fund by the planned percentage point increase in profitability during 1971–75; (4) the norm with respect to labor productivity is set by the ministry, usually at 0.3. These norms are percentages; they are translated into rubles by multiplying them by the total enterprise wage fund in 1970. Ministries may set them individually for each enterprise in the manner explained, or they may set them uniformly for groups of enterprises or sub-branches.

The new rules attempt to give enterprises an incentive to adopt tauter annual plans than those originally set for them in their five-year plans. If an enterprise adopts higher indices for any of the three targets, its incentive funds are increased in accord with the procedure outlined above. Similarly, if lower targets are adopted, incentive funds are decreased accordingly. If planned targets, whether original or revised, are overfulfilled, the incentive funds are increased, but with the use of norms reduced by at least 30 percent. If targets are underfulfilled, the funds are decreased with the use of higher norms.

In addition to these basic rules, the bonus funds of enterprises are increased or reduced in accordance with enterprise performance with respect to three other indicators. They are the plan for production of key products in physical units; plans for the production of consumer goods in excess of those originally set in the five-year plan, where such goods are not the basic output (notably in heavy industry) ; and plans for change in product quality and for new products. The relevant norms are fixed by the ministries. The new incentives for consumer goods production are part of the government's current effort to involve most heavy industry enterprises in producing consumer goods, in order to alleviate persistent shortages of these goods, especially small items such as meatgrinders, tableware, and kitchen utensils. A Council of Ministers' Decree published in October 1971 specified that consumer goods produced in such enterprises were to be counted in plan fulfillment, something that was not done before. Also, the size of incentive funds and the award of bonuses were made to depend on fulfillment of such plans. The new incentive arrangements with respect to product quality are a part of a recent stepped-up effort to improve quality in general and to stimulate production of new kinds of consumer goods in particular. As previously noted, a Council of Ministers' Decree of June 21, 1971, directed the ministries to classify all products into three categories, to specify for each enterprise the share of total output required to be in the top category, and to provide incentives for raising this share and also for reducing the share of products in the bottom category. Systems of price markups and rebates are to be worked out for products in the two categories. The ministries are to fix coefficients by which the so-called "stable norms" that determine the incentive funds will be raised, in accord with the growth of the share of output in the top category and a reduction of the share of output in the lowest category.

New procedures also apply to formation of the enterprise social-cultural fund and the enterprise investment fund. In contrast to past practice, the size of the social-cultural fund is now planned simply as a fixed percentage of the enterprise bonus fund; for the 1971–75 plan period the share is that which existed in 1970. The actual size of the social-cultural fund in each year is affected by the same factors that determine the bonus fund for that year. With respect to the enterprise investment fund, the new rules replace the former complicated procedures with much simpler ones. The funds are formed partly from enterprise profits, and the ministries are now to fix the percentage of profits that is to be allocated to these funds. Although little information has yet been published on the new rules, the size of the funds apparently depends on their size at the start of the plan period and on the amount of planned bank credit to be granted the enterprise for decentralized investment purposes. As before, the major part of these funds will continue to come from a ministry-specified share of regular amortization deductions, and another portion consists of proceeds from the sale of surplus equipment.

Establishment of Centralized Incentive Funds

As noted above, under the new procedures Gosplan fixes the limit for total bonus funds for the ministry as a whole in each year. The ministry is permitted to set aside as much as 10 percent of this total to create centralized reserve funds for itself, its main administrations, and subordinate associations or trusts. Monies for the centralized funds are obtained as planned percentage deductions from total enterprise profits. If the ministry allows the incentive funds of all subordinate organizations to exceed its authorized ceiling, the excess is taken out of the ministry's reserve fund for the year, or for the next one, and paid into the state budget. The ministry reserve fund is to be used for the following purposes: for increasing the incentive funds of enterprises that raise the percentage of highest category product in their plans and that introduce much new technology; for increasing the incentive funds of enterprises that produce consumer goods that are in demand but that have low prices or yield low profits; for replenishing the incentive funds of subordinate units when their indices are temporarily adversely affected by introduction of new technology or major repairs; to add to incentive funds of subordinate units when deemed necessary in order to keep the fund-forming norms stable. The reserve funds formed in associations, trusts, and the like are used for some of the same purposes and also for paying bonuses to their administrative personnel. The formation of this system of reserve funds is regarded as an important step toward achieving one of the original goals of the economic reform, namely, to establish a uniform set of incentive arrangements for all units in the administrative chain, from ministry to enterprise. A further step would place the ministry as a whole on full *khozraschet* and autonomous financing; thus far, this action has been taken for only one ministry—the prestigious and highly profitable Ministry of Instruments, Means of Automation, and Control Systems.

Uses of the Incentive Funds

The original rules of the reform provided that the enterprise bonus funds were to be used for designated purposes, in accord with annual plans for their use worked out between the enterprise management and the appropriate trade union committee. The bonus fund is to be used to pay bonuses to managerial-technical workers and clericals in accord with established bonus arrangements, to grant annual bonuses to all employees in accord with enterprise performance during the year, to give temporary financial aid to employees in need, to award bonuses for victories in socialist competitions, and to reward especially meritorious workers. The reform gave managers broad discretion over the kinds of bonus systems that could be used, circumscribed by a general regulation on bonuses. As a result, a great variety of practices have developed, both on the part of enterprise managers and on the part of ministries, which approve bonus arrangements for the top management of enterprises. Following a barrage of press criticism of the results of such "spontaneity," the rules were amended several times to tighten control over the expenditure of bonus funds. In particular, limits were put on the increase in bonuses that could be given to managerial employees in a given year, and penalties were instituted for permitting average wages to increase faster than labor productivity.

During 1966–70 the bonus funds evidently grew much faster than was intended, and their size varied widely among branches of industry. For example, in 1970, bonus funds were 129 rubles per employee in the building materials industry and 351 rubles per employee in the timber industry. The new procedures adopted for 1971–75 are designed to limit the growth of these funds and to reduce differences in the size of the funds among branches of industry and enterprises. In addition, the Council of Ministers' Decree of June 21, 1971, instructed the ministries, together with the appropriate trade unions, to bring order into the expenditure of bonus funds, and in particular to see to it that (1) bonuses are related more directly to enterprise performance with respect to labor productivity, introduction of new technology, and raising product quality; (2) production workers get a larger share of the bonus funds; and (3) special rewards for outstanding work are given for improving technology and adding new products. On September 28, 1972, an amended bonus regulation was issued to accomplish these tasks.

As matters stand now, enterprise managerial personnel are paid bonuses, within the limits of monies in the enterprise bonus fund, for fulfilling and overfulfilling the plan for sales (or profits) and profitability, as originally specified in the reform. An obligatory additional condition is fulfillment of the physical assortment plan. Ministries are permitted to add additional conditions, if they see fit. As a result, considerable diversity had developed among the ministries with respect to bonus criteria. The Council of Ministers' Decree of October 1971 concerning consumer goods production in heavy industry requires that ministries reduce the amounts of managerial bonuses paid for basic indicators, if the enterprise fails to fulfill its plan for delivery of consumer goods. In accord with the September 1972 amendments to the bonus regulation, managerial bonuses are denied or reduced if the enterprise fails to fulfill its plans for labor productivity and for raising product quality, and if costs are "intentionally" overstated when approval of new prices is requested. Besides the basic bonus, managerial personnel also receive other kinds of payments from the bonus fund, such as lump-sum bonuses at the end of the year. In 1970, total payments from the bonus fund amounted to 31.7 percent of the average salary of managerial-technical workers in industry.

In addition to payments from the bonus fund created out of profits, managerial employees can earn bonuses under a number of other arrangements, e.g., for introducing new technology, for producing consumer goods out of waste materials, and for mastering new facilities ahead of schedule. The total of such bonuses often amounts to several months' average salary. In 1970 the Council of Ministers, by special decree, stipulated that the total of all such supplemental bonuses (except that for new technology) could not exceed four months' salary, but an extra two months' salary can be obtained via bonuses for introducing new technology and for victory in socialist competition.

With respect to the use of social-cultural funds, the new provisions make no essential changes. They spell out some additional ways in which the funds may be spent, and they specify that 60 percent of the fund must be used for the construction of housing and related facilities, such as those for child care. The rules governing the uses of the enterprise investment fund also evidently remain the same.

Two other incentive-related provisions of the Council of Ministers' Decree of June 21, 1971, are worthy of note, however. One of them revises the rules governing the so-called "Mastery Fund" for reimbursing enterprises for start-up costs on new technologies and products, by providing that the funds are to be formed so as to reimburse enterprises fully for all start-up costs, including the higher unit costs in the first (and in some cases second) year of serial production. The other change provides that newly constructed facilities are freed from the capital charge only during a period for their mastery that equals the norm established for the branch. Both of these changes in the rules are designed to deal with the intractable problems of reluctance of enterprises to innovate and perennial delays in getting new capacities into full operation.

IV. CONCLUSIONS

The most recent developments in planning and incentive arrangements, as reflected in the approach to the Ninth Five-Year Plan and now scheduled to continue thereafter, carry out specific proposals made by Kosygin in his announcement of the economic reform in 1965. The nature of these changes and the manner of implementation by the bureaucracy also continue patterns clearly evident in the first several years of experience with the reform. Although there is still much talk in the Soviet press about economic reform, the phrase now has come to mean simply all changes in economic management procedures that are made to improve the existing system. There is little mention of "spontaneity," except to condemn it, or of granting more decision-making authority to enterprises. Instead, emphasis is placed on finding ways to solve the perennial problems with the retention of central planning and as much central administration as possible. As two authors put it, "Raising the role of economic methods of managing the economy does not mean decreasing the role of administrative methods." Indeed, after seven years of the reform, economic methods, or "levers," have been effectively converted into administrative "levers" by incorporating indices in the plans in an increasing amount of detail. As a consequence, centralized planning and administration are even more entrenched, and the developments now in process will continue this trend.

The present emphasis on plans with a time horizon of five years or longer changes nothing essential in the system. However, the mania for long-range forecasting is providing many new opportunities for bureaucratic aggrandizement, particularly for the government organs concerned with the glamorous subjects of science and technology and for the numerous scientific and technical research institutes scattered throughout the economy. The results of the forecasting activities now formally set *en train* ultimately will inundate the planning bodies with a mass of reports. Faced with the urgent, practical task of coming up with detailed operating plans each year, the planners likely will simply continue their established routine. More and better machines will enable them to make more calculations for these plans and to make them faster. Probably, some of the long-range forecasts will provide the planners with information they might not have had otherwise, and perhaps a few more "optimal" decisions, i.e., conducive to less waste of resources, will be made as a result. As is already evident, the idea that directive five-year plans will provide the enterprise with a stable expectational framework within which to operate is an illusion. Annual plans will be changed when current events require it, as were their predecessors that were not developed within such a framework.

The current leadership clearly has given the green light to the cyberneticists, in the belief, or at least with the hope, that esoteric technologies and "scientific," i.e., mathematical, techniques will make the economy perform better. The government bureaucracy has got the message and now seems to be proceeding full steam ahead to take advantage of the situation for its own purposes. The process of assimilating the new computer-based technologies into the bureaucratic routine is in full swing. Resources and people have been allocated to launching the grandiose projects to establish nationwide uniform information systems, data banks, computer networks, and the like, and to computerize everything that seems to be susceptible of computerization. Given the present state of the computer art in the Soviet Union, let alone the present capabilities of mathematical modelling, the ultimate outcome of this vast undertaking is problematic, to say the least. What is clear, though, is that a large amount of bureaucratic activity has now been launched to carry it out, including assignment of specific planning tasks to designated agencies and imposition of bureaucratic controls over fulfillment. The task of coordinating all this activity is staggering. The grand scheme could, of course, be quietly abandoned when the costs mount, as were some of Stalin's canals. More likely, however, the time schedules for the projected systems and their numerous subsystems will merely be pushed continually forward, like the schedules of typical Soviet construction projects. The system's designers will be able to cite the immense, real difficulties and complexities involved, but in true bureaucratic fashion they will also be able to cite their calculations of the large resource savings that the new systems will bring about. Ultimately, a disillusioned leadership may withdraw its political support, in favor of some other approach to economic management. In the interim, some components of the overall scheme may prove practical and be incorporated into planning practice.

The many recent actions taken in the name of the economic reform show that Soviet planners more than ever before are trying to obtain micro-efficiency in the economy over wide ranges of problems by increasing the number of indicators in the plans. Productivity is to be raised, new technologies adopted, new products produced, and product quality upgraded—by devising statistical indicators to measure performance with respect to the objectives, inserting the indicators in the plans, and tying incentives directly to achievements with respect to some or all of them. Thus, planning has become ever more detailed, a process that has been greatly facilitated by the availability of computers. Moreover, the designing and monitoring of the many new plan parameters is being carried out in diverse bureaucratic channels. The more detailed and technical these parameters are made, the more difficult it is to obtain consistency among them. Thus, the task of internal plan coordination becomes more complicated. Finally, the attempt to enforce efficiency and technological progress via plan indicators increases the degree of centralization. More of these indicators are being established centrally for enterprises. Although the original reform reduced the number of such targets from 38–40 to nine key ones, six new targets have been added since 1970. They are labor productivity, gross value of output, assignments for consumer goods production in heavy industry enterprises, tasks for raising product quality, assignments for reducing material and fuel expenditures per unit of output, and the size of basic incentive funds.

This multiplication of plan indicators greatly complicates the task of the enterprise manager in devising ways to get things done and also in deciding which of the numerous assigned chores he should attempt to do. His task is made more difficult by the attendant changes in incentive arrangements. Despite repeated pleas for simplification of the extremely complicated incentive structure, each new change in the rules has complicated them further. The revised methods of forming incentive funds were designed to eliminate specific inconsistencies and perversities in the old rules. The new approach of "planned" incentives is also intended to induce managers to adopt taut plans, that is, to keep them from continuing to conceal real production possibilities from the planners, for fear of the imposition of higher targets in the next year. Also, the traditional reluctance to innovate is supposed to be overcome with the use of the centralized reserve funds and the provisions for extra bonuses. At the same time, however, ceilings are put on total bonus funds and on individual bonuses. Despite all this tinkering with the rules, the root of the problem is not touched. The managers' bonuses still are tied to fulfillment of plans, even more of them than before. This fundamental fact is likely to maintain traditional managerial behavior patterns, as Soviet critics have already started to point out.

In conclusion, the latest round of modifications in Soviet planning and incentives leaves the essentials of the system unchanged, but adds to the degree of centralization and to the complexity of administrative arrangements. The innovations also help to swell the administrative bureaucracy, which has increased nearly one third since 1965. As clearly exemplified in the Ninth Five-Year Plan, the planners' pressure on resources—taut planning—continues unabated. The familiar chronic malfunctions persist, and the problem of devising incentive schemes to remove them continues to defy solution. Finally, the efficacy of monetary incentives is being eroded by the continuing unavailabilities of desired goods and services. The strong current emphasis on "moral incentives" and the heightened pressure for "shock work," socialist pledges, and socialist competitions of all kinds are the familiar and predictable response of the political leadership.

25. SOCIALIST CORPORATIONS: THE WAVE OF THE FUTURE IN THE USSR?

Alice C. Gorlin

In addition to the changes in planning and incentives discussed in the preceding selection, the Soviet leadership decided in 1973 to try to improve industrial performance by reorganizing the administrative structure of industry. "Associations"—similar in some respects to multiplant corporations in the West—have been established as a new middle level of management between the ministry and the enterprise. Although the details are still being worked out as this book goes to press, it appears that enterprises will lose some of their already limited decision-making powers and that the reorganization is on balance another recentralizing move.

In this article, Alice C. Gorlin, Assistant Professor in the School of Economics and Management of Oakland University, analyzes and evaluates the new scheme. She examines alternative possible organizational arrangements, and reviews the previous experience of mergers in the USSR and analogous consolidations in several East European countries. Mergers seek various economies from multiplant operation under common direction, such as greater specialization in production, lower inventories, smaller managerial staffs, and technological transfer from more advanced to backward enterprises. But mergers also create new problems of control, accountability, and incentives—and the net effect of the latest reorganization on industrial performance is therefore uncertain.

ON APRIL 2, 1973, THE SOVIET government announced a major reorganization of the administrative structure of industry. This latest in a series of institutional changes in the Soviet economy will replace the 1965 economic reform which delegated new rights and responsibilities to enterprise managers. Under the new system, major decision-making powers will be vested in socialist corporations (associations), the new middle level of management between ministry and enterprise. An association is a combination of enterprises under a single management, similar to a merged multiplant concern in Western terminology. The association is not a recent innovation, for a merger movement began in the early 1960s. At present there are approximately 1,000 merged concerns.[1] The exact status of the enterprise under the new scheme is unclear, but it will presumably operate as a division of the association and will lose all independent decision-making powers.

This paper has three aims: first, to explain the new arrangements as well as can be done from official sources so far published; second, to summarize the background and development of the merger movement; and third, to assess the significance of mergers and the new associations in improving economic performance and industrial management. The accumulated experience with mergers should provide clues about potential prospects and problems facing the new reform.

THE 1973 REFORM

Responsibility for creating associations rests primarily with ministries, which are obliged to submit plans for reorganization within six months. The new scheme is to be in operation by the end of 1975, but the number of associations there will be is as yet unknown.

The aim of forming associations is to improve industrial performance, especially in the areas of labor productivity, quality, costs, and use of advanced technology.[2] The architects of the reform believe that improvement depends on development of concentration and specialization of production, more subcontracting among enterprises, faster introduction of technical improvements into production, and simplification of the administrative structure.[3] Thus managers of associations are expected to reallocate production tasks to increase specialization and concentration of production at the plant level and to develop reliable supplier-customer ties among member enterprises. Since associations will contain research and development organizations and experimental factories as well as producing enterprises, coordination between research and production is expected to improve. Finally, the reform will abolish most of the *glavki* or main administrations, the old administrative link between the ministry and the enterprise. It is hoped that this will alleviate the problem of an excessive number of stages in the managerial hierarchy.

---

[1] *New York Times*, April 3, 1973, p. 1.

[2] "Resolution on Industrial Associations," *Current Digest of the Soviet Press*, Vol. XXV, No. 14 (May 2, 1973), pp. 1–2.

[3] A major impetus for streamlining of the administrative structure is increasing costs of administration. Employment in state administration fell from 1950 to 1960, but from 1960 to 1969 it increased by 47.3 percent. In several industrial ministries, administrative costs have recently been increasing faster than output.

The reorganization envisages three possible types of managerial structure: two-stage, three-stage, and four-stage. In order to understand these, a distinction must be made between two types of associations. The first is a multiplant concern usually consisting of three to five enterprises located within a relatively small area. This type of association developed during the 1960s and will be referred to as a firm. The second is much larger and extends either over the entire country (all-union association) or over a republic (republican association). This type is so far much less developed than the first, but is intended to be the new middle level of management.

Figure 1 illustrates the possible types of management schemes. In two-stage management, a firm, combine (a vertically integrated multi-

FIGURE 1
Types of Management Schemes

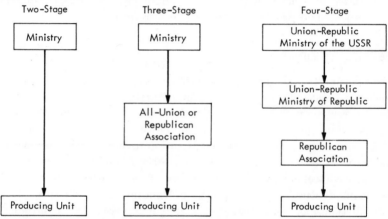

1. The bottom-level producing unit can be a firm, combine, or enterprise. Thus it may contain one or several plants.
2. In the four-stage scheme used in some branches of industry, supervision of producing units is shared by a ministry located in Moscow (union-republic ministry of the USSR) and a ministry located in the republic (union-republic ministry of the republic). The latter sometimes acts as an intermediary for the former, but also has some direct powers over subordinate units.

plant complex), or enterprise is directly subordinate to the ministry. Here the new large association does not play a part. In three-stage management, the firm, combine, or enterprise is the lowest stage, and the ministry is the highest. The all-union or republican association is the middle level. Thus a multiplant concern (firm) can itself be a member of a larger association. The four-stage scheme is retained as an exception in a few branches. Here the stages are union-republic ministry of the USSR, union-republic ministry of the republic, republican association, and firm (or combine or enterprise). Another exception is the retention of a few glavki which have been transferred to *khozraschet* (business-calculation) rather than being budget-financed. (See below for an explanation of *khozraschet*.)

Although the precise rights, responsibilities, and functions of the new associations are as yet unclear, it appears that the associations will gain authority at the expense of both enterprises and ministries. For example, the official statute on the socialist enterprise no longer applies to enterprises which are subordinate to associations.[4] The powers given to the enterprise by the 1965 reform now belong to the associations.[5] Presumably associations will also perform duties now discharged by ministries, while the latter will concentrate on overall planning, investment policy and technical progress.[6] The rationale is that associations are better qualified than central planners and ministries to make planning and resource allocation decisions at the enterprise level, because associations are closer to the sources of information on which these decisions are based.

An example of the expanded powers of the association is the integration of research and development with production; all associations will contain design and research and development organizations, as well as factories. Previously there has been much discussion of this, but very little action. Also associations are expected to study consumer demand, which so far has been neglected at the enterprise level. Another example is the right of the association to redistribute profits as well as material resources among the member enterprises; up to now many firms did not have this right. The role of the association in planning is as yet unclear, but it appears that only the association as a whole will receive a plan and it in turn will divide the tasks, as well as the resources allocated by the plan, among the members. At present some firms do this, while others merely transmit enterprise plans formulated at higher levels. In addition, the association may enjoy greater participation in the formulation of its own plan, since according to the statutes one duty of associations is to construct optimal plans. Finally, the association has the right to establish various funds in addition to those currently formed in the enterprise. The new funds include a fund for research and development, a fund for introduction of new technology, a fund for development of export production, and a reserve of financial assistance to member enterprises and organizations.[7] Most firms do not have such funds, which up to now have been formed at the ministry level.

A curious exception to the expanded powers of the association is the scheme for payments to the state out of profits. In some cases payments are made by the individual enterprises and in some cases by the association. A possible reason for retaining this direct relation between the enterprise and financial authorities is to check on abuses of power by the association, such as exploitation of some members for the benefit of others.

The new association is expected to operate on khozraschet, meaning

---

[4] "Resolution on Industrial Associations," pp. 1–2.

[5] *New York Times,* April 3, 1973, p. 1.

[6] Ibid.

[7] "Resolution on Industrial Associations," pp. 1–2.

that it has a profit-and-loss account and is supposed to cover all expenses and make a profit. The only exception is the financing of research and development and introduction of new technology, which continue to be financed from the government budget. Khozraschet status is a major difference between the associations and the glavki. In the association managerial expenses are part of the costs of member enterprises, whereas expenses of glavki are budget-financed.

To sum up, the new reform involves a transfer of power from the top and bottom levels of industrial management to a new middle level, the association. Since the new statutes contain little or no emphasis on retaining the rights of enterprises, it appears that the essential goal of the 1965 reform, which was to enhance the authority of the enterprise manager, has been abandoned. This is not surprising, since many economists have been arguing that only large enterprises could function successfully under the reform, because only they had the necessary resources and flexibility.[8] The new system is in effect enlarging and giving more power to the basic decision-making unit in the hope that socialist corporations will rescue the economy from its current doldrums.

SOVIET FIRMS OF THE 1960s

The association is not an unknown entity. Merged concerns have been functioning since 1961, and much has been written about their successes and shortcomings.

The first two firms (one producing shoes, the other leather) were formed in Lvov in the Western Ukraine in 1961. They were established at the initiative of the merging enterprises with the support of local Party organs. But what began through local initiative was quickly seized upon by higher authorities; firms were soon being formed by *sovnarkhozy* (regional units of economic administration from 1957 to 1965) and, after 1965, by industrial ministries. The mergers of the 1960s had three goals. First was a transfer of knowledge and resources to small, inefficient enterprises. The typical firm unites an advanced leader (head enterprise) with several small backward enterprises (affiliates). The head enterprise is expected to reorganize production and reallocate resources so that each member can attain its maximum efficiency. The second goal was the realization of economies of multiplant operation, in particular specialization at the plant level, both by product and by stage of production. Because specialization is an important factor in achieving economies of scale, nonspecialization involves cost penalties. However, nonspecialization is rational from the point of view of the individual enterprise,

---

[8] The argument is that large firms have the necessary resources to perform functions such as research and development and market research, resources presumably lacking in small enterprises. The argument also rests on the presumed stability of the performance of firms, achieved by balancing high profits in some affiliates against low profits in others. More stable performance leads to larger investment and bonus funds.

because fulfillment of the assortment plan of final products and provision of a complete assortment to trade organizations are often incompatible with product specialization.[9] Vertical integration of inputs production (lack of stage specialization) protects the enterprise against supply difficulties, a chronic problem in the sellers' market conditions of the Soviet economy.[10] Firms bring the risky market relationships under one roof, making affiliates less reluctant to specialize by product and to discontinue vertical integration. In order to fulfill its plan, management of the firm must ensure regular flows of inputs among members; thus it has a more direct interest in protecting its members against supply difficulties than an outside supplier would.

The achievement of the first two goals of mergers was expected to result in an increase in the growth rate of industrial production and improved economic performance in general. The third goal of the early mergers was less important and was related to the economic reform of 1965. This reform was introduced because it had become clear to the leadership that decentralization of decision making was a prerequisite to continued growth. As the reform progressed, economists began to argue that the firms operated more successfully under the new system than did small, single-plant enterprises. The 1973 reform essentially applies this principle to all of industry, since all enterprises are to be subordinate to associations, the new vehicle of decentralization. It can be argued that decentralization to an intermediate level is a conservative reform, because mergers internalize some market relationships. Decentralization to the enterprise level implies more dependence on the market, since enterprises must then deal with each other.

The number of firms has grown rapidly since 1961, but not without resistance, especially after the return to the ministerial system of management in 1965. By that time there were 592 firms. However, from 1965 until 1969, 240 firms were liquidated and 180 new ones were formed. The major reason was "narrow departmentalism" on the part of ministries and glavki. The ministries began to put firms under the jurisdiction of glavki, and as a result the member enterprises of one firm would often be under the supervision of several different glavki. The glavki either liquidated the firms or interfered in their activities so much that it was impossible for them to operate effectively. Local governmental organs were also a source of resistance to mergers, because after a merger, payments from member enterprises into local budgets often fall, and local governments have less power of procurement for local needs. Other

---

[9] For example, an industrial ministry of a republic may want its subordinate enterprises to produce a complete assortment in order to enhance the ministry's prestige. Trade organizations try to procure a complete assortment from the enterprises in their area so as to avoid reliance on deliveries from other regions.

[10] Because of taut planning and emphasis on high output levels (and until recently little emphasis on cost reductions), shortages of inputs are a chronic problem for the typical Soviet enterprise. It prefers to make rather than to buy and will hoard excess materials.

sources of resistance were managers of affiliates, who often saw their salaries and influence reduced as a result of merger, and local Party organs because they expected their influence over the merged enterprises to decrease.

Implementation of the new reform also is likely to meet with resistance for this reason. Ministries are expected to organize their enterprises into associations, even though the associations will reduce the authority of the ministries. In an environment which breeds interdepartmental competition, the ministries can hardly be expected to perform wholeheartedly actions which curtail their power.

In spite of liquidations and resistance, there were approximately 650 firms by 1971. They merged 2,700 enterprises, or 5.5 percent of all industrial enterprises, and accounted for 8.5 percent of industrial employment.[11] At the Twenty-Fourth Party Congress (1971), Soviet Communist Party Chief Brezhnev declared that firms should become the basic units of production in the future.

Regionally, firms are concentrated in the cities of Moscow and Leningrad and in the western republics of the Soviet Union, including the Ukraine, Latvia and Lithuania. Firms are most important in light industry, food-processing, and machine-building, where the greatest benefits can be attained from multiplant operation.

In general, the number of enterprises per firm is between 3 and 5, although it can range from 2 to 22. Although some firms span administrative boundaries, most are confined within an *oblast* (local administrative unit, similar in size to an American county). The average distance between a head enterprise and its affiliates is 50 to 60 miles. Before the late 1960s, when firms of the association type began to be formed, the average employment per firm was 2,500. Now it is about 4,000. No information has yet been published on how large the all-union and republican associations will be, but organizations spread over an entire republic or the whole country will undoubtedly be considerably larger than the typical firm. Many firms will simply be members of these associations.

The status of the firm with respect to its subordinate enterprises and to higher levels is important, because it determines the flexibility with which the firm can operate and the potential improvements in performance it can achieve. In the early 1960s, the creation of firms usually meant the end of independent status of members. Powers previously vested in enterprises were transferred to firms and the status of members became similar to that of constituent shops of an enterprise. Enterprises no longer received a plan from superior organs. The plan and the resources to fulfill it were given only to the firm, which determined the allocation of tasks and resources among the members. The firm was in charge of sales, supply, accounting, research and development

---

[11] These estimates probably do not include the new all-union and republican associations, some of which already existed in 1971.

(if such activities were carried on), and dealings with financial authorities such as banks and the government budget. The firm had much flexibility: it could reallocate plan assignments, materials, and even profits among its members. Furthermore, savings could be realized through the centralization of functions. In short, the firm itself was now the enterprise, and planners and ministries had fewer enterprises to plan for an supervise.

Another type of firm has existed since the early 1960s, however. In this type, member enterprises retain their independent status. These enterprises can make contracts with other enterprises; they have their own bank accounts; they do their own bookkeeping and keep profit-and-loss statements; and they have direct relations with financial and administrative organs. The only restrictions on their rights are the centralization of some functions formerly performed by each enterprise separately and the centralization of a portion of the three enterprise funds.[12] In some cases, planners continue to formulate detailed plans for these enterprises, and the firm's role is reduced to transmitting plans from one level to another. But often, even in this type of firm, plans and resources are given only to the firm as a whole, as in the first type discussed above. However, the second type of firm cannot redistribute profits among member enterprises. The second type of firm thus has less flexibility in allocation of resources and activities among member enterprises and realizes fewer savings from centralization of functions.

An as yet unanswered question about the new associations is their role in investment. The record of firms in gaining increased authority over investment decisions is not encouraging. The fund for development of production (investment fund) is centralized in most firms regardless of the status of member enterprises, and decisions about its use are made by the director of the firm. The problem is that the fund is too small in most firms, usually between 2 and 5 percent of the value of fixed capital. In this respect firms do only slightly better than independent enterprises, since most investment funds are still centrally allocated to both.[13]

In practice, firms do not always exercise the rights they have on paper, due to interference by higher organs. For example, firms have been prevented from exercising their right to distribute centrally allocated investment funds among members and to introduce measures to increase specialization. Such ministry interference is a potential problem for the 1973 reform. Firms of the second type have often found them-

---

[12] These are the fund for material stimulation (bonus fund), the fund for development of production (investment fund), and the social-cultural fund used for construction of workers' housing, clubs and other purposes.

[13] An equally important question involves the role of the new associations in price formation, so far not mentioned in the statutes on the reform. If price formation continues to be highly centralized, then the amount of genuine decentralization may be quite small. Firms play no role in price formation.

selves in the position of administrative organs without functions, partly due to retention of independence of members and partly to interference from above. This experience raises the question of whether the association too will become a superfluous link.

At present, most firms of the first type (in which member enterprises lose independence) consist of a few small enterprises located within a limited area. The second type is the dominant form, since 61 percent of all merged enterprises retain independence. One explanation for the prevalence of the second type is the importance the 1965 reform attached to increased initiative at the enterprise level. The introduction of the 1973 reform thus represents a major change in the attitude toward the enterprise, because the enterprise statute will no longer apply to members of associations.[14] Perhaps the more positive experience of the first type of firm in achieving economies of multiplant operation has influenced the decision to give the associations more authority than the firms of the second type possess.

The merger experience shows that depriving the enterprises of independence has disadvantages. The problem is similar to one faced by large Western corporations: how to ensure that the interests of the divisions are compatible with the goals of the organization formulated at the top. There are two preconditions for compatibility. First, the divisions of the organization must be made accountable for their actions. Therefore, some performance indicator reflecting their contribution to the overall goals of the organization (usually profits) must be calculated in the divisions. A set of transfer prices with which to value intraorganization transactions is required for calculation of profits in divisions. The second precondition is control of the divisions by the top. Performance must constantly be checked and divisions must be compared with each other. Sometimes in very large organizations there is insufficient or poor supervision, and the top loses control over what is going on at the bottom.

It will be recalled that in the first type of Soviet firm, most accounting is centralized and many indicators of performance are calculated only for the firm as a whole. Thus, profits are not calculated at the enterprise level, and enterprise performance is evaluated on the basis of costs, use of the wage fund, or output. Without profit and profitability (profits in relation to the value of capital) indicators, these enterprises are not interested in sales, quality, or economizing on capital—goals which are important to the firm as a whole.

Incentive problems also arise because in the first type of firm khozraschet does not apply to individual members. These enterprises are not formally obliged to cover costs and earn profits, in short, to be self-financing. It is argued that these enterprises lose financial responsibility

---

[14] This decision is in contrast to the trend in Eastern Europe, where associations have existed for several years. There, the enterprise is gaining increased authority at the expense of the association.

and can overspend without being held accountable. Data are available showing that some enterprises which lose independence borrow too much, overspend on wages, and incur excessive fines for late payments to suppliers and banks.

Enterprises could be made accountable if profits and profitability were calculated at the enterprise level. However, very few Soviet firms use transfer prices.[15] If such prices are used, they are usually calculated on the basis of cost plus a profit markup, similar to the formation of wholesale prices. The problem is that the prices are predetermined to provide a certain acceptable profit level for each member enterprise and therefore are useless for evaluation of each enterprise's contribution to overall profits.

The new associations are certainly going to face the problems of accountability and control. Since the republican and all-union associations will be much larger and more dispersed geographically, these problems can be expected to be considerably more complex than they have been for firms. If associations are unable to control the behavior of their subordinate enterprises to the satisfaction of higher levels, it is almost inevitable that ministries will interfere and begin to deal directly with enterprises again.

THE MERGER EXPERIENCE: A GUIDE TO FUTURE
PROSPECTS OF ASSOCIATIONS

This section of the paper will summarize the positive and negative effects of the merger movement so far. Alternative ways of achieving some of the savings due to mergers will be noted. Finally, a few speculations on future problems of the new associations will be offered.[16]

The major positive results of mergers are the various economies of multiplant operation, chiefly specialization. There is more product and stage specialization as a result of mergers than there would have been without them. This has particularly benefited small enterprises in which vertical integration and lack of product specialization involve severe cost penalties. A second important saving is the reduction of costs of management, mainly due to centralization of functions and a consequent reduction of personnel. There is evidence that managerial personnel account for a smaller percentage of total employment in firms than

---

[15] In general, problems of management within an organization have been neglected by Soviet economists and planners. Now they are trying to catch up, as shown by a proliferation of translations of American books on corporate management.

[16] Most of the conclusions of this section are based on a case study of the Soviet shoe industry. However, the author's survey of the literature on mergers indicates that most conclusions apply to other branches in which mergers have occurred. See Alice C. Gorlin, "Soviet Firms and the Rationalization of the Shoe Industry in the USSR" (unpublished Ph.D. dissertation, University of Michigan, 1972).

in independent enterprises. A third positive result is a reduction of hoarding. When supply operations are centralized by the firm, enterprises can no longer hoard materials. All members share in any reserves available to management, and reserves are thus used more efficiently. This advantage must be weighed against the increased transport costs incident to centralized warehousing. A fourth effect is the transfer of knowledge and resources from the head enterprise to the affiliates. Since the latter have usually been starved for resources before merger, it is probably rational up to a point to redistribute resources away from the head enterprise into the affiliates, where their marginal productivity is higher. There has been a transfer of both equipment and specialized personnel into the smaller affiliates as a result of mergers. Data on the performance of affiliates versus head enterprises indicate that affiliates usually improve faster, narrowing the gap between their performance and that of the head enterprise.

Economies of multiplant operation have in general resulted in superior performance of firms. This conclusion is supported both by data on overall performance of firms compared to overall industrial performance and by performance data for branches, especially the shoe industry. Thus firms normally achieve higher labor productivity, lower costs, higher profits and profitability, and better growth rates than independent enterprises.[17]

It should be noted that some industries have formulated plans to develop specialization at the enterprise level without mergers. The shoe industry in particular has had some success in developing stage and product specialization of independent enterprises. The machine-building industry is another notable example. These efforts have been accompanied by reforms in the supply system which attempt to make deliveries of inputs more reliable, so that enterprises will not be reluctant to specialize. However, as long as taut planning and sellers' market conditions persist, firms will represent a useful organizational approach to the obstacles to subcontracting.

An important question is whether the new associations will be able to extend the economies of multiplant operation to all industry. There are several reasons for skepticism. Since the new associations will presumably be much larger and more spread out geographically than the present firms, it is doubtful that they will be able to provide a secure environment in which to specialize. A few affiliates located close to their head enterprise will be more willing to specialize than will an enterprise located far from a management center which has responsibility for 15 or 20 other plants. Furthermore, centralization of supply is impractical in firms covering large regions, so the problem of hoarding may not

---

[17] Some of this superior performance may be due to the fact that firms, because of their large size, receive relatively more resources from planners than smaller enterprises do.

be alleviated. Centralization of other functions would also be limited in large, far-flung associations, so managerial savings might be insignificant. Finally, there is no reason to expect that the new associations will not be plagued by managerial problems of accountability, control, and incentives which have been experienced by the smaller firms.[18]

The new Soviet reform proposes a managerial structure similar to that in use in Eastern Europe. The East European experience provides certain lessons for Soviet reformers and suggests some problems that the Soviet reform may face in the future.

First is the possibility of monopoly and its abuses, especially if associations receive the right to set prices. Soviet firms do not set prices, and monopoly does not appear to be a problem so far.[19] However, in Eastern Europe, where associations do play a role in price formation, monopoly has appeared, especially in Hungary and in Czechoslovakia before 1968.[20] Because these countries have small internal markets, it is relatively easy for a monopoly to arise. Even without associations, monopolies would emerge in some cases because in various industries a firm of efficient size is a natural monopoly. East European countries contain many more nation-wide associations than can reasonably be expected to be formed in the Soviet Union, due to its much greater size. Thus Soviet republican associations with price-fixing powers would have only partial market power at best. And because of the East European experience, the Soviet reform may move cautiously on delegation of pricing to associations.

The monopoly problem is one aspect of a broader concern facing the new reform: autarky at the association level. Just as ministries and sovnarkhozy in the past have often pursued their own narrow concerns in conflict with overall goals formulated by the leadership, so also may associations. At a higher level, this is identical to the problem of ensuring that the actions of individual enterprises are compatible with association goals, and demands as a solution a mechanism for en-

---

[18] In Eastern Europe, nationwide associations are avoided in some industries, because it is felt that they would have severe managerial difficulties. The equivalent association in the Soviet Union would be much larger.

According to the official statute explaining the new Soviet reform, associations should be formed on the basis of "territorial proximity." However, it is unclear how this principle can be adhered to except in small republics.

[19] Firms, however, because of their large size, do have special advantages over small independent enterprises in the Soviet setting. Firms may exercise influence over planners and industrial administrators in order to get easy plans, favorable prices, and increased resource allocations. There is some evidence that firms are eligible for certain resources that small independent enterprises are not. With all enterprises in associations, there may be a problem of large associations having an advantage over small ones.

[20] In Hungary, monopolistic abuses by trusts were the major reason for their abolition and replacement by voluntary associations (unions). See Michael Kaser and Janusz G. Zieliński, *Planning in East Europe* (London: The Bodley Head, 1970), pp. 45, 87–89.

suring compatibility of goals, accountability of each level for its actions, and control. The market economy solves this problem through competition and the profit motive. If the market is working properly, it rewards those who produce efficiently and in accordance with consumer demand. The Soviet economy lacks a free market and scarcity prices and therefore has no such automatic mechanism to reward good behavior. If planners and top administrators observe undesirable behavior at lower levels, they can impose additional rules and regulations to try to prevent such behavior. The new rules may simply encourage a different kind of undesirable behavior, which, however, is optimizing from the point of view of the lower level. Thus the attempt to control behavior of lower levels, either by additional rules or by creation of new organizations to police lower levels, leads to further bureaucratization of the administrative structure—precisely what decentralizing reforms attempt to do away with.

A second problem in Eastern Europe is resistance on the part of enterprises to an increase in the power of the associations. Now the trend there is toward restoring the decision-making powers of the enterprise. One reason is instances of exploitation in associations run by a head enterprise; management has the ability, in the distribution of plan assignments and resources, to exploit other members so as to benefit the head enterprise. If incentives are structured so that managerial premia depend on overall performance, and not just the performance of the head enterprise, then exploitation should disappear.[21] So far most affiliates of Soviet firms seem clearly to have benefited from mergers, but future resistance is still a possibility.

A third lesson for Soviet reformers is that simply reorganizing enterprises does not necessarily reduce the number of managerial personnel. One of the expectations of mergers in Eastern Europe was a reduction in costs of administration. In at least two countries, Poland and Hungary, the opposite has occurred, because of bureaucratization of the middle level of management. Managing a huge multiplant complex often requires more personnel than are released from higher administrative organs.

CONCLUSION

The announcement of the new Soviet reform raises more questions than it answers. It is not clear that the new associations will enjoy as much success as Soviet firms have had in achieving economies of

---

[21] Exploitation is also a possibility in present Soviet firms because of the incentive structure. In the majority of firms, all managerial personnel of the head enterprise receive their bonuses from the bonus fund of the head enterprise only (rather than from a firm-wide fund for all member enterprises). This creates an interest in improving the performance of the head enterprise at the expense of the affiliates. Counter to this tendency, however, is the fact that the size of managerial premia depends on overall performance. The latter factor is apparently more important, since the literature does not contain complaints of exploitation.

multiplant operation; the associations may simply be too remote from their constituent enterprises. The informational aspect of decentralization (better decisions made at lower levels which are closer to the relevant information) may not apply to very large associations; they may be in no better position than ministries to make decisions on enterprise activities. Finally, the managerial structure may still be subject to problems of accountability, control, and autarky.

It is possible that an incentive structure and methods of effective decentralization within associations will be devised by the reformers to deal with these problems. However, so far the new reform has not been greeted with the fanfare and confidence characteristic of the 1965 reform. Perhaps the leadership does not regard this new reform as an automatic panacea—a healthy attitude not often observed in the past.

Also of interest are the political implications of the new reform, which center around the power of the managerial class. If, as appears likely, the associations are run by former enterprise directors, then the managers will be strengthened by the reform. The question is whether they will challenge the Communist Party's monopoly of decision making. A second question involves the influence of economic development on the political system. Will increased authority for the managerial class lead to demands for political and cultural freedom as well? These questions can only be answered by observing future developments in the Soviet Union.

SUGGESTIONS FOR FURTHER READING

The selections included in this book have been chosen to present, in a relatively small collection, an introduction to various facets of the Soviet economy. For the reader who is interested in exploring the Soviet economy further, there is a wide variety of material to choose from.

GENERAL WORKS ON THE SOVIET ECONOMY

There are a number of textbooks which deal with the Soviet economy from different points of view and at different levels. Harry Schwartz, *An Introduction to the Soviet Economy* (Columbus, Ohio: Charles E. Merrill Publishing Co., 1968) is a brief elementary survey. Robert W. Campbell, *The Soviet-type Economies: Performance and Evolution* (3d ed.; Boston: Houghton Mifflin Co., 1974), is a relatively short, essentially nontechnical book which concentrates on the factors affecting the growth and performance of the Soviet economy. Nicolas Spulber, *The Soviet Economy: Structure, Principles, Problems* (rev. ed.; New York: W. W. Norton & Co., Inc., 1969), considers the organization, operation, and performance of the various sectors of the economy. Alec Nove, *The Soviet Economy: An Introduction* (2d rev. ed.; New York: Frederick A. Praeger, Inc., 1969), emphasizes the structure and problems of the economy, with much institutional information and many specific illustrations from Soviet publications. Howard J. Sherman, *The Soviet Economy* (Boston: Little, Brown and Company, 1969), deals with ideological and historical aspects, as well as contemporary planning problems. Raymond Hutchings, *Soviet Economic Development* (Oxford: Basil Blackwell, 1971) contains both a historical account and a topical analysis of the operation of the economy. Michael Kaser, *Soviet Economics* (New York: McGraw-Hill Book Co., 1970), examines ideological aspects, the operation of the economic system, and growth strategy. Edward Ames, *Soviet Economic Processes* (Homewood, Ill.: Richard D. Irwin, Inc., 1965), is somewhat more theoretical in its orientation and also more difficult, making some use of differential calculus and matrix algebra.

From time to time the Joint Economic Committee of Congress issues important publications on the Soviet economy. The most recent is *Soviet*

Economic Prospects for the Seventies (A Compendium of Papers Submitted to the Joint Economic Committee, 93rd Cong., 1st sess.) (Washington, D.C.: U.S. Government Printing Office, 1973). *The Economic Survey of Europe* and the *Economic Bulletin for Europe,* both published by the United Nations Economic Commission for Europe in Geneva, also contain analyses and statistical data relating to the Soviet and East European economies.

There are several useful periodicals. *Soviet Studies* (published quarterly at the University of Glasgow, Scotland) is an interdisciplinary journal with many articles on the Soviet economy. Its supplement *ABSEES* contains concise digests of important items on the economy in Soviet journals and newspapers. *Problems of Communism* (published bimonthly by the U.S. Information Agency, Washington, D.C.) is an interdisciplinary journal on world communism with nontechnical articles on the Soviet economy and Soviet foreign economic relations. *The Current Digest of the Soviet Press* (published weekly at Ohio State University by the American Association for the Advancement of Slavic Studies) contains translations and digests from Soviet newspapers and magazines, including speeches, reports, and articles about the economy. *Problems of Economics* (published monthly by the International Arts and Sciences Press, White Plains, New York) consists of translations of articles from Soviet economics journals.

HISTORICAL BACKGROUND

There are several important books on the history of Soviet economic development. Alec Nove, *An Economic History of the USSR* (London: Allen Lane—The Penguin Press, 1969), gives a concise account. William L. Blackwell, *The Industrialization of Russia: An Historical Perspective* (New York: Thomas Y. Crowell Co., 1970), is a compact survey from the 18th century to the present.

Eugene Zaleski, *Planning for Economic Growth in the Soviet Union, 1918–1932* (Chapel Hill, N.C.: University of North Carolina Press, 1971), is a concise economic history of the period. Alexander Baykov, *The Development of the Soviet Economic System* (New York: The Macmillan Co., 1947), deals in great detail with the period from 1917 to the end of the 1930s. Maurice Dobb, *Soviet Economic Development Since 1917* (rev., enlarged ed.; New York: International Publishers Co., 1966), concentrates on the same period, although it also discusses Russian economic development before the Revolution and developments immediately after World War II. A more specialized work dealing with the controversy in the 1920s over the strategy of economic development is Alexander Erlich, *The Soviet Industrialization Debate, 1924–1928* (Cambridge, Mass.: Harvard University Press, 1960). Much of the important literature of this controversy has been translated in *Foundations* of Soviet Strategy for Economic Growth: Selected Soviet Essays, *1924–1930*, ed. Nicolas Spulber (Bloomington, Ind.: Indiana University Press, 1964). This material is summarized and appraised in a companion volume by Spulber, *Soviet Strategy for Economic Growth* (Bloomington, Ind.: Indiana University Press, 1964). A detailed analysis of the decisions about the collectivization of agriculture and their implementation appears in Moshe Lewin, *Russian Peasants and Soviet Power: A Study of Collectivization* (Evanston, Ill.: Northwestern University Press, 1968).

HOW THE ECONOMY OPERATES

Economic planning in the Soviet Union is appraised in Abram Bergson, *The Economics of Soviet Planning* (New Haven: Yale University Press, 1964), which presupposes some acquaintance with welfare economics and with the main characteristics of the Soviet economy. Michael Ellman, *Planning Problems in the USSR: The Contribution of Mathematical Economics to Their Solution* (Cambridge, Eng.: Cambridge University Press, 1973), is a more technical treatment emphasizing the "optimal planning" proposals of mathematical economists. A recent discussion of planning problems is Alan Abouchar, "Inefficiency and Reform in the Soviet Economy," and Roger A. Clarke, "Dr. Abouchar and Levels of Inefficiency," *Soviet Studies*, Vol. XXV, No. 1 (July 1973), pp. 66–87. A detailed explanation of the 1966 Soviet input-output table appears in Vladimir G. Treml and others, *The Structure of the Soviet Economy: Analysis and Reconstruction of the 1966 Input-Output Table* (New York: Praeger Publishers, 1972).

A comprehensive survey of the financial system is given in U.S. Bureau of the Census, *The Soviet Financial System: Structure, Operation, and Statistics*, by Daniel Gallik, Cestmir Jesina, and Stephen Rapawy (International Population Statistics Reports, Series P-90, No. 23) (Washington, D.C.: U.S. Government Printing Office, 1968). The basic study of Soviet taxation is Franklyn D. Holzman, *Soviet Taxation: The Fiscal and Monetary Problems of a Planned Economy* (Cambridge, Mass.: Harvard University Press, 1955). Inflation in the Soviet Union is analyzed in Franklyn D. Holzman, "Soviet Inflationary Pressures, 1928–1957: Causes and Cures," *Quarterly Journal of Economics*, Vol. LXXIV, No. 2 (May 1960), pp. 167–88; and Robert M. Fearn, "Controls Over Wage Funds and Inflationary Pressures in the USSR," *Industrial and Labor Relations Review*, Vol. 18, No. 2 (January 1965), pp. 186–95.

Industrial management in the Soviet Union is the subject of several monographs. Joseph S. Berliner, *Factory and Manager in the USSR* (Cambridge, Mass.: Harvard University Press, 1957), based primarily on interviews with Soviet émigrés, is a classic work. David Granick, *The Red Executive: A Study of the Organization Man in Russian Industry* (Garden City, N.Y.: Doubleday & Co., Inc., 1960), is a nontechnical and popular, but solid and well-researched, book which compares the Soviet industrial manager with his American counterpart. These comparisons are extended in David Granick, *Managerial Comparisons of Developed Countries: France, Britain, United States, and Russia* (Cambridge, Mass.: MIT Press, 1972). Barry M. Richman, *Soviet Management—With Significant American Comparisons* (Englewood Cliffs, N.J.: Prentice-Hall, Inc., 1965), is based in part on interviews at 16 Soviet enterprises. Also relevant is Barry M. Richman, *Management Development and Education in the Soviet Union* (East Lansing, Mich.: Michigan State University Institute for International Business, 1967). A first-hand account is Gregory Ryapolov, "I Was a Soviet Manager," *Harvard Business Review*, Vol. 44, No. 1 (January–February 1966), pp. 117–25.

Broad studies of labor in the USSR include Arvid Brodersen, *The Soviet Worker: Labor and Government in Soviet Society* (New York: Random House, 1966); and Emily Clark Brown, *Soviet Trade Unions and Labor Relations* (Cambridge, Mass.: Harvard University Press, 1966). More specialized are S. Swianiewicz, *Forced Labor and Economic Development: An Enquiry into the Experience of Soviet Industrialization* (London: Oxford University Press, 1965); Norton T. Dodge, *Women in the Soviet Economy—Their Role in Economic, Scientific, and Technical Development* (Baltimore, Md.: Johns Hopkins Press, 1966); and Mary McAuley, *Labour Disputes in Soviet Russia, 1957–1965* (Oxford: Oxford University Press, 1969). On wages, see Leonard Joel Kirsch, *Soviet Wages: Changes in Structure and Administration Since 1956* (Cambridge, Mass.: MIT Press, 1972). Social aspects of income differences are discussed in Murray Yanowitch and Norton T. Dodge, "The Social Evaluation of Occupations in the USSR," *Slavic Review*, Vol. 28, No. 4 (December 1969), pp. 619–43; and Robert J. Osborn, *Soviet Social Policies: Welfare, Equality, and Community* (Homewood, Ill.: The Dorsey Press, 1970), ch. 5.

A comprehensive history of agriculture during both the Tsarist and Soviet periods is Lazar Volin, *A Century of Russian Agriculture: From Alexander II to Khrushchev* (Cambridge, Mass.: Harvard University Press, 1970). Erich Strauss, *Soviet Agriculture in Perspective* (London: Allen & Unwin; New York: Praeger Publishers, 1969), is a concise general survey. The formation of agricultural policy is examined in Sidney I. Ploss, *Conflict and Decision-Making in Soviet Russia: A Case Study of Agricultural Policy* (Princeton, N.J.: Princeton University Press, 1965), and Werner G. Hahn, *Politics of Soviet Agriculture, 1960–1970* (Baltimore, Md.: Johns Hopkins Press, 1972). *The Soviet Rural Community: A Symposium*, ed. James R. Millar (Urbana, Ill.: University of Illinois Press, 1971), covers historical, economic, political, and sociological aspects. The organization and operation of collective farms are examined in Robert C. Stuart, *The Collective Farm in Soviet Agriculture* (Lexington, Mass.: Heath-Lexington Books, 1972). Karl-Eugen

Wädekin, *The Private Sector in Soviet Agriculture* (Berkeley: University of California Press, 1973), is a detailed study.

ECONOMIC GROWTH

A comprehensive guide to various types of Soviet statistics is *Soviet Economic Statistics,* ed. Vladimir G. Treml and John P. Hardt (Durham, N.C.: Duke University Press, 1972). Also helpful is *Handbook of Soviet Social Science Data,* ed. Ellen Mickiewicz (New York: The Free Press; London: Collier-Macmillan Publishers, 1973).

Concise explanations and assessments of Soviet economic growth include Raymond P. Powell, "Economic Growth in the USSR," *Scientific American,* Vol. 219, No. 6 (December 1968), pp. 17–23; Abram Bergson, *Planning and Productivity under Soviet Socialism* (New York: Columbia University Press, 1968); and Stanley H. Cohn, *Economic Development of the Soviet Union* (Lexington, Mass.: Heath-Lexington Books, 1970). An interesting comparison is provided by Angus Maddison, *Economic Growth in Japan and the USSR* (London: Allen & Unwin; New York: W. W. Norton & Co., Inc., 1969).

The results of a number of studies measuring different aspects of Soviet economic growth are presented in *Economic Trends in the Soviet Union,* ed. Abram Bergson and Simon Kuznets (Cambridge, Mass.: Harvard University Press, 1963). Basic works on Soviet economic growth include Abram Bergson, *The Real National Income of Soviet Russia Since 1928* (Cambridge, Mass.: Harvard University Press, 1961); G. Warren Nutter and others, *The Growth of Industrial Production in the Soviet Union* (Princeton, N.J.: Princeton University Press, 1962); Richard Moorsteen, *Prices and Production of Machinery in the Soviet Union, 1928–1958* (Cambridge, Mass.: Harvard University Press, 1962); and Richard Moorsteen and Raymond P. Powell, *The Soviet Capital Stock, 1928–1962* (Homewood, Ill.: Richard D. Irwin, Inc., 1966).

Consumption is discussed in Janet G. Chapman, *Real Wages in Soviet Russia Since 1928* (Cambridge, Mass.: Harvard University Press, 1963); and Philip Hanson, *The Consumer in the Soviet Economy* (London: Macmillan, 1968). Detailed recent statistics may be found in David W. Bronson and Barbara S. Severin, "Soviet Consumer Welfare: The Brezhnev Era," in *Soviet Economic Prospects for the Seventies* (A Compendium of Papers Submitted to the Joint Economic Committee, 93rd Cong., 1st sess.) (Washington, D.C.: U.S. Government Printing Office, 1973), pp. 376–403. On Soviet retail trade, see Marshall I. Goldman, *Soviet Marketing: Distribution in a Controlled Economy* (New York: The Free Press of Glencoe, 1963). The purchase and use of automobiles is described in Hedrick Smith, "The Russian Auto Market," *The New York Times Magazine,* October 8, 1972, pp. 18–20ff. On advertising, see Philip Hanson, *The Development of Advertising in the Soviet Union*

(London: The Advertising Association, 1971). Social welfare programs are examined in Bernice Q. Madison, *Social Welfare in the Soviet Union* (Stanford, Calif.: Stanford University Press, 1968).

Recent investment practices and patterns are discussed in Marvin R. Jackson, "Information and Incentives in Planning Soviet Investment Projects," *Soviet Studies,* Vol. XXIII, No. 1 (July 1971), pp. 3–25; and Keith Bush, "Soviet Capital Investment Since Khrushchev: A Note," *Soviet Studies,* Vol. XXIV, No. 1 (July 1972), pp. 91–96. On technological organization, policy, and problems, see Eugene Zaleski and others, *Science Policy in the USSR* (Paris: Organization for Economic Cooperation and Development, 1969), and Gertrude E. Schroeder, "Soviet Technology: System vs. Progress," *Problems of Communism,* Vol. XIX, No. 5 (September–October 1970), pp. 19–29. The contribution of Western technology is examined with detailed case material in Antony C. Sutton, *Western Technology and Soviet Economic Development, 1917 to 1930* (Stanford, Calif.: Hoover Institution, 1968), and *Western Technology and Soviet Economic Development, 1930 to 1945* (Stanford, Calif.: Hoover Institution, 1971).

Studies of environmental problems include Philip R. Pryde, *Conservation in the Soviet Union* (Cambridge, Eng.: Cambridge University Press, 1972), and Marshall I. Goldman, *The Spoils of Progress: Environmental Pollution in the Soviet Union* (Cambridge, Mass.: MIT Press, 1972).

FOREIGN ECONOMIC RELATIONS

Various aspects of Soviet foreign trade are examined in *International Trade and Central Planning,* ed. Alan A. Brown and Egon Neuberger (Berkeley: University of California Press, 1968); P. J. D. Wiles, *Communist International Economics* (Oxford: Basil Blackwell, 1968); and Glen Alden Smith, *Soviet Foreign Trade: Organizations, Operations, and Policy, 1918–1971* (New York: Praeger Publishers, 1973).

Earlier studies of Soviet trade with Communist countries in Eastern Europe include Frederic L. Pryor, *The Communist Foreign Trade System* (Cambridge, Mass.: MIT Press, 1963); and Michael Kaser *COMECON: The Integration Problems of the Planned Economies* (2d ed.; London: Oxford University Press, 1967). Henry Wilcox Schaefer, *Comecon and the Politics of Integration* (New York: Praeger Publishers, 1972), traces political and economic relationships from 1968 to 1971. An excellent analysis by a Hungarian economist is Sandor Ausch, *Theory and Practice of CMEA Cooperation* (Budapest: Akadémiai Kiadó, 1972). Soviet-Chinese economic relations are discussed in Chu-yuan Cheng, *Economic Relations Between Peking and Moscow, 1949–63* (New York: Frederick A. Praeger, Inc., 1964); and Alexander Eckstein, *Communist China's Economic Growth and Foreign Trade* (New York: McGraw-Hill Book Co., 1966), ch. 5.

The possibilities for Soviet trade with the industrial West are examined in Jozef Wilczynski, *The Economics and Politics of East–West Trade* (New York: Praeger Publishers, 1969); Samuel Pisar, *Coexistence and Commerce: Guidelines for Transactions Between East and West* (New York: McGraw-Hill Book Co., 1970); and James Henry Giffen, *The Legal and Practical Aspects of Trade with the Soviet Union* (rev. ed.; New York: Praeger Publishers, 1971). Western experience in joint ventures in Romania and Hungary is analyzed in Robert S. Kretschmar, Jr., and Robin Foor, *The Potential for Joint Ventures in Eastern Europe* (New York: Praeger Publishers, 1972). On Western strategic trade controls, see Gunnar Adler-Karlsson, *Western Economic Warfare, 1947–1967: A Case Study in Foreign Economic Policy* (Stockholm: Almqvist & Wicksell, 1968); and Thomas A. Wolf, *United States East–West Trade Policy: Economic Warfare Versus Economic Welfare* (Lexington, Mass.: Heath-Lexington Books, 1973).

Marshall I. Goldman, *Soviet Foreign Aid* (New York: Frederick A. Praeger, Inc., 1967), considers aid to both Communist and non-Communist countries. A systematic comparison is Robert S. Walters, *American and Soviet Aid: A Comparative Analysis* (Pittsburgh: University of Pittsburgh Press, 1970). Efforts to measure the "burden" to the Soviet Union of foreign aid include James Richard Carter, *The Net Cost of Soviet Foreign Aid* (New York: Praeger Publishers, 1971); Alastair McAuley and Dubravko Matko, "The Real Cost of Soviet Foreign Aid," *Bulletin of the Oxford University Institute of Economics and Statistics*, Vol. 28, No. 4 (November 1966), pp. 261–73; and Franklyn D. Holzman, "The Real Economic Costs of Granting Foreign Aid," *Journal of Development Studies*, Vol. 7, No. 3 (April 1971), pp. 245–55.

ECONOMIC REFORM

Comprehensive discussions include Eugene Zaleski, *Planning Reforms in the Soviet Union, 1962–1966* (Chapel Hill, N.C.: University of North Carolina Press, 1967); and George R. Feiwel, *The Soviet Quest for Economic Efficiency: Issues, Controversies, and Reforms* (2d ed.; New York: Praeger Publishers, 1972).

A concise account of Liberman's proposals in the early 1960s and the ensuing debate may be found in Marshall I. Goldman, "Economic Growth and Institutional Change in the Soviet Union," in *Soviet Policy-Making: Studies of Communism in Transition*, ed. Peter H. Juviler and Henry W. Morton (New York: Frederick A. Praeger, Inc., 1967), pp. 61–82.

Translations of important Soviet articles, speeches, and decrees relevant to the Liberman proposals and the 1965 reform appear in *Planning, Profit and Incentives in the USSR*, Vol. I, *The Liberman Discussion—A New Phase in Soviet Economic Thought*, and Vol. II, *Reform of Soviet*

Economic Management, ed. Myron E. Sharpe (White Plains, N.Y.: International Arts and Sciences Press, 1966).

The implementation of the reform is analyzed in Karl W. Ryavec, "Soviet Industrial Managers, Their Superiors, and the Economic Reform: A Study of an Attempt at Planned Behavioural Change," *Soviet Studies,* Vol. XXI, No. 2 (October 1969), pp. 208–29; Jan S. Prybyla, "Soviet Economic Reforms in Industry," *Weltwirschaftliches Archiv,* Band 107, Heft 2, 1971, pp. 272–313; and Gertrude E. Schroeder, "Soviet Economic Reform at an Impasse," *Problems of Communism,* Vol. XX, No. 4 (July–August 1971), pp. 36–46.

Studies of economic reform in East European countries include Michael Kaser and Janusz G. Zielinski, *Planning in East Europe: Industrial Management by the State* (London: The Bodley Head, 1970); *Reforms in the Soviet and Eastern European Economies,* ed. L. A. D. Dellin and Hermann Gross (Lexington, Mass.: Heath-Lexington Books, 1972); J. Wilczynski, *Socialist Economic Development and Reforms* (New York: Praeger Publishers, 1972); and *Plan and Market: Economic Reform in Eastern Europe,* ed. Morris Bornstein (New Haven: Yale University Press, 1973).